TABLE OF CONTENTS

ABBREVIATIONS

ICE	Islamic Coalition Party
F.Kh.	Fidayan-i Khalq Organization
HMI	Hizb-i Milal-i Islami
IFM	Iran Freedom Movement
INP	Islamic Nations Party
IRP	Islamic Republican Party
MKO	Mujahidin-i Khalq Organization
NAI	Nehzat-i Azadi-ye Iran
NF	National Front
NFLP	National Front for the Liberation of Palestine

A Good Revolutionary Is NOT a Dead Revolutionary

The Memoirs of Ezzat Shahi
Activist and Participant
in the Iranian Revolution: 1978–1979

Translation by

Amir Ali Shirazi

Printed in the United States of America.

Library of Congress Cataloging-in-Publication Data

Shirazi. Amir Ali, translator. A Good Revolutionary is Not a Dead Revolutionary

     p.cm.
Includes bibliographic references
ISBN 10: 1567445810
ISBN 13: 978-1-56744-581-7
1. Iran 2. Islamic Revolution

I. Title. II. Author

Published and Distributed by
ABC International Group, Inc.
3023 West Belmont Avenue
Chicago IL 60618
(T) 773-267-7001
(F) 773-267-7002
www.kazi.org
email: info@kazi.org

Preface

This book narrates the story and adventures of a petit bazaar merchant with strong religious convictions who became a political activist and who devoted the best years of his life to the struggle against injustice and political oppression during the last three decades of the Pahlavi regime. It is a mirror of the mind and soul of a man whose political aspirations and views were deeply rooted in and shaped by Islamic tradition as he understood it. What differentiates this book from many other memoirs and books written after 1979 is the author's honesty in narrating the events and ordeals he went through. The reader will note how his strong faith and dedication to his religious beliefs enabled him to go through many hardships, yet remain loyal and uncompromising to his ideals. Before the Revolution, Ezzat Shahi lived a simple and poor life and associated with common people every day. His humility, selflessness, and life among the ordinary people enabled him to develop a strong sense of political awareness and sophistication that most other activists of his time lacked. He continued the same lifestyle after the Revolution as well, without demanding or even expecting any reward for his many sacrifices. In these qualities lie the reasons for his survival and the uniqueness of the present book. Indeed, in the story of his struggle resonates the utterance of Imam Hossein that "Verily, life is nothing but struggle for the ideal truth" (*inn al-hayat 'aqidat-u wa'l jihad*).

—Abbas, *A fellow political activist and former cellmate of the author*

Translator's Introduction

It is often said that "The only good revolutionary is a dead revolutionary." The case of Ezzat Shahi defies that general rule. Unlike many revolutionaries who died and did not witness the fruits of their struggle, Ezzat Shahi struggled heroically and survived miraculously despite many years of psychological and physical torture in the process.

The Iranian Revolution of 1978–1979 has given rise to a vast body of literature on different aspects of this monumental event, especially in Persian and English, in addition to other European languages. These writings include numerous scholarly books and articles, memoirs of members of the political elite of the monarchical regime, and publications by opposition groups and many intellectuals and individual participants from all walks of life in the process of revolution. Among all these publications, the present book occupies a special place for several reasons. Its author is an ordinary man from the bazaar community with little formal education who learned the complicated art of oppositional politics in the process of his struggle. He is not a thinker or a theoretician, nor does he claim to be one. Unlike many others participants he does not write to defend himself and his accomplishments or justify his failures. Readers may not agree with every statement that he makes, especially on issues that pertain to his role and functions in post-Revolution years. However, he writes with the utmost degree of honesty and documents what he says. His writing represents the views, aspirations, ideals, and dreams of many ordinary participants of similar social and class backgrounds in the process of revolution. It also reflects the frustration of those who were somewhat disillusioned with the claims and behaviors of *post-revolution revolutionaries* who claimed credit for the victory of the Revolution. But unlike many other participants in the struggle, he does not claim personal credit, nor does he expect rewards for his many sacrifices.

1

Ezzat Shahi is one of the few activists who made and/or broke alliances with individual activists or opposition groups on the basis of "his own principles and ideals" as he defined them and did not surrender to pressures from any direction or group. His idealism and selflessness is evident in his lack of any personal ambitions and of a desire to reap the fruits of his sacrifices after the victory of the Revolution. After the Revolution's victory he chose to remain on the margin and only observed the post-revolution developments from a distance. A sense of disillusionment is discernible in his assessment of the post-revolution trends. This account, therefore, is not only a report of the bittersweet stories of two decades of struggle of a single activist; it is also an important historical document that demonstrates the share of ordinary people in the victory of the Revolution.

In narrating his memoirs Ezzat Shahi is frank and honest in expressing his views. Free from all Persian cultural formalities and personal considerations, he criticizes individuals, organizations, prominent politicians, and young and old activists when he observes deviation from the original ideals of revolutionary struggle.

The original Persian version of this book is based on many interviews conducted between 1358 and 1359/1979 and 1980) by Mr. Ibrahim Pur Mansuri, who is a stage-manager, film director, and television producer as a part of The Oral History on Contemporary Iran. Most of the information in this account was collected during the time when revolutionary fever and sentiments were high and before competing groups and factions appeared on the Iranian political scene.

This translation is based on the third edition of his memoirs that was published toward the end of 1385/1986. Earlier in the same year the first and second editions of the book were published in 862 pages that included 64 pages of appendices, notes, and annotations, 164 pages that contained pictures of most revolutionary activists, and 60 pages of an index of names. They provide a wealth of information about many un-

2

known participants and events, as well as detailed information about the inner working of opposition groups and political activists and leaders in prison and on the streets of Tehran. Those pages were not included in this translation as they may not be of interest to English readers of the book.

The translation of a text of this size and caliber was a monumental task. Many parts of the text had to be edited and many terms and proverbs, slang, and slogans had to be rendered into English in a way that would make sense to an English-speaking audience.

This task would have not been possible without the help and encouragement of several friends who chose to remain anonymous. Their support is greatly appreciated. Special thanks are due first and foremost to Mr. Ezzat Shahi who, despite poor health, his characteristic humility, and reluctance agreed to give many hours of interviews and to participate in the process of the preparation of the original manuscript and for his permission to translate the book into English. Sincere thanks are due also to Mr. Mohsen Kazemi, whose painstaking punctuality, remarkable patience, and hard work made the publication of the Persian manuscript possible. His efforts are greatly acknowledged and appreciated. It is hoped that the publication of this book will shed further light on the Iranian Revolution of 1979, which after thirty-five years still stands as one of the most important events of the twentieth century and continues to have profound impact on the course of political and religious developments throughout the Islamic world.

This book is not the account of a single revolutionary. It is the story of a generation that had many dreams and aspirations and was willing to pay the highest price to achieve its objectives. On every page of the book there are invaluable lessons for the future generations of Iran. This book is humbly dedicated to the blessed souls of all those who lost their lives in the process of their struggle.

CHAPTER ONE

Childhood and Early Life

The End of my Childhood

I was born in the year 1325/1946 into a poor family. The major image of my childhood or teenage life that still remains in my mind is the great poverty and hopelessness of the people of the city of Khonsar. When I was growing up, my father used to make wooden spoons and sell them. Afterwards, the nickel spoon came into the markets, and consequently my father lost his job.

He had no other skill, and so he decided to work as a laborer and a bricklayer. As we all know, the profession of bricklaying has its own advantages and disadvantages and is totally dependent upon the weather. So my father would remain jobless during the rainy seasons. This would put my family in the claws of acute poverty and suffering as life would become extremely hard for us.

Both my father and mother were in poor health. Because of our financial condition, we were unable to provide them with proper medical treatment. I was a witness to this situation, and so I had to carry the heavy burden of my family on my small shoulders. I was responsible for sweeping the house and keeping a small barn we had clean. Most of the residents here used to have sheep, hens, and roosters for their primary needs. We also had eight goats.

My older brother worked in a bakery on the outskirts of town. He used to work late at night, until ten or eleven pm. When he returned home from the bakery, he would bring some loaves of bread. My other brother and my father would eat early in the evening and go to bed. Since there was no electricity in the villages at that period of time, people went to bed early. I was a poor sleeper. My mother and I often stayed up late. Despite her illness my mother would read books and stories about the tragedies of "Imam Hossein" and [his half brother] Hazrat Abbas and would lament for hours.

My mother could read but was not able to write. This was because during those days, girls were not taught how to write but only how to read. My mother was able to properly read the holy Qur'an. At the sight of the tears gushing forth on my mother's cheeks, I would ask her, "Why are you crying, Mother? What is written in them that makes you cry whenever you read them?" She tried to help me understand and spoke in such a way that a child my age could relate to. "These books are about Imam Hossein, Ali Asghar, and Ali Akbar. They were oppressively martyred!"

I asked, "What kind of people were these?"

She said, "They were like the saints and clerics and were community and prayer leaders in the mosques. They were very good people. They encouraged people to do good deeds and discouraged them from doing bad things. It was because of this that their enemies killed them."

I asked, "Who were the people who were opposing them?"

She replied, "Shimr, Yazid, Mu'awiyah, and 'Ubeidullah ibn Ziyad were their enemies, and they are the ones who killed them."

I asked, "What kind of people were these enemies?"

She said, "They were like the Shah! They were like the gendarmes[1] and the soldiers of the Shah."

---

[1] The title "gendarme" was used by opposition groups and activists and denoted the most brutal among all security forces. The term "gendarmes" (zhandarm/gendarmarie) is originally a French term denoting the rural police force. In Iran, the gendarmarie was created in the 1920's and was responsible for maintaining peace and order in rural areas. Some of its main responsibilities included control of the border, fighting against drug-trafficking, checking and controlling the traffic, and maintaining peace and order in villages. In post-WWII Iran this term was used by political activists and opposition forces sarcastically to connote the secret police. After the 1979 Revolution the gendarmarie was merged with the police force and the Islamic Revolution committees (Shahbazi, 21).

In our township, there were no police. Maintaining law and order, settling disputes, and solving conflicts were carried out by the *gendarmerie*. Sometimes when the *gendarmes* came to the village to recruit men to serve in the army, they would enter peoples' homes, spend the night there, and cause a lot of disturbance.

Several times I witnessed that whenever the *gendarmes* came to settle a dispute between two people or between two families, they didn't deal with people with justice. They always supported the person who was richer and more powerful. They took the side of the rich and the powerful even on a village level. I was able to understand this despite my tender age and my childish comprehension. I saw that many times the people who were right were oppressed. These incidents that I witnessed closely created a deep hatred in my heart towards the *gendarmes*.

I concluded that if the leader of the *gendarmerie* was not a thief, then his *gendarmes* also would not be thieves. If the king and ruler of the country was not a thief, then his officers would also not be thieves. But since these people are connected like beads on a chain, then they are all the same.

I remember that once before I started attending school, my father asked me, "Suppose you go to school and learn and get educated. What kind of job would you like to have?"

Without hesitation I said, "I want to be a *gendarme*!" This was because I had not seen anyone as powerful as the *gendarmes*. Maybe if I had seen a policeman, I would have said that I would love to be a policeman.

My father asked, "Why do you want to become a *gendarme*?"

I said, "Because I have seen in photos that the soldiers were standing in line and the Shah walked in front of them and saluted them. I want to become a *gendarme* and hold my rifle this way [pointing at the target] and when the Shah walks past the soldiers, I will kill him!"

My understanding of the political and social structure of the country was based on my childish comprehension and the things that I had witnessed closely, and also on the times spent with my family and residents of the village, and on my childhood education. I used to go the mosque regularly during that time. I even became a prayer caller, even though I didn't pray myself. I took some rosaries and *muhr* (stones or small disks made of clay onto which the Shi'ites place their foreheads while prostrating in prayers) from the mosque to our home. My mother advised me to return them to the mosque and I did. My frequent visits to the mosque in my childhood created in me a love for religion and the clergy.

When I started school, since my knowledge was above that of my classmates, I was always appointed the class monitor. I remember that once or twice, when the bell rang for break, I remained behind in the classroom. I tore the pictures of the Shah from the books of my fellow classmates. Not only did I use to do this in school, but also anywhere that I saw the picture of the Shah and his family, I would tear them up with extreme hatred and throw them in the toilet.

I also disliked the children from wealthy families. And in case of disputes, I would always support the children from the poor families. These were the children whose economic situation was terrible. They always came to school in ragged uniforms. Some students did not even have socks in the cold, rainy, and snowy winter season.

As for the children from the wealthier families who had connections with people of power in our township, they always came to school well dressed and clean. During the cold winter season, they wore overcoats made of animal skin and leather boots. When I was the class monitor, I used to help the poor children and would never let the wealthy ones bully them. At times, I took pens and books from the wealthy children and give them to the poor ones.

Whenever I was appointed the class monitor, I had to report to the vice principal those who caused trouble or disturbed others in the class. As a punishment for this, he would hit their hands with a ruler or stick. Sometimes I wrote down the names of the wealthy children to report but would send another student to them to mediate. In return for a notebook I would not report him to the vice principal.

These wealthy children were normally cowards. They took my threats seriously, and so they would send me their exercise books. I gave those notebooks to the poor students. I continued this behavior in all the schools that I attended, and I helped many poor children. Sometimes I was very sensitive because wealthy students bragged about and showed off their clothes to the poor children. My sensitivity went to the point that I sometimes even cut their new clothes with a razorblade. I did this so that they would also taste how it felt to wear patched clothes. Although their parents could afford it, they would not buy them new clothes every month. So they had to wear patched clothes.

I was often punished because of this behavior, but since I was the youngest in our family, I had more freedom. Even though I received a lot of beatings from my father and older brother, I never surrendered to oppression. In fact, my hatred towards oppression, economic inequality in society, and social discrimination increased my desire for revenge day by day. Even whenever my brother beat me up, I never surrendered until I took revenge against him. I would at least hurl abuses or throw rocks at him and run away, but I just had to take revenge by all means anyway.

Later on when I grown up a little bit, I began to work in order to help my family and earn money for my school expenses. For instance during the season of harvesting potatoes I would go to the nearby farms to collect them. During the summer season, I used to work in the brick-burning factory and would earn fifteen or twenty *rials* per day.

The heat and miserable working conditions in the brick factory and witnessing the suffering of the people who worked there and their miserable condition hurt me and pained my heart. It further intensified my hatred toward the prevailing political and economic situation. At times I worked as a porter. I carried the bags of wool from a warehouse in the bazaar to another place and picked up and delivered the payment to the seller and earned one *tuman*. My family did not spend a penny on my education. I supported myself through all possible means. I remember that sometimes I bought some chicks, fed them, and raised them into hens. I would then take their eggs and sell them. By this sort of work I would make some money and buy books, notebooks, and pens.

Apart from this, sometimes I also worked odd jobs. Our neighborhood was divided into upper and lower districts. During our childhood, when the children of the upper and lower districts fought, they always came to me and sought my help. I fought on their behalf and protected them in return for two or three *tumans*. And the group that I fought for always won. The week after the defeated group offered me more money, I fought on their behalf! But in reality, I had no enmity with either of the two groups. The money that I made this way, I gave to the poor people and those who needed it. I didn't need nor did I like the money I earned as a mercenary. I made money for my school expenses by working as a porter.

Even though I was in good standing in school, I changed schools twice. I attended the Chahar Bagh and the Shah school. I used to challenge my teachers a lot. For example, if I saw a teacher beating a student, I cursed at him and ran away. Sometimes teachers expelled me from the class because I was disrespectful and lacked discipline. In the end, I was able to complete the sixth grade in the year 1339/1960. I loved and enjoyed learning and would have loved to continue my education, but because of our family situation and our economic condition it was not possible for me to go to school any longer. The prevailing environment in our town was not conducive to continuing my education.

Lost and Perplexed in Tehran

In 1339/1960, my first suit was made for me. I remember that we gave the material, the lining for the garment, and all other things needed to the tailor. This suit cost me fifty *tumans*, and I was reluctant to wear it lest it would get ruined. Therefore, I preserved it for a day that was to be very important to me. That day came soon enough, and it was the day of my trip to Tehran, or better said, to escape my depressing township where we wore the loose pants. We had heard that it is not possible to walk in loose breeches in Tehran. So the suit was the best thing to wear.

I decided to continue my education in Tehran even though I didn't have the bus fare to travel there, nor did I know anyone there. The only thing that I knew about Tehran was that I had heard people say that it was a big city and that everything could be found there. I was hopeful of studying at the university in Tehran and of serving my community and society in the future.

Because of the pressure from some family members who suggested that I should remain in Khonsar and work, save money, and then later go to Tehran, I remained there for almost a year after completing the sixth grade. I worked and saved around one hundred *tumans*.

One of my classmates, Zabihollah Janabi, who had gone to Tehran before me, used to write me letters. In one of the letters he had written that if I went to Tehran, he would help me and find a job for me. I wrote to him saying he should come to Khonsar on the eve of the *Eid* celebrations so that we could go back together to Tehran. He accepted and came to Khonsar. I took my birth certificate from the house and bought my ticket, and we began our journey to Tehran.

When we arrived in Qom, my friend and I had an argument. Our conflict began from there, and we did not talk to each other. I was thinking that when we arrived in Tehran, everything would change, and that he would welcome me to

11

his home. When we reached the bus station at Mawlavi Square in Tehran, he took his bag and went away. He did not even say goodbye to me. He thought that I was going to beg him. My pride did not allow me to ask him for help or to take me to his house.

I was left alone in a new and strange world not knowing anyone, where to go, or what to do. I neither had an address nor knew anybody or a decent place to stay. I waited at the garage for almost one hour. When I realized that the night was approaching, I had no other choice, so I started to walk aimlessly.

Up to that time, I had never left my hometown. I was an-xiously looking at the doors and walls of the city in a state of shock. Everything was so new to me. Fear and anxiety took me over. I was walking aimlessly as I took one step after the other, shaking with fear. I started remembering all the stories that I had heard about moral corruption in Tehran and the kidnapping of children, and worst of all, terrifying stories about Asghar Qatel, the notorious child-rapist and murderer. This only increased my fear.

I was suddenly standing in front of a grocery store. The store owner was an old man who appeared to be a good person. I had heard that old people are the nicest people. I stopped moving and stared at the old man. He thought that I was a thief. He yelled at me and threatened to hand me over to the police! Why did he think that I was a thief, as I was not even able to cross the road from one side to the other or even pass in between the moving cars? I suddenly lost control and burst into tears, and while I was weeping I said, "No Sir! I am not a thief! I swear by God that I am not a thief!"

The old man came out and said, "Then what are you doing here?"

I said, "I have lost my mother and father." (Of course this was not the case).

He asked, "Where have you lost them?"

I said, "We came to the garage. I lost them there."

He said, "Then sit down on this chair. They might come back and find you here."

I thought that it was better for me to stay there. This would cause the old man to sympathize with me and perhaps take me to his home. I thought that he would not let me remain out at night lest someone come and cut off my head!! In Khonsar, whenever I thought of Tehran, the elders used to frighten us about Asghar Qatel,[2] child-traffickers, and so on.

I stayed for one hour in that grocery store but nothing happened. No one even came after me. Of course nothing was to happen and no one was to come. During that one hour, a lot of thoughts came to my mind. I was so anxious and confused. I suddenly remembered that my father's cousin lived in Tehran, and his home was located in Seyyed Malik Khatun and Mesgar Abad. He had once sent a letter to my father, and I had memorized his address. I pressured my mind until finally I remem-

---

[2] The discovery of three naked and beheaded bodies in the four walls of Shotorkhan from the ruins of Bisim Najafabad (one of the old areas of Tehran) on Sunday, 10-10-1312/12-30-1933, shocked the police headquarters and the Criminal Investigation Department in Tehran. The search for the killer by the Criminal Investigation Department did not produce any results, but instead another body in the surroundings of Jalaliyeh square (Laleh Park) and another beheaded body in Pakand Qanat Aminabad were found. The spread of this news caused great shock to the people of Tehran. Finally, two months after the discovery of the first bodies, the police suspected one person. His occupation was selling a popular sweet known as *bamiyeh* and he was famous under the name of Asghar Bamiyeh. The investigation of this issue led to the discovery of other crimes by him in Tehran and Baghdad. It turned out that he was a certain 'Ali Asghar Burujerdi (afterward known as Asghar Qatil (the Murderer), the son of Ali Mirza, a forty-year-old resident of Burujerd, who confessed to the killing of eight people in Tehran and twenty-nine people in Baghdad and also sodomizing most of the victims. The spread of the news resulted in an uproar from the people of Tehran. Finally, Asghar Qatil was hanged on Wednesday, 6-4-1313/6-24-1934 in the famous Tupkhaneh Square across the Tehran Police Headquarters. This marked the end of the terror of the residents of Tehran. But his name and crimes have not been forgotten in the memories of the people of Tehran. See Seifi Qomi Tafrishi, 148–154.

bered the address. I at once got up and said, "I just remembered!"

The old man came to me and asked, "What has happened?"

I said, "I remembered the address of my father and mother's relatives. If they don't find me, I shall go to that address."

The old man placed his hand on my head and kindly thanked God. He therefore hired a three-cycle motorbike for me, a poor-man's taxi, for two *tumans*, which I paid. He instructed the driver to get me to the address and get a receipt for the old man after dropping me at my destination. We rode for approximately one hour in Mesgar Abad until we finally found my relative's house. I wrote the receipt for the rider and gave it to him. My father's cousin was shocked to see me there. He asked, "How have you found this place?! What are you doing here?!"

I said, "My father told me to come to Tehran, and he will also come after two days."

I lied this way because they would not have accepted me without my father or his permission. After some days when my father did not arrive, I told them the truth, that I had come alone and that my parents were not aware of this, and that I wanted to work in Tehran. Later on, I wrote a letter to my father. I informed him that I was in Tehran and that he should not worry about me.

It took me almost one month to learn how to walk around in Tehran. I finally learned how to cross the roads. Since I had not yet known the roads, I used to mark them with a piece of chalk in order not to lose my way.

The first job that I was able to find for myself was an apprenticeship in a blacksmith shop where they made metal windows and doors. It was located in Samangan in northwest Tehran. I was supposed to earn fifteen *rials* a day. Eight of that would be spent on the bus fare while the remaining seven would be spent on food. Nothing remained at all to save. After two or three weeks, I realized that the job did not really meet my needs. My earnings and expenditures were not proportionate. So I decided to quit that job. Interestingly enough, even though the owner of the shop was one of my relatives, he did not pay me any wages for those two or three weeks. He promised that if I continued to work he would pay me. I accepted but again he never paid me for that period either.

After leaving that place, I worked at a stationery and bookbinding shop where I earned twenty-five *riyals* per day. In my former job, I had to take four buses to get to work, but for my new job, I only had to take two buses to reach the bazaar. I also saved four *riyals*. Later I learned that I could walk from the bazaar to the end of the road and save my fare. Of course I never considered the wear and tear on my shoes and the waste of my time! I remained in the bazaar and worked very hard. My work improved a lot and my employer was also pleased with me and my work. Every once in a while he added five *riyals* to my wages until it reached five *tumans* per day.

At this point, I rented a small room near that place in Atabak Avenue. This room was really small and was hardly the size of a blanket.

A year later, in 1341/1962, my parents came to Tehran, but I didn't want to live with them again because I was aware that living with them would cause restrictions on my life. They would probably prevent me from doing certain jobs. In spite of all this, the persistence of my father and mother, their crying and begging me to stay, I decided to live with them but could not stand them more than one year.

During this period, I had a lot of conflicts with them, and at times they even locked me out of the house at night. My older brother, 'Ali, was really against me. At this time, I worked in the shop of Mr. Hossein Mosaddeqi[3] selling papers.

---

[3] Hossein Mosaddeqi worked in a paper factory in Tehran. In 1341/1962, he struggled against a bill in Iranian parliament that aimed at the establishment of Provincial assemblies. Around fifteen days after the revolt of the 15th of Khordad, 1342/June 5, 1963, he was arrested for cooperating with

My brother out of ignorance and gullibility said, "This Mosaddeqi is that same Mosaddeqi of the oil movement. I will go to police headquarters and report that you are working for him so that you can be arrested."

Later on my parents and brother chased me away from the house. As time went by, my conflict with them intensified even further. This went on until my mother passed away in the year 1343/1964. Before the fortieth day after her burial I left the house. From that time on I lived alone and around the Tehran bazaar until 1349/1970.

My Entry into Political Activity

Working in the environment of the bazaar was an invaluable opportunity for me. Every day I learned something new about society, the government, and the world around me. Dealing with different people from different social classes enabled me to learn more about people. It is not possible for one to stay in the bazaar and remain indifferent to what is happening around there. Moreover, it is impossible to witness problems and afflictions of people and remain indifferent. The bazaar provided such an opportunity for me. It increased my sensitivity towards the political and socio-economic conditions of the people and the government. My sensitivity was manifested for the first time in 1341/1962. This was the time when Imam Khomeini, because of his opposition to the bill of the provincial assemblies,[4] took the lead in fighting against the Shah.

---

the clerics and printing and distributing the declarations. He was again arrested in Isfand 1343/March 2, 1964 for his membership in the Islamic Coalition Party. During his last day in prison, he confessed to have had connections with Ayatullah Khomeini and of being in charge of printing his letters and declarations. Finally, on the 1st of Mordad, 1350/July 23, 1971, he passed away from heart failure. See Seyyid Asadollah Lajevardi, pp. 224–225.

[4] The bill of the Provincial Assemblies was presented to the parliament and was approved on the 14th of Mehr 1341/October 6, 1962 by Amir Asadollah Alam (Prime Minister) in the absence of the majority deputies in the

Of course a year before that and after the death of Ayatullah Burujerdi, in many of religious ceremonies, the name of Imam Khomeini was being mentioned as a Source of Emulation (*marja'*) and chief jurist. This was while the Shah tried to move the center of gravity from Qom to Najaf by sending letters of condolences to Ayatullah Hakim and recognizing him as the Source of Emulation after Burujerdi.

During those days, other people like Ayatullah Kho'i and Shahrudi were favorite candidates for the position of *marja'*. When I was in Khonsar, I asked the prayer leader of the mosque, "After the demise of Ayatullah Burujerdi, who shall be the Source of Emulation?"

He said, "Shaykh Mohammad 'Ali Araki. And as long as he is alive, no one else can be the chief jurist." But the only person who was not seriously considered was Araki. Imam Khomeini did not take any step to fill the position because he had not even written a treatise (*risaleh-ye 'amaliyyeh*) yet. Later on when I was in the bazaar and I was working for Hossein Mosaddeqi, he was the first person to volunteer to publish the treatise by Imam Khomeini. Before this, he did it for Ayatullah Burujerdi.

By becoming involved in political activity, I became very interested in getting more involved in the struggle. I was trying to find something to please and calm down my restless

---

National Assembly. According to Article 1 of this bill, being a Muslim was removed from the conditions for election to the parliament, and Article 2 stipulated that elected members could take an oath of allegiance to the state using their religious books, and Article 3 gave women the right to vote for and be elected for membership in the parliament. After that, the news of the approval of the bill was published in the magazines on the 16th of Mehr, 1341/October 6, 1962. Strong opposition were expressed against this bill, especially from the clerical community. Ayatullah Khomeini was the leader of this opposition on behalf of the clergy. Soon, the student members of the Freedom Movement of Iran also joined the opposition and carried on extensive demonstrations. All this pressure and opposition forced the regime to surrender. On Saturday, the 10th of Azar/December 1, 1962, Asadollah Alam announced the cancelation of the bill.

soul and find peace. The bazaar was one of the most important centers of the activities of the Islamic Coalition Party. I was able to join this organization through my many friends like Mir Hashimi and Lashkari.

After the success in killing the bill for the provincial assemblies, Imam Khomeini ordered the creation of a single organization from many small religious groups in Tehran. He said, "It is a must for us to have an organization. People should come together and should not break up. If people do not make any drastic political move for ten years, but after ten years they do something important, it is better than making yourselves busy with minor tasks. You should neither be fooled by politicians or get close to them. You should first of all train properly and prepare yourself before entering the political arena." What he was alluding to was the National Front and people of similar political persuasion.

Therefore the Islamic Coalition Party began some activities and started circulating a pamphlet called "Resurrection" (Bi'sat),[5] and ideological issues were discussed in it. A number of clergy cooperated with them, for instance Morteza Mutahhari and Seyyed 'Ali Shahcheraghi.[6] As I was in the ba-

---

[5] Shahid Mahdi Iraqi in his own memoirs wrote, "From the beginning of the movement against the Bill the clergy demonstrated against it in Tehran. There were three groups that worked together. Two group were religious and a third group was composed of the youth in Isfahan in the bazaar, commonly known as 'the boys of Isfahan.' All three groups were in contact with Ayatullah Khomeini from the beginning of his uprising. As the opposition intensified they began to compete with one another. According to the advice of the late Haj Sadiq Amani, for the purpose of reducing the damages of competition amongst groups, they formed a coalition and sought Khomeini's approval. He agreed to support them. When we visited Imam Khomeini, I explained the matter to him. Whoever went to seek his opinion, he would say that Muslims need to be organized, for without organization nothing can be accomplished." See Iraqi, 165–166.

[6] The publication of the United Assembly was called "Bi'sat/Resurrection." It was prepared and published by a group of clerics in Qom who were all members of the coalition. It played a major role in informing people of the prevailing political conditions. The first issue of Bi'sat was published in the

zaar, I also joined the Islamic Coalition Party and participated in their meetings.

My First Political Experience: Islamic Coalition Party

By joining the Islamic Coalition Party (*Hay'at-i Mu'talifah*), I began to participate in their meetings. In those meetings, people like Hajj Sadiq Amani,[7] Shahcheraghi, and Seyyed Taghi Khamushi[8] often participated and gave talks.

---

month of Rajab 1383 (Aban and Azar 1342/December 1963). See Islamic Coalition Party, *Badamchiyan and others*, p. 285.

[7] Seyyid 'Ali Shahcheragi, who was the prayer leader of the congregation at the Hosseiniyah Irshad, passed away in the month of Khordad, 1342/June 1963.

[8] Mohammad Sadiq Amani Hamadani was born in the year 1309/1930 in Tehran in an old and traditional neighborhood near the bazaar of Tehran called Pachnar. His father, Shaykh Ahmad, was a jurist, scholar, and businessman in Tehran. After completing his school, Mohammad Sadiq began working together with his father in the bazaar. In the meantime he began studying Islamic teachings (Arabic language, and principles of Islamic laws) in a seminary in Tehran. Politically he was very much influenced by the teachings of Nawab Safavi, the founder and leader of the Fidayan-i-Islam organization. After the oil industry was nationalized in 1952, he formed a Shi'ite group together with his friends (Mohammad Sadiq Islami and Hossein Rahmani), to initiate religious propagation. The centers of the religious propagation of Sadiq Amani were the mosques of Shaykh 'Ali and Larzadeh. Likewise, in the year 1341/1962, they made an alliance with the Islamic Coalition Party under the stewardship of Amani in the mosque of Shaykh 'Ali, and some members from Isfahan. Sadiq Amani was one of the twelve-member committee of the Islamic Coalition Party. He had a close relationship with Imam Khomeini. By Khomeini's orders, he was very active in the movement against the Provincial Assemblies. He played a major role in organizing demonstrations on the day of the tenth day of Muharram ('Ashura and the uprising in 15th of Khordad, 1342/June 5, 1963. Most of the poems that were recited on this day were composed by him.

After the uprising of that year, Amani, together with some of his friends from the Islamic Coalition Party, formed the military wing of the Party. This wing managed to assassinate Hasan 'Ali Mansur (then prime minister) in the month of Bahman, 1343/January 1965.

The most important and effective move of the Islamic Coalition Party was the observance of the mourning during the holy month of Muharram in (1383H/Khordad 1342Sh/ June 1963). The police attacked the Faiziyeh Seminary in Qom where the commemoration of the martyrdom of Imam Hossein and his household was underway under the guidance of the then Hujjat al-Islam, Ruhullah Khomeini. During those ceremonies several speakers delivered sermons and discussed the atrocities of the regime. On the 10th day of Muharram ('Ashura) (13th of the month of Khordad, 1342/June 3, 1963) the Islamic Coalition Party openly expressed opposition to the ruling regime of the Shah.

The demonstration on the day of 'Ashura started from the Mosque of Abulfath.[9] Members of the party were busy overseeing and guiding the demonstrators. They uttered symbolic slogans in relation to the uprising of Imam Hossein, but in reality directing them against the ruling regime. In organizing and leading the demonstration, Hajj Sadiq Amani and Hajj Mahdi 'Araghi[10] played a leading role. I even remember that Hajj Mahdi presented a very interesting lecture before the entrance gate of the University of Tehran. We were handing out leaflets to people during the course of the demonstration.

The result of that demonstration was very important. The Shah's regime was really angered by the movement and the courage of the people. As a result, government agents attacked some religious centers during the night and the next

---

Following this assassination, the assassination team, composed of Mohammad Bukhara'i, Amani, Harandi, Niknezhad and a large number of the group members, were arrested. These four people were sentenced to death by the court. Their sentence was carried out on the 26th of Khordad, 1344/June 16, 1965.

[9] Hajj Seyyid Taqi Khamushi was a businessman in the bazaar and a political activist. He started his political activity against the Shah's regime during the later years of the 1340's/1960's and attended the meetings of Shahid Sadiq Amani.

[10] The mosque of Hajj Abolfat'h is located near Qiyam Square (formerly Shah Square).

day. They arrested a number of the religious scholars who they felt were the propagators of these movements. On the 15th of the month of Khordad, Imam Khomeini was also arrested in the morning in the city of Qom. During that first hour, this news spread to the big cities, and people showed their outrage and opposition to the arrest of these people.

In the city of Tehran, extensive demonstrations took place and turned into a major crisis. The forces of the Shah intervened, and this resulted in a bloody confrontation with the people. I was among the protesters on Shahbaz Avenue (now 17 Shahrivar). I confronted the forces, and a bullet passed by my ear. On that day, we went to different places—Buzar-jumehri (15 Khordad), the bazaar, Khorasan Square, Arak Square, and so on.

In Khorasan Square, there was a truck carrying bricks. Together with three to four people, I stopped the vehicle. We started unloading the bricks onto the road so that people could use them for self-defense if they were attacked. We did this up to Fawziyeh Aquare (now Imam Hossein Square). In this square, the soldiers were present. I managed a soldier's button from him. He followed me with his rifle pointed at me. I lost one of my shoes on the way but still continued to run. Later on when I got tired, I removed the other shoe, threw it away, and continued running barefoot.

When the regime observed people's reaction to what it had done to Mr. Khomeini, it became apprehensive, and perhaps was regretful for doing things that harmed Khomeini. Some of the clerics and religious scholars took advantage of this situation to officially recognize him as the Source of Emulation (*marja'*) so that the regime could not do anything against him.

These demonstration were carried out to warn the regime and prevent it from harming Imam Khomeini.[11] Perhaps

---

[11] Mohammad Mahdi Haj Ibrahim Iraqi (known as Haj Mahdi Iraqi) was born in the year 1309/1930 in the Pachnar area of Tehran. He became a member of the Fadayan Islam at the age of sixteen. He was among the fif-

21

we may say that apart from the clerics who had come from different cities to take refuge in Tehran, it was the members of the Islamic Coalition Party who struggled day and night for the release of Imam Khomeini from prison.

Our participation in these activities increased my courage and wisdom immensely. When General Charles De Gaulle came to Iran,[12] we were present when they escorted him to the

---

ty-three people imprisoned in the Qasr prison because of the arrest of Navab Safavi. He participated in the uprising of the 15th of Khordad, 1342/June 5, 1963. In the month of Bahman, 1343/November 1964, he was sentenced to death for collaborating in Hasan 'Ali Mansur's assassination. Before his execution, the court reduced his sentence by one degree to life imprisonment. He played the role of a father to the Muslim prisoners and used all his wealth outside prison in helping the prisoners and their families. Iraqi was one of the people who had strong faith in the People's Mujahidin Khalq Organization (MKO). He was among the founders of the "Hanifnezhad, Muhsin and Badi'zadegan" group, which constituted the original core of the MK organization and viewed them as free from deviation. However, he stopped supporting them after the organization turned Marxist. Iraqi was forgiven in the month of Bahman, 1355/November 1976, and was freed from prison. Soon he joined the Islamic opposition groups. In the second half of the year 1357/1978, he joined the convoy of Helpers of Imam Khomeini in Nufal Lushatu and returned to Iran in the company of the Ayatullah. After the victory of the Revolution, Haj Mahdi Iraqi was given a position in the Islamic Republican Party of Iran. He was the person in charge of the Qasr prison for some time. He was later chosen as a member of the Central Council and Director of the Mostazafan Foundation of Islamic Revolution (Foundation for the Downtrodden and the Poor). He also was the head of the finance office of the daily Keihan newspaper. He was assassinated by the Furqan group on the 4th of Shahrivar, 1358/August 26, 1979. Imam Khomeini made a powerful statement on his death and said, "He had to be martyred, because dying in bed was too low for him." Iraqi, 15–16; *Cheshm Andaz Iran*, number 30, 15–16

[12] There was no such article in the constitutional laws of Iran and the other civil and penal laws to prevent such a decision. It was only during the premiership of Mosaddeq that, as a result of insulting articles and statements about Ayatullah Burujerdi, a supplementary law was ratified in the parliament. According to that Supplement, those who offended the Supreme Source of Emmulation (the *marja'*) were to be condemned to one month to three years in prison. On 10-5-1334/August 2, 1955 another article was added to that supplement (Article 17) whereby writing or quoting

22

Golestan Palace. One of our comrades was among the spectators and threw a stone towards the General and the Shah, which hit their carriage. The officers arrested a tall man, but he was quite strong and started beating and kicking him. When my friend saw this scene, he decided to run away. He disappeared in the crowd.

Political Inspiration

When Imam Khomeini was released from prison in the month of Farvardin 1343/March 1964, his supporters from all walk of life went to visit him. We also went to visit him.

During those days, often conflicts appeared between students of seminaries (*hawzah*) and those who attended universities. Some of the university students criticized the clerics and labeled them as backward and reactionary. The clerics also condemned university students as irresponsible intellectuals, careless, and anti-religion. These differences were steered by the SAVAK officials, and every once in a while these conflicts intensified.

During one of our meetings with Imam Khomeini in Qom, a number of the university students also came to see him. One of the younger clerics went to Imam Khomeini and told him, "This is the best chance for you to advise these people."

an offensive statement against the *marja'* was punishable by one to three years behind bars for the writer and the head of the newspaper. In the past, the struggle of the high-ranking members of the clergy, such as Ayatullah Hossein Ali Montazeri, to establish Ayatullah Khomeini as the Source of Emulation was expressed in traditional style and on the basis of customary laws. Such verdicts were violated when Shaykh Fazlullah Noori was executed by the Constitutionalists. Some sources argue that based on article 2 of the supplementary constitutional law, the government could not execute a Source of Emulation. However, that article in fact granted only a supervisory role to five qualified jurists to guarantee that laws ratified by the parliament would be—*in principle*—in harmony with Islamic law. See *Kuhestani Nejad*, pp. 424 and 721; and Hosseiniyan, p. 338.

23

Imam Khomeini said, "I do not see anything wrong in them that would need me to advise them."

That person insisted again, "No, sir. This is the best chance. If you say something now, your words will have a great impact on them."

Imam Khomeini asked, "What should I say to them?"

That person answered, "Tell them not to shave their beards!?"

Imam Khomeini looked sternly at that person, kept quiet, and didn't say a word. Contrary to the request from that mulla, Imam Khomeini was very friendly and kind to the university students. It was this kind of behavior that greatly reduced the gap between these two groups of students.

Witnessing this episode inspired a kind of new energy in me. Together with some of my friends, Amir Lashkari and Ahmad Karrubi,[13] I formed a new organization. We named it "The National Front for the Liberation of Iran." Later on we issued declarations in the name of different organizations, such as "The Islamic Students of the University of Tehran" and in the name of other universities. We endorsed and supported the clergy's activities, while at the same time acknowledging and supporting university students in their struggle. If a seminary student was arrested in Qom, we issued a declaration in the name of the students and expressed our support for him. Similarly, if a conflict occurred with the police at the university, we supported the students on behalf of the seminary students.

Even if the leftist university students were attacked, we were not concerned about their ideologies. We used the occasion to issue a declaration. In this way, we wanted to create a sense of comradery and cordial relations between these two groups of students. This situation continued until the year

---

[13] On 24 Mehr, 1342/October 17, 1963 Tehran newspapers reported that General [Charles] de Gaulle, the president of the Republic of France, arrived in Tehran for a four-day visit.

1350/1971 and we regularly issued declarations on important events under a pseudonym or no name at all.

In the year 1343/1964 Hasan Ali Mansur was assassinated by member of the Islamic Coalition Party. This incident took place after the exile of Imam Khomeini to Turkey in the month of Aban/October and was aimed at reflecting the widespread resentment and popular anger towards the regime. But it created a backlash. Members of the Islamic Coalition Party were shortsighted and did not know well the society in which they lived. This was a serious criticism at the time, but perhaps any other group in their position would have acted the same way and done the same thing (i.e. assassinate Mansur) and such action would have been praised as revolutionary. The Coalition argued that if they fought against the Shah and killed him, there was no one to replace him. This would cause chaos in the country, and lives would be lost. But if they managed to kill the people around the Shah who served him, this would wake him up and would persuade him to reform his system. It was because of this that some of the prominent people in the regime, such as Assadullah 'Alam, Hasan Ali Mansur, Doctor Manuchehr Iqbal, and Hasan Sharif Imami were identified as candidates for assassination.

At that time, the Islamic Coalition Party had about 2000–3000 members, but they did not have a well-organized and cohesive organization. Even though these people were faithful Muslims and fighters, they lacked organizational skills. They were totally unaware of the history or anti-colonial and liberation movements in different countries of the world. Their party structure was fragile, and their communication with each other was vulnerable. For example, they did not know that they should have used fictitious names.[14] Because of

---

[14] Ahmad Karrubi (b.1327/1948). He was identified by one of the SAVAK sources for writing and distributing declarations against the coming of the American investors in Iran. On the 22nd of Ordibehesht, 1349/May 12, 1970 together with Hamid Ukhuvvat he was arrested with 4000 copies of the declarations and was sentenced to six years in prison. When Karrubi was

this, when they assassinated Mansur, they were easily identified and arrested because of their naiveté.

They had agreed that Bukhara'i would stand in front of the parliament building and Niknezhad at the front door of the Sepahsalar Mosque (now Shahid Mutahhari). It was planned that after the assassination, Niknezhad should divert the attention of police officers by shooting in the air in front of the mosque so that Bukhara'i would get a chance to escape. However, Bukhara'i was arrested at the Zhaleh Square (now Mujahideen-i Islam). He was taken to police station number nine. He was tortured very much, but he never confessed to anything. After that, his picture was published in the newspapers. Since the Islamic Coalition Party functioned as a religious group and not political, the police went to the family of Bukhara'i and told them that their son had been arrested for possession and use of drugs and especially heroin. His family obviously did not accept the charges, as they knew their son well and were certain that he would not do such things. They told the police that he was always in the company of good people and prayed even the supererogatory night prayers. They also said that he was also friends with religious scholars, for example Hajj Sadiq Amani. From that time on, Hajj Sadiq's telephone was tapped. When Hajj Sadiq called his brother to bring him his sack at a certain place, police agents also went to that place and arrested him. The rest of the members were also arrested in this way. They were arrested so easily because they behaved like a simple religious group and not an organiza-

---

transferred to a prison in Mashhad, he was with Asgar Awladi and Lajevardi. In the prison report of the year 1350/1971, he was described as a religious person, very intelligent, knowledgeable, and a member of the MK. Karrubi's prison term was to end on the 18th of Farvardin, 1355/April 6, 1976 but was extended to the 29th of Isfand, 1355/March 20, 1977 because to his activities inside the prison. After his freeing from prison, he resumed his studies. After the victory of the Islamic revolution, he worked for some time with the Furqan group and was dispatched to Khamseh, where he was killed in the street in an encounter with the police. See Lajevardi, 107.

tion.[15] Among the six people arrested, Sadiq Amani, Moham-mad Bukhara'i, Morteza Niknezhad and Reza Saffar Harandi were given death penalties. The sentences of Mahdi Iraqi and Hashim Amani were reduced by one degree, and they were thus given life imprisonment.

[Abul Fazl] Heidari, Abbas Mudarresi Far, Asgar Aw-ladi, and Kalafchi were also handed life imprisonment. Kalaf-chi did not have a good political disposition, and after four or five years in prison, he was released. Ahmad Shahab (Shah Bodaghlu) was also given a ten-year jail term. After that, the remaining members of the Coalition stopped their armed activ-ities.

Their words and deeds of the members of the Islamic Coalition Party were not in harmony with the general condi-tion of the society and people. They spoke about morality and the fundamentals of religion publicly, and in my opinion, they were a little dogmatic and prejudiced. One of their fundamen-tal rules was that their members were supposed to wear collar-less shirts like those of the clergy. Their younger members were not allowed to go on the streets of northern Tehran lest they be exposed to women who had no proper clothing or *hi-jab*.

Mansur assassination was planned and carried out by the military wing of the Coalition. It would have been impos-sible to have the likes of Hajj Sadiq Amani and others carry out such tasks, as they were religious people and models of etiquette. They were also physically weak. Members of the group had not been trained for that kind of operations, nor were they mentally prepared for such tasks. It was for these reasons that when these people were arrested and a number of them executed or imprisoned, the rest of them did not have the courage to carry on, and so the Islamic Coalition Party fell apart. Those who remained in the Coalition occupied them-

---

[15] Shahid Seyyid 'Ali Andarzgu was one of the few members of the Islamic Coalition Party who, after the assassination of Mansur, changed his name and appearance in order to remain safe from the SAVAK.

27

selves with cultural duties and social services. People like Bahonar and Raja'i ventured into establishing and directing cultural centers while some entered the business world. A number of them returned to their past normal lives. Some of them engaged in building schools and hospitals and helping the orphans. Others continued to offer material support to the groups and organizations fighting the Shah, such as the MKO and Hizbul'lah. Until the end of their lives they did not get involved in political activity directly but offered support to active groups from a safe distance. It was in this situation that a group such as the Islamic Coalition Party ceased to exist until the end of the Shah's regime.

Historical Pictures

I do not remember whether it was after the execution of Mansur's assassins or in the middle of their trial by the military court that I visited a friend who then served at the military court. I do not remember his name now. I asked him if he could bring me the pictures taken at the military court that condemned to death Mansur's assassins. He accepted and later on brought me four or five pictures from the court. I took copies of those photos and then had them duplicated in a print shop and returned the original copies to my friend. I put copies of those pictures in an envelope and gave it to Assadullah Badamchiyan. He sold carpets in his father's store in the bazaar. I was not exactly sure whether he had been arrested or not. I used this as an excuse just to find out how the situation was.

I went to his father's store two or three times. His father (Hajj Mohammad Baqir) was alone at the shop, and Asadullah was not there. I put the pictures in an envelope, sealed it, and decided to give it to his father. I went to the store, and after greeting him, I asked for Asadullah. He asked me what I wanted from him, and I simply said that I needed to see him.

He said, "I do not know when he will return to the store." I gave him the envelope with pictures in it and asked him to give it to Assadullah. He asked me what was in the envelope, and I said that I did not know. I said that it was given to me by my friend to hand over to Asadullah. He took the envelope and checked its weight. He became suspicious. He got angry and started cussing at me: "Hey you son of a——! Get out of here and get lost, and may I never see you again. You have destroyed my son's life." I got up and quickly left the place. After that, I never asked again whether Assadullah Badamchiyan received the pictures or not.

Shaykh Gholam Hossein Ja'fari Hamadani

For a decade between 1340 and 1350/1961 and 1971, the Grand Mosque in the bazaar was one of the main centers of political activities. Since I was working at the bazaar, I went there often. There was a certain Shaykh Gholam Hossein Ja'fari Hamadani, who functioned as the congregational prayer leader (*imam*) in this mosque.[16] He was a brave man and openly preached against the Shah's regime. He was afraid neither of SAVAK, nor of the police and agents of the regime. He performed *istikhara*[17] about whether to talk or not. He was not a

---

[16] Hajj Mahdi Iraqi has a different narration in relation to the arrest of the people who assassinated Mansur, but he rendered valid the view of Mr. Ezzat Shahi. Refer to Mahdi Iraqi, *Nagufteha* (the untold memoirs), Tehran, Resa, 1370/1991.

[17] The practice of consulting the Qur'an when one wants to make an important decision. Ayatullah Gholam Hossein Ja'fari Hamadani was born in the year 1285/1906 in the village of Shahanejarin on the outskirts of Hamadan to a religious family. At the age of twelve, he went to Hamadan for religious studies. In the year 1305/1926, he went to Qom to continue his education. The same year, he went to Najaf and studied for twenty years under such prominent scholars as Seyyid Abul Hasan Isfahani, Mirza Abul Hasan Meshkini, Mr. Ziya Iraqi, Sheikh Mohammad Hossein Kompani, Mirza Ahmad Hossein Nai'ini, and others. He returned to Iran in the year 1327/1948 and settled in Tehran. He began his political activities after Imam Khomeini was sent into exile. He offered sermons against the regime

29

good orator but spoke his mind freely. I was one of his supporters and admirers. A lot of resistant fighters and clerics listened to his sermons. I became so close to him that he would count me as his first child, even though he had two sons who were among my close friends. In 1342–1343/1963–1964 a number of prominent clergy such as Rabani Amlashi, Hashimi Rasfanjani, Shaykh Hasan Tahiri Isfahani, and Morwarid delivered sermons in that mosque and were all arrested. It was here that I became acquainted with these politically active members of the clergy. It was by accident that during that time I found a copy of the magazine *Khandaniha* that was published under the allied occupation of Iran during World War II. In that issue of the journal there was a sermon delivered by Mohammad Reza Pahlavi in which he praised and glorified the clergy. He said, "The Iranian clergy have always defended the independence of the country, and whenever the country would be threatened in the future, it would be the clergy that would save it. And now as always I appeal to the *'ulama* to guide and give advice to government officials and political authorities."

I took a copy of the Shah's sermon and gave it to Shaykh Ja'fari. He read it and found it interesting. During the holy month of Ramadan and especially from the nineteenth to the twenty-third day, the officers came freely to the mosques. On the nineteenth day, the Shaykh gave a sermon and ad-

---

of the Shah in the sanctuary of the major mosque in the bazaar. He was arrested and imprisoned for some months in the Ghezel Ghal'ah prison until Ayatullah Hakim mediated for his freedom. Again he continued with his harsh criticism of the regime until he was arrested and imprisoned again. During celebrations to commemorate the 2500-year anniversary of Persian monarchy, Ayatullah Ja'afari ridiculed the famous phrase that the Shah had made, "Cyrus! Sleep in Peace, because we are awake." He was arrested for the third time and sent into exile to Iraq. He returned after six months and continued with his sermons at the major mosque of the bazaar. He was taken to the SAVAK headquarters several times until the victory of the Islamic Revolution. Ayatullah Ja'fari Hamadani was diagnosed with heart failure in the year 1356/1977. He lived with this disease for years until he passed away in the year 1373/1994.

dressed colonel Tahiri and other government agents present in the mosque and said, "To the officers of the regime, you should bring the tape recorders on the twenty-first day because I have something very important to say then. You should record the sermon from beginning to end and take it to your superiors to listen to."

One day, I was in the mosque and listening to Shaykh Ja'fari's sermon. It was clear that there were some SAVAK agents among the people. Suddenly a cat entered through the window into the mosque. The Shaykh said, "Give way to the cat so that it can go out of the mosque. The devil can come in any shape. Since they are devils, it is possible that the SAVAK have come into the mosque in the shape of a cat. So let it get out." The people laughed aloud and let the cat out of the mosque.

The SAVAK agents were not a match for Shaykh Ja'fari. They did not know what to do with him. They called him "the mad Shaykh"! This was because he would openly speak against the Shah. Once General Moqaddam[18] phoned him and said, "O Shaykh! It is better for you to use your telephone and pen to propagate Islam. You should write letters and give advice, and if you need our help for any purpose, we are ready to assist you. You should write essays, start a magazine, and we shall provide the money for that. Why are you tiring yourself by giving sermons?"

Shaykh Ja'fari revealed the conversation and the General's advice at the mosque and added that he had called the General the same night and said to him, "May God's curse be upon that pen, hand, and ear. May that person who wants to propagate the religion by use of telephone become dumb and

---

[18] General Nasir Alavi Moghaddam was a graduate of the officer's college in France. He was the head of the third wing of the SAVAK headquarters (1342–1350/1963–1971) and the head of the Army Intelligence (1350–1357). He was also the last director of the SAVAK to be arrested after the victory of the Islamic Revolution and was sentenced to death.

deaf! I am a not person to do these things; I will do my own duty."[19]

On the twenty-first day, he entered the mosque with a bundle in his arms. When he reached the pulpit, he said, "If we want to swim, we can't help but get wet. That is why I brought along with me my shroud, because I want to say things that may not please the regime and they might want to kill me." He then bared his chest and said, "If you want to shoot me, shoot here so that I can at least die in this mosque. I have an obligation to fulfill the duty that the Shah asked me to perform. This is because I am afraid that on the Day of Judgment, the Shah shall question me. So I will give my advice now."

The Shaykh started to read the Shah's sermon and said, "When the Shah said these words, *he had a silk handkerchief in his hand.*[20] During those days, he was weak. He neither had

---

[19] In an interview with the Islamic Seminary School magazine Ayatullah Gholam Hossein Ja'fari stated that, "After my last sermon when I was arrested, colonel Afzali wanted to take me to Nasiri, the head of the SAVAK. I told him, that he better not take me to Nasiri because I have heard that he is a harsh person. It is probable that he would offend me. I am not able to control my anger and may say something that would make him angry and do something that may not be good for you and your position. They left me in the car and discussed the matter with Nasiri. He also agreed and they took me to Qizil Qal'ah prison. After some days, I was taken to the office of Muqadam, who was General Nasiri's deputy. He was a kind person. He asked me if I was opposing the Shah, and then began to give me advice and added that he would give me a monthly salary granted that I go to my house and preach through the telephone! He did not ask me to support the regime but only to stop opposing it. I was so annoyed by this talk and I told him to find someone else to do that as I will carry on with my work. He was wondering why I was angry and I told him that he offended me. He thought that we were opposing the regime for worldly gain? *Hauzeh*, the 9th year, number 52, 40–41

[20] This is a metaphoric expression denoting a person flattering and buttering up another person. During the premiership of Amir Abbas Huvayda, a lot of expensive and pompous celebrations were held. These included the art festivals in Shiraz, and the coronation ceremony and the celebrations to mark the 2500th year of Persian monarchy in the Aban, 1346/October 1965.

tanks nor an army or the support of America. But now he has power. He has an army, tanks and guns, and the support of America. So [the Shah] thinks that the *'ulama* have no more roles to play and they have to shut up. Imam Khomeini must be sent into exile. Un-Islamic or even anti-Islamic laws should be enforced. My Lord, be my witness that I have accomplished my duty. I have said everything that I was obliged to say so that on the Day of Judgment, I shall not be questioned."

It was obvious that after this sermon, he would be arrested. We were also aware that the SAVAK agents were waiting for him on Buzarjumehri Avenue (now 15th Khordad). So when he descended from the pulpit, we told him that they wanted to arrest him. He said that he was ready for that and that there was nothing to worry about. We told him that in order to confuse the police, he should come with us via the Mawlavi bazaar. If they arrested him there, that would be fine, and if not, he would be saved for the time being. He accepted and started to leave as people loudly sent benediction to the holy Prophet and his progeny. When we reached the crossroad at Mawlavi Avenue, we saw that government agents were waiting for him in a car. He got into the police car and they drove him away. He was imprisoned for several months before he was set free by the intervention of Ayatullah Muhsin Hakim. During his trial in court, General Khajeh Nuri (the Chief Judge) said, "Whenever the name of the Shah is mentioned, you should rise to show respect!" The Shaykh became angry and said, "You are not qualified to give me orders." He lifted his cane and pointed to the picture of the Shah and said, "I am against this man. Then you say that I should stand up when his name is mentioned! I would not rise if he were present here, let alone when his name is mentioned."

I remember one day the SAVAK officers under the title of The Pious Foundation Organization gave the Shaykh a check in the amount of 100,000 *tumans* (about $20,000 then) to spend for the mosque. They told him, "Take this money by just signing here and then you shall be free to spend it in any

33

way that you like." I was present. The Shaykh looked at them sternly and said, "I cannot be bribed to remain silent. Go and look for people that are in need of that money."

Offers like this were made to him during a period when at times he was in need of daily sustenance for his family. He often said that at times after the noon prayers when he wanted to go home, he would stay in the mosque, for he had no money to buy food for the house. He would sleep and recite the holy Qur'an until evening so that he could receive some money from the community. He once narrated an incident whereby he went home one evening and found his wife crying. When he asked her the reason, she said, "I went to the butcher shop to buy half a kilo of meat with credit, but he did not give me that. Why should we be so poor and our conditions like this when you are an Ayatullah? You are a respected person ..." Shaykh Ja'fari had replied that the butcher had the right to refuse as he did not have any obligation to sell meat on credit for he had to earn a living too. The Shaykh was such a man of dignity and free spirit. Even though all the funds for the mosque were at his disposal, he lived such a difficult life.

In 1345/1966, when SAVAK saw that they could neither prevent this fearless Shaykh nor kill him, they arrested him and sent him into exile to Iraq. During this period, he traveled to Syria. When he returned from exile, he continued his criticism and attacks on the Shah's regime.

Once he shared the following story with the audience in the mosque: "One day in a Damascus market, the Arabs were pointing fingers at me while saying "Brother of the Jews." I found a bench and stepped on it in the middle of the bazaar and asked them why they called me 'Brother of the Jews.' 'We are Muslims like you and we are brothers.' They said, 'No, you are an infidel at war with Muslims!' I asked why they thought so. The replied, 'While we are in a war with Israel, the Shah is selling oil, giving them money and helping them.' Then they were cursing at the Shah. At that point I resorted to practice prudent dissimulation and defended the Shah and said, 'You are mistaken. You have no right to say these words concerning our king. Anyway, no matter how the Shah is, he belongs to us. If he is a Jew, Baha'i, Zoroastrian, or a Muslim, he belongs to us. Have you heard us talk about your president?'"

The Shaykh then added, "I said these words to them but in reality I believed differently. Indeed, if a person helps the enemy who is at war with a Muslim, he becomes an infidel and according to Islamic laws his punishment is death. I really do not know if the Shah was helping Israel then! But if he did, then his action was punishable by the death sentence." Alas, the courageous and fearlessness Shaykh Ja'fari gave this verdict concerning the Shah openly. He was the best example of courage, faith, and wisdom to me. He really left his mark and influence on me. Many times I was taken to the SAVAK and the court simply because of my attendance at his mosque.

One day I was at the store when the phone rang. It was my employer and boss, Hossein Mosddeqi, on the line. He was talking nervously and in a frightened voice. He said, "The SAVAK agents are in the bazaar and ask for your photos." I said, "At the moment I do not have a photo, but tell them that I will send them one soon."

Mosaddeqi was talking to Afzali, the director of SAVAK at the bazaar. He had given him a two-day ultimatum for me to send him six photos. I did not fulfill this request. After four or five days, they came and arrested me at the shop and took me to the SAVAK headquarters in the bazaar. When I arrived there, I realized that the issue was about my attending the mosque of Shaykh Gholam Hossein Ja'fari. Apart from me, they had also arrested some other people. This was because they were not able to deal with the Shaykh directly. They wanted to scatter his followers by use of force. They asked me, "Why do you go to the mosque?"

I said, "Is it a wrong place for me to go? Well, I go to pray and learn about religion"

They said, "There are many mosques in town. Why do you not go to another one?"

I said, "I love Shaykh Ja'fari and have faith in him and not others."

They then advised me against going to that mosque and gave me an ultimatum for twenty-four hours to present my six photos. I teased them and said, "OK, I shall bring them, but why do you not want to pay for the pictures? I am a simple worker who earns two to three *tumans* on a daily basis. I do not have enough money to sustain myself, yet you want me to pay for the photos?"

Colonel Afzali slapped me hard in the face twice and said, "These (two slaps) are the money. Get out of here and bring the photos! If by tomorrow you do not present them, I will arrest you and put you in jail."

When I came out of the SAVAK building, I decided that I had to prove to them that I do not fear them. So I decided to ignore their threats and not take the photos to them unless they came after me. Of course, on that day, I went to the Pelasko building and took the photos. I kept them in my pocket so that in case they arrested me, I would say that I wanted to bring them but had had no time.

I procrastinated and confused SAVAK for almost two months. They kept on calling at the shop and asking about the photos. I told them that I am saving my money to take photos and will do so as soon as I save enough for the purpose. Finally, they phoned my employer and threatened him that if they did not receive the photos in twenty-four hours, they would come and arrest my employer. I told my employer to ask them whether they were interested in me or my photos. They replied, "We are we interested in his photos for the time being, but we shall also arrest this son of a——later."

I kept the photos in an envelope and wrote on it, "To the respected head of the security organization of the bazaar. Please send me a receipt after receiving these six photos!" I gave the envelope to my landlord's son and asked him to take them to the SAVAK headquarters in the bazaar. The young boy accepted and took the photos as I instructed him.

After taking the photos, they told him that he was free to leave. He said, "No, I need a receipt." They said that there was no need for one. The poor boy insisted that he needed a receipt. They officer in charge slapped him twice in the face and said, "These (slaps) are the receipt."

The Front for the National Liberation of Iran

After the break-up of the Islamic Coalition Party, people like me who were young and energetic eventually joined the armed resistance and went underground. After Imam Khomeini was sent into exile in Turkey and later in Najaf (Iraq), we began to copy and distribute his declarations, letters, cassette tapes, and pamphlets amongst the people. We were around ten people, and we carried out our activities under different names such as The Progressive *'ulama, Ruhaniyun Mutarraqi*, Muslim Students Affiliated with the National Front for the Liberation of Iran (*Daneshjuyan Musalman Jebhe Azadibakhsh Melli Iran*), Association of Conscientious Muslims (*Musalmanan agah*) and so on. We were very active and printed declarations and distributed them extensively. The declarations mostly called people to join the armed struggle. By this means, we encouraged and invited people to armed resistance and revolution. We wanted to show the people that there were many others who had already joined the armed struggle.

There were not any clergy present in our meetings. Members read books and gave summaries during the meetings. The aim of this was for people to become acquainted with the context of the book and learn the thoughts and views of other people. We also had regular mountain-climbing events and every Friday went hiking in Tehran or other cities. Apart from physically helping the body and refreshing the mind and spirit, mountain-climbing was also a chance for us to identify and encourage people who might have had an interest in politics and armed operations.

In addition, we also held meetings from time to time and invited people from all walks of life to these meetings so that we could recruit members from among them. Of course after some time, we came to realize that this method was not very fruitful. We stopped the meetings but did not lose the people that we had found. We sought their help in special situations, for instance to host members who lived underground and often did not have a place to go at night.

Although our group had no special name, we distributed the declarations under the name of The National Front for the Liberation of Iran. In 1347–1348/1968–1969, the number of our members reached thirty. These people were from various social classes and places—secondary schools and university students, and simple store workers in the bazaar. The Algerian Revolution had become our model and source of inspiration.

In 1346/1967 during the coronation celebration[21] many makeshift arches were erected in most of the main roads and squares and were decorated with colorful carpets and lamps. We burned three of these makeshift arches. We had made self-exploding Molotov cocktail bombs for this purpose, the likes of which were never made later. In later operations only less sophisticated models of these bombs were used. During that time, the conscripts for the Literacy Corps were given blue bags. We made some similar sacks in the same color and style and loaded them with nails on each side and tied an elastic rubber soaked in benzene. This was a primitive kind of a

---

[21] The Shah was afraid of 'Ali Amini because of his close ties with the United States. In Farvardin 1341/March 1962 the Shah met John F. Kennedy in Washington and asked him to stop U.S. support for Amini so that he could carry on reforms that the U.S. wished Iran to undertake. After removing Amini in the month of Tir, 1341/July 1962, the Shah presented his six principles of the so-called White Revolution to referendum on the 6th of Bahman, 1341/January 26, 1963.

bomb, and we used them in our operations against fixed targets, often in the afternoon when people came out to watch decorations. The mixture of benzene and acid would explode into fire.

The makeshift arches, or "arches of victory," as they were called, were made of a cloth material, a wooden floor, and rubber. The people who had come to watch these decorations would see them burned to ashes. We carried out these operations in many places such as Tupkhaneh Square (now Imam Khomeini Square), Tajrish Square, Firdawsi Square, and another one around the Firdawsi Shopping Mall. For the purpose of speeding up the fire, before placing the sack, one of the team members used a can, in a very clever and skillful way and away from the eyes of officers and people, would pour benzene in the area around the arch of victory. Then the next person's turn would bring the sack and place it at the foot of the arches.

I remember one time when the sack full of explosive materials was placed next to one of these arches, someone came and took it away. Since we witnessed this from a distance, we were worried about that person's life. We went after him until we found him in a deserted street. We knocked him down, took the sack, and then ran away from that place like thieves. I again placed that sack at the base of the arch and threw a lit cigarette on it. The cigarette fire reached the base and immediately exploded. Once the arch caught fire, we saw from a distance the police quickly arrived and arrested one of the people there. They assumed that since he was standing next to the road, he had definitely seen the person or the people that were responsible for that action!

The fact that we were able to fool the police and the regime in that manner made me feel so good and happy. In condemning the coronation celebration, we prepared declarations and distributed them among the people. In these declarations, we asked people to prepare weapons and take part in an armed resistance. During those days, I rented two rooms in the bazaar on the Nurooz Khan Street. My landlord and his family were trustworthy people. I had become a good friend to their son, and I took him to some of the religious assemblies with me. In one of the rooms, I had placed a copy machine under the table. Sometimes, I wrote declarations and duplicated them. At night when I returned home, I covered the table that had the copy machine underneath. I would then light a lamp under it so that the neighbors would not see the light in the room. Since I had the experience of working in a paper factory, I had the necessary tools to make the tools to cut sheets of paper. I designed the declarations with my friend's help, wrote proper text on them, and printed them. Then I handed over the printed declarations to two or three people like Mr. Amir Lashkari. All the members of the group had a copy of these declarations as they went to Lashkari and took them from him and distributed them among the people. Sometimes I gave all the declarations to Mr. Lashkari, and on another day went to him and got a few copies so that my identity as the producer of declarations would net be revealed to all. At that time I only trusted two or three people in these operations. They were Lashkari and Mir Hashimi. I was unaware of the degree of their resistance under torture in case they were arrested by the police.

Since I was the source of and responsible for everything, I skillfully distributed the declarations in order to avoid being arrested. For example, seven or eight of us would go to a movie theater and sit in the balcony or the upper level. When the film was over and before the lights were turned on, we would throw down those declarations from up there to the people below and quickly leave the theater. Because there were many of us, no one would find out which one of us did this. We also distributed the declarations in the Husyniyyeh-yi Irshad, other mosques, and the bazaar, when people were busy praying, and ran away. When Ayatullah Khonsari was on his way home and a group of people were following him, we threw the pamphlets at them and ran away. The people, too, collected these declarations and read them.

Most of the declarations contained statements in opposition to the ruling regime of the Shah and against the American involvement in the *coup d'état* of the 28th of Mordad 1332/August 19, 1953. In these pamphlets we emphasized the dependence of the regime on America. No other group before or after that used our tactics in distributing the declarations. We neither directly handed over the declarations into the hands of people nor did we take anything from the people, lest we be betrayed. For the purpose of distributing the pamphlets, we had divided Tehran into four or five districts. At any given time four people would carry out the task. Each one would come with whatever weapons he had, knuckledusters, daggers, chains, etc. Four people would walk along the road. The persons in front and back had the duty of being on guard and providing security. The two people in the center had the duty of distributing the declarations.

In isolated and less crowded neighborhoods, we glued the declarations to the doors and walls, and the rest would be dumped into the courtyards of the houses in the streets. Whenever the declarations were used up, those responsible would go back and prepare some more. Sometimes we hung up the declarations. We had decided that if a policeman attacked us, we would beat him up in such a manner that he would not die but would be in a very confused state. We would then take his weapon and run away.

We had made some primitive weapons that consisted of a spring and a ball-shaped head. The head was made of lead, while its handle was made of a light wire and was like meat pounder. We always carried these weapons with us. Their handles were in the sleeves of our shirts while their heads were in our hands. The purpose of doing this was that in case of an attack by the police, we would hit his spine and leave him unconscious.

41

One night, I was walking along the Nowruz Khan Street with a bag in my hand. During that time, members of the Islamic Nations Party (Hizb-i Milal-i Islami) had been arrested and the police were suspicious of bags. They would fearfully check whoever carried a bag. Once a policeman became suspicious of me and came to me and asked what I had in my bag. I told him, "It is dark here and you cannot see clearly what is inside. Let us go somewhere that there is light so that you can clearly see what is inside." I took him to a spot where there were four downward stairs and ended up in another street. I opened the bag under the light. As he was busy inspecting my bag, I hit him hard on the chest with the weapon. He fell down from the stairs and fainted. I then took his weapon and ran away.

By 1349/1970 we managed to get some weapons. Of course, we did not really want to disarm the police. Had we wanted to do so, we would have been able to disarm many police officers a long time ago. We only attacked policemen who suspected or attacked us.

Beginning in 1347–1348/1968–1969, confronting police became harder. They went on duty in pairs, and both officers had revolvers with six bullets in each. During these years, because of the increase in our activities, the number of our members had reached fifty. It was difficult for us to control this huge group. At that time I was the leader of this group.

Since I was in the bazaar and familiar with its environment and lived among the people, and in light of my long experience in many years of fighting and avoiding arrest, I was able to properly identify people and comprehend their inner thoughts, ideas, and intentions. Even university students sought my advice in matters related to resistance (for instance, when they wanted to organize a demonstration). All these experiences earned me a place within the leadership of the inner circle of the group. But this did not mean that I was to change my behavior or mode of operation and act like a leader. In fact, I struggled to keep a low profile and not to attract attention.

42

Staying away from the eyes of people and not taking part in some of the public activities enabled me to properly concentrate on planning, organizing, and even supporting the organization in any way I could. During those years I had many responsibilities to fulfill and was constantly preoccupied. I accepted any kind of job that I could. For a while I cleaned pools in people's houses and was curious to see what was going on in those houses. Sometimes I sold new suits while at the same time bought and sold used clothing at the Bazaar of Seyyed Ismael. Since I was not trained in business, I was sometimes cheated. For example one day I bought a ring worth forty *tuman* thinking that it was gold. I later on realized that it was fake and that it was not worth even two *tumans*. Yet I continued this kind of business for a while.

I spent most of my nights on the roads and in parks. I had to sleep along with drug addicts on cartons in the Shush and Seyyed Ismael Squares. I did this so that I could experience the attitude of the police toward these men

One night I encountered police agents along the I'dam Square. At first they wanted to send me to an addiction treatment canter. Of course, I did not oppose this, as I wanted to learn about the condition of those centers. But when they realized that I was not an addict, they asked why I was among the addicts. I told them that I arrived late from the village to Tehran, and since I thought that nobody would expect me at home that late at night I decided to come and spend time here. They were convinced and released me.

I also went to villages like Faridan, Parsesh, Gharbaltaq, and Hossein Abad during the harvest season. In the process of helping the farmers I spoke to them and ask their opinions concerning the White Revolution. At first they never said anything as they feared that I might be a SAVAK agent. So they always praised the White Revolution. But when they realized that I was one of them and like a friend was helping them with their harvest for free, they began to trust me and share their concerns and complaints about the damages that the so-called "land reform" and White Revolution had inflicted upon them

Most farmers complained that their situation deteriorated after the land reform. They said that in the past, there was a landlord, who gave them fertilizers and seeds, helped them, and gave them interest-free loans if they needed them. But now they had nothing. [As a Persian proverb says], now they had rifles but did not have bullets. The lands which they gave the peasants had neither fertilizer nor water. They had invested everything that they had on it. Whatever they got from the land, they had to give it to the [government-sponsored] cooperatives at the beginning of the year, and nothing was left for them.

Villagers lacked medical care and hygiene. I took some simple medicine to them such as aspirin and other painkillers. Sometimes I described the villagers' poverty and poor level of hygiene in our declarations.

After the structure of our organization improved and consolidated, our relations became closer and deeper with the rural population but we reduced sporadic and spontaneous contacts with them. The trips to other cities increased in order to foster our relationship with them. I often visited other cities, such as Aligudarz, Isfahan, Damavand and Qom. In Aligudarz, I stayed at the house of Shaykh Ahmad Karrubi and would give him the declarations. I found out that he was a pious and down-to-earth person. He was among the supporters of Imam Khomeini, and since he realized I also supported Khomeini, he was always helpful and opened his home to me. The father of Mahdi Karrubi was the prayer leader in Aligudarz. He was a courageous man and always delivered frank and fiery sermons, and openly criticized the Shah and his regime.

Since SAVAK was not able to deal with him, just like Shaykh Gholam Hossein, they called him "the mad Shaykh" or "the crazy *mulla*." They could not silence him, so they tried to dissuade people from attending his mosque. It was because of this that when he ascended the pulpit, only a few SAVAK agents were present to listen to his sermon and reported him to the authorities but could not do much more. My most interesting encounter with him was when I gave him declarations. He always encouraged us to set aside these kinds of activities and take arms instead. Despite that he always took declarations to the mosque and distributed them among the people as well as the agents of SAVAK. He even let the head of the police department in town read his declarations but would not leave a copy with him because he did not want to "see the paper wasted"! In those cities I also found people who were able to help us in some of the tasks such as temporary housing, armed activists, and finding weapons.

The Ideological Weakness of the Front

In the year 1348/1969, I realized that we were making some mistakes in some of our tasks. We were preparing and training people on how to get weapons and kill people, but in the ideological domain, people were very ill-prepared. We never did enough for them, and we failed to answer many of their basic ideological questions.

This was a great weakness. Of course we read the holy Qur'an frequently. Some of our friends were well acquainted with the translation and commentaries on the holy Qur'an. These were the friends of Sadiq Amani and were among the members of the Islamic Coalition Party. They were somewhat aware of the military aspects of the struggle as well.

In the religious domain our knowledge was mostly based on Mehdi Bazargan's writings and some other books published in Arab countries and translated into Persian. Therefore, our knowledge of religion was minimal and limited to what we had traditionally learned in the family and/or heard in religious gatherings conducted by the clergy. Having such limited knowledge, no one could claim to be the "ideologue" of the group. We were never able to deal with ideological question or claim to be able to respond to such question.

It was possible for us to connect to any of the active political groups like the National Front (Jebhe-ye Melli), Iran National Party (Hizb-i Mellat-i Iran) under Daryush Foruhar), the People's Mujahidin Organization of Iran (MKO), and the group led by Bizhan Jazani, which all knew our group. Yet we chose not to do that. The Jazani group had really pleaded us to join them, but we did not accept their request. We believed that religion was the most vital principle for us, and the members of our group had to be completely religious. Some groups like the Mujahidin-i Khalq (MKO) believed that their main objective was struggle against the regime. For that reason they even accepted communist elements to their membership. This was one of the main causes of their deviation, which became obvious in 1354/1975. They said that religious resistance was important to them since the people of Iran were religious. In order to attract the interest and support of the people, they needed to use religion. They had even succeeded in weakening the belief of our members in our views and positions and attracted some of our members to their group. At times, the text that we prepared for declarations was altered, and I was aware of this. Knowing our ideological weakness, we realized that it was vital for us to take measures to fill this big gap in our group.

I talked about a pamphlet in Arabic titled "Commanding Good and Forbidding the Reprehensible" (*Amr bil ma'aruf wa nahy 'an ilmunkar*) with Lashkari and Lajevardi.[22] It was a

---

[22] Asadollah Lajevardi was born in the year 1314/1935 in Tehran. He completed his primary education and then attended the classes held by late Hojjat al-Islam Seyyid 'Ali Shahcheraghi. He worked in the bazaar of Tehran for his livelihood. He became a committee member of the Islamic Coalition Party in 1342/1963. A year later, he was arrested in connection with the assassination of Mansur and jailed for eighteen months. After his freedom, he began selling headscarves and handkerchiefs in the Ja'fari Bazaar. He was again arrested and sentenced to four years in solitary confinement in connection with the commotion created on the day of the match between Iran and Israel and distributing declarations against the coming of the American investors to Iran. Lajevardi was set free in the last days of Far-

summary of sermons of Imam Khomeini. They suggested that Jalal al-Din Farsi[23] should be given the pamphlet to translate into Persian. We contacted him and he accepted and translated it. I duplicated the pamphlet and held several sessions during which we discussed its content with Mr. Farsi. He formed a group with the collaboration of other people like Assadullah Lajevardi. They did not know anything about our group. We just asked them to give us instruction on theoretical and ideological issues and had several sessions with them.

---

vardin, 1353/March 1974 and continued with his political activities. He was arrested for the third time in the month of Isfand, 1353/February 1974 and sentenced to eighteen years' imprisonment. He was finally set free on the 27th of Mordad, 1356/August 18, 1977 and joined the committee to welcome Imam Khomeini's return to Iran. After the victory of the Islamic Revolution, he worked in several positions as the judge of the Revolutionary court of the Islamic Republic and the director of all prisons. He was assassinated by the MK organization in 1377/1998. *Memoirs of Ahmad Ahmad*, 269–270;

[23] Jalal al-Din Farsi was born in the year 1312/1933 in Mashhad. He came to know of Dr. Ali Shari'ati in his first year of secondary school. In 1339/1960 after Abdul Karim Qasim's coup, he went to Iraq but was arrested and imprisoned. After his freeing, he went to Syria and then came to Iran. He was arrested and taken to Qizil Qal'ah prison until Mehr, 1341/October 1962. In the years 1342–1349 he distributed declarations about the benefits of a revolution. In 1349/1970 he went to Lebanon and was appointed as the representative of Imam Khomeini in the al-Fath organization. After the victory of the Islamic Revolution, Jalal al-Din Farsi, together with Yasir Arafat, came to Iran. He became a member of the Islamic Republic Party Front for the Republic of Iran. He was elected to the parliament after the victory of the Islamic Revolution. He has written several treatises and books, which include *Zawaya-ye Tarik* (*The Dark Corners*), *Chahar enqelab va do geryesh-e maktabi dunya dolati* (*The Four Revolutions, Two Movements, and the Worldly Governance*), *Falsafeh enqelab-e Islami* (*The Philosophy of the Islamic Revolution*), *Farhange Vajeha-e Enqelabe Islami* (*A Dictionary of the Islamic Revolutionary Terms*), and *Enqelab-e Islami va sazmandehi-ye ijtimai* (*The Islamic Revolution and the Social Mobilization*).

We were willing to learn from their experiences and planned to collect some of their instructions in the form of pamphlets without allowing them to interfere in our affairs. We had some joint meetings with them as well, but they had differences and conflict amongst themselves. Some believed in struggle outside Iran while others advocated collaboration with the Palestinians. They had different opinions concerning fighting against Israel, for or against the Syrians and Egyptians. Others among them did not belong to any specific group or movement and worked without any particular objectives, and we tried to unite them. Our collaboration with them did not last too long. As internal conflict among them grew, we ended our relationship with them. Other than Mr. Jalal al-Din Farsi, we also tried to have Mr. Ma'adikhah teach us Islamic history and Imam Ali's *Path of Eloquence* (*Nahj al-Balaghah*), but unfortunately this too was not followed regularly.

To promote a spirit of camaraderie we went hiking with other members of our group regularly. During those trips we exposed ourselves to physical hardships and tried to endure the harshness of nature and ate little. The mountains provided a pleasant environment to speak about the resistance and revolution and talk about the lives of heroes of Islam such as, Ammar Yasir, Salman Farsi, Bilal, Abudhar Ghifari, Malik, and Hujr ibn 'Adi al-Kindi, as well as contemporary freedom-fighters like Che Guevara, Ho Chi Minh, and Jamilah Bou Pasha.[24] We also discussed the experiences of other freedom fighters and their experiences and exchanged books. Hiking trips helped us to identify and recruit individuals with revolutionary potential. One time, twelve members walked to the Caspian Sea region and walked back. During that trip, two of

---

[24] Jamila Bou Pasha was an Algerian revolutionary who was born on the 9th of February, 1938 in St. Lushon in Algeria. She was one of the members of the Algerian National Liberation Front. She was arrested and tortured by the French for participating in several operations against French forces. After the victory of the Algerian Revolution she sued the French government and asked for reparation. Her suit received much attention and publicity and caused a great deal of tension in Europe.

48

our members participated and were given the task of recruiting the best candidates who showed special talent in team-work and were willing to accept difficult tasks.

In terms of the financial needs of the group, we did not have any immediate problems because our expenses were minimal. Each person paid his own expenses during hiking trips. The group also agreed to pay to purchase paper and cover printing costs. Most members worked and had good income. Members like me who were not married spent most of their money on the group. My weekly wages during the time I was a simple sales clerk at the bazaar were around one 150 *tumans*. This was while the monthly salary of a teacher was around 350–450 *tumans*. With this kind of income, my economic condition was good. I had my primary needs for a good living, including carpet, refrigerator, and library.

Later on when my economic situation worsened because I had to go underground I sold most of my belongings, even my rugs, to avoid spending public funds. Then Mr. Kachu'i offered me a part-time job. He had a book-binding shop in Imam Zadeh Yahya Street. I worked there two to three hours a day. I had to manage my life in accordance with the wages that I received there and dropped all the extra expenditures in my life. During those days I rarely ate cooked food. All my food was simple: bread and yoghurt, fried eggs and omelets, bread and watermelon, or bread, tomato, and cucumber, etc. Every once in a while when I desired to eat Persian food like *ghurme sabzi*, I would invite myself to a friend's house and asked for *ghurme sabzi*. So I did not have a lot of expenditures.

In the year 1347–1348/1968–1969, the price of each bundle of five hundred A-4 papers was 11–12 *tumans*. During this period, some of the workers stole the papers in bundles from their workshops and sold them in the bazaar at half price. The movements and activities of our group were being supported by religious scholars such as Ayatullah Sa'idi and Rabani Shirazi. Some of my friends and I who were known at the bazaar had the advantage of collecting financial help from people. I always tried hard to use the collected money the way the donor wanted it to be used. If he wished to give it to poor people, I would give it to the poor families that I knew. If he wanted me to buy charcoal for the winter season, or to buy new clothes for them for *Eid* or to buy rice, oil and provisions, I would do as he had said.

One day, one of my friends had gone to my house while I was away and had brought some fruits and prepared some food. He then looked at the wall cabinet and saw that there was money placed in glass jars, vases, and cabinets. When I returned home, he asked me the reason I kept money in different places. I told him that each of those funds were for a special purpose such as buying food, medicine, shoes, clothes, charcoal, and so on. I kept them separately for those purposes. My friend was so surprised. Sometimes my own money would get mixed up with the group budget, but I do not remember any time mixing those funds with my own money, or even spending a penny for my personal needs from that fund. This was while the Mujahidin-i Khalq Organization was paying its members on a monthly basis. They offered housing and food to their team members. They provided for those who had escaped and were living underground. Although I lived underground too, I never allowed myself to use people's money for my own personal needs. I believed that God would not be pleased by such action. Some people offered money to us for fighting, provided that we did not reveal the donor's identity or the source of the money. We went to small towns and villages to fight. Apart from helping people, I benefited politically from those contacts. This method of working was greatly criticized by the Mujahidin-i Khalq Organization. They believed that all the funds should be put at the disposal of the organization and spent in accordance with their instructions. They argued that offering money to the people to comfort them or to please them was a way of seeking a comfortable life. They claimed that this sort of relief weakened the poor man's incentive for class struggle and reduced people's suspicion and negative view toward the policies and operations of the regime. According to them the aim of the struggle was to spread further the hatred towards the regime.

The EL-AL Operation

In the year 1347/1968, there was a soccer match between Iran and Israel in the Amjadiyeh (now Shahid Shirudi) stadium.[25] A lot of Israelis had come to Iran. We were not aware of this but some groups held demonstrations to boycott this match and opposed the entry of Israelis into Iran. They also prepared slogans to use during these demonstrations. They had made one-eyed dolls to mock Moshe Dayan. Some of the Jewish homes in Tehran were attacked and set on fire. We considered these actions as childish activities and condemned them strongly. But in the year 1349/1070, when the Asian soccer games were being played in Iran,[26] the Israeli team also was invited and agreed to come to Iran.

---

[25] In the year 1347/1968, the fourth tournament of the AFC Asian cup of nations was conducted in Iran. Iran and Israel met in the final on the 29th, Ordibehesht, 1347/May 19, 1968. At the end of the game, the score was one to one. But during the overtime, Iran managed to score the winning goal. Before this, the national team of Iran had faced Israel three times, and their last encounter was in the year 1353/1964. In the first tournament of the AFC Asia Cup, in Tokyo, Japan, on Khordad Israel scored four goals and won (Mordad 5, 1337/July 25,1958). In the qualifying matches of the second tournament conducted in Kerala, India on Azar 14/December 6, 1959 Iran scored three goals and won. In the second qualifying matches conducted in Kerala, India, the two teams tied. In the final of the fourth tournament held in Tehran, on 29/2/1353/May 19, 1974 Iran managed to beat Israel two goals to one and received the AFC Asian championship. In the seventh tournament conducted in Tehran on Shahrivar 24, 1353/September 15, 1974, again Iran managed to beat Israel by one goal and was crowned the champion. After 1353/1974 the Iranian national soccer team did not face the Israeli team again.

[26] For more information on Iran's political condition during those years see, *The Memoirs of Tahireh Sajjadi.*

51

We were aware of this invitation two months in advance. Because we were so angered by the burning the al-Aqsa mosque,[27] we saw this soccer match as the perfect opportunity to revenge and condemn the relationship between Iran and Israel. We thought of doing something like the Munich Airport operation where nine Israelis were killed.[28] This became our dream for a while. Therefore, since we had no interest in the games, several of us went to the Amjadiyeh Stadium to view the environment and compare it with our capabilities. In the

---

[27] On the 30th of Mordad, 1348/July 20, 1969 the al-Aqsa Mosque, the first Qiblah (direction of prayer for Muslims) and one of the holiest sites of Islam respected by all religions, burnt down. Most Muslims of the world viewed this as an act of the Zionists.

[28] In 1351/1972, a Palestinian military group called Black September took hostage members of the Israeli teams at the Olympics games held in Munich, Germany. The efforts of the German police to save the hostages resulted in the bloody killing of eleven Israeli athletes and all members of the Palestinian group. Two years before that date in 1970, the conflict between the Palestinians and the government of Malik Hossein came into the open. Subsequently, the Jordanian government declared martial law in the country. On the 16th of September, 1970, the Jordanian army carried out extensive operations as a result of which many Palestinians were killed. Palestinian refugees appealed to Yasir Arafat (Abu Ammar) to help them and take revenge. Therefore a militia group known as Black September was formed, and many Palestinian resistance groups joined it. The U.S. foreign minister claimed that this group was connected to and had ties with the Palestine Liberation Organization. Although Yasir Arafat expressed his support for this group, he denied having any ties with it. Black September was an armed organization with a four-person team composed of men and women. They did not know the members of the other teams and carried out their activities for years without having a major leader. After the event in Munich, Golda Meir, then Prime Minister of Israel, gave orders to Mossad to destroy this group. By 1975 Mossad succeeded in assassinating eight members of this group. The leader of one of these groups, called Ali Hasan Salamah, also known as Shazdah Sorkh (The Red prince), was also assassinated in a bomb blast in Beirut. In his biography titled *From Bayt al-Muqadas to Munich*, Abu Dawud, one of the remaining members of the Munich massacre, wrote, "Mahmud Abbas (Abu Mazan) was the head of the budget of the Munich operations but I had no knowledge of how the money in the group was being used. Yasir Arafat did not participate in the Munich terrorism but authorized this event."

course of assessment and analyzing our capability from the bases of installations and the entry gates of the stadium, we came to the conclusion that we could not carry out any operation like the one in Munich by Palestinians. This was because we lacked experienced and professional sharpshooters. This action would only have resulted in our own destruction. Therefore, we decided to abandon this terrorist operation and started preparing declarations against the occupation of the Israel and in support of the Palestinians. The tournament lasted ten or twelve days. From the first night that the tournament began, we started printing around ten thousand declarations. We placed four people in different places in the Amjadiyeh stadium to distribute the declarations.

Each person was supposed to carry the number of declarations he could distribute. A person would carry one hundred or two hundred declarations and drop them at once, just in case he was caught, so that he would have no more declarations with him. At every exciting moment in the game, people would cheer, and their voices would dominate the space of the stadium. We would then take advantage of those moments and throw the declarations among the crowd. At first people thought that these papers were being thrown to support the Iranian team and cheer them up.

The members of the Mujahidin-i Khalq had deceived some of my friends. The word *khalq*/people is mentioned in the Qur'an frequently, but Marxist groups used it in its non-Quranic context to denote their own ideological orientation. These groups insisted that we should use this term in our declarations, especially to express the support of the Iranian people (*khalq*) for the "People of Palestine." We rejected their request and instead used terms in accordance with our understanding of the term. I particularly insisted on this point and threatened to stop production of declarations. Two of my friends finally convinced me to do it the way I thought appropriate.

On the first day of the tournament, the stadium was decorated with participating nations' flags, including that of Israel. We decided to burn Israel's flags. We formed ourselves into four groups. We filled several water containers with benzene and carried them to the stadium. During the moments when the people's excitement was high, we set fire to Israel's flags. The next day, the authorities took away all the flags except the Iranian flags. The only place all flags remained was in the V.I.P. area, which was tightly secured, and we did not have access to it.

The final match was between Iran and Israel. We had made some banners raised by two poles specifically for this day and placed them next to the church[29] close to Amjadiyeh stadium. We encouraged people to take the banners. The slogans on the banners were against the Israeli and Iranian governments and their policies and in support of the Palestinians.

People's emotions were intensified by the slogans that were being voiced. During that time, the prime minister of Israel was Golda Meir, and Yasser Arafat was the leader of the Palestinian movement. Slogans were against Golda Meir and in support of Yasser Arafat. On that day, General Tahiri, the head of the Special Forces of the army, was also present in the stadium. When the game ended and there was commotion, one of our friends hit the general on the head with a piece of wood and disappeared among the crowd. Tahiri and his angry officers could not find the person. So they arrested another person and started beating him up there, and threw him into the vehicle and drove him away. Tahiri was truly shaken and embarrassed in front of his officers and bodyguards. He looked like a wounded tiger. He was a cruel and frightening man and eventually was assassinated by Mofidi in 13251/1972.

This tournament was of great importance to the regime. Prior to the tournament they had prepared double-decker buses from the Tehran Bus Company to transport people immediate-

---

[29] The Orthodox Church is located on Shahid Mufatteh Avenue on the south-west side of the Shahid Shirudi Stadium, near Talaqani Street.

ly after the match. They did not want people to congregate or demonstrate after it. These buses were lined up in front of the Amjadiyeh Stadium. The people punctured the tires of most of the buses by taking advantage of the situation and confusing the policemen and drivers. I had prepared to burn some of the places, and so I carried some Molotov cocktails in my pocket. It was because of this that our group members called me *Yan Palach*.[30] According to our plans, I was supposed to wait at the B. B. Cinema[31] to distribute the cocktail bombs to the members when the match was over. During this time, I had stationed myself next to a stream so that in case one of the bottles caught fire, I could throw it into the water and under the bridge.

To prepare these Molotov cocktail bombs we poured benzene and acid into the bottle. We then poured paraffin in it and washed it so that it would not settle. We would then pour chlorate into the bottle. After the bottle broke, the benzene would react with the chlorate and fire would start.

In that tournament, we really wanted Israel to win in order to take advantage of people's anger. In the first half, Iran had scored one goal. In the second half, Israel made a goal. The game went overtime, during which Iran scored the winning goal.[32] People celebrated this victory. This was not what we had wished. If Israel had won this match, our job would have been easier. We would have easily used people's rage

---

[30] On the 16th of January, 1969, by the command of Leonid Brezhnev, the Warsaw Pact forces, with the support of the Red Army of the Soviet Union, arrived in Prague to suppress the freedom fighters of Czechoslovakia. Yan Palach, a young university student, set fire to himself and then threw himself under the tank of the armies and committed suicide

[31] The B.B. cinema (now Payam) is located off Firdawsi Square across Lalehzar Avenue.

[32] In Farvardin, 1349/March 1970, the third tournament of the AFC champions league of Asian soccer clubs was held in the Amjadiyeh stadium now (Shahid Shirudi) in Tehran. In the final match of the tournament (12/1/1349) the Iranian team Taj (now Esteghlal) and the Israeli team (Hayoel), played together. Esteghlal defeated Hayoel two to one during overtime. *Keihan Varzeshi*, number 807, p. 2.

against Israel and the regime of the Shah. All in all, we did not lose hope and were optimistic about our future plans. Finally, at eight p.m. the match came to an end. Since the tires of city buses had been punctured, people took to Roosevelt Avenue (now Shahid Mofatteh). At the end of that avenue, they were divided into three groups. One group went towards Fawziyeh Square (now Imam Hossein) and another group walked towards Mokhbir al-Dawlah Square. The largest groups walked towards 24 Isfand Square (now Inqilab) and the Firdawsi Square.

I distributed the Molotov cocktail bottles among the members of our group. They threw one along Firdawsi Square, and another one into a police car and burned it at Hasan Abad Square. I was together with Karrubi and Lashkari and we joined the largest crowd. When we reached Villa (now Shahid Ustad Nejatullahi) Avenue, we tried to lead some people onto this avenue where the office of EL-AL airways was located.[33] We had earlier identified that place and had drawn out a plan for it. When we reached the end of Villa Avenue, Karrubi, Lashkari and I attacked the office.

Two policemen were guarding that building. We chased them away, and we broke all the glass and boards of the airline office. I had two Molotov cocktail bombs. I threw them into the office and ran away. It didn't take too long before the office caught on fire. Soon the police sirens could be heard. That was a night to remember for all of us. We were successful in actively carrying out these operations. It was not until late that night that the police were completely able to disperse the people. Luckily enough, no one was captured by the

---

[33] El-Al is the Israeli national airlines established on the 15th of November, 1948. The first flight was the transferring of the first president of Israel—Chaim Weizman—from Geneva to Israel in the year 1948. In 1950, this airline transported more than 47,000 Yemen Jews from Yemen to Palestine in an operation called "Magic Carpet." One of the distinguished attributes of El-Al airlines was their adherence towards the Jewish traditions and culture. By the order of David Ben Gurion, El-Al was to serve only Jewish kosher food on board. And there was no flight on the Jewish Sabbath.

police on that night. For more precaution, we decided to all depart, and each of us took different routes home.

I Am a Fan of the Shah!

During the end of the month of Farvardin, 1349/March 1970, we heard that a number of American capitalists and investors like Rockefeller wanted to come to Iran. The aim of their visit was to investigate fields of investment in Iran.[34] The clergy had expressed their opposition to this visit and their aims. Ayatullah Sa'idi[35] gave sermons against the visit of the American capitalists. Our group also decided to produce declarations against this visit. We decided that we had to put the names and signatures of prominent people in these declarations. To make the matter clear, since this was open opposition, in case we were arrested, our only crime would have been distribution of declarations, and the people who had singed them would have been responsible for their content. We went after some famous politicians like Allahyar Salih,[36] but he did not agree to collab-

---

[34] For more information concerning the disruption of soccer matches and the torching of the office of EL-AL airlines, see *Memoirs of Mohammad Hashim Baig Lashkari and Hasan Kolahduzan.*

[35] On the 1st of Ordibehesht, 1349/April 25, 1970 the Iranian press reported that a group of American investors led by John Rockefeller and Lilian Tel would arrive in Tehran soon to examine the possibilities of investment in Iran, *Haft Hezar Ruz,* vol. 1, p 403.

[36] Ayatullah Seyyid Mohammad Reza Sai'idi was born in Nughan, Mashhad on the 2nd of Ordibehesht, 1308/April 26, 1929. He received religious education in Qom and Mashhad and studied under Ayatullah Burujerdi and Ayatullah Mirza Hashim Amoli, and later under Imam Khomeini. After the exile of Imam Khomeini from Turkey to Iraq, Ayatullah Sai'idi went to Najaf, and upon his return to Iran he was appointed as the imam of Musa Ibn Ja'far mosque. Ayatullah Sai'idi played a major role in producing some of the declarations in opposition to the Shah from the point of view of the clergy. His signature was seen at the bottom of most the letters and declarations. Finally, he was arrested on the 11th of Khordad, 1349/June 21, 1970. He passed away after ten days as a result of severe torture in prison.

orate with us. Daryush Furuhar[37] said he would agree to sign on the condition that the declarations would be under the name of his party, the National Party of Iran. This was not an acceptable condition for us, so we failed in this bid. Ayatullah Sa'idi decided to issue a declaration of his own in which he criticized the regime in a strong tone. The declarations that he produced were very strong and caused strong reactions. Immediately, SAVAK[38] arrested and tortured him severely. He fell

---

[37] Ilahiyar Salih, the son of Mirza Hasan Khan Mubassir al-Mamalik, was born in Kashan in the year 1276/1897. He studied in a school established by the Democrat Party of Kashan. He attended the French school before entering the American School in Tehran. He worked as a translator at the U.S. Embassy in Tehran for a short time. During the reign of Reza Shah he functioned in important positions such as the Inspector General of the Ministry of Justice, Chief Justice in Isfahan, and Director of vustoms office. Under Mohammad Reza Shah he was appointed as Minister of Justice, Minister of Finance, member of parliament, and Ambassador to Washington. He was the founder of the Iran Party and one of the leaders of the National Front. Salih passed away abroad in the year 1360/1981.

[38] Daryush Furuhar was born in Isfahan in the year 1307/1928. He graduated from the School of Law and Political Science at the University of Tehran. He joined a nationalist group called *Maktab*. He was arrested in 1329/1950 because of his activities in the movement for nationalizing the oil industry. In the year 1330, when Maktab changed its name to Hizbe Mellat Iran (the Party of the Iranian Nation), Furuhar was elected as the secretary-general of this party later that year. He was again arrested on the 29th of Khordad, 1331/June 19, 1952. He participated actively in the events that resulted in the nationalization of the Iranian oil industry and subsequent event until the coup of the 28th of Mordad, 1332/August 19, 1953. For a while he published the *Arman Mellat* (*The Aspirations of the Nation*) and then was exiled to the Qishm Island. When he returned to Tehran, he led the formation of the National Resistance Movement. Furuhar was elected as a member of the Central Council of the Second National Front. Two months later he was again arrested. In 1343/1964 he met Imam Khomeini through his son Mostafa Khomeini. He was arrested again and imprisoned. But after his release in the year 1345/1966, he continued with his opposition against the regime of the Shah. He spent time in prison several times until Aban 1357/October 1978. After his release, Furuhar went to Paris and joined Imam Khomeini's aides and returned to Iran with him on the same flight. Between 1353 and 1357/1974 and 1978, he worked as a lawyer in the court, but he continued his opposition against the Shah's re-

ill in prison and finally died under torture. Despite that loss, we distributed our declarations together with those of Ayatullah Sa'idi. But distributing declarations caused much trouble for us. One of the members, Ahmad Karrubi, carried some of these declarations to the university in his bag and gave them to his friend, whose name was Fatimi.[39] Fatimi gave the declarations to his friend. He did not know that his friend was a SAVAK agent and the plan was thus leaked. The SAVAK agents watched Fatimi and his close friends and monitored his calls. After some time, he was arrested along with four or five of his friends, including Ikbatani,[40] Okhovvat, and others. The surveillance went on for some time, and as a result, Ahmad Karrubi, Mostafa Sattari,[41] and Hasan Kolahduzan were arrested in a meeting at 24 Isfand (now Inqilab Square).[42]

---

gime. After the victory of the Islamic Revolution of Iran, Furuhar served as the Minister of Labor and Social Services. He later on turned into a critic of the Islamic Republic. At the end of the year 1377/2008, Furuhar and his wife, Parvaneh Iskandari, were killed in a horrible manner in their home. Later on, the Ministry of Information connected the assassination of these two and other people to the leaders of that ministry. See *Bomdad*, number 203, 12; *Etela'at Muhaqiq*

[39] For more information concerning the content of the poster, *Gam-i digeri dar rah-e tashdid Gharatgari'* ("Another Step in Expanding Robbery"), refer to the context of the poster in index III.

[40] Seyyed Mahmud Fatimi, known as Fereidun (b1329/1950). He was very well-read and was a good writer and published essays in *Negin* and *Firdawsi*, two of the most widely read journals published in Tehran. He also wrote articles for a column in the *Kayhan* newspaper. In 1349/1970, while he was a freshman in the School of Economics at the University of Economics, he was arrested and imprisoned for his activities with Lashkari. The SAVAK reported that he was a Marxist. In his interrogations he admitted that in his discussion with Karrubi and Mahdi Rajabi concerning communism, he stated that some of the views of communism were appealing to him. Fatimi was released from prison on Isfand 6, 1349/February 25, 1971 and went to the university to continue his education. In the reports of the SAVAK in 1350/1971, they identified him as a religious-socialist student. See Shahid Seyyid Asadollah Lajevardi, 114–115.

[41] Ali Asghar Ikbatani, known as Nasir, was born in Tehran in 1327/1948. In 1349/1970, he was a junior in the department of geology at the University of Tehran when he came to know of Lashkari through Seyyid Mahmud

Amir Lashkari owned a weaving factory in I'idam Square (Mohammadiyeh) near Khani Abad street and had turned it into the storage house for our declarations. One afternoon I went to his shop to talk about issues pertaining to our budget and declarations. From the moment that I rang the doorbell I noticed that the situation was not normal. There were several young men working in this shop. I asked them where Amir was, and they said that he had gone to the bazaar and that he would soon be back. This was an unusual time for him to go to the bazaar. So after waiting for about half an hour I repeated my question, one of his workers laughingly said, "Today at noon, they came. They slapped him in the face and took him away."

I asked, "Who else did they take?"

He placed his index finger on his mouth, and pointing at one other young worker, he said, "They also took that boy."

I realized that Ni'matullah Hajj Amiri had also been arrested. I felt that I had walked into a dangerous trap. I had to leave that place as quickly as possible. But before I went out, it occurred to me that I should find all books, pamphlets, and

---

Fatimi. He was arrested on Khordad 2, 1349/May 24, 1970 for his participation in the attack on the El-Al airline office and jailed for nine months. He and Rajabi were not very religious and had their differences with Karrubi, Lashkari, and Lajevardi. On 14 Azar, 1352/November 30, 1973 he was arrested and jailed for three days because of his communist activities and his connection to a revolutionary communist group. After the victory of the Islamic Revolution, Ikbatani continued his relation with communist groups. See Lajevardi, 116–117.

[42] Mostafa Nejad Sattari was born in Isfahan in the year 1328/1949. He knew Lashkari, Karrubi, Mir Hashimi and Kalahduzan through Mohammad 'Ali Ashraf Khorasani. He was in charge of providing the financial cost of the meetings. In 1349/1970, he was sophomore in the meteorology department at the Technical University of Iran He was arrested on the 24th of Ordibehesht, 1349/May 14, 1970 and jailed for one year because of his involvement in the El-Al airline incident, and for preparing and distributing the declarations in opposition to the coming of the American investors to Iran. After completing the sentence, he was released from prison on the 20th of Ordibehesht,1350/May 10, 1971.

60

declarations that he had hidden in his shop and take them away and burn them. Before I set to go downstairs, suddenly the doorbell rang. I returned to the upper floor and looking out through the window. I saw three SAVAK agents at the door. I knew them very well. During the time that I was in the bazaar, they had taken me to the police headquarters for interrogation many times for my involvement in bazaar politics, and my affiliation with the Friday mosque. They were aware of my previous arrests and short-term imprisonment. After seeing the police, I wanted to escape, but there was no way out. I was not in such a dangerous situation that would warrant committing suicide to avoid arrest. I decided to get ready for anything that the hand of destiny planned for me. I told myself, "If worst comes to worst, I shall go to prison for one year or two!" The only thing that I was able to do was to throw books and pamphlets into the garage that was behind the workshop. I also threw some papers containing telephone numbers into the toilet. At that time, I was not brave enough to throw myself out of the window. So I hurriedly threw myself into the lump of clothes and fabrics and hid myself and pretended to be asleep. I told the workers that no one should know that I was there. At last they opened the door for the police. Because of the delay in opening of the door, the agents entered by force and immediately started searching everywhere.

On the upper floor, there were three or four rooms. My plan was that if they entered one of the rooms, I would use the corridor to escape. But they also had their plan. One of them remained in the corridor as the other two went into the rooms. I was able to see their movements from my place of hiding. I pretended to be asleep until they entered the room where I was hiding. Suddenly, they pulled away the pile of clothes. They were shocked and perhaps even frightened to see me there. I never woke up and continued to snore. It was as if I was asleep for hours. The two looked at me and then called their third fellow. One of them said, "He is the one. This is the real culprit! I know him." He had recognized me. He asked, "Are you not one of the workers of Mosaddeqi? You are the one responsible for printing the declarations. You are the leader of these people."

I realized that the situation had gone wrong. I tried to remain calm, yet I pretended to be asleep. They continuously cursed at me, but I did not pay attention. They kicked me in the back, took my hand, pulled it, and lifted me. I pretended to be asleep and confused as I said, "Are you mad? Why are you beating me? What are you doing here?"

I then pretended that I was coming into consciousness little by little. They were annoyed, and they said, "Oh! What are *we* doing here? What are *you* doing here?"

I said, "That is not your business!"

The policeman who had identified me again asked, "Tell me, are you not one of Mosaddeqi's employees?"

I said, "Of course I was, but not any more. I had an argument with him over my salary and I left."

He said, "Stand up, you idiot! Whatever the case, you are responsible."

I said, "Mind the way you speak or else....."

He asked, "Or else what? Wake up and stop this drama. We are SAVAK agents."

I started cursing Lashkari (whom they had already arrested). I then turned to the young workers, and in a state of drowsiness said, "Why did so-and-so not come? Today marks the end. If he comes tonight I will teach him a lesson. Why doesn't he pay his debt! When I find him I will report him to the police and get my money back!" I went on with my drama in another way. The police men said, "What! Why are you annoyed?"

I said, "The person I am talking about is the owner of the workshop. Three months ago he borrowed several thousand *tumans* from me but doesn't want to pay me back. He keeps on telling me that he will give my money back to me tomorrow. Go and come back tomorrow! Next day it's the same: In short I am frustrated and exhausted. I also came this afternoon and waited for him to come so that I could take him to the police headquarters. I still don't understand why he hasn't showed up yet! I got exhausted and fell asleep in this pile of clothes and I did not hear you come in!"

One of the agents said, "Silly! You are the one! You are the fool. Did you want us to believe you? Of course not!"

They laughed and said, "Since you have been printing the declarations, you must have been tired, so you fell asleep in this place!"

I asked, "What are these declarations that you are talking about? I don't understand what you are talking about. This man owes me money, and I just came to collect my money. And of what concern is it to you?"

They said, "Stand up! You are tired! Stand up, it is over now. We shall give you a lot of time to sleep so that you will be tired of sleeping. Stand up man, you are under arrest!"

I asked, "What for?"

They said, "Don't you want to see your friend? He and your other friends have been arrested and are now at our headquarters, and they have confessed. This place is for producing and storing the declarations."

I pretended to be unaware and innocent and not comprehending these words. I said, "How wonderful it is that he has been arrested! Long live the Shah! Our king is a good one and the people who do these kinds of things are traitors."

I went on, "In fact where are these people? Give me the address. I will come and prove to you that I have no role in this work. I will come to prove my innocence to you."

One of them said, "Wow! What a nice boy!"

Another one said, "This is a trick." He faced me and said, "You are the idiot yourself! Let's go!"

Then they pushed me to another room. They wanted to search my body. I asked them to show me their ID cards before they could search my pockets. They realized that I was aware of some things. They said, "If you haven't done these things, then how did you find out that policemen are supposed to have and show their identity card to you?"

I realized that I had made a mistake and so I quickly rectified it by saying, "It is obvious since I work in the bazaar environment. I have a very good reputation here. Some policemen come and put heroin and opium into the pockets of the certain people; then they arrest them and take them to the police headquarters and charge them with possession of drugs and get them into trouble. You too are saying that you are police agents. Well, then, you have to show your identity cards to give me peace of mind."

They pretended that they believed me and showed their cards and later on inspected me. They found nothing! One of them asked, "Should we put handcuffs on him?"

Going ahead with my drama, I extended my hands and said, "Lock me properly. I shall come forward myself. I want to prove my innocence, because I love the Shah! A true patriot! A person who has done nothing wrong should have no reason to be afraid of judgment. You don't have to arrest me sir, I will come on my own two feet; so let us go!"

It noticed that they probably did not have any handcuffs with them, and they had not thought that they would find themselves in such a situation. One of them said, "No! This is a good boy. We do not need handcuffs. He will come!" Then, one of them held my left hand and the other my right and we moved. We came out of that workshop as the workers looked on. We walked toward a car that was parked on the road. I was thinking I would be imprisoned for two years, and the idea of escaping from the police was totally out of my mind.

One of the police officers began to drive. The other one let go of my hand and sat in the rear seat of the car so that I could sit between them. At that moment an idea came to my mind: Escape! I did not waste a second. I had not quite entered the car yet, so I took a shoehorn from my pocket with my free hand and hit as hard as I could on the wrist of the police officer who was holding my hand. He shouted and let go of my hand, and I started running as fast as I could. Before the agents could understand what had happened, I was already many meters away. They ran after me as they cursed at me. They were shouting, "Catch him! Catch him!"

I was also running and shouting, "Catch him! Catch him!" The passers-by too were perplexed as they wondered which one of us should be caught! They followed me from I'dam Square to the small bazaar known as Sa'adat. I was a teenager, a mountaineer, strong and with high spirits. I was really running fast. It was around nine o'clock at night that I managed to escape from them in the streets of the bazaar. They lost me. Perhaps they were tired and so decided not to run after me. Later on I read in their reports that they "had freed me since they had not found any document proving [my] guilt!" Making such reports was a normal thing for them. Of course they had to do this in order to cover up for their weakness.[43]

An Escape within an Escape

When I was sure that the police no longer were following me, I went back to my workplace in the bazaar. I was convinced strongly that the police did not have my home address, but they knew my place of work. I had earlier had an argument with my employer. He knew most of my friends. In those days, the bazaar remained open until late at night. Mr. Mosaddeqi performed the evening prayers in the bazaar mosque and then went back to the store and would stay there for another hour or two before going to his house. So I went after him and took him to a secluded and quiet alley. I told him in a very serious and assertive way that some of my friends had been arrested and the police might come tomorrow to his shop or look for me and ask about me. I told him to say to the police that we had had a quarrel over my wage and that I had quit working

---

[43] For more information concerning the manner in which the El-Al group was betrayed and arrested, refer to the memoirs of Lashkari, Mohammad Reza Moqaddam, Hasan Kalahduzan, and Hamid Okhovvat, Index # 2.

there. I made it clear to him that if he said anything else to the police and I ever got arrested, I would hold him responsible for everything and for providing the money for the paper and the production of the declarations. Since he had been jailed before, he got scared and complied. I made sure that he understood that this was not just about me, but also applied to my friends. He complied and assured me that he did not know anything about my friends to begin with.

The plan worked. The next day, he was taken to the police station three times. He repeated exactly these statements. It was this plan that set him free from this trouble and ended in his favor. On the first night of my escape, I was thinking that they would never leave me in peace, and the situation would deteriorate and become increasingly harder.

I had two guns that I hid under my pillow at night. I had had these weapons since 1347/1968. One of them was confiscated from a policeman, while the other one had been given to me by one of our members from Kermanshah. So when I left the bazaar and arrived home, I collected the weapons, some of the documents, and my personal belongings that I needed daily and put them in a bag and took the bag with me. I told my landlord that I was going to travel around for one month. I told him that if someone came to ask for me, tell him that I no longer live there. And so I did. My landlord's son who was my friend realized that I had run away. At first I had a room close to the stairs. But after they got to know me and my relationship expanded and improved with his family, they gave me two rooms on the same floor.

The next day, the police went to that house. My landlord and his son only showed them the first room close to the stairs. After the police had gone, they went into the other two rooms. They found copies of books by Ayatullah Taleqani and Mehdi Bazargan, which they destroyed out of fear of the police. After leaving that house, I put my belongings and documents in another house. I then hired a taxi-cab and went to see several friends at their homes. I told them everything that had happened and informed them that our place had been identified and that they should not go there.

I had the habit of listening to foreign radio every night. The most interesting thing was that a night after my escape, while listening to Baghdad radio (the Patriots Radio Station), I heard them talking about the discovery of a workshop used for storing the declarations and reported my escape. I never found out who had transmitted this report to Baghdad within twenty-four hours, and I still do not know. Many political activists as well as politicians listened to this radio every night. It was obvious that some of my friends had also heard this report, but since my name had not been mentioned, they were still unaware of what was going on.

Mir Hashimi was a close friend of mine who had just joined the army, as all high school graduates were expected to serve for two years. I had to inform him of my situation. He was a good and talented young man but had fallen into the trap of the Marxist groups. Although he pretended to be religious, he was closer to and associated with Marxist activists. One early morning I put on a black shirt and went to the air force base where he served and requested to meet him. I told his senior officer that his mother had passed away, and since he was the oldest child in the family, I thought he would want to see his mother for the last time and to attend her funeral. Several officers, including a major and a colonel and a few soldiers, came and paid their condolences to him. I requested of his commanding officer a few days off for him and he granted them. We came out of the garrison around eight o'clock. It did not take long for SAVAK to go to the garrison and find out that he was not around. We went to our friends' house for two days.

We then decided that we must leave Tehran and go to places far away from the capital. I suggested the cities of Mashhad and Qom because we could perform pilgrimage there at the holy shrines and also to take advantage of the presence of huge crowds and mix with them and avoid being identified.

During this time, some of our friends and members of our groups who lived and worked in cities like Tabriz, Behbahan, and other cities were in contact with us. Lashkari had their letters, which contained their names and addresses, and kept them at his store. When the police raided his shop, they found these letters and arrested about fifteen of them. When our arrested friends realized that I had escaped, they told the police that that I was responsible for everything, including the purchase of the copy machine, writing the text of the declarations, and preparing them, as well as burning the makeshift arches. The police then held me responsible for all of these acts.

Sometime before these incidents I received a number of key chains that were produced by armed Palestinian groups such as al-Sa'iqah, al-Asifah, and al-Fath with their names engraved on them. I gave one to every member of our group, and when they were arrested, they told police that I had given those key chains to them. Perhaps they thought that I would never be captured and by blaming everything on me and holding me responsible, charges against them would be less serious.

Mir Hashimi did not agree with my suggestion to go to Qom. He suggested another far away village in Arak. His aunt lived in Arak and another relative who was a retired colonel lived in Mashhad. The colonel's house was neither trustable nor safe. The police had my photos from my files that SAVAK had created for me after my arrests. They also had pictures of Mir Hashimi taken from his file in the army. Therefore, it was not wise to waste more time in Tehran, and so we headed for Arak. That village was about forty kilometers from Arak. It seemed a good place to hide because of its distance from urban centers.

On an early morning around the end of the month of Urdibhesht/April, we started our journey and arrived in Arak around noon. The only means of access to the village we planned to go to was a daily mini-bus service that took passengers from Arak to the nearby villages. Before taking that bus, we bought some sweets for Mir Hashimi's aunt. We also had a sack full of books and clothes. We thought that we would stay in the village for at least twenty days or more until the situation cooled down. At one o'clock we took the bus toward the village. We were overwhelmed with joy on our way to the village as we had found a good place to hide. After two or three hours, we arrived at the village hungry and thirsty.

When we got off the mini-bus, we asked for the aunt's address. It was obvious to the locals that we were strangers. One of the boys, who was stuttering, came close to us and said, "Last night, Mahmud came looking for you!" and he kept on repeating this statement. At first we did not understand what he was trying to say. I told Mir Hashimi that I had a feeling that something was wrong.

Finally, we found the aunt's house. When she opened the door, she became hysterical and started crying and saying, "My dear, why have you come to this place? I am ruined! Last night, the *gendarme* and the district officer came looking for you. He was saying that you committed crimes and killed people! Is this true?"

We looked at her in bewilderment. We then understood that what that stuttering boy meant by saying that Mahmud was looking for us.

We said, "No Auntie! What crime are they talking about? We did not want to serve in the military and so we ran away from that. They are lying!"

It seemed that after my friend had escaped from the garrison, from the documents found in Lashkari's shop, they discovered the relationship of my friend with our group. They went to his home, arrested his brother, and tortured him, and he revealed the names and addresses of his relatives, including his aunt and all the others who might be involved. So they assumed that we might come to this village. It was terrifying to imagine what would have happened if we had arrived in the village just a day earlier.

Struggle in the Swamp

The situation was critical, and we couldn't afford to procrastinate or delay a decision. I told my friend to get ready to leave. The aunt noticed and changed her tone a little and began to insist that we should eat supper and stay overnight and leave the next day. She even prepared food for us, but we could not accept her invitation to stay and eat. My friend ate a little. Just about the same time a person came and called the aunt out of the house. It was obvious that they were planning something against us. We left the sugar cones we had brought for her and left the house immediately.

There was no transportation, and waiting until the next day was risky. We had no choice but to travel on foot. We left the village and were walking along the road next to the wheat farms. We did not use the road for fear of being followed by the police. We were also not well acquainted with the road. We were just guessing that we were following the road to Arak, and we did not know what lay in store for us.

After walking for a while, we arrived at a muddy area. There was no indication that this was a swamp. But as we stepped there, our legs sunk into the mud up to the knee. It had a very deceptive appearance. We thought that if we went three to four meters ahead, the mud would end, and therefore, we did not feel like returning and taking another route. As we continued walking, the swamp became deeper. Everywhere was dark and cold, and we did not have warm clothes because we never thought we would fall into a situation like that. Every once in a while, the lights of a passing car lit our path and we threw ourselves in the wheat field until the car passed us and disappeared in the dark.

It seemed that the farmers had pumped water into the wheat farm that afternoon. All my clothes were wet and muddy. The cold weather was also unbearable. Sometimes we had to embrace each other to stay warm. Sometimes we slapped one another so as not to fall asleep. We put on all the clothes that were in the sack.

The combination of the cold weather and the dampness of the ground really took its toll. We could neither stand the cold nor could we fall asleep. Every once in a while, the voice of a barking dog reverberated in the air and could be heard. Everything was lined up to kill our morale. If we had lost hope, then everything would have been over. We could not afford to stop. We had to move by any means.

Sometime in the course of walking our shoes would get stuck in the mud and our bare feet would feel colder. To find them, we had to put our hands into the mud at the bottom of the swamp and find the shoe with great effort. Our eyes were tearful. The tips of our fingers and feet were completely numb. Our ears and noses had also frozen. We could hear the sound of teeth knocking together. At one point my friend almost gave up and surrendered to the situation. He fell into the mud and didn't want to stand up again. I forcefully took his arms and lifted him out of the deep mud. A little later and after struggling to get out from the swamp, we arrived at a ditch. We approached it and saw that a big river was passing in the middle of the swamp. It seemed to be very deep. We could neither cross nor jump over it. We had reached a dead end. For some minutes we stood in despair and confusion. It was as if we had reached the end of the rope.

In that darkness of the night, I looked at the sky. Stars were shining as though smiling at us. I silently prayed to God and appealed to Him to help us and show us a way out of that situation. I asked myself if there was a way out in this dark night! We turned back from the ditch to the edge of the road. The river had also crossed the road, but there was a bridge over it. We passed it, but we were not supposed to walk along the road. So we returned to the wheat farm.

It was around 2 a.m. when we arrived at another village. The dogs attacked us, and the people came out to welcome us with their clubs and bats! We hid in the rows of wheat. When the dogs became quiet, we crawled and then stood up and went ahead without any noise. We continued until we became totally exhausted and our knees could no longer carry our weight. We reached a point that we could not take one more step ahead. Just at the moment of despair, suddenly I saw the city lights, and that seemed like a miracle. We felt a renewed energy. The joy and happiness of that moment is beyond description. But as we started walking toward the city, we were overwhelmed by fear again. We thought that at this time of the night, the city was not a safe place for us. Because of our unusual appearance and condition, any policeman would become suspicious of us and might arrest us. I warned my friend of my fear.

We knew that in a short distance to the city there was a shrine (Imam Zadeh) where a descendent of the Prophet was buried. We headed toward that but before getting there we had to go through a dried up riverbed covered with soft sand. It was already five o'clock in the morning. We chose a soft spot and decided to take a nap. The warmth of the sand was soothing and relaxing and soon we fell asleep for two hours. It was seven or eight o'clock in the morning when we woke up and went to the edge of the road. We cleaned our clothes and waited for transportation.

After a few minutes a truck carrying tomatoes and cucumbers stopped and offered to give us a ride to the city. The driver was transporting fruits and vegetables from Ahwaz or Abadan to Tehran. He agreed to take us to the city of Qom in return for five *tumans* fare for each of us. We agreed and started our journey toward Qom. The warm air inside the truck compartment was pleasant and soon we fell asleep. Sometime my head would fall on the shoulder of my friend and sometimes his head would fall on mine. The driver, who also seemed to be sleep-deprived, must have fallen asleep because several times the truck swerved, once so bad that it went off the road. We were afraid and so we tried to stay awake.

The driver had become suspicious of us, so he started to ask questions as who we were, where we were from, and where were our destinations and other questions. We made up a story and told him that we had attended our cousin's wedding, and that as he might know, villagers usually partied and danced all night during the wedding. So we had to stay up all night. And now we were late and were very much in rush to get to town.

We were sure that the driver did not believe our story. So about 2–3 kilometers to Qom we asked him to stop the truck. He asked for the reason, and we told that we had some relatives in that neighborhood and now that we came there, it was appropriate to pay a visit to them. He replied, "No! You have to come to Qom. You have paid your fare to Qom!"

We said, "We want to get off here, and it is not your business what we wish to do from then on." He continued to insist. But fortunately, by divine providence, there was a traffic jam right at that spot and no car moved. Our truck was forced to stop as well. We paid his fare and got off the truck. We washed our hands and faces in the river and walked alongside it and reached Qom. We ate breakfast in the morning and when we were sure that no one was following us, we started our journey to Tehran.

Escaping to the Caspian Sea Region

My financial condition was not bad at all. In Tehran, we went to Pahlavi Crossroad and to the house of one of our friends to eat lunch. After changing our clothes, we went to Karaj at around two o'clock in the afternoon. We intended to go to the Caspian Sea region. We did not want to travel directly there but planned to use an alternative route and catch anther bus to our destination somewhere on our way. At eleven o'clock at night we arrived in Rasht. The hotel receptionist asked for our identity cards. We did not have a place to sleep. So we decided to go to Pahlavi (Anzali) harbor and spend the night in the plaza. But at that time of the night, there was no car that was going to Pahlavi harbor. We went to another hotel. The receptionist in that hotel also asked for our identity card. We told him that we were from the Tehran bazaar and came to visit our friend but he was not home. Since we had no plan to stay in a hotel we did not bring our identity card. Again he said that it was impossible to check us in without an identity card. Only after I tipped him generously he agreed to give us a room. We gave him two fake names and he wrote them down. He gave us a room on the upper floor. My friend and I had agreed that we should not spend our money lavishly, because if we were going to live for four months in hiding, then we needed to save. Before arriving in Rasht, we ate a big meal on the road that cost us five or six *tumans*. At night when Mir Hashimi was no longer worried about finding a place to sleep, he suggested that we should go out and eat. But everywhere was closed at that time of the night except a very expensive restaurant. I had an appetite for beef stew but it was nowhere to be found at that time of the night. My friend suggested that we should go for lamb liver Kabob and we did.

At that time in Tehran, the price of a skewer of lamb liver was about 2–3 *rials*. I told my friend that if we wanted to buy those kabobs in Tehran, it probably would have cost two *tumans* each. He believed that since this was a small town, it must be much cheaper. I told him to ask the price first, but he said it wouldn't be wise because people would know that we are strangers in town. So I left it to him and he ordered fifteen skewers of kabob and four loaves of bread. Neither I nor Mir Hashimi was very hungry, so we just ate six skewers of kabob. I was guessing that the price of six kabobs was two or at most three *tumans*. To my surprise, it cost much more. To avoid looking like fools, I decided that since we needed some change I gave him a fifty *tuman* bill. When the kabob house owner gave me the change I realized that we had been ripped off. This was a lesson for me that whenever and whatever I wanted to eat, I should first ask for the price first. The next morning

74

we collected our belongings and went to Bandar Pahlavi (Anzali). During those days, the weather was still cold and few tourists were in town. They said that tourist season in the Caspian Sea region started in the middle of Khordad/June. We arrived there before the high season so the city and harbor were empty. We walked for almost five kilometers away from the harbor towards the plaza where they said that the unlicensed and illegal fishermen were active at night. We met a few of them there. We told them that we were businessmen from the Tehran bazaar and we had taken a short vacation because business was slow, and that we didn't like to come in summer because the beaches are crowded and women were in their swimming suits. We rented a room in a beach house for ten *tumans* per night, and we paid it all in advance. During the day we did not have anything to do other than eating and resting. The plaza owner and Mir Hashimi became friends from that first day. Every day, our landlord came and took Hashimi to the sea, as he knew how to swim. But I did not know how to swim, so I lay down in the sand and waited.

Sometimes I went back to our room and rested. Some other times we just went back to the beach and took a boat and went to the middle of the sea to watch the sunset. Watching the sun set created a feeling of hope in my heart and always made me hopeful for the future

Our five nights' stay turned into twelve nights. I felt that the landlord was growing suspicious of us. Our appearance at that time was unusual. We had long beards and wore straw hats. We mostly resembled wandering dervishes rather than businessmen. The people there thought that we were foreign tourists. At times they teased us or threw curse-words at us. Of course we just ignored them.

We had to escape from Bandar Pahlavi before we were caught. We went towards Rudsar, Babolsar, Shahsavar, and Ramsar. It was not possible to remain in one place. We had to stay near the Caspian Sea and away from the eyes of people. There were no beach houses in these cities. We stayed in Ramsar for two or three nights and then went to the village of Chamkhaleh in Langaud.

In Chamkhaleh, the beaches were very clean and the water was pure, unlike Bandar Pahlavi, which was muddy and polluted. While in Chamkhaleh, we heard that Ayatullah Hakim had passed away. We had gone from the village to the city for a walk and found people commemorating his death. We remained there for ten days. It was not possible to continue our journey. We had no source of income, and we were running out of cash. We assumed that the situation might have improved in Tehran somewhat so we decided to return to the capital.

The End of the El-Al Group

I contacted the family members of a few political prisoners whom I had met in prison and with whom I had become good friends. These families had visited their children in prison and were able to bring some information about their condition for us. It turned out that my friends had held me responsible for everything. This story repeated itself many times, and any of my friends who were questioned had said that I told them what to do and what not to do and that I gave them all the declarations. A special dossier was created for me in SAVAK on the basis of their confessions. In the eyes of SAVAK I was that monster. They searched for me from house to house

SAVAK called for interrogation anyone who they thought had information about me or my whereabouts. This caused a great deal of unjustified fear of me among the police officers. As I was fully aware of this matter, I tried in every way possible to stay away from them. Each day I would put on a different appearance. One day I dressed like a cleric of the bazaar with a long beard and a rosary in my hand. At times, I dressed like a porter, carrying a sack on my back. At other times I spoke in praise of the Shah and expressed support for the programs of the regime to the extent that some were suspicious of my sermons and the seriousness of them. Sometimes when some of our members were arrested by SAVAK, my friends would jokingly say, "Ezzat! How much do you charge to report these people? How is it possible that everyone else was being arrested while you still remained free!?"

To be more cautious, I had cut off relations with my family. Neither my father nor my brother was aware of my exact address. All my calls to my friends or anyone else were one way, as I was always the one who would call. I had prepared ways and planned different scenarios to play at the time of my capture, which could be at any time. Approximately twenty days before the capture of some members of our group, a cleric called Shahcheragi passed away. He had been involved in political activities. I decided to hold him responsible for everything that my friends attributed to me. He was no longer alive to contradict or refute my claims. I had planned to stand on this claim even if it cost my life.

I had too many tasks and responsibilities and functions to perform in Tehran to worry about Mir Hashimi and his mistakes all the time. After some times, his was too much of a burden for me to bear. Of course, I had had some differences with him in the past. He was one of the group members who had relations with Marxist activists. Sometimes when he tried to modify our declarations to include his Marxist friends, we came into conflict.

However, whenever he was with me during our friendship and prayed or perhaps pretended to be religious, I knew that he was not serious about religion. His mother had told me that Mir Hashimi did not pray at home. Whenever Mir Hashimi was in our presence, he prayed and followed his religious duties. When he was with his Marxist friends, he would be influenced by them and would become negligent of his religious duties. When we were at Bandar Pahlavi, sometimes he prayed and sometimes did not. Since our return to Tehran, I had lost hope in him because he had completely thrown himself to the side of his leftist friends.

When we returned from the Caspian Sea, we went to visit some of his Marxist friends in order to learn about the prevailing condition. They had rented a room around the Fawziyeh (now Imam Hossein) square. We visited them and got introduced to one another. It was the first time I saw Faribraz, Khashayar, and Kiyumars Sanjari,[44] all three of whom became members of the Fidayan-i Khalq Organization. Mir Hashimi introduced me as an engineer. Because of the type of glasses and the briefcase that I carried, they believed him. We did not have any particular purpose in visiting that house. Its residents had come from other cities and were studying in Tehran. In that house, they spent their time playing cards and backgammon. I was neither a player nor was I interested in such things. I kept myself busy with books. At night, they insisted that I too should join them and play. Mir Hashimi thought that it would be an embarrassment if I didn't play! Finally, I was forced to play cards, and we were in groups of two to three people. Those four nights that I had watched them play, I understood that the object was to pick cards that added up to eleven. I was always confused on the difference between six and nine in Latin numbers. Sometimes I picked cards with the numbers six and two and at times the numbers nine and five. At first they thought that I was cheating them. They told Mir Hashimi that my game was suspicious. He too, had forgotten that he had introduced me as an engineer, and so he told them that I did not know English!

They asked, "So then how has he become an engineer?"

I saw that things were getting out of hand, and so I did not waste time. I said, "I am an expert in the field of printing

---

[44] Shahrak Chamkhaleh is located ten kilometers from Langurud. It is also very close to the mountainous areas of the Caspian Sea region. This area is very rich in two natural features. On the side it faces the Caspian Sea and in the back are the mountains. It is always green and appeasing to the eye. In addition to this, due to the presence of villas and hotels, Chamkhaleh is a major tourist town.

and repairing printing machines. But I have not gone to the university. I have gone for training and I have experience in this field. This is why my friends call me engineer."

After five or six days, we went back to the house that we had rented in Mesgar Abad. Since that day, however, I have carried the title of engineer.

I pitied Mir Hashimi and his friends. They had a plan to go to Babol and Amol by foot and come back. They had asked me to join them. I had accepted initially but changed my mind. There were twelve of them! The movie *Twelve Angry Men* had just come onto the screen in Tehran. So they called themselves the "Twelve Angry Men"! They went to Babol and Amol and returned. This was the first step in my separation from Mir Hashimi and his friends.

I was disappointed of the possibility of working with Mir Hashimi. I had the intention of separating myself from him, but since he was aware that I had ten thousand *tumans*, if I had left him in this condition, he would have thought that it was because of the money. That would have not been right. I decided to be patient because I wanted to influence him by setting an example of good conduct. I had no regrets in helping him as much as I could. I even found him a part-time job to support himself. But his reaction was very interesting. He said, "Ezzat! We are not supposed to work. Our duty is to adopt a strategy for struggle and revolution, and the people ought to help us; if not they will force us to steal."

I told him that I did not agree with his argument. I said that we have to earn money for our faith and for activities. I cannot eat people's money or steal people's belongings in the name of revolution. I have to struggle, work, and make money. Even though we have chosen to free people from oppression and restore justice, we cannot live and depend on people.

With the kind of ideas that he had, I had no choice but to separate from him. I told him in a friendly and sincere manner that it was no longer possible for us to remain together, and we had to separate, but we could continue our friendship. He did not expect such a gesture, and so he was annoyed and insisted that we had to remain together.

I told him, "I want to go to Bandar Abbas and buy some materials and bring them to sell them here in Tehran."

He said, "Let us go together. I am also coming."

I told him that it was not possible for us to leave Tehran together and that he should remain behind so that he could continue his duties if I were arrested on the way. I insisted that he should stay in Tehran and if he liked, he could work.

During those days, our rented room was in Mesgar Abad. He said that he would be lonely there. Without electricity, it was too hot for him in the house. He added that he would remain in Sanjari's house while I was gone and our belongings could remain in their house, and when I came back, we could still go to that house.

I agreed and gave him some money. He went to the house of Fariborz Sanjari in Fawziyeh Suare. I did not travel and of course I also did not go to the house. Four days had passed since our separation. I knew that Mir Hashimi was at Sanjari's house. I had to phone him because of a mission I had for him. I had some documents that were in the hands of my friends and I had to take them back. It was either on the fifth or sixth of the month of Shahrivar/August that I called Sanjari's house. The person who answered the phone said, "Yes! Please!"

Because of my numerous encounters with SAVAK I was familiar with their voice, tone, and manner of speech. I realized that there was something going on.

I said, "I want to talk to Khashayar."

He asked me, "Who are you?"

I said, "I am engineer Khonsari."

He said, "Hold on for a moment. I'll call him."

He then told his friend, "He is the one, the engineer!"

When the waiting period became too long, I hung up the phone. I then called another friend. Muhsin Rashidi picked up the phone and said angrily, "Sir, this is a wrong number. Khashyar is not here."

I realized how bad the situation was. I hung up the phone and again called the Sanjaris from a different number. I begged one of the neighbors to tell me the situation there and in the neighborhood. He told me that SAVAK was present in the area. I then phoned another one of my friends and asked him about Khashayar. He told me that he did not know them and that I had phoned a wrong number, and he hung up the phone. I realized that they had been arrested. The danger had come really close. There was the possibility of all kinds of developments. I went to the house at Mesgar Abad and collected books and documents that were there and told my landlord that I was traveling.[45]

When Mir Hashimi was arrested, just like my other friends, he turned everything against me and held me responsible for all others who had been arrested. This was because we had all agreed that if a person was arrested, he should put all the blame on those who were not arrested. The arrest of

---

[45] Faribrez, Khashayar, and Kiyumars Sanjari are from Malayar region. All of them were active members of the Fidayan-i Khalq organization and were under SAVAK surveillance for over a decade. Faribrez was arrested in 1350/1971 and sentenced together with thirty-two other people including Mas'ud Ahmad Zadeh Heravi. He was released from prison in 1357/1978 and married Rubabeh Ashraf Zadeh Dehqani, commonly known as Ashraf Dihqani. After the victory of the Islamic Revolution he opposed the Islamic Republic and then fled the country. Currently he lives in France, and his signatures can be seen on some of the declarations in opposition to the revolution.

Khashayar was born in the year 1327/1948. He was a student at in the Technical School of Narmak studying in the faculty of arts and sciences. Because of his participation in political activities, he never completed his studies. Khashayar was killed in the month of Farvardin 1354/March 1975 by SAVAK agents.

Kiyumars was born in the year 1329/1950. Like his brother he was a student at the Science and Technology University of Narmak. Their mother, Mah Munir Farzaneh, passed away in Paris in 1382/2003. Her memoirs were published in France under the title of *Surud Payedari* (*Eternal Anthem of Resistance*).

Fariborz Sanjari was also connected to me, and so it added another page to my already thick dossier in SAVAK.

At the same time the news of the martyrdom of Mr. Sa'idi and Nikdavudi under torture reached us. Their martyrdom under torture resulted in an uproar against the of Shah's secret police. It only took ten days from the arrest to the martyrdom of Mr. Sa'idi. He was severely tortured in the Qizil Qal'ah Prison.

The total number of the people arrested from our group was fifteen by then. The responsibility of all the activities of our group such as burning the makeshift arches, producing and printing the declarations, bombing the office of the El-Al airways and so on had been blamed on me. During the trial of our group members in the military court, they referred to us as "the El-Al group." They identified me as the leader of this group. But fortunately for me they mistakenly wrote my name as Arab Shahi instead of Ezzat Shahi. Most of the people arrested including Lashkari, Mir Hashimi, Hasan Kulahduzan, Lajevardi, Khorasani, and Karrubi were sentenced to prison terms ranging from one to four years. With the arrest of Mir Hashimi, I did not run away, but I began to be more cautious. Meanwhile I continued with my political ties with other groups as I became more serious in the fight against the Shah's regime.[46]

---

[46] Ahmad Ahmad in his memoir wrote, "After completing my military service in Mehr, 1349/September 1970, I needed weapons to prepare for military operation. Mr. Javad Mansuri introduced me to one of the brothers named Ezzat Shahi to obtain weapon from him. His alias was Khonsari. I spoke to him several times. Once, I went mountain climbing with him. There, he assured me that he would deliver weapons within the next two to three days. Days passed but there was no news from him. One early morning I went to his house located near Khorasan Square. He was not at home. When the landlord and the neighbors heard me calling him by the name of Khonsari, they guessed that I was one of his closest friends. So they said, "We do not know where he is. People have been looking for him for some days!" Upon hearing this I realized that he was under SAVAK surveillance. So I left that place cautiously and when I was far enough to feel safe I in-

Ezzat Shahi: A SAVAK Agent or a Madman?

After Mir Hashimi was arrested, almost all the members of our group were arrested except me. I really wanted to know to what extent my friends had revealed information about me. So I went to visit them in prison once or twice. I was a friend of Mir Hashimi's family. I had a close relationship with his brother, sister, and mother. I joined his family, and we visited him together.

During the Persian New Year holidays (*nowruz*) in [March] 1350/1971 one day I changed my appearance and put on a new suit and tie and a hat and went to visit Mir Hashimi as his brother in the prison. I talked with Lajevardi, Lashkari, Taleqani, Anwari, and others behind the bars, but I was able to speak with Mir Hashimi face to face. The families of Amani and Hajj Hadi had also come to visit their brother Hajj Hashim, who had been given life imprisonment. I knew both of them. I went to them and greeted them. Hajj Hadi was surprised but unhappy to see me. He turned his head and looked away, avoided eye contact with me, and did not return my greeting. Then at the bazaar, explaining what he had witnessed, Hadi revealed that Hashimi had told the people in prison that this guy (Ezzat Shahi) is either a madman or a servant of SAVAK! Otherwise, a person in his right mind who is being sought after would never come to prison on his own to visit his friends![47]

---

formed my friends about Khonsari's situation and told them to avoid going to his house." *Memoirs of Ahmad Ahmad,* p. 213

[47] In his memoirs Morteza Alviri wrote about the activities of the group and of another organization under the command of Ezzat Shahi, whose name he did not remember. He only recalled that he had a relationship with Alviri and was with him on the journey to Damavand and Lake Tar. He took part in the distribution of the declarations. Alviri wrote, "I came to know of Ezzat Shahi in the year 1349/1970. At that time he had not yet joined the Mujahidin-e Khalq and was well-known among political activists. He also worked in the bazaar. He and I, together with two to three other people, decided to form a new organization. With the growth of the activities of

83

On another occasion I went to the prison with Mahdi Maliki. He asked Mir Hashimi where he had hidden the book that had the formulae. What he meant was the book containing the chemical formulas for making the bombs. Mir Hashimi was shocked and looked at me and could not say anything. During such visits, a police officer was present in the meeting room. That day a prison guard named Namiyan was present there and could hear our conversation. I noticed that everything was about to be ruined. I jokingly told Maliki, "How could you have forgotten? That mathematics formulae book is in my possession. If you need it for the final exam to get your high school diploma come and get it." Moments later when the prison guard went to write the report, we quickly left the place and never went back.

Collaboration with Hossein Jannati

Lajevardi and Lashkari were introduced to Hossein Jannati in prison where they shared a cell together.[48] Reportedly, a cer-

---

this organization, we could educate people about the weaknesses of the Shah's regime and prepare the ground for an armed resistance in order to fight against the regime in the future. The founders of this organization were five or six people including Ezzat Shahi, Mohammad Ali Khalili Niya and Katouzian, who unfortunately joined the MKO. Reportedly, he was killed in an internal armed conflict with his own group. We held a lot of meetings to plan our activities. This was when the MKO was very serious in carrying out their activities." *Memoirs of Morteza Alviri*, p. 27.

[48] Amir Lashkari narrated the following story about the coming of Ezzat Shahi for a visit to prison: "We had just been recently arrested. So we had to be very cautious so we never contacted anyone. Ezzat, too, was a courageous and fearless man. It was on the Eid day in the year 1350/1971 when he came once or twice to visit us. This was the same time that the police were looking for him. I told him behind the bars, 'What a courageous person you are! The SAVAK agents are searching for you door to door, yet you come here on your own two feet!' Anyway, we knew who he was." (An interview with Amir Lashkari, 3/10/1383)

Mohammad Reza Moqaddam was one of the members of the El-Al operations who was arrested while in service in the Literacy Corps in Kerman. When he was taken to the prison, he said, "Ezzat came to visit us

tain *mulla* named Shaykh Golru had disturbed Hossein and gave him a hard time in prison. Hossein complained to Lajevardi, who then volunteered to intervene and settle their dispute. Soon at lunch time Lajevardi started an argument with Golru over a silly excuse as to who should get the best utensils just before lunch. Lajevardi became physical and began to beat up Golru. With the intervention of prison guards, Shaykh Golru was taken to solitary confinement for one month and was released at the end of the month. Hossein, too, was released after a short time, and as Lashkari and Lajevardi had told him, he came to see me. From then on, regular contact started between us. From that day I started regular trips to Qom to establish connection with other individuals who might be potentially interested in joining us.

Hossein was a high school student in his senior year. Together we would often visit many *'ulama* and some Sources of Emulation *(maraji')* in Qom. For example, we once visited Mr. Mohammad 'Ali Gerami[49] at his house and took some of

---

two or three times so that we could assess the situation and find out to what extent the SAVAK had collected information about us.

"On New Year's Eve of 1350/1971 they did not place restrictions on visitors. I suddenly saw Ezzat Shahi wearing funny clothes. He had put on a suit, a tie, a cap, and a pair of glasses. That was at a time when the SAVAK was searching for Ezzat door to door. His presence in prison at such a moment was a very surprising thing. I remember that some of us did not recognize him at first. He went to Mr. Hashim Amani and greeted him. Amani at once recognized him. He was really shocked. He turned his head and started walking around in his cell, pretending that he did not know Ezzat and saying, 'Is this Ezzat Shahi a servant of the SAVAK or a madman! Is it possible for someone who is being searched everywhere by the SAVAK to walk to this place on his own feet!' In short, this was one of the actions of Ezzat who was the only person not yet arrested in our group. Probably, he lived in a situation in which he actually needed to know the level of information about him that had been given to the SAVAK." *An interview with Mohammad Reza Moqaddam,* 5/11/1383.

[49] Mohammad Hossein (b. 1330/1951). He began his political activities in high school, and when he graduated, he was arrested for selling copies of letters, Imam Khomeini's works in Qom. He spent six moths in prison. In prison, he kept in contact with members of Islamic Coalition

our declarations for him. In our subsequent visit we discussed the possibility of armed resistance with him. We requested that he turn his sermons to political issues and frank discussions about the political condition of the country on the pulpit. Mr. Gerami's reply was very interesting. He said that a few nights before our meeting he had a dream of the Prophet. The Prophet had said that Ayatullah Khomeini has one foot in Heaven and therefore he (Gerami) must focus all his time and energy on his religious duties and the affairs of the Qom seminary and prepare for the leadership of the community! We left him at that point so that he would carry on the duty that he was supposedly instructed to carry on.

Party and attended Mr. Asgar Awladi's teaching sessions. After his release from prison he was connected with Ezzat Shahi, and produced and distributed declarations issued by Imam Khomeini and others. In 1325/1973 SAVAK was after him because of his association with Ezzat Shahi and also his membership in the MKO. Under different names, such as Abdullahi and Ahmad Zamani, he pursued an underground life. On Mordad 28, 1354/August 19, 1975 he was arrested as a result of confessions of Vahid Afrakhteh and was sentenced to life imprisonment. He was released from prison in the month of Aban, 1357/October 1978, and resumed his activities in the MKO. For a while he was the leader of the MKO headquarter in Isfahan. Along with another MKO member known as Fazlullah Tadayyun he ran for the parliament but was not elected. In 1359/1980 he married Fatimeh Sururi, a student in Isfahan University and a member of MKO. After MKO declared armed resistance against the Islamic Republic, Hossein and his wife intensified their activities. In the autumn of the year 1360/1981, his house was besieged. According to Ayatullah Musavi Tabrizi, the date of this event coincided with the assassination of Musa Khiyabani and Ashraf Rabi'i on 19/Bahman, 1360/February 7, 1981. When Hossein realized that resistance was futile he tried to escape and jumped out of the window of their building and died. When his wife, who had gone shopping, returned home, she was suspicious of the situation and escaped from the scene. Later on, she left the country and continued with her activities in the organization. Hossein and Fatimeh had a son named Muhsin. He was raised by his grandfather, Ayatullah Ahmad Jannati. At the age of seventeen or eighteen, while he was working in the office of *Munkarat* (in charge of Commanding Good and Forbidding the Reprehensible), he was killed in an auto accident. See Asadollah Lajevardi, 223; "telephone conversation with 'Ali Jannati," 28-11-1383/2004; in *Cheshm Andaz Iran*, number 22, 41.

My friendship with Hossein, his brother Ali,[50] and their father was very precious. Sometimes when I went to Qom, even when Hossein was not present, I settled in their house and had interesting conversations with his father. Of course, I was always careful not to reveal myself and never talked about politics and political struggles. During this time, I taught Hossein the basic rules and principles of political activity, how to pursue an underground life, and even how to make a bomb. We went to Darband and Ushan for hiking several times with him and his brother 'Ali. My friendship with Hossein became very close and we distributed declarations in Qom several times. When I took Sadiq Katouzian to Qom several times, he stayed in Hossein's house as well.[51]

Sadiq and I were friends for several years. He was young, and in the beginning he did not know much about political activities and its requirements and implications. Through his participation in the religious sessions of the *Ansar* group, he was introduced to its members, such as Hasan Hossein Zadeh, Amir Hosseini, and others. Therefore, his name was mentioned in the SAVAK agents' reports about this group. I got to

---

[50] Mohammad Ali Gerami (b. 1317/1938) received his elementary education and before graduating from high school entered the seminary in Qom. He actively participated in the events of 15 Khordad, 1342/June 5, 1963. He was arrested in 1344/1965 and exiled to Gunbad Kawus. His memoirs were published under the title *Yek Tab'idi* (*An Exiled Man*). After teaching for a while he was arrested again in 1347/1968 for condemning death penalties given by the regime to the founders of MKO. At first he was imprisoned in Qom and later on transferred to the Ghezel Ghal'ah prison. He published several books including *Khoda dar Nahj al Balagheh* (*God in* Nahj al-Balaghah), *Shenakht-e Qur'an* (*Knowing of the holy Qur'an*), *Sharh Urve* (*The Explanation of Urve*), *Negahi be Bardegi* (*A Look at Slavery*), *Dowlat Jumhurie Islami* (*The Islamic Republic*), and *Barresie Melak-ha-ye Ravani dar Islam* (*A Look into the Psychological Criteria in Islam*).
[51] In his memoirs, 'Ali Jannati wrote about his connection to Ezzat Shahi and stated that he received many of the educational pamphlets and declarations from him and knew that he was a member of a secret armed group because he lived underground. See, *Memoirs of 'Ali Jannati*, p. 89, Tehran, 1389/2010.

know him in the gatherings of this group as well. After that he visited me from time to time in the bazaar. He was still very young, somewhat spoiled, and not yet ready for political activity. He was always very well dressed and clean-shaven. Even in the winter season, he preferred to stand the cold and never wore a heavy sweater to remain safe from cold. He always went out in a shirt and an overcoat. I told him repeatedly to dress warmly, but he did not heed my advice.

On the basis of what I knew of him, I decided to work on him and his way of thinking and include him in some of the activities such as distribution of declarations and letters of Imam Khomeini as well as participation in some of the meetings. It was for these reasons that whenever I went to Qom, I took him to the house of Mr. Jannati. His relation with Hossein Jannati evolved in this manner. With the help of Jawad Mansuri, we established an institute to teach in order to identify and attract other youths to our group.

Imprisoned Because of Me

During the period of living underground, gradually I sold everything that I had, including my furniture and library, and spent the money on my daily needs. When I was about to run out of money, I went to one of my friends, Mohammad Kachu'i, who had a book-binding business. He was aware of my political activities and the difficulties of my underground life. I asked him to give me a job in his shop so that I could make some money and meet my expenses. He agreed to give me money but did not want me to work. I told him that I was not asking for charity and could not accept money unless he allowed me to work in his shop because I was skilled in printing and bookbinding. Finally he accepted and gave me a job. With my being at his shop, Kachu'i had peace of mind and could take a break from his responsibilities. Hardly had I begun to work in the shop than I found out that the police had discovered my whereabouts. One day when Kachu'i was not in the shop, they came in, but did not recognize me. They asked me about Kachu'i and I told them he was around. When I asked them what they wanted they said that they just wanted to place an order for several albums. I recognized them and asked them whether they had a sample, but they said that they didn't have one. I placed some albums in front of them. One of them chose a sample and said that he wanted one like that but insisted that he had to speak with Kachu'i himself. It was two o'clock in the afternoon, so I told them to come later in the afternoon.

They asked me where he had gone and I said that since it was Thursday he had gone to collect payments for some orders. He could be anywhere, only God knew where he was! I told them if he was done with collection, he might come back soon. I showed courtesy by welcoming them to sit down and sent one of our workers to bring them tea. After drinking the tea they stepped out of the shop and began to stroll around and said that they would wait until he came. They strolled back and forth in the middle of the street but came back after half an hour. I took this opportunity to shred some of the documents and declarations and stuff them under the photocopy machine.

They asked me for Kachu'i's telephone number and I said that Kachu'i was not an organized person and that I did not have his number. Just as I was talking, Kachu'i arrived on his motorbike with Hasan Kabiri. They wanted to get off the motorcycle but I made a gesture for them not to do so! They did not understand and immediately entered the shop. Before they even said anything, I placed two books in front of them and started shouting, "Hey Sir! You are making fool of us! Last night you made us wait for you here until nine o'clock to come and take your books, but you never showed up. Now take your books and go away and let me never see you again here. We will never accept orders from you again."

They both understood that I was playing a game and that things were not all right. They gave me some money as a payment for the books and left the shop as quickly as they had come. Before they left, at a very brief opportunity and away from the eyes of the policemen, I told Kachu'i that I would go to the Khorasan Square within two hours, and if I didn't show up then he would know that I was arrested. I then asked them to quickly disappear from that area. After they left, the policemen asked why Kachu'i would not come back to the shop, and I reminded them that he was not a predictable fellow and perhaps would return by late afternoon.

My task was already over there. I had a feeling of relief after helping Kachu'i escape. The police officers again left the shop, and in their absence I told the two younger workers that I had to leave and if the officers came later they should just tell them that Kachu'i did not show up and that he would be at the shop on Saturday. I instructed them to close the shop and go home and not open it on Saturday unless we give them instruction. I then picked up my coat and left through the back alley. During this time, the officers had asked the neighbors about us and tried to get information about Kachu'i and his whereabouts.

The neighbors had told them that Kachu'i was here a few minutes ago with his friend on a motorbike, and Mr. Mahmoodi should have told him.

They asked, "And who is Mr. Mahmoodi?"

They said, "He is that person whom you were talking to in the shop!"

They understood that they had been completely duped. They had lost both Mr. Kachu'i and me.[5253]

---

[52] Mohammad Kachu'i (b. 1329/1950). After graduating from sixth grade elementary school started a book-binding shop in the bazaar to support his family. He started his political activities by participating in classes held by Ayatullah Khamene'ie in the Ansar al-Hossein mosque. He also attended Arabic language classes in the *Maktab al-Qur'an Institute.* He was arrested in 1351/1972. SAVAK tortured him to reveal the whereabouts of Ezzat Shahi. He was then sentenced to one-year prison term. After his release from prison, he continued his activities and was again arrested in Azar, 1353/November 1974 and was given a life imprisonment. He was released because of to the pressures by the Human Rights Commission on the Iranian regime on the 28th of Mordad, 1356/August 19, 1977. He was an ardent

When Kachu'i decided to marry, I advised him that if he wanted to be part of the struggle, then he should not marry because none of us was wealthy or had anyone to take care of the wife and children in case we died or got arrested in the course of the struggle. Unfortunately, he never listened to my words and said that he would marry a girl from a family who were aware of his beliefs and were involved in political struggle themselves. In any case, he married the sister of Hasan Hossein Zadeh. Hasan was a fighter and had already been jailed. His father, too, was a follower of Ayatullah Kashani. Kachu'i felt comfortable that he had formed a relationship with a family of fighters. He thought that in case of a problem, the girl would be cared for by her own family. His wife was not happy about his political activities. Of course she was right because she had witnessed some of the hardships her father's family experienced as a result of their involvement in political activity and did not want her life to go through the same kind of difficulties.

Later in the afternoon of the same day that I had helped Kachu'i and Kabiri to escape, I went to Khorasan Square and met Kachu'i. His wife was pregnant at that time. I reminded him of my advice not to get married if he wanted to be involved in political activity and that now that he had gotten married he had to separate from his wife and child and leave them in God's hands! Just like the rest of us, he had to start living an underground life. Otherwise, he should go back to his life because sooner or later the police will come after him. He said that his wife was about to deliver her baby any day and that he could not leave her in this situation but promised to

---

enemy of the MKO and the Marxist groups. After the victory of the Islamic Revolution he was appointed as the security chief of Khomeini's temporary residence at the Refah School compound. When the Ayatullah moved to Jamaran, Kachu'i was appointed as the Director of the notorious Evin prison in Tehran. Finally, he was assassinated by Kazim Afjeh'ie by the order of Moḥammad Reza Sa'adati.

keep low profile and stay away from the eyes of the police. He then left me and took his wife and went to live in the house of his brother-in-law who lived near the Khorasan Square. After two days, his child Muhsin was born. The police went to his father's house. *His father, Mohammad, was a police informant* and was completely against political activities against the Shah's regime. He took the police officers to Kachu'i's house and said, "My son is here; arrest him!"

When the police entered the house, Kachu'i was praying. After he concluded his prayer, they arrested him. They were so annoyed that he had once escaped from their hands through me, the main suspect. But Kachu'i did not give any information about me. It seems that they really tortured him, but he remained quiet. Of course it was not possible for him to give them my address, because he did not know my whereabouts, and my phone calls were different public phones each time. Although he could have betrayed me and given some of our friends' names and addresses, he never did so and underwent the torture for my sake.

After a year and some months, after realizing that Kachu'i had not revealed any information, they freed him on the condition that he stop all his political activities and report the people who visited him. After some time, a number of our friends went to him and told him that they wanted to go to Mashhad to bring weapons and that they needed his help. Kachu'i advised them not to do so because those weapons are hand-made and fake. He even told them that they could buy weapons from some SAVAK agents who were corrupt and would do anything for money! They listened to his advice and so did not go to Mashhad. Soon they were arrested and they confessed that they were in contact with Kachu'i. The police arrested Kachu'i again because of his refusal to cooperate as an informant and his failure to report his meeting with those friends. He was charged for repeating the same crime knowingly and was sentenced to life imprisonment.

On the Shores of Lake Tar

One of the main centers of political struggle was in Damavand. A number of activists in our group like Hossein Shari'atmadari, Morteza Alviri, 'Ali Reza Kabiri, Muhsin Hajj 'Alibaigi, Asghar, and Sadiq Nuroozi went to Damavand once a week and held meetings there.

One of my brothers-in-law was an employee in the Bureau of Registration and Records and worked in the Damavand office and lived there. I visited Damavand once a week and went to my sister's house. I also participated in the meetings of my friends, which were held in the house of Mr. Tavassuli and where speakers presented lectures on different topics. This house had a big courtyard and was on a street close to the SAVAK office in Damavand. SAVAK had complete control over the area.

The meetings were held in the house during the winter season and outside in the courtyard during summer. Different preachers came to these meetings and gave talks. I remembered having seen and listened to Mr. Imami Kashani and Shahcheragi. Mr. Mohammad Jawad Sharafat (who was martyred in the bomb blast in the office of the Islamic Republic Party) was then a teacher at the city of Masjid Suleiman. He had been sent into exile in Karaj. He taught exegesis of the holy Qur'an in these sessions. Sometimes I took declarations and distributed them among people who attended these sessions.

One day my friends told me, "We would like to go to Lake Tar. Would you like to come with us?"

I said that if I came, I would have to bring with me four or five people. They agreed and so we were almost thirty people in total who traveled toward the north. For a quite a distance, the SAVAK agents followed us. At night, I went to them and said, "Look, we know who you are and you also know who we are! So don't bother yourself aimlessly. We shall go on our own and come back on our own. Don't bother in the middle of the dark night to follow us."

93

They laughed and got scared of the darkness of the night seriously so they turned around and went back. We remained for two or three days beside the lake and the plains of Damavand. The weather was warm and there was no need of putting up the tents. But for the sake of avoiding mosquito bites, we put them up anyway. In that place Mr. Sharafat and others gave their sermons, and then we returned. We separated right in front of the SAVAK office.

*   *   *

CHAPTER TWO

Drill with Weapons

Together with the Hizbul'lah group

Early in the month of Bahman, 1344[54]/February 1965 an article with bold headings reported the arrest of an armed group called The Islamic Nations Party (Hezb-i Milal-i Islami). The leader of this group was Seyyed Kazim Bujnurdi,[55] whom I met and became friends with in prison.

Other important members of this group were Mohammad Javad Hujatti Kermani,[56] Abulqasem Sarhaddi Zadeh,[57]

---

[54] Seyyid Mohammad Kazim Bujnurdi (b. in Najaf 1321/1942) came to Iran in 1339 and attended Sepahsalar (now Shahid Motahhari) seminary. In Isfand, 1340/March 1961, he established the Islamic Nations Party (Hizb-i Milal-i Islami). Its purpose was to start armed resistance against the Shah's regime and establish an Islamic government. However, the group was discovered by the police, and its members were initially sentenced to death, but with THE mediation of Ayatullah Mohsin Hakim they were given life imprisonment. While in prison, Bujnurdi translated the book entitled *Iqtisaduna* (*Our Economy*) written by Shahid Seyyid Mohammad Baqir Sadr. After the victory of the Islamic Revolution, he served in the following positions: governor general of Isfahan, a member of parliament in the first Islamic National Assembly, director of the Center for the Great Encyclopedia of Islam, director of Iran National Library, and cultural advisor to the office of the President Khatami

[55] Hujat al-Islam Mohammad Jawad Hujjati Kermani (b. Kerman 1311/1932) was arrested in the month of Bahman, 1343/February 1962 when he gave a sermon in support of the assassination of Hasan Ali Mansur and was jailed for a few months. He was again arrested in the year 1344/1965 because of his membership in the Islamic Nations Party (Hizb-i Milal-i Islami) He spent ten years in prison until the autumn of 1354/1975. Again in 1357/1978 he was arrested and jailed. After the victory of the Islamic Revolution, he remained active in the country's political, social, and cultural life and held several important positions.

[56] Abolqasem Sarhaddi Zadeh (b. 1324/1945) joined the Islamic Nations Party (Hizb-i Milal-i Islami) before the events of 15th of Khordad 1342/June 25,1963. He was arrested in 1344/1965 and given life imprisonment, but his term was later reduced to fifteen years. After the victory of

Arabshahi,[58] and Javad Mansuri. The Islamic Nations Party [59] advocated armed resistance against the Shah's regime and was

---

the Islamic Revolution, he joined the Revolutionary Guard Corps and held positions as the director of the Downtrodden Foundation (Bunyad-e Mostaz'afan), Director of National Prisons, membership in the Central Cadre of the Islamic Republican Party, the Director General of *Subh-i Azadegan* Newspaper, Minister of Labor, and several terms membership of the parliament.

[57] Mohammad Mawlavi Arab Shahi was a university student studying engineering, and a member of Islamic Nations Party. When the party was discovered by SAVAK, he escaped to Najaf and lived many years there as well as in Lebanon and Syria. From there he went to East Germany and continued his education. Currently he is affiliated with the Center for the Great Encyclopedia of Islam and is the editor-in-chief of the science department.

[58] The Islamic Nations Party (Hizb-i Milal-i Islami) was a political organization and advocated the armed struggle and revolution that was established in 1340/1971 by Seyyid Mohammad Kazim Bujnurdi. It advocated the establishment of an Islamic government. Its constitution contained sixty-five articles that dealt with the party's economic plans, judicial and cultural structures, and foreign relations of the state. In 1344 after the arrest of a member, Mohammad Baqir Senobari, fifty-five other members of the party were also arrested

[59] In his memoirs, Bujnurdi, who at the age of sixteen joined the Islamic Propagation and Dissemination Party (Hizb al-da'wah al-Islamiyyah), wrote, "In *hizb al-da'awa* despite the fact that I was only a teenager, I was appointed as the head of three units of the organization. This was done perhaps in consideration of my education and my humble knowledge and political consciousness, while many members of the organization were older than me.

"It was obvious that they counted on me. I had developed a taste for politics and an insight into political matters and was able to present fresh analysis about the current events. Once I told one of my superiors in the party that the popular reception of Abd al-Karim Qasim's *coup d'état* killed all the possibilities for an Islamic revolution in Iraq. However, in light of the objective conditions brought about by the *coup d'état* of 28th Mordad/August 19, 1953, an Islamic revolution was possible to take place." (Bujnurdi, 15, 16)

It is possible to say that Bujnurdi was aware of the political conditions in Iran after *coup d'état* of in 1332/1953. Inspired by *Hizb al-da'wah* and the political events in Iraq and the rest of the world, he planned the establishment of an organization in order to fight and topple the regime of

in the process of organizing the base of their operations and activities. The biggest shortcoming of this group was its lack of deep knowledge of Iranian society, as its leader was born and raised in Iraq. They held meetings and used fictitious identities and names.

Reportedly, some members of this group collaborated with members of similar groups in Arab countries such as the Muslim Brotherhood (Ikhwan al-Muslimin). Perhaps the name they had adopted for the group was to highlight this connection.[60] Even though they were sincere and honest people, they were weak in organizational skills and the necessities of oppositional political activities. They had come together because of their long association and friendship. Some of them had decided in Iraq to start their political activities when they came to Iran. They conducted classes, practiced shooting, and recruited members to distribute pamphlets and declarations. However, they were not very lucky and were all arrested before any sig-

---

the Shah through armed resistance and replace it with an Islamic government.

[60] In 1346/1967 Abbas Aghazamani (known as Abu Sharif), Javad Mansuri, Ahmad Ahmad, and Ali Reza Sepasi Ashtiyani, who were all former members of Islamic Nations Party (Hizb-i Milal-i Islami) formed a group to prepare individual members to face challenges and threats from the Shah's regime and use their past experiences in their struggle against it. Inspired by the Qur'an (*Beware! the party of Allah, they are the victorious* 5:56) they named the new organization The Party of God (Hizbul'lah). Their goal was to fight against the regime of the Shah and topple it. This group adopted the Islamic monotheistic worldview as the ideology of the group without much publicity. They intended to provide ideological training and education to their members before carrying out any activity and remain a secret underground organization. After the terrible blow that SAVAK inflicted upon the MKO in Shahrivar 1350/August 1971, the Mujahidin members tried to infiltrate into Hizbul'lah organization and attract their members to their own group and incorporate the Hizbul'lah into the MKO and use them for their own purposes in their organization. Some of the founding members of Hizbul'lah, such as Javad Mansuri, were not willing to merge with the MKO. They left the group, and that was the end of the Hizbul'lah group.

nificant operation due to lack of experience. After their release from prison, they formed a new group and called it The Party of God (Hizbul'lah).[61]

In 1347/1968 they began their activities and concentrated on theoretical and educational programs. They organized Arabic language classes for people, especially the youth. They also identified and recruited students from universities and other learning institutions and guided them to these classes in groups. The teacher of most of these classes was Javad Mansuri.

These classes focused on the holy Qur'an, prophetic sayings (*hadith*) and narrations from the *Nahj al-Balaghah* with the main theme of struggle against injustice and oppression through armed resistance. These classes were publicized, and even the regime's agents were aware of their activities because they appeared like any other class in an educational institution.

I also attended these classes for a time and established contact with some of their members. Some of the connections were in fact established through similar gatherings where members were recruited. In these centers, there were some people who could be easily identified by the manner of their fiery speech and behavior. For example, in a class that Ayatullah Khamene'ie taught I could easily identify those who asked fiery questions and those who were more compromising, and

---

[61] In the Hizbul'lah group, Abbas Aghazamani started Arabic language classes in the Hajj Ahmad Mosque and later on in the mosque of Amir al-Mu'uminin. These classes adopted new teaching methods and were free of charge. Aghazamani wanted his students to memorize verses of the holy Qur'an, especially those dealing with the issue of *jihad*. After some time, Jamal Nikoo Qadam, Javad Mansuri, and Abbas Duzduzani started other classes. These classes met in a three-story building adjacent to Amir al-Mu'uminin Mosque. They hoped to achieve three objectives: (a) Propagate Islam and expand cultural activities; (b) Identify and attract new members to their group; and, (c) Control and make good use of people's talent and capabilities. See *Memoirs of Ahmad Ahmad*, 3–172.

some people never asked any questions and always remained silent. It was through these gatherings that I came to know members of Hizbul'lah. In their religious activities, their political objectives were hidden but easily discernible.

From the ideological point of view Hizbul'lah faced a major dilemma. Even though their faith and belief in religion was firm there were some contradictions in their words and deeds that did not correspond with injunctions of religion. For example, they condoned robbery and stealing for the sake of the group's objectives, while this is forbidden in religion. In fact, there were two currents of thought in Hizbul'lah at that time. The first advocated theoretical and ideological training and preparation through teaching the Arabic language, the science of Qur'anic commentary, and the *Nahj al-Balaghah.* Javad Mansuri[62] and Abbas Aghazamani were in this group.[63]

---

[62] Javad Mansuri (b. 324/1945) received his education at Alavi High School. Then he joined the Hujatiyyeh group followed by membership in the Islamic Nations Party (Hizb-i Milal-i Islami). In Mehr 1344/September 1965, Mansuri was arrested along with his brother Ahmad and spent six years in prison until his release in Isfand 1347/February 1968. That same year Mansuri became a member of the Central Committee of Hizbul'lah group. When Hizbul'lah and the MKO merged in the second half of 1350/1971, he left the group. He received his B.A. degree in economics at Tehran University. He was released from prison in the month of Azar 1357/November 1978. After the victory of the Islamic Revolution, Mansuri served in the following posts: Commander of the Revolutionary Guard Corps, Deputy Foreign Minister for Cultural Affairs, Iran's Ambassador to Pakistan, Vice Chancellor for Cultural Affairs at the Azad Islamic University, and several other positions. Mansuri wrote and published several books, including *National Independence* (*Esteghlal*)*, Culture and Development* (*Farhang va To'se'eh*), *The Development of the Islamic Revolution* (*Sayr-i Takvini Enqelab Islami*) and *The Uprising of the 15ᵗʰ of Khordad, 1342* (*Qiyam 15 Khordad 1342*). See *Memoirs of Ahmad Ahmad*, 134–135).

[63] Abas Aghazamani, known as Abu Sharif (b. Tehran, 1318/191939), obtained membership in the Islamic Nations Party (Hizb-i Milal-i Islami). Abu Sharif was arrested in 1965 and imprisoned for two years, to be released in 1346/1967. He earned a degree from the School of Foreign Language Translation, followed by a degree in Islamic Law from the University of Tehran's School of Theology. In 1346/1967, Aghazamani, in collabo-

99

The second current supported more emphasis on military training and formation of an armed force; Mohammad Mufidi, Baqir Abbasi, and Ali Reza Sepasi were notable members of this current.

Members of this faction were often very proud and even arrogant, and this attitude rendered them careless and negligent of organizational efficiency and safety, and they rarely observed rules of security. This was at a time that protecting security of every fighter was the most important task. They did not observe the most basic rule of security. For example they carried large grenades on the back of their trousers and walked in the street. It could be easily detected even if one wore a jacket. Sometimes their guns could be seen through their coats. This degree of carelessness showed how little they knew about the secret police and their power and modes of operation.

Another example is that they were careless about time and never attended a meeting on time. In certain situations, being five minutes early or late for a meeting could be a matter of life and death. At times they would come early and at other times with a half an hour or longer delay. Sometimes they would not even show up. I had told the Hizbul'lah members

---

ration with Javad Mansuri, Ahmad Ahmad, and Ali Reza Sepasi Ashtiyani, established the Hizbul'lah group as an underground organization. But he left the group when it merged with MKO. After spending time in Palestine and Lebanon, Pakistan, and then in Europe he joined the Muslim Students Association there. In the autumn of 1357/1978 Abu Sharif joined the supporters of Imam Khomeini and returned to Iran after the victory of the Islamic Revolution. He served at the Refah School and was in charge of security at the compound. He was one of the founders of the Revolutionary Guard Corps and in Ordibehesht 1357/May 1979 was appointed as its Commander of Operations. Aghazamani played a major role in defeating opposition groups in Kurdistan and Tabriz and restoring order there. Finally he was appointed as the Commander-in-Chief of the Guard in 1359/1980. Then he was appointed as Iran's [military] attaché in Pakistan, to be promoted soon as Iran's Ambassador, and retired two years later. He has been living there ever since. See *Farhang Nomravan*, vol. 2, 91–94.

that since I had been under the surveillance of SAVAK for years, I kept a low profile and live in hiding most of the time. Therefore, nobody should come to my house without advance notice or arrangement. Whenever they wanted to have a meeting with me, we held it somewhere far away from my house, and then we would go to the house together. This is the degree of care and caution I observed. At times I had to threaten them that if they came to my house and got arrested by the police, they should blame themselves because they put my life and their own at serious risk. I told them that I was under constant surveillance and might be arrested any day. We did not have to have regular meetings, but if I was arrested, I would not be able to resist torture too long. Apart from that, I could escape from SAVAK in the streets, but one day I might fail, and they would be able to find out where I lived. In such a situation they could locate and arrest anyone who came to that house. Therefore, I insisted that if they wished to come to my house, they should make sure to coordinate with me in advance and should not bring a new person without my knowledge because, for security reasons, I might not always be interested in meeting and knowing new people. Sometimes I felt that some of the members of the group came to my house out of curiosity to check whom I met and what I did. Therefore, when a person knocked at the door without advance notice, I did not allow them into my house, to teach them a lesson. Even if the landlord opened the door, I made up an excuse and turned them away. Unfortunately, they were curious to know any person who came to my house. This was to disregard one of the most fundamental principles of security. Of course, later they chose fictitious names for themselves on the advice of experienced activists.

It was due to these weaknesses that when I encountered them, in a short time I learned many of their secrets, and therefore was not willing to support them or introduce other activists to them. Some of them were aware of my background and were aware that I knew many activists and was in contact with them. They insisted that I should introduce some people to them, and I always refused and made different excuses. Since I could not count on their security measures, I performed my duties alone and without their knowledge.

Members of Hizbul'lah, like those of Islamic Nations Party, were young, and there was hardly anyone among them who was older than twenty-five years of age. As a result, they were immature and lacked experience and knowledge about society on one hand, and on the other hand, they were very emotional and zealous. Moreover, they did not respect the older and more experienced activists and claimed that the older ones did not intend to bring change and therefore were counter-revolutionaries.

Similarly, they did not seek advice on security matters from the older activists on the grounds that they did not know much. They were too proud of their own accomplishments and did not give credit to others. Among them there were some elements that were against the clergy and did not wish any role for them in the struggle. Even when they cooperated with others, they wanted to do everything their way, and they ended up at a dead end. Those who did not agree with them left the group.

I also left them in 1349/1970. Of course, they never wanted to accept that I left them because of their attitude. They thought that I left them because I did not respect them or acknowledge their qualities. They were, however, certain that I would not abandon the struggle.

Critic of the Hizbul'lah Group

Even though I separated from the Hizbul'lah group I occasionally met some of their members here and there until the month of Shahrivar 1350/August 1971. They always warned me to carry a weapon with me, but I always argued against the idea. I tried to convince them that if I were to be arrested unarmed, I might get a two- or three-year prison term, but if I were armed,

I would be given a life-sentence in prison. I intended to surrender if the police caught me and not resist.

At times I also tried to scare them and warned them that if I were ever arrested, I would reveal information about them to the police. I said this so that they would leave me alone and disturb me less. However, after long discussion and because of their persistence, I agreed to carry a weapon, and they promised to bring me one.

I was familiar with the route they would take to meet me at 2:00 p.m. the next day. We decided to meet at Ziba Street (now Shahid Mohammad Mahdi Mashhadi Rahim) on Khorasan Square, and I could easily go there from the Tehran bazaar.

When I arrived at Adib Street on Rey Avenue I saw a person who was from their group, but he was not the same person that I had agreed to meet. He had put on a shirt and from the back pocket of his pants I could see a grenade he carried. He also had a big grocery bag in which he had two guns on the pile of grapes. He was walking carelessly and was not at all conscious of his surroundings. I walked a few steps behind him, and at a proper moment I hit him in the head, and at the same time I placed my other hand on the grenade. He was terrified. He dropped the grocery bag and the weapons, and all grapes dropped on the ground. I quickly collected them from the ground before anyone arrived at the scene. He was shocked at the way I acted. I blamed and strongly criticized him for not observing safety rules and security measures. We then started walking. I had a meeting with someone else other than him, and I found out he also was supposed to meet another member somewhere else. Following meetings with a number of people, I was supposed to receive the weapons.

He was so naïve that he walked me toward his destination where he was to meet another member. Finally, he went to Ziba Street, and Mohammad Mufidi[64] came with a bicycle,

---

[64] Seyyid Moḥammad Mufidi (b. 1327/1948-Tehran) graduated from Dar al-Funun School. He participated in religious gatherings and Qur'anic

wearing a torn shirt. He was carrying a sack full of grenades on his bicycle. Greatly angered, I did not know what to do with them and their carelessness. I cooled my anger in order to deal with them at the appropriate time later. We went to another street where Ali Reza Sepasi[65] was waiting for them and

commentary classes held in their house under the guidance of his father, Dr. Seyyid Ibrahim Mufidi. Through his brothers and their friends he was introduced to members of the Iran Freedom Movement (Nihzat-i Azadi-ye Iran) while in high school. He was admitted to the College of Translation in Tehran, but he accepted a teaching position while holding religious and educational classes. Because of his acquaintance with Moḥammad Baqir Abbasi and Ahmad Reza'ie, he became a member of the MKO. In his memoirs Ahmad Ahmad mentions that at first, Mufidi was attracted to Hizbul'lah through Ahmad, but after the month of Shahrivar 1350/August 1971 when Hizbul'lah merged with the MKO, Mufidi too joined this group. Mufidi was a man of action and participated in numerous missions along with Moḥammad Baqir Abbasi and 'Ali Reza Sepasi Ashtiyani. The most notable of these missions was the assassination of General Tahiri in Mordad 1351/July 1972. He carried on some of his missions with the adopted names of Moḥammad Lutfi and Moḥammad Amini. Once in 1350/1971 he was arrested by mistake but released shortly afterwards. After General Tehiri's assassination in Shahrivar 1351/August 1972 he was arrested and after much torture was executed on Dey 5, 1351/December 26, 1972 See,*Memoirs of Ahmad Ahmad,* pp. 184–190; Moḥammad Mufidi, pp. 1–6.
[65] Ali Reza Sepasi Ashtiyani (b. 1323/1944, Arak) entered the College of Fine Arts and Architecture. Through Asghar Qurayshi he became a member of the Islamic Nations party (Hizb-i Milal-i Islami) in 1343/1964 but was arrested a year later and remained in prison until 1346/1967. After he was released, he established the Hizbul'lah group in collaboration with Ahmad Ahmad and Abbas Aghazamani. He wrote many of the educational treatises and was the political analyst of the group. During this period, he managed to complete his studies and receive his college degree. After the merging of Hizbul'lah and the MKO in 1350/1971, he joined the organization. In the month of Mordad 1351/July 1972, together with Moḥammad Mufidi and Moḥammad Baqir Abbasi, he carried out the assassination of General Tahiri. After the arrest of his comrades he went underground. Reza was emotional, highly ambitious, proud, brave, and hot-tempered, and had a sense of grandiosity. Due to his discipline and serious attitude, he advanced the MKO ranks very quickly and in 1353/1974 became a member of the central committee of the organization. In 1354, when a group of members of the MKO adopted Marxism and defected from the organization, Reza joined the new faction and its leader Taqi Shahram. They assas-

three people who were to join them soon. We went together to another street across a sports and recreation center. Mostafa Javan Khoshdel was waiting for us there. All of them were from the military wing of the Hizbul'lah. Time was ripe to teach them a few security principles. I criticized them strongly and blamed them for their carelessness.

I said, "Do not think that if you are killed in this movement you shall be counted as a martyr. But rather you shall first of all be considered traitors by us, by your group and by the people. Your action is no different from betrayal because you are endangering the life of a group whose aim is to fight for the people. If you are arrested, this will be a great setback to the resistance of the people. You have taken carelessness to its limit, and you do not seem to know the danger of this. You have underestimated the power of the police. I cannot take weapons from careless people like you." After a few more words in their criticism, I left them.

In Shahrivar 1350/August 1971 the MKO suffered a heavy blow from SAVAK. Most of their leaders and members were arrested. In the process of preparing for celebration and commemoration of the 2500 years of Persian monarchy, SAVAK carried out an unprecedented series of operations during which it attacked several safe houses of the MKO and arrested many its key leaders and members of its central cadre. This was accomplished as a result of the betrayal of an activist named Shahmurad (Allahmurad) Delfani. These operations continued until the end of October and the arrest of the MKO's

---

sinated a number of MKO members who did not comply with their order to join the Marxist faction. He continued his activities until 1357/1978 along with Taqi Shahram in his organization, known as the Organization for the Struggle for the Liberation of the Working Class (Sazman-i paykar dar rah-i azadi-ye tabaqeh-ye kargar). After the victory of the Revolution the group openly opposed the Islamic government. Reza was arrested in 1360/1981 and in prison often insulted sacred symbols and beliefs of Islam and quarreled with security officers. Finally, when he attempted to escape prison, he was shot and killed.

founding members such as Mohammad Hanifnezhad. As a result of this setback the status of the MKO and its leadership as well as its strategies and plans changed drastically. Ahmad Reza'ie, who had managed to escape from this operation, tried hard to reorganize what was left of the MKO and its remaining members. Mostafa Javan Khoshdel[66] was one of the active members of the MKO. He collaborated with Hizbul'lah and oversaw their activities and at the same time recruited its qualified members for the MKO. In other words, the Hizbul'lah became a recruiting ground for the MKO. After the great blow in 1350/1971, he struggled to utilize the potentials of Hizbul'lah in the service of the MKO. In the course of two or three years of his collaboration with the Hizbul'lah, he was able to recruit Baqir Abbasi, 'Ali Reza Sepasi, and Mohammad Mufidi for the MKO. He used this connection to distribute the MKO's declarations and writings among Hizbul'lah members. However, Javad Mansuri and Abbas Aghazamani were critical of Hizbul'lah and soon both of them left. Aghazamani (Abu Sharif) went to Lebanon, and Javad Mansuri was arrested after a short time.

Mufidi, Sepasi, and Baqir Abbasi, contacted Ahmad Reza'ie[67] and Reza Reza'ie and increased their cooperation

---

[66] Mostafa Javan Khoshdel was born into a religious family in 1325/1946. He developed an interest in politics at a young age. He was one of the active members of the Hizbul'lah group and then the MKO. He was arrested in August 1974 and was executed on Farvardin 29, 1354/April 19, 1975 along with eight other resistance fighters. The regime claimed that they were killed when they attempted to escape from Evin prison.

[67] Ahmad Reza'ie (b. 1325/1946, Tehran) His father worked in the bazaar and was among the supporters of Dr. Mohammad Mosaddiq. Ahmad Rezai was one of the few MKO leaders who dropped out of high school in his senior year and never attended university. He started his political activity in the Iran Freedom Movement (Nihzat-i Azadi-ye Iran) and at the same time entered the army for military service. Ahmad participated in the events of 15 Khordad 1342/June 5, 1963. He played a leading role in the reorganization of the MKO after the defections of 1971. When he was to meet another MKO member in Ghaffari Avenue in southern Tehran, he encountered the

with the MKO. Early in 1351/1972, they took measures that resulted in the merger of Hizbul'lah with the MKO. Of course in addition to the defection of Mansuri and Abu Sharif, this merger caused many other problems. On the one hand, the MKO no longer respected Hizbul'lah members, and on the other hand, people like Mufidi were not willing to settle for any role less than membership in the central committee of the organization. There were also some other problems. The military wing of the MKO was leaning more and more toward intellectualism and was increasingly blurring the line between religious members and non-religious members of the organization. They gave priority to fighting and struggle over anything else.

Baqir Abbasi had already turned Marxist since 1350/1971 and his political perspective was based on his new ideology. He no longer prayed, and even if he did, he never used a *muhr* and prostrated on the ground or carpet. He argued that this is necessary in order to bring unity between the Shi'ites and the Sunnis. Sepasi followed his wife's lead in daily prayer. He claimed that by doing this, he had resolved inherent problems in gender relations.

Mufidi's situation was not any better than that of Abbasi and Sepasi. I had placed a prayer mat and several *muhrs* in my room that I had received from my mother. These were very precious memorabilia from her. There was also an emerald ring and a rosary (*tasbih*) made from the clay of Karbala.

Sometimes on Friday nights when I remembered my mother, I prayed on that mat, recited the Qur'an, and also prayed for her soul. Always a very special spiritual state descended on my soul when I prayed for her. One day, Mufidi came to my house and wanted to pray. He made the ablution and spread out the mat to pray. That night, however, he set aside the mat and used only a *muhr* to pray.

SAVAK agents. Fighting broke out, during which he killed three agents and was finally killed himself. He was in fact the first martyr of the MKO.

When he completed his prayer, I asked him why he used the mat. He considered the mat a luxury that only the "capitalists" used! I lived with him for almost a year and often noticed that he hardly performed the obligatory daily prayers. Even if he did, he prayed so quickly, like a crow that eats food from the ground. I must mention that Mohammad's father was a physician and had a different life style. Mufidi's prayer was so shallow and mechanical on the one hand, and on the other hand, he was so rigid to the extent that he believed a simple prayer mat was a capitalist luxury. Despite that he never stopped performing the supererogatory night prayers and he recited the holy Qur'an regularly.

Another problem with Mufidi was that he insisted that whoever we wanted to recruit, we must first know him well and test his sincerity and honesty. Yet, he always wanted to have the final decision to accept or reject the candidate[68] as he claimed to know the aspirants better than anyone else did. Several times I criticized him and told him that by doing this he was in fact committing treason because he knew many people, and if he were ever arrested and tortured, he might reveal their identities to the police. This would be the biggest blow to the group. And he would always assure me that "even if they

---

[68] Ahmad Ahmad, one of the members of Hizbul'lah, had a different opinion about Moḥammad Mofidi, as he wrote, "In my many visits to the garrison in Karaj a tall young man attracted my attention. I became very curious and after a few days I noticed that he recited Qur'an very well. In the political environment of those days, one's familiarity with the Qur'an was a good criterion to identify potential recruits from among religious elements. Therefore, I began to approach him and we became friends. After a while I began to discuss politics and religion matters with him and realized that he was quite experienced and mature, and a politically minded person. Many days afterwards we spent most of our free time talking about politics. After about three months we began to develop trust in each other. He shared some of his political activities with me, and in return I introduced him to Abbas Aghazamani so that if he saw him appropriate, he would be recruited for membership in Hizbul'lah group. Moḥammad held several meetings with Abbas and after that he was accepted as a member of the Central Cadre of the organization." See *Memoirs of Ahmad Ahmad*, 186–187.

cut me to pieces, I will never give information to the police about any member."[69] He said, "No, even if they cut me into pieces, I shall not even say a word."

I said, "This is where you are wrong. You overestimate your capacity. Give it a try. Let me whip you a hundred times on your feet and let us see if you can tolerate it."

These people had never been tortured, so they thought that even if they were cut into pieces, they wouldn't say a word. They claimed that they would do what Bilal Habashi did when he was tortured. I always reminded them that Bilal and all other Companions of the Prophet were able to stand tortures by the grace of God and the presence of the Prophet. Seeing the holy Prophet was a powerful blessing and strengthened their faith, and that enabled them to resist all kinds of difficulties. How could we compare our time and ourselves to the time of the holy Prophet and his Companions? We did not live in such a time and environment

The Assassination of Brigadier Tahiri

After extensive debates and discussions, it was decided that Hizbul'lah would form a coalition with the MKO. The organization gave the order to assassinate Brigadier Tahiri as the first test of joint operation. Mohamad Mufidi, Baqir Abbasi,[70] 'Ali

---

[69] Javad Mansuri also made the following remarks concerning Mufidi: "His extensive connection with different people and groups gained him access to a lot of information which he then passed on to the Central Committee. Through some friends, he was in contact with the members of the Fidayan-i Khalq organization and brought their publications for us. One of the people whom he recruited for Hezbullah was Mahdi Eftekhari. After the arrest of Mohammad Mufidi, Eftekhari also was arrested and jailed. Mahdi was very much attracted to the MKO and was accepted as a high ranking member of the organization. When the MKO settled in Iraq, he was promoted and became a member of the Central Cadre of the organization." See, *Memoirs of Javad Mansuri*, 88.

[70] Colonel Sa'id Tahiri was one of the main police commanders who played a leading role in crushing the popular uprising on Khordad 15/June 5, 1963, and other popular protest movements such as the demonstrations during the

Reza Sepasi, and Mostafa Javan Khoshdel were chosen to carry out that mission.

Preparations were made to carry out the assassination, and a few days before the operation the rest of the members in the group were informed of the plan. If they went to the house of an acquaintance, they would say that in the following two to three days, something important would happen! Thus, these four people were putting the group in danger. On the night of the operation one of them even went as far as visiting two or three houses of the other members and informed them that they would carry out the mission the next day and asked for prayer. They also told others that if they did not return home by nine o'clock, others should conclude that they had failed and were killed in the process. Many of the people who had thus been informed of this operation did not even have the capacity and integrity to hear this information. This kind of carelessness was a reflection of their pride and arrogance and continued even after the operation. The four people carried out the assassination successfully and they returned safely. Obviously they should have remained in hiding for a while and removed all evidence that might give their traces to the police. But they appeared in public places the next morning. In the afternoon, they went to the famous ice cream shop of Akbar Mashadi and celebrated and ate ice cream. Later on Abbasi and Mufidi went

---

funeral of Ayatullah Fumani, demonstrations against Israel during the soccer match between Iran and Israel in 1349, attacks on the cotton factory workers and students at Tehran and Sharif Universities. In return for these services he was promoted to the rank of brigadier-general and appointed as the deputy commander of the Tehran police and director of police prisons in 1349/1970. In 1350/1971 he was appointed as the commander of the "anti-terrorist" committee that was established to deal with and curb anti-regime groups. Together with General Khatai, he interrogated and tortured many members of opposition groups. Finally, at 6:10 on a Sunday morning on Mordad 22, 1350/August 12, 1971 he was assassinated by Mohammad Mufidi, Mohammad Baqir Abbasi, and 'Ali Reza Sepasi Ashtiyani. See *Memoirs of Ahmad Ahmad*, 80–81; See also, "Chera Tahiri Terror Shod," in, *Bayaniyeh Sazman*.

to the neighborhood of Ab Mangal (now Shahid Seyyed Abdullah Razavi and Ziba Street and Shahid Mohammad Mahdi Mashhadi Rahim Avenue). Sepasi and Khoshdel too, went to the bazaar. In Ab Mangal, Abbasi and Mufidi talked openly about the assassination that they had carried out. They even made jokes about the police and said to a traffic police officer that they "assassinated his commander." When the officer heard this and decided to question them, they shot and killed him, too. Observing this scene, people began to chase them. Abbasi and Mufidi were forced to separate. Mufidi escaped towards the south, but Abbasi was caught at Ab Mangal. He shot into the air and also shot at a certain Agha Reza Najjar, who reportedly was a police informer.

Then a police cadet followed Abbasi on his motorcycle in the street. Abbasi knocked him down and then shot him. By then he had lost the chance to escape. The police patrol number 14 arrived at the scene and arrested Abbasi. But Mohammad Mufidi managed to escape. All of this could have been avoided if they had observed the basic rules of secrecy. Unfortunately, Mufidi committed more mistakes. Even though he knew that his friend and partner had been arrested and was alive, he remained careless and did not follow the most basic principles of security. After moving from one place to the other, he was arrested by the police. There are two different narratives on his arrest.

One report indicates that Mufidi was in contact with his sister, whose husband was Dr. (Abbas) Shaybani. The police invaded Dr. Shaybani's house and arrested Mufidi there. Another story reveals Mohammad's complete carelessness and lack of precautions. Reportedly, early in the morning he went to a crowded restaurant that served the traditional Persian cuisine made of lamb head for breakfast. He did this at a time when his photo had been printed and distributed widely by the police. The police identified him there and arrested him.[71]

---

[71] Mohammad Baqir Abbasi (b. Om, 1325/1946) started political activity in his teenage years and joined the Islamic Nations Party (*Hizb-i Milal-i Is-*

Both of the above stories show his lack of precautions. Mufidi, a person who used to carry a weapon, was not armed then. He also carried a small amount of cyanide pills, but he did not take one when he was arrested. Things happened so fast that he was not able to make a quick decision. He knew that if he remained alive, the death penalty was waiting for him. The only advantage of killing himself by taking cyanide was that he would have not revealed the identity of his comrades and would have saved many lives. Furthermore, had he committed suicide then, it would have given much publicity to his cause and exposed the nature of the regime. He did not have time to waste and should have made a quick decision because his fate was not predictable once he was arrested. But sacrificing one's life is not an act that just any activist can undertake. Thus, lack of concern for security and indecision at the time of crisis resulted in the arrest and execution of Baqir Abbasi and Mohammad Mufidi. In 1351/1972, Khoshdel was also arrested, and three years later executed by the regime in 1354/1975.

As for 'Ali Reza Sepasi, he was not arrested. He continued his activities along with the MKO. In 1354/1975 he became a Marxist and got a high position in the organization, and later he joined ['the Maoist group] Paykar and continued his activities with that organization. He also established ties with the Soviets.[72] He delivered to the Soviets the briefcases of two

---

lami). When this group was discovered by the police in Mehr 1344/September 1965 he was arrested and imprisoned for two years. When was released he joined the Hizbul'lah group. Abbasi became a Marxist in the year 1350/1971 and came into serious conflicts with the Hizbul'lah. Shortly after that he joined the MKO. He participated in many of this organization's activities, including the assassination of General Tahiri. He was arrested and executed in Dey 1351/Deceber 1972.

[72] Mas'ud Haqqgu was a cellmate of Mufidi in prison in 1351/1972. He recorded the details of Tahiri's assassination that Mufidi shared with him and how Mufidi and Abbasi were arrested. Ror details of this account see *Memoirs of Ahmad Ahmad*, 189–190.

Americans advisors[73]who were killed and were carrying important documents.

With the assassination of Brigadier Tahiri in Mordad 1351/July 1972, the Hizbul'lah organization was completely destroyed and its office closed. As for Mufidi's torture, there are a lot of rumors. It is said that he died under torture before being executed. However, this was not the case. He told everything and confessed that he had carried out the assassination in collaboration with several other members.

He even revealed the identities of people that he had known ten years before that date, including the name of a person who had paid him twenty *tumans* to purchase charcoal! His betrayal was so damaging that when he was executed the MKO was not willing to announce it and count him as one of the fighters. After a while when they realized that they could use his execution to propagate their cause, they made an idol of his name. They exploited the deaths of Mufidi and Abbasi to claim credit for their organization. They claimed that in his trial Mufidi had defended the MKO, whereas in reality the court did not even permit him to defend himself.

The statement that he presented in court in his defense was recorded in his file, and he was taken from his cell to the committee and shortly after was executed. He did not spend time in public prison cells to tell anyone about his defense in the court. The military court was not open to the public and no one heard of his defense. If such a statement ever existed, then we would doubt the chief prosecutor of the court as a sympathizer. It is obvious that this story about Mufidi's defense statement is a story that the MKO made up.

---

[73] The date of this incident was taken from the interview of Ezzat Shahi that was conducted in the month of Bahman, 1358, when 'Ali Reza Sepasi was still alive.

The Struggle and the Fragile Resistance

SAVAK always claimed that they did not arrest political prisoners in the streets, but rather comrades in fact revealed information about each other! One person can bring five people while another can bring ten and another fifty people. It all depends on the person. What SAVAK meant was that negligence and carelessness of opposition activists about their own and their comrades' security resulted in their arrest.

The reason for Mufidi's weakness in the interrogation, in prison and in court, was due to certain characteristics and his lack of sincerity that manifested in prison. He revealed the identities of all people inside and outside of prison who were connected to him. A person who was raised in an affluent family and never experienced hardship, and as we say in Persian, his foot was never pricked by a thorn, cannot endure torture and whipping. The lack of strong faith makes resistance even more difficult.

I always wondered why the number of communist and Marxist inmates is much greater than that of religious activists. This difference was always noticeable. From a qualitative point of view, however, they were less prepared for struggle. This probably explains the reason non-religious elements were willing to change their position in the court or in prison and confess and repent on national television. The conditions that prevailed in prison, during interrogations, and in court were very different from the environment outside prison and in the society. An activist's arrest could have meant his life and death. If he did not believe in religion and rejected the Hereafter, he would give up easily. Since he did not believe that he would be rewarded in the Hereafter for the torture he received in prison, a single lash of the whip was enough to make him confess and give all the information about his comrades to the police. At that point individual safety and interest would become the main concern. It was often in situations like this that twenty prisoners were arrested because one activist had a single [outlawed] book, or a minor mistake or action of one person would lead to the arrest of an entire group. For an activist who had no faith in God or did not believe in rewards in the Hereafter, prison meant deprivation from life's bounties and pleasures. Therefore, when such an activist got into trouble or faced hardship, he would conclude that resistance was futile. He would then not be willing to endure hardships, and would surrender; even worse, sometimes he would begin to collaborate with the police. In short, he would not be willing to sacrifice himself for the sake of others and the cause. This was one of the reasons their number was always greater in prison. Of course, one must always avoid gross and unjustified generalization, and I should—in all objectivity and fairness—emphasize here that this rule did not apply to all leftist activists then. One must give credit to individual activists such as [Khosrow] Golsorkhi, [Mas'ud] Ahmad Zadeh, [Khosrow] Roozbeh and many others like them and appreciate their heroic resistance. Similarly, leftist prisoners also acknowledged that members of religious groups endured more under torture and did not reveal information easily. Otherwise, considering their large number of members outside prison, there would be more arrests and a lot more members of religious groups in prisons. These qualities, they explained, are not understandable through science or scientific means, but are personal and depend on individual character, capacity, and the strength of faith.[74]

SAVAK was also more comfortable with non-religious activists and claimed that they are more *rational*. It was enough to talk to them a few minutes and they would be convinced and willing to open up and reveal information! In contrast, religious activists—from the point of view of SAVAK—were *irrational*. They were like the followers and disciples of Hasan Sabbah, who took hashish and sacrificed their lives easily and carried out assassinations by his command. The reli-

---

[74] At 6:40 a.m. on Wednesday, Ordibehesht 31, 1352/May 21, 1973 two American Military attachés, Shafar Joyce and Lieutenant Colonel Jack Turnerwill, were assassinated by the MKO.

gious activists were indifferent to promises and pleasures of this world and resisted torture in the hope of union with virgin *houris* in heaven. The belief in the rewards of the next world turned them into *irrational* people and made it impossible to talk logically with them at all.

Another major problem with resistance groups such as Hizbul'lah and the MKO was in their strategy. I believed and still do that political activists must live in the society and interact with the people so that they can understand and analyze the social condition and political environment. A person or a group that claims to be a vanguard or wants to lead ideological and political struggle against a regime like that of the Shah cannot and must not hide in his ivory tower and lead the movement from above. Such a strategy is doomed to fail. Whenever these resistant groups found a person who was talented and prepared for political activity, they would quickly lead him to underground life and hide him, assuming that he would be safer, not realizing that such a measure would create backlash as it might attract unnecessary police attention, and increase the pressure from the candidate's family on him/her. When a person went into hiding and did not return home for a few days, his/her parents usually contacted the police and filed a missing person report. The police then would inform all the family members and seek help of their relatives and friends to locate the son/daughter. Naturally, in such situations SAVAK then concluded that he/she was either a fugitive or lived underground [for political reasons].

In addition, when members of a group started underground life, their connection with the society became limited, and the possibility of collecting aid and weapons was reduced. Since they did not interact with people from whom they could get information about the political condition, they were unable to properly analyze the situation. This strategy distanced political activists from people, and as a result, they became isolated and out of touch with the society. They could not participate in social activities or attend public meetings, and after a while they even feared their own shadows. Consequently, their understanding of the realities of the society became entirely subjective and theoretical.

The other problem was that adopting an underground life required measures and preparations that these groups usually did not pay attention to. Emotional dependence of the new members on their parents and siblings did not allow them to continue under those conditions for a long time. Therefore, after a period of time, they reached a dead end. They had alienated their parents and relatives, while at the same time created resentment in the group because of their inability to continue underground life.

When a political activist adopts underground life, he/she must constantly receive ideological, intellectual, and political feedback. Since none of those groups was able to provide such training, after a while members became disillusioned and felt useless. In such situations, a new member only hoped to be arrested so that after a couple of months in prison he could go after his own life. After a while, leaders of these groups realized that there were inherent problems with their organizations and sought to address and resolve these shortcomings. However, they were not honest and sincere; so instead of seeking proper solutions, they began to use scare tactics. They frightened those members who had gone underground by telling them that they should avoid arrest under all circumstances, because if they were ever arrested, they would be severely tortured and then executed. Thus, they would convince members that in order to survive they should always be prepared to carry out terroristic missions and be willing to kill, or else they will be killed anyway. Those tactics intimidated those members who were not prepared for military operations and pushed them against the wall. They were not prepared for such dangerous missions, but were not courageous enough to reject the leadership's orders and convince them that they were not capable of performing such missions. To avoid disagreement and conflict and resolve some of those challenges the leadership of such groups tried to brainwash members and create a mindset that they would believe that under no circumstances they should betray the organization and give information to the SAVAK, even if the police tortured them and "cut him into pieces," as they said.

I had come across such cases quite often. Many activists claimed that if they were cut into pieces or burned, they would not betray me and reveal my name. In response, I would turn to them and say, "But if I am arrested, I will reveal your name and give information to the police." My objective was that individuals would accept responsibilities that they were capable of carry out, and if not, give the least amount of information away. Despite that, individuals would brag and exaggerate about their ability to resist torture and their commitment to remain silent.

In a closed circle of activists, members tend to reinforce in each other's mind the illusion that if they are arrested they can all resist to the last breath and not betray the cause and their comrades. Unfortunately, upon the arrest and after just a little torture, many disclosed the names and identities of others, and as a result many people got arrested. Then in prison they argued and blamed each other for their weaknesses. Worse was the fact that some activists revealed the identity of all members they were connected to even without receiving a slap in the face. Ironically, the very same individuals were praised by their friends as the symbol of resistance! Sometime an activist who had been very weak and scared before the police turned into a hero in prison. Often such individuals started arguments and fights with the guards and were sent to solitary confinement. When he returned from his cell, he would be treated like a hero. A case in point was Mas'ud Rajavi who was arrested in August 1350/1971 but was never tortured until 1352/1974. Yet he defended himself in the court and created an impression in others' mind that he was a truly a hero. He was one of those members of the MKO who were arrested as a result of the mindset explained above. As a result, all their information and documents fell into the hands of SAVAK. Among those members of the MKO who were arrested, only Ali Asghar Badi'-zadegan was beaten up and somewhat tortured. The reason for that was that during those years SAVAK and the police worked independent of each other and there was no coordination between them. The Joint Committee (*komiteh-ye moshtarak*) had not been established yet to create cooperation and coordinate their activities. Those who were arrested by SAVAK were taken to Qizil Qal'ah Prison and interrogated there, while those who were arrested by the police (*shahrbani*) were taken to police headquarters or Qasr Prison. When Badi'zadegan was arrested, the conflict between SAVAK and the police came out into the open.

Badi'zadegan was arrested by the police, whereas his comrades had been arrested before him by the SAVAK. They had revealed their affiliation with the MKO and given all the information they had. The police tried to get Badi'zadegan to confess, but he continued to resist torture, not realizing that his friends had already given SAVAK all the details of their activities and members' identities. Finally, he also broke under torture and confessed and gave some information to the police. This coincided with a bitter rivalry between the police and SAVAK. The police were always behind in identifying activists or in arresting them. That was the reason that when they arrested Badi'zadegan, they tortured him so severely, hoping to get new information from him. Finally the police concluded that SAVAK knew everything and there was no point in torturing Badi'zadegan further. They delivered him to SAVAK.

The degree of torture that the arrested MKO members received in 1350/1971 was limited to slapping in the face, kicking, and mild beating up. The reason was that most of the information had been given out to SAVAK earlier by a member named Shahmurad [Allahmorad] Delfani. SAVAK no longer needed any information from them. After realizing that their information had been given out, the Mujahidin-i Khalq members saw no reason to resist. At one point, I asked Rajavi

119

if it is true that such-and-such sympathizer of the MKO claimed that in 1350/1971 that he was severely tortured. Rajavi denied that and said that although he was a member of the central cadre of the organization, he only received 24 lashes of the whip, and even that in two sessions.

The sentence that was handed to Mas'ud Rajavi was quite surprising. At first he was sentenced to death, but at the second hearing his sentence was reduced to life imprisonment. Some observers said that since one of Rajavi's relatives was a member of the parliament, he intervened and used his influence so that he would not be tortured. This is not true. Such an intervention might have been effective before or during trial in the court, but once interrogation started, SAVAK did not show mercy to anyone. They just wanted information, and anyone who would give information would remain immune from torture. SAVAK could not allow any authority to intervene in the manners in which they extracted information from a prisoner. Moreover, rarely did any authority dare to interfere and mediate on behalf of a political prisoner. I cannot, however, deny the effectiveness of intervention in the process of trial in the court.

Rajavi came from a wealthy family, some of whom also were influential figures abroad.[75] One of his brothers was a

---

[75] In his own memoirs Mohammad Kachu'i states: "When an activist who was not a religious person was arrested he would easily give information to the police. Such people would say that they do not see any reason why they should suffer while their comrades outside of prison were happy. Some Marxist elements revealed the identities of over 200 of their comrades to the police. I always was happy to be tortured so that my friends outside prison remain safe. It was on occasions like that when I realized the role of faith in God. A believer never wished another person to be tortured for his sake or separated from his parents, or wife and children. It really did not matter for a Communist to betray his comrade and have them arrested and imprisoned. For us it did, and for God's sake." See *Interview with Mohammad Kachu'i*, Tehran, 1358–1359/1979–1980.

Ashraf Dehqani (Robabeh Ashrafzadeh Dehqani) was one of the leaders of the Fadayan-i Khalqe organization. She was arrested in the summer of the year 1350/1971. In describing the memoirs of her impris-

university professor in Switzerland. He organized demonstrations and appealed to the United Nations and the Human Rights Organization. They pressured the Iranian regime to reduce Rajavi's sentence from execution to life imprisonment.

There were a lot of unsubstantiated rumors and a great deal of exaggeration about the relationship between these individuals and such groups. Many of these assertions were based on personal love or hate relations between individuals. Under those circumstances, even if a person were weak or a traitor, if he took measures that were in the interest of a group, he was praised and became their hero. They applauded him and cheered him up, but if he disagreed with them and wished to maintain his independence of opinion, then they blamed him and labeled him as weak and a traitor. Even if he were the greatest thinker and strongest person, they would start attacking his personality and terrorize him.

My activities with Hizbul'lah, or my relation with any other group, did not prevent me from having my own independence of mind and actions. During those years I was in contact with my friends such as Kachu'i[76] and Ahmad Mahdavi, and with their help continued to produce declarations and

---

onment, she writes, "The whip was a reality and it was impossible to endure it. I needed to prepare myself mentally and understand and accept that as a reality. Each time, the pain of the whip became more intolerable. I called out the names of my comrades, Ipak, Raihan, Robab, Qasim, and so on. These people were some of the hard-working villagers where I was a teacher." She then adds, "When the torturers tied me up onto the wooden bench and went away, I felt an excruciating pain. And the fact that there was no longer anyone around that I could curse and forget my pain, I started reciting a poem by Comrade Mao titled 'Hanging Leaves.'" See, Dehqani, pp. 22, 24.

[76] Part of the interview took place in the month of Bahman, 1358/February 1979, 25. This interview took place in Bahman 1358/February 1979 while Kachu'i was still alive.

.

121

carry out political and military missions. The main reason I maintained contact with other groups was that I wanted to get information and feedback from other sources as well.

Of course, we did not have many financial problems but were poor in our theoretical knowledge. Most of the members of our group were freshmen or sophomores at the university, or had quit high school before completing their education. Some others were simple laborers and had much less education. Therefore, we always sought to recruit educated and intellectual members who also believed in and were willing to engage in political struggle, or at least produce educational pamphlets, books, or weapons.

*   *   *

CHAPTER THREE

Serving the Mujahidin-i Khalq Organization

Mysterious Connection

Every Friday I usually went mountain-climbing and only took some bread and dates to eat. One day I came across a person in the mountains who seemed very nice and friendly and was praying and reciting the holy Qur'an. He also appeared to be very lonely. After seeing him several times, I concluded that he was an enlightened and knowledgeable person. I asked him to teach me how to recite the Qur'an and he agree. His name was Ali Reza Beheshti.[77] He was affiliated with the MKO and through him I became interested in and felt sympathetic to this group.

I had separated from Hizbul'lah before its collapse. At that time, I had a friend by the name of Mehr Ayin.[78] He was a

---

[77] Ali Reza Beheshti Zadeh was one of the Muslim members of the MKO who encountered the police in 1352/1973 and was killed after a fierce fight with the police in the streetd of Tehran. He was a skinny young boy with red hair and shining face and was very honest and brave.

[78] Mohammad Mehr Ayin (b. 1318/1939). Due to his physical strength and talent in sports like judo and karate, he offered self-defense classes for members of groups such as Hizbul'lah, the Islamic Coalition Party and the MKO. Taking as a hostage Prince Shafiq, the son of Ashraf Pahlavi, was one of the operations in which Mohammad Mehr Ayin played a major role. In the course of his struggle he was arrested three times, and was interrogated and severely tortured. He stayed in prison until 1356/1977. Mehr Ayin's other name was Davud Abadi. But he used other names like Davudi, Mohammad Jawad, and Mohammad Motori. After the victory of the Islamic Revolution, he served in different posts in the political, cultural, and athletic clubs. Some of his important positions included the Director General of the Logistical Support of the Revolutionary Guard Corps, the Director General of the National Federation of Physical Education, and Governor General of Logistical Support for the National Parliament. Mehr Ayin played a leading role in the expansion and institutionalizing of disabled sport teams and arranged Iran's participation in international and Olympic games for disabled athletes. His two sons, Mohammad Reza and Nasir,

123

master judo and karate teacher and had a black belt. He trained me and a number of other political activists in self-defense and martial arts. The MKO also had connections with him and frequently visited him in his house or at his club, where they identified potential recruits.

After the month of Shahrivar, 1350/August 1971, Mehr Ayin, who at that time was known by the name of Davoodabadi, invited me to his house and introduced me to an uneducated young but very religious and knowledgeable man. In matters related to security and also experience in politics, I realized that he was much more knowledgeable and more qualified than I. I had the impression that he was a university student. In terms of his organizational experience, his piety, and religiosity also, he was far superior to me. Mehr Ayin told me that he was a good and pious young man and that I could work with him. At first I thought that he meant that I should recruit him for collaboration with me in political activities, but soon realized that he meant exactly the opposite.

I never asked him any questions concerning matters related to security, although I met him and spoke with him several times in Mehr Ayin's house. It was in this manner that I was introduced to a person whom I later found out was Ali Reza Zemorrodiyan,[79] who was known [jokingly] as the Muja-

---

were martyred in the war between Iran and Iraq. See "Fasl Nameh-ye Mehr Ayin," in, *Mutale'at tarikhi*, number 2, 283–284.

[79] 'Ali Reza Zemorrodiyan (b.1331/1952, Tehran). He joined the Mojahedin Khalq Organization while at the University of Tehran. Strictly following the Shari'ah, he was well organized and responsible, ate and slept little, hard on teammates. He dealt toughly with the people who acted contrary to the rules and regulations of the organization. Among the members of the organization he was called "the Cardinal" because of his punctuality and discipline. In his memoirs Lutfullah Maysami quotes Ayatullah Rabaani Shirazi as follows: "I have never seen a fighter like Zemorrodiyan amongst the old fighters." Zemorrodiyan was arrested by the SAVAK and jailed for fifteen years in Adil Abad prison in Shiraz. Finally he deviated in 1352/1973 and joined the Marxists. In 1357/1978 he was freed from prison and joined the Maoist group Paykar. Finally he turned into an ardent enemy of the Islamic Republic and was killed in a street clash with the Revolu-

hidin's cardinal. After the first or second meeting with him, I realized that I would not be able to work with him. So I told Mehr Ayin that I have a feeling that Zemorrodiyan was affiliated with or had his own group, and as long as his affiliation was not clear I would not be able to work with him. I came to that conclusion when I observed his behavior. If he expected to have my support and collaboration, then he should have been honest and truthful with me. He continued to act mysteriously, so I could not honestly continue to work with him. I decided that I had better end my connection with him. So I did not meet him again. During this period a few more activists were arrested, and that was how I found out that he was a member of the MKO.

The MKO did not leave me alone because of the assets that I had at my disposal. Since I was still in contact with Mehr Ayin, perhaps he used other people to keep in touch with me. Perhaps upon his recommendation, Morteza Alviri came to me and asked to have a meeting between me and one of the members of the MKO at Buzarjomehri Avenue. It was there that for the first time I met and came to know Vahid Afrakhteh. Initially, I was not introduced to him by my real name but used a fake one.[80] Alviri told Vahid that I was a friend and a supporter of the resistance. After he introduced us to one another, Alviri left us.

At first, Afrakhte gave me a couple of short treatises that contained commentaries on chapters eight, nine, and forty-seven of the Qur'an.[81] We later went for a walk, passed

---

tionary Guards. See *Memoirs of Mas'ud Haqgu*, tape number 4, 2–8. See also Maysami, *Tarikhche Mukhtasar Guruhak'ha* (*A Short History of the Petit Resistant Groups*), p. 148.

[80] According to available documents it becomes clear that Ezzat Shahi did not want to identify Vahid Afrakhteh to the SAVAK. It was for this reason that he used the fictitious name of Hossein Mohammadi.

[81] The full names of the pamphlets were as follows: "Lessons from Chapter Nine"; "Lessons from Chapter Forty-Seven"; "Lessons from Chapter Eight" [of the Qur'an].

through Budharjomehri Avenue to I'idam Square and then Ark Square. We spent two or three hours walking and agreed to meet again later. In fact, we did meet several times afterwards. Later on, I read in a SAVAK document that based on the confessions of Afrakhteh, Manuchehri [the notorious SAVAK interrogator] had reported that Alviri connected me to Vahid Afrakhteh. Of course I did not speak a word concerning Alviri in my interrogations except an allusion to a trip to Lake Tar in Damavand, and that was not an important piece of information.

After Afrakhteh, several Mujahidin members like Mohammad Yazdaniyan, Mohsin Fazil,[82] Abbas Javdani, and Hasan Abrari, who were all among early leaders of the organization, became my liaisond one after the other. Farhad Safa and Bahram Aram attended our meetings to examine us and get accurate assessments of our conditions. I, too, continued my cooperation with them and used my own judgment and assessed them. If I found any of the sympathizers especially talented, I tried to take some of them out of the organization and work with them. If I found them qualified, I provided more resources for their activities. The MKO as an organization faced pressure and suffered from limitations of membership and resources, and out of desperation would turn to anyone who could help them, and all the more to me whom they knew well.

---

[82] Muhsin Fazil (b. 1328/1949, Mashhad) joined the MKO while he attended the Arya Mehr Technical University (now Sharif University). A friend of Hadi Rushan Ravan and Ḥossein Mosharzadeh, escaped prison in Shahrivar 1350/August 1971, and was under the surveillance of the police afterwards. He became a Marxist and was sent to Iraq, Syria, and Lebanon in 1353/1974. Fazil had a high position in the al-Fath Organization and went through extensive military training. Because of his blond hair and fair skin, he looked like an Englishman, hence his nickname "John." Fazil resigned from political activities in 1357/1978, but in 1359 he joined the Maoist group Paykar. Finally in 1359 while he tried to escape the country, he was arrested and jailed and eventually executed in Khordad in 1360/June 1981.

126

Growing Criticism against the Organization

After the destructive blow by SAVAK in the month of Shahri-var 1350/August 1971, the MKO developed a new policy in light of which they began to recruit just about *anyone who wished to struggle against the regime*. As a result of this change, a considerable number of irresponsible and unqualified individuals found their way into the organization. Gradually, therefore, the MKO began to resemble more a political organization than an ideological organization; something like the Palestinian organization al-Fath, which was a military-political organization, but neither a religious nor a fully a secular organization.

The MKO adopted the al-Fath model but faced a dilemma and much limitation. On the one hand, it was operating in a social environment that was deeply religious, and the MKO had to appear as an Islamic group. Otherwise, it would be ostracized. On the other hand, if it identified itself as an organization that only advocated struggle against capitalism, dictatorship, and colonialism, people would not pay much attention to it, and it would not receive any portion of financial support or a share of religious taxes and charities. It was only for these reasons that they pretended to be religious so that they could enjoy the support of the people and have access to religious resources. From the beginning [of my acquaintance with them] I was suspicious of their behavior and personal character and the way they talked and presented themselves. Therefore, I never introduced anyone to them and went alone to meet with them so that I could get to know them properly.

Most of my contacts in the organization were with Vahid Afrakhteh. Through him I met some other members. Whenever I went to meet him, I noticed that he was engaged in conversation with someone else. When he saw me he would leave that person and come towards me. Most of the time, I knew the individual that he was talking to. Perhaps Vahid

127

wanted to show us to each other. This was not a wise move from a security point of view.

In my dealing with the MKO members I had made it clear in advance that if I ever noticed discrepancies or contradictions in their words and deeds, not only would I leave the group, but I would also disclose everything that I knew. I made it clear that I would not allow them to abuse the people, and added that I would educate others about their true nature. When they understood my position, knowing that I had close ties with and a good reputation among the bazaar merchants, they were careful to hide their non-orthodox and deviated views from me. If something came up and I did not approve of it, they tried to minimize or justify it. For instance, whenever I asked them to come and recite the Qur'an together or read other books, they tried to change the subject and made all kind of excuses. They often complained of lack of knowledgeable members who could recite the Qur'an, but also argued that their priority was to train people for political struggle. Sometimes they also tried to butter me up by complimenting me and praising my humble knowledge about Islam. They would always say that they needed four people like me who could teach all members of the organization. In response I always told them that I had no claim of knowledge, but I had the courage to be actively involved in military operations and to use my experience in organization-building, and for these reasons I needed and had the right to be informed of their political position and the trends that prevailed in the organization. They always dodged my question and praised me in a flattering language, saying that "...we do not have time to respond to that kind of demands and need to spend our time and energy to train new members to bring them up to *your* level! And we will address your demands when we will have more time."

As the days went by I began to notice serious flaws and weaknesses in the political views and ideology of the MKO. Whenever I brought those issues to their attention, they tried to convince me [that I had misunderstood]. When they realized that those are very serious issues, they did not react and tried to avoid confrontation. Gradually they began to hide things from me and kept me uninformed. After that they would make sure that I didn't get much information so that confrontation would be prevented.

One day, we had a discussion about a short treatise that they had written on chapter forty-seven ("Muhammad") of the Qur'an. In that pamphlet they discussed martyrdom and mentioned the names of some of their members who had been killed as the *Supreme Symbols of Martyrdom*. This was quite a controversial writing, as they had introduced Che Guevara and Ho Chi Minh as some of those examples. I criticized them for doing that and mentioned that we do have in our culture and religion many of the best examples in human history, and that it is not right to choose Marxist elements and communist leaders to present as symbols of martyrdom. I added that ultimately God will be the One who will judge these people, although neither they nor their followers perceived martyrdom in the manner we understood in our culture and religious tradition. I mentioned that it would be better to mention Muslim martyrs like Bilal, Abudhar Ghifari, Ammar Yasir, and the like rather than Che Guevara and Ho Chi Minh. In response, they would say that those individuals belong to the past. We must introduce and focus on contemporary champions of struggle who have been killed in the course of fighting for freedom in our time so that people can relate to them. Early Muslims like of Bilal Habashi, Abudhar, and Ammar were never engaged in armed struggle like contemporary strugglers. To them I would reply that contemporary activists like [Ayatullah] Sa'idi, who was killed under torture, or the founders of the MKO, who were executed, have priority and must not be forgotten; or at least those individuals who struggled in Islamic countries and were martyred, like Jamilah Bou Pasha. However, they always dodged my questions and never gave an answer.

This kind of mindset prompted me to distance myself from them and limit my relationship with them. They also tried, on their part, to avoid me so that I would not learn about their relationship with the communists and other deviated currents, or if I found something they tried to distract me from paying attention to it. In the final days of 1350/1971, they distributed a declaration and I did not receive a copy of it. I felt that the MKO deliberately kept me in the dark and did not want me to see any of their writings after that. In any case, I finally received a copy of that declaration in which they had provided religious justification for armed robbery of the banks by members of the Fidayan-i Khalq organization and compared the Fidayan's action with that of early Muslim fighters in the Battle of Badr when they confiscated the properties of Quraysh caravans. They argued that the Fidayan's action was like that of the Prophet when his forces attacked the Quraysh caravans and distributed their belongings among the poor. I expressed strong objections to their comparing the action of the Fidayan with that of the Prophet and added that Muslim forces attacked Quraysh caravans only once under Sa'ad ibn Abi Waqqas without the permission of the Prophet, and that the Prophet criticized him for that action.

These declarations were produced at a time when the Mujahidin organization had not adopted an official name or emblem and there was no signature on the declarations. During that time, Vahid Afrakhteh was my liaison with the organization. I showed him the declarations and expressed my objection. Since he could not justify its content, he had no convincing answer but claimed that he had not seen that declaration either. To prove his claim, he took that copy from me and promised to give me an answer soon. Perhaps he thought that I would forget the whole matter after a few days. But whenever I saw him, I asked him for an answer and he always said that he did not know the reason why armed robbery was justified. I was sure that the declaration was issued by the Mujahidin and that he too was aware of it. This went on until one day he came to my house for a meeting. He took off his coat in the house and threw it into a corner. We spent some time talking and

130

drinking tea. When he put on his shoes and was about to leave he asked me to hand him his coat. When I picked it up, suddenly more than fifty copies of that same declaration fell onto the floor. I collected the copies one by one and put them in his side pocket and asked him to leave. It is interesting that he never gave up or felt embarrassed. In our next meeting, Vahid brought me ten or fifteen of those declarations and said, "Believe me, I had not seen the declarations before. The coat that I had that day did not belong to me. Others had just duplicated these declarations and I was not aware of them." I gave him back those declarations and said, "It is no longer important and I have no use for them. I will not distribute declarations for Marxist groups."

Early in 1351/1972, the regime had planned to execute a number of political activists and members of the opposition groups and was only looking for an excuse to carry out this plan. To that end the regime had called for a public demonstration. The MKO and the Fidayan-i Khalq organization issued a declaration and asked the people not to participate in such a gathering because the regime had planned to place bombs in the midst of the students and ordinary people and hold the resistance groups responsible for killing ordinary people. There was a precedent for such actions as the regime had taken similar measures in 1350/1971 as a result of which a cab driver had been killed.

One day, I met Vahid Afrakhteh to discuss this issue. He had a bundle of declarations with him and gave me a package, and when I opened it, I saw that it contained around one hundred copies of the same declaration. Fifty of them belonged to the MKO and the rest to Fidayan-i Khalq. Without any hesitation I tore up the declarations of the Fidayan-i Khalq group. I threw them away and told him that we had agreed not to have anything to do with the Fidayan. Vahid became nervous and said that he had made a mistake and that he was not supposed to give me the Fidayan's declarations. I said that it didn't matter who distributed those declarations because we had agreed not to work with the Marxist groups, and I took this as evidence of his dishonesty and lack of transparency, and this was a violation of our agreement.

On another occasion I learned that the MKO had given money to the Fidayan-i Khalq. When I questioned them about this, first they denied having given money to Fidayan. I continued questioning them about this issue for a couple of weeks, and they continued to deny it. Finally, I provided enough evidence that they could no longer deny it. When they realized that the matter had already leaked, they claimed that they had given them the money as a loan. I was not convinced and criticized them for giving the money collected as religious charities to a group that was against religion. Again they argued that this kind of collaboration had a historical precedent in the early days of Islam and that the Prophet also lent money to infidels to capture their hearts and attract their support. They argued that this should not be a problem, as all opposition groups must help one another against a common enemy in all matters, whether related to security issues, organizational experience, or any other relevant situation because they were all struggling for the same cause. No matter how much I argued that our objectives were different from Fidayan's and that our war was to save religion, whereas they saw religion as the "opium of the masses," they were not convinced.

Prudent Attitude toward the Mujahidin Khalq

In the early days of my cooperation with the Mujahidin, I had provided some logistical assistance to them, including some weapons, a printing machine, a typewriter, and some money. But from the moment I became aware of their dishonesty and hypocrisy, I stopped providing them with assistance. Several times they approached me and asked for more help, but I refused, even though I was able to provide help to them. Since I became aware of their dishonesty and lack of transparency, I refused and informed them that I could no longer help them.

They contacted me several times and asked for the reason for my refusal, and I told them that the people I knew among them were no longer qualified to carry out the task and I could not count on them because of their ties to other groups. At best, they could only be good for distributing the declarations but not for armed struggle.

My justification for this attitude was that in the past the situation was different, but as the objective conditions changed I was convinced that I could not count on them, and any help to them would mean betraying other efficient and sincere groups. I was certain that if this type of activist were arrested, they would sell us out to the police and disclose all the information they had because they were immature and inexperienced. This would be a heavy blow to us and the struggle because many of them did not even believe in, nor did they condone, the armed struggle.

With that kind of explanation, I avoided them and refrained from further assistance to and cooperation with them. Gradually, I lost my trust in them even more. Therefore, I tried to get to know their views and positions by any possible means. I wanted to learn the truth of the matter. The problem was that on the one hand I no longer believed that the communist and Marxist groups were weak and vulnerable before the regime; and on the other hand, I did not wish to see them harmed by the regime. But I could no longer tolerate the hypocritical games the MKO was playing. Because of many connections and information I received, I was aware of many issues that they did not even know anything about. For example, on occasion I would receive information that such-and-such an area in town was under the surveillance of SAVAK, and if any activist went there, it would be a high probability that he could be arrested. On other occasions I would be informed that such-and-such a member was under the watchful eye of the police and they would arrest him if they could find him. This situation posed a serious dilemma. On the one hand, I had to be careful that no one would go to certain suspicious locations or contact suspicious elements where SAVAK was present, and on the other hand, if I informed anyone of such dangers, I would be asked the source and authenticity of my information and expected to introduce such a valuable source to the MKO leadership. So I had to provide convincing reasons for my refusal to do so. Therefore, I had to make different excuses. Sometime I told them that I received information from a friend in the bazaar when I met him by accident; sometimes I had to say that I hadn't been in contact with my source for a while, or had met so-and-so by accident and I would introduce him to them if I saw him again; or that I heard such pieces of information from two young men on the bus; and similar excuses. Of course, they did not like, nor were convinced with, my explanations, but I had to be very careful what kind of information I gave to the MKO. Sometimes in our conversations they asked me questions that I had to dodge, and sometimes I gave very general responses. One day Hasan Abrari complimented me sarcastically and said that I treated them as if they were SAVAK agents and wouldn't give up information easily, and that they must pressure me like SAVAK interrogators so that I would reveal information! This was because I had a lot of information that I did not want to share with them. They too were certain that I had a lot of information that I was hiding from them. I did not deny that I had a lot of information but told them that it might not be of any use for them, nor would it be of any help to their activities. One time I also told them frankly that I did not trust them lest they might reveal them to the police under torture. Therefore, it was appropriate not to bring up this issue again and save many troubles for them and me.

The MKO considered me a threat to their political and organizational activities. They had no choice but to assign me to military missions and operations. Therefore, they tried to keep me preoccupied with making bombs and planning assassinations so that I wouldn't have time for other duties. This trick did not work, however, because I was able to fulfill the duties that were assigned to me quickly and efficiently and still have time for my own responsibilities.

The information and experiences that I gained from the organization were very beneficial to my own activities. In order to keep me under control, they even wanted me to provide daily report of my activities every twenty-four hours. This attitude indicated that they did not know what to do with me, and our relationship had come to a dead end. Yet I performed any task they assigned to me, and they could not find any flaws in my actions. Those assignments ranged from making bombs to investigating the safety of meeting locations and the like. I would do all those tasks with the utmost degree of efficiency and care, and they could not find any shortcomings in my work. I tried to make it clear that my criticism was not aimed at the way they operated but at their questionable positions and deviated views and lack of transparency. By showing my utmost effort in performing the task they assigned to me, I wanted to show them that my objection was not out of fear for my life but was based on my beliefs. I wanted them to understand that I am a man of action and accept all dangers in the process.

In order to accomplish the many tasks given to me by the organization and also attend my personal duties, I was forced to work harder and sleep less. For example, to make a bomb, I would stay up until late at night. In my report to them, however, I told them that I went to sleep at ten o'clock and spent the next morning completing the job. In reality, however, by morning I was at a different place performing other tasks. At times when we were supposed to meet, I would tell them that I would be at home, and since they did not have my address, they could not find my whereabouts. On other occasions I would continue my work regardless, because I was not certain that we would be able to meet the next day. Sometimes in between the meetings I went to Qom or Damavand and returned in the afternoon to meet them. Therefore, it was never possible for them to find out where I was or when I was in any given location or whom I met.

My ability to and courage for acting the way I did was simply because I had strong faith in my ability to resist torture. Otherwise, there was always a danger that if I were to be arrested, all those who were connected to me would also be arrested. I was certain that such a danger would not exist, as my arrest would not harm others in the group.

Bomb Explosion in the Shah Abbas Hotel in Isfahan

In the month of Khordad 1351/June 1971 the president of an Eastern Bloc country paid a state visit to Iran. The organization decided to carry out a few terrorist acts in Isfahan in order to reflect popular grievances and demonstrate the regime's incompetence. This city was chosen because that president was to visit Isfahan as the special guest of the governor-general. Until that time our operations had not received much publicity. This was an opportunity to force the regime to acknowledge public grievances and reflect the news of operations in the media. Hasan Abrari, Vahid Afrakhteh, and I were assigned to carry out this mission, and we went to Isfahan. We rented a room in a hotel. Muhsin Fazil also traveled to the city separately. We went to his hotel room to prepare the bomb. He was alone and had brought the materials we needed to make bombs. It was the first time that I made a bomb out of TNT. Until then, I had used benzene and sugar to make bombs. TNT smelled bad, and its odor burned our eyes. I never knew of this, and my collaborators did not tell me anything. Perhaps they wanted me to get used to this smell. The TNT rolls looked like candles, and I had to mix them to make a ball-shaped bomb. As a result its smell intensified, and it really burned my eyes and gave me a terrible headache. For two or three days after that I did not feel well.

First, we placed a bomb under a bus that exploded across the headquarters of the Isfahan main police station on Chahar Bagh Square. The governor-general had planned a reception in honor of his guest at the Shah Abbas Hotel. So we decided to plant a bomb next to the hotel building. We made the bombs with TNT and decided to program them to explode as the reception was underway. In the sidewalk next to the hotel building there was a garden covered with grass and flowers where we planned to place the bomb in a green bag. To distract police attention and to have enough time to place the bomb there, we cut a rosary and spread the beads on the ground. Then we sat on the ground pretending to collect the beads so that we had enough time to hide the bomb between the flowers and went away. We programmed the bomb to explode at one p.m. and waited somewhere else in the city for it to explode. However, the bomb did not work. This problem occurred on other occasions and different locations as well. Since the police were on high alert after the first blast, we decided that everyone should return to Tehran except me so that I could analyze and report the reasons for our failure. I did not return to my hotel that night. Instead, I went to the house of a friend and supporter by the name of Ashraf Khorasani[83] and spent the night there. Until that time, there was no news concerning a bomb explosion. I guessed that the bomb had been discovered and detonated. For obvious security reasons it was not right for me to go and find out why the bomb had not exploded. After the explosion of the first bomb we placed under the bus, the entire city and its police forces were on high alert.

Next morning I realized that there was no news about the bomb, so I decided to return to Tehran. To be cautious I decided not to take the main road[84] but to take another route[85] to Tehran. It was around ten o'clock in the morning when I went to the garage and suddenly heard an explosion. I returned right away to the city and took a taxi and went toward the Shah

---

[83] Mohammad Ali Ashraf Khorasan i was arrested twice and jailed before the victory of the Islamic Revolution. After the victory, he was killed in a motorcycle accident.

[84] The route of this journey was in the following order: Isfahan—Shahin Shahr—Meimeh—Delijan—Salafchegan—Qom—Tehran.

[85] The journey was in this order: Najaf Abad—Khonsar—Golpeigan—Qom—Tehran.

Abbas Hotel. I did not stop the taxi but noticed that the bomb had exploded. The windows of the hotel had shattered, and a part of its building had also been destroyed. I heard that one of the cleaners had been injured and was taken to hospital where he passed away.[86] The Isfahan radio station announced the news of the bomb explosion, and city papers also reported the incident. I was very sad and distressed for the death of that worker. Apparently he had found the bomb under the bushes and picked it up, so it exploded in his hand. I was especially heartbroken because we were so careful not to injure innocent people. After receiving the information about this incident, by the order I received from the organization, I made a call to the police headquarters and told them that the Mujahidin-i Khalq Organization claimed responsibility for this explosion.

The Discovery of the House on Arif Avenue

I had rented a room on one of the streets of Arif Avenue (now Shahid Seyyed Kamal al-Din Mukhbir). The landlady lived in the house with her daughter. The rest of her children were all married and were living somewhere else. This lady and her daughter spent most of their time traveling. That was an ideal place for me to live. In their absence, I had the opportunity to live and carry out my activities freely and without any fear or concern.

Most of my meetings with the members of the organization took place in the vicinities of my neighborhood where my residence was located. Out of precaution, I avoided meeting in my house. Even if I wanted to take someone to my house, first I would meet him outside and then go to the house together a little later. One day I had a meeting with Hasan Abrari. He said that he was not feeling well and wanted to come to my house so that we could cook and eat together. We

---

[86] The worker killed was called Abdul Rasul Yusufi, twenty-six years of age, and was an employee of the Shah Abbas Hotel in Isfahan.

returned home around 11:30. Hasan prepared the food and I went to the neighborhood store to buy yoghurt, vegetables, and potatoes. The store owner asked where I was earlier in the evening, and when I asked him the reason for his curiosity, he said, "Your friends came and wanted to see you." I had no friends who would want to come to my house without advance notice and arrangements. I asked him how many people there were and what questions they asked him. When he said that your friends thought you were in Mashhad I realized that they probably were police agents and wanted to attack the house and arrest me. Because of the fact that Javad Mansuri had been arrested a short while ago, I thought of him immediately, be-cause only he knew where I lived.[87] Perhaps he had given up the address of my house to the police under torture. In any case, I was certain that the police agents were in the neighbor-

---

[87] In his memoirs Javad Mansuri described the details of the discovery of the house located on Arif Street by the SAVAK. According to him, "As a result of confessions of Hossein Javanbakht, on the morning of Aban 3, 1351/October 13, 1972, I was arrested and taken to the Ghezel Ghal'eh prison. When Abbas Shahrudi confessed before the police, then they trans-ferred me to the Evin prison. This incident prompted the SAVAK to pres-sure me even more. For about a month, they took me for interrogation and torture on a daily basis. They kept me in solitary confinement This went on until Jalal Ganjeh'ie revealed the names of comrades (among them Ezzat Shahi) who attended Thursday night meetings. After that day the SAVAK intensified my torture in order to get the names and addresses of the houses of my friends. One night they interrogated and tortured me until 1.30 am in one of the underground chambers. While torturing they continuously said that 'You are capable of helping us in the arrest of Khonsari' (the fictitious name of Ezzat Shahi). I was sure that Ezzat Shahi was aware of my arrest after nearly two weeks and that he had already changed his address. I told the police the address of the house. They immediately prepared two cars with armed police men. They carried me up to the Ghiyathi Road while I was blindfolded. They opened my eyes upon reaching there and I showed them the house. The police approached the house in fear and after waiting for a while, they realized that no one was in the house. The SAVAK offic-ers were very angry as they thought that I had lied to them. After a couple of hours, they took me back to prison." Memoirs of Javad Mansuri, pp. 116–125).

hood expecting to see me. Without buying anything, I left the store. I returned home immediately and found Hasan sitting in his pajamas. I told him that the situation was critical. He got dressed quickly and before leaving the house we designated a place to meet later. He said that if he didn't show up I should conclude that he had been arrested.

After Hasan left I had to destroy the documents that I had kept in the house or take them with me. Hasan looked much older than his age and had lost his hair, and that made him look even older. Therefore, he was able to avoid the eyes of the police. Five or six minutes after he left, there was a knock on the door. *It was the police.* There was no more time to do anything with the documents, and I only could collect a few of them. I did not even have time to put on my clothes. I jumped over the balcony and then climbed up to the neighbor's roof. From there I jumped onto the street behind many houses while the police were in front of the house. Later I heard that the police had knocked for some time and when there was nobody to open the door they kicked and broke the door and forced their way into the house. Reportedly, they stayed there for two to three days waiting for me or others who might come to visit me. Meanwhile, they were able to search the house and found some documents. These included my identity card and some declarations. As I mentioned before, like SAVAK agents they reported the failure of their operation in such a way not to be embarrassed or questioned by their superiors. They reported that they had entered the house and found no one there! Obviously, they did not say that we fooled them and escaped.

After escaping and as soon as I had a chance I phoned another member of the MKO—Hasan Farzaneh—from a public phone booth and told him that my house had been discovered and neither he nor anyone else should go there. I called two other people and informed them of the situation. One of the relatives of Hasan Farzaneh lived in the vicinity of my house. Out of carelessness or curiosity Hasan went there.

When he was passing by, the police stopped him and questioned him and the reason he went near my house. He told them that his brother lived in the neighborhood and he just wanted to visit him. The police asked him more questions and luckily he was freed. Hasan Abrari escaped wearing his pajamas and carrying his trousers in his hand. As for me, I never had this chance to even take my pants. After I called a few friends, I decided to go to a relative's house located on Ahmadiyeh Avenue just a short distance from Arif Avenue. When they saw me in such a situation they wondered why I was not properly dressed. I had to make up a story and tell them that I had had a fight with someone on my way and my clothes got all torn. I also asked them to give me some clothes so that I could go to the police station. Incidentally the brother-in-law of that relative served in the military police force and insisted that we should go to the station so that he could take care of the perpetrators and have them punished. The situation was about to turn into a fiasco, so I convinced him that I had no time because a couple of friends were waiting for me to go to the police station together. I assured him that I would call him if I felt there was a need for his intervention and he agreed. To make the story short, I wore the clothes he gave me and went to a barber shop and got a haircut, then went to meet Hasan Abrari. We were happy that we had managed to save our lives and hadn't fallen into police trap.

I was still worried about some of the documents I had placed in different corners of my residence. Since I knew that the store owner in my neighborhood went to the wholesale market early mornings to buy fruits and vegetables for his store, I decided to go and meet him there. I wanted to ask him to go to my residence, find all documents, and destroy them. I changed my appearance and wore a chapeau hat and together with Kachu'i, who had a motorcycle, we went to the wholesale market.

We found the man and greeted him. He did not recognize us at first and wondered what we wanted. When I introduced myself, he asked me about the reason that the police were after me. He also said that I had lied to him because the police told him that I had killed a man and that I was involved in criminal acts! I assured him in an assertive tone of voice that all these were nonsense allegations. He warned me that that at least five police agents were waiting in my house to arrest me even as we spoke. I knew that he was a religious man and had been scared by all these events. So I explained to him that I had not killed anyone and that I had only participated in distributing declarations. When I noticed that he was frightened I changed my mind and decided not to ask him to go to my house and destroy the documents.

I had placed some of the writings, pamphlets, and hand-written notes, and a number of key chains engraved with the emblems of the armed Palestinian groups such as al-Fath, al-Sa'iqah, and al-'Asifah in the cabinet. The police had found some of these key chains and declarations. Since I lived in hiding for several years and was in fact a fugitive, they had concluded that I had been in Palestine for some time. They also thought that I was armed. In addition, my birth certificate, which had my picture, was among the documents that were then in SAVAK's hands and they knew well what I looked like. It was, therefore, very easy for them to identify me if they ever saw me again.

Hossein, the Pickle Vendor

After my house on Arif Avenue was discovered by the police, with the help of my friend, Akbar Mahdavi, I found another house on Sahib Jam' Street and rented a room on the first floor of a house that belonged to Hossein Sha'bani. He was a sympathizer of the Mujahidin-i Khalq Organization. Vahid Afrakhteh also checked the house and approved of it. He came there occasionally and spent time there.

Mr. Sha'bani had a shop where he sold pickles and vinegar and helped us a lot. Even though he was a simple man and illiterate, he was politically aware and had an interest in current affairs. He was a good and pious person. He had only one problem, and that was his excessive curiosity. He wanted to know every detail of our business. Although he was the owner of the house, occasionally he caused trouble and disturbed us. For example, without advance notice or permission, he entered my room to see what I was up to. Of course, he had no ill intention and wished to help us. In a sense he had sympathy toward me. Sometimes he came in because he felt bad that I was lonely and wanted to make me feel good. Since I was single and most of the time ate very simple food like bread and yogurt or cheese and grapes he would bring a bowl of soup or his dinner to share with me. Some evenings his wife would make tea and he would bring it to my room to drink together. He had a son and I taught him how to recite the Qur'an. Occasionally he attended those sessions to observe his son's progress and enjoyed watching him learn the Qur'an.

This situation brought us so close that he used to sit with me and discuss politics, and he would give his opinion. Since his store was located adjacent to the Hosseiniyyah Irshad he often listened to sermons that were delivered there and had learned a few things about religion and social issues. He often complained about the moral corruption in the society and lack of women's *hijab* and blamed all these on the American presence in the country! Gradually I opened up to him a little. I told him that there were a lot of people who thought and felt like him and opposed the prevailing conditions; and that some young people had started fighting against the regime and had agreed to pay the price, too. As a result of this relationship, little by little Mr. Sha'bani became interested in political activity and developed sympathy for the opposition groups. He particularly insisted and was eager to know those young activists so that he "would sacrifice his life for them." He even offered to send his family to his village or sell one of the two houses he owned and donate the money to these groups. His words were really sincere, and he meant what he said. He was sin-

143

cerely ready to sacrifice all of his property and even his life. But he was a novice in political activities. At forty-five years of age he was not fit or prepared to get engaged in armed struggle. Moreover, I was also not willing to let him sacrifice his life for a group and organization that I had full knowledge about. In response to his insistence I told him to go and get an education. I promised to help him in such an undertaking, and once he received some education, then we could talk about making a decision. With my encouragement he registered to attend night classes in Akhbari School and got busy with his studies. He was quite talented and performed very well in school. Once, he brought around ten thousand *tumans* that he had saved and gave it to me to deliver it to the MKO as [religious] charity donation (*zakat*). I didn't want him to give that money to the MKO. I told him that there is no need for him to give this money to that organization. Instead, I suggested that he donate that to Imam Khomeini's representative and they would spend it as they saw fit. Because of Sha'bani's admirable qualities I always welcomed him to my room. When I felt that he might come, I covered my weapon and declarations with an old blanket I had so that he wouldn't see them. One night Afrakhteh come to spend the night at my house. As was taking off his weapon from his belt, suddenly Sha'bani opened the door and came in and saw the gun in the hands of Afrakhteh. Vahid became very nervous and scared. To his surprise, when Sha'bani saw him and his weapon, he was jubilant and said, "I was looking for you in heaven. But now I have found you on earth and in my house." Without hesitation or asking for permission he came in, sat down, and started talking. From that time onwards, he indeed became even closer to us. For a whole month, he was insisting that we should accept that money he had offered and told us to spend it as we wished. I did not take it. Later on, he gave the money to Vahid, who also passed it on to me, and I spent it to the last penny in the course of the resistance.

144

Sha'bani had a storage room. He gave us permission to take a few barrels of acid we had and store them there. The buckets that contained acid were white, while his containers of vinegar were blue. Apart from these, I also stored a motorcycle, some books, and pamphlets in that storage house. Because of this relationship and the trust that developed between us, I continued to produce declarations and pamphlets with peace of mind. He was convinced that we were on the right course. Sha'bani was really sincere to us and the organization, but since he was such a simple man, we could not fully utilize his services in our operations or tell him about matters related to organization. Even the degree of information that he acquired from our work in his house created major problems for him and us later on.

An Explosion on Firdawsi Avenue

In the summer of the year 1351/1972 when my house on Arif Avenue was discovered, the police waited days and days for me to return and to arrest me, but that never happened. They searched the house, and among all documents they found my birth certificate that had my picture on. They duplicated that picture and handed it to the undercover police agents so that they could find me dead or alive.

In the early days of the month of Mordad/July a taxi-cab exploded at the Istanbul-Firdawsi intersection. Reportedly, two people had gone to place a bomb near the National Iranian Oil Company headquarters (NIOC) located a mile from that intersection. When they saw a large crowd in the street or perhaps for some other reasons they decided not to place the bomb. However, they forgot to disconnect the wires and defuse the bomb. Then they took a taxi, and one of them got off at the Istanbul-Firdawsi intersection, and the second man stayed in the cab. A few minutes later the bomb exploded. The explosion was so devastating that one of the doors of the taxi was thrown away near the Pelasko commercial highrise.[88] A piece of the car was thrown inside the Turkish embassy. The driver and the person carrying the bomb were both killed on the spot.

SAVAK agents had been searching for me for over three years and had failed to arrest me. They were frustrated and tired of continuous search and wanted to close my file. When the explosion occurred, they thought that I had been carrying the bomb, and because of the resemblance of my photo to the body, they concluded that Ezzat Shahi had been killed in the explosion and announced that news. Since SAVAK thought they had accomplished their mission, they were relieved and happy. That night the national TV and the next day Tehran press reported that Ezzat Shahi, a well-known terrorist, had been killed while carrying a bomb in a taxi.[89] I did not hear the news that night, but the next day at two o'clock when I was at a bazaar restaurant eating lunch with Hasan Abrari (now my liaison with the organization), I heard the news from national radio: "Yesterday afternoon in a bomb explosion on Firdawsi Avenue, a terrorist by the name of Ezzat Shahi was killed."[90] Thus, I found out that I was killed! Since Hasan Abrari knew me only by my fictitious name, he did not realize that the person who had died was meant to be me! I pretended that I did not hear the news.

After lunch Hasan and I went to the bazaar. I should admit that this was a mistake because I should have not gone to the bazaar where everyone knew me. We passed by Bayn al-Haramain bazaar and went through the Shah Mosque (now the Imam Mosque) to go out through Nasir Khosrow Avenue.

---

[88] The Pelasko building was by far the first and tallest building that was built in Downtown Tehran in the 1960's.

[89] On Mordad 5, 1351/July 15, 1972 Tehran newspapers reported that "Ezzat Shahi and 'Adil Jismi (the taxi driver) escaped the scene by a taxi-cab but were killed in the taxi as a result of the explosion of the bomb they carried."

[90] The SAVAK went ahead and even issued a death certificate for for Ezzat Shahi.

146

In the bazaar, a few people recognized me, but I pretended that I did not know them. In the Shah Mosque, I also came across two people that I knew. One of them was Morteza Kashani.[91] He was a very clever and fine young man. When he approached me, I made a gesture to him telling him not to say anything. He never said a word and went away. The second person was Mohammad Khalilniya.[92] He saw me from the window of the mosque and came to me. No matter how I tried to avoid him, he never paid attention. He hugged me and became emotional, uttering my name and wondering where I had been and what had happened to me, because a couple of hours ago he had heard that I was killed. This was a disaster, as at that moment Hasan Abrari found out my real name and identity. Until that time, the organization referred to me by fictitious names like Hossein, Mahmud, Khonsari, Mohammadi, Abudhar, and the like. I had to explain to Khalil Niya that the news report was a mistake. The person killed only looked like me. Hardly had the words come off my tongue than Hasan

---

[91] Morteza Kashani served at Sanduq Qarz al-Hasaneh Bank (the interest-free bank) after the victory of the Islamic Revolution. He passed away in 1381/2002 because of heart failure.

[92] Mohammad Khalili Niya (b. 1319/1940, Tehran). He completed his elementary and secondary school studies at Sorayya and Marvi Schools respectively. He joined the National Front (Jebhe-ye Melli'), then the People's Party of Iran (Hizb-i Milal-i Islami) and became its liaison with the bazaar. He was arrested several times, the last time in 1355/1976, and was imprisoned for seven months in a prison that was under The Joint Committee for Anti-Terrorism. Before the victory of the Islamic Revolution, Khalil Niya owned a shop in the bazaar and sold photo albums. Then he started to buy and sell iron and steel. During this time, he financially supported the families of those activists who were arrested. After the victory of the Islamic Revolution, he served at the Ministry of Labor under the late Daryush Furuhar and was in charge of handling labor disputes, a position he held also under President Bani Sadr. He was also the Director General of two companies that belonged to Mostaz'afan and Victims of War Foundation. At the moment he is in building and construction. He has been engaged in construction business since then. *Interview with Khalil Niya*, Tehran, Azar 5, 1383/December 15, 2004

Abrari told the organization everything. He explained to them that the Ezzat Shahi that had been reported dead was our own Hossein. From that day on the organization said that I had no permission to go the bazaar because I was already known and my going there was dangerous for me and for the organization. I pretended to accept their order but in reality I never observed it and often went to the bazaar to visit my friends. When the organization found out about my breach of promise, they decided to punish me. One day, Abrari and Afrakhteh informed the members that we would go hiking the next day and I gladly welcomed the idea.

Early next morning, we went mountain-climbing in the north of Tehran. While hiking we were all happy and talked and laughed together and did not discuss any serious issues. When we reached the peak and stopped to have lunch, Afrakhteh asked for my weapon, pretending to check it. I gave it to him. Then he and the others began to criticize me, saying that I had become arrogant and disobedient and did not care for the chain of command and the orders of the organization and acted as I wished. I was told that my behavior put myself and everyone else in danger. They asked me if I were going to stop acting the way I was and work within the rules of the organization. They blamed me for going to the bazaar despite the organization's order.

Of course they were right and were telling the truth. Since I was working with them, I should have obeyed all the rules of the organization to avoid any harm to them and to myself. While I listened to their criticism I tried to deny having gone to the bazaar or anywhere near it and asked them where they got their nonsense information from. It turned out that they knew exactly when I had gone to the bazaar and that I had gotten a haircut there. I realized that they had appointed someone who followed every move I made. I tried to explain that it was cheapest to get a haircut in the bazaar, but they were not convinced. The argument went too far. One of them said that in other liberation movements and organizations in the world, this kind of behavior and disobedience was counted as a treason, as for example among the Viet Kong, and the violator would be condemned to death. I felt that the situation was getting out of control, so I changed my tone of voice and told them, "I have enough experience to know what is what, and I have always obeyed the orders of the organization. And even if I went to the barber, it was because it was cheaper than the other places." To make the story short, as we continued to climb in the Darakeh Mountain hills and they continued threatening me, I pretended that the issue was not so serious. When we returned to town in the afternoon, they did not give me my gun back. For over three weeks I had no gun and no longer went to the bazaar, as I knew they would follow me. Two weeks later, they gave me a better gun than my own and I took this as a sign of appeasement.

The Assassination of Sha'ban Bimokh (the Brainless)

We stopped all our activities for about a month. The organization started to identify unpopular and oppressive individuals within the regime to punish them. Sha'ban Ja'fari, commonly known as Sha'ban Bimokh, the Brainless[93] was one of those

---

[93] Sha'ban Ali Ja'fari, known as Sha'ban Bimokh (the Brainless), was born in Tehran in 1300/1925. He was unable to complete his studies because of his troubled lifestyle and turned his attention to traditional Persian sports. In 1319/1940 he joined the military for two years. In 1326/1947 he and his gang attacked a theater that was directed by Abdul Hossein Nooshin, a member of the Tudeh Party. As a result the government became interested in and recruited him. He was then sent to Lahijan for one year to keep him away from his political activities. In Lahijan, Sha'ban caused much trouble for the people. During this time, he attracted the attention of M.I.6 Intelligence Service. He sought financial help from the Rashidiyan brothers. With the help of his group, on Azar 9, 1330/December 1, 1951 he set fire to the offices of several leftist newspapers: *Chalangar*, *Besuye Ayandeh*, *Mardum*, and the headquarters of House of Peace. As a result, he was imprisoned where he met Khalil Tahmasabi and thus became a supporter of the Fidayan-i Islam organization. After his release he became a supporter of Ayatullah Kashani for some time. Then he joined the supporters of Dr. Mo-

individuals identified as a traitor to the nation. His negative role in the *coup d'état* of 28 Mordad, 1332/August 19, 1953 followed by his assassination attempt on the life of Dr. Seyyed Hossein Fatimi [Mosaddiq's Minister of Foreign Affairs] had made him a much hated man in the country, especially among the youth and political activists of all persuasions. The Organization had condemned him to death, and now it was his turn to be assassinated.

Vahid Afrakhteh and I were chosen for this task. We assessed the situation for two weeks and gathered all necessary information, and then decided to carry out the mission. Sha'ban had a routine schedule every day. Every morning at six o'clock he would start to walk from the intersection of Pahlavi and Sepah Avenues toward the Hasan Abad Square, and from there he would walk to Park-i Shahr and finally to his club located at the north of the park. Sometimes he used his personal car, a Land Rover, and some other times he walked

---

saddiq. In 1331/1952 when he heard that the Shah was permitted to leave the country, he mobilized Tehran thugs and attacked Dr. Mosaddiq's house. He was arrested again and remained in jail until the afternoon of the *coup d'état* if 28-5-1332.There, Sha'ban, with the help of Parvin Azhdan Qizi, joined the *coup d'état* forces along with his club-wielders and the mob of south Tehran. He attracted the royalists' attention and became one of the closest friends of Mohammad Reza Pahlavi. As a reward for his work during the coup, the Shah gave him a piece of land in the northern part of the City Park through the approval of Development Bank for him to build a sports club. The building of this club took three years and was opened by Mohammad Reza Pahlavi. On Isfand 22, 1332/March 13, 1954 Sha'ban assassinated Dr. Seyyed Hossein Fatimi, Mosaddeq's Minister of Foreign Affairs, who died as a result of his injuries a few days later. During the uprising on Khordad 15, 1342/June 5, 1963 demonstrators attacked and set fire on Ja'fari's club, but he managed to escape. As one of the closest men to Shah, Ja'fari often traveled to Israel, Japan, Turkey, and Europe throughout the Shah's reign. He escaped the country before the victory of the Islamic Revolution to Israel before joining the forces of General Bahram Aryana to bring the Shah back but failed. He finally settled in Los Angeles and died there. He narrated his memoirs to Homa Sarshar in 1999, who later published it. See *Memoirs of Sha'aban Ja'afari.*

towards the Hasan Abad Square. From there, he went to the city park, and finally to his club via the road to the north of the park. Occasionally, he used his Land Rover to drive to his club.

It was early morning on the fifth or sixth of the month of Mehr/September 15 that Vahid and I left my house on Sahib Jam' Avenue on a motorcycle and began to drive towards the designated place. There were a lot of potholes on Sahib Jam' Avenue, and the road was in bad condition. It had also rained the night before and made the road condition muddy. I was driving, and Vahid sat behind me.

As we were driving, suddenly an old lady jumped in front of us. At that moment, I stepped on the front and rear brakes in order not to hit the old lady. As a result of this, the motorbike turned over and we were thrown onto the side of the road. I felt some pain in my shoulder but did not take it seriously. So I got up and took the motorbike from the ground, and we continued our journey towards the Hasan Abad Square. My weapon was an old one, but Vahid's was new and the kind used in the army, so he was supposed to shoot Sha'ban. Apart from this, we also carried two smoke and teargas bombs.

We waited for a while at the Hasan Abad Square, and before too long we saw Sha'ban coming. As we approached him, we chanted revolutionary slogans. Sha'ban noticed that the situation was not normal. As he was terrified, he started running away and took out his gun to defend himself. When Vahid wanted to shoot him, we heard the siren of a police vehicle. Vahid got frightened and shot a few bullets toward Sha'ban, and I also shot several times. Sha'ban was frightened but managed to run around and shoot at us. I believe his weapon was a revolver handgun. I had once told the members of the organization that Sha'ban was always armed, but they did not believe me. In any case, we exchanged several rounds of bullets, and some hit the target. Sha'ban fell to the ground. I ran out of bullets. Vahid tried to finish him off, but he probably got nervous and shot a bullet from a distance that missed the target.

The siren of the police was getting nearer and nearer every second. We had to leave in a hurry. We did not even have a chance to use our teargas bombs and had to leave the scene quickly. I was sure that Sha'ban had died. But this was not the case. Reportedly, they took him to the Sina Hospital that was in that area, where he received treatment and survived. Although he was hit by two or three bullets and his hand was also injured, he recovered but never went to the club after that. In any case, we failed and he survived. If Vahid had not become nervous and had shot the last bullet at the target, then Sha'ban would have been killed.[94] Vahid and I as well as the organization were so certain of the success of our mission that they had prepared and distributed announcements on the day of the terror.[95] When we left the scene, I noticed that Vahid was bleeding on his shoulder where a bullet had hit him. When I brought it to his attention he assured me that it was not serious.

We were trying to decide what to do next and where to go. We could not return to my own house because my landlord was so curious. An idea came to my mind that we should go to the house of my friend Akbar Mahdavi that was located on Adib Street. When we arrived there first we treated his injury temporarily and had breakfast. Akbar suggested that we go and have a doctor treat Vahid's wounds before it got infected.

I knew Dr. Hossein Ali, who was a member of the Freedom Movement of Iran, and I trusted him. I decided to

---

[94] In his memoirs, Ja'fari narrates the story in a different manner.

[95] I contacted Dr. Ali's house on Ordibehest 13, 1382/April 23, 19, 2001. His wife said the doctor was ill and could not talk, and was also suffering from Alzheimer's disease and did not remember anything. She said that she would talk to Dr. Ali and describe the story for him and if he remembered anything, she would let me know. The next day Mrs. Ali called and said that the doctor only remembered that he had treated an injured man after the assassination of Sha'ban Ja'fari, but he did not remember how he treated him.

take Vahid to his office, which was located in southern Tehran in a neighborhood known as Tir Doqolu. We went there. For security reasons I did not even tell Vahid that I knew the doctor. I only told him that he was a Muslim and a good person. Before we entered the doctor's room, I asked Vahid to stay out for a few minutes so that I could go in and check to make sure everything was all right.

I entered and greeted the doctor and told him that I had a friend and we were playing together in the house when suddenly a bullet came out of nowhere and hit him. It passed from one side of his shoulder and came out from the other side. I want you to check and make sure that it would not cause infection. Apparently, the doctor had heard of the story from the radio as he said he knew the story of my hero! I laughed and said that I didn't know and it did not matter what the incident was. Whatever it was, he'd better not be curious and just treat him if he could. The doctor asked me to go and bring him in and I did. He treated him and added that thank God it was not serious and asked us just to keep it covered and clean. He also said that since he did not trust his assistant, we had better get injections and bandages in another place. So he prescribed some penicillin shots and I performed all the other treatments myself, including giving Vahid his injections. I never wanted Vahid to find out that I knew this doctor, so I went to the counter, and like the other patients, I paid his fee.[96] Later on when

---

[96] Akbar Mahdavi remembered the day Sha'ban Ja'fari was assassinated: "Apparently, that day was the second time they went after Sha'ban because the first day he didn't show up, but they accomplished the mission the second day. Sha'ban also had used his pistol during the conflict and one of the bullets had hit Afrakhteh's shoulder. When they went to our house that morning, I sent my brother (Asghar) out so that he couldn't find out anything, but he later on found out what had happened. First I cleaned Afrakhteh's bleeding shoulder and bandaged it to stoop the bleeding. Then we had breakfast together. We needed to check the neighborhood to make sure that nobody had followed them so I sent Ezzat Shahi out to do that. Once we knew that it was safe for them to leave, they went to Dr Ali's office." See *Interview with Ali Akbar Mahdavi*, Tehran, Azar 26, 1383/December 16, 2002.

Vahid was arrested and confessed to all of these, the doctor was not suspected and remained safe because of my ordinary behavior in his office. Soon Vahid's shoulder was healed. For over six months, however, I had pain in my arm and could not move it easily.

My Encounter with Dr. Javad Manaqebi

One of the tasks that Mohammad Kachu'i and I were assigned to perform was to disrupt the sermons of Dr. Javad Manaqebi[97]and to set fire to his car. He was known as a [royal] court appointed *mulla.*

Manaqebi was the son-in-law of 'Allameh [Seyyed Mohammad Husayn] Tabataba'i and brother-in-law of Ayatullah Ali Quddusi. But I do not know how he chose to side with the regime. In addition to traditional religious education, he had also attended the University of Tehran and received a degree from the School of Theology where he was hired as a lecturer. In his sermons in the mosques, he praised the Shah, and many supporters of the regime attended his mosque and listened to his sermons. I remember that one day when he went to the pulpit in the bazaar mosque [Prime Minister Amir Abbas] Huvayda was present. Addressing him, he said, "Oh, Mr. Amir Abas! You did not come here on your own. Fatimah Zahra, peace be upon her, welcomed you here, and Imam Zaman [the Mahdi], peace be upon him, is also pleased to see you off!"

---

[97] Dr. Javad Nava'ie Manaqebi (b. 1309, Tehran) Studied in Qom and Tehran University, earned a doctoral degree in Islamic studies and joined the faculty of the School of Theology at the University of Tehran. He was reportedly in contact with the U.S. Embassy staff in Tehran. He was arrested as a result of his association with [Sadeq] Qutbzadeh and involvement in a plot to overthrow the Islamic government. He lost his clerical status and garb as a result. After his release from prison he continued his anti-government activities, but as a result of the mediation of some friends he was given back his clerical garb. He passed away in 1382/2003 after a long illness. See Khorasan, #9586, p. 4; and, Sharifrazi, pp. 404–406.

154

Then he recited the following poem: Your Excellency Mr. Amir Abbas Huvayda should know that,

Only a pure soul is worthy of [divine] emanation
For not every mud brick will turn into a shining pearl.[98]

He then attacked Ayatullah [Ali] Meshkini and [Hossein Ali] Montazeri, who had written a review of a book titled *The Eternal Martyr* (*Shahid-i Javid*). Kachu'i and I decided that whenever he went to the pulpit to deliver a sermon, we would disrupt his session. On one occasion we gave money to a madman and told him to go to the bazaar mosque and sit there and listen to the shaykh's sermon and when the shaykh began, start to act out and make faces and strange sounds. At first the shaykh pretended that he did not see the man but soon realized that he could not continue with that situation and asked people to take the man out of the mosque because he didn't seem to be normal. Suddenly the madman began to scream and use foul language, cursing the shaykh. The situation became so chaotic that the shaykh came down from the pulpit and left.

Toward the end of the 1340's/1960's, Manaqebi attended a private residence on Cyrus Avenue regularly and delivered sermons. He had a chauffeur who would stay in the car while the shaykh went into the house to give a talk. Kachu'i and I decided and planned to set fire to his car. After taking the necessary measures and at a proper moment, Kachu'i sprayed benzene on the front tires, and I did the same to the two rear tires. I lit the match on the wheels where we had already poured benzene, and in a moment the car was on fire. I then joined Kachu'i, who was waiting for me on his motorcycle to get away from the scene. The driver noticed this and started the car and drove fast for a short distance, and the wind killed the fire. The car did not burn, but the tires were completely destroyed. It is interesting that when Kachu'i and Hasan Kabiri were arrested later, Kachu'i never mentioned my name as his

ور نه هر خشت و گلی لؤلؤ مرجان نشود [98]   نطفه پاک بباید که شود قابل فیض

collaborator in that operation. He only mentioned my name as a provocateur.

Another time we thought of attacking Manaqebi and pouring acid on his face. We did not wish to blind him, so instead we poured ink on his face and dress. The ink covered his head, face, and clothes and made a mess. Despite all this he never changed his behavior, nor did he give up his defense of the regime, and continued to deliver sermons in praise of the Shah.

Once in 1350 or 1351/1971 or 72 a few friends and supporters of Shahid [Seyyed Ali] Andarzgu pretending to need the shaykh's service for a funeral session. They drove him to the outskirts of Tehran in the south of the city near a remote well and began to beat him to death. The shaykh started to beg them not to kill him, admitted his wrongdoings, and promised not to say anything in praise of the regime again.[99] So they stopped beating him. Once he was set free he continued preaching in support of the regime as he had done in the past.

The Team House in Mashhad

The attitude of Vahid Afrakhteh and the MKO, and the limitations they imposed on me, bothered me, so I decided to ask them to define and clarify my official status in the organization. Up to that time they only used me and my services as one of their many sympathizers and for their own objectives. Even though I had a good record and was quite successful in operations, they never involved me in any political or ideological discussions or decision-making and never shared anything

---

[99] On Aban 6, 1351/October 28, 1972 SAVAK issued a press release that stated that "Two unidentified men invited Dr. Manaqebi to conduct a funeral. They picked him up and drove him out of town where two other men joined them. They beat up Manaqebi and left him in the middle of nowhere."

with me. They allowed themselves to read any books, pamphlets, or declarations I had but never shared their own publications with me. I was not pleased with this situation. After some time, I wanted them to clarify my position and the nature of our relationship with them. A few days after that conversation they came to me and said that I should get away from Tehran for a few months because the situation in the Capital was critical and I might be in serious danger.

The Organization had rented a team house in Mashhad. So I went there together with Hasan Abrari, Vahid Afrakhteh, Abbas Javdani, Mohammad Yazdani[100] (Yazdaniyan), and Mohsin Fazil. Abbas Javdani, Mohsin Fazil, and Vahid Afrakhteh were all from Mashhad. They went to other places and did not always stay in Mashhad. Once a month I also took the train to Tehran and stayed there for a few days and met some of my contacts. I had a friend named Murad Nankali. He used to work in the Safyad Metallurgy Factory. Reportedly, the shares of that factory belonged to Mr. Mehdi Bazargan and

---

[100] Mohammad Yazdaniyan (b.1327/1948, Kashan) a graduate of Sharif University in chemistry, fluent in English, he joined the MKO and went underground in 1350/1871. In 1354/1975 joined the Marxist branch of MKO and was sent abroad where he declared the new Marxist orientation of a branch of MKO in Europe and the Middle East and then established its headquarters in Paris. He used several fictitious names including Mohammad, Ayyub, Mas'ud, Umar Khattab, and Mahdi. He failed to convince Mohammad Yaqini, the representative of MKO in Paris, to accept Marxism and sent him back to Iran. Yaqini was later assassinated by his former comrades who had adopted the Marxist ideology. In Paris, Yazdaniyan married Mahbubeh Afraz. She refused to accept the Marxist ideology and was poisoned and died. Yazdaniyan announced her death as a suicide. Mohammad Taqi Shahram and Mujtaba Taleqani, who were in Paris then, were accused of having killed Mahbubeh. On the eve of the Revolution, Yazdaniyan, in collaboration with Javad Qa'idi and Firuzkoohi, established the organization known as Unity for the Aspirations of the Working Class, known commonly as "Arman." He joined the opposition groups against the Islamic government and was arrested and executed in 1362/1983. See *Tarikhche-ye Mukhtasar Guruhakha*, p. 133, Nejat Hosseini, pp. 356–357, *Interview with Marziyyeh Hadidchi*, pp. 163–165, *Interview with Behjat Afraz*, and *Interview with Ja'far Yazdaniyan*, 1383/2004.

Dr. [Yadullah] Sahabi. Murad took advantage of his position and made hand grenades in the factory. Each time I went to Tehran, I collected a number of those grenades and took them with me.

In my opinion the time that we spent in Mashhad was a waste of my life. We spent a lot of time in discussions and debates that were purely speculative and theoretical. Each team member was appointed to identify the streets and surroundings in his neighborhood. We even produced a blueprint of important landmarks and roads. It was necessary to acquaint ourselves with the city as much as possible. This was the only task assigned to me even though I was not able to use my left arm properly, which had been injured in the operation to assassinate Sha'ban Ja'fari. I had several doctors check my arm, but they couldn't do anything.

This situation continued until one day Mohsin Fazil gave me the name of his brother-in-law who was a neurologist and recommended that I make an appointment and see him. He insisted that I should see the doctor like an ordinary patient and never mention Mohsin's name to him. He did not want his brother-in-law to find out anything about my relationship with him.

I went to see that doctor's office two or three times and he ordered x-rays of my shoulder. When I went to take an x-ray the technician asked for my name and I said it was Hossein Mohammadi. He placed the x-rays in a large envelope and wrote my name on it. When the neurologist saw the x-rays he prescribed some medicine and a few injections. So I bought the medicine and one syringe and took it to the doctor's office and he injected me in the shoulder. After some time, my arm was healed. But every once in a while, when I exert myself or do a little heavy work, the old pain comes back. I kept the large envelope of the radiologist and used it to store some documents. Later on when I was arrested this envelope indeed became very handy and useful.

Ten Explosions on the Tenth Anniversary of the White Revolution

Living in Mashhad and spending time in the team was indeed a waste of our time, and we did not accomplish much there. With the month of Bahman 1351/February 1972 and the tenth anniversary of the White Revolution approaching, the organization decided to carry out some terrorist activities during the commemoration events. As the most experienced and skilled operation team, we were ordered to return to Tehran. In Tehran I rented a house on Imam Zadeh Yahya Street and began making bombs and explosives. This was a very dangerous and risky job that no one in his right mind would have agreed to do. From the process of preparing the explosives and making a bomb until the time of using it, my life was in danger at every step. It was difficult to find supplies, and I did not even have access to TNT, and had to use alternative materials.

We had to make explosives by mixing sugar, chloride, and phosphate. This combination did not have much destructive impact and often was used as a sound bomb. At best, its impact was limited to breaking glass windows and doors. Of course we were able to make bombs with more destructive materials like nitrate ammonium. For this task, we usually bought at the bazaar three or four kilos of ammonium, which is often used as fertilizer in agriculture. We extracted nitrate ammonium from the manure. We would then put it in a container and pour water on it and then pass it through a drainer. At the bottom of the drainer small particles settled that resembled powdered glass. We would then put them into a sack and make some holes at the bottom of the sack for any remaining water to drip away. The material that settled in the sack was nitrate ammonium, which worked like TNT. Thus, we obtained around 150g of nitrate ammonium from every kilo of manure. With this method I made around 30 kg. of nitrate ammonium and 30–40 kg. of chloride in my house at Imam Zadeh Yahya

Street. I also had twelve bombs in this house that were ready to fill in.

Of the total number of bombs I made I placed one in a mall called Firooz located next to the police headquarters building on Takht-i Jamshid (now Ayatullah Taliqani) Avenue. This building belonged to an Iranian Agro-Business Company owned by Sabet Pasal. The store sold agricultural machinery. I placed another bomb under the bridge across the same building so that some minutes after the first explosion when the police arrived at the scene to investigate the degree of damage, the second one would explode and kill the police or at least create fear in them. In order to avoid injury to innocent people, we set out the bombs on the Friday afternoon when the city was less crowded.

I was the person in charge of this operation. I was supposed to analyze the level of the destruction and loss, the number of the injured people, and the probable casualties after the two explosions. The bus line ran on time on that day on Takht-i Jamshid Avenue. I took a double-decker bus several times back and forth between two stations that were located on the two ends of this road and waited for the bombs to explode. The first bomb exploded as planned. The glass windows broke, the building was shaken, and a pedestrian was thrown down and the hat on his head was thrown into the air. Luckily apart from minor injury this person was not seriously hurt.

It did not take too long for the police to arrive at the scene. I was waiting anxiously for the second bomb to explode but it never did. I could not figure out what went wrong. Perhaps the same problem that occurred at Shah Abbas Hotel at Isfahan had occurred again and the connection of the explosives was bad or it failed to respond. After waiting for half an hour for the second bomb to explode, fearing a repetition of what happened to that hotel custodian at Shah Abbas Hotel in Isfahan, I went to a nearby telephone booth. I called the police headquarters and told them that another bomb was planted in such-and-such place and that they should quickly go and de-

160

fuse it so that no one would be injured. Later I left the scene. Reportedly, they sent their specialists to defuse the bomb. This kind of phone calls to the police to claim responsibility for planting the bombs and informing them of the bombs that failed to explode was an order of the organization and a kind of showing off of its power. Hasan Abrari and I also set off a powerful bomb in the Army Department Store located on the Sepah Avenue (now Imam Khomeini) near Qurkhaneh Street. All in all, the team set off ten bombs in Tehran on the tenth anniversary of the White Revolution.[101] In order to prepare Akbar Mahdavi spiritually and psychologically for these kinds of operations, I wanted him to come to the surrounding area at the time of the explosion and see the scene. I do not remember whether he came or not.

The Dungeon of Scholars (*dakhmat al-'ulama*)

On the third floor of the shopping complex located at the Mohammadi Crossroad across Pamenar District, Mr. Mohammad Mostafavi had his bookstore. It was a place where underground or semi-underground clerical elements would hang out and meet friends. Jokingly, we called this store the Scholars' Dungeon (*dakhmat al-'ulama*). Many members of the clergy such as Mr. Khamene'ie and Ayatullah Morvarid frequented the place. They exchanged messages or passed on declarations to their team members or collaborators and friends. I also went there occasionally when I had a thing or two to exchange. I am not so sure that SAVAK was unaware of that bookstore and

---

[101] Ali Akbar Mahdavi (b. 1312/1933). He grew up in a poor family and was unable to continue his education and started his own business but failed. He joined Ayatullah Sa'idi's classes where he was introduced to Ezzat Shahi. He opened a small grocery store in south Tehran and turned it into a meeting place for political activists. After Ezzat Shahi was arrested, Mahdavi also was imprisoned for eighteen months. A short while after his release, he was arrested again and remained in prison until Aban 1357/October 1978 and the victory of the Revolution.

161

what went on there. My guess is that it was aware, perhaps indirectly by sending spies or watching people who frequented the store. A couple of times when Mr. Mostafavi was arrested, he was freed by the mediation of one of his relatives named Musavi, who was a clergy affiliated with the royal Court. A student who attended one of the seminary schools named Ziya'i was often seen there as well. He was then employed by SAVAK and abandoned his clerical garb. I met him a couple of times, and each time I snatched his hat and made fun of him.

One night, I went to that "dungeon" with Sadiq Katouzian to deliver the latest declarations of Imam Khomeini that we had duplicated for Mr. Mustafavi. On our way back, Sadiq and I walked to the Shah Square (now Qiyam/Uprising) before we departed in different directions. Sadiq's residence was located on Ziba Avenue. When he approached his house, the police were waiting for him and ordered him to freeze. Sadiq tried to run away, but the police started shooting, and a bullet hit him in the leg. He was unable to run and the police arrested him. Apparently, Sadiq was scared, and during interrogation he became helpless and gave all the information he had to the police, including all his contacts, my trips to Qom, and staying in the house of Mr. Jannati. Another page was thus added to my already thick dossier.[102]

After this incident I had a feeling, a kind of consciousness and certainty like the feeling that may descend on one's heart before death: a feeling that the journey to God is approaching and will end all hardships. This feeling often prompts man to assess his life, achievements, or failures, ask

---

[102] Some of the most important activists who had information about others always carried a cyanide capsule that contained about 200 milligrams of cyanide. They were instructed to take it and commit suicide when they were arrested so that others would remain safe and secure. Many members of our friends in MKO committed suicide by taking these capsules. See Nejat Hosseini, p. 366.

for forgiveness from those he might have hurt and resented, pay his dues, and make up all the prayers he has missed.

It may be difficult for the reader to believe this story, but a few nights before my arrest I had a dream. I dreamed that I had fallen in the street. A bullet had hit me in the leg, and my face was injured, and blood covered all around me. I then felt lightheaded and weightless. I was flying in the air like a free bird, and the wind was carrying me. I felt very much at peace. It was like an out-of-body experience. This dream greatly influenced me and created a special state in my soul. I was certain that something was awaiting me. Therefore, I visited some of my friends and relatives and bid them farewell.

The Friday Mosque of the bazaar was one of my favorite places. I had not gone there for a quite a while. I really loved Hajj Gholam Hossein Ja'fari. He was the prayer leader of that mosque, and I used to visit him often. Next morning after I had that dream, I longed to see Shaykh Gholam Hossein. Around noon I went to the mosque and prayed behind him. After the prayer I went to him and we greeted one another. He was upset that I had gone to the mosque and was worried about me. He said that the mosque is like a beehive! And the police are looking for me there. He was not happy that I exposed myself to danger just to visit him. He then prayed for me.

After the dream that I described I felt that my days in this world were numbered and these were my last days. I went to see a few of my friends whom I owed money and cleared my debts. Indeed during those days, I had a very exalted state of soul, and a special joy overwhelmed my heart. I was totally intoxicated. In my thoughts I forgave all the people who had bothered or hurt me or talked behind my back. I also called some people and bid them farewell and asked them for forgiveness. Some friends, when they heard me saying farewell, would pull my leg and would recite the famous Persian proverb, "No pest can digest the eggplants from Bam (*bademjan-i Bam afat nadarad*)." They meant to assure me that nothing

163

will happen to me, and I had better stop saying farewell to them. Despite that, a very strange and unfamiliar feeling took over my heart, and I thought perhaps it was the feeling of the spirit of martyrdom, and the fact that I did not consider myself worthy of martyrdom felt very strange to me

I even went to pay a visit to my father. He usually performed prayer in a mosque that was located on Atabak Avenue. I went there in the evening but did not enter the mosque. I stood in the dark behind the glass window until the prayer finished and people started coming out of the mosque. I walked a little bit behind my father and then called him. He was so happy to see me. I also cried out of joy. We walked through the labyrinth of streets and alleys for about half an hour. He asked me with a kind tone of voice when I should stop these [political] activities before I caused trouble to myself. I told him that life and death is in God's hands and perhaps we should not necessarily expect to see one another again. I also asked for his forgiveness. At the end he told me not to "do anything that will not please God and His Prophet." He then cried, and I cried too. I bid him farewell and left him. After walking for a distance, I turned back and saw that he was still standing on the same spot and watching me. It was obvious that he also felt that this probably was the final farewell. Some people may blame me and assume that I was knowingly walking into danger and trouble. The truth is that I never took safety measures lightly, nor did ever make a mistake in observing security matters.

My Arrest

It was during the last days of the summer or the first days of autumn in 1352/1973 when Hasan Farzaneh was arrested. He showed his weakness during the interrogation and confessed and accepted responsibility for all he had done and gave up all the information he had. Concerning me, he said to the SAVAK agent that Ezzat Shahi was not the person killed in the taxi explosion in Istanbul Avenue, and that the person who had died was someone else. He also said that he had seen me with Akbar Mahdavi several days ago on Ziba Avenue. Therefore, the police went after Mahdavi and arrested him. Akbar resisted arrest and denied any ties with me.

When the police encountered Akbar Mahdavi, they thought that Hasan Farzaneh had made a mistake. So they showed him Mahdavi through a glass window, and he again reiterated that he had seen him with Ezzat Shahi. The police resorted to a different strategy. They freed Akbar in order to have him and his calls under surveillance. We found out about this change of strategy, and so nobody ever called him again. I only sent one man to his store in Khorasan Square to pretend that he wanted to buy cheese and asked him to give a message to Akbar instructing him to be careful and not to make any calls to anybody and not to respond to calls that were made to him. After some time, SAVAK realized that such a strategy would not work so again they arrested Akbar in the month of Bahman/February. This time they beat him up really hard and tortured him severely, but he did not open up. After more torture, he admitted that he had had contact with me, but that it was only a one-way contact. He denied knowing where I was or what I was doing and added that I was the one who always called him and that he never tried to contact me.

Around that time on several occasions I came into conflict with the Mujahidin because through Vahid Afrakhteh they pressured me to give them all documents. I told them that I had no access to documents because they were stored in a place that was too dangerous to go to, and that the only person who had access to them was Akbar Mahdavi. They insisted that I should go and bring them the documents because Akbar had been in prison for over a month and had not revealed any information. So they argued that it was not dangerous to go and bring the documents for them. I had earlier explained to them that Akbar was once arrested in the summer of 1351/1972, and had resisted and denied all connection with me. That was the

165

reason SAVAK freed him after forty days. I told them that when the [false] news of my death was announced during the explosion of the taxi, and Hasan Farzaneh was arrested, he told SAVAK that I was alive and he had seen me on Ziba Avenue with Akbar. That was the reason they arrested Akbar again.

Akbar Mahdavi was in contact with me and Abdullah Mahjum, who had a small textile factory on the Cyrus Crossroad where we kept some of the documents. When Akbar was arrested for the second time, I warned everyone not to go to Mahjum's shop because it was too dangerous. The more I insisted, the more MKO members denied the existence of danger. Finally, a month after Mahdavi's arrest, we decided to get hold of those documents we had stored in Mahjum's shop. In any case, after a few days I went to pick up those documents, but it was not clear where he had stored them and he kept on procrastinating and finally he told me they are not in his shop, but he promised to deliver them to me within a few days. However, many things happened during those few days. Mahdavi was beaten up badly and tortured severely but did not give up any information until his cellmate, who was an agent, fooled him. He told Mahdavi that he would be freed in a few days. The prison guards also played a tricky game by treating Mahdavi's cellmate like other [political] prisoners, cursing him to make things look natural. This fooled Mahdavi, and he began to trust his cellmate and opened up. Mahdavi told the man that I (Ezzat) often go to Mahjum's factory on Cyrus Crossroad and asked him to go there and tell me to leave the country because whoever was arrested talked about Ezzat!

That man accomplished his mission very well and reported to SAVAK word for word what he had heard from Mahdavi. After that they tortured Akbar even more harshly and forced him to come out and identify me. Those days that I went to Mahjum's factory to get the documents, the police also brought Akbar to a house across the shop and watched through the window. Mahdavi often saw me but never showed me to them. Although the police had distributed copies of my photograph widely, they could not identify me either, because I had totally changed my appearance. I found out all these details later in prison. In any case, Mahdavi did not collaborate with the police.[103]

Around the same time, another man by the name of Khan Ali was arrested. He was a friend of Hasan Farzaneh, and they had met in prison. I had gone to his shop with Hasan several times to exchange declarations. SAVAK promised him that if he could find and identify me, they would reduce his five-year prison term. He was a weak man, and since he had a big family he agreed to collaborate with the police. They took him to the bazaar several days and searched the places I used to frequent. They failed to find me there. Then they took him to the same house across Mahjum's shop and waited for me.

The 5th of Isfand, 1351/February 24, 1973 was the fourth or fifth day that Farzaneh had me under surveillance. I had spent some hours in the streets, but I thought that instead of wasting time, it would be better if I went to Mahjum's shop. Therefore, I went down Rudabah Street disguised as a pool-cleaner wearing a shaggy coat and worn-out trousers and wore a hat on my head.

The night before I was arrested, Vahid Afrakhteh visited me at my house. In the morning, he told me that his gun needed repair and he had taken it for repair. He asked if he could borrow my gun and promised to return it to me in the evening when he came home. I gave him the weapon without any question.

I had set a sign with Abdullah Mahjum that if the situation was normal in his shop he should hang a piece of red cloth on the window of his shop. Otherwise, if the situation was abnormal or dangerous he should hang nothing in the window. Rudabah Street is located on Cyrus Avenue toward the south

---

[103] The Tehran press reported that one of the opposition members was killed in a clash with government forces. Also, a ten-year-old girl named A'zam Fard Amiri was killed in this conflict.

167

and behind the Bahbahani Technical School. It was a narrow street and as I entered I saw the red cloth in its place. A lady had taken the water hose out of her house and was busy washing dishes. The red cloth was also hung on the window. Everything seemed to be normal. I entered the shop, went upstairs and sat down. 'Ali Reza Kabiri was also there. While I was reading the book entitled *Zardha-ye Sorkh* by Mao Tse Tong [translated into English as *The Little Red Book: Quotations from Chairman Mao*]. A man came up and asked if we knew a man here named Hossein. We said no. He checked the room and excused himself and left.

Suddenly, my heart started pounding and I became very nervous and anxious. I stood and looked around the building, but everything seemed normal. I ate lunch, but I was still anxious. It was already 1:30 p.m. and I had to go and meet Vahid. Apparently, as soon as I opened the door of the shop to leave, Khan Ali saw and identified me. I closed the door quickly. But I was caught by surprise. The police started shooting from a small opening on the door of the house in which they were hiding. Before I could think of running away, I was already on the ground. At that moment, I did not know from where exactly I had been shot. I looked around but I did not see anything. I took a small piece of paper on which I had several phone numbers of my contacts and swallowed it. I also placed the cyanide capsule in my mouth. As I had given my gun to Afrakhteh, I did not have any weapon to use. When the police opened the door of the shop to come in, I was almost getting unconscious because of bleeding. One of them had a gun in his hand as they came two steps ahead of me shouting and ordering me to have my hands over my head and throw my weapon on the ground.

Meanwhile a lot of people had gathered around the factory. They had heard the shooting and police noise and were wondering what had happened. People condemned police action for "killing the nation's children," and blamed them for

168

killing the "innocent young man." They ordered the people to stay away.

I do not know whether it was out of fear or hate at that moment that I suddenly placed my hands on my waist and with a loud voice told the police that I had a grenade and if they came any closer I would explode that and kill them all. In reality, I had no weapon and all I wanted was to frighten them and force them to shoot and kill me instantly so that I would not be arrested alive. They believed my words. Even though there was a large crowd of people there, they again started shooting rampantly. They shot me twice this time. Reportedly, one or two people were also shot. A lady was also injured while a girl named A'zam Fard Amiri was killed.[104] The news that was broadcast the next day did not mention my name because SAVAK had once announced my death before in a bomb explosion. So after arresting me and realizing that I was alive, in order to avoid embarrassment and save face SAVAK reported that "a terrorist was arrested after shooting and killing an innocent girl." They never mentioned my name. At that moment, the only thing that I was able to do was to chew the cyanide capsule. I had lost all my strength. I lifted my bloody legs with my hands and faced the direction of the Qiblah. I started uttering the formula of the faith (*Shahadatayn: I give testimony that there is no god but God and Muhammad is His Messenger*). I do not remember anything after that. I must have passed out. I do not remember how long after that I regained my consciousness. Police officers shoved a hose in my mouth and ran the water on and off as I was choking. Where I fell was a narrow street and inaccessible to police cars. So after a few minutes they carried me to the main street and threw me in the police ambulance. In the process my head hit the ground several times and I realized that I was being carried. When they threw me into the ambulance, it seemed that people did not care for the police siren because the traffic did not clear the

---

[104] A'zam Fard Amiri was only ten years old when she was martyred. Unfortunately, we were unable to locate her family after the Revolution.

road. I lost consciousness again. Occasionally, I regained consciousness, noticed the traffic lights, heard the siren, and fell unconscious again.

I had gone through many difficult experiences in my eventful life marked by many ups and downs from my childhood until that day. I will never forget two exceptional instances in my life. The first instance was when the second series of bullets hit me and several times I shouted, "O [Imam] Hossein, I am coming to you!" It was during those last breaths that I felt so selfless and free, just as in my dream. That was an amazing experience, like the feeling that descends on one's heart when one falls in love. I thought that my death was imminent and that I had at last reached the end of hardships and pais. I felt it was time to go! It was during that moment that I really understood the meaning of martyrdom. Even though I felt so weak, I felt an indescribable state in my soul. I became so certain that if died, I would attain felicity in this world and the next; in this world because my death would mark the end of all hardships and torture in the hands of the interrogators, and in the Hereafter, I would attain eternal happiness. It was immersed in these thoughts and feelings that I must have fallen unconscious again. When I regained consciousness and opened my eyes it was 10:00 p.m. and I found myself almost naked on the hospital bed, an oxygen tube inserted into my mouth and an IV tube injected into my arm. Again I lost my consciousness. For a while, I continued losing and regaining consciousness, and the last time that I regained consciousness I saw seven or eight people surrounding me.

The moment I saw these men around my bed, I choked and burst into tears. I began to cry louder and louder while I was saying "O my lord, I knew that I did not deserve to attain martyrdom. I gave You all I had and whatever I did was to please You! Didn't I deserve to be a martyr? Why did You allow me to fall into the hands of these people?" This was the second incident that I will never forget in my life. It was a dark and painful moment. I did not believe that I was alive. I felt cold in my entire body. I was taken over by anger and felt that I was burning. Then weakness overwhelmed me and I fell unconscious again.

I asked myself if the bullets did not kill me, why didn't the cyanide pill that I took work? I remembered how they shoved a hose in my mouth. Since I had seen and or heard members of other groups betray their friends, I got scared when I realized the amount of information that I had. Heavy streams of thought went through my head lest I were not able to resist torture. I was afraid that I might break down and say everything! Even though I was not so well educated, I was afraid because of the amount of information and many connections that I had with people and members of different groups. Mentally I was going through a very difficult time, but I was still strong physically, thanks to those days of mountain-climbing. I felt that I could stand any kind of torture, but mentally I was not so sure! I was depressed and angry. As I was immersed in these thoughts, a question came to my mind. It was not clear whether a person who is shot and killed with a bullet while in the resistance movement is considered a martyr, or the person who takes a cyanide pill and commits suicide so that he would not be captured by the enemy. I wondered if God would count both as martyrs. Then I realized that perhaps it was God's will [that I didn't die]. I said to myself that people who are mentally or physically weak and take cyanide pills to kill themselves are not real men to fight and get martyred. Only God knows that these people cannot resist, and therefore He takes away their lives in an easy way. Similarly, God knows who can resist and endure torture, so He saves them and allows them to live a little longer in order to undergo torture or get martyred in the process. That kind of death would be more precious than just dying by a bullet or cyanide pills. During those moments I was totally perplexed, confused, and dizzy. I was lying on the hospital bed naked and only a bed sheet was my cover. My wounds were somewhat treated but my injuries mattered the least to them. They had only stopped the bleeding and were washing my wounds to prevent the cyanide poison from spreading. In such a condition, I told them that I wanted to pray. They wondered if I felt better but said that it was not necessary to pray. So without allowing me to make ablution I made an intention and started praying. I performed my prayers in that state.

While praying I also recited some supplications: "O my Lord! Since You did not will to see me killed by the bullet or by cyanide pills, perhaps this is what You willed. If You are pleased to see me in this pain and suffering, I surrender and am pleased with pleasing You! But I beg You for one request. Do not let me down! Do not let me fail under torture. Take me before I become the cause for the arrest of others. I beg You grant me strong faith to resist these agents and fool them."

Soon I felt a light in my heart that lifted my spirit and took me to a higher and more exalted state. By the time I finished my prayers, I felt very calm. I was no longer unhappy. I was feeling a kind of courage in my heart. This was completely different from the weak state that I had experienced just a little earlier on the same hospital bed. I was feeling a kind of strength that made me ready to resist any kind of pressure and torture. So I decided to resist by all means and ways, no matter what kind of torture was inflicted upon me. This lightness and calmness in my heart gave me amazing strength. *Whenever I think of that day and that moment, I comprehend perfectly what it means for God to take hold of his servant and guide him.* In that state, the powerful hand of God took hold of my weak hand and prevented me from falling. Other than God no one else was able to save me from the condition that I was in. My morale was strengthened by that experience. I just wanted the agents to torture me and beat me up. I wished to pull their legs and make them tired. The police were extremely happy that I had survived and regained my consciousness. They probably thought that being alive, I would be very useful for them and that they would get a lot of information from me.

Torture in the Hospital

From the first moments after I regained consciousness and prayed, the police started beating me right there in that hospital bed. They could not afford to wait because getting information from me in the early hours of arrest was vital for them. They began slapping and punching me in the face. They then started using matches and cigarettes to burn different parts of my body, especially the shoulder, navel, and nose. Then they slowly started beating me up with the electric cable. They beat me for a while and then rested for some time to give me time to think and answer their questions. Since I was not answering them, they would resume beating. I mentioned before that when I was shot I kept on screaming *"Ya Hossein! Take me, I am coming to you!"* and my interrogators thought that Hossein was one of my contacts and they continuously asked me who this "Hossein" was! No matter how hard I tried to convince him that I meant *Imam Hossein* they never believed my words. They insisted that I tell them who this Hossein was that I was calling him like I would call my son! They wanted to know what kind of relationship I had with Hossein and why I was calling his name at that place! I told them that they had arrested me by mistake and I was not who they thought I was and that I have no information to give them, even if they cut me into pieces I have nothing to tell them.

Because I had escaped from them once at Lashkari's shop and another time from my own house that they had surrounded, and the fact that I had not died in the shoot-out, all meant that I was important to them. My first interrogator was Kamali.[105] He was one of the oldest and most experienced po-

---

[105] Farajullah Sayfi Kamangar, known as Kamali, was a retired army officer who joined the SAVAK primarily for personal gain. He was transformed to the Anti-Terrorism Committee upon its formation. After the victory of the Islamic Revolution, he went into hiding in the Caspian Sea region for a while. In Azar 1358/October 1979 he went to Revolutionary Prosecutor's office and introduced himself to him. Ezzat Shahi narrated that, "Once the storm of revolution settled, Kamali went to the Prime Minister's office to collect his unpaid salary. He was told to go to the Revolutionary Prosecu-

licemen and was very tough and cruel. I believe he was a Kurd and a Sunni. He was really curious about me. To prove to him that I was a good and simple man, I did something very creative and interesting. I pretended that I was very afraid of Kamali, and he really thought that this was the case. One night when he didn't come for interrogation and other officers replaced him I told them, "You are referring to that fellow as Dr. Kamali although he is not a doctor. He is a colonel." They asked me how I knew that he was a colonel, and I said his face looked like Colonel Afzali who was the Chief of SAVAK in the bazaar.[106] I said that I was certain that Kamali was the head of SAVAK at the bazaar because when I worked there I was taken to him several times, but I fooled him and made fun of him, and I think that he wanted to get even and take revenge.

The policemen were laughing at my stupidity for taking Kamali for Colonel Afzali. The next morning when Kamali came in, one of the officers went to him and whispered in his ear while Kamali was gazing at me. It was obvious that they were telling him that I was confusing him for Colonel Afzali. They had actually believed that I was telling the truth. I was trying to persuade them to believe what I said. When he was coming to me, I pretended that I was scared and that my whole body was shaking and I was unable to talk.

Kamali was a nervous man. During the interrogation he often personally beat up and tortured prisoners. After a while he would get tired and pass on the duty to his colleague. He could not manage to do the interrogation, beat, and torture more than an hour.

In that hospital, there were four other agents. They referred to two of them as "captain" even though they were sim-

---

tor's office and obtain a clearance form. After several times going back and forth, finally one day Kachu'i saw him in the Evin prison courtyard and arrested him."

[106] Colonel Mohammad Ali Afzali was the commanding officer of the tenth police headquarters. Between 1353 and 1354/1974 and 1975 he was the director of SAVAK in southeast Tehran and after 1355/1976 was the director of SAVAK in Shemiran.

ple guards. The two other people were in charge of torturing me. I spent thirteen days in the police hospital where I was continually tortured. Different agents from different police departments came to see me. This showed that arresting me was very important to them.

Whenever they came to see me, they called me a giant monster. The night that they began to torture me, I quickly lost consciousness, but not for too long, and after ten or fifteen minutes I regained consciousness. Sometimes they beat me up while the oxygen tube was in my nose and I had an I.V. tube in my arm. They also injected blood because of excessive bleeding that I had gone through. My body had become very weak because of the torture and I had pain all over, especially where I was shot. Several times I came so close to death. In such situations they stopped the torture and left me alone and waited for a while. As soon as my condition improved a little they would start the torture all over again. They burned sensitive spots on my body, the soles of my feet and my genitals and my navel. Since they had completely covered my mouth, I couldn't scream and was only able to move my body. Whenever they took their hands off my mouth, I would scream deafeningly.

As a result of the torture I received that night, I became very irritated and aggressive and found new courage. I made myself numb and insensitive to torture and made fun of my torturers. I pretended to be confused and asked them why were they beating me up if they were practicing Muslims! I wondered what I had done that deserved to be beaten up by another Muslim and wondered why they were not afraid of the fire of Hell! My torturers also were confused and wondered whether I was playing a game or I was serious. But that did not deter them from torturing me more. They only wanted information from me and didn't care if I died or survived. I passed those nights with all kinds of torture but stood firm on my claim that I had done nothing wrong.

Early next morning they brought some photos from the office of the Joint Committee for Counter-Terrorism (JCCT) and asked if these were my pictures and I nodded that they were indeed my pictures. They shouted that I couldn't fool them and that they were after the person in these pictures and that was me! I was not willing to surrender, so I admitted that those pictures were mine but they didn't prove that I had done something wrong! The interrogator was so annoyed that he shouted at me, "*You fool, these are your photos, and then you are saying that you have done nothing. You have to say everything that you know!*"

As I continued to say that I was nobody and had no information to reveal, my interrogator became angrier and shouted at his subordinates to "*beat this foolish man. He doesn't seem to understand our language. Beat him until he starts talking!*" With his order they intensified the torture. In that situation I asked if it was a crime to sell Imam Khomeini's treatise or emulate (*taqlid*) him, and added that if being an emulator (*muqalliad*) of Imam Khomeini was a crime, then I confessed that I was his follower and supporter and they could do whatever they wished. They became even angrier when they heard my words, and they hurled curses at Imam Khomeini. They said that they were aware of all this and asked for more about my "*terroristic activities, assassinations, and other crimes!*" I said that how I could accept responsibility for things that I have not done? What was it exactly that they wanted from me! What bomb? Which assassination? What crimes?"

Then they asked, "When did you go to Palestine? Which people and groups did you establish contact with? What is the name of your group? Who are your other friends and where are they? Where is your team house located?" They especially insisted on finding out about the location of our team house. They also asked about Mofidi and Sepasi and wondered where they were. I had no choice but to go on with the way that I answered their questions before. I pretended that I was completely unaware of what they were talking about and insisted that I was just a simple man. I must have done this in such a way that the policemen began to doubt and wondered whether I was truly the person pictured in the minds of SAVAK.

It was two or three nights after my arrest when they came to my room in the hospital and began to lecture me about moral corruption in the society, asking how many times I had been to Tehran's Red Light District (*Qal'eh*) and whether or not I was married. They insisted that I should have gone there and relieved myself [of sexual tension] because I would be in trouble on the Day of Judgement anyway. They promised to help me before I died and provide means of pleasure for me right there! Then they brought in a young lady wearing a mini-skirt to please me and have a good time with. They asked me to have her in a temporary marriage (*mut'ah,* or *sighah*). I do not know where they found her. Perhaps she was one of the patients or employees of the hospital or their agent. Whoever she was, I was shocked when I saw her. It immediately oc-curred to me that these people had set up a trap for me. I guessed that they had placed a camera in a hidden corner of the room and that they wanted to take photos and use them against me. They were aware that I was a religious person, so even if I remained silent, they wanted to use this woman to ruin my reputation among revolutionaries and religious activ-ists.

As I was lying on my bed half naked and covered only by a sheet, I decided to ignore that woman. I was well aware that my smallest mistake could lead to the biggest fall in a dreadful valley of scandal and humiliation. I remembered Prophet Joseph (Yusef) and how the Pharaoh's wife fell in love with him and when he rejected her, she tried to ruin him and his reputation but God saved Joseph. I also prayed to God to have mercy on me and save me from this trap and tricky sit-uation. When that woman came to the right side of my bed, I turned my face to the other side of the room, and when she came to the left side I turned to the right side. I treated her in a very despising and harsh manner. I cursed her and told her to get lost and assured her that she could not tempt me, and even told her that I preferred to sleep with a dog than with her!

This statement annoyed her very much and killed her feminine pride, if she had any. For almost two hours she had tried in whatever manner she knew to make me fall into her trap, but every time she failed. The harder she tried, the stronger my resistance became. This went on to an extent that she was overwhelmed by anger and realized that she could not break my resistance. I was aware that this lady was desperate and had been forced to do what she was asked under police pressure. So by despising her I was able to make her stop trying. Perhaps this was my trial and God helped me to save myself from this trap. Indeed, if it were not for God's help, it would have been impossible to save myself from such temptation and trap. This is because later I heard that many activists failed to resist torture and sold themselves out for a single pack of cigarettes. I can only say that with the help of God, this was the most precious moment in the whole course of my struggle.

At one point, we agreed that I confess and give them information. Since I was lying on the bed and had handcuffs, I was ordered to talk so that the interrogator could write down what I said. The information that I gave them was of no particular value or importance to them. Two agents wrote down the information I gave them on two different sheets of papers. They would then tear one paper up in front of me to tell me that my information was of no benefit at all and that I was supposed to talk again. Since I knew that two people took notes of my statement, I tried to repeat what I had said before so that I would not contradict myself.

After a while, I admitted that I was a supporter of the MKO. Now I was supposed to tell them how I came to know the MKO, the members of the group, and where and with whom I lived. I had to make statements in such a manner that I would be held responsible for everything, or to hold responsible members who had already died or names that did not even

178

exist. In my house located on Imam Zadeh Yahya Street there were around thirty kilograms of explosive materials, twe;ve ready-made bombs, and a number of documents. Therefore, I was afraid of this house's being discovered by the police. I had to kill as much time as possible because it was not possible for the group members to have cleared everything from that house quickly. I had to think of another plan so that just in case that house was discovered by the police, I could give a convincing explanation and save my other comrades from trouble. I had to be very alert and careful and use caution. Since those members of the El-Al group who had been arrested had accused me of planning and carrying out the operation, I knew that my interrogators had a lot of information about me, and in fact their decision to torture me and extract information was based on their knowledge of my involvement in those operations. Therefore, in my next interrogation, I discussed issues that had no consequence at all or were irrelevant. My contact with 'Ali Reza Beheshti[107] was cut off nearly after our acquaintance, and throughout the time that I was in the organization I had no contact with him. I was convinced that he was either out of the country or had been killed in a confrontation with the police. So I told my interrogators that I got to know and was connected with the MKO through Beheshti. This was not true because it was through Ali Reza Zemorrodiyan that I was introduced to and connected with the MKO.

I told the police that after the El-Al group was arrested, I was alone and was afraid of making contact with anyone. Since I was not that educated, no one took me seriously, nor did I have any desire to get involved in other people's business. Beheshti was a university student, and after a while he came to me and said that he had graduated and wanted to go to Isfahan for military service. He also added that another person

---

[107] Ezzat Shahi was introduced to Ali Reza Beheshtizadeh during mountain-climbing trips and through him found his way to the MKO. Ali Reza was killed in a conflict with the police in 1352/1973.

179

named Hossein Mohammadi would replace him as my Qur'an teacher.

What Beheshti said about going to the military service was true, but a person named Hossein Mohammadi did not exist at all. I made up all these stories. On some occasions in the past I even used that name as my fictitious name. But I was able to convince them that a person by that name, in fact, existed. They started asking about Ali Reza Beheshti. They wanted to make sure that I had no information whatsoever concerning his whereabouts and that I was telling them the truth.

I told them that after that conversation with Beheshti I never saw him again. The last thing I know about him was that I had heard that he went to Isfahan. The police too, just like me, were pretending to be fools and continued to ask where Beheshti was and wondered if he really was in Isfahan. I told my interrogators that as far as I knew and as Beheshti told me he must be in Isfahan and serving in the military and added that I believed he had said the truth because he had no reason to lie to me as he did not have to tell me where he was going. I added that later on Hossein Mohammadi began to come to my house to teach me lessons from the Qur'an and we also talked about politics. Often he argued that the people the regime was arresting and executing were good and mostly educated people who sacrifice their lives and everything else just for the sake of God and His religion. I was a simple and uneducated man and was fooled easily and told him that if what he said was true, I might help him in distributing declarations and cooperate with him at that level only. My intention in telling them this story was to convince them that my only crime was distributing declarations and nothing else. I wanted to save myself from other charges such as bombing and preparing weapons. Therefore, I took the first step in making up this story with confidence. I made sure that everything I said was either related to me personally or to the deceased members of the organization or people who did not actually exist.

It was only twenty-four hours after my arrest that I thought of different ways to ease the torture and stress of prison. Once I gave them a wrong address in Isfahan. I told them that I was in Isfahan and I left that city for Tehran to go to my father's house when they arrested me. Giving them the address of my father's house was not to cause a problem for me because my family and I had different views on different issues and I usually did not discuss my activities with them. So there was no danger in giving the police my father's address. It took them two hours to contact SAVAK headquarters in Isfahan and ask them about the address that I had given them. This was a chance, however small, for me to rest a little bit from the torture. The SAVAK center in Isfahan confirmed that such an address did not exist at all. They came back at me and beat me up even more severely. I realized that the situation was now getting out of hand. I started crying and pretending to be afraid of them. I begged them not to beat me and admitted that I lied and am ashamed because a Muslim must never lie and that a liar is an enemy of God and shall go to Hell. I asked them to stop beating so that I could tell them the truth. They rejected my plea and continued to beat me up with a metal cord on my feet and hands so that my finger nails and toe nails came out. The next morning the chief interrogator of the police, a man named Niktab‘, came to my room. When he saw how my face and body were swollen, he said, "See how nice and fit *you* look, just like a groom on his wedding night." He then took the leg of a broken chair that looked like a cane and started beating me with it from the forehead down to the toenails. He beat me on the forehead, eyes, nose, mouth, chest, and stomach, and everywhere in between. It was as if he was hitting a sack. The whole of my body had become swollen and black. Blood clots began to form under my skin. Niktab‘ stayed in the room for two hours. He was truly a cruel and hard-hearted man. When he left, the police, who were worried about my health, brought me water to drink. For several days I was bleeding from the mouth and nose. After three days, these parts of my body turned yellowish. They were afraid when they saw my skin turning yellow. They brought a specialist doctor to examine me, and he assured them that there was nothing to worry about and that my body was absorbing the blood, and that was the reason my body had turned yellowish. The doctor ordered the police to monitor my condition carefully. So for a couple of days they stopped beating me up. They only whipped me on the feet and burnt different parts of my body with cigarettes, including my nipples, testicles, and armpits. They surrounded me and constantly smoked and poured the ashes of their cigarettes on my body.

In the hospital they had inserted a hose inside my genitals so that I could urinate because I was not able to go to urinate myself. Sometimes, the hose was blocked and I could not relieve myself easily. This was very painful and I constantly screamed. Then they would clean it and open the blockage. Taking off and replacing this hose for dialysis was so painful, even more painful than the whipping. Indeed I suffered greatly because of this. One day, a doctor changed this hose in a way that was less painful. I realized that the pain was caused by the nurse's lack of skill or care. Either out of ignorance or anger the nurse did this procedure in a manner that caused a lot of pain. Sometimes when they wanted to insert the hose it would get stuck. They would pull it out in such a harsh manner that I would scream loudly because of the pain that it caused. Sometimes they applied Vaseline on it and made it oily in order to insert it smoothly. Unfortunately, this same Vaseline was the cause of the blockage. This process was done once every two days. There left a bottle under the bed that I was to use to urinate in through the hose. They used to empty it when it was full. During the first ten days, the only kind of food that they offered me was chicken soup so that I would not need to have a bowel movement. But during my last three days at the hospital, they gave me a piece of chicken or a bowl of yoghurt with the soup. On the last day, they offered me a little rice, which I ate.

Throughout the thirteen days that I was in the hospital, I was continuously interrogated and tortured. After the police realized that the address I gave in Isfahan was wrong, they intensified their torture. Thirty hours had passed after my arrest when I gave them the address of my house that I had rented in Mashhad, because it had been almost two months since we had evacuated that place and had come to Tehran. I did not anticipate this as causing any problem. I had told them that the landlord worked in a railway station. They became very happy as they thought that I had given them a very important piece of information. They again asked their contact officers in Mashhad to investigate that address. They investigated but found out that everything had been evacuated and that nobody was there. So they came back after me, this time much more angry. I tried to explain that I had told them the truth and that a few days before I returned to Tehran I lived in that house. I added that I was not aware of why the tenants had moved out of the house, and that perhaps they are still in Mashhad. I assured them again that what I had told them was nothing but the truth; otherwise, I would have not given them the address of the house.

My landlord in Mashhad had told the police that four people lived in that house and that they had many visitors. In reality five of us lived there, including Vahid Afrakhteh, Hasan Abrari, Abbas Javdani,[108] Mohammad Yazdani, and me. They asked me about the identities of my housemates. I told them that the landlord was wrong and that only three of us lived there: Hossein Mohammadi, who was our leader, Hossein Ja'fari, and me. I also told them that I had left the envelope that contained the x-rays of the injuries to my shoulder in that

---

[108] Abbas Javdani (b.1322/1943, Mashhad) graduated from Mashhad University in the School of Science and Engineering, where he started his political activities and finally joined the MKO and participated in several military operations. In 1354/1975 he joined the Marxist wing of the MKO. In 1355/1976 he was killed in a street clash with the police in Baharestan Square. See *Tarikhche-ye Mokhtasar-i Guruhakha*, p. 128.

house (that I suffered during operations to assassinate Sha'aban Bimokh). Luckily, I had erased the name of that doctor from the x-rays. The police took this envelope, and they were then certain that a person called Hossein Mohammadi in fact existed. They believed him to be our leader but asked for my name. I said that my name was also Hossein (my fictitious name). The landlord too called me by this name, and if they showed him my photo he would have definitely identified me as Hossein. In reality, none of these three individuals named Hossein actually existed but they became "persons of interest" for police investigators. Thus, I was able to save Abbas, Vahid, Mohammad, Muhsin, and Hasan from the hands of SAVAK. The fewer the fake names I mentioned, the fewer problem I would face. If I had mentioned more names of people who did not exist, it would have been more difficult for my stories to be consistent, so the fewer names I mentioned, the easier it was for me to create stories about them.

The police decided to continue investigation and brought my landlord from Mashhad to the hospital just to confirm our number. He stood in front of me and was saying that we were four people. I kept on insisting that we were only three people, and persisted that the man could not remember and was probably confused because we used to go in and out frequently and he could not keep track.

A new problem appeared after this encounter. SAVAK had a lot of photos of the people whom they were looking for. They showed these photos to my landlord, and he identified Hasan Abrari as the person who had originally rented the house. With this piece of new information, the police came back to me again and asked about Hasan. Things were getting out of hand, but I had to remain firm with my words. I therefore denied any kind of acquaintance with him. No matter how much they beat me up, I denied that I had ever seen that person in my entire life. I said that perhaps he had rented this house before or after we left because the house was rented before us and when we moved in, this person was not there. Finally, they had to accept my claim. Then they asked where I lived after leaving this house. At that point I was forced to reveal the address of my real house located on Imam Zadeh Yahya Street.

The Discovery of a Team House and the Explosive Materials

According to the rules of security and discipline in the organization and the necessities of underground lifestyle, any member who was arrested was expected to resist under interrogation and torture for up to twelve hours. During that period other members were responsible for noting the absence of their comrades and were expected to realize that something suspicious had happened. Therefore, they were supposed to clear the team house as fast as possible when they became aware of or suspected any threats. When I was arrested at one o'clock in the afternoon, obviously I was not able to go to my three o'clock meeting with Vahid Afrakhteh, which was supposed to have taken place at my house. As a rule, my comrades should have become suspicious when I didn't show up to meet Vahid and even couldn't make it for another meeting I had later that day. They were supposed to take security measures and clear the team house. Apart from this, I also had another meeting that I missed. So when I didn't show up for that meeting, the organization must have realized that something had happened to me. Now, thirty-six hours had passed since my arrest, and I was able to use different means to preoccupy the police and kill time. I expected that by then my friends would have already cleared the house. There were no more lies or excuses that could I could make and be effective to calm the police under those circumstances. At the same time, I realized that I could not resist torture any longer. I also knew that by telling more lies and giving other excuses, I could easily spoil my next round of fabricated stories. So I said, "Just like I never lied to you on the matter of Mashhad, I am not lying on the information that I am about to give you." I then gave them the address of my house located on Imam Zadeh Yahya Street on Buzarjomehri Avenue.

Upon receiving this information the SAVAK agents did not waste a moment, and around 3:00 or 4:00 in the morning went to that house, but because of darkness in the neighborhood or other unexplained reasons, they were not able to locate the house. So they returned and started beating me until morning. They had become frustrated and complained of constant headaches. They went to take painkillers, and after a few minutes came back to torture me again. When they were whipping me, I screamed but deep down in my heart I was cursing them. Sometimes I made faces behind their backs to forget my pain, and once or twice the guard saw this and reported it to the torturers. They intensified their torture and continued beating me up. As I mentioned before, upon my arrest I made up a story about Hossein Mohammadi who became my liaison after Ali Reza Beheshti. During the course of this interrogation, I resorted to tricks to confuse them more, and it worked. One of the tricks was shouting Hossein's name. I continuously shouted *"O Hossein, I am coming!"* The story that I made up about Hossein Mohammadi always worked.

After so much torture, the next morning I was forced to give the address of my house located on Imam Zadeh Yahya to the police, thinking that my comrades had cleared the house by then. Unfortunately, it turned out that they had not evacuated the house despite the rules of the organization. As a result, all the documents, pamphlets, declarations, around twenty kilograms of explosive materials, and twelve ready-made bombs were discovered in the house by the police.

There must have been some reasons that could explain why that house was not cleared. Perhaps my comrades were afraid that Mofidi's confession to the police that had resulted in the killing of Shamekhi[109] would be repeated. They might

---

[109] Mahmood Shamekhi (b. 1325/1947, Tehran) attended the Alavi School in Tehran, and entered the School of Accounting affiliated with the National Iranian Oil Company (NIOC). In 1349/1970 he and five of his comrades

also have thought that I had been killed and that there was no longer the need to clear that house quickly and that they should wait to do it at a more appropriate time. In my opinion however, my comrades showed weakness in this incident. Since there were a lot of explosive materials and documents in that house, they should have realized the gravity of the situation and paid more attention to clearing the house as quickly as they could when they did not hear from me after thirty-six hours.

I had left several telephone numbers of my contacts in the house, but fortunately they were coded, and the police could not find out what they were. We had posted a newspaper on the wall in my room and through multiplication and division we could find the telephone numbers. We wrote the most important numbers by interchanging the numbers and left them in the cracks of the walls in the house or on the street walls. This helped us to avoid future problems in case of arrest. After the discovery of the important things in that house, the police were now sure that I was involved in these operations. So they again came to me and asked me about the explosive materials. I pretended that I did not know anything about the explosives. One of the agents slapped me in the face and said, "Don't

---

were on their way to join the al-Fath training camps in Lebanon but were arrested in Dubai. On their way to Iran they hijacked the Iran Air plane and landed in Baghdad. From Baghdad, Shamekhi went to Lebanon and joined the Abu 'Amer group and received training in Palestinian camps there. As a result of heavy losses by the MKO in 1350–1351/1971–1972 Reza Raza'ie wrote and asked for help from chapters of MKO abroad. Shamekhi immediately returned to Iran and collaborated with Reza'ie, Bahram Aram, and Kazim Dh'ulanvar for about a month. During this time he wrote an essay titled "The MKO in Crisis." In 1351/1972 Mohammad Mofidi was arrested and taken to the Anti-Terrorism Committee and under severe torture released information about team houses of the MKO. Police surrounded the house of the Kabiri family. To avoid arrest, Shamekhi took his cyanide pill and died. Mostafa Javan Khoshdel was arrested. See Nejat Hossieni, p. 128–154. See also *Tarikhche-ye Mokhtasar-i Guruhakha*, p. 69, and *Tarikhche-ye Mokhtasar…*

make a fool of yourself! We are talking about the explosive materials that were in the sack."

I said, "What materials? I never opened the sacks to see what was in them."

He said, "What a surprise! You mean you were not aware that those were explosive materials?"

I said, "No! And why should I have known?!

They asked, "What do you have to say concerning the ready-made bombs?"

These bombs resembled in shape and structure to the bomb we had placed in the Firuz building and they had discovered and discharged. They then started beating me severely so that I would admit that I was the person responsible for placing that bomb in that building. No matter how hard they beat me, I kept on denying my involvement and said, "In fact I do not possess any knowledge of carrying out such tasks! I am only responsible for distributing a few of the pamphlets!"

In short, I did not admit any involvement in those operations and denied categorically knowing anything about the explosive materials and bombs. I did so because I was well aware of the consequences.

Then they asked what those explosive materials were doing in my house and where I got them from.

I said, "Up to this moment I have neither touched a weapon nor dealt with explosive materials. I haVE never advocated the killing of a human being."

One of the agents said, "Should we believe the carpet or the rooster's tail?" [110]

I started cursing Hossein Mohammadi and said that he fooled me and that all these explosiveS must have belonged to him, and I was not aware of what was in the sack. He brought them to my house and said that he would come back and take

---

[110] This is a famous Persian proverb denoting the denial of an obvious truth. The text reads as followS: "Should we believe the rooster's tail or you swearing to Hadrat-i Abbas?"

them in a day or two. I did not know what was in those sacks. I placed my full trust in this guy and he abused my trust. Had I known about the content of the sack, I would not have allowed him to bring these dirty things into my house. The beatings, whipping, and torture did not change my stance on this fabricated story. I put all the blame on Hossein Mohammadi and Hossein Ja'fari. In my confessions, whatever I did, I placed the responsibility on Hossein Mohammadi. The police tried hard to get the address of this person from me and I continued to repeat what I had said and denied that I had any trace of the man and did not know where he was. I added that he was my superior in the organization. Therefore, I could never ask what he did, where he went, or with whom he met.

Then they asked me to describe his physical appearance. They had asked for this before going to the house. So without changing any part of my earlier story, I said that he was a heavy-built student with a big belly, and he had big black eyes and a heavy Isfahani accent. Of course, none of this was true.

The interrogators wrote down what I said. They went to all university campuses, military garrisons where university graduates served their military service, and any other possible place in search of this person, and obviously they never found such a person. They had developed a feeling of hatred and frustration toward this [imaginary] person and relieved their hatred by beating me up even more. In fact, I had become their punching bag. I knew that I had made up all these stories about myself, and they could not find such a person and bring him to me for verification. Whenever I made up stories like that I stayed firm in what I said, and they had no choice but to believe me. I had given them so many lies that they wanted to know every other detail of my life, where I had lived all these years, and what I had been doing since 1349/1970, so that they could discover contradictions in my statements. During those years, I had lived in several cities and changed homes frequently so that the police could not trace my whereabouts and cause trouble for other comrades. In every house that I had rented I stayed a very short time, but gave them false information about the length of my stay in each residence. If I stayed in a rented house for four months, I would report a year and a half. Sometimes they brought the landlords to face me to verify my statement and they would always say that this man is illiterate and could not remember exactly the length of his lease. When I insisted that I was right, the landlord—perhaps out of sympathy—would accept what I said. Then they would release him and bring another landlord, and the process repeated frequently. When they added all the months I reported, they concluded that there is a gap of two months in my claims and insisted that I should tell them where I was during that period. It was a very difficult process but I played my role so well and pretended to be so stupid that they accepted my report when I said that I lived in a tent in the mountains during those two months. Luckily, in their search of my room the police had found a tent and they were convinced that I told them the truth.

I am sure in their hearts the interrogator did not believe me. They always said, "Whatever you say is a lie. None of your words is true." But to save themselves of their own pain of further torturing me they accepted these lies. Once one of them said, "Frankly we know YOU have done all these; you made the bombs, you placed the bomb, you had weapons, and you distributed the declarations. But anything else that you did is no longer important. Just tell us the people you had connections with. Give us the names of your comrades and collaborators. We only need their names from you." They really wanted me to give them the names of my comrades. In response, I played the victim and told them "I was not crazy to accept all this torture for nothing and indeed it was my religious duty to tell them if I knew of the 'terrorists'' whereabouts, and that Islam is against violence and the killing of the innocent and those who commit these crimes are traitors and deserve punishment. I insisted time and again that I was in contact only with Hossein Mohammadi and Hossein Ja'fari and I didn't know where the hell they were.

This kind of defense was a good strategy under those circumstances. But after 1353/1974 political activists were unable to resist and give such a defense. Their defense was only ideological. My strategy was correct only at the time of my interrogation. Unfortunately, after that date whoever was arrested easily confessed and accepted responsibility for everything that had done. By then the situation had completely changed. Everything was open and a number of the people who were arrested confessed and gave invaluable information to the police. They argued that a person's resistance had limits. Sometimes the arrested comrades would claim that they were misled and fooled and asked for forgiveness. In such cases the regime took advantage and publicized their confessions in national newspapers and broadcast the "repenting activist's" confession on national television. But during the years I was in prison the situation was different. Until that time SAVAK did not have accurate and reliable information about our activities, and therefore, it was easier for us to refute charges and play thevictim.

The Final Treatment

During the thirteen days that I was in the hospital, I received no special medical treatment. In fact my health was not at all important to them. Even if sometimes they gave me treatment, it was only to keep me alive so that they could get as much information as possible. During the confrontation with the police I had received seven bullets. Five were in my right leg: one of them next to my big toe, another one above the knee, another one below the knee, and the two other in my hips. The sixth bullet hit my waist, and the seventh one hit my shoulder. Three of these bullets remained in my body while the other ones had passed through. The injury below my knee had gone all the way to the bone and caused excruciating pain. A few days later a part of my leg turned black. They insisted that my leg should be amputated to prevent it from spreading to the rest of my body. I refused to have this done and threatened them that if they amputated my leg I would commit suicide because I knew that they would kill me anyway and I wished to leave this world with my leg intact. No matter how much they insisted and reasoned, I did not accept. In the final days, without even taking an x-ray, they put my leg from my toe up to my waist in cast. These bullets remained in my body for a year or two before they removed them.

The cast on my leg was tight and placed much pressure on me and caused a lot of discomfort. I was in pain because my leg was crooked. Then the next day they came and removed the cast and put on a new cast. They took me to the Central Committee [of SAVAK] while the cast was still wet. After two or three months, my leg was healed. They took the cast off while I was limping. After this incident I always wondered how many hands and legs had been amputated unnecessarily before my turn came.

*   *   *

CHAPTER FOUR

Inside the Women's Prison

A History of the Formation of the Joint Committee for Counter-Terrorism[111]

Before 1350/1971 a joint committee to deal with the regime's opponents did not exist. The police and SAVAK worked independently from one another. They worked separately and carried on their own investigation and arrested the activists as they wished. Similarly, the intelligence department of the army worked independently from the other two organs. Sometimes both SAVAK and the police worked on the same case without being aware of the other one. This situation caused a great deal of confusion and conflict. For instance, in the case of arresting people who were accused of kidnapping the son of Ashraf Pahlavi, there was no coordination between the police and SAVAK. When the police arrested and tortured Badi'zadegan to obtain information, it turned out that everything that he had said had been related to SAVAK earlier by other activists.

After several unexpected incidents that revealed total lack of coordination and harmony between SAVAK, the po-

---

[111] Toward the end of 1340/1971 as armed guerrilla groups' activities expanded the Joint Committee for Counter-Terrorism (JCCT) was established. The SAVAK was in control of this committee, and its agents who worked there received training by Iranian and Israeli instructors. It first director was General Ja'far Quli Sadri. Parviz Sabeti, known as *maqam-i amniyyati*, was its chief of staff. Most types of torture were carried out by this committee. Among its most famous torturers were Nasser Nowdhari, Mohammad Ali Sha'bani, Bahman Naderpoor, known as Tehrani, Fereidoon Tavangari, know as Arash, Mostafa Hirad, and a few others. Among their well-known prisoners were Ayatullah Khamene'ie, Ashrafi Isfahani, Rabbani Shirazi, and Mohammad Ali Raja'i, Khosrow Golsorkhi, Dr. Ali Shari'ati, Ezzat Shahi, Zahra Javaheri, Tahereh Sajjadi, Fatemeh Hosseini, and a few others. This building was converted to a museum after the Revolution. See Ahmad Ahmad, *Khatirat*, pp. 283.

lice, and the army intelligence, the Shah issued an order to establish a joint committee to monitor and suppress the opposition groups. Before the formation of this organization, the SAVAK headquarters were located at the Evin and Ghezel Ghalaeh Prisons, where the accused were interrogated and kept. After they were tried in court and condemned, they were then taken to the Qasr Prison. After the JCCT was established by the direct command of the Shah, these three units started cooperating and coordinating their duties together. After the formation of the Joint Committee for Counter-Terrorism (JCCT) beginning in the month of Ordibehesht, 1352/May, 1973, all interrogation of the political dissidents was conducted in the JCCT Headquarters and if necessary, was followed up in Evin Prison. Of course, those activists who were interrogated for the first time or were referred to Evin were not quite known to SAVAK. It was therefore necessary to keep them away from the other prisoners for some time without permission to meet anyone or have visitors. Incidentally, a number of the less-known political prisoners disappeared after they were transferred to Evin!

In the early days after its establishment, the JCCT had its special prison in the basement of the police building located near Tupkhaneh Square (now Imam Khomeini Square). It was an old and dark building with a low ceiling and damp air, and it had no ventilation. There were twenty-two cells in this basement, one toilet, one sink for washing hands, and a small pond for washing the utensils. It was also used to wash up and make the ablution. The cells were on both sides of the basement, and a corridor separated them. Each cell was approximately 2 meters by 1.8 meters and was made of concrete and bricks. These cells were originally for solitary confinement but were often used to house two to five prisoners. There was no special area for torture. Prisoners were usually interrogated and tortured in a single room. They wore their own personal clothes. The only things that were taken away from them were things like belts, shoelaces, pens, and paper.

When the number of the armed opposition groups began to increase, the number of political prisoners as well as the activities of the JCCT also increased correspondingly. It was no longer possible to keep prisoners in this basement, and the authorities had to think of another alternative prison. There was another prison nearby in the center of the city known as the Women's Prison. From the month of Tir/June or Mordad/July they began to transfer some of the political prisoners from the JCCT to that prison. This was a three-story building, and each floor had about twenty-two cells. Each of the cells opened onto the corridor. At one end of the corridor on each floor, there were three toilets, a number of sinks, and a small pond for washing and making the ablution. On the third floor, there was a 3-meter by 3-meter room, which was used for interrogation and torture. After a while by Ordibehesht, 1352/May 1973, even this prison could not accommodate the rising number of prisoners under JCCT. Therefore, they added another building, which later came to be called JCCT's anti-terrorist building. This three-story building constructed in a circular shape was located to the south of the Women's Prison. It was said that both of these prisons were designed and constructed by engineers from Germany. In the two uppermost floors of the JCCT Prison, long metallic bars had been installed to prevent the prisoners from throwing themselves down. Each floor had twenty-five cells that had been divided into sections. Sections one and two were located on the right and left side of the entrance door of the first floor. On the second floor sections three and four were located, and finally sections five and six were on the third floor. On the ground floor past a circular courtyard, there was a pool at the center, and on the left side of the room, there was a medical center. The shower rooms were located on the first floor and at the end of the corridor. There were also one or two rooms that were set aside for VIP prisoners. These were prisoners who were willing to go on national television for confession. Their rooms had special accommodations such as a radio and a TV, and they received high-quality food and service. They provided political analysis and comments for the JCCT interrogators. Vahid Afrakhteh and Khalil Faqih Dezfuli were among the VIP prisoners after they made confessions in the later years. The other rooms in this corridor belonged to the prison chief and the night officer, and a room was set aside to receive the accused activists and store their belongings. In the medical center they treated the prisoners' injuries and gave them pain-killers and other medications after they were tortured. Often they gave the same medications for different ailments. They applied a yellow ointment to all the types of injuries and band-aged their injuries, and they changed their bandages every day or every other day. There was no medical doctor in this center, but prisoners addressed each other and even the interrogators as doctors! There was also an old man in prison in charge of injections who was also referred to as the doctor. He carried out all these tasks. On the second and third floor, there were rooms for interrogation and torture. On the second floor, past the stairs and near the circular entrance, there was a room on the left that reportedly was used as a third torture chamber. On this floor, more experienced interrogators like Kamali (my first interrogator at the hospital) and Isma'ili worked. I do not have enough information about this floor and what was going on there. As for the third floor there was a place where the first-class interrogators were active. On the right side of the circular entrance Mohammadi and Vahid shared an office. The second office belonged to Aresh and another interrogator. Rasuli and Tehrani had the third and fourth offices respectively. Another interrogator named 'Azodi had his office in front of the stairs, and on the left there were two offices where Manuchehri and Hushang Tahami and Sa'idi worked. All these individuals were in charge of interrogation and torture.

Mr. Guerrilla

They transferred me from the hospital to the JCCT prison while I had many injuries all over my body and my left leg was in a cast up to my waist. The cast was still fresh and wet and very painful. This prison was so dark and infested with mold and smelled so bad that even the prison guards could not endure the condition of this place. They had no other choice when they were sent here by the authorities.

At first they pulled me to a cell that was near the basement. I had already gone through very difficult situations and was in a terrible condition both physically and mentally. I was constantly in a state of fear and anxiety and my morale was low. The slightest noise would cause my body to tremble, fearing that that they were coming to take me for interrogation. For instance when the phone rang and the commanding officer put it on hold, I thought that he was uttering my name. This is how terrified I was. Physically, I was unable to stand. The cast that had completely covered my left leg to the waist caused an unbearable pain. Despite that, interrogation and torture continued even in such conditions. Whenever they took me for interrogation, they would drag me on the floor like a corpse. As they moved me up the stairs, my head would hit stair after stair and was always swollen. Interrogation was carried out in a hall where several people surrounded me and harassed me. One of them would spit on my face, another one would pour cigarette ashes on my face, and another would blow his nose on my face! When they arrested me and took me to the hospital, my clothes were all bloody and dirty because of injuries I had received. They had to tear my clothes to remove them from my body. Before they took me to the JCCT, they gave me a shirt and a pair of trousers from the hospital. The shirt that they gave me had no buttons and the pants did not fit me, as I had the cast on my left leg, so it got torn off in my cell and I took it off and threw it away. Whenever they took me for the interrogation, because I had no proper clothes they dragged me and

197

made me sit on the cold floor. No matter how much I begged them to give me at least a piece of paper or cardboard to sit on, they didn't care. Sometimes I sat on the cold floor from morning until noon. Indeed, I suffered a lot from this as cold would penetrate the whole of my body. But they were not content even with all this torture. Sometimes, one of them would come and open up my legs to display my genitals and then laugh and make fun of me. One of them would say, "How are you, Mr. Guerrilla?" and the other one would say, "How are you, Mr. Wrinkled Guerrilla?" They violated me and my dignity in any way they could and did not spare me of any kind of torture they knew. They treated me worse than animals and totally inhumanely! They wanted to destroy my self-respect and break my character. Since it was still winter and cold, the darkness and dampness in the basement made it feel even colder. I had only one blanket in the cell and had to keep warm with it. Often I tried to skip meals and only had soup and drank water so that I wouldn't have to use the toilet often. During that time, I performed my prayers in that condition, and since it was not possible to remain ritually clean and make the ablution, I preferred to drink water and soup to reduce my trips to bathroom.

In the cell, other than one blanket, I only had a bowl which I used for three purposes. I ate my food in that bowl, washed my hands in it, and sometimes used it to urinate in when the guards didn't allow me to use the bathroom. This shows how harshly the guards treated me and perhaps in some ways were also afraid of me because they had been told that I had killed two police officers. So they treated me like a murderer. Sometimes they beat me up severely without the order of a superior just as revenge. They never paid attention to any of my needs or requests whatsoever. They did not allow me to visit the toilet more than twice a day, and when I had permission to go I carried the bowl to the toilet and emptied it there. Once when I was taking the bowl to the toilet, as the bowl was full to the brim the urine spilled on the corridor floor. The prison guards came and poured the rest of the urine over my head. I was so angry and humiliated at that moment. This action was so disgusting and inhumane that I didn't know to weep or scream at him. The pain from the humiliation and anger I felt in my chest was too much for me to bear. This incident was repeated one more time later when the urine spilled on the corridor floor and the prison guards came and poured the rest of the urine on the corridor floor. They then rolled me on the floor like a cleaning rag in order to dry the urine. After this incident I felt so humiliated and my morale was totally crushed. So I never repeated that act again. I began to pour the urine in the bowl into the corners of the cell or apply it to the brick wall to absorb and dry. As a result, after a short time, my cell began to smell so bad and unbearable to the extent that no one could stand it. Every morning when the shift officer came to take the report and check attendance, as soon as he opened the small window of my cell and noticed the disgusting odor, he started cursing at me and calling my mother and sister prostitutes. Ironically, when he entered other prisoners' cells he would greet them and talked to them politely. I had to and did perform my daily prayers in such a horrible condition. I had no other choice. It was not possible in any way for me to observe the [Islamic] rules of cleanliness and perform the ablution.

The Wedding Night

After my cast dried up, I was able to lean on the wall and stand on my feet with much difficulty. Since no one had been yet arrested who was connected to me, the police could not find evidence to prove their claims, and my interrogation and torture continued as normal. It didn't matter whether it was day or night; sometimes they came at night and took me for interrogation. During the first two months after my arrest they beat me up on a daily basis. After that they would take me two or three times a week and would beat me up. It was as if this was my weekly ration. I was now used to this situation, and if a day passed by and they forgot to beat me, I felt something was missing! The results of these beatings trained my body in such a way that I learned to resist harder situations, and I no longer had any fear of them.

When they took me to the JCCT prison and put the cast on my leg, no trousers fit me over my cast. The shirt that my interrogators gave me did not have buttons in front. They took me with this appearance from the hospital to the prison. The prison guards too had no permission to bring me clothes. Perhaps they wanted to put me under more pressure this way. The prison guards were very mean to me and hated me. They treated me harshly and never paid attention to my needs. They kept me naked in the cell just like Adam and Eve and no matter how much I appealed to them to give me a piece of cloth or shorts to cover my private parts they did not care and they never listened. There was a small window on the wall of the cell near the ceiling where a lightbulb covered with a metal screen spread a little light in the cell. Fortunately, most of the time the light bulb was out of order and the cell was dark so no one was able to see my private parts. The trouble came when I wanted to go to the toilet as this was a great embarrassment and torture. So whenever I wanted to go to the bathroom, I covered my rear end with one hand and my genitals with another and walked backward. Because of this embarrassing situation, I tried to use the bathroom less often.

Most prison guards were mean and careless but after a while I realized that one of them was a better person and more humane. It was during one of the days of the month of Ordibehesht 1352/May 1973 when I called him and asked if he could change the lightbulb as my eyes were losing sight. He brought a new bulb and installed it. When he turned the light on he was taken aback by the scene he saw. He could not believe his eyes, so with an angry tone of voice asked me why I was in such a situation and where my clothes were.

I said, "Don't ask me, ask the prison guards!"

He became angry and said, "I asked you a question, and you answer me properly. I asked you why you were naked."

I said, "From the first day that I was brought here I only had shorts. They were torn and very embarrassing so I threw them away." I then asked him if it was possible for him to give me at least proper underwear!

He went away and half an hour later came back and said that they do not have any other kind of clothes except the prisoners' uniforms, but he did not think that political prisoners like me would wear these clothes. "This is what we have," he said, "a pair of shorts and a prison shirt. Will you take them?"

I said, "We are prisoners and we have not come for a party. This place, too, is not a hotel. Give the clothes to me."

He said, "We also have a shirt and a pair of trousers. Do you want them?"

I said, "Yes, of course, may God bless you!"

He brought me a shirt and a pair of trousers. The trousers were tight but I managed to put them on. When I wore these clothes, I had a great feeling and was really pleased. It was a special moment. Initially I felt strange but soon I got used to my new outfit. The next day when the police came to take me for interrogation they saw me in new clothes. They cheered for me and applauded and congratulated me, saying, "Here is the groom!" Of course they were making fun of me and breaking into laughter. All this was psychological torture to break my morale. I also started laughing at them and said, "Wow! I have new clothes! Finally, I too have become a groom and have a wedding outfit."

Until that time, only criminals and thieves were given special prison uniforms to wear, whereas political prisoners wore their own clothes. Perhaps I was the first political prisoner in the history of that prison to wear the official prisoners' clothes. This experience prompted the authorities to give the same clothes to other political prisoners as well. Probably, I was also the first prisoner to be blindfolded. Until 1352/1973 they never blindfolded any political prisoner. Rather, they walked them through the corridors and allowed them to greet other prisoners and even meet them in their cells. In my case, however, the situation was different. When they took me for interrogation they blindfolded me and then walked me through the corridor. They did this to prevent my contact with other prisoners so that I could not recognize them lest I find out which of my comrades who were in contact with me had been arrested. That is the reason they blindfolded me and walked me through the corridor to the interrogation room.

Longing for Sugar Cubes

With the passing of time, I was able to mingle with the prison guards and establish closer relationships with them to the extent that we could sit together to have a chat and even crack jokes. They came to understand that what they were told about me was all lies. They also realized that I had not killed a person and that I was not an infidel and that I performed my [daily] prayer regularly. Gradually, I was even able to explain to them that the reason I was in prison was because of my struggle for their sake and for the sake of the people. I could explain to them that they were also part of the same people, the poor and the deprived for whose sake I fought. I would assure them that I knew they were believers and that if they could find an honorable job that pays 500 *tumans* more per month, they would leave their jobs in prison. As a result of this relationship a number of these prison guards became my friends. But the interrogators never changed with the passing of time, and in fact they became even worse. They constantly threatened to kill me and said that nothing could stop them, especially because they had announced in the press that I had been killed in a bomb explosion that occurred on Firdawsi Avenue inside a taxi! In a way they were telling the truth. In the situation that I was in, fooling them as I was with my contradictory and false stories, it was likely that they would decide to kill me and no one could find that out. They could have killed me and then announced that I had been killed in a confrontation, or died as a result of severe injuries or even illness. They could also choose not to announce anything at all. Therefore, this threat on their part was logical, and I took it seriously. But all in all this was not a reason for me to get worried or give up. I was firm in my stance with God, and I was least afraid of death. To me, death was sweeter than living with humiliation or betraying my comrades. Therefore, I remained firm in my resistance while at the same time was expecting these threats to be carried out sooner or later.

One morning they came after me and asked me if I wished to write to my parents or prepare my will, because it was my time to go! I said that I did not have to prepare my will. They asked me if I wished to meet my father or mother in these last minutes of my life. I said that I did not wish to have a visitor, and if they wanted to kill me innocently, then they should just do it without my visiting any of my relatives. I truly felt that my time was over and that now they were taking me to execute me. They raised me from the ground and tied my hands and blindfolded me. They then took me to their commanding officer, whose name was Colonel Abbas Zamani.[112]

Colonel Abbas Zamani inspected me from head to toe, and then he stared at my face. Suddenly at that moment a man came and slapped me on the face. Colonel Zamani protested and asked him why he had slapped me. When the man said, "He is a terrorist and a member of the MKO," Colonel Zamani replied, "He is just a suspect accused of terrorist actions, and as long as his crimes are not proven, no one has the right to beat him up!" Since I had been brought here to expect my execution, I was heartened by what I heard and pulled myself to-

---

[112] Colonel Abbas Zamani was the deputy of General Zandipoor in the JCCT. He was not related to Major Zamani who was the Director of Qasr prison.

gether. Soon I realized that they had started a new game to win me over by pretending to care for me and wanted to be kind to me to get information. I reminded myself that I needed to be even more careful.

Then Zamani ordered a cup of tea for me. Two more people joined us in his office. It had been over three months since I had had a cup of tea, and I was really longing for a good cup or two. But I controlled myself and rejected his offer of tea. The general said that if I didn't desire tea, then they would use the whip to make me drink it. This was exactly what I wanted. On the one hand, I really had a great appetite for tea, and on the other hand, I didn't want them to know that. I did not want them to use that as leverage against me. I wanted them to force me to drink the tea. They offered me two cubes of sugar. I drank the tea using one cube and kept the other cube in my pocket to break it into smaller pieces in my cell and eat it whenever I felt the urge to do so.

Colonel Abbas Zamani said, "I will not allow them to beat you, but you also have to behave like a human being. I want you to sit down and tell us everything. Otherwise, these interrogators will start beating you again."

I replied that I had said everything that I knew, and I did not have anything more to say, and that they should not beat me up, because I was innocent. So interrogation by the colonel was not successful as they had hoped. I stood up to go back to my cell, and they asked me where I was going and wondered what I had done with the other sugar cube. I told them that I had used it with my tea. Obviously, they didn't believe me and started searching my pockets and found it. They threw it on the floor and crushed it under their feet. I looked at them with anger and regret. I really felt bad. They evoked a very bad feeling in my heart with the crushing of the cube. I felt that along with the sugar cube, my dignity and pride has also been crushed.

Unity, Resistance, Victory!

As a result of the severe torture that I had received, my body was injured all over. My hands were burnt and injured, my face was swollen, and my body was bruised. In addition to all these forms of torture I was also subject to other forms of abuse. Gradually, the interrogators reduced the severity of the beatings and torture upon me but increased their threats and verbal abuse. For instance, when the interrogator gave orders for a hundred round of whipping, the person in charge would only whip me twenty times. He would ask me to keep it to myself and never reveal that he hit me less. He would also ask me to scream and complain of pain so that they would think that I had received a hundred rounds of whipping. I was completely aware that these kinds of favors and kindness toward me were new tricks. In reality, they were aware of what was going on. I pretended that I believed them and showed them that I was grateful and that I believed their words. I did so in order to make them believe that they had succeeded in fooling me. This made them happy.

Sometimes I gave information to my torturer while he beat me, and that made him happy. I made him feel that the torture was working, and he then reported that to his seniors. In reality, what I told him were the same things that I had told another interrogator. This would create rivalry among the torturers as another one would come and hurl curses and abuses at me, complaining that I did not give him any information. He would then begin to beat me. I would also give him some information that in reality was just like the information I had given to the one before him. He, too, would become pleased and stop beating me. I was convinced that they had believed that I was just a simple and uneducated man so they easily accepted my words.

Even when they realized that everything that I said was not true they viewed my lies as insignificant and unsophisticated. They attributed these lies to my simplicity. They could not even think that from the beginning of my arrest I was determined to lie and fool them. If they had concluded that I was sophisticated, intellectual, and educated (that I truly was not!), they would have probably treated me differently and would have made a deal with me. But in dealing with me, the interrogators were not concerned about my rights as a human being with basic human rights. They did not show any sign of respect and treated me worse than an animal. As an example of this kind of treatment, I should mention that they left me fully naked for almost two months in my cell. Although the round building of the JCCT was fully operational at this time, in Khordad 1352/June 1973 they transferred me from the basement of police prison to the third floor of the Women's Prison. This prison had been administered by the JCCT for over eleven months. For about a month I shared a cell in this prison with Manuchehr Moqaddam Salimi,[113] who belonged to the Golsurkhi group, and with two other prisoners. Every morning when the night shift's commanding officer or interrogators came for inspection to take the report, these fellow inmates stood up as a sign of respect. But as for me, if I was sitting I would pretend I was asleep. If I was facing the door, I turned my back on them and never paid attention. My cellmates always criticized me and insisted that I should stand up and show respect to these agents.

Salimi especially insisted on this issue lest my behavior cause trouble for them. But I never changed my manners. Even when General Zandipoor came in, I never stood up for him.

---

[113] Manuchehr Salimi Moqaddam (b. 3124/1935) was a former member of the Tudeh Party. He was a painter and sculptor and became a close friend of Golsorkhi and Shokuh Mirzadegi. He was arrested after a plan to assassinate the Shah failed. He collaborated with the SAVAK extensively and disclosed information about many of his comrades. He was condemned to fifteen years in prison but expanded his contact with the SAVAK, applied for membership in the Rastakhiz Party, and wrote letters and appealed. Finally, he was freed, in 1355/1976. See *Terror-e Shah*, pp. 586, and Salehi, 132–135.

One day my cellmates insisted that I stand up when General Zandipoor came. Yet when he came in, I placed my hands on the wall and pretended that I wanted to stand up but had difficulty. The general understood that I was playing game and pretending, so he told me to sit down.

Manuchehr Moqaddam Salimi loved to be asked how he was doing. He loved to be addressed as "Aqa Salim" ("His Excellency Salim") and be offered a cigarette. But this was not my style. If somebody offered me a pack of cigarettes, I didn't accept and said that I was not a smoker. I didn't ask for anything from the officers of the JCCT, not even for permission to have a visitor. I did not feel I needed anything from them, so I never asked for a favor to show respect in return. In my conversation with the agents I always insisted that they had arrested me for nothing and that I had no obligation to respect them.

After one month, they moved me to cell number 11, which was across from the torture chamber, where we could hear the voice of every prisoner who was brought to that room for torture. Each prisoner, after receiving enough torture, was asked to reveal "his connection with Ezzat Shahi." They tried to trick them by saying that Ezzat had given all the information about them and they should reveal what they knew too. At the same time they came to me and used the same technique. I always insisted that I had shared everything I knew with them. Since I knew that they were bluffing. I remained firm in my words. I knew that if they received a document or someone gave information about me, they would never leave me alone and would make life miserable for me. I just knew that they were trying to fool me, so I never paid attention to their threats. When they said that with new confessions my trick no longer worked and I would pay for my stories, it was quite obvious that these were mere bluffs and threats. Sometimes they even went inside the torture chamber while there was no one in it and cursed and screamed as though they were torturing someone. I could hear them say that Ezzat was also here and he had given all the information about you and that your con-

207

fessions could save your life or else you would regret the day you were born, while in fact there was no prisoner in the chamber. At other times they asked for eggs and a police baton to "rape" the prisoner. At that point another agent would pretend to intercede on behalf of the prisoner and promised that the prisoner would reveal what he knew about Ezzat! Of course at times they indeed took someone to the chamber and beat him up.

One day they arrested one of the leftist activists. They brought him to the torture chamber and started whipping him. While he was being whipped, he shouted, "*Unity, Struggle, Victory.*" The torturers also repeated this slogan and added to it many curse words. This kind of abuse was a normal thing among the interrogators and the torturers. When he was being whipped and was shouting this slogan, in my heart I praised him and wondered who he was who could take whipping and torture and at the same time shout this kind of slogan. They whipped him twenty times and still he was shouting the same slogan. I kept the door of my cell ajar by putting a book of matches in the crack of the door so that it wouldn't completely close. It was from this crack that I saw a person was sent to bring a bottle or an egg. He returned carrying a tray containing tea, a drink, and a bottle to the torture chamber. The prisoner who was shouting such heated slogans drank the tea, and a few minutes later he left. Within twenty-four hours, twelve people were arrested as a result of his confession!

I really wanted to know who this person was who within a few minutes changed 180 degrees and whom the guards saw off with utmost respect. Unfortunately, I never found out his identity. The interrogators always came to me after incidents like this. I always told them that they should not bother to come to me and ask me about books, cassettes, or declarations, as I had admitted my involvement in producing them and had accepted my responsibility for everything in relation to this matter. I told them that for two years I had distributed books and declarations among the people, but I could not recall their faces one by one. I carried out this task for over two years at intersections or on the streets and gave out declarations or [Ayatullah Khomeini's] treatise. Two years was a long time, and obviously I could not remember all those faces. Moreover, some of them met me and received declarations from me only once. I wondered how they expected me to remember all of them with just one meeting. It was possible for some of them to recognize me, but I could not recognize them. Even if a person claimed that he had received a declaration or a treatise from me, I could not tell whether or not he was lying because I could not remember. This was a very interesting game that I started with the interrogators. I pretended to be an honest and truthful person and wanted them to believe that my crime was very minor and that they might have forced some of the arrested activists to lie about me in their confessions.

This strategy proved beneficial to those activists who had lied about me in the sense that the interrogators never followed up with them. Nor did they refute their confessions unless they lied about someone else and caused trouble for him. Some of the people arrested said that they got the declarations in the Hosseiniyyah-ye Irshad or in such-and-such mosque. The declarations were either placed in different sections of the mosque or in between pages of the Qur'ans or in boxes used to store prayer clay (*muhr*). To give credence to their confessions, I admitted that in fact I had placed the declarations where they described. Actually, I had gone to Hosseiniyyah-ye Irshad several times and placed declarations where people could see them, but did not personally distribute them myself, because the audience there was attentive and alert, and it was possible for them to recognize me. It was also possible that I knew some of them, and this would have caused further problems in case of arrest.

From the beginning I never admitted to having carried weapons. The police did not have any evidence against me for possessing weapons. But it was three months after my arrest that they arrested someone and brought him to prison. After he was tortured, he told his interrogators that such-and-such a person [Ezzat] had "stayed in his house for two nights, and when he wanted to sleep, he hid his weapons under his pillow." The torturers then came after me and started beating me, saying, "You fool! Are you not the one who was saying that you never had a weapon? So what is this guy saying? Tell us about the weapon. What did you do with it?"

I said, "I am still saying that I never had a weapon because I am afraid of weapons. The weapon that this guy is talking about was not even mine. It belonged to Hossein Mohammadi. He wanted to go to Isfahan. Since he was afraid that the police might catch him with a weapon, he asked me to keep it for him for a few days. I was afraid of keeping a weapon in my own house lest the police find it if I were arrested. Moreover, I thought that if I was ever arrested or my house was raided by the police, having weapons at home would make my crime more serious. Therefore, for two nights I did not go to my house and stayed in that friend's house. On the third day, Mohammadi returned and took his weapon. You can ask the man if he ever saw me again with the weapon after that."

It was very difficult to persuade the interrogators to believe this story. They tortured me more, but I remained firm in my words. This went on until finally they accepted my words, but despite that they still added the possession of a weapon to my file.

The late Mr. Shahcheraghi had passed away two years before I was arrested.[114] Concerning the tapes, I told the interrogators that I had received all these tapes from this cleric who had brought them from Najaf. We did not know how and where he got these tapes and the speeches of Imam Khomeini. It was not necessary for us to know, either. We only got the tapes and transcribed them and used them to write pamphlets and produce declarations. Then we photocopied and distributed them among the people.

---

[114] Hujjat al-Islam Sayyid Ali Shahcheraghi was the prayer leader (*imam*) of Hosseiniyyah-ye Irshad. He died in 1349/1970.

210

I had accepted my responsibility in distributing pamphlets and copies of [Imam Khomeini's] treatise. I was aware that the presence of these confessions in my file would hurt neither me nor anyone else. These activities were very insignificant in relation to the crimes of the setting and exploding of bombs, assassinations, and possession of weapons. In the course of the operations there were only a few people arrested, and none of them knew anything about my other activities. So I really tried as hard as I could to hide this matter.

The arrest of these people was not important, and their confessions could not add anything to the charges against me. Being aware of the degree of their political consciousness and the nature of their confessions, I could guess that their confessions could not hurt me much. If the police could ever arrest an experienced activist or a well-trained guerrilla who was aware of my activities, I could expect commotion and more interrogation. However, judging from the behavior of the interrogators, it was easy to conclude that the recently arrested activists were not so important. Yet, all in all this was quite a headache for me, since each time they arrested a person, I had to go through more interrogation and answer more questions. Even when I was being whipped, I was thinking what I should say and what not to say—how I should articulate my thoughts so as not to get into trouble in the future if somebody contradicted me and proved I was lying. I carefully watched every statement that I made in front of the interrogators, which they were recording. I thought that if I mentioned the name of such-and-such a person and he got arrested, what would he do? How much could he resist, or whom would he sell out? I was constantly careful to talk in such a way that I could predict the consequence. Fortunately, most of the people I mentioned in my confessions were either imaginary characters or dead, or I was talking about myself but with another identity.

My Encounter with Ahmad Jannati [115]

When Sadiq Katouzian was arrested two or three days before me, he had confessed and revealed my connection with Hossein and Ali Jannati (the sons of Ahmad Jannati). He had given information about my meetings with Hossein. The police had gone after Hossein Jannati, but he had escaped. Therefore, they arrested his father in his place and brought him to prison. When he was brought to me, I was still naked and had my leg in a cast. Kamali stepped on the plaster on my leg and caused excruciating pain. Mr. Jannati was also behind the window watching this incident. I knew that everything between his sons and me had been shared with the police. They asked me if I knew him, and I admitted that I knew him and his sons. I was aware that Hossein Jannati's name was already in my file, as they had asked me about him before. Now they wondered what kind of relationship I had with Mr. Ahmad Jannati and what kind of operations we carried out together. I just said that he was like a father to us and denied any kind of special relationship with him. I then turned the question to the interrogator and asked him what kind of ties he expected me to have with Mr. Jannati, other than the fact that I respected him, but we could not work with clerics. When they asked me why, I said that these clerics used the pulpit to voice their grievances and did not observe the rules of safety and security, and for that reason we could not talk to them much, let alone collaborate with them in our operations.

Then they asked me how I knew him, and I simply said that his son was my friend, and I had gone to their house for dinner a few times. They also asked Mr. Jannati if he knew me, and he gave the same answer, that [this man] is a friend of

---

[115] Ahmad Jannati (b. 1305/1927) received his education in Qom, joined Ayatullah Beheshti and Sadooqi, and started his political activities in 1342/1963. After the Revolution he was appointed chief judge in Tehran, Isfahan, and Ahvaz, and then served as MP. He is currently a member of the Guardian Council.

my son and had come to our house for dinner a few times! I had a feeling that Mr. Jannati had been questioned by the police earlier. When I said that I had no special connection to him other than friendship with his son, he got the message and confirmed what I had said, that I was only a friend of his son and that I had gone to their house twice. The police thought that I had planned to infiltrate Mr. Jannati's house and recruit his family members, so they asked me why I went to his house. I told them, "After my escape from prison, I was exhausted and was thinking of quitting political activities. When his son and I became friends, I learned that his father was an instructor at Haqqani Seminary School in Qom. Since I knew that the students of this school were enlightened and that unlike other seminary students, they were not closed-minded and dogmatic, I asked Hossein to beg his father to admit me to that school. I was disappointed to learn that it was not possible, and that to be admitted there one had to hold a high school diploma or at least have completed junior high school. Therefore, I could not be admitted there because I only had a sixth-grade education certificate."

They asked Mr. Jannati if I was telling the truth, and he responded that he could not remember well. Perhaps his son had told him something, but he did not recall anything!

I told all these lies to prevent any harm to Mr. Jannati and save him from more trouble, lest he end up in prison, as he was already an old man. In such a case I would have felt guilty for the rest of my life for causing more trouble for a member of the clergy. I really struggled to prove his innocence and to show that he had nothing to do with my activities even though I had given him many pamphlets, had consulted him about my activities, and had frequent discussions about matters related to struggle and revolution.

Finally, the issues related to Mr. Jannati were wrapped up after this single meeting. Even though we saw one another in the JCCT prison, we behaved like two strangers and pretended we did not know each other and never spoke to one another. After fifteen or twenty days, he was released from prison and I felt a sense of relief.

With the Khosrow Golsorkhi Group[116]

To intimidate Islamist activists in prison, the authorities assigned Marxist prisoners to share a cell with them. Some of them were very intelligent and cultured. They talked with others, expressed opinions, exchanged views, and were very considerate of us. Some others were less understanding, and their company was torture for our morale and spirits. For instance, there was a person who did not wash up sometimes for a week or two. He did not observe the basic rules of sanitation when he used the bathroom, much less observe ritual cleanliness and purity. He did not even wash his hands after using the bathroom and before joining us to eat. Most of the time, he slept under a filthy blanket in his cell. Every morning I told him that and he need not pray but at least should wash his hands and face. When prisoners talked to each other, he nagged and complained that we were distrubing his sleep.

Sometimes SAVAK put us in the same cell with leftist activists hoping to extract information through them. I was aware of this trick from the beginning. In situations like that I always warned my cellmate that I was under interrogation and did not wish to be beaten and warned him not even try to get information from me. So my cellmates understood and did not try. Sometimes we killed time wisely and tried to learn from each other, especially teaching each other our local dialects or language if our cellmates were non-Persian-speaking.

---

[116] Golsorkhi's trial in November and December of 1973 was one of the most controversial trials during the reign of the Shah. He did not play a leading role in the group known after him, but his courageous defense in court earned him much respect and recognition. A gifted poet and writer, he joined other leftist activists who planned the assassination of the Shah. He was executed in Bahman 29, 1352/February 8, 1974. See Tayarani, pp. 649–708, Salehi, 131–157, *Kitabil Mehrab*, # 3.

When I was taken to cell number 17 on the third floor in the Women's Prison, I was sent to share a cell with Manuchehr Moqaddam Salimi and a couple of other prisoners. I was stunned to see how they buttered up the prison authorities. When I was in the JCCT's prison, members of the Golsorkhi group were also there. They did not receive much torture, and they were strong and steadfast in their resistance. Among them only Golsorkhi and Karamatullah Daneshiyan were strong. Both of them were executed. Of course, Abbas Samakar[117] and Teifur Bathai were also beaten up quite a bit. This is because a member of the group, Shokuh Farhang, in her confessions gave the names of all the members and other information to SAVAK agents. As a result of her confessions the trial of members of the group was open, and some parts of it were broadcast on national television. Among the survivors of this group only Abbas Samakar and Teifur Bathai remained loyal to their principles and maintained their position in prison as well.

Golsorkhi and Moqaddam Salimi were both arrested in the month of Farvardin 1352/March 1973. Until that time, their activities had not been discovered by the police. After their interrogations ended, Moqaddam Salimi was taken to the Ghezel Ghal'ah Prison while Golsorkhi was taken to the Qasr Prison, where he stayed with us for two months until Mehr 1352/ September 1973. But after some members of this group betrayed their comrades and decided to collaborate with the police, Golsorkhi was transferred to Evin prison where he was tortured severely. Shortly thereafter they executed him because of the statements he had made during his trial.

---

[117] Abbas Samakar (b. 1325/1946) was a poet and a writer, graduated from the School of Communication, and specialized in radio and TV production. He was active along with Golsorkhi and Daneshiyan, arrested, and condemned to death, but his verdict changed to life imprisonment. He was again imprisoned after the Revolution for a short time, and when he came out he left Iran for Germany, where he has been living since. See Samakar, p. 429.

The Types and Magnitude of Torture in the JCCT Prison (1352–1353/1973–1974)

The torture chamber was on the third floor in the Women's Prison building across the hall from room number 11. I spent most of the months of Tir and Mordad 1352/June and July 1973 in that chamber. It measured approximately 3 meters by 4 meters. There was a metal bed, some ropes to tie up the prisoner's hands, a number of whips of different sizes and lengths, and a battery for powering the electric-shock batons.

When a prisoner was taken to the torture chamber, if he was an important person, he was surrounded by a number of interrogators. They either whipped him altogether, or one whipped, the other ones kicked him, while a third one slapped him in the face. They would also use foul language and verbally abuse the prisoner in a loud voice to scare the other prisoners and give them the impression that the man under torture might be one of their own comrades.

When the interrogators were busy beating and torturing the prisoner, with all the noises they made, the rest of the prisoners in other cells were emotionally tortured and distressed. They felt terrible for the person who was being tortured, but also for themselves. Often interrogators opened the doors of all the cells and cursed so that other prisoners could hear them and feel threatened.

The type of torture of most prisoners during those years (the first six months of 1352/1973) was mostly limited to burning a part of the body with a lighter or a cigarette. Kicking and slapping in the face was routinely done. The harshest type of torture was whipping with an electric cable. Some people quickly surrendered under lashes of the whip and confessed. The torturers called the whipping the "Problem Solver." The pain of the whip was unbearable, especially on the nerves of the foot. With each whip, the pain would reach the brain. The repetition of the whip would cause tremendous swelling on the foot, which would not go away for a long time.

Hanging prisoners upside-down was also practiced quite frequently. Of all the types of torture, the tying of the hands in a crucified position was the hardest to endure. In this kind of torture, they would tie the person's arms and nail him to the wall or on a ladder and hang him upside-down. The weight of the body caused the arms to stretch on both sides. As a result, unbearable pressure would cause excruciating pain in the hands, elbows, and shoulders. A person in this position felt as if all his veins are about to rupture. It was impossible to endure this torture for more than twenty minutes because the hands would become swollen, blood circulation would become slow, and the hands would turn black. After a while the torturers would place a stool under the feet of the person, and if he confessed, then he would be left alone. If he remained silent they would pull away the stool and he would be hung again. A year later when they took me to the main building of the JCCT, they tortured me in the manner described above. In this prison, they placed me on the metal ladders and tortured me almost to the point of death.

Another means of torture was the electric baton. They used a car battery to power it. It was just like an ordinary police baton except that it was made of rubber and was electric and had a button on its end. By pressing the button and pointing the baton toward the prisoner, high voltage from the battery powered the baton and caused shock waves throughout the body. It didn't burn but caused the body to shake and shiver.

One other form of the torture that was extremely hard and painful was the "Apollo" that was adopted in the JCCT headquarters in 1352/1973. When a prisoner was subjected to this type of torture, he experienced severe headache that ruined his entire nervous system. The psychological effects of these tortures were much more harmful than their physical pain. Hearing exaggerated stories about these tortures and aggrandizing their effects disheartened and demoralized and killed the spirit of resistance of many prisoners. Fear of and anxiety about torture broke the back of many prisoners and killed their ability and will to resist.

I neither saw nor heard anything literally about pulling out the toenails of prisoners by using pliers for that purpose. However, when they whipped people on the nails, the nails would crack and separate from the fingers. Sometimes they even inserted a few needles half way under the nails and then lit a candle or a lighter under the needle. The needles became hot and burned the skin and caused excruciating pain. After a while the flesh under the nail would shrivel and the nail would fall of shortly afterward.

I do not believe the rumors and allegations that SAVAK used broken bottles as an enema. At least I did not see or hear of it. It is not right to say that SAVAK committed immoral acts such as forcing prisoners to perform oral sex on agents or similar acts to violate the prisoner's dignity. I never heard someone claim that such an act was done to him. If such an incident had occurred, people would have definitely talked about it, and nobody would have hesitated to publicize such heinous acts. Accepting such torture would have been seen as a sign of utmost resistance and not as a shameful action.

Even what was said about raping female prisoners is not true. The interrogators threatened to rape women, but they never carried out the threats. If one asked members of other groups like the Marxist activists or the Tudeh Party members—if they were honest—they would confirm that after 1325/1973 the degree of torture was not that bad. Before that date most activities were limited to the distribution of leaflets and pamphlets, and for such activities the police never resorted to sexual abuse. Even if one asked members of the MKO[118] that were involved in armed struggle, they would say that whipping with cables was the common torture, and it was enough for a person to confess to everything.

---

[118] Those interviews were conducted during the first year after the victory of the Revolution.

They rarely beat up female prisoners unless the interrogators were certain that they had important information and were not willing to disclose it. However, they never forced a female prisoner to be naked and stay in such a condition for any amount of time. Of course, there were special cases among female prisoners like A'azam Ruhi Ahangaran and Fatemeh Amini who died under torture. Amini was even taken to a hospital, but she passed away there. There was also another woman who was executed along with Vahid Afrakhteh.[119] Of course, I should mention that Vahid and this woman acted very poorly during their interrogations.

Since they frequently took me for interrogation, I noticed that they also brought female prisoners there and most often put Arash and Rasuli in charge of interrogating them. Arash beat them up, pulled their hair, and tied it around their necks, kicked them, and cursed them, but never raped them. There could have been some exceptions, but I was not aware of them. Women wore prison uniforms. Those who claimed that agents tore women's uniforms and abused them sexually were not truthful. They never did such things. Sometimes it happened that they stepped on women's chests, but actually they never went beyond the threat of rape. There is no evidence to prove otherwise, and if someone claimed differently I couldn't accept such claims. However, whether there were some exceptions to the rule, or violations took place and the victims chose to remain silent for different reasons, is another question altogether.

Some people also have claimed that interrogators forced them to perform oral sex with them and then urinated in their mouths. This is also not true at all. Occasionally some agents poured water and salt in a prisoner's mouth and claimed it was urine. But it really was not. In fact SAVAK was careful not to tarnish its image by committing such acts. It is possible that in exceptional cases they treated a prisoner very harshly and tortured him in an extremely brutal and sadistic manner

---

[119] That lady's name was Manizheh Ashrafzadeh Kirmani.

and violated all the rules. This was the way they treated some prisoners who misled SAVAK or JCCT by giving wrong information and inflicting damages to their reputation. In such cases sometimes the victim died under torture as a result of the agent's personal hatred and vengefulness. I was treated in such a way several times. The second time they took me to the JCCT headquarters, they tied me to my bed in a crucified position for about two-and-a-half months and used the Apollo torture technique to force me to confess and disclose information.

*   *   *

CHAPTER FIVE

Memories of Qasr Prison

Not Worth a Penicillin Shot

It was around the month of Mordad 1352/July 1973 that, hearing the tone of conversation and the type of questions my interrogators raised, I got the impression that my interrogation was completed. They complained that they had not been able to receive any useful information from me. I was at peace with my conscience that not a single activist, from the Mujahidin-i Khalq Organization or any other resistance group, was arrested and imprisoned as a result of my interrogation.

I knew many activists among the opposition groups, but I did not cause an iota of trouble for any person. Therefore, I felt confident, proud, and at peace with myself. There was no one who could claim to have experienced trouble or arrest as a result of my confessions. In contrast, there were many activists who, when they were arrested, talked a lot about me and my activities. I had to lie in order to refute their claims, but I never surrendered under torture and never disclosed any information about my activities except that which I had admitted myself. Had I done otherwise, their charges would have been heavier. Whenever I was brought face to face with any activist, I told my interrogators that so-and-so had lied about me under unbearable torture. I would appeal to them not to torture the poor man further and ask me so that I would accept all charges but would not accept charges that were not true. I did not care, because my charges would have not been any more serious than what they already were. This gave assurance to other prisoners and boosted their morale. They admitted that I was telling the truth and stated that they had been forced to lie under torture. In short, from the tone and complaints that the interrogators expressed about their failure to reach a conclusion in my case, I guessed that my interrogation was over. I tried to convince

221

them to take me to another prison, but they would not listen to my appeal.

One day, prison officials said that General Zandipoor was planning to come for an inspection.[120] The guards told me to ask anything I wanted from him. The day before this, the interrogator gave two apples to every cell. Apparently, they had decided to give fruit to the prisoners once a week. General Zandipoor was the director of the prison compound and occasionally would visit the cells for inspection. Unlike other times, this time when Zandipoor came to my cell, I got up and greeted him and asked him if he had a son.

He said, "Yes. And why are you asking?"

I said, "Suppose your son did not return to your house for two nights. How would you feel about that?"

He said, "I would be very unhappy."

I said, "I also have a father and a family. It has been several months since you brought me and kept me here without any crime. No one has any information regarding my whereabouts. Is that fair? I just hope that my father has not yet died out of sorrow! Please decide about my case; if I deserve to be executed, please do so, and if you plan to set me free, I would appreciate if you did so now. I haven't seen the daylight for months, and my eyes are going blind. I have spent five of my six months of prison time in solitary confinement. During all this time I have not been allowed to take a shower. If I committed a crime by distributing a few leaflets, the torture that I have undergone is enough for me. I appeal to your son's life to decide my case."

Although he knew me, still he asked my name.

I said, "My name is Ezzat Shahi!"

---

[120] He was the second director of the JCCT, educated in Iran with periods of training in the U.S., England, Italy, and France, he held positions in the SAVAK, including the chairmanship of the Committee for the Celebration of 2500 years of Persian Monarchy, and the directorship of the JCCT. He was assassinated by a ten-man team of Mujahidin in Isfand 1353/March 1974. He was described as a dignified, cool, and friendly officer. See Khosrow Tehrani, *Memoirs*, and Ahmad Ahmad, *Memoirs*, p. 298.

He said, "Oh! So you are the famous Ezzat Shahi?"

I said, "No! I am not famous. It is these police officers who made me famous. There is nothing wrong that I have done to them to suffer such awful conditions. The police have arrested me and made my famous to impress you and please the authorities. I am a simple and uneducated laborer who only distributed a few leaflets and nothing more."

Zandipoor asked his men, "What is the status of his case?"

They said, "His file is complete."

He said, "Then, take care of the rest of the paperwork of his file and take him out of here."

After this episode, it did not take more than four days before a couple of officers came to me and asked me to take my belongings and go with them. I did not have much belongings, so I only picked up my worn-out shirt and left that place. At the time of my arrest, I had a fake birth certificate, 250 *tumans* in cash, and some change. What was interesting was that those who arrested me never took my birth certificate so they could steal the little money I had. They had recorded only thirty-three *rials* as my belongings. Therefore, when I was freed they only gave me that amount, and when I complained, the man in charge said that there was nothing more, and if I wished, I could file a complaint and they would follow up. The truth was that prison guards had stolen that money and he probably knew. I never followed up that matter again.

By the day of my departure from the JCCT my health had somewhat improved, but the pain and the traces of injuries on the soles my feet and especially my ankles were still there. I was also limping a little on the leg that had been shot earlier. I could hardly bend my knee. Yet I was very grateful to God the Almighty who helped me not to allow hospital authorities to amputate it, even though I had endured a lot of pain from this leg.

It was during the last days of the month of Mordad 1352/July 1973 while I had the prison uniform on, and flip-flopping my slippers, I entered the Qasr Prison. Even though I had undergone a lot of torture and suffering, my appearance had not changed much to show signs of my ordeal.

The Free Zone for Guerrillas

The Director of the Qasr Prison was a man named Colonel Moharreri.[121] He was a highly organized, disciplined, serious, and to some extent even cruel. He had assigned political prisoners to Major Pour Kumayliyan. Unlike the Colonel, he was polite, flexible, and down-to-earth, and had a good attitude toward prisoners. He dealt with prisoners in a very kind and personable manner and avoided conflict. He associated with them and sometimes even ate with them. His deputy, Captain Ta'ziyehchi, was also a nice man. In Qasr Prison torture was rarely used and even in some cases that a prisoner was tortured, it was not very harsh. Thanks to such a leadership, Qasr Prison was more like a school playground than a prison. The officials of this prison had not yet really been integrated into the SAVAK system. Their explanation to us was that they were only guarding us and were responsible for our safety and security, and were not concerned with our political views and ideas, and were responsible for maintaining order in the compound. Simply put, we were prisoners serving our terms and they were prison guards, so to speak.

There were some of the prisoners who took advantage of and abused this state of prison. They were rude and they presumed that their behavior was revolutionary! In my opinion this was a mistake. If a political activist could not understand the nature of his environment and conditions of his enemy,

---

[121] Promoted to the rank of brigadier general, he was the director-general of Iran's prisons. He was a disciplined and powerful manager and tough, yet obedient to the regime and trusted by the national police department. He fled Iran in the company of Hozhabr Yazdani and settled in Costa Rica, where he was put in charge of the Baha'i organization. See Javad Mansuri, *Memoirs*, pp. 146 and 157–158.

then he/she would be prone to commit irreparable mistakes in reaching his/her objectives and goals. The political prisoners in Qasr did not understand the environment and conditions of their enemy. They lacked a clear and thorough knowledge of their enemy and were underestimating the power of the police and their captors. They did not appreciate, nor did they understand, the power of the police at all. As a result of their miscalculations and inappropriate attitudes and behavior they assumed themselves to be in a sort of autonomous and free zone rather than in a political prison. They expected prison authorities to seek their opinion and take their advice in prison affairs. In short, these activists assumed that they, and not the police, were in charge of the prison! In such an environment, they sang revolutionary songs and national anthems several times a day. These included revolutionary songs against the regime, religious, and even communist songs. Each group composed its own songs and sang them together. Each prisoner acted in accordance with the demands of the group with which he was affiliated.

Thus, during those days the police did not have an active part in the management of the internal affairs of the prison. Each ward was under total control of its commune and had its own spokesman. The police did not communicate directly with the prisoners. Rather, they would call the representative of each group to ward 8 and through him would give the message to others. These spokesmen then informed individual prisoners to appear, for example, at the military court or JCCT prison. Before sending a prisoner to such places, each group performed its own rituals and sang revolutionary songs to see him off. As a result, sometimes the officers in charge had to wait for a couple of hours to transfer a prisoner from Qasr to another location. It was because of this situation that the Baghdad radio called the Qasr Prison a "university" where prisoners received political education and training and resumed their anti-regime activities with more experience and in a much better form. Thus, some activists entered prison with little or no experience, but when they were freed, they acted as though they had become political philosophers and thinkers!

Most of the political songs were composed and sung inside prison. Political debates and ideological discussion sessions played an important part in shaping and nurturing the thoughts and minds of political prisoners. Often individuals got together and organized discussion groups, read books, and wrote pamphlets on history and ethics, and wrote memoirs and diaries. It is for these reasons that many prisoners who were released after a year or two continued these and other forms of political activities. SAVAK understood the significance of this situation and often complained that they spent much time and resources to identify and arrest political activists, but once they went to prison, the police gave them the opportunity to undergo all types of training, and when they were released, they recruited and trained many more new activists. Therefore, SAVAK pressured the police to put an end to this practice and threatened that unless prison conditions were reformed, they would take political prisoners from the police and bring them under their own control. The situation grew very tense before 1351/1972 and prior to the formation of the JCCT, and caused conflict and sometimes confrontation between the two organizations. This was one of the many reasons for the formation of the JCCT. From the beginning of 1352/1973 the JCCT consolidated its power and increasingly coordinated the behavior of the two institutions. Gradually, more and more restrictions were placed on the "free zone" of the guerilla groups and their activists.

The police department inspected the cells once every twenty or thirty days but was not able to discover anything important. Always a few days before each inspection, prisoners would find out the date of the inspection and would hide all their books and documents. Sometimes prison officials announced the day of inspection a day or two before the coming of the police inspectors, and this gave prisoners ample time to hide their sensitive documents, books, and writings.

In 1352/1973, SAVAK agents came to the prison unexpectedly. They entered all the wards and began their inspection. Prisoners were caught by surprise and did not have enough time to hide their books and documents. Agents found all their records, books, pamphlets, papers, and other writings that had entered the prison secretly. They also discovered the hiding places of these items behind closets and cabinets. The discovery of these documents prompted SAVAK to file a complaint against the police department. SAVAK argued that they had arrested these activists for possessing a single declaration and condemned them to five-year prison terms or more, while the police department allowed them to collect illegal books and documents! As a result, beginning in Khordad 1352/June 1973 the police department gradually but in a friendly manner warned prisoners and asked them to be careful, observe prison rules, and let them do their job. The police wanted to convince prisoners not to bring books and documents into prison and cooperate with them to keep peace in the compound. They did not forbid them to sing songs or give slogans but asked them at least to decrease the frequency of such demonstrations. They warned prisoners that if they failed to observe the rules, SAVAK would take over and treat them more harshly. The police department was trying to keep peace in prison and strengthen its own position *vis-à-vis* SAVAK. But the prisoners refused to accept their suggestions and did not retreat. They were determined to resist and refused to compromise.

In the beginning of the month of Tir/July, the Police department came for another inspection of Ward Four of the Qasr Prison but encountered prisoners' defiance and protest. SAVAK was informed of the situation and brought the special forces into compound. Despite that, a few days later when a prisoner was to be released, the police department appealed to prisoners not to hold the usual rituals they observed on such occasions and to keep quiet, and warned them that the special forces were prepared to suppress them if they did not comply.

However, prisoners ignored the police warning and went ahead and performed their rituals, clapping hands and singing revolutionary songs. Suddenly, police officers entered the prison and attacked the prisoners, injured a few, and confiscated some of their belongings such as watches, money, and lamps. In response, prisoners went to the courtyard and threw bricks and broke windows and a few trees. They also fought the police, and several people were injured on both sides. In short, this incident marked the end of the honeymoon with the police as well as the little freedom the prisoners enjoyed. Reportedly, the chief of prison police transferred two of the better-known prisoners, namely Mas'ud Rajavi and Bizhan Jazani, from ward 3 to ward 4 and asked them to mediate between the police and prisoners and make peace. As a result, the police department agreed to pay compensation to damages done to prisoners' belongings. This measure taken by the chief of police of the prison was seen as a sign of his weakness. He was removed from his position, put on trial, and demoted. He was then replaced by another officer named Mansur Zamani, who had the rank of major. He was the son-in-law of General Kamangar, the president and general director of all the prisons in the country. To establish his firm control over the prisons, Major Zamani addressed the prisoners and said, "Prison is not a hotel, and your party is over. You are only prisoners, and we are prison guards. There exists no other type of relationship between you and us. You ought to observe the rules and regulations of the prison; otherwise, you'll regret it." Zamani was very serious and harsh in his tone. The prisoners reacted and showed resistance, went on strike, and avoided accepting visitors.[122]

---

[122] "In Tir 1352/July 1973 a liberalization policy was initiated by the regime. In the new environment prisoners often clashed with prison guards and sometimes beat them up. As a result the Shah personally appointed Major Zamani as the director of Qasr Prison. He was a shrewd, tough, and rude officer and placed much restriction on prisoners' activities." For details see Abbas Duzduzani, *Recorded Memoirs*, tapes # 4, 7, and 10.

From Quarantine to the Wards

It was during the days of the prisoners' strike that I entered Qasr Prison. At first, they took me into the "quarantine" room. I was supposed to remain there for twenty-four hours, but because of the prevailing condition in prison, the strike, and the unrest among the prisoners, I remained there for ten days.

During this time, they brought in about twenty more prisoners there in separate groups. Their charges were much lighter than mine, and so they were quickly transferred to their wards before me. Whenever I asked the reason as to why they would not send me to my ward, the guards would say, "You are more comfortable here. Do not think that if you go to your cell you will have a better time than here. Do not think that you are falling behind and missing something, because at the moment, there is a crisis and fighting in all cells. It is better for you to remain here and enjoy the comfort of this place."

I told him that I just wished to go there in this situation so that I could share the ordeals of my brothers and help them in their hardship and troubles. After all, we did not come to this place to rest. We came here to serve our prison terms. You'd better be aware that I am one of them, believe in what they believe, have faith in them, and say whatever they say." During the time in quarantine, I associated with drug addicts and dealers at that place. We didn't have blankets or good food. Therefore, I decided to go on strike right there. I confronted the police and insisted that they should give me a blanket and good food.

Khosrow Golsurkhi and I were together in a cell for a while in Qasr Prison, along with Dr. Rashidiyan and a number of secular activists who were transferred there. They suggested that I should avoid conflict with prison authorities because my situation was different from that of other prisoners, as I had not been put on trial yet and I was once declared dead in an explosion. Otherwise, I would be in a disadvantaged position. I said, as the saying goes, "Black will take no other hue." If worst comes to worst, they will condemn me to death. I will take it. In fact, I would be pleased to be executed."

I have another interesting memory from my days with Golsurkhi. He was my cellmate in Ward Four for a while. When they wanted to take him for interrogation for the second time, he came to bid me farewell. I could read in his eyes that this was probably the last goodbye we would exchange. It was quite clear that he was consciously accepting death like a real man. He was in a special state. *After a few moments of greeting and exchanging jokes, he handed me his suit. I was in pain and choking, and he just gazed at me. He was quiet. I took the suit from him. Through a friend I gave the suit to a poor man in town, but I really wished I had kept it for the sake of history.*

It did not take more than two or three days before Golsurkhi and a few others were transferred to their cells. But I was kept there for around ten days under terrible and unbearable conditions. I do not remember whether it was because of strikes and chaos or just to calm down the situation in prison that they transferred me to Ward Four in Qasr Prison. Before taking me to my cell, however, they took me to another room where Captain Zhiyan Panah, Colonel Zamani's deputy, was for yet another round of interrogation. He asked me if I knew why I had been arrested and what the court verdict would be if they put me on trial.

I told him that I did not know why I was arrested as I only had two declarations with me, and that I believed I would be cleared of all charges if I went on trial, but with the prevailing environment that I witnessed, the judge might condemn me to a two-year term in prison. If the police had believed my statements, they would have been kinder to me. Often if they knew an activist well, they controlled him more than others, but if I could make them believe that I was a simple, uneducated laborer and that I did not know much about politics, they would have been much less sensitive to my case.

Zhiyan Panah then advised me to behave like a "good kid," and not talk to or listen to anyone, to go to my cell and mind my own business.

I told him that I had to see what kind of environment I was entering into and how others would treat me, for after all, I had to live with them.

Zhiyan Panah again warned me to listen carefully, and try not to cause any trouble; otherwise, he would send me to solitary confinement. He also forced me to sign an agreement to respect and obey the rules and regulations of prison. After this exchange of words with Zhiyan Panah I convinced myself that no matter what the police wished to do, I would do what I intended anyway, and even if I were to receive a few lashes of the whip, it would be fine because it would instead raise the morale of other prisoners.

Khosrow Golsurkhi and others who had gone into the ward before me were not welcomed by the usual rituals because of the control of the police, but they had informed other prisoners of my imminent transfer to the ward. Therefore, despite the suppressive environment that had been created there and in spite of the prohibition of rituals to welcome new inmates, when I entered the ward, everyone lined up and cheered for me. While I was limping, I greeted each one of them shook hands and we hugged and kissed each other. Among the leftist activists there I remember Rajabi, Azarniya, Hasan Khalili, Rahmani, and Jowhari. Of members of Islamist groups a few members of the Hizb Milal-i Islami and [Mostafa Javan] Khoshdel, whom I knew before, were also present. I climbed on a bench and introduced myself as a member of the MKO and said that I had been arrested because of my participation in operations conducted by this group. Charges against me in police files, however, were described as *distribution of declarations*, letters, and pamphlets, and nothing more.

With this introduction, my political orientation and religious identity became known to everyone. Since there was a clear demarcation among members of different groups, gradu-

231

ally the leftist activists distanced themselves from me. As for members of religious groups, individuals such as Kazim Zulanvar and Mostafa Javan Khoshdel were always close to me. They informed me of everything that had taken place in prison over the last two months. They advised me to rest for a few days and not to speak with just anyyone who would wish to talk to me until I had learned more about the prison environment. Since I had not been tried yet, they also strongly recommended that I not associate with people so that police attention would not be directed at me.

Commune and Anti-Commune

The Qasr Prison compound had several buildings, and each building had numerous rooms where religious activists lived side-by-side with secular and leftist prisoners. Each group had its own commune. Soon after I went to this prison, I realized that political prisoners had no right to express their opinions. With more observation I noticed that a strong reign of censorship and suppression of opinions dominated the environment.

I felt that there were some restrictions and conditions that were imposed on the prisoners. Since I opposed any kind of forced conditions on prisoners and the prison environment, I tried first to gather information on prison conditions in general. Prisoners were generally composed of leftist and religious groups. The Left itself included members of Tudeh Party, the Fidayan-i Khalq guerrilla organization, Kar, Setareh-i Sorkh, Shafaq-i Sorkh, and a group affiliated with Cyrus Nahavandi. Religious groups in prison included the Islamic Coalition Party (Hay'at-i Mu'talifah-ye Islami), Islamic Nations Party (Hizb-i Millal-i Islami), and the Mujahidin-i Khalq Organization (MKO).

In 1350/1971 the MKO and Fidayan-i Khalq groups in Ghezel Ghal'eh Prison had decided to claim the leadership position in the struggle against the regime inside prison and outside. These two groups considered themselves the symbols and leaders of the Revolution. They believed that any individual or group that wanted to fight against the regime must acknowledge their leadership and follow their lead. Otherwise they would be defeated and destroyed. They were convinced that to prevent deviation, all groups must accept their leadership so that others would not attract them to their camp.

Before 1350/1971, living quarters of Islamist and leftist groups were separated. Each group had their own kitchen and cooked their own food, and their activities and political objectives and positions were different from one another. They had cordial relationships with each other, talked to and treated each other well, and occasionally got together. But each group maintained its own independence. There was no "grand commune," so to speak. Leftist groups had their own "commune" in accordance with their ideological orientation. Some were pro-Soviet, pro-Chinese, and pro-Cuban, and the like. In brief, each group had its own views and position, and there was no harmony and coordination in their activities. Islamic activists too had their own camp.

According to an agreement between the MKO and the Fidayan-i Khalq, different groups got together in their own commune. Therefore, anyone who entered prison, if he was religious and performed daily prayers, had to accept the leadership of the Mujahidin-i Khalq Organization and become one of them. And if an individual identified himself as a leftist, then he would be counted as a member of the Fidayan-i Khalq group. No group had the right to be independent and express its own views and positions. Specific affairs that pertained to prisoners, such as choosing a representative or a spokesman, or issues related to the daily needs of the prisoners, were under the control of the group with which each prisoner was affiliated. If a person acted or said anything outside of these frameworks, he would be quickly labeled as a *SAVAK agent, policeman, opportunist,* or *traitor.* The last label referred to these who were not willing to accept all commands and positions of one of these two groups. These two organizations openly declared that anyone who was not one of them was not a revolutionary; rather, he was a counter-revolutionary element and hence a traitor. They identified as an opportunist anyone who did not obey the decisions of one of these organizations but took a position in consideration of the overall interest of struggle in mind.

The individual Islamist activists such as those who had been condemned to death but had not been executed yet, a number of activists from the bazaar, and those who were affiliated with the Islamic Nations Party (Hizb-i Millal-i Islami) and were condemned to long prison terms, whose number exceeded fifteen, observed this condition but were disturbed. They were under constant pressure by these groups, but since their number was small, there was nothing that they could do, and they never joined the commune, and lived in isolation.

Other non-religious individuals did not like the communes and had their own independent opinions and positions. They did not approve of the leftist groups' dominance of the prison and formed their own small groups. They were in fact boycotted by the "grand commune." Rarely did anyone talk to them because the Fidayan and the Mujahidin dominated prison and isolated them.

Members of the Tudeh Party, as the oldest leftist organization, did not bother this group and were not strong enough to oppose them. They were few in number in prison, and outside prison, the party had sent its members to different cities, with a few members left in Tehran. They were weak inside prison, too, because those who advocated armed struggle were in control of the prisons. Tudeh members were in the minority, and their votes did not count in matters where voting was necessary. They had no choice but to remain silent.

It could be mentioned that the condition just described above prevailed in all wards of Qasr Prison where political prisoners were classified into different categories. Those who had been given five-year terms lived separately from those who had been handed longer terms. Each category was put in different cells. Ward Four was for the prisoners who were waiting for their trial but for whose appearance in court no date had been decided.

News, information, and decisions made in prison or outside [about resistance] would be exchanged between prisoners and their family members when they visited them. On the basis of this information, prisoners of different wards would then meet briefly and exchange opinions and take or change political positions. For instance, all shower rooms were located in Ward Five. Therefore, all prisoners had to pass through Ward Two and Ward Three in order to reach Ward Five and take a shower. Thus, during the short period those prisoners stood in line to take a shower, they exchanged information or assigned duties to others, or planned future actions. In addition to pressure and control by prison authorities, this situation placed much stress on the prisoners and created a suppressive and dictatorial ambience in prison.

Major Zamani, who was appointed as the commanding officer and director of political prisoners' section, was not prepared to show any flexibility or kindness to prisoners. He tried to prevent unity among the prisoners and struggled to break the communes. He argued that a political prisoner must not rely on anyone else but keep his independence in thought and deeds. He persisted in this idea. If a person talked about the unity in his presence, he would have them beaten up by his officers. All his efforts were to break the spirit of unity among the prisoners. He was successful in his attempts to some extent. His father-in-law, General Kamangar, fully supported him in his efforts. He brought into Qasr Prison a number of his friends, such as Captain Zhiyan Panah, Captain Ne'emati, and Captain Sarimi, and replaced many old guards. Zamani and Kamangar were both originally from Kurdistan. Therefore, most of the new prison guards they brought in were also Kurdish. Zamani was also able to promote sectarian differences between Sunni and Shi'a prisoners. He had told the Sunni prison guards that these Persians were Shi'a, and allies of communist groups, and they wanted to start a war against the Sunnis! With this type of allegations, he provoked the prison guards and the police against the prisoners and promoted hostility against the prisoners among them. Of course, prisoners too developed anger and hatred against Major Zamani as a result of the restrictions he introduced. But petit-officers and guards became the target of their revenge. They boycotted the prison guards and considered them their enemies and did not even greet them. The poor guards spent entire days and nights in the cells and were bored to death, and nobody even talked to them for a moment. In fact, the prisoners never even maintained eye-contact with them, and if they looked at them, it was with deep hatred and anger. Sometimes when prisoners encountered a guard, they would spit in front of him. Unfortunately, there was no ethics and piety in the prison. Even if out of sympathy a person greeted the guard, the rest would quickly label him a policeman or a SAVAK agent. Even if there were some people who never wanted to follow and observe the rules and regulations of the commune, they had to remain silent and do nothing out of fear of being shunned and labeled as traitors or collaborators with the police. Therefore, it was logical that in such a situation Major Zamani's allegations made sense to the guards and officers and planted the seeds of bitterness in their hearts against the prisoners. Zamani acted in such a way that authorities considered him an exemplary officer who knew his duties well and served the system with utmost loyalty. I am not sure whether he had received training abroad but could see that he was a talented officer, capable of carrying out his duties in accordance with standards set by the regime. To kill the spirit of unity and teamwork and prevent group activities in prison, he did everything possible to break the prisoners' spirit and subject them to all kinds of abuse and torture. For example, if we needed thread to stitch or patch up our clothes, we had to ask several times in order for him to respond to our request, and even then, we received only enough for the job we were asking. His excuse was that we might use the extra threads to make a rope and climb up the prison walls and escape! It was obvious that such excuses were another tactic to torture prisoners psychologically and break their spirit.

When Major Zamani was appointed to lead the political prisoners' ward, he removed books and all exercise equipment from there. The prisoners' strike and their refusal to meet their visitors had failed, and all privileges they had earned were taken away from them. In order to regain some of those privileges, we had to appeal several times and send written requests to Zamani to return some of the equipment to the ward. He even did not allow prisoners' families to bring these items for them. When he approved some of these requests, he would only give permission to purchase them from the prison store at highly inflated prices. His response to prisoners' objection was straightforward and simple: "Take it or leave it!" The books that were sold there were mostly novels and educational and foreign language texts, and prisoners did not have many choices. Despite all these, one should admit that those groups that dominated the prison and their insistence on the absolute validity of their views and behaviors also played an equally important role in creating an oppressive and dictatorial atmosphere in prison.

When I entered the Qasr prison, there were about 300 to 350 political prisoners there. However, the number was on the rise gradually, and soon there was not enough room in the third and fourth wards to accept the newcomers. The cells were all full, and prisoners had to sleep side by side. Sometimes there was not enough space even in the hallways, so authorities brought some bunk beds there and prisoners had to take turns sleeping. Lack of space for political prisoners prompted the authorities to evacuate Ward One, which was for ordinary prisoners, and send political prisoners there. In Azar 1352/November 1973 one-third of the space in Ward One was assigned to political prisoners from Ward Three. By the end of the same year, all inmates from Ward Four were also sent to Ward One. This part of the Qasr compound was composed of a triangle-shaped courtyard and several sections, and each section had its own small backyard. It had enough space to house 1000 to 1200 prisoners. By the middle of 1353/1974 it also became full and could not admit new prisoners.

In 1353 all prisoners lived together and mingled freely with each other. Some of the restrictions placed by Major Zamani were removed gradually, and some degree of freedom and certain privileges returned to prison life. But authorities constantly warned us not to form communes or even use that term, and simply to live together. Of course, the police dealt directly or indirectly with the prisoners' desire to live like a commune. If in the past prisoners received money in large bank notes from their visiting family members, by Zamani's order they were supposed to accept only coins. The objective was to prevent circulation of money in prison. Authorities justified decisions like that because in the past on a few occasions a couple of prisoners collected money from others and wanted to escape, but they were stopped. Sometimes they said that prison laws did not allow prisoners to keep money in prison. Some other times they said that some prisoners insulted the Shah's picture on the banknotes. They made similar excuses. In short, police rule aimed at promoting an individualistic character among the prisoners so that each person would only speak for himself, shop for himself, and provide for his own needs. But prisoners did things the way they wished anyway. For instance, each prisoner would go and buy half a kilo of sugar and then bring it and put it into a big sack and share it together with others. The shortage or unavailability of some items of daily life such as refrigerators and fans was resolved by the inmates themselves, even though sometimes it cost a lot. We had to do all the plumbing repairs. Sometimes a special fund was allocated for this sort of expense from sources outside prison.

Strike: Refusal to Accept Visitors

When I was in quarantine, prison authorities asked for my family's address, and I told them that I did not have the address of any of my family members. I had no choice but to say this because earlier I had told them that I had lived underground for so many years and that I had no ties with anyone during this period. I intended to inform my family about my whereabouts through other prisoners' visitors once I settled in my ward so that my family could come to visit me. However, when they transferred me to Ward Four in Qasr Prison I noticed that after the police invasion of that ward, prisoners were on strike and refused to accept visitors. Prisoners in my ward had not been tried yet, and indeed they needed to meet their families and have them hire attorneys to represent them. The MKO and the Fidayan-i Khalq Organization had declared that the strike was permanent and that it would go on until prison authorities fulfilled their demands. Some of their requests were simple and included soccer shoes, dumbbells, and cooking facilities. The police had limited the prisoners' access to these facilities or confiscated them when they encountered their rebellion. At first the leaders of these organizations stood firm in their demands and were not willing to request, much less beg, for the return of the items that they had been entitled to in the past. They therefore wanted to achieve their requests by putting pressure on the authorities through strikes. Continuation of this situation was so difficult for some prisoners. Therefore, I approached Kazim Zulanvar, Mostafa Javan Khoshdel, Dadizadeh, and Hasan Mehrabi,[123] the leaders of the religious wing of the MKO. I told them I personally did not care to accept

---

[123] Hasan Mehrabi was a member of the Political Bureau of the MKO in 1346/1967. He came into conflict with Rajavi after the so-called Ideological Revolution and the latter's marriage with Maryam Azodanloo. He was ostracized to the Ashraf Camp in Iraq, but eventually managed to leave and settled in Paris. He has never talked or written about his life and activities in the organization.

visitors because I had been disconnected from my family for over ten years and that I did not have a wife or children to expect a visit from, except an elderly father whom I last saw a long time ago. But the rest of the prisoners are in different situation and some of them had wives, children, and parents and were worried about them. Some of them had serious problems. At the end I asked them to set a ten-day, fifteen-day, or thirty-day time limit for the strike. The two groups had already declared that whoever accepted visitors would be kicked out of the group, and their membership would be revoked. I tried to convince the leadership of the two groups that those who were against the strike were not a small number of prisoners, and that their number was on the rise. Therefore, it would be very difficult to control them then.

They argued that they could not afford to give prisoners a choice, for if one of them broke the strike, then the rest would follow them. Right now they were under group peer-pressure, but if one broke the strike, all would lose. I advised them to find a better strategy because prisoners might be able to put up with this situation for ten, twenty, or thirty days, but in the long term they would get tired, and the number of strike-breakers would rise. In such a situation they might oust the leadership or boycott them, and then they would be in a majority, and the leadership would lose its legitimacy, and the commune would then be divided. The more I insisted, the more they resisted the idea of ending or limiting the length of the strike.

Finally, two prisoners broke the strike and accepted their visitors. As usual families brought them fruit, and when these two brought fruit to share with others, everyone rejected them because "they had acted against the wishes and decisions of the commune." But a few days later around twenty prisoners decided to accept their visitors. They also prepared a list of their comrades and invited others to join them. They threatened that if they were kicked out of the grand commune, they would form their own separate commune. This was what I had initially predicted and had warned the MKO and Fidayan leaders about. The police also anticipated this and hoped to break the unity of the grand commune. The authorities even offered strike-breakers separate cells and other privileges on the condition that they disregard decisions of the leaders of the grand commune. But the inmates were too clever to accept police conditions, but declared their willingness to accept their visitors.

The MKO and Fidayan leaders became apprehensive. On the one hand, they realized that prison authorities were not willing to retreat, and on the other hand, they recognized that the prisoners were divided and wanted to break the strike. They therefore decided to end the whole fiasco in a face-saving manner. So they appealed to Abdul Ali Bazargan, the son of Mehdi Bazargan [the respected leader of the Iran Freedom Movement], for mediation, as he was respected by all activists as well as by the police. He accepted and appealed to prison authorities to restore some of the earlier privileges, and in return the prisoners would end the strike.

Being aware that the prisoners were no longer able to continue their strike, the police rejected Bazargan's mediation and advised him to mind his own business and added that whoever wished to accept visitors could do so, and those who refused could continue their strike!

Major Zamani also gathered prisoners in the courtyard and offered a long lecture to prisoners, saying, "It was your right to accept or reject visitors, not ours, and if you did not care about your families who came here to visit you and waited for hours in the cold, how could you be kind to your nation? How could you claim to lead this nation while you are so insensitive to your parents and disappointed them! So if anyone wishes to accept visitors, come to us and give your request, and I personally will call your parents and ask them to come and visit you! You must have independence of mind. I do not believe in collective actions and therefore will not change my position even if the strikes were to last for a year."

Major Zamani's speech had its own effects, and a few more people joined the list of strike-breakers and wished to allow their families to visit them.

The MKO and Fidayan leaders realized that they were fighting a losing battle and expected the imminent end of the strike. One more time they appealed to Abdul Ali Bazargan and sent him to mediate between them and the police. Bazargan asked Captain Zhiyan Panah to give him an appointment to see Major Zamani, but was told that he had to respect the chain of command, and if he had any request, he must discuss it with Zhiyan Panah first and if he judged it to be appropriate, he would then refer Bazargan to Major Zamani. Finally, Bazargan had to convey the demands of the prisoners to Zhiyan Panah, who told him that prison authorities could not promise to fulfill the prisoners' demands, but if they ended their strike, they would report to their senior officers that the situation was back to normal and that the prisoners had learned their lesson. Zhiyan Panah added that if peace returned to the prison, authorities might gradually restore the lost privileges. But as long as the situation continued as it was, no concession would be given to the prisoners.

This strategy finally broke the resistance of all the prisoners. They ended their strikes, and the next day they announced that they would accept visitors. Prison leadership justified this decision by announcing, "Since we were informed that the police planned to break our strike and end our unity, and because some comrades wished to accept visitors, we negotiated with the authorities, who accepted our demands and promised that they would restore the concession we enjoyed previously."

This statement was nothing but a justification to claim victory, while in fact it was a total defeat. In short, the strike ended, and in the days that followed, prisoners started accepting visitors, but no concession was restored. The only outcome was that in the process a few prisoners became scapegoats and were ostracized from the commune and were criticized for their willingness to retreat before the police and even for collaborating with them! During the visits, the police were very careful not to allow the exchange of dangerous items or information. During a visit by my brother, the police reported that I had asked him about books that I had hidden in storage in the roof of our home. All in all, a very difficult and unbearable ambiance dominated the prison environment after that event.

A Plan to Assassinate Zamani and Zhiyan Panah

The way the situation evolved in prison prompted us to find solutions and change the prevailing conditions. After consulting a number of friends, we reached the conclusion that to change the situation we should eliminate the two individuals—namely Major Zamani[124] and Captain Zhiyan Panah[125]—who were responsible in the first place for creating such an unbearable and oppressive situation. We concluded that they had to be assassinated. So I had to find a way to convey this decision to members of the MKO outside prison. I checked to find out who was to be released from prison soon, and identified Ali Mohammad Aqa, who was to be freed in Mehr–Aban/September–October. I wrote the plan to assassinate Zamani and Zhiyan Panah on a piece of paper and gave it to him so that he would pass it on to Hamid Nankali's sister (Hamideh) who in turn would deliver it to MKO members in town. I do not remember now why we could not do it through her.[126]

---

[124] Mansur Zamani was the director of Qasr Prison between 1352 and 1357/1973 and 1978 and ruled over the prison with an iron hand. After the victory of the Revolution he was arrested and executed by firesquad in Isfand 1357/March 1978. For more details on his period in Qasr see Javad Mansuri, *Memoirs*, p. 158.

[125] Qasim Zhiyan Panah was convicted by the revolutionary court and executed in Isfand 1357/March 1978. For more detail on his life and career see Mansuri, *Memoirs*, p. 159, and Safar Khan, *Memoirs*, 335–336.

[126] On Nankali and his sister Hamideh, see *Interview with Ali Mohammad Aqa*, Tehran, Bahn 11, 1383/February 4, 2005.

The next person to be released was Hasan Hosseinzadeh.[127] He had been in and out of prison several times and suffered a lot. We decided that he should take several messages out, one of which was about the plan to assassinate Zamani and Zhiyan Panah. I also had another message for Hossein Jannati. The first message was given to my brother Ni'mat[128] through Mohammad Kachu'i. Murad Nankali and I had introduced Ni'mat to Hamideh. Therefore, after my brother received that message, he passed it on to Hamideh. Apparently, Hosseinzadeh gave the other message to Asadullah Lajevardi.

Before Hosseinzadeh agreed to carry the message, he said he didn't mind doing that but stated that he had been in and out of prison several times and had suffered a lot under torture, and he might no longer be able to take more torture. He assured me that if he was arrested, he was going to resist as long as he could, but was not sure how long he could resist. He left the decision to me. I weighed Hosseinzadeh's honest confession, and since I concluded that they might execute me anyway, I must make sure that Hossein Jannati would not be arrested so that he could continue his activities; and if he was arrested, he would know what to do.

My reason for insisting that the letter should reach Jannati was because a few nights before my arrest, Sadiq Katouzian had been arrested and had disclosed my connection to Jannati. I therefore had no choice but to inform him of the dan-

---

[127] Hasan Hosseinzadeh (b.1331/1952) started his political activities when he was sixteen. Several times he was arrested while distributing opposition declarations and spent several years in prison, where he got very ill. He became disillusioned with the Mujahidin. In 1357/1978 he was released from prison and did not engage in politics for several years. When his brother-in-law (Kachu'i) was assassinated, he entered the Revolutionary Guard Corps and participated in the Iran–Iraq war. He was captured by Iraqi forces. It was believed that he had been killed but was released at the end of the war. See Mansuri, *Memoirs*, pp. 190–191.

[128] See *Interview with Ni'matullah Shahi*, Tehran, Azar 26, 1383/Dec. 4, 2004. See also *Interview with Hamideh Nankali*, Tehran, Aban 21, 1382/Nov. 12, 2003.

gerous situation. I asked Hosseinzadeh to write my message on a piece of paper when he was released and give it to Lajevardi. This was the text of my message to Lajevardi: "Katouzian had already informed the interrogators of his connection to you. So in case you were arrested, do not resist." Hosseinzadeh handed the letters to those he was supposed to, but later this matter was disclosed before the police and caused a lot of problems for me.

Major Zamani and the Mourning Procession in Muharram

It was the holy month of Muharram of the year 1352/1393 (H)/1973. Inspired by the philosophy of Imam Hossein's uprising against the Umayyid Caliph (Yazid), we had initiated our struggle in Muharram. Therefore, during this month we always became emotional and zealous. Major Zamani, who was cunning and very clever, was aware of prisoners' feelings and sentiments. To capture the hearts of the prisoners and persuade them to collaborate with him, he took advantage of this situation and prepared some mourning processions during the month.

It was on one of the first ten days of this holy month that we noticed that the police came to our cells and wrote down the names of all members of the clergy and anyone who had a beard. They did not mention why they wrote down these names. They also wrote my name. The situation was very suspicious. I went to one of the guards and asked him the reason for their action. I found out that Major Zamani was planning to organize a mourning session in Ward Eight on the following day, which was probably a Friday. So that night I went to all the cells and informed everyone that there was a plan to conduct a mourning session tomorrow and warned them not to attend, because attending such a session would only show our willingness to follow Zamani's commands. I even warned the prisoners that the police might film the session and use that to

245

claim that these prisoners were remorseful and ask for a pardon.

Then I went to see Mr. Mohammad Taqi Shari'ati (Dr. Ali Shari'ati's father) who said, "I will excuse myself and tell them that I am an old man and sick, and that I cannot attend the session."

Hasan Lahuti said, "My son is awaiting his trial, and if I refuse to go, they may treat him more harshly."

I advised him not to go because they might film him and use that to ruin his reputation. He did not listen to my advice and stated that he would go only on one condition, and that was if they gave him his clerical garb. He thought the authorities would not give him his attire, but I was certain that they would and told him so.

When the time for the ceremony came, the guards came after Lahuti. He told them his condition, and the guards said that they would give it to him in Ward Eight but would take it away at the end of the session. Lahuti became agitated and did not know what to say next. An idea came to his mind, and he said, "I will only participate if you don't take back the attire from my possession." They did not accept this condition and left. Thus, Lahuti got out of this trap.

On that eventful day, I went to see Seyyed Mahdi Tabataba'i in the court yard. Instead of a turban he wore a cloth towel on his head and was walking around. I told him that there was a mourning session for Muharram, and they wanted someone to conduct it, and added that he should go and hide lest they found him in that appearance and pulled him to the mourning session. He was not informed of this event when I told him about it. Contrary to my expectation, he deliberately walked toward the entrance of Ward Eight so that the police would see him and invite him to conduct the ceremony. I went after him to persuade him to change his mind to no avail!

In contrast to his case, I also witnessed respectable and principled behaviors from other prisoners. Once while I was taking a walk with Seyyed Nur al-Din Alavi Taleqani [Ayatullah Sayyid Mahmood Taleqani's nephew) in the courtyard, Major Zamani and Zhiyan Panah came after us. They called him "Hajj Aqa," but Taleqani told me not to pay attention to them and to keep on walking. After calling his name three times, Zamani got angry and shouted, "O Mr. Taleqani! I am talking to you."

We stood still. Seyyed Nur al-Din turned to them and said, "Are you talking to me?"

They said, "Yes."

He said, I am not "Hajj Aqa." My name is Seyyed Nur al-Din Alavi Taleqani."

Zamani wanted us to attend the ceremony, but Taleqani courageously said, *"Since when did you become a pious Muslim to hold a mourning session in Muharram?* If you are truthful and serious about Muharram, then let us conduct our own mourning for Imam Hossein in the courtyard of the prison."

Zamani said, "Well now that you resist coming willingly, then I will force you to attend this ceremony!"

Taleqani courageously said, "I will not, because I signed an agreement in the military court not to participate in any public gathering. I can therefore not take part in this ceremony and break my promise."

Members of the Mujahidin-i Khalq Organization were young and barely had their beards long enough. Their names were not on the list. But there were some leftist prisoners who had beards and whose names had been written on the list. They rejected our request and took part in this ceremony together with some other prisoners. Seyyed Abdul Reza Hejazi went to the pulpit and narrated stories on the tragedy of Karbala.

Discipline and Hygiene in the Qasr Prison

In the Qasr Prison, prisoners were not tortured. It was only in the JCCT prison that torture was used. After interrogation of a prisoner was completed and he entered prison, there was no torture any longer. Sometimes when a conflict emerged between the guards and a prisoner, his punishment would be solitary confinement. Occasionally the prison director would slap a person who was rude to him or did not greet him. Normally, the guards did not interfere with matters related to disciplinary affairs in prison. Of course, political prison had a clean and hygienic environment. We swept and mopped the floor of our own cells on a daily basis. Each and every prisoner had his own part to clean. Political prisoners were clean and maintained a clean and sanitary environment, even though in every cell there were a few careless inmates who often hid their mess under their beds. We also had general cleaning every weekend, when we removed beds and cleaned underneath. Sometimes when they took us to a dirtier cell, before too long we had cleaned and organized the place so much that the prison guards would jokingly say, "If they took you to Hell, you would turn it into Paradise."

There were no bedbugs in our cells and quarters. Occasionally some prisoners developed fungus and scabies and some of these diseases were contagious. But by keeping personal clothing clean and observing general rules of sanitation, these diseases could be prevented. In general, there was no serious illness in the prisons and no attending physician in the compound. Once or twice a week a doctor would come to Ward Eight and treat ten to twenty patients from one cell. If a prisoner's illness was serious, then he would be sent out of the prison for treatment. Specialist doctors never came inside the prison.

Most of the sicknesses in the prison were simple colds and headaches. The headaches were due to tension and stress. There were no other serious illnesses among the prisoners. We rarely had serious backaches or appendicitis. Among the prisoners there were also doctors, but association with them was based more on political considerations than on medical needs. One of them was Dr. Shaybani, who opposed the MKO. He had been practicing medicine for a while and was involved in political activities as well. There was also Dr. Sarukhani, who was a well-known physician who had a clinic in town. He, too, was against the MKO. It was because of this that prisoners affiliated with the MKO and the Fidayan-i Khalq groups never went to these two doctors for treatment. They preferred to be treated by a second-year medical student in their cell rather than visiting Shaybani and Sarukhani.

The nights that they served beef stew or soup for dinner, some inmates didn't eat. They claimed that they had ulcers and that they would get sick if they ate those dishes. They managed to buy butter and honey, cheese, or eggs and make their own dinner. Of course if anyone was truly sick, then it didn't matter whether they ate with everybody or not. But their problem was that they were picky and hard to please. Sometimes the very same individuals who claimed to be sick ate with those who were truly sick. Prisoners who belonged to religious groups never did so. They felt embarrassed to disturb the sick when they ate. Even if they became sick, they preferred to eat alone in a quiet corner. I became sick occasionally and felt terrible. In such situations I would either eat by myself, or if I chose to join others, I would eat the same food as others did. I might add that a number of religious prisoners, especially the group that had assassinated [Hasan Ali Mansur], separated themselves from the commune and usually ate together and away from the rest.

The Mujahidin, Dictatorship, and Boycott

In the Qasr Prison, Islamist and leftist prisoners lived in the same ward together. In continuation of their past leaders' claims, the MKO and the Fidayan groups considered themselves the vanguards of the struggle. Taking advantage of the atmosphere of prison they inherited from their past leaders, they resorted to unethical and oppressive measures to establish their control over the prison.

Of course when Major Zamani took control of the prison, he took the situation lightly and dealt with it in a shallow manner, even though prison authorities considered his policies sophisticated. Zamani and his colleagues took aggressive measures to establish order in the prison. He transferred some of the MKO leaders and those of the leftist groups such as Mas'ud Rajavi and Bizhan Jazani and even a few other groups including Mahdi Iraqi of the Islamic Coalition Party to solitary confinement. He clobbered some others and had their hair shaved. Some prisoners were forced to admit that they had committed mistakes and promised not to ever violate prison rules and regulations. Rajavi[129] personally promised that he would never again sing revolutionary songs, and if others want to do so he would stop them. Major Zamani was well aware that if he could teach a lesson to the leaders of these groups, then the rest of their followers and other inmates would fear further reprisals and shut up.

These measures resulted in an end to the free environment that had prevailed in prison a short while ago and that was replaced by a very restrictive and oppressive atmosphere after Mordad 1325/July 1973. In spite of this situation, the Mujahidin and Fidayan continued to impose their views and decisions on others and did not tolerate others' expressions of their views and opinions, hence leading to further restrictions on the prisoners. Anyone who opposed their views was isolated and suppressed. The unfortunate and sad reality was that communist activists and groups behaved in a much more democratic manner, thanks to their numbers, maturity, and organizational structure, than the Mujahidin, who were very authoritarian and acted in a dictatorial manner. It was in Qasr Prison and under such circumstances that I truly experienced the meaning of the term "boycott" and understood that it meant restriction, isolation, killing of self-confidence, corruption from inside, and the like! Their domination over the prison environment has given a free hand to the Mujahidin to boycott

---

[129] This interview was conducted in Bahman 1358/Feb. 1980,

their opponents. Whoever expressed a different opinion was immediately kicked out of the group, and others were not allowed to contact him.

They even treated the prison guards in the same manner because they considered them as their enemies and therefore boycotted them too. I was against this behavior that in my view was unethical and inhumane. I believed that the guards should be treated with dignity and respect. This was also an exceptional opportunity for us to impress them by our good Islamic and human behavior. I believed this would in turn encourage the guards to treat the prisoners better and might even encourage them to disregard some prison rules and provide for our needs. In any case, the new situation that was created was not beneficial to anyone. Unfortunately, ethical values and piety were rare commodities in prison. The environment was highly politicized by the MKO and the Fidayan, and polarized as a result of lies and accusation and counter-accusation. Any opposing voice was silenced immediately by one of the two organizations. Supporter or opponents of each group only had two choices: either hide their real opinions and practice prudent dissimulation, or leave the commune, submit to isolation and boycott, and face labels such as the "traitor," "police agent," and "remorseful."

The prevailing oppressive condition in prison, filled with lies and accusations, forced some prisoners not to express their views and ideas and maintain their independence. This was the real meaning of a "prison within a prison." For some prisoners, boycott was a very painful experience. Isolation and collective punishment seriously harmed the victims psychologically. Treatment of an inmate in boycott was a collective act of punishment. The decision to boycott a person came from above. Without any advance notice the leadership could decide that so-and-so must be boycotted. The next day even one inmate from among over 200 prisoners would not greet that person. During mealtime no one would sit at his table, and he would not be allowed to participate in any other group activity.

A person who was boycotted had only four choices to make. If he was patient and strong, he had to accept and tolerate the situation. The second choice was to completely separate himself from the MKO and reject the notion of "revolutionary Islam" once and for all. Such individuals usually joined the leftist groups. The third choice was that if a person was weak and did not have strong faith and firm belief in struggle, he could abandon activities and sometimes join the regime. The argument of this group was that "if these organizations are the symbols of freedom fighters and represent the future regime, compared with them, may God bless the Shah's regime! I am not willing to live in prison for the sake of people like them." He would then write a petition, express remorse, and ask to be pardoned. In some cases such individuals even collaborated with the regime and became SAVAK agents. Some of those remorseful petitions that were written in prison had their origins in the circumstances that I described. Finally, the fourth choice was that the ostracized member would write letters to the leadership of his group and ask for forgiveness, and admit that he was had been fooled and did not realize what he was doing. He would then go through a period of self-criticism and accept responsibility for his "errors." He also shared everything he had done and every thought he had entertained and would even share his most personal "secrets" with the group.

For example, if an activist left the Mujahidin organization and began to cooperate with the police, then leaders exploited that and justified their attitude toward him. They also tried to convince others that the leadership's judgment was sound and objective and they knew all along that the defecting member was not a fitting candidate to become a good revolutionary. Sometimes they even claimed that they knew he was a SAVAK agent and did not trust him. If the same person left the MKO and joined the leftist groups, then they would take it as a proof of their claim that the man did not have strong faith and was not even religious, and that we were suspicious of him and were concerned that he might spy for the leftist groups, and that was the reason we asked everyone to boycott him. Yet if the very same boycotted person returned to them and admitted that he was wrong and made a mistake and asked for forgiveness, the same leadership claimed, "This man is a revolutionary who has seen the truth and chosen the right path!" Alas, it was a strange situation; a person who was subject to attacks for a whole month and was called a traitor and a police agent suddenly became a true revolutionary, a comrade, and a brother. To justify these actions, the leadership would announce that the information they had received about so-and-so (the defecting member) was wrong. Sometimes they claimed error in recording names, and some other times they said the defecting member's last name was similar to that of another person who was suspected of being an agent! The major reason for and objective of this kind of behavior was to convince members to obey the organization's commands and leadership's decisions without any question. There was no opportunity to think, investigate, challenge, and question. No member could ever investigate to find out for himself whether or not whatever Rajavi said was true and valid. The organization and its leader thought and decided in his place. The only thing members were expected to do was to be obedient and submissive and accept all decisions and plans of the organization. The leadership and many members of the MKO were more obedient to the command of the organization than to the beliefs and observation of the principles of Islam. In other words, they were revolutionary first and perhaps Islamist second. From the point of view of the MKO and its leadership, a good revolutionary and a true *mujahid* was a person who turned to the organization for every question and blindly obeyed what the central cadre of the organization ordered him to do. For him the organization was his religion, his intellect, his faith, and in short, his life and his whole being. He no longer had his own will power. The organization had taken away his right to think and make decisions. It had become everything in his life. Of course let me also make it clear that most prisoners were very annoyed by this situation, but they detached themselves and found peace of mind by thinking that they would stay in prison for a year or two, and that when they were released, they would never look back and leave political activity once and for all.

As to my situation and reaction to the prison environment, it was obvious that I disagreed with the spirit that dominated the prison and expressed my opposition. But the MKO leadership did not dare to boycott me. Had they tried to boycott me, it might have turned against them, and they would have been boycotted by others. There are three reasons for my claim. One was because of my reputation and the fact that everybody knew me well. I respected everybody, and those labels would not work against me. The other reason was that I was still waiting for my trial, and the MKO leaders were certain that I would be executed. The third reason was that they knew I was well known in the clerical community and in the bazaar, and also had many connections in other cities. Therefore, I had nothing to lose, but their disagreement or open hostility toward me would have cost them dearly. Therefore, they tolerated me, or perhaps sometimes ignored me, hoping that sooner or later I would be executed and they would no longer have to worry about my opposition to them. In such a case they could declare me a martyr and claim credit for the organization. In other words, I was more valuable for them dead than alive.

My interrogation went fairly well. In fact, it was better than that of all the other prisoners. I did not yield and never showed any weakness. I suffered more torture than most other prisoners. While the number of operations I carried out was more than every other activist, I had not disclosed any information, nor had I left any records behind in the hands of the police. Of course, the announcement of my death in the taxi explosion at Firdawsi Square, which had been announced in 1351/1972, convinced me that the regime definitely planned to execute me. Yet none of this was enough to convince me to remain silent when I observed how the MKO treated other prisoners. On every occasion I resorted to different excuses to oppose the dictatorial and oppressive behavior of the MKO leaders. I maintained contact with those individuals who were boycotted by the MKO, listened to their grievances, and tried to help them as much as I could. Sometimes I mediated between these victims and other prisoners and urged them to treat them well.

The oppressive environment and dictatorial behavior was not limited to prisoners in Ward Four. In other political wards of Qasr Prison also the same situation prevailed, but the main center of control was in Ward Three, where Mas'ud Rajavi and Musa Khiyabani were present. In 1352/1973, however, these men, along with many other political prisoners, were transferred to Ward One. Ward Three was then assigned to ordinary, non-political inmates.

The MKO's domination and control over the prison environment continued until 1353/1974, and the prison situation deteriorated steadily. I pressured them to open communication with those inmates they had boycotted, but they rejected my suggestion. They also avoided direct contact with me because I constantly criticized their behavior, questioned their decisions, and pushed them to provide convincing reasons and justifications for their actions and decisions. As a result they avoided me and preferred not to have any interaction with me. Since they could not convince me, they always made excuses. Sometimes they complained of lack of time; at other times they argued that it was not in my interest to get involved because of my imminent trial, and that my association with them could endanger my situation! No matter how much I insisted and assured them that I was not afraid of being executed, they did not pay attention.

The most interesting thing was that they played games with me. On the one hand, they warned me about the gravity of my situation, and on the other hand, behind my back they told others that charges against me were serious, and since my trial was pending, everybody should stay away from me. Ward Four in Qasr Prison was assigned to those political prisoners who had not been tried yet. To frighten others they told them that association with Ezzat would have a negative impact on their situation, and the guards reported on them every day, and they should therefore avoid me.

I had thorough knowledge of the MKO and Fidayan leadership and knew what kind of people they were. Therefore, I never paid attention to what they said about me, and associated with everybody, talked to all kinds of people, joked around, and even wrestled with some of the prisoners. Of course, because my mind was always preoccupied, I did not try to get too close to anyone but hoped that my friendship would boost other prisoners' moral. For instance, since I limped, whenever I ran, I stumbled and poured water on their faces, and we burst into laughter. At some other times despite my physical condition, I wrestled with them, and this made them happy and they laughed.

Some prisoners found it rather astonishing to see me in such a joyful mood with such a high morale while I was expecting to be executed soon. Perhaps many of them expected that I should be in a sad and depressed state, whereas I had trust in God, the Almighty, and believed that my life or death was in His hands. I was not afraid of death, and in fact I considered it a rebirth and the beginning of a new chapter in my life. I was preparing myself for that eventuality. Therefore, in addition to all other activities that I explained, I spent most of my time in prayer, fasting, and supplication. I felt responsible for acting in this manner in front of other prisoners because in the unbearable environment of prison that Major Zamani had created and the leaders of the MKO had made worse, I had to boost the morale of the remaining prisoners and defend them before my death.

Future Leaders

It was during this time that I realized the true nature of our leaders in prison. Before my imprisonment, I did not know any of the leaders and symbols of revolution. But when I went to prison and observed them closely, I realized that they lacked piety, ethics, and sound faith, and did not possess any other quality or competence that qualified them for leadership. Being in prison gave me an opportunity to recognize quickly the shortcomings of the future leaders of our nation. I personally witnessed how Mas'ud Rajavi[130] made his decisions and imposed his dictatorial control over the organization. He was truly egotistic, totalitarian, and thirsty for power. I was so concerned that individuals of this caliber would become the future leaders of our nation and take the destiny of the people into their hands. I was so apprehensive that their behavior would result in such a situation that people would become nostalgic for the days of the Shah's regime.

The leaders of these groups, on the one hand, did not permit their followers to read and reflect or learn about the prevailing political conditions; and on the other hand, they did not have much to teach to the prisoners. As a result, they kept them busy and occupied them with meaningless activities so that they would not become passive and disillusioned. They created responsibilities to boost their self-worth and confi-

---

[130] Mas'ud Rajavi started his political activities when he was admitted to the School of Law and Political Science at the University of Tehran and joined the MKO. He graduated in Khordad 1350/June1971. He received training in the al-Fath Organization in Jordan. He was arrested in 1350/1971. He put a lot of information at the SAVAK's disposal during his interrogation. As a result of this and thanks to the activities of his brother, Kazim Rajavi, who was a professor of political science in Switzerland, his sentence was reduced from the death penalty to life in prison. After the victory of the Revolution in 1979 he was released and began to reorganize the Mujahidin organization. He came into conflict with the revolutionary government and fled to Paris in 1361/1982 and established the organization's headquarters there. For the detail of his character and his activities see, Lutfullah Maysami, *A History of the Formation of the MKO*, Gholamreza Nejati, Memoirs, pp. 395–407, Mehdi Khanbaba Tehrani, *Memoirs*, p. 469.

dence. For example, they appointed one to be in charge of tea, another one to be in charge of the nail-clipper. One person was put in charge of the newspaper, another one in charge of pens, food, and soap, and somebody in charge of the kitchen. They created as many false functions as the number of prisoners. They imposed these responsibilities on prisoners and created such a false pride in them to the extent that when, for instance, somebody called the person in charge of the nail-clipper, he would feel as though he were the president of the nation! That man kept the nail-clipper in his pocket, and whoever needed it had to see him. He would write down the name of the person that borrowed it, and after half an hour he would go to collect it. He would later on give his duty report to his master! Indeed, this is how they used to waste and kill people's time. Thus, the main preoccupation of the prisoner was to keep his position, and he could never understand that his position was indeed worthless. This type of relationship gradually killed a prisoner's identity and made him completely subservient to the organization and its leadership.

I constantly criticized the MKO and Fidayan leadership. My argument was that if they struggled against the regime's bureaucratic rules and wasteful administrative procedures, why did they emulate the regime and create 300 posts for prisoners and cause unnecessary rivalries among them? This was a paradox, and it created unnecessary rivalry among the prisoners. This was harmful to the prisoners' characters and ruined their self-confidence. In return for my criticism, they always justified their actions and argued that what they did was part of building revolutionary spirit, and in the process people could learn how to be responsible and perform their duties well, regardless of the nature of their functions!

The funniest and most regrettable attitude was that the prisoner in charge of the nail-clipper considered his responsibility very important and took it seriously. He was told that the nail-clipper was a form of weapon, and the police must never find out that such a weapon was in his possession! Unfortunately, many prisoners were preoccupied with these illusions, which were planted in their mind by the leadership, who warned them constantly lest the guards find out about the nail-clipper, and that protecting that secret was part of one's revolutionary duty, as if the guards cared about a nail-clipper at all. Whenever I remember those attitudes and arguments, I can't help but laugh, and at the same time feel sorry for them. I often asked myself how tragic it would be if these people one day become the leaders of our country and nation. These observations were priceless for me to learn the reality of the situation. Sometimes I became disillusioned and pessimistic and asked myself what the would future hold for us. In such moments I comforted myself by realizing that I would be executed soon and would not have to worry about the future, but wished that God would help those who had to remain in prison for a long time and associate with this kind of leader and organization.

During the last years of my term in Qasr Prison, I witnessed some really unfortunate and disgusting incidents. There were two brothers in prison who shared a cell. One of them was a supporter of the MKO while the other one opposed that organization. Their relationship had deteriorated to such an extent that not they did not talk to each other, but in fact had become blood enemies. If one of them could have had a chance, he would have killed the other one! The sad thing was that when their poor father came from the town to visit them, the two brothers would not go together to meet their father. One week the old man had to come and visit one son and the week after to meet the other. Of course, these types of quarrels were not limited to prison; rather, they were quite common outside prison as well. Often members of a single family were divided in terms of their affiliation with one organization or the other. These kinds of quarrels, disagreements, and fighting were very common in various families.

In such a situation, the leaders of any organization could never claim leadership of the entire nation because they did not know the reality of the society. Many prisoners were frustrated and I usually tried to comfort them and boost their morale and tell them that it might take many years for our revolution to attain victory, and in the process, new generations would rise, and their mindsets and characters would be very different. Leaders would also be replaced in the process, and the present leaders would not be able to muster support and would lose their popularity. By making these kinds of statements I wanted to tell the prisoners not to assume that the current leadership of these organizations would be in power in the future. I insisted that they should not identify the MKO and Fidayan leaders with the noble ideals of revolution and never question the legitimacy of their own struggle. I also tried to share some of my experiences in relation to SAVAK and the police and how to mislead them and continue resistance.

Everyone including the police knew that I did not trust anyone in prison, nor outside of it. In general, I hardly trusted anyone or any group easily, and at no time did I ever reveal everything that I knew to anyone or to any group. Some prisoners were inclined to exaggerate about the nature of their activities and impress others, while I always said that I had been arrested for distributing declarations and books. Interestingly, no one believed me! They were convinced that my activities were more serious, and I always denied it. Rajavi always insisted that he knew what I had done but had refused to disclose the information. They knew very well how much I had helped them since1350/1971. They also knew that I was a guerrilla and had participated in many operations. They were upset that I never shared with them the operations that I had been involved in. My answer was always the same; "In case you are arrested and show weakness under torture, it would be in your best interest not to know much about me." Of course I also tried not to ask other prisoners about their own operations. In fact, I tried as much as possible to avoid knowing anything about them. It had happened that some activists did not reveal so much information during the first interrogation. But when they were arrested and were taken to the JCCT prison, they revealed a lot of information.[131]

The Interactions between Islamist and Secular Groups

Some prisoners who turned their backs on religion and adopted Marxism as their creed pretended to be religious in front of their families whenever they visited them. To cite an example, there was a prisoner named Dr. Gholam Ibrahimzadeh whose father visited him from time to time. Before Gholam went to meet the father, Mr. [Ayatullah] Anvari[132] also went to meet his own visitors. Dr. Ibrahimzadeh's father told him to take advantage of Mr. Anvari's presence and learn from him. The doctor replied that he attended Mr. Anvari's classes every day and learned a lot from him! The poor father did not know that his son had become a Marxist and that he had no faith at all in Mr. Anvari and his teachings. Those prisoners who did not have strong ties with their families were indifferent toward them. But there were some prisoners who continued to pretend to have kept their faith intact. To convince them they even carried a copy of the noble Qur'an, a rosary and a prayer mat, and a copy of [the well-known] prayer book] the *Mafatih al-Jinan*. But inside prison, they were hostile to us and called us the "reactionary elements." However, in reality I believe they were more reactionary than we. They observed certain Persian traditions that in our view were reactionary such as the last Wednesday eve of the year (*chahar shanbeh soori*), Persian

---

[131] See Behzad Nabavi, *Memoirs*, recorded in Tehran, tapes # 12, 21, and 22.

[132] Mohammad Baqir Anvari (b. 1305/1927) received his education in Qom where he studies with Ayatullah Ashtiyani, Mutahhari, Sha'rani, and Rafi'i Qazvini. He joined the Islamic Coalition Party and was arrested and imprisoned until 1350/1971. After the victory of the Revolution he was appointed as Ayatullah Khomeini's representative in the *gendarmerie*, served as MP from Hamadan, and is currently a member of the committee that oversees the activities of mosques throughout the country. See Ahmad Ahmad, *Memoirs*, vol. VI, pp. 257–258.

New Year's Eve, and the 13th day of the new year (*sizdeh bedar*) as the symbol of national culture. Interestingly, on those occasions they replaced the Qur'an (which is traditionally part of these ceremonies) with a copy of the book titled *Social Transformation and Change* that was compiled by the MKO and indeed was their manifesto. [133]

The Marxist groups were also divided despite many slogans they preached on the necessity of unity. They did not respect and recognize each other. Of course, these conflict and quarrels among them also prevailed outside prison but to a lesser extent because they were scattered throughout the country and interacted very little with each other. The limited space of prison left them not much to do except meddle with one another. Outside prison, sometimes they met once a week or so and did not have much time to deal with ideological differences or minor issues; in prison they had plenty of free time and all they did was to watch other people and analyze their actions. They were always apprehensive lest other groups should plot against them. If a member of one group talked about personal issues to someone in another group or organization, or intended to resolve differences, others in his group would lose trust in him and sometimes would even suspect spying. In fact, they spent their days and nights in plotting against each other to attract a few members to their own groups. Ironically, even though many Marxist activists were from the upper classes of society and wealthy families, they called Islamic activists and especially those from the bazaar *petit-bourgeois* and used other communist slogans when they addressed them. I always told them, "If you are honest and consider yourselves revolutionary proletariats, just let us know what kind of profession your fathers were in. If you were of poor and working-class backgrounds, you could have hardly

---

[133] *The Social Transformation and Change* was the manifesto of the MKO that examined historical materialism in detail. It was translated in prison by Mansur Pour Kashani. See Maysami, *Memoirs*, p. 279.

attended universities, whereas I notice that you are all educated engineers and doctors."

For example, Bijan Jazani was an investor in the film industry. I think he owned a movie production company known as Tabli Film. Cyrus Nahavandi, Akbar Izadpanah, and Mansur Nahavandi, who had established the Front for the Liberation of Iran, owned a very large and well-established construction company. Apart from this, they had also invested in many projects. Some of the Marxist activists who came from religious backgrounds had serious problems with their families. In general family ties and relationships among leftist groups were diluted and much weaker, and compared to Islamist prisoners they usually had much fewer visitors. But they collected all the gifts, foods, and fruit that visitors—religious or leftist visitors—brought to prison in one place and distributed them equally among all inmates even though Islamist prisoners' families often brought a lot more than others did. Leftist groups in fact took advantage of this situation and felt entitled to share other prisoners' food and fruit because, they argued, those visiting families who brought more things in fact were capitalist *bourgeois* and could afford it.

In addition to the money those leftists spent to buy milk and other dairy products, they paid over 300 *tumans* per month just to buy cigarettes. Many of them smoked a pack of cigarettes a day and sometimes more. Interestingly, I heard that when the families of some of them insisted on giving them money, they refused to accept it and stated that they did not have any expenses in prison. They expected the bazaar merchants [of Tehran] to bring them money, but did not spend their own money or that of their organizations because it belonged to the people. I often heard that they said that "...those bazaar merchants are wealthy capitalists. Let them bring money for us to spend. We will have to confiscate their money in the future anyway." Their shrewd and opportunistic behavior had no limits whatsoever. The money collected from visitors was kept in one place. The contributors to this fund were Islamist inmates. But often they allocated funds to their friends in other wards as well. Whenever one of their comrades was released from prison, they gave him 200 to 500 *tumans* for travel expenses so that they would not feel ashamed before their families. In such situations they did not treat everyone equally and often acted in a non-ethical and discriminatory manner.

One day, one of our friends, who was originally from Qom, was released from prison. When he wanted to leave, we did not have money to offer him. There was only eight *tumans*, and we had to borrow another two *tumans* from an inmate for him. That amount was barely enough for him to get home. Just a few minutes after his departure, the spokesman of one of the leftist groups came to me. He was angry over why we had given him ten *tumans* while he needed only six to get home. I was really annoyed by his reaction. I told him that if we had had more, we would have given it to him. I expressed my anger and reminded him that they usually gave their released comrades 200, 300, 500, and sometimes 700 *tumans*, but when it comes to Islamist prisoners, they get upset over ten *tumans*! The MKO members too shared their views and argued that they only took the money that belonged to the wealthy capitalist! This kind of discrepancy was not important to them. Whether it was because of a sense of entitlement or other flaws in their character, they spread this kind of attitude. The MKO also thought in the same manner, and the similarity in their mindsets was the most important reason for their collaboration with the leftist organizations.

Some of the funds that we brought to prison came from religious charities (*wujuhat*) collected by the mosques or other religious organizations. When I complained that those funds were offered in the name of religious charities and were collected in the name of the Twelfth Imam (the Mahdi) and that should not be used in such an irresponsible manner, the Mujahidin called my argument nonsense! They argued that these funds have no bearing on Islam and we must share them with the leftist groups to win their friendship and support. However, from the point of view of Islamic law (the *Shari'ah*) this was not permissible. Because of it ideological identification with the Left, for the Mujahidin, religious law was not important at all. All they said was that the money was extracted from the wealthy capitalist and must be confiscated. This sort of argument by the MKO was not accepted by all, and gradually many religious elements began to express their opposition to these policies. They threatened that they would stop contributing to the prison fund. One argument was that none of the Islamist inmates were smokers, but they had to share the burden of the leftist prisoners, most of whom indeed smoked. The leftist groups in fact spent most of the available funds while contributing a lot less.

For a few weeks I took charge of the accounting of the funds brought in and carefully kept track of expenses. I appointed another person to be in charge of the accounting records, who accurately controlled incoming funds and expenditures. At the end of the period, it turned out that the Islamist inmates brought in the most amount of money, while the leftist groups spent the most. We shared our findings with the other prisoners, who were very upset to learn the truth. I decided to talk with the leaders of the leftist groups. I expressed my dissatisfaction with the situation and told them that they should also pay their fair share of the expenses for the smokers and the sick and threatened that we would stop contributing to the prison fund. I also insisted that the available fund must be equally divided among all groups, and that they should stop paying their comrades when they were released, and our comrades should get a bigger share when they were released because our members were smaller in number and had family commitments. Leaders of the leftist groups then promised to contribute more money to the prisoners' fund. But the leaders of the MKO were very annoyed by this decision that I had made and criticized me, arguing that what I did was in sharp contrast with the spirit of revolution and that we should share

265

everything because we all struggled against a common enemy and should not quarrel about money. I replied that if our relationship was based on justice and equality, we did not have any problem, but the truth of the matter is that neither were our objectives re the same as theirs, nor were our values identical, for they spent their days and nights plotting against us, and their aim was to do away with us even before they did away with the regime. However, the MKO was not prepared to listen and accept our logical answers.

In comparison with the Islamist groups and the Mujahidin, the leftist organizations had very few daily programs, and most of their time was spent idly. The Islamist groups, in contrast, had organized daily programs and carried out at least three or four different programs on a daily basis. For example, they assigned a person the responsibility of reading and analyzing the newspapers, while another one was given a particular book to read. So they were always busy, whereas the leftist groups spent most of their day time on debates and useless discussions or were assigned childish functions that I described before (nail-clipper officer!). Our people really had no time to waste. The night curfew began at ten p.m. The leftist prisoners usually woke up at six a.m. They went for exercise first and then had their breakfast. But the Islamic inmates always woke up earlier and before the sunrise. They prayed first, but rarely did anyone go back to sleep after the prayers, except some who held night vigil.

As I explained before, ironically and in comparison with the MKO, the left was more democratic and behaved in a more democratic manner. Some of these traits came from the ethical teachings and mottos of Marxism. For this reason, some prisoners who were frustrated and fed up with the dictatorial attitudes of the MKO developed a liking for the leftists and considered them more logical individuals and better fighters. Since the Mujahidin were ideologically weak and intellectually shallow, often they felt inadequate before the Marxists and developed a sense of inferiority before them. To make up

266

for this shortcoming they resorted to suppressive and dictatorial measures in their treatment of others. In general, because of their dictatorial attitude and inferiority complex, the MKO often praised the Marxists so that they wouldn't leave any stone unturned to attract their support.

Among religious inmates some suffered from severe back pain. They needed to place two blankets under their legs to reduce the pain so that they could sleep. But the MKO leadership did not allow this; they argued that that the leftists would criticize them and say that the Mujahidin were comfort-seeking *bourgeois*. This argument was so annoying at the time that many Marxists had bought themselves comfortable mattresses from the prison store for lucrative prices paid from the commune's budget that was contributed to by Islamist inmates. So, if a person stood against the leaders of the group, rejected their reasoning, and bought a second blanket, the leadership called him a *petit-bourgeois*. As a result that inmate became subjected to boycott and overnight was transformed from being a revolutionary to a comfort-seeking, pleasure-loving *bourgeois*! In defiance to their argument the person would sarcastically responded, "*Yes indeed! My grandfather, my father, and myself are all* petit-bourgeois."

The most appalling thing was that the MKO along with the Marxists considered the bazaar merchants and the clerics *bourgeois* and *petit-bourgeois* while the very same people provided them with money. They took their money and in return labeled them with these epithets. Unfortunately, most religious prisoners did not have much education and did not have much knowledge about politics. They were mostly young and opposed to the clerics and were not willing to learn or interested in learning about the teachings of Islam from the clergy. To read and understand the Qur'an and books like *Nahj al-Balaghah* (*Peak of Eloquence*) and collections of Hadith, some knowledge of the Arabic language is essential. But these youths were highly Westernized and strongly anti-Arab and considered any connection to Arabic as a sign of *Arabtoxica-*

tion, like *Westoxication*. Their interest in and knowledge of Islam was limited to what they learned from books written by Dr. Shari'ati and Mehdi Bazargan. Even Mas'ud Rajavi[134] himself, who is currently the leader of the MKO, did not know Arabic. When he wanted to translate the holy Qur'an or *Nahj al-Balaghah*, he used Arabic-Persian dictionaries and translated them word by word. He then added his own views and claimed that he had written commentaries! The Mujahidin had their own comprehension and interpretation of the Qur'an and *Nahj al-Balaghah*, which they offered to the people as their ideology. Their translated verses often dealt with anti-imperialist struggle and support of socialism. For instance, they interpreted verse 213 in chapter 2[135] of the Qur'an to denote the existence of a *commune* in the early phases of creation! And later some appeared among them who exploited others and created slavery, whence colonialism dominated over the world!? They never accepted any other translation. They said that if the young people learned Arabic, they would not accept their translations and interpretations. In fact the Mujahidin themselves were among the most ardent opponents of teaching the Arabic language. Of course these issues were never discussed openly, but each member had a mentor whose function was to make sure that he would not go beyond the frameworks decided by the organization. A case in point was deciding which books a person was supposed to read and which ones he was not.

The Qasr Prison Library

The library had a vital role in prison. An example of special treatment of the Marxist groups by the Mujahidin was in the management of the prison library. They decided the rules of

---

[134] This portion of the interview was conducted in 1358/1979.
[135] Qur'an 2:213: "Mankind were only one community."

the library, which only had one shelf, and always appointed one of their own to run that.

To justify this policy, the MKO claimed that the library was really not important to them, and that they never had enough time to take care of such matters, as they had more important things to do. The funny thing was that they stated that they had created the theory of "revolutionary culture" and claimed that their work was on the same level oasf the Qur'an and *Nahj al-Balaghah*! Since these two books were available in all rooms they didn't feel any need to keep them at the library. The effect of such special treatment of the Marxists was that the books found there were limited. Books by religious scholars like Mutahhari, Seyyed Qutb, Allameh Tabataba'i, or even Ayatullah Taleqai's commentary of the Qur'an (*Partovi az Qur'an*) were available for check-out. Even though many religious books contained political discussion, the Marxist in charge never lent them out. There was a book titled *The Sarbedaran Movement* (*nahzat-e sarbedaran*) written by a Russian scholar. This was one of the most popular books available at the library. It was on the history of a national movement originated from Western Khorasan. Sarbedaran established a dynasty in 1337. Its center was the city of Sabzavar. The dynasty ruled over most parts of the province until Tamerlane conquered it in 1381. This book was always either lost or was checked out, and whenever we went to the people who had borrowed it from the library they would give all kind of excuses to keep the book longer.

When I first went to my ward, I was not aware of the situation. An inmate came to me and showed me a book titled *The Earth, the Heaven, and the Cosmos in the Qur'an* (*zamin, aseman, va setaregan*). Its author was a scholar by the name of Dr. Sadeqi. The Marxists did not allow this book to be placed in the library. They organized the books on the basis of their topics. They placed any books that dealt with a religious subject on a "black list." We were not aware of this list. They did not give any book to Islamist inmates or to ordinary religious

269

prisoners. Furthermore, they told their members that this book was not good reading because it was a reactionary book, and they were not supposed to read it. They had made some other statements that friends informed me of. This went on until two religious prisoners came from the JCCT prison to the Qasr. The head of the library thought that these two prisoners were Marxists and so explained to them about the black-listed books. He warned them not to read those books. He also told them other things that these two fellows related to me.

I was very sensitive and felt responsible for this situation. I began to question the MKO and Fidayan leadership. I told them that we did not struggle for communism, that we were believing and practicing Muslims and had every right to have access to books on Islam; and from here on I would see to it that any book that came into the library was available to all prisoners. It was interesting that for those funny functions that I described before, their joint leadership had appointed two people, one from the MKO and one from among the Fidayan members. It was only the library that was under the control of the leftists. It was as though supervision over and the control of nail clippers or soap was more important and needed two officers, but the library could be controlled only by one librarian. I insisted that the leadership should explain the reason for their decision and demanded that we alternate weekly and manage the library between Islamist inmates and the leftists. The Mujahidin gave me a hard time and wanted me to mind my own business. I insisted that what I asked for was legitimate, and I believed it was just and that you could not force me to change my mind. I decided to do as I thought right whether they liked it or not. There were also some prisoners who supported me and asked me to form our own commune and separate the camp of Islamist groups from the leftists. I was not in favor of creating our new commune and did not want to deal with anyone except Rajavi and Khiyabani to see what explanations they had. They were both in Ward Three. In truth, I did not recognize any of their supporters as true *muja-*

270

hid, but *sympathizers* of MKO who now decided to call themselves *mujahid*.

For about one and a half months I negotiated with Marxists until they agreed to honor our demands. They agreed that the books on religion must be kept in the library, and religious inmates should share its management. But there were some of the Mujahidin members who opposed this idea, and they went to their leaders and provoked them. They claimed that a reactionary trend was taking shape in the prison, and that if the leadership did not resist their demands, it would not be able to control it in the future. Even Mas'ud Rajavi sent me a message saying, "Ezzat! Do not bite off more than you can chew!" Therefore, the Marxists did not fulfill their promise and were not ready to include religious books in the library and catalogue them like other books, nor did they share with us a role in the management of the library,

However, despite this, we did not retreat, and discussions continued for the next two and a half months. There were only three options. One option was what we had agreed upon two months ago, which they were not ready to honor. The second option was to arrange an alphabetical list of all books and separate religious books from the rest. The third and last option was to divide the library into two sections and assign one section to religious inmates to keep their books in, and the other section for the leftists and their books. They rejected the third option because we had more books and would get more space. Accepting the first option would have meant defeat for the Marxists and the MKO. So they chose the second option, which required them to create a catalogue and arrange the list of books in alphabetical order. Besides this, they also agreed that the responsibility of the library would be shared between them and us. But when they prepared the list of books and displayed it on the wall, people came and realized that the way it had been prepared was confusing. So a number of leftist inmates complained about why such a list was made and asked who had prepared it. The leaders of the MKO and the Left

271

blamed religious inmates for that. When they heard that religious inmates had prepared the list, they came and questioned us. I explained patiently and they realized we were right. In short, the leadership came to a dead-end and could not do anything. So they appealed to us for help to resolve the crisis. Finally, they accepted the arrangement we had proposed some three months before. The list remained in that order for one good week. Then they came to us several times and complained until we agreed to arrange the books according to their subjects, and we accepted their request. After that, any book that was brought into the prison was taken straight to the library.

The MKO was not pleased with the fact that we had reached an agreement with the Marxists. At times they prevented the books that were brought to the prison from being taken to the library. And if the books made their way to the cells, they tried as hard as possible not to let them get out and be added to the collection. If the Marxists allowed it, the MKO always opposed this arrangement. When the leaders of the MKO failed to succeed with this means, they resorted to non-ethical and dictatorial measures. They prepared their own separate list, which contained books that they never allowed their supporters to read. Among the books that were not allowed to be read, in view of the leaders, were books and other writings by Mutahari, Shari'ati and 'Allameh Tabataba'i. Usually none of these books were ever read by other leftist inmates, as well as by the members of the MKO. The leadership and those affiliated groups other than the MKO read these books regularly, often at night. To prevent anyone from seeing what they were rading, MKO leaders and members usually covered the book with newspaper and nobody dared ask them what it was. Their purpose of reading these books was to finds flaws in them so that they could raise them when the opportunity arose.

My Trial and Sentence

Toward the end of 1352/1973, that is, around one year after my arrest, my first court session was conducted. The whole process only took two hours, and my sentence was announced. Before the court procedure they wanted me to hire a lawyer who would be able to defend my case. But I knew that my case was decided already, and hiring a lawyer would make no difference at all. They already had decided my sentence, and nothing was going to change that. Apart from this, I was supposed to pay the lawyer, which at that time cost approximately 5000 *tumans*. I could not afford such fees so I told them that I would not hire a lawyer on my own. Therefore, I was given a court-appointed attorney. Once or twice I went to hear charges against me as my file was read. The lawyer told me that I should be remorseful and express regret for being involved in terrorist activities, as I was young and fooled by others. He also asked me to write a letter, apologize, and praise the Shah and the Queen, and ask them for mercy and forgiveness, and this might change my punishment from execution to life imprisonment. I told my lawyer that I was an uneducated man and did not understand the legal implications of my activities, and I left my defense in his hands, and said that he could do and say anything he deemed appropriate and I would sign it at the end. He said that he was confused and insisted that if I were truly regretful I should admit and ask for forgiveness. I told him that I had done nothing wrong to apologize for and whatever my case might be, they would give me a sentence proportionate to my crime. The more he insisted that I should appeal to the Shah, the stronger became my conviction not to do so. My own impression was that if they were going to hand me a sentence based on the hatred and vengeance of the police and SAVAK, then my sentence would be nothing short of execution. But if they wanted to hand me a sentence based on the existing documents, they would condemn me to a year or two in prison.

The trial was carried out in a very simple manner. I pretended and claimed to be innocent so that in case they did not condemn me to death, they would not be able to give me more than a year or two in prison. I said that since I was an uneducated man, I was not able to defend myself and that I gave my attorney full authority to represent me. The lawyer talked about my youthfulness and ignorance as the main reasons for my actions. He said that I was born into a religious family and that people took advantage of my beliefs. He emphasized that I was a simple, ignorant, and a gullible young man who was easily fooled. He then went on and appealed to His Imperial Majesty, the King of kings, and the Light of the Aryans, to pardon my guilt.

My silence at the trial helped to kill two birds with one stone. One of them was that I said nothing. Secondly I gave my lawyer full authority to do and say as he wished. The court was very sensitive towards me. It was walking on eggshells. The slightest mistake was enough to make my sentence very serious. It was not at all necessary for me to reveal my revolutionary beliefs and emotions in that situation. The best defense was my silence. I did not feel any need to make a big deal of my case or defend myself and deny or reject charges against me. After all, none of my complaints and defense could affect the outcome of the case.

When they read charges against me, which included possession of weapons, carrying explosive materials, forging identity card and birth certificates, and funding the MKO, the chief prosecutor asked me if I accepted those charges. I said that I accepted the charges but none of those have anything to do with me.

The chief prosecutor then asked for an explanation. I said that the weapon he talked about (as I had said before) belonged to a person called Hossein Mohammadi. He wanted to go to Isfahan. He came to my house two or three days before his journey and left a sack in my house. I was not even aware of the materials in the sack but since I trusted the fellow, I did not ask him about it. He just asked me to keep the sack for him in my house for some days. Concerning the identity card, in fact he was the one who made it for me but I never used it. The funding of the MKO is also not as it was reported. When they came to my house, I prepared food for them. You could realize that it is not possible not to host guests when they come to your house.

I never read a defense statement that one of the inmates wrote for me in my notebook. I knew that he did not have good intentions but wanted to provoke me so that I would disclose all I knew in court and receive a maximum sentence. In short, at the end of the trial the chief prosecutor read a statement, and then the judge issued a verdict. Contrary to my expectations, I was sentenced to a fifteen-year prison term!

Before my trial I had convinced all the prison authorities that I was innocent. But the two prison guards who accompanied me to the court reported to the court that I had been involved in many terrorist operations, and had ties with terrorists like Mohammad Mofidi and Baqir Abbasi, both of whom were involved in the assassination of Brigadier-General Tahiri. With this report, the police became more suspicious of me and began to monitor every step that I took and everything that I did. If I ever talked to an inmate, they would go to him and ask what I had been talking to him about. Sometimes when I spoke to a person, they interrupted us and would ask us what the other person had said. If we gave contradicting answers, they would harass us. When I saw that the police had become more suspicious of me, I realized that I had to be more careful.

One day one of my friends, who was to be released soon, came to me between two prayers. We spoke about future plans outside prison. To mislead the guards and prevent curiosity about our meeting, I placed a copy of the Qur'an in front of us and pretended that we were discussing verses of the holy book. A guard came and interrupted us and asked me what we were talking about. I said that the young man asked me the meaning of this verse, and I was explaining it to him. The

275

guard then asked, "Who was Abu Lahab?" and I said that he was the uncle of the Prophet of God. He asked my friend the same question, and he offered the same answer. These answers did not convince that guard, so he went ahead and wrote a report saying, "These two prisoners were speaking to one another; when they saw me they opened the holy Qur'an and pretended that they were reading it." We had decided on what we were going to say in this circumstance.

On that very night, Major Zamani asked for me. They had me wait in Ward Eight and every once in a while he would come smile or throw out a few curse words and go away. Once when he came again I asked him if he would let me go back to the cell, and he told me to wait. As I waited and occasionally stretched my legs to get rid of the pain, Major Zamani came. He shouted at me and said "Are you not ashamed of yourself?"

I asked, "Why should I be ashamed?"

He said, "You are crazy! I have been here for almost one year and I never even knew your name. But a few days after your trial when you came back to prison, the police have reported all your activities that you are inciting the prisoners to, recruiting membership and so on." As we were talking, some officers came in and told Zamani that the prisoner they were torturing fell unconscious after 100 lashes! Major Zamani ordered them to continue beating him up and then take him to solitary confinement until he could go and find out what his problem was. I was sure that all this talk was nothing but drama and unreal. I was bored with this talk and finally I asked him what it was that he wanted to tell me. He said that I was a fool and was trying to recruit members and he was wondering what exactly I planned to do! I told him that what he said was totally irrelevant and I did not know what he was talking about. He asked me again once or twice and I gave him the same answer as I had given to that policeman. When Major Zamani realized that he would not get any other answer, he sat down and said in a soft tone,

"Look! You are a poor and simple worker who was fooled by these people. Tell me, how much did they pay you to get into this work?"

I said, "No one paid me anything. In fact, I was the one who offered all the money I made to the MKO and its members. I never received a penny from them.

He became annoyed, raised his voice, and shouted, "Why were you giving them anything? Were you mad? Those people were doctors, engineers, and university students. They had ambitions to become prime minister, lawyers, and judges. But look at you, the unfortunate and poor man! What did you want to become? You have no education, and I wonder why you entered into such an organization. God forbid if this regime falls, the new regime will not give you a job higher than a simple prison guard! Even for that position one has to have completed junior-level high school. You are even far from that!"

I said that I never joined this organization for the sake of money or anything else. I even gave whatever I had to the organization. On the path of struggle when some people sacrificed their lives, money and position had no value.

Major Zamani's tactic failed again. He then asked, "Why don't you write a letter?"

I was well aware of what he meant by that statement but pretended that I did not know, so I said, "I don't have anyone to write a letter to; my father is alive and he normally visits me once a week. So I do not see any need to write a letter." Of course by a "letter" he meant a letter to apologize and seek pardon from the regime.

He said, "Stupid! I am not talking about that type of letter. I meant that you should write a letter to the Queen or the Shah. If you wish I can send such letter personally for you to assure that it will be delivered to them. Beware! We have had prisoners who were condemned to a five-year term but long after their terms ended, we did not release them. In contrast, we have also had prisoners who were given life terms but after two years we set them free."

I told him that my trial was not completely over yet and although I was given fifteen-year term, I was sure in my appeal I would be cleared of all charges and acquitted because the chief prosecutor noted that they had made a mistake and stated that I would be acquitted when I had a second trial. After all, I did not commit any crime to write a letter and ask for forgiveness for. If my innocence was proved, then I would be set free, and if I was found guilty I would remain in prison.

Again Major Zamani said, "If you don't care for yourself, at least think about your old mother. She came to me several times and begged me to release you because she needed someone to take care of her and there was no one else to do that. I tried to comfort her and promised to do my best to have you released."

To make the story short, Zamani talked about five more minutes about my mother and praised her character, and I was silent all that time. When he stopped talking I said, "Major Zamani, I do not have a mother. My mother passed away some years ago."

Since he never expected such an answer from me and because I had embarrassed him, he really got angry and said, "Ah! Wait and see how I will find your mother and we will talk of your father!"

I said that my father did not contact anyone and was aware of my activities and knew of my affiliations, and that he never asked anyone for anything. I added that I hadn't even talked to him for several years.

We did not interfere in each other's life and business. In short, after the forty-five minutes he had talked he realized that he could not get any information from me. He then told me that they had another prison that served better food and had better facilities and they would send me there soon, but wanted me to promise not to cause problems until I was transferred.

I asked if it were possible to send me right away because I had nothing to do in Qasr and got bored. I would still be serving my sentence in that place and it would not be different from here. I would be able to survive there, too. I neither wanted to propagate anything nor to have any business with anyone. I assured him that I would only try as hard as I could to protect myself and stay occupied. He ordered me to leave his office until he could decide about my situation.

Transformation of the Mujahidin Organization

After a couple of days they transferred me from Ward Two to Ward Four, where higher ranking members of the Mujahidin such as Sa'adati, Eftekhari, and Dr. Turshizi stayed. My cell was located between Wards Four and Six. The environment in this cell was suffocating and unbearable. Those who were with me in the previous ward had a cold attitude toward me and treated me in an unfriendly manner. Initially, they respected me because they were certain that I would be sentenced to death and hoped to get rid of me quickly. So when they heard that I was sentenced to fifteen years and thought that at worst it would change to a life term, they became disappointed, and in a sense were upset. After that their attitude changed drastically, and they no longer respected me as in the past. Shortly thereafter they appointed Ahmad Banasaz Noori as the head of the ward. This man was recruited by Asghar Badi'zadegan in 1349/1970. He was a Marxist from the beginning who was arrested in 1351/1972 and showed a remarkable degree of resistance under torture. The effects of the torture were still visible on his body when I met him. The organization had a high regard for him and treated him with much respect. With this mindset he took charge of propagating and teaching religious prisoners in Ward Four. Mas'ud Rajavi and other high-ranking members of the MKO remained in Ward Six. Banasaz was openly defiant and never performed daily prayer but surprisingly, fasted during the holy month of Ramadan! When I entered this ward, I noticed that he was the in charge and often caused a lot of trouble for everyone.[136]

Before prisoners were transferred to Ward Six, they recited the Qur'an and read *Nahj al-Balaghah*. In the new ward those books were replaced by Marxist literature and books like *How Man Became a Monster, Book of Evolution,* and other Marxist books.

Another tactic the MKO leaders used in this ward was to appoint younger inmates to spy on others. I confronted them for this behavior because I believed that such behavior would kill the spirit of friendship and camaraderie among the prisoners and would eventually work against them. I asked them to stop this behavior and especially criticized them for appointing a Marxist to run the affairs of the ward. I particularly confronted Abulqasim Reza'ie (Mohsen).[137] However, they did not have a convincing answer. Reza'ie even admitted that my criticism was logical and valid, but since Mas'ud (Rajavi) and Musa (Khiyabani) had decided that, all others had to obey because they were not in a position to oppose the orders from the organization. I continued to express my frustration and advised them to use their intellects and rely on their own judgment. But they never listened. They recruited some of the known communists in prison like Mehdi Rajabi and Hadi Mansuri and were pleased with such decisions. When I asked them where on earth a communist party ever recruited religious elements for membership, they had no answer. I even suggested that they should try to re-educate Marxist elements and introduce them to Islam, but their reaction was thoroughly insulting. They argued that as long as the Marxist inmates were firm in their own beliefs and collaborated with them, their presence in

---

[136] In his memoirs Behzad Nabavi states that "Noori openly declared that he was a Marxist. Mujahidin acknowledged that but argued that he accepted their ideology and hence we can have a Marxist member." See his *Memoirs,* recorded in Tehran, tapes # 12 and 16.

[137] Abulqasim Reza'ie, known as Mohsen, is the youngest son of Mr. Khalil Reza'ie. He became one of the main leaders of the MKO and currently is the General Secretary of the National Council of Resistance.

the organization was acceptable. They even bragged and claimed that the presence of Marxists in their organization was a proof that they were democratic and progressive.

The source of this kind of attitude and reasoning was the very same factor I described before, that is, lack of confidence and a sense of inferiority before the Left. I knew very well that they were not sincere in their justification and that their faith was not based on a solid foundation. They did not advocate an Islamic government but believed in the ideals of a National Liberation Front where all anti-imperialist forces and people of all ideological persuasions could be recruited. The only goal of the MKO, too, was struggle against imperialism, but they did not have the courage to inform the people of their real intentions. I warned them several times that once the truth of their nature became evident, people would no longer support them, and the clergy and bazaar merchants would no longer fund them. They claimed that they were aware of that and were moving in a direction such that they would no longer be dependent on the bazaar merchants and the clergy. They said, "We know that we have to confront them in the future because we do not believe in their jurisprudence at all."

There were a lot of double standards and hypocritical attitudes in the MKO. They were negligent toward daily prayer and took it lightly. Some of them did not even make the ablution properly, nor did they know how to pray correctly. Clerics like Rabbani Shirazi and Anvari criticized them and advised them to perform the prayer correctly.

In its classification of the society the MKO identified the clergy, bazaar merchants, and in general religious members as "second-echelon," less important, and as sort of "second-class citizens." They often made fun of them by warning everybody to "pray correctly" if you pray with them, but to be careful before you recruit them and make sure you know their reactionary characters and beliefs. I always criticized them and warned them that they might fool the clergy, but they could not fool God. Their response was to warn others not to confront me because I might use their arguments against them. At least they told everyone that I was courageous and truthful and they should avoid arguing with me.

Another reason that the MKO justified their collaboration with the Left was their understanding of the struggle that was intellectual and not revolutionary. They openly stated that their struggle was intellectual-centered and if they could not get along with the Marxists, they would become isolated by intellectuals. They believed that since Marxist groups dominated the scene of the struggle it was important to have their friendship. Otherwise, the intellectual community would isolate the MKO. The strangest thing was that acceptance and recognition by the Left was so important for them that they were prepared to sacrifice their faith and their religion. In fact, they didn't even care if the clergy or the bazaar turned against them; rather they would brag that they were closer to the Marxists than to the religious activists, and whoever confronted and criticized them, they would immediately label him as reactionary, capitalist, and the like. The MKO believed that the Marxists were true revolutionaries, and the Islamist groups would not remain steadfast in their struggle. It was these kinds of attitudes and positions that paved the way for the ideological transformation of MKO and the adoption of the Marxist ideology by a large group of their members that came out into the open in 1354/1975.

Against the MKO Position

As I mentioned before, the MKO had placed a leftist inmate in charge of propaganda and the educational program in the ward. The organization had lost its ground to the Marxists. For instance, it had been decided before that for cleaning and related chores in the Ward, four people from each organization were to be selected for the function. On such days the names of the team members were written on the announcement board. During the month of Ramadan the Mujahidin-i Khalq members were supposed to reduce their work load as they all fast. During that period they worked as hard as on other days, even during lunchtime, and assigned more people for the chores. I opposed this decision because people who fast have to wake up in the middle of the night to eat and then pray. My argument was that those who were fasting did not get enough sleep and therefore had to take a nap during the day. It was impossible for them to work as hard as on any ordinary day. So I suggested that the leftist inmates must also accept responsibility and do their share of chores. The leadership in response defended its decision lest the leftists think the "we were lazy. We should act in a revolutionary manner"! It was interesting the leftist inmates were more fair and realistic and were willing to take their share of the chores. But the MKO leadership just wanted to please them. It seemed that the only thing that did not matter was religion and faith, even thought there were many inmates who supported my argument and respected my views on the issue.

One day Ahmad went to one of the inmates who agreed with my position and threatened him that if he refused to help with the chores of the ward, he would expel him from the commune. The fellow refused to work during the day because he was fasting. Ahmad verbally abused him, called him worthless, and again threatened to kick him out of the commune. I was informed of this encounter, and I was greatly disturbed. The next day, I confronted Ahmad and told him that his behavior was not acceptable and if he claimed his words represented the MKO's position, then I was not a mujahid; in fact, I refused to be part of such an organization and opposed it strongly because those attitudes were in sharp conflict with everything that I knew about Islam and its injunctions. I also warned him that if he insulted any of my brothers in Islam ever again, he should be prepared for consequences, and if he didn't like what I said, he could ask to be transferred to another ward. In short, I made it crystal-clear that I would no longer tolerate or allow his insults to any Islamic inmates in that ward.

Ahmad reported this incident to the members of the Central Committee of the MKO (Rajavi and Khiyabani). He complained that I disturbed him. They wrote a note to me and said that I should mind my own business! After that on many occasions even when I was taken to the court for my trial they repeated this message one way or the other. To make sure that I got their message they sent Mohsen Reza'ie to negotiate with me. After long discussion in the presence of two clerics, we reached an agreement whereby working during the day should be optional for those who were fasting. Whoever volunteered to work was free to do so, and if an inmate chose not to work, no one could pressure and force him to work.

Early the next morning after eating *suhur* and washing my dish, I went to sleep. On my way to my cell I encountered an inmate who was busy preparing breakfast for the Marxist inmates. He told me how displeased he was to prepare breakfast for those inmates, but he had to do so because the organization had threatened to kick him out of the commune if he refused to comply. He asked me to inform Mohsen Reza'ie that he was sick and that someone else must replace him for the duty. When Mohsen Reza'ie heard of this encounter early next morning, he came to me. He was angry and asked me to stop discouraging inmates from working, mind my own business, and let them do their job. I reminded him that I did not incite anyone not to work but that he breached our agreement. Again he insisted that everyone should work. It seemed that logic and reason were not acceptable to them, and I told him that if they did not respect our agreement and resorted to threats, then I would not allow such a thing to happen. In short, we argued back and forth until several inmates joined us to mediate between us. At the end, he agreed to have some of his own men share the chores on a voluntary basis. Some other inmates were unhappy and continued to express their anger and criticized them for pleasing the leftist inmates. The MKO still insisted that what they did was part of their revolutionary duties.

284

Continued Fighting against the Destructive Policies of the MKO

My conflict with the MKO went on. Even though they pretended to respect me in my presence, behind my back they continued to talk and act against me. For instance they claimed I was never a member of the MKO but was always a simple sympathizer and supporter. They also claimed that I was never a political element and was only involved in some military operations. Since in prison there is no place for such operations, and all activities were concentrated on theoretical knowledge and politics about which Ezzat had no knowledge, therefore, if he opposed the MKO it was because he wished to impress others and gain respect. They didn't realize that I had my own supporters who reported these sorts of allegations to me. In my heart I laughed at the MKO reasoning. Ironically, some of those inmates who spread these sorts of charges knew exactly who I was and what I had done, but dishonesty, subjectivity, and lack of piety prevented them from seeing the reality of the situation. They closed their eyes and opened their mouths, as the saying goes.

In any case I maintained my relationship with many inmates who were unhappy with the prevailing situation in prison. I held discussion sessions with some university students and talked to them about contemporary historical and political developments like the oil nationalization movement and the August 19 *coup d'état* in 1953, and shared some of my practical experiences with them. As a result the MKO's allegations against me created backlash, and my relationship with those students became even closer, and they looked up to me and asked me to teach them what I knew and lead them. This caused a great deal of anger among the leaders of the MKO, and they tried to end my relationship with those students. My advice to those students was that they should keep their independence of mind and never follow anyone or any organization blindly and always verify what they heard through grape-vine.

Once an inmate who was in charge of shopping for the commune asked me to recommend two men whom I trusted to help him in his duty because the MKO refused to accept those two inmates and accused them of buying food secretly for their own consumption. It turned out that what they ate "secretly" was some biscuits brought to them by their families on one of their visits to prison!

There was a master sergeant in prison from Hamadan by the name of Khodadadi. He was a sincere man, and the inmates loved him and often used a term of endearment (*Dada*) to address him. When he received a promotion he celebrated that with the inmates and bought some suits for them from the prison shop. When this story was leaked, the MKO made a big story out of that to prove the "dishonesty" of some inmates who supported me.

I went to those people who were spreading this story and told them that I was aware of the whole story and that the accusation was baseless and that they must apologize. When they heard my criticism they promised not to act like that again and asked me to mediate and end that incident right then. When I insisted that they should apologize, they refused and argued that if they did so, others would lose trust in them. They accepted their mistake yet still refused to apologize. When I threatened that I would tell everybody of their allegations, they begged me not to do so, and in return they promised to apologize on a more appropriate occasion. It was in this manner that they destroyed Lajevardi's reputation. When I confronted them in defense of Lajevardi, they admitted their wrongdoing but refused to apologize because they were afraid that an apology would enhance the reputation of Lajevardi and many more would join him.

Lajevardi was a self-made man. He was a firm activist and had a solid personality in terms of faith and commitment to struggle. We collaborated in some operations together. He never accepted the MKO's ideology, their objectives, or strategies. As a result, the MKO allowed itself to criticize and attack him. They even accused him being a SAVAK agent and openly cursed him. No one had the courage to investigate his background to find out how true the allegations against him were. The dictatorial grip of the MKO had killed objectivity in the minds of all their members. Members were to obey the orders of the organization blindly and without any question.

One day, one of the MKO commanders complained that prison guards constantly reported on them to higher authorities. He warned me to be alert. I told him that they a job to do and they should just perform their duty. He complained that the guards beat up prisoners, but when I asked him if he had seen it personally, he said he had heard from other people! This was the judgment of an educated man. I advised him to verify before believing such assertions.

In Ward Four some cells had a small storage-like that inmates used as a reading room. It was possible for a guard to pass through the cell and see a prisoner reading or writing. But they never disturbed anyone and quickly looked inside and went away.

Bizhan Jazani and His Doctrine[138]

The presence of diverse groups of political prisoners in the Qasr Prison provided an opportunity for me to know them and some of their leaders. Bizhan Jazani was one of these leaders

---

[138] Bizhan Jazani (b. 1316/1937) started his activities in the Tudeh Party of Iran where his father was also a member. A high-school drop-out, he established an advertising company known as Persepolis and was quite successful, followed by a film production company. He then completed his high-school education and entered the department of philosophy at the University of Tehran, where he formed his own political group. In 1346/1967 he was arrested and sentenced to fifteen years in prison, where he wrote two books titled *A Thirty-Year History* [of Iran], and *Everything that a Revolutionary Must Know*. He was executed on Farvardin 29, 1354/April 18, 1975. See, *Negah-i Now*, # 11 and 16, 1355/1976.

who claimed to be the leader of the Fidayan-i Khalq Organization, although the Fidyan did not acknowledge him as their leader. One day I received a pamphlet written by Bizhan in which he had presented an interesting analysis of the sociopolitical condition of Iran. According to him the most important duty of revolutionaries in the society was dual struggle against the regime on the one hand, and against religion on the other. Inside prison, however, it was important to fight against religion alone and identify those sincere and honest elements among the religious youth and protect them [against religion]. In his definition, "honest" and "sincere" referred to uneducated and simple masses among prisoners. He called anyone who knew something about religion "reactionary" and claimed that they lacked discernment, did not understand, and were not good for the revolution because they had "class connections" and were anti-revolutionaries, and therefore true revolutionaries had nothing to do with them.

Jazani believed that to become revolutionaries, the "honest" and "sincere" activists must become Marxists! And his real mission in prison was to turn prisoners into Marxist elements. It was on the basis of this argument that his supporters approached younger inmates and taught them Marxism, and engraved in their minds that "religion is truly the opium of the masses." In short, they did everything they could to persuade the youthful inmates to turn their backs on religion. When that happened the person stopped praying and fasting, but he didn't become a revolutionary. Indeed, after that all he cared about was playing soccer or chess and backgammon. At best, he would start learning a foreign language.

The strangest thing was that this kind of ideology was acceptable to the MKO as well. They argued that as long as a person was engaged in struggle, it did not really matter if he was an Islamist or a Marxist. In his analysis of the society, Jazani wrote that those activists who came from the *petit-bourgeois* class might continue their struggle up to a point, but when their own class interest was threatened, they would join the counter-revolution. He used this argument in persuading the younger activists to embrace Marxism. Since Jazani was determined to fight against faith and religion, he wrote that the most important duties of his comrades in prison were to set aside inter-group conflicts and unite against religions and religious forces.

There were more Marxist groups in prison than Islamist (Fidayan-i Khalq, the Red Star, Tudeh, Saka', Palestine, Tufan, and so on). Every four or five of them formed their own groups, but despite Jazani's doctrine they were far from being united. Each group was concerned about its own interests. The only sign of unity among them was during mealtimes when they sat together to eat. They could never be politically united, because each group viewed itself as the center of the universe. For example, Paknezhad claimed the leadership of the Palestine group, whereas many members did not acknowledge him as their leader.

The Sho'aiyan Group

The only Marxist group that never openly opposed the Islamist groups was the People's Democratic Front of Iran. It only had a few members in prison. The leader of this group was Mostafa Sho'aiyan,[139] who was killed in a fight. Some members of

---

[139] Mostafa Sho'aiyan (b.1315/1936) a graduate of Tehran Polytechnic School of Engineering, started his political activities with his interest in Marxism. Along with Nader Shaygan he founded the People's Democratic Front of Iran and later joined the Fidayan-i Khalq Organization, but as a result of ideological differences he left the organization and started independent activities. He was a diligent writer and produced more than twenty books, the most important of which include *A Thesis for Struggle Today, Dr. Mosaddeq and the Tudeh Party, On Revolution, The USSR and the Jangali Movement in Iran*, and *Let us Not Kill Self-Criticism in Marxist Ideology*. He was wounded in a conflict with the police in Bahman 1354/Feb. 1975, and before they could arrest him committed suicide by taking a cyanide capsule. On his life and activities see Hooshang Mahrooyan, *Mostafa Sho'aiyan: The Lonely Thinker*, Tehran: Baztab Publishers, 1383/2004.

this group, like Bizhan Farhang-Azad, Akbar Pur Ja'fari, Abdullah Anduri,[140] and a few others maintained cordial relationships with the Islamist prisoners. One reason was that other Marxist groups did not consider the Sho'aiyan group to be Marxist, but Trotskyite, and therefore were not on good terms with it. They were isolated from other Marxist groups. I often talked to some of the members of the Sho'aiyan group. In general they had a good attitude towards me and their behavior was cordial and respectful. In contrast to other Marxist groups they never insulted Islamist inmates, nor did they express dislike toward them. Of course, this group agreed on one principle with the other Marxist groups in that "religion was the opium of the masses." They were all in agreement in their fight against the Islamist forces, but their styles and tactics differed. Some of them believed that religion must weakened and set aside in a slow and long process, while some said that it must be fully destroyed after the [victory of] revolution. Others thought that religion would automatically become extinct with the development of knowledge, while still some others believed that the tree of religion must be destroyed from the root.

Cyrus Nahavandi: Banging Your Head against a Brick Wall

Cyrus Nahavandi[141] was the leader of the People Front for the Liberation of Iran. SAVAK forced him to collaborate with

---

[140] Abdullah Anduri was a petroleum engineer and political activist who was arrested in 1352/1973.

[141] Cyrus Nahavandi was originally a member of the youth organization of the Tudeh Party who studied in Germany. Reportedly the party sent him to China and Cuba for training. He returned to Iran and founded an independent group called the Liberation Organization of the Iranian Peoples. He was arrested in Azar 1350/November 1971, could not tolerate SAVAK torture, and allegedly began to collaborate with them. As a result many members of the group were thus arrested, executed, or killed in street clashes with the police. Later, Tehrani (Bahman Naderi), the notorious interrogator and torturer of SAVAK, revealed in his trial that Nahavandi in fact had collaborated with the SAVAK. Nahavandi fled Iran and reportedly went to the U.S. Some observers believe that currently he lives in Europe and is writing his

them. As a result of his treason, between 150 and 200 activists were introduced to SAVAK. This was the first group that resorted to armed operations to confiscate money from the Irano-British Bank. They had also planned to take hostage the American ambassador in Tehran in 1349–1350/1970–1971. But after a while they abandoned political activity and with the money they had stolen went to Reza'ie'yyeh (Urumiyyeh) and started a cattle farm. They claimed that they wanted to work with the masses and ordinary people! Toward the end of 1350/1971 and during 1352/1972 members of this group were arrested very easily. SAVAK spent a lot of time re-indoctrinating them. Some members of the group such as Akbar Izadpanah, Manuchehr Nahavandi, Rahim Banai, and Cyrus Nahavandi, who had returned from abroad, were well known figures. Among them only Rahim had a political agenda and remained steadfast until the end.

In the beginning when they were arrested, their number was not more than forty or fifty. SAVAK managed to quickly get a confession from each one of them and collect a lot of information. Their trial was open to the public. Although, on the basis of their confessions, the court could have condemned some of them to death, none of them were. Instead, the death sentence was reduced to life-imprisonment. During their trial they condemned armed struggle and stated that in Iran armed struggle was like banging your head against a brick wall. That was the reason their sentence was reduced. However, none of them spent two or three years in prison and were released. Interestingly, the leader of the group, Cyrus Nahavandi, was released before his trial. Rumor had it that he had escaped from the hospital.

After that for some time he collaborated with the Fidayan organization and reportedly passed on some information about them to the police. The great blow that the members of

memoirs. See Koorush Lasha'ie, *Memoirs*, pp. 179–181; Iraj Kashkooli, *Memoirs*, pp. 163–168, Kamalvand, *Seven Thousand Days*, vol. II, pp. 279–282.

the Fidayan-i Khalq group suffered during those years was because of him. Yet, when he could not continue to work with the Fidayan, he tried to revive the People Front for the Liberation of Iran and recruited 200 to 300 members, among them some people who had received military and ideological training in Cuba, Vietnam, and other communist bloc countries.

In 1354–1355/1975–1976 some members planned to carry out operations, but Cyrus Nahavandi opposed them. The members gradually began to be suspicious of him and realized that he was not trustworthy. The Central Committee concluded that Cyrus was not a reliable member and planned to assassinate him. But a member who was present in that meeting and had feelings for Cyrus informed him of this decision, and Cyrus in turn informed SAVAK. SAVAK attacked the groups team houses, killed eleven and arrested eight of the members. This incident was publicized, and the arrested members were put on trial. This trial also was open. All those arrested were remorseful and asked the court to pardon them. It turned out that some of these individuals were police agents and caused much trouble for inmates in Qasr Prison. I think Cyrus fled the country and is still abroad.

My Ultimatum to the Mujahidin-i Khalq

My appeal court was scheduled nearly a month after the first hearing. It involved a re-examination of my file and answering questions from the prosecutor and the presence of a lawyer. In this hearing, all procedures went on just like in the first one with the only difference being that now it was shorter and more summarized. My lawyer made the same statement he had in my first hearing and I, too, went on pretending that I was innocent. At the end the initial verdict was reiterated and I was sentenced to fifteen years in prison.

I described the environment that the MKO had created in prison before. It turned out that they classified members of the organization into three categories. The first group included

292

those who pretended to be religious, but in reality they followed the Marxists. The second group was real Marxists and its members were steadfast in their Marxist beliefs and ideology. They included people like Mohammad Hayati, Mahdi Rajabi, and Hadi Mansuri. The third group was a small number of members who were pious, but out of fear of being boycotted they practice prudent dissimulation (*taqiyah*). They normally refrained from openly criticizing the organization. At the head of this group were members of the central cadre of the organization that included Rajavi, Khiyabani, Zulanvar, and Khoshdel. The last two were very pious and religious. They opposed and avoided attitudes and policies that weakened the organization. As for Rajavi and Khiyabani, their main concern was to establish and impose their leadership and control over the members. Their criterion for being a true revolutionary was unquestioning obedience to the order of the organization. This policy contributed to the weakening of the foundation of the faith of younger inmates and the strengthening of the position of the Marxist groups. They believed in the primacy of anti-imperialist activities even if it required collaboration with the Marxist groups. After my sentence was finalized in my appeal court, I knew that I would be in prison for a while, and the disagreements and objections that I had toward MKO leadership's dictatorial rule and its policies came into the open.

I was still considered a member of the MKO and continued to express my opposition to Ahmad Banasaz Noori, the Marxist who was the head of the MKO in Ward Four and Ward Five. In response, he spread accusations and rumors about me with the help of his friends. I requested that the Central Committee of the MKO appoint two people to investigate the charges he spread against me. Since MKO leaders were aware of my honesty and truthfulness, they never paid attention to my request to prevent embarrassment for Ahmad. After all, they had appointed him to the position. Even after that several times I requested to meet Rajavi and Khiyabani so that I could discus my grievances with them without any intermediary. Again they avoided me. They stated that they had a lot of work and not much time, and would leave this request to a more appropriate time. There were other reasons they avoided talking to me. They feared that I might use their own words and excuses against them. When they interacted with other people in the ward, they used unfamiliar vocabulary and sophisticated and difficult language. Since their audience often was unable to understand such words, they remained silent. But in relation to me they could not do that. Even though I did not have the same level of education as they did, since I read most of their books and pamphlets, I was familiar with their views and their language of discourse. Therefore, they were not able to use the same tactics and fool me. Whatever they said, I answered them with their own logic and reasoning. The Central Committee said that I should listen to and obey Ahmad, as he was my superior. Even if he made a mistake, I was not supposed to confront him directly and openly. I should keep quiet and bring it up with him later at an appropriate time. This was how the organization worked. I asked them when I faced trouble, what is the point of criticizing him, and said that if we did not stop this current from mistakes and deviations before it is too late, we would have to be prepared for a tragic end tomorrow; therefore, I did not approve of this style of policies for the organization.

Later on in Evin Prison, Rajavi, Khiyabani, and Hayati would get together and under a dim light secretly read some analysis that SAVAK had put at their disposal. I was certain that if that situation continued for another year, definitely Mas'ud Rajavi, just like Parviz Nikkhah, would surrender to SAVAK, and possibly would enter into the service of the regime.

One day I took Kazim Zulanvar[142] to a quiet room and talked with him for about an hour. Since he was a member of

---

[142] Sayyed Kazim Zu'lanvar (b. 1326/1947) was born into a religious family, received early education in religious sciences, graduated from the School of Agricultural Science of the University of Tehran, and became a

the Central Committee of the MKO, that meeting was important because some issues came out into the open. I told him that people in society identified the MKO members with the early heroes of Islam like Abudhar (Ghifari) Salman Farsi, Miqdad, and 'Ammar Yasser who spent day and night in prayer and were very pious. But when they realize that they spend their whole day playing chess and flirting with the Marxists, the masses will withdraw their support from them and the clergy and the Source of Emulation (*maraji'*) would stop funding their organization. Zulanvar told me the truth was that the MKO did not recognize the authority of the clergy and the *maraji'* in the first place. They did not believe in the practice of emulation (*taqlid*). In fact they considered religion to be an obstacle in their struggle. This was an eye-opening conversation for me.

In any case Zulanvar was the only person from the Central Committee of the MKO who was at least willing to talk to me and tell me the truth. The rest ignored me. It was around the end of Shahrivar 1353/August 1974 that coincided with the beginning of Ramadan that I had a meeting with Mohammad Mohammadi Gorgani, who was a high-ranking member of the organization. I told him that despite my frequent requests, Rajavi made excuses and avoided meeting with me. I gave him a message to convey to Mas'ud and warn him that unless he listened to what I had to say and came to an agreement before the end of Ramadan, I would leave the commune and the organization on *Eid*. This was a serious threat on my part. However, since they did not have convincing answers to my questions and criticisms and did not intend to come to an agreement, they resorted to playing new games. For example, they tried to use the help of those friends whom I loved and respected to change my mind and stop the criticism. One day

---

member of the MKO in 1347/1968. He was arrested after he was injured during a clash with the police and sent first to Qasr and then to Evin Prison. He was executed along with eight members of the Mujahidin on Farvardin 29, 1354/April 18, 1975.

Mostafa Javan Khoshdel came to me and said: "Ezzat! You are our pride and the symbol of our reputation. You are known in the bazaar and among the clergy, and it will have a destructive effect on the organization if you separate your path from us. Be patient! All of us have questions and criticisms from time to time. The inmates of the wards are not homogeneous. They also have differences with each other. One must be flexible in a situation like this. See for example Dr. Shaybani,[143] who also disagrees with us but doesn't disclose his position before the others. Follow his example." I told Mostafa that our friendship would remain intact, but he should not expect me to accept and follow the irrational and anti-religious style of the organization. I liked Dr. Shaybani and believed he was a very pious person and had a peaceful life. I also knew that he believed there were deviations within the MKO, yet he continued to remain silent. I did not support these tactics because he had a duty to enlighten others about it. It was his duty to spread the word and inform others. In my opinion if he remained silent he committed a big mistake, but that that was his problem, not mine. As for me, if the leaders came, talked with me, and accepted their mistakes, then that would be fine. I would be ready to help them in any way I could to improve the situation. But if they refused, I would separate my path from the organization. I would also declare in prison and in town that I no longer belonged to any group and organization. I would do my best as an independent and would accept responsibility for the consequences of my actions.

---

[143] Dr. Abbas Shaybani (b.1310/1931) graduated from medical school at the University of Tehran and started his political activities and joined the National Front, and was one of the leaders of the national movement in the 1950's. Arrested in 1335/1956, he was sent to exile in Mashhad where he attended Mohammad Taqi Shari'ati's circle. He spent thirteen years in prison until 1978. After the victory of the Revolution he held important posts such as membership in the Revolutionary Council and chancellor of Tehran University and served five terms in the national parliament. See Ahmad Ahmad, *Memoirs*, p. 178.

In any case Mostafa could not convince me and returned to his friends without success. Next, they sent Hajj Ezzat Khalili, who was often referred to as Hajj Khalili[144] He adopted a different strategy and warned me that I was unknowingly on the verge of committing treason, that the outcome of my actions would be disarray and factionalism, and that that would destroy the unity of Islamist forces. At the end he wondered if I were in a sound state of mind! On the one hand he blamed me, and on the other hand, tried to fool me and said that he also agreed with much of what I said, but invited me to be patient and remain with the MKO for one or two more years until I learned more about them, and then if I wished to leave them, I would do so with full knowledge of the nature of the organization and its leadership. I told him that he couldn't fool me. I told him that he knew damn well that I was not a traitor and never ever would betray the organization, but would face the leadership like a man and abandon them like a principled revolutionary.

I asked him why I should remain with the organization and act like a spy and change my mind a year or two after. I assured him that he could not force me to change my mind and that I made such a decision with full awareness of its consequences because the direction that the MKO was heading toward was crystal-clear to me, and that by doing so I could at least save my faith. I did not see any convincing reason to set aside my legitimate demands and wait for the unknown future. I asked him to leave me alone.

When these intermediaries failed to achieve their objectives and change my mind, they turned to their vain play and began a campaign of character assassination and spread

---

[144] Ezzatullah Khalili (b. 1311/1932) joined the Islamic Coalition Party, arrested in 1343/1964 and sentenced to eighteen months in prison. He was arrested later for collaboration with the MKO and imprisoned for another three-year term in prison to be released in 1355/1976. In 1978 he went to Paris and met Ayatullah Khomeini. After the victory of the Revolution he and all members of his family joined the MKO. He passed away in 1382/2003 after a long illness. Asadullah Lajevardi, *Memoirs*, pp. 27–28.

stories about me and claimed that I was thinking of leaving the organization for childish reasons and joining the assassins of [Hasan Ali] Mansur and having a good time with them. With these kinds of assertions they wanted to ruin my reputation and hurt my relationship with the Islamic Coalition Party. I mentioned earlier that some of the members of the Islamic Nations Party (Hizb Millal-i Islami) and assassins of Mansur had left the commune and carried out their duties separately without any interference of others. Since some of them were bazaar merchants and well-to-do, they received what they needed in terms of food and other things from home. In general, they had a better life than the rest of the prisoners. For these reasons, the Mujahidin had a hostile attitude toward them and cleverly worked against them behind the scenes. Fortunately, they could not use these kinds of assertions against me, because unlike the bazaar merchants, my family and I were not wealthy, nor did I have any visitors to bring me food and other things from outside. Even when occasionally my father and brother came to visit, they never had money to give me. Everybody knew from the beginning that I never bought anything from the prison shop. I used to eat prison food only and used whatever was available to all prisoners. Even when the prison served lentil soup for dinner and some prisoners refused to eat it, I ate it willingly.

When the Mujahidin continued to spread their story about me, I assured them that even if I left them I would never join the bazaar merchants to eat with them. When they failed, they came up with other allegations and claimed that the police would be more sensitive of the loners and would watch them more carefully. They argued that such a prisoner would be boycotted by others, and his only choice would be to turn to the police and collaborate with them. I assured them that I would never be alone and there would be many among the prisoners who thought like me, and they would live with me. This response frightened them even more as they worried that I might form my own group.

In the process of all these exchanges and before they could decide what to do about my ultimatum, I was transferred to the JCCT prison in the middle of the month of Ramadan for the second time and in an unexpected manner.

*   *   *

CHAPTER SIX

Nights in the JCCT Prison

Caught in Purgatory (*barzakh*)

The disputes and conflicts between members of the MKO and me, along with their unethical and cruel attitude towards me, disillusioned me and caused much emotional stress and psychological exhaustion. The sad thing was that all these disturbances and difficulties were inflicted upon me by people that once claimed to be my comrades and ideological brothers and friends. Even though my level of patience and tolerance was very high, sometimes I became so stressed out that I wished they could send me to a far-away prison in another city, or transfer me to solitary confinement for a few years.

In the middle of the month of Mehr 1353/September 1974 they transferred me from Qasr to the JCCT prison along with Kazim Zulanwar, Mostafa Javan Khoshdel, Mohammad Sadiq Katouzian, and a few others. This transfer took place when I was emotionally traumatized, and this measure only made my condition even worse. Of course, the main cause of this stress was my anxiety and fear that new information about other activists would fall into the hands of the police, or other connections would be discovered. Before my transfer from the Qasr Prison, I had heard that a few members of the MKO had been arrested. I was afraid that the new prisoners would reveal more information about me to the police. The other possibility was that my transfer to the JCCT Prison might have been decided as a result of the information a new prisoner who had been transferred from the JCCT Prison to Qasr had put at police disposal.

During the time that we were in the team house in Mashhad, I often came to Tehran to get hand grenades from

301

Murad Nankali,[145] who had also provided a handgun for me. Murad was arrested in 1351/1972 just about one hour before my arrest. He was interrogated, tried, and imprisoned in Qasr. By Isfand 1353/March 1974 when only a few weeks of his term remained and he was supposed to be released soon, he was again transferred back to JCCT Prison. This was two to three weeks before our transfer.

Nankali's two friends from Hamadan who had been arrested disclosed much information about me to the police. They said that in 1350/1971 they had sold weapons to Murad in Mashhad. It was logical for me to conclude that my transfer to JCCT Prison was connected to their arrest. In fact I was right. Even though Nankali resisted bravely under torture, he had to admit that he gave the weapons to someone. He could not endanger other activists' safety, and since he was aware that I was in prison and that I had already been tried and convicted, he had decided to disclose information about me. It was true that I had taken the weapon from him. So my situation became even more complicated and critical. Nankali had been really tortured badly and had resisted well. Apart from giving me a gun, there was nothing else that he confessed. Anyway, I was not in a good situation.

It was around noon when we arrived at the JCCT Prison. But our interrogation was not to start until the next morning. All my preoccupation during those hours was to decide what the best strategy would be to adopt so that like last time I would not give any information about others and be consistent in repeating the false information I had given before. That night, I did not sleep at all. I kept on walking around that small cell. Since I had gone through so much psychological stress

---

[145] Amir Murad Nankali (b.1328/1949) started his political activities when he joined small religious organizations like Ansar al-Hossein and Khamsah Tayyibah. He was introduced to Akbar Mahdavi, Kachu'i, and Ezzat Shahi and joined the MKO. He was arrested in Isfand 1352/March 1972 and was sentenced to a two-year prison term. He died under torture on Shahrivar 19, 1353/August 9, 1974.

and my mind was so exhausted, I thought perhaps I had better give the interrogators misleading information or tell them that I had committed a murder, or something like that so that they would quickly try me and execute me and I would be free of all troubles and tragedies I had been facing.

There were nine of us together in that cell. Other than myself, Zulanwar, Behruz Shuja'iyan, [Javan] Khoshdel, two or three members of the Jazani group had come from Qasr Prison, in addition to three or four prisoners who were already there. When they saw me so preoccupied and distressed, they asked me what was wrong, and I denied that there was any problem. Mostafa [Javan Khoshdel] tried to comfort me and said: "Ezzat! I know that you are afraid neither of being beaten nor tortured. But tell us, why are you so unhappy? I am sure that it is not because you are afraid. Anyone who comes to prison expects to receive his share of beating and torture. Obviously the degree of tolerance and endurance before torture varies from person to person. So even if two people are arrested and brought to prison because of the weakness of others, it is not a big deal."

I assured him that I was not disturbed or stressed out because of those issues and that the dilemma I was facing was about life and death. I told him that I was stressed out because I was trying to make a decision about my life or death.

Even Mostafa never understood what I was trying to say and what my intention was. In short, that night I stayed up until four a.m. thinking about and reviewing the challenges and issues that I faced. Near dawn I felt a breeze of fresh air in my heart and soul and once again I felt that God showed me the light at the end of the tunnel. God took my hand and saved me once more. I realized that I was not responsible for all members of the MKO and should stop worrying about them. After all, I knew I did not owe them anything. If I was concerned, it was because I was worried about their lives, but I had done my duties toward them and the organization. I had also warned them whenever I felt they might be in danger. So it was now up to them to either follow or not. I had warned them several times that if they continued their style of leadership and activities, people would turn away from them and they would be destroyed. So if they chose not to listen, let them do what they wished and see the consequences. It was no longer my business.

My own duty was to remain steadfast in my actions and not to disclose any information. If I was to die under torture, I would have reached my goal. And if I remained alive and was taken to the non-political prisoners ward, I would pick up my little belongings and isolate myself in that ward and live a quiet life. Anyone who wished to talk to me and accept my position could follow me, and I would bring him/her into my world. I would not interfere in other people's affairs. I would let others do as they wished. I did not have any personal interest in anything that I had said up to that point. If I made any recommendations, it was for the sake of the preservation of the organization and its members.

Early next morning they brought breakfast that consisted of bread, cheese, and eggs. It was either the sixteenth or seventeenth of the holy month of Ramadan. I didn't eat anything because I was fasting. It was around eight o'clock that someone came and asked me to go with him. Before I left my cell, Mostafa (Khoshdel) said goodbye to me. And he added that we might not see each other again! Perhaps he had a feeling that I would not return to that cell again.

When the interrogation began, they separated all of us from one another. During interrogations they often tortured prisoners, and when they returned to their cells, most were injured and suffered pain. They covered my head with the overcoat that I wore and took me to the interrogation room. When they took the cover off my face, I saw the interrogator. I greeted him. The interrogators were not the ones who had been present in the previous year (1351/1972). They were much younger. One of them asked, "Why have they brought you here?"

304

I said, "I do not know the reason. You asked me to come here."

He said, "Don't you think that you have not yet disclosed everything that you knew?"

I said, "In fact some of the things that I said in the past were lies."

He angrily said, "Why did you lie?!"

I said, "What did you expect me to do with all that beating and torture?! I was beaten to such an extent that I had no choice but to lie. When a human being can no longer take torture and stand the pain, he will do anything to stop the torture. I, too, when I realized that I could no longer put up with the beatings, I told myself that it was no longer a significant matter to lie and accept responsibility for some of the things that I had never done, even if it meant four more years in prison rather than dying in the hands of the torturers. Anybody in my position would have done the same, even you, Mr. Interrogator! Beating is good to tame a donkey, not a human being!" I said these words because of the decision I had made that morning. I was determined not to disclose any information even if that meant dying under torture.

The interrogator pulled his chair in front of me and sat down. He spread his legs and placed them on my knees. I threw his legs down and told him, "Excuse me! I am also a human being just like you are. In fact, my leg is in deep pain!

He said, "Oh! So you have also tasted pain?"

I said, "I was shot six or seven times in my leg and it broke. It still hurts because it is not quite healed yet. So if you have something to say, tell me, and if not, there is no reason for you to place your legs on my knee!"

He said, "We received the revelation last night that you have not yet said everything you know, and that is the reason we have brought you here so that you talk! If you lied earlier, you have a chance to correct it now."

I said, "I do not think that you are in a position for an angel to come in your dream and give you a revelation."

He said, "And why is that so?"

I said, "The angels only go to the infallible people, the Prophet and Imams. Neither you nor I am infallible."

He replied, "Anyway, we are aware that the things that you said in the past were nonsense, much less true. Now I want you to assume that you have just been arrested this moment. You must sit down and write your life story from the beginning until now. The more you pay attention and write the truth, the better for you."

I said, "The things that I said earlier on and wrote are no longer in my memory. So if you wish, you can bring my file for me to write it again. I have nothing new to add to my previous statement."

He said, "So, you shall not write?"

I said, "No, because I have nothing to write!"

Suddenly he exploded: "Your activities are not limited to one assassination or two. You have committed so many acts of terrorism. You participated in many explosions, and you recruited many people for your organization! You had your own group, you exchanged and bought and sold weapons, and much more!"

I just broke into laughter, and this made them so angry. He slapped me on my left and right cheek before kicking me until he got tired. He said, "You fool and son of a fool! Do you think you are dealing with children here? Like a good child, sit down and talk. Tell us who you gave the weapons to that you received from Nankali. He told us everything."

The man thus played his last card. I said, "Nankali lied to you. You tortured him so much that he lied and made up stories against me!"

He said, "The game is over. Why don't you say everything you know?"

I said, "I have already said everything that I knew."

A man named Mohammadi[146] was my main interrogator, and Manuchehri, Rasuli, and Arash were his collaborators. When he finished, another one took over. In the past, there was only one interrogator at a time and I only provided answers to him, but this time there were several of them together. Perhaps the reason was that each of my friends who had been arrested disclosed some information about me to their interrogators. Therefore, all four of them wanted to question me together. When one let go of me, the other one took over and started questioning me. When they realized that their efforts were useless, they decided to form a round table and question me. They asked me to sit in the middle of the room, and they surrounded me and started to question me more.

Just like a frog that first the hunter confuses and then captures, each of the four men asked a question, but before I answered him the next interrogator would throw his question, but none of them ever waited for my answer. From the type of their questions and the way they questioned me, I realized that some things must have happened and a lot of information must have been leaked to the police. Even though they bluffed a lot, it was clear from their tricks that they knew more than what Nankali had told them. In this session, I said nothing. They called the guard to come and take me back to my cell.

Before I left the room I addressed Mohammadi and said that I did not have anything new to say and that he had better leave me alone and not bother me, unless he wanted me to lie, and if that were the case I could make up stories as much as he wished and save him the trouble of beating me up. I added that when the truth did not matter, there was really no difference between accepting responsibility for two assassinations or ten. I even added that I was willing to accept the responsibility for *all* assassinations by all revolutionaries. I would write whatever he wished and put my signature under it.

---

[146] Mohammad Tafazzuli, known as Dr. Mohammadi and "The Handsome Mohammad" was the interrogator at JCCT who later was promoted to Chief Interrogator.

Mr. Mohammadi replied, "Stop talking nonsense. Just write what is true."

I said, "If that is the case, then I do not have a thing to say, and in fact my emotional and psychological state is bad. My concentration is poor. I have nothing to tell you."

He said, "I will give you some time to go and think properly then come back."

I said, "If I remember something that I had not said before, I will write it down."

He said, "How much time do you need that you expect us to give you?"

I said, "One week."

I had realized that a lot of things had been disclosed to the police up to that point, and if these things could be proven, then matters would be even worse. I asked for one week in order to plan and find a way to commit suicide. Then Mohammadi called the guard and told him to take me to Mr. Hosseini and tell him to give me one week and a bed so that I could think clearly and let him know if I remembered anything.

Hosseini, the Torturer[147]

Until that date I had not met the famous torturer, Mr. Hosseini, but I had heard about him and his cruelty. I knew that my case could have not ended just so easily and that these people were not naïve so as to be easily fooled. But I tried to comfort myself by keeping my hopes high that they had other priorities, and a week's delay to get back to my case was not a big deal for them. I convinced myself that since I had been in that prison for over a year and a half, therefore, I was not their imme-

---

[147] Mohammad Ali Sha'bani, known as Dr. Hosseini (b. 1302/1923), the notorious interrogator and torturer, entered the army at a young age and transferred to SAVAK in 1336/1957. In 1352/1972 he moved to the JCCT. He was the most ruthless torturer of SAVAK. He committed suicide after the Revolution and died in 1358/1979. See *Kayhan Daily Newspaper*, # 10663, Ahmad Ahmad, *Memoirs*, p. 249, Muhtaj, p. 35.

diate priority, and I decided to believe that they indeed had given me a whole week to think! How naïve I must have been!

Anyway, the guard put my overcoat on my head to cover my eyes and took me to the lower floor next to the entrance to Hosseini's office. I noticed that there was a long line of prisoners waiting to be admitted. The strange part was that there were some prisoners who were so scared of Hosseini that they had already wet their pants even before seeing him. Some of them were crying. When it was my turn, Mohammadi addressed Hosseini with a loud voice and said, "Mr. Hosseini! I have just sent your friend to you. Please take care of him before the others and let him go and rest afterwards." It was there that I realized that they had a plan for me.

Hosseini took the overcoat off my face. He looked at me and I also looked at him. He was a Dracula! For those who were not prepared, just seeing his scary face was a torture in itself. His eyes, beard, teeth, and everything were just horrifying. He was like a wild animal and not a human being! I was also shocked when I saw Hosseini face to face. I knew then that everything had changed.

Hosseini greeted me warmly and said, "Wow! My intimate friend, Mr. Ezzat! How are you?" I answered that I was fine. He took my hand and pulled me inside the room in a very respectful manner. He asked me to lie down on the bed and I did. Then he tied my legs to two sides of the bed and my hands over my head and said, "Don't say a word. Let me also not hear your voice. Whenever you want to talk, it is enough for you to shake your thumb." He then started to slowly whip me in cold blood. Every stroke was like a shock that took my breath away, and I felt excruciating pain even in my bones. Mostafa Khoshdel had told me that Hosseini was a stupid man and that he could be easily fooled. He told me that I should pretend to faint after a few strokes of the whip and he would leave me alone after that. After I had received about forty strokes of the whip, I started screaming and realized I could not take more. I remembered Mostafa's advice and pretended to faint. But he still continued whipping me, and I received another round of lashes, perhaps twenty or thirty more.

Hosseini was annoyed seeing the soles of my feet not swollen. Since I was a mountain-climber most of my life, and also walked barefoot during the whole time that I was in prison, the skin of the soles of my feet had hardened in the course of time. So no matter how hard he whipped me on the solse of my feet, they never got swollen. He became angry and said, "With these feet, you have really exhausted me! Why are your feet like this?"

I said, "Well, what can I do if they have hardened?"

During the short moment I pretended to have fainted, I no longer cried. Hosseini kept on whipping me and saying, "You will bring yourself back to consciousness! I am well aware that you are not the type of person who can faint. So do not fool yourself."

After receiving enough strokes of lashes I realized that this animal was not going to stop. So again I started to scream. I heard Hosseini saying, "See! I told you that you would bring yourself back to consciousness!" I continued to scream and when I ran out of breath and could no longer scream because of the pain, he said, "Well, do you now have anything to say?" I answered that I still did not remember anything, and if and when I remembered, I would definitely let him know. He then took me out of his torture chamber and asked me to jump up and down on my feet so that my feet would not get swollen. Normally, after a person was whipped, he would be forced to run around so that his feet would not swell up. I was still in this condition when Mohammadi came from the upper floor and asked Hosseini why I was allowed to come out of the chamber and added that only my corpse should be allowed to come out of that room.

Hosseini often worked alone in his office, but sometimes other interrogators came there too. This time Mohammadi joined Hosseini in his office. They threw me on the floor, and Mohammadi stepped on my face with his full weight and pressed his shoe on my mouth so hard that two of my teeth broke. This inhumane treatment of another human being was truly cruel. Many prisoners cried in such a situation, but I couldn't even cry, as though the tear glands had dried up and there was no longer any fluid in my body. Hosseini and Mohammadi whipped me so hard that my toe nails burst and came off my fingers. They also pulled out my fingernails on both hands. While I was in pain they threw me on the floor soaked in blood and forcefully poured water in my mouth. I spat in their faces. They never stopped their horrible acts. Then they became even wilder and poured some grains of rice in my mouth. They imagined that by doing so, they could force me to break my fast. In order not to give that pleasure I said that no matter what they did, even if they urinated in my mouth, still my fasting would not be nullified because breaking fast by force is not acceptable from the point of view of the *Shari'ah*. Finally, Mohammadi and Hosseini got tired of dealing with me, and Rasuli stepped in to "mediate" on my behalf. He said, "You have nearly killed this unfortunate guy. Let him rest a little. I am sure he will get up and disclose what he knows soon. In fact, I will talk to him myself." In situations like this usually one of the interrogators played the "good guy" and the other played the "bad guy." One of them pretended to play the role of Imam Hossein while the other played the role of Shimr. The ironic thing was that the one who pretended to be the good guy was the same man who had tortured me in the other room! I was not so stupid as to be fooled by their tricks. Finally, when they failed to force me to talk, they did not return me to my cell. In fact they just left me behind that door and I fell asleep with a mountain of pain all over my body.

Interrogators' Night of Power

That night interrogators and torturers returned and said that they could no longer continue and tolerate the situation and that they had to finish me off and warned that tonight would be the night of my martyrdom! So they took me out again, and after beating me up, they tied my legs together and hung me upside-down. After a while they came back and untied me and threw me on the floor. They then forced me to stand on a stool and tied my hands to long nails on the wall. They then pulled away the stool and left me there in a hanging position. My two wrists had to stand and support the full weight of my body. The ropes that were used were sinking deeper and deeper into the skin on my wrists every moment. Blood was no longer reaching my hands and they were turning numb. As though this was not enough, they began to whip me on the soles and the tops of my feet. They tortured me in this manner for around one hour, and then took me back to Hosseini's office. When they failed to get any words out of my tongue, they untied me and took me to the back of the cell. I fell half-conscious and lay there for the next twenty-four hours.

On the 19th night of the month of Ramadan (*Laylat al-Qadr*/the Night of Power) they came and took me away again. There were two or three new interrogators in the room. Their attitude had changed, and they dealt with me in a friendly and respectful manner. My hands and legs were severely injured and were dressed in bandages. I was unable to walk. I kept on crawling on the floor. They asked me a few questions, which I answered briefly. One of them said that they did not intend to torture me but only wished to ask a few questions related to religious matters and the *Shari'ah*. I said that I was not a jurist (*faqih*), nor a Source of Emulation (*marja'*). He said that he had heard that I had a treatise and hoped to become a Source of Emulation. I said that I would have been happy if that were the case but that was not possible because I did not have enough education. I am not a member of the clergy, but I have read the treatise Imam Khomeini wrote, and I am his follower. He then said that he was certain that I could answer his question. Then he raised a silly question: "If we get lost in the mountains and the weather is cloudy, how can we find the direction of the Ka'bah (the *qiblah*) to pray?"

I said that "a practicing Muslim can always find the *qiblah* if he only knows north and south. Moreover, why should you be concerned where the *qiblah is as you do not pray?* But if you decided to pray, any direction you faced would be fine and your prayer would be accepted."

He said, "You idiot! I am asking you a religious question. Even if I do not know what prayer is, I want to learn the injunctions of religion about my question."

I said, "OK! I shall explain it to you. If you have time, you are supposed to pray in all four directions. And if not, you should pray in a direction that you strongly feel is the right direction."

He said, "Very good. Suppose we want to slaughter a sheep in this condition. What shall we do? You are aware if we don't slaughter it in the direction of *qiblah*, consumption of its meat will not be permissible. We can pray in all the four directions, but is it also possible to slaughter a sheep in all the four directions?!"

I said, "As for you, in whatever direction you slaughter it, it becomes lawful for you."

He asked, "How is that so? Why should it be lawful?"

I replied, "A person who eats pork that has been prohibited for him should not mind if the sheep is slaughtered in a religiously sanctioned way or not!"

He asked, "Do you mean that we eat pork?"

I said, "Is it not so? The sausage that you eat has been made out of pork."[148]

He said, "Why are you talking nonsense? Give me a proper answer to my question."

I said, "Come on! You neither want to pray nor slaughter a sheep. But you should know that if you want to slaughter

---

[148] Production of hot dogs and baloney started in Iran in 1307/1927 by a Russian subject named "Afunsa." His main customers initially were foreign residents of Tehran, Armenians, and other religious minorities. Later several factories began production, such as Arzuman. See *Donya-ye Taghziyeh*, # 1, pp. 29–31, and *Goftegoo ba Jouzani*, 1384/1985.

a sheep, then you ought to slaughter it in the direction that you strongly feel is *qiblah*. This makes it lawful for you."

The other interrogators who witnessed this conversation were laughing. They said, "Look at the way this idiot answers questions! He is already an ayatullah himself! Imam Khomeini should come and ask this fellow about these legal matters."

I told them that they could not insult Imam Khomeini and I was proud to emulate him and be one of his humble followers.

Hosseini was not present during the early stages of this interrogation that night. They phoned him to come and he immediately took a taxi and after twenty minutes arrived there. They then took me to his room.

Hosseini started talking. He said, "Tonight you are the son of Ali [ibn Abi Talib] and I am the son of Ibn Muljam [Muradi, who assassinated Ali]. Tonight is the nineteenth night of the holy month of Ramadan (*Laylat al-Qadr*) on which Ali (a.s.) was struck with a poisonous sword by Ibn Muljam. So tonight is your night! We shall also strike you tonight. If you have a will to write, you can say it now!"

I said, "I do not have a will to write. I do not have any wealth to divide. I have also prayed and fasted at the appropriate times. So you are free to do as you wish."

That night they took all my clothes off and I was naked. They lit a candle and poured drops of melted paraffin on my skin. It burned and pierced my skin. At times they put the candle under my testicles or used a lighter and burnt my body hair. I was in excruciating pain. But as the fire burnt me, a good feeling began to descend on my heart and calmed me down. I felt an ocean of light in front of my eyes.

In the meantime, my torturers continued to pull out my hairs one by one with a nail clipper, saying, "*Tonight is your last night.*" They put on a tragic show that was ironically also comic.

There was a cabinet in the room where they kept first-aid kits. They would take a cotton ball, soak it in alcohol, and tie it around my big toe and then light it! It probably took two minutes for the cotton ball to burn around my finger. They would also take a piece of cotton, put it on my navel, and burn it. At times they would pour the cigarette ashes on my body.

There was nothing that I could do other than scream. I was screaming from the depth of my lungs, and in a way this reduced my agony and pain, but it was annoying the torturers. I had a feeling that the pain was good for me because somehow it brought peace and serenity to my soul. It was such a strange state. On the one hand the pain was killing me and taking all my strength, and on the other hand my soul was in deep and great joy and contentment as though it was about to unite with my beloved. The torturers called me a beast. They continued to keep me naked and in a hanging position. Sometimes they even whipped me on my genitals, which were so swollen as a result that they referred to me as a donkey!

In light of this situation I felt that I had nothing to lose, so I became very aggressive and talked back to my torturers and defied them at every moment. I even exaggerated in treating them with the same degree of insult they treated me with. As a rule, in early phases of interrogation one was to act with caution. I did not need to impress anyone and play the role of a hero. I was in a phase of my life when nothing really mattered and was beyond all considerations. I was at a point of no return and saw death imminent. I was determined to break the soul of my torturers, and they wanted to break mine. The outcome was not what they expected.

On that night of the nineteenth of the holy month of Ramadan I really drove my interrogators crazy to the extent that they all got severe headaches. They took pain-killers one after the other. Finally, one of them said, "You Son of a——! You have driven us all crazy!"

I was aware that my interrogators had received a lot of new information from the other prisoners who had confessed, but they never wanted to tell me anything. So I decided to play their game as well, and told them that since they planned to use force, I would accept everything they accused me of committing.

They constantly cursed at me and insisted that they know everything. I told them but they wanted me to tell them something new. They claimed they already knew everything I had told them as to who printed and who distributed declarations and books, but wanted me to tell them what they didn't know. They also claimed that as a rule they only have 30% of the information about individual activists at the beginning of an interrogation. The remaining 70% was always put at their disposal by the prisoner himself. They were so desperate that they even said they did not expect 70% of the information from me and that they would be happy if I gave them only 20% of what I knew.

Hooshang Tahami was one of my former interrogators in the JCCT Prison. When I was being transferred from JCCT to the Qasr Prison, he told me that he liked and admired me because of my resistant under torture. On the night of the nineteenth of Ramadan, again he interfered in my case and wanted to play the role of a friend and a mediator. In short, he wanted to improve my relationship with the other interrogators. They tortured me in every way they wanted until two a.m. When they realized that conventional torture would not work on me, they took me to the Apollo room. All interrogators left the room. Apollo was an arm-chair with a wide seat, and when I sat on it, my legs from the knees remained hanging down. I spread my arms on the armchair, and they used nuts and bolts and tightened my hands on it. As they were tightening the strap on my hand, the screws also pierced my hands and legs and really squeezed my nerves. The pressure on my arm was so bad that I thought blood was going to gush forth from the tips of my fingernails any moment. This time the pain was even much more than that of the lashes of the whip. My hands kept on aching, and all my nerves from the tips of my toes to my brain were in deep pain. They reduced the pressure on my right hand because it was going to swell and there was no way I could write my confession with a swollen hand.[149] After fastening my hands and legs, they placed a cone-shaped cap on my head that hung over my face and touched my throat. Then they started whipping me on the feet. When I screamed, the echo of my own voice would reverberate and bounce back into my head, and this deafened my ears. I was neither able to endure the pain of the whip nor to stop screaming. There was no other opening in the cap to let the sound come out. Sometimes they banged the cap on my head. The sound and echo from the cap gave me an unbearable headache and made me dizzy.

Torture on the Apollo[150] was real and very painful as they continued to adjust the screws on and off. After I had been under Apollo torture for a while, Hooshang came and said, "Ezzat! I am your friend. I did not allow them to continue with this torture."

I was angry and told him that I did not have a friend in that place and that he and everybody was my enemy there. In fact I told him that he was the worst because he claimed to be my friend, yet he wanted to kill my soul and destroy me. I also added that if he were telling the truth, then why was he allowing them to torture me to this extent? I said, "The things that you were doing to me were things that an animal could not do to another animal. Why are you beating me when I have done nothing? To tell the truth, there is nothing wrong that I have done."

These words really angered him and brought out his true nature. As he began to curse he said that I had a lot more

---

[149] In an interview Ezzat Shahi stated, "After three decades I am still unable to use my left hand properly, and whenever I remember those days, I get panic attacks and feel the pain."

[150] Apollo was one of the most painful torture techniques used in prisons during those years. They put a long metal hat on the prisoner's head and hit on that. The noise that was thus created was deafening. When they added electric shocks to it it became even more painful. This instrument was made in Sweden.

information to give, not just a piece here and there. The he pulled back and tried to control himself so that he could play the role of a mediator again. He said that he wanted to help me: "Tell other interrogators what I tell you now, but they should not find out that I told you these things. This is just between you and me." He was aware that I was not a fool and that I could read his mind and knew his plan, but he still tried, hoping that he could convince me. Again he said the reason he wished to help me was that he liked and admired me for my resistance. He added that if other interrogators found out what he had told me, it would cost him dearly. Again I told him that I had nothing more to say but would listen to whatever he had to say, and if any of that were true, I would admit my guilt. Again he cursed me and called me a bastard but did not continue the conversation.

The interrogators spent a lot of time with me that night. After whipping and putting me on the Apollo, they took me out of Hosseini's room and forced me to run around so that I would not get blisters on the soles of my feet. Then they hung me upside-down as before. It was around three or four a.m. that they got tired and were falling asleep. To pretend that they were religious and intended to fast, they ordered *suhur*. Rice and kabob and beverages were brought for them. As they ate, I was still hanging upside-down, very weak, and half-conscious so much so that I didn't notice when they wrote things on my belly with a ball-point pen. When they finished their food, they rested a little. Since they were also exhausted and realized that they would not get any information from me in this condition, they whispered and loosened my hands and threw me on the floor. They wanted me to eat their leftovers, and no matter what they did, I refused. Finally, they forced me to lie on the floor and pushed a spoonful of rice in my mouth, but I spat that into their faces and said that I preferred to die but would not eat their leftovers. Although I was weak and powerless, I felt strong and I never showed weakness. Even if they had given me good food, I would not have eaten it anyway, unless

318

they had given me the same food those other prisoners were given.

In any case, eventually they took me to room number 22. The floor of this room was wet and was uneven. I was fully naked. They showed me the room and ordered me to write. I sank to my knees, covered my genitals with one hand, and held a pen with the other. The room was very cold, and my lips and teeth were shaking. Hot air that came out of my nostrils and mouth spread steam through the room. My hands and body were trembling. The cold weather affected my whole body, including my brain. It was impossible for me to write. As I was shaking, I told them that I couldn't write. So they started asking questions, and I answered them, and they wrote down my answers. When they saw that my information was nothing new, they became angry and tore up the papers. They cursed me more and hit me with a few more lashes of the whip on my knees and feet. Then they took me to the lower floor, threw me into a cell, and covered me with a blanket. Covered in wounds, my entire body was swollen and in excruciating pain. I covered my head with the blanket, but I was still shivering. After a while, my body became a little warm, and despite all the pain that I felt, it didn't take long before I feel asleep. This was how I spent the nineteenth night of the holy month of Ramadan. That night I truly experienced the meaning of the *Laylat al-Qadr*.

The Interrogators: Their Character and Morale

Hosseini, Manuchehri, Mohammadi, Arash,[151] and a number of other interrogators spent the nineteenth night of Ramadan

---

[151] Fereidoon Tavangari, known as Arash (b. 1329/1950), was employed by the SAVAK in 1352/1973. He was the commander of operations and special interrogator in the JCCT. He was brutal and exaggerated in torturing his victims, many of whom were female. He sexually abused many female prisoners. After the victory of the Revolution he was arrested and executed in Tir 1358/July 1979. See Iskandar Deldam, *Memoirs*, pp. 129–131, Muhtaj, *Memoirs,* pp. 35, 62–63, 74–75, & 141.

torturing me! Arash was not my interrogator, but he just came to be involved in my case. Once I yelled at him and said that my case had nothing to do with him and he had no right to beat me up. He said, "So you don't know, but do you want to know who I am and what my job is?"

I said, "You are one of those spoiled gigolo boys who wanders the streets from morning to night just to pick up girls. I don't care who you are, but know that my case is none of your business because you are not even qualified to question me!"

So it was because of this exchange of words that he developed a deep hatred toward me, and whenever he came across me, he disturbed me one way or the other, even if it were simply pinching and pushing me or spitting at me, or anything else that he could do. I always reacted whenever I saw him and argued with him. Often he said that he hated how I looked. In response, I told him that I couldn't care less.[152]

Since my information was no longer important and urgent for the interrogators, they often took me to torture when there was no other suspect in line. They wanted to deal with me without any disturbance and when they had nothing else to do. Therefore, they often came to me on Friday or other holidays and in the middle of the night. On all those occasions, they kept me fully naked to break my dignity and kill my morale. I tried to be strong and never reacted in an emotional way and even belittled them for their behavior. When they ordered me to remove my trousers, I removed my underwear as well. I knew that in those situations if I showed sensitivity to exposing my body, they would become more aggressive and would harass me even more. Therefore, I showed no emotion, and in

---

[152] In an interview in Bahman 1358/February 1979 Ezzat Shahi stated, "The fact that in his trial Arash said that he was ashamed to look at my face and asked for forgiveness was because Ezzat Shahi had witnessed many of his victims under torture." Arash said, "Ezzat Shahi was one of the prisoners whom we tortured for over six months but he never revealed any information. I hope he would forgive me." See *Kayhan*, #10737.

fact I was relaxed. When they ordered me to get undressed, I removed all my clothes, and they would say that I had no shame and was willing to get undressed whenever I was asked! Once Mohammadi threatened that he would call the guard to come and rape me!

I said, "Why should you call the guard? Why don't you do it yourself!"

He became helpless and whispered, "Ezzat! How condescending you are!

I told him, "*You and your torturers have forced me to be like this! Otherwise, I would have not been where I am now.*"

This was the best way of answering them to make them feel ashamed. They knew very well that this was not my normal behavior, but they still got annoyed with my answers. My answers made them mad.

The interrogators had different characters and personalities, but in general they were all cruel. Occasionally, some of them became uncomfortable during torture. Sometimes, I felt that they ignored certain things. Some of them did not bother to spend too much time and energy with a prisoner and get exhausted. Instead, from the beginning they brought a person who confessed face to face with other suspects. They went straight to the point without beating about the bush.

Rasuli was among the political interrogators and performed his duty with a strategy and tricks of his own. Some others like Niktab'[153] (from the police department), Mohammadi, Manuchehri, and Arash had grown so wild and ruthless that even calling them blood-thirsty animals did not do justice to describing their characters. These were people who really enjoyed torturing people. Almost all the interrogators suffered from psychological problems and tension, and to relieve themselves of these pressures they drank alcohol heavily or used

---

[153] Bizhan Niktab' was another ruthless torturer from the police, especially famous for sexual torture. He was killed when his car was blown up by the Fidayan in 1352/1974.

drugs. All of them were chain-smokers. Judging Hosseini's ruthless behavior, it was obvious that he had a bad upbringing and a very difficult past. He would get angry if a prisoner uttered the name of Fatimah Zahra under torture. He would say, *"You can mention any name you want but do not mention her name. If you mention it, I will whip you to death!"*

There was also a division of labor among the interrogators. Religious prisoners were mostly interrogated by people like Mohammadi, Manuchehri and Rasuli. The Marxists were often interrogated by Tehrani and Arash.

The Scarecrow at the JCCT Prison

The next morning around eleven o'clock my interrogators again came after me. They started afresh with their work, whipping, torturing, and burning me. Their eyes were still red and puffy. It was obvious that they had not had gotten enough sleep. It also seemed that they had not had enough of torturing me. Again they forced me to run around the hall to prevent my feet from swelling. In front of each door, there was an interrogator standing with a whip in hand, and each of them hit me as I passed them. While I was running, the guards also ran after me. I could no longer walk because of the bullets that had been shot at my leg, the broken bones in my leg, and all the whippings that I had received. In the fourth round, I couldn't take it any more and threw myself on the floor and came down on my face. My lips and nose were injured, and blood gushed forth. The other prisoners who had been brought for interrogation could no longer see me because they had their backs toward the hallway. But of course some of them knew that I was being tortured and that the person screaming was no one else but me.

When I fell on the ground, the interrogators tried to lift me up. No matter how hard they whipped my back, I told them that I couldn't stand. At last they took my hands and legs and pulled me back into the interrogation room. There was no more strength left in my body. All I wished was to die. I was totally fed up, and to whatever Mohammadi asked me I replied in defiance. Again he slapped me in the face and shouted, "You son of a——! What is wrong with you? Answer my questions properly." But none of this worked. He threw the whip at me. I grabbed the whip with both my hands and gave it back to him. This really annoyed him. He again began cursing me. I thought that I had hit the target and had made him even angrier. An idea came to my mind that I should irritate them more so that they would whip me even harder and send me to my grave and I would be free from all these troubles. Perhaps this was the best idea.

Then something happened. I stood and threw the chair towards Mohammadi and it hit his face. He stood facing me. I broke the big glass window on the door and held a piece of that in my hand and shouted, *"You son of a——! Do you dare take one step forward? If you are man enough, then come on and hit me."* Suddenly several guards entered the room and everything changed. I injured the hand of one of the guards. They kept on shouting and saying, "This animal has become wilder than before. He has turned mad. Let us stop him." I was so angry and was sweating and breathing with difficulty. Several guards overpowered me and then tied my hands and legs. They were really afraid. Mohammadi's face was swollen. He attacked me and kicked me hard. When I felt that these were my last minutes alive and I would soon be free from all these pains, I really had a happy feeling. But this happy feeling did not last for long because they stopped beating me!

From that moment on, they never came near me again because they were afraid. Three or four guards carried me to the interrogation room again. When they saw that I had turned into a dangerous person and attacked them like a wild rooster, they decided to change their strategy and style of torture. On the third floor, there was a circular room with a broken box-spring in it. They took me to that room and tied me on that bed in a crucified position. They tied my legs from below the knee and locked them. They also cuffed my hands on both sides.

They covered my eyes and inserted cotton into my ears. Since my feet and hands were swollen, these straps really hurt me. There was neither a mattress nor a blanket underneath. I was just lying on the box-spring and they covered my naked body with a blanket. I spent that night, the next day, one week, two weeks and more in that position! I lost hope that my ordeal was to come to an end. The days and nights came and went by, but I still remained in this situation. They turned me into a scarecrow.

Whoever was brought for interrogation for the first time was brought to see me and learn a lesson. They would remove the blanket so that he could see the condition of my body. Of course they never let anyone see my face. I was supposed to act as an example to them. They told the arrested activists that if they wished not to go through my experience, they should speak up as quickly as possible. This way, they forced them to confess and accept all charges. I never said a word and never moved my body. To show the new prisoners that I was not dead, they would whip me twice in front of them and say, "You fool! Shake your body for these people so that they will believe that you are not dead!" I would then move my foot a little bit. I was ready to be beaten instead of new prisoners and was able to endure my beatings. But I could not stand seeing other people being beaten because that made me more nervous and irritated. The interrogators realized that this was my weak point. So when they wanted to torture some guys, they did it in front of me. This really made me sad and I begged them to take new prisoners away from my sight.

Among the people who were tortured in front of my eyes was Ali Reza Kabiri's mother.[154] 'Ali Reza was a mem-

---

[154] Ma'sumeh Shadmani (b. 1310/1931) was a housewife who became involved in political activity because of her sons (Hasan and Ali Reza). This family became members of the MKO in 1350/1971 when Mostafa Javan Khoshdel introduced them to the organization. When she was arrested in 1351/1972, she was tortured severely. After the victory of the Revolution she returned to the MKO along with her two sons and revolted against the Islamic Republic and was finally executed in 1358/1981. She was a legend-

ber of the MKO and one of my friends. Personally, I did not support Mrs. Kabiri ideologically because she was a tool of the MKO and they used her. But I have to say that in terms of resistance under torture, this lady surpassed many of the leaders of the organization. She was severely beaten but took it all very well. When she was being beaten, I felt so bad. I actually would have been happier to be beaten in her place. Anyway, they kept me tied to that bed under these awful conditions for around two months. During all that time, there were two guards appointed to keep an eye on me. They only opened my hands and legs once a day to take me to the toilet. Taking a shower was a luxury that I was deprived of. Throughout that period I performed my prayers in that condition. Every two or three days, they would come and beat me, torture me more, and burn me and then go away.

Contemplating Suicide

One day, an interrogator came and told me that it was my last day! The interrogators had decided that they were going to kill me. They had decided that either I would talk or face death! There was no other option left for me. I believed these words and thought that they wanted to do to me what they did on the nineteenth day of Ramadan. So I decided to end my life myself and not let these guys set their filthy hands on me. I had decided to commit suicide. To accomplish this, I checked the condition of my room and the way to the toilet. The only thing that was available to carry out this plan was the electric socket in the room. I doubted that it was working because there was a water cooler placed there that never worked. So I guessed that the problem must be the socket. I once asked the guard if the water cooler worked. He was wondering why I asked that question. I simply said that I never knew if it worked and he assured me it did. He plugged it into the socket and switched it

---

ary figure among female fighters for over two decades. See Muhtaj, *Memoirs*, pp. 311–312, *Zan-e Rooz*, # 756, *Babdad*, #240, pp. 9.

on and it started working. He then unplugged it. I realized that the socket in fact worked. So I planned what to do next.

During the day when they took me to the toilet, I did not waste any time. I kept the guards preoccupied, and while one of them faced the window I took advantage of the moment and quickly returned to my room. I broke that socket and grabbed the wire. The electricity shocked me and threw me on the bed. My hand was itching and I felt terrible. When I fell on the bed it made a loud noise. The guard came in and saw the situation. He started shouting and calling others to come and see what trouble I had put myself into. Several guards, officers, the interrogators, and even Zandipoor—the prison director—all came to see me. My interrogator Mohammadi was very angry. He said, "If you are a real man, stand up and go and touch the live wire again." I stood up and went to touch the wires again, but this time they stopped me. Mohammadi began to curse "You fool! Did you by any chance think that the electricity is not working here and that it cannot shock anyone?"

I wondered how the water cooler worked but the electric current did not kill me. Later I found out that Mohammadi was lying and I was not electrocuted because I wore a pair of plastic slippers. When they saw this condition, they attacked me with fists and kicks again and said that I could no longer go to the toilet and use the bathroom! But they could not put up with the mess I created in my room because whenever I relieved myself, their work doubled. So they decided to change their ways. One day they even gave me a cigarette to smoke. I told them that I wasn't a smoker. They acted in contradictory manners. One was kind to me while the other was cruel and rude. Another guard would come and comfort me, saying that even the interrogators were human beings and not wild animals. He added that if they knew that I was telling the truth, they would not harass me. Still another guard came and asked me questions. I only answered those that I felt were worth answering. Those questions that I deemed worthless, I only answered by saying that I did not have an answer and denied having any information to answer him. In short, I was quite alert.

During those two months that I was crucified on the bed, they brought me food on time. I ate very little in order to avoid going to the toilet frequently because I had a lot of doubts in my mind. At the same time it was difficult for me to clean myself and attain ritual purity. I therefore took soft food and liquids. Sometimes when they pitied me, they placed a blanket for me on the bed. Otherwise, I just lay directly on the springs with nothing separating my body from the bed.

It was during this situation that I began to talk to the guards. Some of them came close to the bed and spoke with me and asked questions about the religion of Islam. Some of them sympathized with me and advised me to talk to avoid more beatings and torture. On one day, one of the guards told me, "Ezzat! *Your friend is gone.*" I asked who he was talking about.

He said, "Murad. Was he not your friend and collaborator?"

I said, "Of course he was."

He said, "That is why I advise you to talk and free yourself from all these troubles. In short, this guy was beaten and tortured, and I don't know what happened to him that he died!"

I was really shocked to hear that news. Out of despair and hope, I doubted the authenticity of the story. One day, another older guard named Sattar, the one who was closer to me than the rest, came to shave me. I asked him to tell me more about Murad.

He replied, "Don't ask me!"

I urged him to talk and he said, "This guy was beaten and kicked many times in the stomach. It was as if his intestines were torn out, and he died."

I still didn't want to believe his words, even though there was no reason for him to lie to me. I thought for a moment and said that was is possible that these guys were trying to fool me. So I decided to be cautious and wanted them to bring him in face to face with me. Later on they pressured me to tell them what connections I had had with Murad. I told them that Murad was in their custody but they pretended that Murad was no longer in that prison and that he had been taken to Qasr Prison. I insisted that they should bring him to face me and I wiykd disclose everything and accept whatever he said.

Rasuli asked if I had any news about Murad's whereabouts. I said that I was in Ward Four or Five or Six, and Murad was in Ward Three. Manuchehri tried to confuse me and said, "You fool! Don't you know where Murad is?"

I said, "Well, if he is here, the better for me. He is close to me. So bring him here in front of my eyes and let him say everything."

Manuchehri laughed and said, *"You will never see him again. Never! But if you keep going in this way, you will soon join him."*

I said, "Then if that is the case, write that I confess to everything that he said." Thus, *I knew with certainty that Murad had lost his life under torture.*[155] Later on I found out that they had severely beaten him on the head and chest. They removed his eyes and crushed his teeth.[156]

---

[155] Hamideh Nankali, Murad's sister, claimed that they were unaware of Murad's whereabouts until the victory of the Revolution. She was in prison after 1353/1974 and there was no way she could contact her brother. Later she said that she had seen Murad's death certificate that recorded the cause of his death as stomach bleeding. *Interview with Hamideh Nankali*, Tehran, Aban 21, 1382/October 30, 2003

[156] Lutfullah Maysami was injured and arrested when a bomb exploded in his hand. He was taken to the hospital and placed on a bed next to Nankali's bed. In his *Memoirs* he wrote, "Nankali was beaten so bad that he fell unconscious and could not talk. He died in his bed next to mine." Maysami, *Memoirs*, vol. II, pp. 444.

The Night Party

One day, Mostafavi[157]—the head of the interrogation department —and my interrogator, Mohammadi, along with Arash,
Kamali, and two or three other interrogators came to have a
night party. They untied my hands and legs and invited me to
join them. They greeted me warmly and pretended to be
friendly. Mostafavi wanted to take advantage of my ignorance.
He said, "According to the information that I have, this guy
[Ezzat] is a good guy. Don't torture him more than this. We
really respect him for his dignity and character."

Mohammadi said, "Mostafavi spoke the truth. Even
though we are enemies and I am the person in charge of his
interrogation, and sometimes I beat him and he becomes angry
at me—yet despite all this, he is the suspect that I love the
most." He then cited an example and said, "Have you ever
seen that a person has ten friends but he only chooses one of
them to walk around with and go to the movies or parties
with? I too, have a lot of respect and love for Ezzat, out of all
the suspects who have been under my charge."

I started laughing sarcastically and said, "You are so
kind. May your kindness never end! It is in fact because of
your kindness and love that I am here. Were it not for that I
would be in the ward just like the other prisoners."

Mohammadi was shocked at my response. Mostafavi
changed the subject. They tried in vain to use my religious
sentiments against the communists or the MKO. Mostafavi
said, "Ezzat! You are aware that I do not lie, and I also know
that you are not a traitor but very patriotic, in fact, especially
you and other religious groups who are not dependent on any
outside power. We know that what the media report—that you
are the tools of foreign governments—are all lies and that in
reality you are very sincere and honest. We also have a duty to

---

[157] Mostafa Hirad, known as Mostafavi, was a SAVAK interrogator and
torturer who worked at the JCCT headquarters. See Sardar Sarfaraz, *Memoirs*, throughout.

329

accomplish. If our country does not ally itself with one of the superpowers, it cannot stand on its own feet. If the regime did not have a foreign source of support, it would have definitely fallen a long time ago. We also know that some of the people in high positions are thieves, corrupt and filthy people. We are all aware of these realities, but we are not in a position to do anything against them because they depend on the same foreign supporter that has protected the country [he meant the United States]. Well! Now in this situation you want to have guerrilla organizations and fight the regime. Let us assume that you take half of Iran under your control, and the Soviet Union comes to your help. Do you think that America will sit idle? The Soviets will attack us from the north, and America will attack from the south. In such a battle, it is only the poor people who will get killed."

Mostafavi's analysis was long and too shallow. He thought that I was simple-minded person and a fool and he could influence me by his words. He continued, "Whatever you do, consciously or unconsciously, will cause the Soviets' intervention and dominance over this land. The United States also will follow suit. So why do you want to have innocent and poor people pay the price and get killed because of your thirst for power? We cannot allow things to reach this point. I admit that there are a lot of shortcomings and weaknesses in the regime. You can go and write essays, criticize the government, and do anything else, but do not take arms to fight the regime. This is exactly what those foreign powers want you to do. So if you do that, we have a duty to stop you."

Mostafavi was showing off his knowledge of politics to impress other interrogators, but his analysis was baseless and shallow. I was not willing to answer him, and in my heart I was laughing at his simplicity, but had to control myself and maintain a serious attitude. Still I had to say something, and so I told him, "*You do not even possess the power to tolerate criticism.* Out of all these political prisoners, only a handful of them are involved in armed struggle, while the rest were only involved in distributing declarations, lecturing, and criticizing the regime, and keeping a few pamphlets. So why have you locked them up? You are only liars. As for me, there is no difference between America and the Soviet Union. I am not the puppet of either of them. I support neither of them. However, if this country is attacked by the Soviets or the U.S., you guys will be the first to run for cover. We are the people who shall remain behind and fight them."

I then pointed out the role of Iran in the Second World War and told him that it was the Iranian army that ran away. and that it was the people that fought the enemy and killed many Russians, and the government could not do anything. Nothing had changed, and if Iran were attacked, they would definitely run away. It would be the same poor people who would remain behind, fight, and prove their patriotism. "We are the people who love our country and cannot allow a part of it to be taken by anybody. We are not like you who say that you shall protect Bahrain and after two days you give it away! So we are not the ones that are the instruments of the superpowers, but it is you and the regime you support that are their tools and puppets. If I were in the government, I would not allow even a drop of our oil to be given to anyone. All our problems come from this oil. They are selling this oil, and the money that we get from it has to be spent the way they [foreign powers] want. Why should we—a third-world country— buy shares in German companies while our country needs this capital?"

Mostafavi said, "His Imperial Majesty in one of his speeches said that we have a duty to take care of the Western economies, because if we don't, they will collapse, and if they collapse, our economy will also collapse."

I said, "Yes, you are correct. They have already collapsed. They cannot stand on their own, and that is why you have to give them money so they can rise again and carry on their colonial policies. Isn't this stupidity, that for the sake of drilling oil, we have to seek help from foreign countries and

331

invest money in Britain so the British companies can drill oil wells in the North Sea? Does that mean that America and Britain do not have enough capital of their own to invest? So now tell me, is it we the people who are dependent on foreign powers, or you and the regime you support and defend? So admit that we have the right to fight this regime!"

I knew very well that my explanation would land me in more trouble. I also tried to make them believe that I was an ignorant person and that I just said these words without any intention. I kept on telling them that I was not an educated man, and so I did not want to be the president or prime minister by saying those words, and no one was going to give me a high position in the government, and I was just doing all this because of my religious obligation.

One of them tried to compliment me and said that all educated people, the doctors and engineers, should "come and learn from an *uneducated* man like you. You are a teacher to all of them. If you are the *uneducated* man of this nation, shame on all the educated ones."

Many discussions of this kind took place between the interrogators and me while at the same time they beat me up and tortured me. Since I often confronted them assertively, they always conducted the interrogations while I was lying on that bed so that other prisoners could not hear me and become aggressive. Sometimes they brought a chair and told me to sit on it. They would tie my left hand and place a paper on the arm of the chair on the right so that I could write while I wore the prison uniform that they gave me. I was always firm in my statement. If I decided that I didn't feel like writing, I would not change my mind. They were not able to keep up with me and left it to me to write whenever I wished and stop when I got tired. They would also tell the guards to let me go to sleep when I got tired. I wrote down the same things repeatedly as I had before: that we went mountain-climbing regularly, ate soup or dates, played games, went to movies, in such-and-such a place ate beef stew, etc. etc. I told them nothing new that

332

would be useful information. They then read my writings and took questions from the answers and asked for more explanation.

I had prepared my answers to their questions as far in advance as I could predict. They thought they were skilled and would finally extract useful information from me, but in reality I just made up stories and confused them even more each time. Sometimes they really got annoyed and became frustrated that an uneducated man like me could confuse them so badly. They knew that if they asked the same questions from an educated activist he would organize his answers in a systematic way, but they could not get anything from the answers I gave them. My answers were always vague and confusing so that I could justify them if and when somebody else gave them information about me.

One night, Mohammadi came to me and said that he had two questions, and I must answer them convincingly, and I accepted. I sat down and wrote the answers. Then they brought supper. It was a traditional Persian dish, a sort of beef stew with potatoes and garbanzo beans (*abgoosht*). After writing for about half an hour, I got tired. I asked the guard for my supper before it got cold. While I was eating the potatoes, the interrogator came and asked, "Is eating your supper more important than answering those questions?"

I said, "Obviously, supper is more important because I can write until tomorrow morning, but if this food gets cold, I can no longer eat it!"

He kicked the plate and everything in it spilled on the floor. He then said, "Now writing is more important."

I told him that I could no longer write. No matter how much he insisted, I refused to write. He got very angry and cursed for a while, and before leaving the room he told the guard to let me sleep and I went to bed.

The next night, the same scene was repeated. They brought me food and a piece of paper to write. This time I didn't eat but continued to write. It was around eight-thirty p.m. when the interrogator came in. He saw me writing. He took the paper and looked at it for a while, and then in an angry tone of voice said, "You are again writing nonsense. These are things that are of no help to us. You had better go to interrogation room and write there."

I said, "Even if you take me there, I have nothing more to write."

He wanted to leave the room, but I asked him to give me the bowl of beef stew to see whether I could eat it or not.

He asked, "Haven't you eaten your supper yet?"

I said, "No. Tonight it was important to write first."

I looked at the bowl and saw a thick layer of fat over the food. I put it aside and didn't eat. He insisted that I should eat but I refused. He took the bowl outside and gave it to the guard and told him to go to the kitchen and bring his food for me to eat. I insisted that I would not eat anything other than the food that is given to other prisoners. Mohammadi didn't listen to me, and the guard brought his supper for me. It was two skewers of Kabob, a piece of bread, some vegetables, and a bottle of 7 Up. He also ordered them not to give me onions. It had been almost two and a half years since I had last tasted meat and chicken. When the aroma of kabob filled the room, my mouth watered. I really wanted to eat, as I was very hungry. But just to frustrate Mohammadi, I controlled my desire for kabob and refused to eat. Even though I really wanted to eat the food, the joy of defying him was sweeter for me than eating. He insisted more, but I said in a sarcastic tone, "For me to eat that a kind of food, I would have to be an interrogator, while I am nothing but a humble prisoner who must only eat what other prisoners are given." Finally, Mohammadi got very angry. He placed his hands on his testicles and said, "To my testicles that you cannot eat these!" He then gave the food to the guard and said that I did not deserve it. I picked up my bowl of beef stew ate two potatoes from it and went to sleep.

Thirty Birds: The Case of Thirty Comrades

My attitude toward my interrogators angered them immensely, as few people had the courage to act as I did. Sometimes when a prisoner was arrested and wanted to resist, they severely beat him and warned him not to follow the example of "Ezzat." My interrogators, who were sick and tired of me, did anything they could to force me to give up and surrender. Sometimes new prisoners who in the past were connected to me or who had disclosed a bit of information about me were brought before me. Even if the information they disclosed about me was valid, I would deny everything to prevent others from being dragged into my case. I always reiterated what I had said before.

One morning, Mohammadi came and took me to the interrogation chamber. He slapped me on the cheek and asked me how long I wanted to continue this game. He insisted that my case was not closed until I told them everything I knew. In response, I always repeated that I had nothing more to say. Mohammadi said that there was also something that he was going to discuss with me and I should admit it if I did not wish to be beaten up again. I told him that if there was anything new about what he wished to say, I would definitely talk.

He said, "Tell me about the thin guy. Who is he?"

I was really shocked. I quickly realized that Mahdavi had been arrested again. Akbar Mahdavi had been sentenced to one and a half years in prison earlier. During the last days of 1353/1974, when he was scheduled to be released from prison, I had told him about my case. I had also given him a message to take it to Vahid Afrakhteh. The message was to inform Vahid that the thin guy had been introduced to the police by someone else, not me. By not mentioning the name of Hasan Abrari and our landlord in Mashhad, who had identified Hasan, I intended to prevent possible troubles for Akbar. I emphasized that if he were ever arrested again, he shouldn't mention anything about this message because I planned to deny everything. Particularly, I told him that even if he were tortured and forced to say something, or if he were brought to face me, he must claim that it was a lie. We took every precaution in order to save ourselves and also Akbar. They severely beat and tortured him, yet he told them nothing of great importance. But he was forced to confess that he knew about this message. Anyway, I told Mohammadi that I did not know what he was talking about.

He said, "Mahdavi has said everything."

I said, "Then he has lied to you."

He said, "OK! We shall see!"

They tied my hands behind my legs, and I could not stand. My back was also hurting. I slept in that posture in the corner of the room. Mohammadi tried to force me to stand, but I couldn't. He ordered Mahdavi to come in. We spoke for a while and then Mohammadi asked him to tell everything about that "thin guy."

Akbar said that he didn't know him, but this man (Ezzat) had told me him that if he saw Vahid, he should tell him that the "thin guy" had been arrested.

I said, "He is telling lies."

So after talking with me for one and a half hours, Mohammadi untied my hands and placed me on a chair. Mahdavi also sat on another chair. Then they gave each of us a whip and asked us to hit each other so that in the end, it would become clear which one of us was telling lies.

I told Akbar that I had made his life miserable and caused all these troubles for him. I was dead wrong to get him into this mess because he had a wife and a child, and therefore he had every right to hit me now, but I wouldn't hit him. I also repeated that he knew in his conscience that I had never told him anything, and that I knew he had been forced to tell lies. So I asked him to go ahead and whip me and I would not mind. This was the arrangement that Akbar and I had decided on before. We had agreed that when he was arrested again, we should say that he was lying. Akbar Mahdavi became angry and said, "Everyone else has given up. Resisting torture has no benefit at all! Just tell the truth! Tell them that you said these words and make my life easy!"

Under the pressure of the interrogator, Akbar slapped me on the face softly, but I didn't slap him back. They told me to beat him, but I told them that even if they cut off my head I would not do so!

They had told us to look down and not to look each other in the eye during all this time. We were both looking down when I abruptly lifted my head and looked at Akbar's face. I signaled him to say that he had lied. Otherwise everything was going to get spoiled. They started kicking me and beating me up with more lashes. When Mahdavi saw me being beaten, he changed the story and said, "Mr. Mohammadi, I lied to you."

Mohammadi asked, "Did you lie to me?"

Akbar said, "Yes! I saw that if I didn't lie, I would be killed under your torture. So I was forced to lie."

At that moment Mohammadi asked me to leave the room. After I left, he whipped Akbar about twenty times. Later I learned that Akbar told Mohammad that he had told the truth initially, but when he saw me being beaten, he felt sorry for me, and that was the reason that he said he had lied.

A few days later they took me back to the interrogation room. Mohammadi had a work habit of his own. Whenever a tortured prisoner revealed information, Mohammadi would disclose a little bit of it and gradually discussed it in full. He called me in to go to his office, and when I got there, he had a photo in his hand and showed it to me and asked me what I had to say about it. I looked at the picture, and it was a picture of Ali Reza Kabiri.[158] He had been arrested and apparently re-

---

[158] 'Ali Reza Kabiri (b. 1331/1952) entered political activity in 1351/1972 and joined the MKO, where he received military and guerrilla training. After participating in a series of operations, he was arrested in Azar 1352/December 1973 and was sentenced to life imprisonment. He married the niece of Abbas Agah and as a result of his activities in the MKO against the Islamic Republic he was executed in 1359/1980.

vealed some information about me. From the number on the picture and its condition, I realized that it had been taken at the JCCT Prison. Mohammadi said that they had finally arrested Kabiri! I told him it really didn't matter, as anyone who got engaged in political activity expected to be arrested and/or executed sooner or later. Anyone who joined our movement must have thought about the consequences before starting his struggle. He insisted that I tell him everything I knew about Kabiri.

I said that I never worked with him, as he was young and inexperienced. He was not mature, nor was he prepared for armed struggle.

Mohammadi repeated my statement and asked, if he was so unprepared, why did I have so much interaction with him, and what was the basis of our friendship?

I said that I used to attend a mosque and so did he, and that was where we met.

He cut me off and said that I was not telling the truth because Kabiri had said a lot about our contacts and relationship. I denied that there was anything more than what I said and repeated that I never worked with him. I told him it was up to him to believe me or not.

Mohammad then said that the issue was not just Kabiri but that there were as many as twenty or thirty people who were reportedly recruited by me.

As I was being whipped I tried to remember some of the statements that I had made during my earlier interrogations. I wanted to remember if I had talked about thirty people or not. I thought about it but nothing came to my mind. It was only one day in 1349/1970 that we went to Lake Tar in Damavand in a group of thirty people. There is the probability that Kabiri and Mahdavi were present and that they had mentioned that to the police.

I did not know what Akbar Mahdavi had told Mohammadi after I had left them. I told Mohammadi that like Akbar, who had lied to him about me the other day, chances are that Ali Reza also lied like him. Perhaps he was unable to stand torture and was forced to tell these lies. At the end I told Mohammadi that if he didn't believe me, he could bring Kabiri to an encounter with me.

He just said "Do you think I am a fool like yourself! After you left the room the other day, Akbar told me what you had said to him." I continued to deny everything he said. Then they brought in Mahdavi. He said "Ezzat! I can no longer lie to these people. You said these things! If you don't admit it, they will take me to the torture chamber again." I still denied everything.

Mohammadi said that now both of us were in deep trouble. He had alluded to thirty people in his statement, and I pretended I did not hear that. I assured him that he could not force me under torture to admit that I had anything else to say, and he threatened and assured me that he would torture me so much that I would talk. I said, "Go ahead and try."

They took us to Hosseini's torture chamber. They tied Akbar on the bed and tied me on the Apollo. They whipped us thirty times in turns. Akbar was screaming that he was telling the truth and should not be beaten, and it was I (Ezzat) who was lying. It was truly an unbearable and tragic situation. My friend was being beaten for nothing and I had to stand and suffer seeing it. Indeed, it was a very difficult moment for the two of us. We were two sincere friends, like two brothers, but were placed in a situation such that we had to refute each other and curse one another When they whipped him, he screamed that I was lying and that he had told me these words himself and he had told them the truth.

To further mislead my torturers when they whipped me, to convince them that I was telling the truth, I would react in a more aggressive manner and curse Akbar. They tortured us for over two hours, but I said nothing. They were already tired. Mohammadi was really exhausted and cursed our sisters and mothers, using the dirtiest language one could have used. Despite all this I did not confess to anything.

Their harassment and torture went on until one p.m. Then suddenly Rasuli appeared. As it appears, Rasuli was their savior. He came and mediated on my behalf and asked them to let me go and guaranteed that I would eventually talk. Whenever I was under torture and Rasuli came to save me, I never refused and promised to write if I remembered anything new. So we were freed as a result of Rasuli's intercession. When the guards carried us upstairs, our interrogators walked behind us in full anger. Suddenly, I burst into laughter! The interrogators, who were already angry enough, became angrier and wondered why I was laughing, as they felt I had made a fool of them.

I said, "And why should I not laugh?" I then told Mohammadi, "*Didn't I tell you in the morning that I would say nothing under torture?* At long last I have proven my words. Now do you want me to tell you what you want to know right now that I am not being whipped?"

He conceded and I said, "You wanted to know about the thirty people that I recruited?"

He nodded.

I said, "I discussed this issue in my file. I told you that in 1351/1972 when I was arrested I said that we were thirty people that had gone to Lake Tar in Damavand, and that our trip was purely for mountain-climbing and totally unrelated to politics, and I never recruited any of those people because they were all young and inexperienced. A few of them had been imprisoned from time to time, and some of them may still be in prison. I reminded him that I had told all of this to him before, and he could read all of it in my file, or ask those people to believe me.

I had made a fool of Mohammadi by saying that I had never said anything under the torture. He started beating me on the stairs, cursing my sister and my mother because I had wasted his time and energy and made a fool of him.

Asghar Mahdavi—the brother of Akbar Mahdavi—was also arrested after the arrest of Ali Reza Kabiri.[159] Together with Hamideh Hayati[160] and Seyyed Ali Hosseini, they decided to form a group. They planned to carry out armed operations, so they wanted to get some weapons from Mashhad. They discussed their plan with Kachu'i, who advised them not to buy those weapons because they were hand-made in Afghanistan and were not well made. So when these individuals were all arrested, they mentioned the name of Kachu'i. Even though Kachu'i had warned them against buying these weapons, he was arrested because he had failed to inform SAVAK. He had been condemned once before, and this time he was sentenced to life imprisonment. Asghar Mahdavi also disclosed two pieces of information about me in his interrogation. One was about Hossein Sha'bani and the house on Sahib Jam' Avenue. The second was about the assassination of Sha'ban Bimokh.[161] Until this time, I had really refrained from mentioning anything about that house and its owner (Hossein the vinegar-seller). I mentioned earlier that before I went to Mashhad, I had cleared out that house. But I had left some items in its storage because I had the sympathy and support of Hossein. After I was arrested, he went to see Asghar Mahdavi and told him that since his brother Akbar Mahdavi was in prison, he should ask him to find out if I had said anything under torture about his house. It was almost a year after my arrest that Akbar talked about this issue with me. I realized that the house was

---

[159] Ali Reza Kabiri's arrest led to more arrests. The SAVAK issued a special memorandum about his involvement in a series of operation and claimed that many of his collaborators were identified and arrested. See *Special Bulletin*, #13408/Isfand 26, 1352/March 16, 1974.

[160] Hamideh Hayati (b. 1337/191958) married Hasan Kabiri and through her mother-in-law she was introduced to other political prisoners and joined the MK. She showed a remarkable degree of resistance under torture. Later she joined the Marxist branch of the MKO and along with Vida Hajebi fled the country.

[161] Asghar Mahdavi wrote to Ezzat Shahi and advised him to spread activities like formation of reading groups, hiking, and writing declarations.

341

no longer suitable for our purposes and from prison informed other members of the organization not to visit that house because it was no longer safe. Unfortunately, some members did not pay attention to my warning and assumed that I had given that message to protect myself. So they never cleared out the house. I suffered quite a bit because of their negligence. The interrogators pressured me to say anything I knew about that house and its location, but I never surrendered to their pressure.

In order not to disclose any information about that house and its owner, I decided to commit suicide. Once when they wanted to escort me from the third floor to the second floor I threw myself from the third floor, but unfortunately, or perhaps fortunately, I survived but was unconscious for an hour or so. I started feeling some pain in my shoulder. Finally they took me to the room that they had intended and asked me why I wanted to commit suicide. I said that I did not wish to live because they tortured us, and I could not put up with it and with these filthy and intolerable conditions. They tried to comfort me a little and later on went and got the address of the house from Mahdavi. They also brought Sha'bani for a face-to-face meeting. I said that I didn't recognize him and denied everything. Hossein the vinegar-seller was a really simple and ignorant person. He said, "Hossein! It is me, Sha'bani! How could you not remember me, I was your landlord." He told his interrogator, Hooshang, that I was his tenant but he had no other relationship with me and never received anything from me. They beat up the poor man a little and because he was old and weak he fainted every once in a while. They never wanted to beat and torture him but their aim was to torture me by torturing him. They wanted me to feel sorry for him and confess everything. They brought him to me one more time and again I denied that I knew him or had ever dealt with him.

I looked at him and said if there was anything that he knew about me then he should say it, and he said that there was nothing that he knew about me apart from renting his house to me. They then made me lie in front of him and started kicking and whipping me. He became emotional upon seeing the scene and asked them to stop and added that he would talk and say whatever he knew. He talked a little but some of his statements were not true. Hooshang said, "Only a stable-boy understands the language of the donkey! Do you see what we did to this poor man! Now tell him to speak." And I said that it was not my business to tell him to speak or not!

The second issue that Mahdavi had disclosed about me was about my involvement in the assassination attempt on Sha'ban Ja'fari's life. He had said that after I and my friend had assassinated the man, I had returned with my wounded partner to the old man's house and that he had cleaned and dressed my partner's wound. This was new information for the interrogators. When they got this information about the assassination of Sha'ban Bimokh[162], they got angry that I had kept this matter from them all this time. They started beating me very hard. Akbar—the brother of Asghar—was also severely beaten since he never confessed anything about this incident and his involvement in it. His beating was very painful to me but I had no choice except to be patient and remain silent.

The Recess Time

On 16 Azar, 1353/December 6, 1973 a number of political activists were arrested. In fact, during the second half of 1353/1974, the number of political activists that were arrested was on the rise. The officers at the JCCT prison decided to change my ward and transform my cell into an interrogation and torture chamber. They pretended that my interrogation was over and that they had received enough information from me.

---

[162] Before Azar 1353/November 1974, Ezzat had refused to give information about his involvement in Sha'ban Ja'fari's assassination and other activities. After the arrest of Ali Reza Kabiri and Asghar Mahdavi he revealed some obsolete information to the SAVAK. See *Special Bulliten*, #13408, Isfand 26, 1353/March 16, 1974.

They said, "Ezzat! Your interrogation is complete. You have said everything that we needed to know, and what you have not yet told us is no longer important. So get up and get lost and wait until your leg is

completely healed so that we can send you to Qasr Prison." They wanted to make sure that I would no longer think of committing suicide in my cell. They took me to a cell where two non-religious inmates were kept. They did this intentionally to punish me. In most cases, they never put me in the same cell with other Islamist activists. They thought that it would be the best torture for a person like me who was very religious to live with non-religious prisoners in one cell. On such occasions I really tried to make a positive impression on my cellmates and perhaps influence them by proper behavior. Most often the non-Islamist prisoners were impressed and embarrassed by my humility, and they asked me to live in their cells. I always tried to boost their morale and help them get over their depression. Even though my own condition was worse than theirs, I still helped them as much as I could. Sometimes I helped those who could not walk because of torture to go to bathroom or even carried them on my back to take them to the toilet and helped them wash up. I did all these things because of my faith, and I wanted to show them that it was my religious conviction that commanded me to help others.

I did not want them to think that religion was a reactionary set of beliefs and that religious people were all reactionaries. Sometimes we discussed ideological issues. Obviously, they were against religion of any kind, but they never took positions against me. They knew that I was being tortured because of my religion and that it was my faith that enabled me to remain steadfast and withstand all hardships. Whenever I was beaten up and whipped, I would scream, "Ya Hossein! Ya Ali! Ya Zahra!" But those prisoners did not have a leg to stand on. They had no one to appeal to. They could not shout, "O Marx! O Lenin! O Stalin! Come and help us!" In contrast, I always resorted to the Imams, and at times even the officers were impressed by this appeal.

One day after several days had passed in my new cell, someone opened the gate of my cell, and to my surprise, I saw Hossein Sha'bani—the vinegar-seller—thrown in! He had been arrested on the charges of renting his house to me. Twice they had brought us face to face to have us confess that we knew each other and I had denied everything. He was a simple man and had sympathy toward me and the organization, but I was afraid of his presence because it was possible for him to say things to the other prisoners, and his statements could cause more troubles for me. I told the guard that this man was arrested because of me and should not be in the same cell with me. But the guard said that it was not his business, and he was ordered to bring him in. In any case, when he entered the cell, he tried to comfort me and said that I should not worry or feel guilty because of the troubles I caused that resulted in his arrest. He added that although it was true that he was a simple man, he had enough experience, and that his arrest was not a big deal! Then he asked if my cellmates were members of the organization and trustworthy. I told him that they were decent people and trustworthy, but as a rule he should not trust anyone in prison. Then he wondered if there was any camera or tape-recorders in the cell and whether or not it was safe to talk.

I realized that he might ruin everything. I stood up and called the guard. He opened the small window and asked what my problem was. I told him to go and ask the interrogators whether it was the right decision to send this man to my cell. The guard knew me and understood that things were not all right. He went and asked. The night officer admitted that Mr. Sha'bani and I should not stay together in one cell. So they came and transferred me to cell number five.

In this cell, there were two members of the Marxist Tudeh Party. One of them was Mahdi Ma'afi Madani, who was from the Caspian Sea region, and the second one was Hasanpour, who was an Azari Turk from Tabriz. They were both

345

in low spirits. Mahdi was also corrupt, but the other was not corrupt despite his weakness. These two did not have much work to do in the cell and spent most of their time in the cell sleeping. They never spoke a word to me. They rarely washed up, sometimes for as long as a week! Hossein always placed his hands in his groin. What bad luck I had! I had just jumped from the frying pan into the fire! I really suffered a lot because of these two cellmates. These never cared for cleanliness, much less for ritual purity, and did not wash their dishes. I was the one who did everything. Madani wanted to make me talk. I told both of them that I had nothing new to say, as I had told the interrogators everything that I could tell. I also said to them that I did not wish to know anything about them, and that they should not tell me anything about themselves.

Ordinarily, in all the cells they took me to, I would act this way and tell everyone at the outset that I had nothing to say about myself nor any interest in knowing anything about others because I might be tortured and forced to share with the torturers what they told me and this might cause a lot of trouble. I also told them that if I shared anything about myself with them, they were free to report it to the interrogators and that I didn't mind. I emphasized that they should not tell me anything that they had not told the interrogators before. Later on in order to keep these fellows a little bit busy, I asked them to teach me Turkish and the northern dialect, and in return I would teach them my Khonsari dialect.

Give One, Take One

Around the last days of the month of Azar/November at about midnight, torturers came to take me to the torture chamber. There was a young girl around 14 or 15 years of age in the room. They asked whether I knew her or not, and I said that I did not know her.

My torturers pretended to be taken by surprise and asked how it was possible that I did not recognize my friend's

346

sister! I asked which friend they meant, and they said Murad Nankali. They insisted that I should tell them about my relationship with the young girl, and I denied that I knew her or had had contact with her, and said that I had seen her two or three times when she and her other brother had come to visit Murad at Qasr Prison. She had been arrested because of the message Kachu'i had given her to pass on to the organization.[163] They asked her if she knew me and she said that she had met me once when she visited her brother in prison. They asked me about the message that was sent out, and I denied that I knew anything about that. They then started beating me in front of that girl. They were more sensitive about that particular message than about many other messages that had gone out of prison. This was because in that message we had asked the organization to assassinate Major Zamani and Captain Zhiyan Panah. This message was taken out of the prison with a lot of difficulty.[164] But the plan failed and we did not get the desired result. SAVAK and the police were very angry about this message but tried to prevent an incident like the death of Amir Nankali, who had died under torture. So after severely beating me, they did not take me back to my cell. Instead, they returned me to a hall behind my cell. I remained there until noon, when they came and asked me to tell them everything that I knew about *my brother!*

I told them that my brother had nothing to do with this.[165] I was actually telling the truth because despite our close relationship I never wished to drag him into political activity

---

[163] See *Interview with Hamideh Nankali*, Tehran: Aban 8, 1382/October 18, 2003. See also *Interview with Kachu'i*, 1358–1359/1979–1980.

[164] Ni'matullah Shahi (Mutahhari) was arrested on Azar 21, 1352/November 13, 1973 and imprisoned in the JCCT headquarters.

[165] Ni'matullah Shahi reported, "In one of my visits to my brother [Ezzat] he told me to go to Mr. Mir Hashimi's residence and take the copy machine to my house and he would tell me later where to take it from there. I did not have a car so my nephew drove me to Mr. Mir Hashimi's house and we took the copy machine and left it in the basement of our house." *Interview with Ni'matullah Shahi*, Tehran: Azar 26, 1383/November 6, 2004.

because he was already married and had children. Despite that, the police had gone to his shop one afternoon and arrested him. In his house they found only a copy machine, and that was his crime!

The story of this printing machine goes back to the time of our activities in the El-Al group. Some members of that group who had been arrested in 1349/1960 had informed the police that they had used that machine to duplicate declarations that were distributed. They were also forced to confess that this machine was in my house. When I was arrested in 1351/1972, the police asked me about that machine. They wanted to know where I had purchased it and what I had done with it. I told them that I had purchased it from Mr. Shahcheragi (the imam of the Irshad mosque who had already passed away) and I gave it to Mohammad Mufidi (who been executed already). I explained the story starting from a dead person and ending it with a dead person. The truth is that I had hidden it under the stairs of the house of my brother's friend—Mr. Mir Hashimi—and built up a wall in front of the stairs. In 1349/1979 Mir Hashimi lived underground like myself. While I was in Qasr Prison, I was informed that he had completely changed and deviated and was even drinking alcohol and that he had been arrested several times for the being drunk in public. I was therefore worried that the copy machine would be discovered by the police. It was during a visit by my brother that I asked him and my nephew (who owned a car) to go to Mir Hashimi's house and take that machine to my brother's house. They went and brought the machine and placed it in a box where I used to store the used paper and old newspapers. After the discovery of that message and the arrest of Hosseinzadeh, Kachu'i, Hamideh Nankali, and my brother, the copy machine was found in my brother's house by the police.[166]

---

[166] Ni'matullah Shahi (b. 1320/1941) was born into a poor family in Khwansar. He did not receive an education beyond elementary school and was forced to work to support the family. In 1353/1974 he was arrested because of assisting his brother [Ezzat] in his activities and sentenced to

They took me into a room, and I saw my brother standing like a scared boy. Manuchehri was standing beside him and was playing with his beard. Mohammadi was also present, standing with his hands on his hips while Hosseini was preparing his whip. They had prepared this dramatic scene for us. I was unable to walk because of the injuries caused by whippings on my feet. My interrogator asked me not to tell my brother what to say and what not to say, but just tp tell him to disclose all he knew or say nothing: "*Ezzat! You surely know that we are going to make him talk in the same manner that we made you talk.*"

It was obvious that they were afraid of me. I had already told my brother during our visits that if one day he was arrested and brought in front of me and was ordered to say everything, that meant that he should not say anything, as each sentence would add a year to his prison term. I had also warned him that even if my friends came and greeted him, he should still not say a word to them. In that meeting with the police I told them that I was not sure if my brother had anything to say, but I certainly had nothing to do with him and whatever he might say. When the police saw that I had given guideline to my brother despite their prior warning, they started beating me again

My brother was a simple and emotional man. I could tell that he felt terrible but was able to control himself. Then they began to beat him up. To prevent his feet from swelling, they made him run around. Ni'mat had a lot of family problems. He was married and had a child, and was in debt. These problems were his priorities and he felt responsible. He was sensitive to issues that pertained to his family life. Despite these difficulties, they kept him in the JCCT Prison for ten

seven years in prison. In Isfand 1356/March 1977 he was released and returned to the bazaar to resume his business. His eighteen-year-old son, Mohammad Mehdi, was martyred in the war with Iraq. See, *Interview with Ni'matullah Shahi*, Tehran: Azar 26, 1383/November 6, 2004.

months. He was not allowed to have any visitors. During this time, we were both unaware of what was going on outside of prison.[167] When he was being beaten, I really felt sorry for him because he was being beaten and tortured for nothing. When out of frustration I asked them to beat me up instead of him, I realized that it was a big mistake. With this mistake, they realized that I loved my brother, so they beat him up and whipped him even worse than before in order to torture me psychologically. To make up for my mistakes I decided to show them that I had no feelings for him and asked them to give me the whip so that I could whip him myself. I said that I was so pleased that they had arrested him and brought him to prison. The torturers were surprised and asked me why I made that statement.

I said, "Because this man did not know you until now, but now that he knows you he will develop hatred toward you. You will execute me but he will be jailed and finally he shall be free and will tell the world how you treated me and will ruin your reputation." Yet they continued beating us up so that one of us would start talking. They made me lie on a bed and Mohammadi stepped on my face with his shoe. We were blindfolded so we could not see one another. When they whipped me I screamed. They would then ask my brother who was this screaming man, and he would answer, "My brother"; and when they whipped him they asked me the same question, and naturally I would say, "My brother." Then they would say, "Tell your brother to talk. It is clear that you are not going to say a word, but tell your brother to do so to get a break."

I would say "It is none of my business whether you beat him or not."

---

[167] Reza Attarpour, known as Dr. Hosseinzadeh, was a SAVAK interrogator and torturer. He was directly involved in the arrest and execution of nine members of the Fidayan and Mujahidin organizations in 1354/1975 at Evin. He was trained in Israel and after the Revolution he fled there and was given a job. Later, rumor had it that he started a carpet business in Washington, D.C. See General Hossein Fardoost, *Memoirs*, vol. I, pp. 463–474, Seyyed Jalaeddin Madani, *Memoirs*, vol. 2, pp. 158–160, Shams Aal Ahmad, p. 67, and Koorush Lasha'i, *Memoirs*, p. 191.

They told my brother that he seemed to be less stupid than I, so he should ask me not to be fool and talk. So my brother said, "O Brother! Tell them whatever you know."

I said, "I have nothing to say. I have already said everything that I know."

To make the story short, beating up two brothers next to each other was a tragic scene.

It is indeed very hard for anyone to see his brother being tortured. It was unbearable for a brother to witness his brother being tortured to the point of death and not be able to do anything. Every once in a while, a police officer came to me and said that they knew my brother was innocent. In one episode Manuchehri said *"Give one, take one."* He wanted my brother to give information about one of his comrades if he wished to be released; or I should introduce one of my comrades so that they would release my brother. They gave me this advice several times, and reminded me that he had a wife and a child, he was in debt, and it was not fair at all for him to remain in prison because his wife and children would suffer. When I realized that they would not stop making those kinds of statements, I said, "As far as I am concerned, none of these issues are important for me because they were not applicable to me. As to my brother, he is just one of the thirty-five million people in the country and must have his share of misery and hardship. Even though his entire life has been filled with pain and suffering, he should accept all this pain and torture at your hands. I am not willing to make a deal pver him." To convince them not to expect anything, I added that I was not worried—nor should they be—about my brother's family, for they will survive, as other prisoners' families do. They would be happier to see him in prison for political charges than for selling drugs, or dying in a car accident. My elderly father would support my brother's family even if he were to go begging in the street. When one of the interrogators said that they will arrest my father too, I said that in that case my brother's wife would have to go and beg herself. So in short, they realized that they couldn't accomplish anything by threatening me.

My brother was truly a pure-hearted and simple man. He only minded his own business. When I was at Evin Prison, two Marxist prisoners came to me and praised my brother and said that they liked him very much. When I asked them the reason, they said because he was such a simple man and was not disturbed by life in prison or worried about his family. His only concern was that he had borrowed ten thousand *tumans* and worried that he might not be able to pay his debt on time, and people might think that was the reason he was imprisoned. He cared so much for his reputation in the society.

After he was in prison for three or four months, officials came and told me that they intended to put my brother on trial and they could either release him or execute him. I told them that it would be better if they executed him. They were surprised and asked me the reason for that statement. I told them that my brother had four or five children, and when they grow up, they would definitely follow their father's footsteps. This was better for us since we would be in great need of people who could replace those who were executed. So they put my brother on trial. In the first phase of his trial, he was sentenced to a four-year term in prison, and the appeal court condemned him to seven years behind bars. He remained in prison until the month of Isfand, 1356/March 1977, when he was released.

Crucified

It was thus that whenever a political activist was arrested and said something about me or my brother or had any ties with me, the police would make conditions more unbearable for me. As the days went by, I got weaker and weaker and my health declined. I was low on energy and lost quite a bit of weight. As a result, again the thought of committing suicide began to haunt me and I decided to go ahead and end my life before I was forced to surrender as a result of physical and mental weakness. One day when I went to the toilet, I cut off a piece of rusty metal from the bathroom door. I brought it into the cell and tried as hard as possible to sharpen it by rubbing it on the floor tiles. It was around midnight when I cut a vein in my leg and wanted to cut another one in my arm. I thought that by losing blood until morning, I would die before they could catch me. But unfortunately, it wasn't more than a quarter of an hour, and before I could cut the veins in my arm, the police came into my cell to take me for yet more interrogation. They were not aware that I had cut myself on the leg. While conducting the interrogation they realized that blood was dripping from my leg. They quickly took care of the situation and tied a bandage to my leg and stopped the bleeding. This incident made them more sensitive and watchful of my every move. They must have concluded that I really had important information to give them, and that was the reason I wanted to kill myself.

One of the interrogators said that even if I attempted to commit suicide a hundred times, they would do anything to save me, and that I had no choice but to talk. In response I told them that I had nothing important to tell them, and the reason for committing suicide was that I was only tired and could no longer put up with torture, and that I wanted to kill myself and set myself free from all the pain and suffering. After treating my leg, they beat me again but did not return me to my cell. Instead, they took me to Ward Five across the hall. They also brought there that same bed that they had tied me on for one and a half months in my cell and tied me to it again. This time they positioned me in such a way that my head faced towards the cell, and my legs were tied towards the courtyard.

I remained there for around two months and witnessed many incidents of torture. In my new position, the interrogators were not interested in further questioning me but wanted to torture me psychologically. There was a metal door that was opened and closed perhaps a hundred times in a day. Even

353

though I was blindfolded and my legs were tied to the bed and they had placed cotton balls in my ears so that I could not to hear their steps when they entered, the sound of the door was nerve-racking and disturbed me a lot, but there was nothing that I could do. The torturers came every other hour and hit me whether I was asleep or awake and then went away. Every moment I expected a kick, slap, or punch. Sometimes they came in and slapped me four times on the cheeks and then went away. Other times they would punch me hard on the nose. Sometimes I thought that I was dreaming, but when I saw blood dripping from my nose I realized that I was awake. Before I could scream, the torturer would leave the room. One time I was in a deep sleep when one of the torturers came in and kicked me in the stomach and left the room quickly.

A few guards especially treated me harshly, but most of them were friendly and took care of me. Some of them wondered why I was beaten up so much and insisted that I should give them any information I had. As always, I would tell them that I had nothing more and that the interrogators only tortured me because they hated me and wanted to take revenge on me for my endurance. Most of these guards were from rural areas and I dealt with them in their own way. Some of them befriended me and sometimes would inform me of new arrests and ask me to be prepared for more interrogation. At times they would show me the names of the people that were called for interrogation and ask me if I knew them. To be on the safe side, I always said that I did not know any of them. I feared that they might go and tell the interrogators that I knew some of the newly arrested activists and make my situation more difficult.

Sometimes a guard allowed me to visit the toilet several times, and in such situations I went to use the bathroom several times between morning and noon time. Once Major Vaziri—the prison director—had seen me going to the bathroom several times and wondered why. I was trying to find a convincing answer when one of the guards saved me the trouble and said that I was suffering from diarrhea! He made me laugh, and I nodded in the affirmative.

Sometimes I spent up to an hour in the bathroom and the officers would come and ask the guards where I was. The guards would tell him that I had gone to wash my clothes. To show that he told the truth, I would take my underwear into the bathroom. I would turn on the tap and wash it and then show it to the officer so he could see that I was truly washing my underwear.

These little episodes were much better than sleeping on that metal bed. I was really tired of sleeping. My health had actually deteriorated. My back was in pain and I had become lazy. Sometimes when I went to the toilet, I would exercise for half an hour or so. In most cases, I prayed outside the bathroom. At times when this was not possible, I performed my prayers lying on that bed. I was unable to take a shower for over three months, and my body was filthy, but I still prayed in that condition.

Once when I was praying outside the bathroom, Manuchehri came and pushed me away. He cursed at me and didn't allow me to complete my prayer. He said that I was not a Muslim and wondered why I prayed! He was not my interrogator, but he hated me deeply. Wherever he saw me, he would harass me and give me a hard time. Arash, Rasuli, and others also harassed me in different ways. I had become an international figure!

Whoever came to me wanted to bother me in one way or the other. I had totally given up and no longer cared to behave in a proper manner. One night one of the prison officers came to me and started a conversation. He talked about the White Revolution, SAVAK, and the regime. He spoke against them and pretended that he opposed everything that they did. He claimed that SAVAK's duties pertained to foreign intelligence, and domestic issues were within the authority of the police department. I told him since they were incompetent, SAVAK felt free to take everything under its control. He did not expect this answer from me. He then said, "At least say something so that when I return to your interrogators, I can intercede on your behalf and convince them that you do not remember anything else to talk about."

I was fully aware that he had been sent to me by my interrogator, so I told him that I really did not have any more information to share, and even if I had something to say, I would definitely not tell him and would only talk to my interrogator. It was not appropriate for me to debate about the White Revolution with him. I had earlier told Zandipoor—the head of the JCCT prison—that I was against the White Revolution because it brought to our people nothing but poverty and misery. Whenever I debated with them about political issues and gave my analysis, they would curse me because I was not educated! When we talked about constitutional law, I rejected their argument that we had any constitutional law, and said the law of jungle prevailed in our country. They claimed that they knew better than I and they were the ones in charge of implementing the law and that it was none of my business to talk about the constitution.

My new location in the hallway had some benefits and some disadvantages. I was pleased because I did not have to deal with inexperienced and untrained activists. I was alone and all by myself. The disadvantage was that I could witness the suffering of other prisoners and was greatly disturbed. Moreover, my back was injured and tired from lying down on the bed and my health was seriously deteriorating. I was growing impatient day by day.

Despite all this I was still happy that I could see the other prisoners like Rajavi, Khoshdel, and other friends as they were moved from one place to another. Their physician treated me as well. Even though I had my own differences with Rajavi, whenever he saw me in that condition, he always expressed admiration and respect, saluted me, blew a kiss to me, and wished me good luck.

Most of the Marxists also saw me there. Sometimes on Friday afternoons, I would see the guards escorting Dr. Shari'ati to take a shower. The guards treated him in a respectful manner. On his way back to his cell, the guards allowed him to rest under the sun. He knew me well. On his way he always looked around, and when he was certain the guards were not watching him, he would greet me and wave at me. Some good-natured guards realized that I knew him and would give him time to greet me. We could not talk, and he could just wave at me, and I would reply by moving my fingers and rolling my eyes. I could only move my arm a little. Once he asked me why I was in that situation. I replied by sign language that I was involved in armed struggle. Again he asked me whether I had done something, and I answered him. Then Shari'ati put his hands on his neck to ask whether I was going to be executed. I lifted my hands slightly to show that nothing was clear and that I was not sure if they are going to execute me or not.

At night the guards covered my face with a blanket so I could not to see other prisoners who came to mop the floor in the hallway. When the guards left the corridor, the cleaning crew pulled the chains on my feet to signal that the guards were not present there. They would ask me who I was, and I talked to them while I was under the blanket. Some of the guards who were kind to me realized what was happening and would tell me to choose the cleaning crew myself.

Sometimes when the guys were busy mopping, I would call the guard and tell him that I wanted to go to the toilet. He would untie my hands and legs and then leave. This was a great chance for me to greet other prisoners who were mopping the place and tell them to tell others that I was still alive. This was important, since the interrogators had said that I was dead. Witnessing this situation made many prisoners very hopeful and boosted their morale. They understood that it was possible for them to put up with the torture if they wanted. After all, the worst part of being tortured was before the torture began, but after it started, it was no longer as frightening an

357

experience as before. Before a person was tortured or beaten, he was so afraid, but once he was beaten up, he did not fear it any longer.

Sometimes Zandipoor came to see me and asked me how I was, and I always said I was fine and never complained. Some other times he leaked some information. When he saw my terrible condition, he would criticize the interrogators and blame them for torturing me so much. The torturers would insist that I still had much information that I had not revealed, whereupon Zandipoor would urge me to talk, arguing that several activists who had been arrested had spoken about me, and that I had better talk, too. He blamed me for subjecting myself to so much torture and was worried that I might die under torture.

The Price of a False Oath

My biggest problem in the JCCT Prison was when they arrested a new activist and he gave information about me. I had to refute his statements by accepting more beating and torture. Then another person was arrested and disclosed new information. No matter how much I swore to God and on the Qur'an that I had nothing more to say, they would not believe me. In the condition that I was in, I could not say that I had nothing more to disclose, but insisted that I didn't remember anything. If there was anything that happened, then I could not recall. It was during the interrogation concerning the letter that I sent to Hossein Jannati that they tortured me almost to the point of death, until Hosseinzadeh came to my rescue. He asked me if I recognized him and I acknowledged that I did. Again he asked me if I really had told the interrogators everything I knew, and I told him that by God, I had said everything that I knew.

He said, "Don't swear by God and the Prophet that you do not believe in! They are not here to defend you if your oath is true or false. Swear by my name so that just in case it happens that you lied, then you will know what I am capable of doing." I thought for a while that I should take an oath and free myself from all these troubles and then later on figure out what to do. So I said, "Mr. Hosseinzadeh, I swear by your life that I have nothing more to say. I have said everything." Then he ordered the guard to untie my chains. Until that moment I did not had breakfast and was very weak. So they gave me a cup of hot tea and half a glass of milk. On a piece of paper I wrote again the same things that I had told them before. Hosseinzadeh ordered the guards to take me away. I thought that at that moment they would leave me alone and would let me just sleep on the bed. In less than ten minutes they came back to me and said that I was a fool to take a false oath in the name of Hosseinzadeh! They took me again and told me that I had not yet said anything about the declarations. It was obvious that the whole thing was just a bluff, and in reality they only wanted to test me. I said that I could not remember anything. Then Hosseinzadeh came in followed by a few others and claimed that I had sworn in Hosseinzadeh's name, but I was still lying! They all jumped on me and beat me until I accepted my responsibility about issuing the declarations. When they had gotten tired of beating me, they took me to the office of Hosseini, the torturer. Hosseini said, "The other time you swore by the life of Hosseinzadeh and you lied. This time swear by my life."

I said, "I will not swear on the life of anyone again, Mr. Hosseini! I am not saying that I have nothing to say. What I mean is that I have forgotten everything. I assure you that I could not recall anything."

When Hosseini realized that I had no intention of speaking, he hung me on the wall and began whipping me. One lash of the whip after another and one injury after another…

This episode was repeated time and again, and they continued to beat me up mercilessly. Most of my body was injured. The flesh on my feet was falling of and all they did was to dip a piece of cloth in oil and insert it in my wounds. I had got used to being beaten up and tortured to the point that if I was not beaten for a day or two, I would become disoriented! I would do something to cause them to beat me. Practically, my interrogation was over and they had no reason to torture me other than personal hatred and desire for revenge. They just wanted to break my spirit and torture me emotionally and psychologically.

A year before that, in 1352/1973, Kamali was my interrogator. One day when I fell behind the door of my cell, he came to me and said, "Ezzat! Last year you made a fool of me and never said a word. See what kind of a mess you have put yourself into! These people will kill you. Allow me to save you from the claws of these torturers and talk to me so that I will have a reason to take over your case." In fact, he was trying to fool me, and I knew his plan, so again I told him that I had nothing more to say and mentioned that everything other prisoners said about me was untrue and that they tortured me to lie to please their egos. I added, "Mr. Kamali! I have nothing more to lose and no matter what I say or don't say, they will execute me anyway and I want to let them do as they wish and let them write whatever they want so that my ordeal can end as quickly as possible because I am so tired of this situation." Thus, I was able to escape Kamali's trap, and he returned empty-handed.

The End of the Turbulent Night

As the days passed, the frequency of torture decreased. They also reduced the number of times they took me to Hosseini's office. Instead, they conducted interrogations and beat me up in my cell. I prioritized the questions they posed and accepted simple charges but refused to accept responsibility for important activities or operations. When I was busy writing something on the paper, Mohammadi would curse me and ask me to reveal the name of the person who had paid for the copy machine and other issues related to that. I laughed at him because I knew that they were aware of the full story. When a matter was not so important I would write a few sentences about the person who sold the copy machine to me or the person I gave the machine to. In reality, none of these people existed at all, but the interrogators would carefully write down this information. After that, whenever the interrogators came for other matters, I would tell them not to bother or pressure me, and that I would tell them whatever I could remember. I reminded them of what I had shared with them about the money and the copy machine and promised to tell them if I remembered something else. So this attitude created a more positive image of me and enabled me to fool them.

One day, Mohammadi came to me and said that if I told him the truth and accepted all charges, he would be lower than a pimp if he did not transfer me to Qasr Prison and end my ordeal here. He thought that I would love to go to Qasr Prison, but I told him that it didn't make any difference for me whether I was sent to Qasr or stayed where I was, as they are all prisons for me. I added that in fact I liked it better at the JCCT Prison. But he still thought that I was so anxious to go to the Qasr Prison, so he insisted again that I should admit my connection with the newly arrested activists and tell him about them so that he would transfer me to Qasr Prison. I said that I neither recalled anything, nor did I want to go to Qasr Prison, but if he wished to do me a favor, he should send me to Evin Prison. He found this request interesting because every prisoner was afraid of being transferred to Evin, yet there I was begging to be taken there.

Two months had passed since they had tied me up in a crucified position behind Ward Eight. During the last days, the interrogators no longer beat me up, but rather greeted me warmly and asked kindly about my condition. One morning, Mohammadi came and said, "Ezzat! Do you think that I am an animal? I am also a human being! I really have a heart! I have feelings! I am a true human being and not a wild animal like you! Do you think that I sleep peacefully when I leave this place and go to my home? No! This is not the case for me. I am always thinking about you! I swear to God that last night I dreamed about you. I saw you in a bad condition. Just tell me the purpose of your life. Every human being wants to live well. This is not life that you are subjecting yourself to. Why on earth are you doing these things to yourself? You are a miserable fool who wants to sacrifice himself for people who disclose information about him so easily when they are arrested!"

I broke into laughter as I heard him talk in that tone and said that I just did what I thought was the right thing to do, and it was not my business what other people did. They, too, were responsible for their own actions. Again he wondered why I behaved so. He said that it was not fair the he rested peacefully at his house every night while I was crucified in that prison. I said that this was the question that he should ask himself, since he was the one responsible for putting me into that terrible condition, and if he were truly a good human being and had a conscience, he would not treat me in that manner!

Whenever the interrogators came to see me, they felt sorry for me and wanted me to ask them for a favor such as a cigarette or visitation by family members. In fact, they even went as far as sending mediators to ask me if I wanted to have visitors or wished to be saved from that condition. Several times they asked me if I knew that my brother was also in prison and if I wished to see him. I always said, "The hell with my brother! In fact, bring him here for me to beat him up." They also asked me if I wished to see my elderly father, and I said that I did not, because that old man opposed my political activities altogether and that I had not seen him for twelve years, and even if they brought him to my cell, I would refuse to talk to him. Of course, I knew in my heart that I missed him badly and wished to see him even for a few seconds.

Sometimes the guards brought me a pack of Winston cigarettes, but I refused to accept it, although I really had the urge to smoke just one cigarette to ease my pain. If they brought me milk, I did not drink it and told them that I didn't like milk at all. I refused to eat whatever they brought me. Whatever they wanted me to do, I would do exactly the opposite. Every once in a while, my interrogator set conditions and say that if I met them, he would take off my chains and take me back to my cell. He wanted me to beg him to take my chains off. Even though I was so tired of the metal bed, I defied him and told him that I was comfortable out in the open space and enjoyed the fresh air and did not want to go back to that overcrowded, filthy, and smelly cell. When the interrogator could not win my heart by his kind gestures, he came and jokingly asked how I was and said that whenever I wished to see him I could go and talk to him. I told him that I was always available and did not see any reason to talk to him, but he was always welcome to call me if he wished to talk. He really wanted me to beg him to free me from that bed, but it was a futile attempt, and I never asked him for anything.

It was toward the end of the month of Bahman/February when the prison director and the night officer came to see me. The tone and manner of their talk had totally changed. The prison director said that he had fought on my behalf with prison officials and guards several times, and he wanted me to know that *he* was the boss and responsible for the management of the prison, and that no one else had such authority to treat me the way they had. He asked me to go back to my cell and promised to send me to either Qasr or Evin Prison soon.

After him Mohammadi came and said that he wanted me to go back to my cell, as he had no hope of changing me and making me a decent human being. He said that he planned to go on vacation during the Persian New Year holidays to enjoy himself and wanted me to have a good time too in prison and rest in my cell! He also promised that when he returned, he planned to meet me so that we could talk. I told him that I never asked him for anything, but I wanted to make a request!

For a moment he probably thought that I had an important request. He said that it was my fault that I did not ask him for what I needed, but now I could, and promised to fulfill my request, whatever it might be. I said that I did not want anything important, but now that the spring was around the corner and there would be no more interrogation, and also the weather was turning mild, I wished to stay out where I was. I was very anxious in my heart and wished to get rid of that bed as soon as I could, but I asked him to leave me where I was because the air inside the cell was not good and I always felt short of breath there. He became very angry and cursed me again and insisted that I must go back to my cell! It was a Wednesday, so I asked him to let me go to my cell on Saturday. He refused and ordered the guards to take my chains off and take me back to cell number eighteen the very same moment!

The Final Days in the JCCT Prison

During the first few days I was alone in cell number eighteen. Several times I tried to contact the two cells next to mine. Even though the guard walked very quietly outside my cell, I knew where he was by placing my ears on the holes of the door. When the guard went far away in response to a call from a prisoner in another cell who asked for a book of matches or to escort him to the toilet, I took advantage of the opportunity to make contact. I started hitting the wall to the next cell to communicate with prisoners there and tell them who I was and what I was doing at that cell.

I managed to talk three times with the prisoner in the next cell. The fourth time the guard realized what was going on and came behind the door to eavesdrop on our talk. He took some notes. It was during this time that the prison director arrived for inspection! When he did not find the guard in the hallway, he asked the person who had the keys to quietly open the door. He entered and saw the guard standing behind my cell and asked what he was doing there. The guard became embarrassed and said that prisoners were communicating with each other. The director became angry that the guard had not stopped them and had allowed them to talk to each other. He came in and started to beat me up very hard. He went to the next cell and beat them up too. He then called Mr. Mohammadi to come and see what Ezzat wanted to say!

It didn't take long before Rasuli, Arash, Tehrani, Manuchehri, Mottaqi, and Hooshang all came and started beating me. They did the same to the prisoners in the next cell and then left. But unfortunately enough, one of the most malicious guards said, "Ezzat will not learn to behave properly, and we have to take him to Hosseini's room."

I was blindfolded as we were all taken to Hosseini's chamber to receive some lashes of the whip. When Mohammadi and Manuchehri were far away from us, I told the other prisoners to remember that they did not talk to me and I was the only one who talked to them. I also repeated to them the part of the speech that I suspected that the guard had heard. In Hosseini's office, he started whipping me again. He asked me why I sent signals to the next cell. I told him, "I only wanted to introduce myself to them because I am convinced that you are going to execute me but other prisoners will remain alive. I wanted them to inform people when they are released that so-and-so was alive up to such-and-such a date." I remained steadfast in my claim because I did not want those prisoners to be beaten because of me, and that was the way I could save them from being whipped.

In that cell there were a few activists from Qom, such as Mohammad Reza Fatemi, Mohammad Ali Baqiri, Abbas Farnam, and Mohammad Ali Muvahhidi, who had killed a policeman in order to confiscate his weapon. Later on three or four of them were executed. They were fine young men who had formed a separate group for themselves and carried out many operations.

This incident convinced my interrogators that I still had a lot of information that I refused to share with them. So my ordeal started all over again. After this they brought two prisoners to cell number eighteen. One of them was a religious man, while the other was from [a communist] organization known as Toofan.[168] The religious man's name Seyyed Ahmad Hashimi Nezhad, and he was from Mashhad.[169] He was to be released very shortly. He liked to get information from me, and several time he asked if I had any message for my comrades outside the prison. He said that he planned to join the MKO when he left prison and insisted that I should help him in his plan. I told him that he need not join the MKO, but instead he should go to school and study to become a member of the clergy so that he could guide people to the straight path. I denied that I knew anyone in the MKO to connect him to and told him that if he really wished to join them, they would find him. A few days later they came and took him away.

The second prisoner was a Marxist who was a member of Toofan organization. He had studied abroad and was a member of the Confederation of Iranian Students abroad. He had a degree in engineering and had served in the army for two months. When he was arrested, his ties with the Confederation outside the country were discovered. He had not been beaten

---

[168] During the second half of 1340/1961 there was a split in the Tudeh Party that resulted in the formation of Toofan, a Marxist organization and the revolutionary organization of the Tudeh Party. Initially Toofan resorted to using religious slogans and often quoted passages from *Nahj al-Balaghah* in its declarations, but gradually focused on reviving the Tudeh Party by the very same leaders who were responsible for all deviations and treasons of the party in the past. It did not contribute in any way or form to the enrichment of the revolutionary experience of the activists. In fact, Toofan was stillborn. See, *The Armed Struggle and the Opportunists*, vol. I. See also www.ashrafdehghani.com.

[169] Seyyed Ahmad Hashimin Nezhad (b. 1328/1949) after the ninth grade attended seminaries in Mashhad, where he started his political activity. Arrested in 1351/1972, he was imprisoned several times after that. In prison he joined the MKO but turned against them after the Revolution. He held several positions afterwards in the Ministry of Roads and Transportation. He has left a vivid description about Ezzat Shahi's torture in prison. See, *Interview,* Tehran: Ordibehesht 2, 1383/April 12, 2004.

very much. His presence in the cell was a kind of torture for me. When I leaned on a wall, he would warn me against that lest I would send messages to the adjacent cell and therefore invite the guard and cause trouble for both of us! This young man was very emotional and sometimes even cried. He missed his family and his fiancée, whom he took to the movies when he was out and wondered what would happen to now that she was alone. He was so emotional that he could hardly eat his food, and sometimes I had to force him to eat something small. I often tried to comfort him because his interrogator was Rasuli. I assured him that his interrogation was complete, and if he made the request they would transfer him to a group cell.

In this cell, we ate our food with our hands because we did not have forks and spoons. Our hands were dirty, and our blankets were very filthy and smelly. I had experienced situations like this before, so I made spoons by taking the dough in the bread, drying it, and using it as spoons. I could use them even for beef stew and soup. The young communist was not able to do that. One day I decided to pull his leg and make a joke with him. I said that these cells were meant for people who were still under interrogation and whose cases had not been tried yet. It was obvious that his interrogator had no information about him and that he was not supposed to be in this cell but in group cells, where they would give him stainless steel forks and spoons, a clean personal blanket, and even a nice carpet, and he could have visitors regularly. He asked me what he should do to be transferred, and I told him that a simple request would be enough.

After I gave him this guidance, I became apprehensive lest he tell his interrogator that I was the one who told him what to do. So I told him "Just forget what I have told you, and in fact don't tell your interrogator anything!"

He asked, "So what should I say now?"

I said, "Just find another excuse. Tell them that Ezzat bothers you in the cell and that you cannot sleep peacefully because he always snores. Ask them to change your place or take you to the public Ward Five. Be careful and do not let them find out that you are doing this, because you want a stainless steel spoon and an extra blanket. This will only make them keep you here longer."

The young engineer quickly believed my words, and he soon started asking to see his interrogator. The guards went to his interrogator a few times until finally he was able to meet Rasuli. He told Rasuli exactly how I had told him and requested that he change his cell. Rasuli, being very intelligent, understood that this fellow had been fooled. He told him, "No, Sir! This is a plan made for you by Ezzat." The young man was so simple that right then he confessed that Ezzat had given him the idea for this request and had told him that in the communal ward, they gave prisoners stainless steel forks and spoons, nice carpets, and so on. Rasuli, too, made fun of him and told him, "What a poor fellow! Ezzat has fooled you. He only wanted to get rid of you, and that is why he told you these things. In this place, all the cells are the same. There is no difference at all. Ezzat is a just a cunning fellow who wanted to make fun of you. Don't let him do this to you again."

When the engineer returned to the cell, he was very angry. He argued with me and said Rasuli had told him everything and that I had made a fool of him.

I said, "You are a simple man who quickly believes things. Oh, poor guy! Why should I lie to you? Rasuli has lied to you because he doesn't want to transfer you upstairs. If you want to find out who is telling the truth between the two of us, then tell your interrogator to take you to the general cells for you to see for yourself."

I just wanted him to be separated from me in any way possible because he really irritated me. I wanted to talk with the prisoner in the adjacent cell, especially that man from Qom. But the presence of the engineer in my cell was a great hindrance that I could not put up with. The other guys were also afraid to make contact with me because of what had happened earlier. However, I never lost hope. I had reached a point that I wanted to make contact with the other Islamist prisoners. I did not have a good relationship with the guards in cell number eight. Whenever they escorted me to the toilet, I talked with them in a loud voice. I told them things that I wanted the other prisoners in the adjacent cells to hear. Sometimes when the guard called me to take my food, I would talk to other prisoners the moment I placed my bowl in front of the door of the cell. Sometimes I asked the guards to assign me to the task of cleaning the hallway and mopping the floor at night. Some of them agreed while others refused. When I did the mopping, I would sneak a look into the cells and sing. Thus I could find out which prisoners were in each cell.

One day when my cellmate was taken for interrogation, I spoke with the person in the adjacent cell. The guards found out what I was doing and took me to the torture chamber and beat me up along with the prisoner in that cell. I told Mr. Manuchehri that I was tired and frustrated and that was the reason I was trying to talk to someone. I asked him to transfer me out of that cell or send a religious cellmate for me. Of course the police in the JCCT Prison was also tired of me. They had nothing else to do with me, and all their efforts to force me to talk had failed. Beating and torturing me had become completely useless. It was because of this that they decided to get rid of me. So they transferred me to Evin Prison. This transfer really angered my interrogator. He cursed me constantly and did not know what he should do next.

*   *   *

CHAPTER SEVEN

At the Evin Prison

The Evin Prison—1354/1975

I had identified every corner of the Evin Prison in advance and was well familiar with it. This prison was located in the northwest of Tehran in the hills of Evin. It was surrounded by tall walls that could be seen from the National University of Iran (now Shahid Beheshti). I once went there with a friend to identify the details of the prison. There was a river flowing by it, so we walked in the opposite direction of the river. Behind us, a soldier in the guard's tower saw us. He came down and asked where we had gone and why we had come up to this place. We told him that we had gone hiking and offered excuses so that he would let us go our way. He warned us that we should never be seen again anywhere near the prison compound. The Evin Prison was a garrison before it was converted into a prison and was under army's control. There were no buildings in it, only some old structures. Between 1350 and 1352/1971 and 1873 they kept spies in that place, and no political prisoners or criminals were taken there. But after 1352/1973 it was taken over by SAVAK, converted into a prison, and assigned to political prisoners.

The Evin Prison had an old and a new section. The old section contained some individual cells that were under the control of SAVAK. It was small and simple. The new section was constructed in 1352/1973.[170] They built ten wards there that could house a total of eighty individual cells. There was a

---

[170] General Manuchehr Hashimi was the director of the counter-intelligence department of the SAVAK during 1352–11357/1973–1977. He claimed credit for initiating the construction of Evin compound. It was initially intended as a temporary residence for dissidents and in mid-1350/1979 was officially converted into Evin Prison. See Manuchehr Hashimi, *Memoirs*, pp. 523–527.

ward there that right now is[171] known as ward number 209 that contained eight cells that were all assigned for solitary confinement. These cells were quiet, dark, always locked, and all underground. It was commonly known as "five by seven," denoting that to get there one had to take five steps down and then three steps up. Beyond that was the torture chamber. Whenever a prisoner was taken there, other prisoners would say that "So-and-so was taken to five down and three up." This room was located through the lower entry door where Hosseini tortured prisoners.

The new cells were made American-style, measuring 2 by 2.5 meters. Each of these cells was assigned to a single prisoner. They did not place two prisoners in one cell except in special cases. For instance, two prisoners facing execution would be placed in one cell. Each cell had a European-model toilet, a sink with warm and cold water, and a small ventilator, which often did not work. High above the wall of the cells, there was a window protected by a metal railing and screen. This window was the source of light for the cell. The sun reached the cells for around two hours in the morning. There was a light behind the door, which was also covered by a metal screen and controlled from outside the room. Inside the cell there were a mattress, a mat on the floor, two military blankets, and a small trash can. Other items in the cell included a spoon, a plastic cup, a bowl, a plate, and a tray. The soldiers brought breakfast, lunch, and dinner to the hallway outside the cell. Through a small window on the door of the cell every inmate passed his plate to the guard and received his food. They would also provide every prisoner with three cups of tea and three cigarettes daily. In most cases, they gave tea to the prisoners after every meal. When a prisoner was ill and was under medication, they would also bring him his medicines. Prison authorities did not give the medication bottle to the patient to keep. Rather, soldiers usually kept their medications.

---

[171] This interview was conducted on Mehr 7, 1379/October 21, 2000

The sanitary conditions and medical services at Evin were much better than at Qasr and JCC. They provided aspirin to anyone who suffered from a headache or toothache. There was a soldier who was in charge of dressing the wounds and injuries of prisoners. In the past he had worked for some of the torturers where he learned how to take care of the wounded prisoners.

In the Evin Prison cells, there were many insects and bedbugs. Sometimes we could even find scorpions. Bedbugs bit us frequently. The clothing of the prisoners included a t-shirt and underwear, a shirt, and a pair of pants. The floor of the prison was covered with tiles. Since soldiers and guards wore tennis shoes when they walked around so it was not possible to hear their footsteps. They normally allowed prisoners to take a bath once a week upon request. There was one shower room in every corridor and each had one small shower. The time assigned for the shower was only 10 minutes. Once a month they gave us three soap bars, one for washing hands and the other two for shower. Each ward had a small backyard the size of the cells, and a sheet of metal constituted its roof. Every once in a while, they took one of the prisoners to that backyard to get some fresh air. That too could only happen when a prisoner requested it. At most, the period for enjoying the fresh air was between ten and fifteen minutes.

Every week or every other week they took prisoners to the barber shop and gave them a haircut. This barber shop was in the hallway, and the prisoners were taken there blindfolded. At the Qasr Prison a prisoner's hair was shaved the moment he entered before taking his photos. But at Evin, prisoners could grow long hair if they wished, but everybody had to shave his beard. In Evin Prison, every prisoner was given a set of underwear, a shirt, and a pair of trousers. The uniforms at the Evin Prison were much better than those of the Qasr and the JCCT Prison. They did not give towels or toothbrushes to prisoners, but those items were available in the prison store for purchase.

373

At least up to 1354/1975, they did not bring newspapers or books to prison. But after that year and as a result of the insistence of the prisoners, the authorities allowed four months of old newspapers to be brought in, mostly pages that contained advertisements and reports of accidents. This went on until gradually, authorities allowed newspapers be delivered daily. They also gave us books by authors affiliated with the regime, such as Hashimi Qauchani, who had written against the Communists. They did not allow a copy of the Qur'an and *Nahj al-Balaghah* to be brought in. It was nearly impossible for someone to sneak a copy of the Qur'an into prison.

Each person had his own way of killing time in prison. Some spent most of the time in bed sleeping, and some of them did not even come out of bed to eat. Even when they were awake, they would pretend to be asleep. Since there was not much to do, those who did not have physical activity grew lazy and developed depression. After a while their bodies began to swell and ached. But there were also other prisoners who had their own daily schedule that included exercise and games. Some sang revolutionary songs, some recited poetry, and those who knew Qur'an by heart chanted the verses they knew.

My Life at Evin Prison

It was in the early days of Farvardin 1352/April 1975 that I entered the Evin Prison. First they took off all my clothes before giving me a prison uniform. They then took me to a cell that was located between rows seven and eight. The first thing that caught my eye in the cell was a European-style toilet. The guards were more polite than those in the JCCT Prison and had a kind and respectable attitude and greeted me warmly. Although I arrived at night and they had already served supper, they still brought me food to eat. It was a dream to sleep on a mattress and have two blankets, and this memory will remain in my mind forever. I slept that first night in a very relaxed and peaceful state and with many hopes and dreams. The next morning, they brought breakfast for me along with three cigarettes. I had to use the European toilet, but I had no experience using it. The European toilet was not suitable for us. If I sat on it in an ordinary way, I would not be able to cleanse myself and thus attain ritual purity. At first, I could not sit on it since my legs were still in pain. Also, I was obsessed with being ritually clean. I tried as hard as I could not to pray while my body was ritually impure. Since the guard was watching my every move through the window of the cell, I was forced to go for a long call only during the nights and it was very difficult. The noise caused by flushing the siphon disturbed and awakened prisoners in the adjacent cells. So to avoid waking up others prisoners, I did not flush the toilet. This made the whole cell smell very bad until the morning. The next day, when everybody else was awake, I flushed the toilet. If I wanted to go for a short call, I would do that in a standing position and then clean myself with water. At times when I could no longer wait until the night to go for a long call, I would collect some of the old newspapers, cover myself under a blanket, and relieve myself. I would then throw that into the toilet. This situation was not a difficult thing for the Marxist prisoners, who were used to wiping and cleaning themselves using newspapers, but for an obsessive religious person like me, it was really cumbersome because ritual purity was very important to me.

They had given us a piece of sponge for cleaning our own dishes. Washing and drying our clothes was also very difficult because we only had one set of uniform. Whenever we washed our shirts and trousers, we only had the underwear until the other clothes dried. When we washed the underwear we only had the shirt and the trousers to wear. There was a radiator located at the back of my cell that was covered with a metal screen. I cut a string of the blanket and tied one end to the radiator and the other end to the door handle and used that to hang my clothes on. If the guards saw this, they would instantly cut the string. So I had to do this at night and early in the morning. Then I took away the string and hid it under the mattress. I struggled as much as I could to always remain clean and in a state of ritual purity. Sometimes I hung the washed pair of trousers on the door handle.

One day two guards along with the prison director opened my cell and greeted me. They asked if I needed anything, had any message for my interrogator, or wished to have visitors. I told them that my interrogation was not yet over and I did not expect any visitor. They thus closed the door and went away. On that same day, they changed my cell and transferred me to cell number one. In the cell next to mine, there was a prisoner who talked excessively, and I was suspicious of him. My suspicion was not baseless because, in contrast to the other prisoners, they used to bring him newspapers on a daily basis and give him special treatment. Sometimes he would shout and ask for dates or other things. The guards treated him warmly and were very friendly toward him. He tried hard to initiate communication with me by hitting the wall of the cell. But since I was suspicious of him, I never answered back. And whenever I did answer him, my answers were short. I didn't tell him anything concerning my interrogation and other important matters. I guessed that this person must have been Ahmad Reza Karimi. Often they transferred him from one prison to another so that he could collect information from prisoners. After some days, he was transferred to another cell, and I never found out who he really was. When I was in solitary confinement, I knew nothing about the group cells. Sometimes I could hear voices of unknown people playing games in the yard. I was not sure if they were prisoners or the guards playing games.

Time really moved on very slowly. It was necessary for me to draw up a schedule for every day to avoid getting lazy and tired. I exercised for an hour. I set myself to walk from one corner of the cell to another corner 1500 times a day. I would count 750 rounds in the morning and another 750 in the afternoon. I even decided to flush the toilet to enjoy listening to the sound of the water! In the quiet environment of prison, this was the most pleasant music that a prisoner could listen to. I just had to find a good way to spend time. Sometimes I sat down and counted the holes in the metal screen of the heater. I would then multiply them in order to find out the number of the total holes. Sometimes I memorized the telephone numbers from newspaper advertisements. And on the accidents page, I counted the names of the people who were involved in or had died in accidents. This is how I came to know about the death of some people I knew.

Sometimes I got myself busy with ants and bedbugs and placed small bits of food on the ants' nests. When the ants came out of their hole, I would close it and then begin to count them. After counting them, I would again open up their nest and let them go in. I used to do this two or three times a day. If I was in a good mood, I would pick up the ant and place it on my hairy arm. The ants got stuck in the hairs of my arm and were not able to move. When they managed to come out of the haris on my arm I would place them on my other arm and would repeat this process sometimes for over two hours. Whenever I saw that an ant was not capable of carrying a whole grain of rice, I would divide it into three particles.

The walls of the cells were made of concrete, and insects were able to climb up easily. When the bedbugs reached the roof of the cell, they would fall down to the floor. I would pick them up from the floor and place them again on the wall. In the beginning, I did not know that we should ask for permission to take a shower and thought that they would inform us. They had changed the wound dressing on my leg and my leg was now healed. It was either on the 24th or 25th of Farvardin, 1354/April 14 or 15, 1975 that Major Afshar and General Vaziri came to my cell for interrogation. I was performing my prayers, and so they had to wait. Vaziri said, "This is what we refer to exactly as an Islamic Marxist!"

377

Afshar said, "No sir! This one is different from the others."

They greeted me and wished me a happy New Year. When they wanted to leave, they asked if I needed anything, and I said that they allow me to take a shower.

Afshar asked, "How long have you been here, and how often have you taken a shower?

I said, "Almost one month now."

He did not know that the guards had not yet taken me for a shower. He looked at the guard and said, "Now that the weather is hot, you should let him take a shower once a week." He didn't want to embarrass the guard and show that it was his mistake. He pretended to show that this was the prison system and that it was only due to the cold weather that they did not allow me to take a shower. So from that time on the system changed. I also developed a friendship with the guard. I told two or three of them who prayed that I was also a Muslim, and sometimes we need to perform a greater ablution (*ghusl*) to be able to pray. We cannot just rely upon the prison schedule to shower only once a week. They said, "Whenever you want to make your greater ablution, just knock on the door and let us know. We shall take you to the shower room." So I took advantage of their kindness and favor that they extended to me, and every two or three days told the guard that I needed to go to take a shower. They made a list of those who wanted to take a shower to prevent people from taking a shower more than once in a week. Sometimes the guards would reject my request, but I always argued and convinced them that I had not taken a shower for over a week, and therefore they let me go. At last they would accept my excuse.

I tracked the passing of time by following the sunrise and sunset and the rays of sun that flew through my cell window. I also used the food-serving schedule to guess the time of the day. By following the size of the area that the sun light covered, it was easy to find out how long remained till noontime or sunset. I woke up early in the morning at the sound of

378

the crows. This prison had a lot of trees. The crows had their nests in the branches of those trees. In the morning they used to sing in a very harmonious and beautiful way and then fly away as though they were trying to tell me that it was time for morning prayers.

Sending Morse Code with an Egg

The solitary cells in Evin Prison were very quiet. For me it meant loneliness and silence. For others it was an eternal darkness and death! It was only me and me alone! I reviewed each moment and all events of my life one by one many times. I was dying to have a companion to talk to. There was no way to have contact with prisoners in other cells. The guards walked back and forth quietly in the hallway, and we noticed their presence only when they opened the small window to check on us. Some prisoners tried to break the silence of prison by knocking on the concrete wall and sending Morse code to the person in the next cell, but often they were caught and severely beaten up.

I finally found another means of communicating with the person in the next cell. This was through the ventilation pipe of the toilet. The ventilation pipes of the two cells were close to one another. So if a person wanted to talk, he had to place his mouth on the pipe and speak through that. Since the pipe was located beyond my reach, I had to step on the handle of the door and place the other foot above the toilet. To share this great idea for communication with others, whenever they took us out to get some fresh air, I wrote instructions on the walls for prisoners to talk to each other through the ventilator in their cell. Occasionally the guards noticed my writings on the walls and erased them. To punish us they changed some prisoners' cells and beat us up, of course not as hard as in the JCCT Prison.

Every day I spent a few hours making up my lost prayers. In the four and a half months in Evin I probably made up for all the prayers I had missed for four or five years. I also fasted secretly every other day. I kept my lunch for dinnertime and my dinner meal for the *suhur*. When I had leftovers, I did not throw them in the trash can, lest the guards think that I was on a hunger strike. Instead I dumped them in the toilet and flushed.

They offered us hard-boiled eggs for breakfast some days and I usually kept them for my *suhur*. My cell was located at the end of the corridor, and it was next to the cell assigned to Fazilat Kalam's father.[172] He was a hot-tempered man, and I had known him since we met in Qasr Prison. In order not to disturb him when I wanted to eat my *suhur*, I often peeled the hardboiled egg in advance. One day I forgot to do that, so I had to knock the egg on the wall, and this created a Morse code-like rhythm. The guard heard this sound and thought that I was sending some messages to the old man. He opened the door of the cell, cursed at me, and threatened to beat me up. I yelled back at him and said that he had no right to insult me, nor any authority to beat me up, and all he could do was to report me to his superiors.

As a result of this dispute, he reported me, but to prove he had misunderstood me, I did not eat the egg so that I could present it as an evidence of my innocence. The next morning, the senior prison officer called me to his office and reminded

---

[172] Abbas Fazilat Kalam (b.1303/1924) started his political activities in the 1320's/1940's with his membership in the Central Council of the Labor Division of the Tudeh party. He was arrested in 1325/1946 on the charges of recruiting members for the Democrat Party of Azarbaijan that was backed by the USSR. In 1334/1955 he defected from the Tudeh party and in 1350/1971 he joined the Fidayan-i Khalq Organization through his son. His three children, Mehdi, Shirin, and Anusheh, were killed in clashes with the SAVAK in 1351/1972, 1353/1974, and 1355/1976 respectively. After the Revolution he joined the minority branch of the Fidayan but soon fled the country, settled in Paris, and joined the Society for the Defense of Prisoners of Conscience. He passed away in 1377/1998 at the age of 78. See www.Ettehadfedaian.org/yaran/Albomyadeyaran ri-1.htm.

me that I caused trouble at Qasr Prison, was unruly at JCCT Prison, and that there were many complaints against me.

He said he wondered why I was doing this to myself and added that he had to report my conduct. I told him he could do as he wished. After a short time, Major Afshar, the Deputy Director of Evin Prison compound, called me and asked for an explanation. I told him the story that I was simply trying to peel a hard-boiled egg and had not sent anyone a message, and showed him the egg as evidence. I also said that I was fasting and did not have a chance to eat this egg for *suhur* because the guard started cursing and threatening me. Major Afshar realized that the guard was mistaken and tried to wrap things up and advised me to act properly and respect the rules of the prison.

I was very isolated in solitary confinement and did not know what was going on in the communal ward. Sometimes I heard the voice of a few people playing games in the courtyard but could not tell if they were prisoners or prison guards.

Peaceful Co-Existence in Ward Two

I stayed in solitary confinement and the isolation cell for almost three and a half months until the last days of the month of Tir 1354/July 1975. Then one day, prison authorities decided to switch some prisoners from their cells to other cells. They also told me to gather my belongings. I knew that they would not take me for interrogation because my interrogation had already been done at the JCCT Prison. When they told me to gather my belongings, the first thought that came to my mind was that they wanted to take me back to JCCT Prison. But I was wrong and this was not the case.

It was not clear to me whether they wanted to bring in new prisoners or not. Anyway, they took me along with four or five other prisoners to the office of the head of the prison. Rasuli was also present there. In addition to working at the JCCT headquarters he was also the head of the interrogators at

Evin Prison. When he saw me, he got up, greeted me in a very friendly way, and extended his hand to shake hands with me. When he took charge of a prisoner and wanted to make him comfortable, he usually made a joke. His favorite term that he used in such cases was "pimp." So he said, "You pimp! Your interrogator was not willing to take you to the group cells, but because of my friendship with you, I have decided to take you there. So be careful that just in case they take you to the JCCT Prison, don't say that you were in the communal ward." I was aware of his intention and knew what he meant by friendship with me. This entire maneuver was nothing but a game, but I had to remain silent. I assured him that I would not say anything.

They took me to the communal ward number two. In this ward, the Islamist inmates were housed on the upper floor, while the leftists were kept on the lower floor. Each group cell had two windows that had been fixed to the wall with nuts and bolts, and it was impossible to open them. It was only the upper window that could be opened. Yet it was still not possible to see the outside through it. They had applied white paint to that window so it was impossible to see anything through it. We were not pleased with this, so we used nails and erased a large part of it, and that made it possible for us to see the outside world.

One of the rules in Evin prison was to house prominent members and leaders of each group in one cell. They would also assign ordinary and often shady inmates to live among them in order to control them. To torture me psychologically they always put me in one cell with the leftist inmates in JCCT Prison. They decided to do the same in Evin, so they sent me downstairs to be with prominent leftist inmates and their leaders. Since I had a good reputation among the leftists, they treated me with respect. I tried as hard as I could not to come into conflict with them. I told them at the outset that we had different and conflicting strategies and ideologies and we should not expect support from each other. I believed that one of us was legitimate and the other one was wrong, that I believed I was right and they thought they were legitimate. If it were any other way, then we would be in the same boat. That meant that if I were to support you, I would have to accept that I am on the wrong side and vice versa; and that they were against God and believed religion was the opium of the masses and struggled to establish a communist government, whereas I struggled to create a just Islamic government. Despite these differences, we both shared a common enemy. There was one thing that united us, and that was our common enemy. Our main enemy was the regime, and the regime knew that and would be happy to see us fight each other. Therefore, I made it clear that I was against any dispute, which would only benefit our common enemy. I emphasized that we needed to maintain a good working relationship with one another but could not come to political unity. You take care of your duties as I take care of mine. Let us not involve ourselves in one another's business so that respect and mutual understanding between us can be maintained.

The leftist groups liked this position of mine, which was based on honesty and integrity, unlike that of other Islamists like Rajavi. In fact, they considered him and his comrades opportunists who were eclectic in their ideology and opportunistic in their behavior. They believed that people like Rajavi were hypocrites because they told the leftists one thing and religious people different things. It was interesting that leftist groups called Rajavi and his associates the hypocrites before anyone else and even defended me when I came into conflict with him. They always said, "Ezzat's position was consistent, honest, and transparent, and his arguments were logical, and therefore we accepted what he said."

This situation was not liked or approved of by Rajavi and his comrades. He criticized me for establishing a friendly relationship with the left. I tried to convince him and his associates that inside prison we should not come into conflict with the leftist groups and let the police take advantage of the situa-

383

tion; rather, we had to be united in our struggle against the regime. Because if we fought with the left, the police would exploit our differences, and if any one of us preferred the police over the leftists, then he was either simple-minded at best or a traitor at worst.

My Marxist cellmates who knew my position always said that they were aware that SAVAK brought me to their cell to give me a hard time and torture me, but they all respected and accepted me. The police really pressured me to talk against the Marxists. They wanted me to declare my opposition regarding the leftist groups' ideology and political behavior. But I told the police that our own differences were our business, and that the undeniable truth was that we were both enemies of the regime. Each of us had his own reasons and it is because of this that we had both received a lot of torture and beatings from the police. The police insisted that there iwass a great deal of difference between Islamist and leftist groups and that we were true believers, whereas the communists were infidels, and wondered how we could get along with them. My answer was that they were more understanding and respectful toward us than the regime was. I questioned the regime's honesty when it treated the Islamist activists much more harshly than the leftist prisoners. There were in fact moments that I actually defended a communist against the police.

An Encounter with the Two Shaykhs

One day I was summoned to the office Mr. Rasuli, who was then the chief interrogator. A few minutes later they brought Shaykh Ahmad Karrubi and Shaykh [Hasan Ali] Montazeri. I was facing the wall. When I saw both of them, I said to myself, "Oh, Lord! Everything will be ruined now." I had my head down looking at the floor.

Rasuli asked if I recognized these two people, and I quickly said that I did not.

Again he said that these two gentlemen were well known and asked how it was that I did not know them. I told Rasuli that he knew that I did not have a good relationship with the *mullas* and had no ties with them. Rasuli obviously did not believe me and asked me not to play games and said that Montazeri was too famous for me not to know him. I said that I had just heard his name, but I never had anything to do with him. Of course I knew both of these gentlemen very well. I prayed that they would reiterate what I had said and deny that they knew me.

Rasuli asked Shaykh Ahmad if he knew me, and he said, "I am not a SAVAK agent, and even if he knew him I tell you that I do not!" Then he asked Shaykh Montazeri, and he said that he didn't know me.

Rasuli became angry, and addressing Montazeri, said, "This is Ezzat Shahi! How is it possible that you do not know him?"

At that moment Shaykh Montazeri turned and asked me, "O Ezzat! Is that you! I can't believe it!"

I was really flabbergasted by his reaction. Rasuli asked Montazeri, "You said that you didn't know Ezzat! How is it that you recognize him now?"

Shaykh Montazeri realized that he had spoiled everything, and so he tried to correct himself. So he said, "I really don't know him personally and just remembered that last summer I read in the newspaper that a taxi exploded on Firdawsi Avenue and a person by this name was killed. Right now my biggest surprise is that the same person who was reportedly killed is alive and standing in front of me."

Rasuli understood that there were some connections between us but pretended that he believed Montazeri's explanation. He then asked if we smoked, and Montazeri said no, but also advised him not to smoke either, because it was harmful to his health and his wallet, as he could use the money for better purposes. A few minutes later Rasuli left us alone and we started talking.

Chief Interrogator Rasuli, the MKO, and I

Rasuli,[173] the Chief interrogator, was a very skilled, sophisticated, and politically astute man, and a number of interrogators worked under his command. His style of interrogation was unique and shrewd. First he sent a prisoner to his subordinates, who beat him up really well. Then he stepped in, interfered, and criticized them for the inhumane way they had treated the prisoner and questioned them as to who gave them the authority to beat and torture. From that point on, he would take charge of the interrogation. He treated the prisoner kindly, offered him cigarettes and chocolate, and arranged family visitation for him. By doing so he tried to capture the heart of the suspect. If the prisoner was fooled and began to talk and gave him information, his interrogation would end quickly. But if a person recognized Rasuli's trick and refused to believe him or share information, then Rasuli changed his position and gave the suspect back to his subordinates to beat and torture him.

Still he tried to play the "good guy" and said that he opposed torture and regretted sending the prisoner back to his previous interrogators, but this is the choice that he made, and he must be prepared for its consequences. Some prisoners were prepared to make deals in order to avoid torture. The tactic used by Rasuli was very effective in most cases. He claimed that there were many prisoners who never said a word

---

[173] Nasser Nowzari, known as Dr. Rasuli (1319/1940), started his career as a teacher, joined the SAVAK in its infancy, and for over twelve years in the guise of math teacher was in charge of surveillance against the people in Khuzistan. When the guerrilla organization emerged in the 1960's, he was transferred to Tehran and joined the JCCT. With his short and bulky appearance, and always well dressed, he was the most articulate interrogator in the JCCT headquarters. He was responsible for the execution of nine activists in Evin in 1354/1975. He held several important administrative positions in the SAVAK and received much recognition and many medals of honor from the regime. On the eve of the Revolution he sensed the danger and fled the country, first to Israel, then Greece, and the U.S., and finally settled in France. See Christin De la Noua, "200 Portraits in Ebrat Museum," in Kaman, #7, 195

under torture. But when they met and talked with him once or twice, they revealed everything. But I often pulled his leg and fooled him and got rid of him.

My leftist cellmates warned me not to deal with Rasuli because he would turn against you, but I did not pay attention to what they said. Whenever Rasuli entered our cell, everybody got up to show him respect, but I remained in my bed and even covered my head with my blanket. My cellmate thought this behavior was rude and criticized me for that lest they would also pay the price for my rudeness. I assured them that they would not be punished for my behavior because authorities would never treat them the way they treated me, and that I have never showed respect to police and SAVAK agents and never will.

Sometimes Rasuli noticed my disrespectful attitude toward him and warned me not to ruin our "friendly relationship," or else he would beat me up. I always replied to him and said that no matter how hard he beat me, it would still be less than what I received at the JCCT Prison, and that being beaten had become part of my normal daily life in prison anyway. Sometimes he pulled up a chair and sat next to me and claimed to be a good human being and my friend, a believer in God and the Prophet. Of course he was an educated person. I never thought so, and always told him that he was not different from the rest, and all those who were in the service of SAVAK were the same, and only their styles might differ.

As a member of the MKO, I maintained communication with the Mujahidin members on the upper floor through a crack in the door and other means. In the month of Ordibehesht 1354/May 1975 they transferred around 200 religious and not-so-religious members of the Mujahidin to the Evin Prison. The transfer of the Mujahidin members to the Evin Prison was done after the assassination of Majid Sharif Vaqifi and Samadiyyeh Labbaf. This was the first public sign of the deviation of the MKO and their attraction towards Marxism. The police had transferred these prisoners because they thought that they had ties with the assassination of Sharif Vaqifi. These prisoners were not given visitation rights for a period of one full year. Those among them who had been in Qasr Prison before thought that I was dead because they had heard rumors that I had been killed in the JCCT Prison. They had been told that I tried to commit suicide a couple of times and that I had cut the vein in my hand. These rumors were everywhere. Some had concluded that even if I did not die before, I would have been killed along with nine other people in order. When they were transferred to Evin during the last days of the month of Ordibehesht, 1354/April 1975 they realized that I was still alive. It was in the afternoon when Rasuli came after me and asked me to go with him so that we could talk. In fact it was for this reason that he had brought me to the communal ward. I refused to obey him, and he threatened to send me to the basement where he would teach me a lesson.

That same night, they took Rajavi, Hayati,[174] and Ganjeh'ie[175] for interrogation. I saw this from the crack in the door. Rasuli told them that they were all communists. He also bragged that he had done me a great service and saved my life when everybody wanted to execute me. Mas'ud pretended not to know that I was in the communal ward at Evin and dis-

---

[174] Mohammad Hayati (b. 1326/1947) received his B.A. degree in physics from the University of Tehran. Initially he joined the Hujatiyyeh group and was close to its founder, Shaykh Mohammad Halabi. Toward the end of his education he joined the MKO. He was arrested in 1350/1971 and was condemned to seven years in prison. After the Revolution he turned against the Islamic Republic and fled the country, first to France and then to Iraq in 1365/1986 where he settled at the Ashraf compound and was one of the deputies of Rajavi. Javad Mansuri, *Memoirs,* pp. 25 and 274, Nejad Hosseini, pp. 299–303, Lutfullah Meysami, *Memoirs,* vol. II, pp. 92–95, *and Tafsir-i Khoshunat* at *www.Irandidban.com.*

[175] Jalal Ganjeh'ie was the religious theoretician of the MKO. He was initially invited to teach Islamic Culture at the Ansar al-Mahdi mosque. His lecture attracted much attention because of his new approach. He was arrested in Khordad 1351/June 1972 and released two years later, to be arrested again in 1355/1976. After the Revolution he joined the MKO. For more information about him see Javad Mansuri, *Memoirs,* pp. 104–106.

missed what Rasuli had said because Ezzat was dead, and what Rasuli had said was related to the past and no longer relevant!

The more Rasuli insisted, the more Mas'ud and the others refused to accept that I was alive unless they could meet me. This prompted Rasuli to prove his point by calling me to meet them. So cleverly Rajavi encouraged Rasuli to arrange our meeting. It was around midnight when a guard came after me, woke me up, and took me to Rasuli's office. I saw Mas'ud, Hayati, Ganjeh'ie, and Rasuli sitting there. I greeted them coldly and treated them all without emotions. Rasuli offered me a handshake and said, "Oh, my little pimp! How are you? Do you recall how I saved you from death?"

I said, "You should have not done that!"

He asked why, and I said because I just want to die and be free from your oppression.

He said, "Don't be silly and don't make a fool of yourself. If you are willing to die, then let me send you to be executed right away."

I said, "This would be really a great favor to me, and it is my only wish. It would be so nice if I could die at your hands and not by my own. I am so exhausted and fed up with this world."

Rasuli then offered me a cigarette, but I told him that I did not smoke and added, "I do not want anything from you. The whipping I received from you was enough for me."

He said, "You fool! Was I the one who whipped you?"

I said, "It makes no difference! You never whipped me personally, but you ordered, and the interrogators under your command carried out the order.

He said, "These fellows (showing Rajavi, Hayati, and Ganjeh'ie) thought that we had killed you. I simply brought you here so that they could personally see you."

He then looked at them and asked, "Now that I have proven to you that I told you the truth, are you satisfied?"

I greeted and hugged Mas'ud and the others and sat close to Mas'ud. He thanked Rasuli and said, "Mr. Rasuli! We are very grateful. We never thought that Ezzat was alive. We are very pleased to see him alive."

We stayed together for around twenty minutes. I noticed that Rasuli was proud of what he had done and was bragging. I said that I had a bad headache, and I saw that Rasuli kept heaping much praise onto himself. I said, "Mr. Rasuli! I have a headache. If you have nothing else to do with me, please allow me to go to bed."

He said, "Shame on you! Where do you want to go?"

I said, "I am not feeling well at the moment. I have no mind to listen to this conversation. Let me go and sleep."

He said, "Do you want me to send you to Mas'ud's cell so that you can have a talk with them and catch up?"

I said, "I have no business with these guys. They are prisoners here and so am I. Being on the upper floor or lower floor makes no difference to me. I will be fine wherever you place me."

Rasuli said, "Listen, you fool! These men are all leftist, whereas you are Islamist.

I said, "It makes no difference to me. I keep my faith and perform my duties, and they never disturb me at all. Even if I am transferred to the upper floor, I will do the same thing. A prison is just a prison, and there is no difference between its lower and upper floors."

Before I could complete my sentence, Rasuli called a guard and told him to take me upstairs with my belongings. He didn't even give me a chance to bid farewell to my cellmates.

Being a Cellmate with Rajavi

They took me to a room where Mas'ud Rajavi was also placed, and a little later the guard brought my belongings. This room was on the second floor in Ward Two. Mas'ud and I talked about my interrogations and the state of my case as well as the issues related to the JCCT Prison. Rajavi explained to me,

"When Hasan Kabiri[176]was transferred from Qasr to the JCCT Prison, he said to him that Ezzat Shahi had given Kazim Zulanvar the address for Niktab'. Kazim too, was brought to the JCCT Prison, and he said that he had given that address to a person named Ibrahim Davar,[177] who had been released from prison and was a fugitive. Kazim also said that he had held discussions with me [Mas'ud] concerning Niktab' and his assassination and received my approval. I had rejected the idea. When interrogators at the JCCT Prison heard my rejection they showed me what Kazim had written. I said, 'I can recall that one day Kazim talked about this matter and I told him that it was not my business and we are not in charge of the things that are happening outside of prison. If Kazim did something on his own, then it is up to him, but it does not concern us in any way or form.'"

For this reason Mas'ud was beaten in the JCCT Prison two times. Since he was physically weak, he had stomach bleeding and was hospitalized and after a few days transferred to Evin. During the few days that I was with Rajavi, I criticized him on several issues and complained about the Mujahidin's dictatorial behavior in Qasr Prison, and questioned him about the influence of the leftist forces in the organization.

After listening to me, he said, "Ezzat! This is not the time for these issues. You have just come out of a stressful situation. Take a little bit of rest, and when everything else cooled down, then you can address these issues again."

---

[176] Hasan Kabiri (b. 1327/1948) started his activities when he joined Ansar al-Hossein, and shortly afterward the MKO. He was arrested in 1351/1972 and spent four years in prison. After the Revolution he began to fight against the Islamic Republic and was finally killed in an encounter with [SAVAK] agents.

[177] Hajj Ibrahim Davar (b. 1330/1951) entered the University of Tehran to study economics, but joined the MKO. He was one of those members who split in 1354/1975. He apparently committed suicide. According to another report he died under torture. See Haji Ibrahim Davar, *Tarikhche-ye Mukhtasar-i Gruhakha*, p. 131.

I said, "No! I am still the same person and my position has not changed. I speak my mind and I am neither concerned about what so-and-so may say nor afraid of the probable pressures by anyone."

We talked a lot about these issues, and I realized that he and his comrades suffered from lack of confidence before the Marxists elements. I also found out that he had a lot of issues and problems with the clergy and especially the Source of Emulation (*marja'iyyat*). I remember how much pain I had suffered in Qasr Prison because of the MKO and their behavior. They frustrated me so much that sometimes I thought of accepting responsibility for a murder so that I would be condemned to death and be free from all these pains. But by His grace, God guided me to respond to the call of duty. If I got killed, I would have been content. Otherwise, I would return to prison and live happily ever after.

I told Mas'ud that I could no longer collaborate with him and the MKO because I did not approve of their policies and behaviors, that I was firm in my decision and could not play games and just wanted to serve my prison term.

Mas'ud said, "Ezzat! You are not feeling well, and your wounds are not healed quite yet. Do not make a hasty decision, and you must stay with us."

I said, "Your position is not transparent, and you must clarify your position first so that I can decide whether I could work with you or not." Mas'ud spoke a little more about his positions. I noticed that he did not speak frankly. He neither approved nor disapproved of the leftist groups. He did not see a problem admitting Marxist elements for membership in the organization. I told him that we share some ideas and positions and we differ on some others, and each of us should pursue his own path. He categorically rejected this idea and said that we should talk about this issue more extensively later on.

After four or five days, a guard came and called me during lunch: "Ezzat! Take all your belongings and let us go."

*   *   *

CHAPTER EIGHT

The Genuine and the Fake

Futile Resistance

Although I spent four or five days with Rajavi, we did not get another chance to discuss our positions further. I had to gather my belongings and move back for the third time to JCCT headquarters. They blindfolded me and cuffed my hands and I was escorted by several bodyguards to the JCCT Prison. When I entered the night officer's room, the prison officer said, "Here we go again!! You have come back here again?"

I said, "My destiny is intertwined with this prison and as long I am alive, I remain yours truly, and would come and go as you please." He asked me who brought me there and I said I had no idea. He phoned the interrogators, and when he returned he said that Tehrani[178] had asked for me. I told him that my interrogator was Mohammadi, and this was not Tehrani's business. He said he had no idea but was told that Tehrani wanted to see me. I told him that it did not make any difference anyway.

---

[178] Bahman Naderipour, known as Tehrani (b. 1324/1945), joined the Tudeh Party when he was a student at Tehran University School of Law and Political Science. Soon he abandoned political activity and the left. In 1347/1968 he was employed by the SAVAK as a clerk but soon transferred to the intelligence department in charge of communist groups. Under the patronage of Abbas Ali Shahriyari and his guidance, Tehrani infiltrated the Tudeh Party organization and played a leading role in the arrest of the Jazani group and some members of the Siyahkal movement as well as the destruction of the MKO in 1350/1971. After the Revolution he was arrested and confessed and asked for execution. In his trial he addressed his wife and said, "I have committed many crimes and deserve to die. What I did even Shimr did not do [to Imam Hossein]. I must be killed, or else I am too embarrassed to look people in the eye." He was executed on Tir 3, 1358/June 24, 1979. See, Iskandar Deldam, *Tarikhche-ye SAVAK*, p. 115, *Kayhan*, #10736–7, and *Sharq*, # 207–208.

393

There was no vacancy in any of the cells. There were two girls in one cell, and I waited until they were moved to other cells so that I could take their cell in Ward Two, cell number nine. When I was passing through the courtyard, I saw my interrogator, Mr. Mohammadi. He cursed me and warned me that this was my last chance and I was finished. I did not show any reaction. The guards knew me and they greeted me. After a week or two, they came and took me to Hooshang Khan's office for interrogation. The first question he asked me was about production and distribution of the declarations in 1349/1970. I realized that new information about me must have been revealed to the police, so I said I was alone in that activity.

He didn't believe me and told me to keep thinking.

Again I said that I was alone and no one else helped me.

He asked who in the year 1349/1970 on Arif Avenue helped me to produce declarations.

I said that I didn't know what he was talking about.

He mentioned the name of the landlord—Behrooz Shuja'iyan![179] He then asked, "Doesn't that name ring a bell?!"

Behrouz Shuja'iyan was one of the activists in contact with me in 1349/1970. Sometimes I stayed at his house overnight. Once he told me that someone wanted to print declarations but did not have a copy machine. Since I had full confidence in him, I took the copy machine to his house at night, and with the help of a third person printed the declarations. The third person was Khalil Faqih Dezfuli,[180]who had placed

---

[179] The late Behrouz Shuja'iyan was one of the most courageous activists and participated in Arabic language classes. In addition to Tehran, he was also active in Zanjan.

[180] Mohammad Ali Faqih Dezfuli, known as Khalil (b. 1332/1953), joined the MKO in 1325/1973 and went underground. He advanced quickly to the leadership cadre of the organization but was then demoted because of his differences with other leaders. He adopted Marxism for a while but was arrested in 1354/1975 and began to collaborate with the SAVAK. In a series of televised interviews, Khalil unveiled some of the crimes committed

the order for the job. We finished the job that night, and the next morning we went about our own business. Then Faqih Dezfuli was arrested and confessed that we had done the job together. I was not aware of his arrest and his betrayal. Therefore, I thought Behrouz, who had been arrested in 1353/1974, had said something as he had been transferred with me from Qasr to the JCCT Prison. So I said, "I am not saying that I never went to Behrouz's house. I might have, but what I am saying is that I do not recall anything."

Well! these interrogators knew that they would not be able to get any information from me by those means. So they did not want to waste time and took me straight away to Hosseini's office. They gave me forty lashes of the whip.

Hooshang said, "Ezzat! You fool! You stop f—ing with me. This matter is no longer important to us. It is a matter of the past. It is also not necessary for you to mention the name of a person because the same person you wish to protect has already been arrested and has confessed everything about you. I am not making it up. Use your senses and do not subject yourself to torture for nothing. Believe me! I do not want to leave you in the hands of your interrogator. I want to have a good relationship with you. So if there is anything you know about this fellow, just write it down and free yourself from all these unnecessary trouble."

I still didn't believe that Khalil had been arrested. I thought that the whole story was nothing but a bluff, and that they had just made it up to set a trap for me. I was aware that apart from me, there were only two people who knew about this, Behrouz and Khalil. I thought that Khalil was in hiding and had not yet been arrested. So it had to be Behrouz who told everything. Therefore, I said, "I swear by my life! Hooshang Khan, there is nothing that I remember about this

---

in the MKO during their internal conflict and purges such as the assassination of Sharif Vaqifi, stealing, and illicit sexual relationships among its members. Mansuri, *Memoirs,* pp. 172–173, *Tarikhche-ye Mokhtasar-e Guruhak-ha*, pp. 126.

matter." My purpose for making such a statement was to protect Khalil and not reveal his name. Hooshang said, "Behrouz is here."

I said, "I know that very well, since we were together in the Qasr Prison."

He said, "Get up and leave, but promise me that you will write something."

I agreed and again they brought me the album and showed me some pictures.

Hooshang said, "Ezzat! Look here! Don't bother yourself. Just tell us the person who helped you to print the declarations in Behrouz Shuja'iyan's house. Just show us which one he is in the picture."

The page of the pictures that he showed me as we were talking was the page that had the picture of Khalil. He wanted me to look at his picture so that I could recall everything. I then started to look at the pages of the album. Hooshang kept on telling me to pay more attention to the pictures. He also asked me whether I remembered anything or not.

I looked quickly at the pages that contained the pictures of the people I knew in order to avoid evoking suspicion while I took time looking at the pictures of people I didn't know. I looked at them from different angles and looked at the album again from the start to the end and told them that I could not recognize him.

Hooshang became very angry, and finally he showed me the picture himself and said, "You fool! Don't you know this person?"

I said, "No I don't know him. You cannot force me to know him!"

He realized that he had no choice, so he asked for Khalil's picture and his file to be brought to him. He showed me what Khalil had written about me and said, "These are the things that he wrote about you! Do you still deny that you know him?"

In order to change the topic and give an excuse for not saying anything, I said, "I do not recall if this person was at Behrouz's house that night. I am not saying that I never printed the declarations. My point is that if there was another person in the house other than Behrouz, I don't remember if it was this man."

He showed Khalil's picture and said, "He is the one."

I continued with my drama and said, "Even if he is the one, I only remember that someone came to the house wearing pajamas. He had also completely shaved his hair. But in this picture I see that he has put on a suit and a tie and looks very different from the man in pajamas. He doesn't look like the man I saw that night."

In short, I did not admit anything, and I just wrote down things that were in my mind, that "One night BehroUz Shuja'iyan came to me and said that there was someone who wanted to print the declarations and that he needed a copy machine, so I took the printing machine to his house and we printed the declarations." Then I described how the "man in pajamas" looked that I had mentioned earlier, but I never said anything about his identity because I was unaware that Khalil had betrayed us. Had I known, I would have tried to avoid being beaten up because of him. Later on I learnt that Khalil had conducted a television interview and had confessed a lot of things in relation to the organization. His betrayal was so open. He had even gone to the extent of working and collaborating with the police. He walked around with them in the streets and identified members of the organization when he saw any of them.

Making a Conspiracy Obsolete

After that incident they took me back to my cell. This time I was no longer tied to the metal bed. They just told me that at night I should sleep facing the door so the guard could watch me every moment lest I commit suicide. There was a lightbulb in front of the door of the cell. Its light penetrated into my cell through the small window on the top of the door and disturbed my sleep. So I faced the dark side in the cell so that I could sleep.

I was content to sleep in such a situation, but the guards did not leave me alone in my cell and constantly watched me. Every fifteen minutes or half an hour, they opened the little window and looked inside or knocked on the door just to check on me and then slammed it. They continued this several nights and frustrated me.

I asked Hooshang why they disturbed me like that and requested to be transferred somewhere else so that I could share a cell with others and not suffer and they could have peace of mind. I complained that what they were doing was not fair and that I was losing patience. My complaint was effective. It seemed that they no longer wanted to treat me as in the past and transferred me to the communal Ward Six. There were around twenty-three prisoners there with me. They were all good people. We sat there from morning to night and sometimes I narrated stories for them. We were happy, played games, and performed plays. A few times thing got a little out of control, and the inmates gave the guard a hard time. Once he became angry and wanted to ask for punishment for them. Since he knew me as his old prisoner, I mediated and the inmates apologized, and he accepted and the crisis ended.

A couple of times Manuchehri came and yelled at me and said, "You asshole! You are the source of all this trouble."

I told him he was using me as a scapegoat because he could hold anyone else responsible, and that I had nothing to do with what went on.

Then he turned to all the inmates and said that he was appointing Ezzat as the chief of the ward responsible for everything that might go on, and told them to communicate with him through me (Ezzat). He also made it clear that if anything illegal was found in the ward at the time of inspection, then I would be responsible for that.

398

This was a very crafty step to ruin my reputation and convey to the inmates that I was collaborating with the police. So I rejected his idea and said that I did not accept responsibility for anything, and he could give me whatever punishment he wished. I was certain that this was a conspiracy and that I must keep my alertness at all times. So I decided to counteract and make their plot ineffective. The prisoners, too, did as they wished, and I did not place any limitations on their activities.

They took me for interrogation a few more times. They cursed me and said, "You asshole! Who the hell do you think you are? Do not even think for a second that you are a hero! Don't you push us to do something to have you ostracized by all the prisoners so that nobody will talk to you and you will have no choice but to beg us to listen to your confessions. You'd better remember the last time that we placed you on that metal bed. We think that you really don't want to be tied to that bed again. We could do that again!"

I broke into laughter, and then said, "How I wish to see that day! You can do as you wish. I am ready for that day! Whatever you might do is nothing better than death." This arrogant answer resulted in a lot of beatings and whipping.

Vahid Afrakhteh's[181] Arrest

It was on either the 8th or the 12th of the month of Mordad, 1354/July 30 or August 3, 1975 when I was taken to the interrogator's office. I had an excruciating pain in my feet, so I placed one on the other to rest and ease the pain. The interrogator of the day, Hooshang Tahami, was a tall and heavy-set man with curly hair. Before asking me any questions, he slapped me very hard on my cheeks. Then he placed an album in front of me and asked me to identify the ones whom I knew.

I reviewed the pages of the album from the beginning to the end and even though I knew most of the people in the album, I told him that I did not know any of them. While he insisted that I must recognize some of them, the phone rang. Apparently, someone on the other side of the line was asking him if he should bring a suspect to Tahami's office. He said that he should bring the suspect. After a while they brought a man in while his face was covered by his shirt. Tahami told the suspect to remove the shirt from his face.

When he did, I recognized Muhsin Khamushi.[182] I had met him at the bazaar before and knew him. Of course, I never

---

[181] Rahman Afrakhteh, known as Vahid (b. 1329/1950), joined the MKO while he attended The Aryamehr Technical University (now Sharif), advanced quickly, dropped out of school in 1350/1971, and went underground. He participated in numerous operations including the assassination of Sha'aban Bimokh and the explosion in Isfahan. In 1353/1974 when the MKO split into two factions, he joined the Marxist faction under Bahram Aram. He also participated in the bloody purges within the MKO including the assassination of Sharif Vaqifi and Samadiyyeh Labbaf. After the assassination of an American military adviser the regime started an extensive campaign to arrest activists. Vahid also was arrested and showed much weakness in his interrogations and started collaborating with the SAVAK and identified many revolutionaries for the SAVAK, including Hasan Abrari. He was finally executed by the regime on Bahman 3, 1354/January 23, 1976. See *Tarikhche-ye Paydayesh Guruhak-ha*, Rouhani, Hamid, *Nihzat-e Imam Khomeini*, vol. III, Tehran, 1372/1994.

[182] Seyyed Muhsin Khamushi (b. 1334/1954) joined MKO through his brother. He was a member of a military operation team and was instrumen-

400

worked with him, nor did I collaborate with him in political activity. He was a classmate of Javad Musaddeqi (the son of Hossein Musaddeqi) in the Alavi School. Both of them had been admitted to Shiraz University and both of them frequented the paper shop. They talked with each other, and I never interfered in their affairs. Now they had arrested Khamushi and had him in prison uniform. He wore a pair of slippers, and there were no signs of torture on his feet, hands, or face. Reportedly, a person named Muhsin Batha'i reported him to the police.

Hooshang asked Muhsin, "Do you know this fellow?"

He said, "No!"

I don't think he remembered me or even knew who I was. Hooshang asked me whether I knew him or not. I said, "No! I do not know him."

He said, "Have you ever seen this man in your life?"

I said, "No, Never!"

Hooshang turned towards him and said, "How is that possible? This guy is from your organization. He is called Ezzat! He is one of those sons of——, and has been here for three years now. He has given us all kinds of trouble and tried to commit suicide several times but failed. He has been beaten like a donkey from morning until night. Look at his condition now! After three years he is still here in prison."

He again asked him, "Are you sure you don't know this guy?"

He said, "His name is quite familiar to me. I think I have heard his name being mentioned in the organization, but I have never seen him."

I became a little suspicious of this arrest. Vahid looked fine and did not seem to have suffered torture or beating. The

---

tal in the ideological transformation of the MKO and its split into a Marxist and an Islamist faction. He was arrested in 1354/1975 and was condemned to death and executed on Bahman 4, 1354/January 24, 1976. Rouhani, pp. 424–425, *Tarikhche-ye Paydayesh...*, *Malik Ashtar-e Dowran: Ayatullah Taleqani*, vol. ii, pp. 41 & 540, Tehran, 1382/2003.

interrogators treated him kindly. I was in doubt over whether he had been arrested or had surrendered himself just as Saʿid Shahsavandi[183] had done. During the last several months, the MKO members outside prison had been disillusioned, and some of them collaborated with the police and SAVAK agents. They disclosed the time and location of the meetings to the police. From the moment I saw Muhsin Khamushi, I had a feeling that he had started collaborating with the police since he was arrested.

Hooshang said, "Muhsin! Pray to God that this guy comes to the meeting place this afternoon. Otherwise you will see fire!"

Muhsin said, "Do not worry, Sir! Our meeting is so important that he will just have to come."

Hooshang said, "Just pray and be hopeful that your meeting does not fail!"

Muhsin said, "I can assure you of that, Sir!"

Hooshang then called ʿAzodi and said, "Their meeting is very important. You have to siege that place and control everything in an extended radius."

Hooshang then ordered another police officer to take Muhsin away and give him back his clothing so that could go to such-and-such a place on time. So they took him away, and I never knew what happened next. After Muhsin was taken away, Hooshang turned to me and said, "You are in trouble! We have set a trap today and will arrest your leader!" He was in a really great mood and talked to me for a while, saying at

---

[183] Saʿid Shahsavandi (b. 1339/1950) joined the MKO and after 1350/1971 went underground. He was arrested in 1354 and was sentenced to life in prison, but was released a few days before the victory of the Revolution in the month of Dey 1357/February 1978. He resumed his activities with the MKO. After the Revolution he went to Kurdistan first to launch a radio program, and then went abroad. He continued his activities against the Islamic Republic until he was captured in Mersad operations in 1367/1988. After four years in prison he was released and left for Germany, where he opened a bookstore. Interview with *Iran-e Azad,* on *www.Iran-azad.edu.*

the end, "Today, we will bring to you your dear friend Vahid Afrakhteh." Then he asked me to leave.

I went away and realized that the meeting place with Afrakhteh had been discovered by the police. The time of the meeting was four o'clock in the afternoon, and it was supposed to take place in the area surrounding Iran Avenue and 'Ayn al-Dowlah. I was very anxious and worried about friends. When I went back to my cell, I shared the news with three of the inmates whom I trusted. It was half past four when I noticed a lot of noise in the JCCT Prison. I really wanted to know as quickly as possible what had happened. After half an hour, thanks to the friendship that I had with one of the guards, he came and told me, "Ezzat! I want you to go and wash your dishes." So I went to the washroom for this purpose. On my way to the toilet, he told me, "Ezzat! Be very careful," and when I asked him why, he said, "Because Vahid Afrakhteh had been arrested."

I was really shocked. This was indeed very bad news for me. I did not believe that he had been arrested. He was not a person who could be easily arrested in this manner. I said, "No! This is not possible!"

He said, "Yes, it is. He has been arrested, and so you must be very careful."

I took his advice and returned to the cell totally disoriented and sad. I didn't want to believe it, but because of my encounter with Muhsin a few hours earlier and by recalling his statements, I feared the worst. This was the worst thing that could have happened to me after all these years. I had spent one year working with Vahid, and we had done a lot of things together. He had a lot of vital information that was very useful for the regime. I was very restless and anxious and could not calm down. I was just counting the minutes before they came after me. On the one hand, I was trying to comfort myself and hoped that even if Vahid was arrested, he was not a person who could be easily forced to confess and give away vital information. It was impossible to expect him to do so. I tried as much as I could to control myself and hide my anxiety and emotions. I kept myself busy by recalling all the lies that I had told the interrogators and find convincing reasons for the things that I had not yet confessed or the issues that I was hiding from the police. Unfortunately, there was nothing that I could do. I had no choice but to wait.

As the days passed, I became more hopeful. Of course I expected that Vahid too would resist torture. This silence continued for a few more days, and there was no more news from my interrogator. I prayed the situation would continue like that. On the twelfth day after the arrest of Vahid, they came and counted us and again transferred me to Evin Prison without any interrogation. I was very happy, but I was also anxious as I thought it was possible that no one would come after me. But the truth of the matter was different. The situation was very suspicious, and the reality was the complete opposite of what the JCCT authorities pretended it to be. They pretended that Vahid had said nothing. But one day at Evin Prison, Rasuli came to me and scared me. He said, "You fool! You'd better be careful and talk about many things that you have avoided so far. There are a lot of questions that you have to explain to us. Most of the things that you have kept away from us and avoided sharing are now disclosed by others."

In the meantime, while I was transferred to Evin, the news spread and reached the prisoners who were kept on the second floor. They, too, were very anxious. This time at Evin Prison, I had a chance to follow up on my discussion with Rajavi. It was the same old story, and at long last Rajavi said, "Look here Ezzat! We are still the same people as we were and have not changed a bit." (He meant they were Islamists.) I also assured him that I too was the same person he knew in the past and nothing has changed.

I read about the televised confession made by Khalil Faqih Dezfuli about the organization in an old newspaper. I was therefore certain of his betrayal. In these days, the environment of the prison had changed drastically and was very tense. The information concerning the assassination of Sharif Vaqifi and Samadiyyeh Labbaf, the arrest and confession of Khalil Dezfuli, and now the news of the arrest of Muhsin Khamushi and Vahid Afrakhteh had really destroyed the morale of all prisoners. When I was in the JCCT Prison, I was always up-to-date about everything that took place outside prison. It was there that I found out that the organization had publicly announced its transformation into a Marxist organization. This news confirmed once more the validity of my views about Rajavi and his ideological orientation. I remembered that from the outset I had opposed recruiting and involving Marxist elements in the organization and allowing them to influence the leadership. But the leaders were not willing to listen to my warnings. After a short time at Evin Prison, I was again taken back to the JCCT headquarters on the first days of the month of Aban 1354/October 1975.

Naked in the Cell, Dressed up for Interrogation

When I entered the JCCT Prison, I was shocked by what I saw. There were three blankets and a carpet on the floor. I had been sitting on the floor for an hour when a guard came and asked if I had an extra blanket. I told him that there were three blankets in my cell. He told me to give him one of them, and I did. After twenty minutes, he again came and said, "Throw the carpet outside so that we can exterminate the cell, as there are many mosquitoes and ants in the cell." This was surprising since I knew that whenever they wanted to spray, they started from the first cell before coming to mine. I guessed that there was something suspicious going on. After another half an hour, the guard came back and asked me to remove my clothes so that they could give me new ones. I told him that I didn't want new clothes, but he said that I didn't have a choice, and that I had to give him my clothes. I gave him my clothes, and he ordered me to also give him my underwear! I asked him to give me something to wear before I took off my underwear, but he refused and said that I should first take off the underwear and give it to him. I didn't insist any longer and took it off and gave it to him. The guard took the clothes, closed the door, and went away after leaving a pair of shorts in front of the door in a plastic bag so that I could wear them whenever I wanted to go to the toilet. Jokingly I said that he might as well take the shorts away and set me free altogether.

It was toward the end of autumn and the weather was gradually getting cold and the cold wind blew into the cell through the broken window on the wall. This was very hard on me, so during the day I covered myself with the two blankets I had, and at night I wrapped them around my body until I fell asleep after much struggling. I tolerated these conditions but never asked to meet my interrogator and never complained about anything. The guard now knew me, and he sympathized with me. They blamed those prison officers who treated me in that manner. Often they apologized that they had no choice but to follow orders of their superiors.

The Deputy Commander of the prison was a fat man and knew me well. He was truly a hypocrite. When he saw me, he shook hands with me and treated me like a brother and ordered the guards to treat me well, because "He is different from the rest. Give him anything he wants. If he is in need of cigarettes or tea, don't hesitate to give them to him."

It was this same person who would tell the guards behind my back that I was a dangerous person and should be watched carefully. He would even curse me and my family. Since I maintained good relationships with the guards, they always told me what he said behind my back and that he intended to disturb and hurt me. So when I ran into him, I had an indifferent attitude and just ignored him. If he ordered cigarettes or tea for me, I would refuse to accept them and told him that I did not need anything and always asked him to leave me alone. It was on a Friday when they asked me to go for interrogation. I started walking, naked as I was, but they said that I couldn't go like that and I had to put on something.

406

I said that I had been in that condition for a month, and now that I had to go for interrogation, they told me to wear something! Didn't the interrogator say that I should not be disturbed? So just take me to him naked as I was. The officer repeated that I had to wear my clothes! They brought me a shirt and a pair of trousers, and I put them on. They then took me for interrogation, this time to Rasuli's office. After greeting me, he offered me tea. He then said, "Ezzat! When did they bring you here?" He pretended that he was not aware of my transfer. I was familiar with his trick, so I said, "I have been here in solitary confinement for a month."

He said, "I was not aware of this. I was busy attending to my sick mother. I kept on going to and from the hospital every day, and she passed away yesterday. Of course, I had seen your name on the list the day before yesterday, but I did not have the chance to call you and talk to you. I asked my colleagues who sent you here, but no one answered. So I decided today—being a Friday—I should come and see you and have a talk with you. Today also is the memorial ceremony for my mother, and I have to leave early."

He went on with his cunning behavior and pretended to dial the Sorkheh Hesar Hospital and thanked the hospital authorities for taking care of his mother at the end of her life.

I also offered him half-hearted condolences. He thanked me and then said, "Look Ezzat! Are you interested in having a meeting with me in the afternoon so that we can talk about some issues?"

I said, "I have nothing to do other than eating and sleeping and am free from morning till night time."

He said, "Of course Dr. 'Azodi and Mr. Hosseini are also willing to come and have a talk with you."

I told him, "I swear by God that I have no business with these fellows. I have nothing to tell them. I am not in the best psychological mood to go through this again. I have hardly any control over my nerves and am afraid of losing control in front of them and using foul language. This may be harmful

407

for your reputation as well. If these gentlemen have something to say, let them tell you so that you can share with me, and I will answer their questions."

He said, "No! They want to directly talk to you. We have made a decision to pay your brother five thousand *tumans* per month beginning next month (Azar/December)."

I asked, "What for?"

He said, "Well, you may not be concerned about your brother's wife and child, but we are thinking about them."

I said, "Impossible! When my brother was outside prison and had a job, he hardly made 1200–1300 *tumans* per month and even saved some of that money. Now are you telling me that you want to give him 5,000 *tumans*? My brother does not need this money." I then sarcastically laughed at him and he said, "You pimp! You are so rude. You do not have any feeling and sympathy in your heart."

I said, "I do not expect anything from you and your colleagues. Why don't you just leave me alone?"

He then openly said, "Look, Ezzat! We are not asking you to come and talk on our behalf, have an interview or anything else. I have to admit that we have some information that is lost. You are the only person who can help us to connect the dots and retrieve this information."

I said, "You have made a big mistake in your calculations. I am not a person who does this sort of thing. I hope that after these three years you have realized this reality."

Again he said, "I did not ask you for an interview or a confession. The only thing is that right now you are the only person who is trusted by everybody. The religious and the non-religious prisoners all trust you and regard you as their hero. They all believe in you and your words. Rajavi and the rest trust you and, in short, you are the leader of everyone in this prison. You are the unifying factor of all these groups, and they tell you everything about themselves. I am not asking a lot by requesting that you tell us what these fellows tell you."

I said, "Do you think that you are dealing with a kid?! It seems that you have not known me quite well yet!"

He got very angry and said, "I will kill you. I will crucify you and make you an example to the rest."

I realized that he was talking nonsense and there was no logic in what he said. So I decided to express my anger too and started talking rudely to him and remained firm in my words.

He said, "I will destroy you and make you obsolete! I will do something that will make you the subject of boycott. You have grown a tail, and I am going to cut off that tail. Anyone who becomes arrogant here, we can label him as we wish easily.

I said, "You are free to do as you wish."

The interrogators wanted nothing else but to use me for their plans. They wanted to take advantage of two factors. One was that they were aware that I was under a lot of pressure in prison and knew that my relationship with Rajavi was tense and I opposed Rajavi and his faction. But the problem was that I did not know how they found out about our differences. When Rasuli brought up this issue, I said that I had no dispute with them because they said they were Muslims and I believed in them. Of course, whenever I made such claims, I pretended that I was an uneducated and simple man. I told him that Islam judges man by his outward actions and not what is in his mind and heart. Members of the MKO pray, fast, and chant the Qur'an, and as long as they perform these duties they are orthodox in my view, and whenever they stop, then they shall become Marxists.

He said, "You are a very simple man. These people are lying to you."

I said, "God forbid! I am not God to make such a claim. Only God is aware of what is in the hearts and souls of people. In any case, I have no business with the leftist groups whatsoever, but I respect them and they respect me.

The second factor was that the interrogators tried to take advantage of my religious orthodoxy and whatever Vahid Afrakhteh had said about me. They were aware that I was a serious religious man and that there were certain things that had taken place in the organization that were against my beliefs. They told me, "There is no doubt that you are not a Marxist. You are a serious and practicing Muslim, and we also acknowledge this. Other prisoners have always admired your strict observance of Islam and praised your steadfastness."

Lest my interrogator think that I would believe his admiration, I said, "If you praise me more for observing my duty to my religion, then I will go and become a Marxist because I do not wish to follow the religion that *you* approve of!"

Rasuli continued: "You have worked so hard throughout your entire life, and as you said, you have struggled on the path of God, His religion, and His Prophet. Now see what the result of all this struggle has been. Everybody has become a communist. They have struggled against each other, have violated each other, raped each other, and the entire organization has become like a whorehouse.

I said, "I have no updated information about the prevailing situation in the organization. I also do not accept everything you have said about it. When I was working with the organization, all the members were orthodox Muslims, pious, and pure. And I believe that those members, who are in prison, are good and pious Muslims."

After he listened carefully to what I said, he asked me to leave and return in the afternoon to talk.

Embarrassing Rasuli

I returned to the cell and they let me keep my clothes on, and the guard did not show any objection. Nobody came after me for interrogation that afternoon. In the cell adjacent to mine there was a prisoner named Manizheh Ashrafzadeh Kermani,[184] who was later executed. She was working with Afrakhteh. Her morale was low and she did not show strength in her interrogations and disclosed all information she had. Several times even the guards told me that they were suspicious of her and warned me to be very careful around her because she was even reporting them to the authorities. The guards often talked to me, but they tried hard to keep Manizheh away and not to let her know about our conversation. Manizheh received special care and had all kinds of medicine, including pain-killers and cough syrups in her cell. Sometimes the guards got medicine from her and brought it to me. Sometimes they pretended that I was sick and came to my cell to bring medicine, and we chatted all night. So if Manizheh ever reported them or me to the authorities, both of us had enough reason to justify our long conversations, and that was the reason I often and deliberately complained of pain and pretended to be sick.

As the days passed we continued with this game. I was happy that I had some clothes to wear until Rasuli called me for another round of interrogation. Once I sat down, he started:

"Ezzat! I have never been your interrogator, have I?"

I said, "Of course not."

He said, "Now I want to be your interrogator. I am not going to beat you, but I am going to do something that will make you say everything."

I said, "I have nothing to say."

'Azodi came in and greeted us. He placed his hands on my belly and said that my belly was big because I had just been eating and sleeping and obviously I did not do any work.

'Azodi's stomach was also very big. I said that my belly had not grown big out of my laziness and asked why he had such a big belly.

---

[184] Manizheh Ashrafzadeh Kermani was initially a Marxist activist and worked with Hamid Ashraf. After she was introduced to the MKO, she joined the organization and went underground. She was involved in the assassination of American advisers and Sharif Vaqifi. Finally she was arrested in 1354/1975 and executed on Bahman 4, 1354/January 24, 1975.

411

Rasuli interfered in our talk and said, "My Little Pimp! Don't talk to him like that. He is Dr. 'Azodi."[185]

I said, "I don't care who he is. Why are you defending him? By the way, I am talking to him and not you."

'Azodi said, "We have also arrested your friend!"

I said, "Which friend are you talking about?"

He said, "We have arrested Afrakhteh!"

It was for the first time that without beating around the bush they told me that they had arrested Afrakhteh. I pretended that I had no knowledge concerning this arrest and said that it was impossible and that Vahid would not so easily fall into a trap and get arrested alive. I still did not know how extensive Vahid's confessions had been and how significant his treason might be. I had to make them bring Vahid to meet him face to face. 'Azodi said that they had arrested him alive and he was here in the compound and asked if I wished to see him.

I said, "It is impossible. This is a bluff, but if you are telling the truth, then bring him on."

Another interrogator went and came back and said, "Right now he is not here!"

I said, "You see? I told you it is not possible to arrest Vahid alive!"

Rasuli said, "All right! Don't be so rude now!"

'Azodi then asked the other man where Vahid had gone.

---

[185] Mohammad Hasan Naser, known as Dr. 'Azodi, started his professional life as a political activist but soon changed and found employment with the SAVAK. He was a graduate of a school of law and a member of the youth branch of the Tudeh Party. In the SAVAK he was appointed as the chief interrogator. His mission was to infiltrate political groups, especially the National Front and student group. Once he was identified by students and beaten up badly. He was extremely clever and was able to flee the country just before the victory of the Revolution and settled in Los Angeles, where he owns a fabric store. See Koorush Lasha'ie, *Memoirs*, pp. 191, Tahereh Sajjadi, *Recorded Memoirs*, tapes # 8, 21–22. Deldam, p. 130, and Kalamvand, pp. 60.

He said, "He has been taken out by his interrogator and the police to locate street prostitutes. They are just driving around in the streets."

This meeting did not produce any results, so they returned me to my cell. My going back and forth between my cell and the interrogator's office increased. I asked three of the guards to tell me about the situation of Vahid. They said, "Do you know a person by the name of Ahmad Reza Karimi?" I said that I knew him. He had leaked the names of about 200 activists in the past.

They said, "Ahmad Reza Karimi cannot even match Vahid in terms of his betrayal. Vahid Afrakhteh disclosed so much information that no one would believe. Now he drinks alcohol, he has become a womanizer and lives a very dirty life. The police used him to locate and identify the activists outside. He is currently in Isfahan. You should be certain and believe that he has betrayed you and the organization and not subject yourself to torture and beating for his sake."

I could not believe that Vahid had become so corrupt in such a short time, but I was convinced of his treason. However, this was not a reason for me to say anything against him. I was preoccupied with my thoughts about the time we collaborated and was trying to find excuses and justifications that I had to present to my interrogators. During the next round of interrogation Rasuli said, "Just assume that you have been arrested right now. We shall also assume that we know nothing about you. Tell us everything from the beginning to the end. I am going to ask you one general question and you are supposed to answer me in a detailed manner." I agreed and Rasuli wrote on a piece of paper, "Mr. Ezzatollah Shahi! Your identity has been confirmed. Describe in detail every operation and activity that you have been involved in since you joined the MKO." This was another futile attempt by the system. Once again I wrote the same stories, half true and half lie, that I had written in the past.

I was well aware that for the time being beating was not in order although Rasuli constantly warned and frightened me of my interrogators. Once he said that Mohammadi planned to whip me, and Manuchehri [186] also had some plans for me, and other similar threats. I pretended that I was afraid. When we were in the interrogator's office, we heard Manuchehri's voice from the hallway. Rasuli asked me to cover my face and head with my shirt and I did. Then Manuchehri came in and joked around with Rasuli, engaged with him in a fist fight, and left. Rasuli then asked me to remove my shirt from my face. He said, "This God-damned Manuchehri wants to crucify you. He hates you and just wants to beat you up constantly. Be careful and avoid coming across his way."

After a while I got tired of Rasuli and his threats, so I decided to test him and see how true his claims were. One day I took a risk and told the guard that I wanted to see my interrogator. The guard went away, and after a few minutes he returned with Mohammadi. It was the first time that I had made such a request. Mohammadi too was very happy that I had requested to meet him. Instead of coming to my cell, he went to the guard's room and called me there. When I went there he greeted me and asked me about my health and whether my feet were healed. I told him that they were fine and he asked what I was doing. I told him that I was not doing anything in particular and no one disturbed me.

Mohammadi asked if Rasuli was still my interrogator, and I confirmed that he was. He then told me to leave, and I did, but I was sure that what Rasuli told me about him to

---

[186] Manuchehri Vazifeh Khan, known as Dr. Manuchehri (b.1319/1949), graduated from high school and was hired by the SAVAK. He was devoted to the regime and received extensive training, especially in techniques of torture with Apollo, crucifixion, nail-clipping, and all kind of psychological tortures. He was the most ruthless interrogator, and many activists were tortured severely by him. He retired on 16 Bahman 1357/February 5, 1979 and fled to London. Rumor had it that he committed suicide in London. See Ahmad Ahmad, *Memoirs,* p. 295, *Kaman: bi-weekly journal* # 7: Tir 16, 1383/July 6, 2004, p. 195.

frighten me was baseless. I also had to find out about Manuchehri's position, so I requested a meeting with him. This time he came to see me. He was in good mood and greeted me and welcomed me into his office. He ordered tea for me and treated me with respect. He asked about my health and wondered if I was in Qasr Prison or at Evin Prison and I told him that I was at Evin.

He said, "Now I will tell them to take you to Qasr Prison." I stayed in his office for about ten minutes, and when he realized I had no other demand he said goodbye and left. I concluded that Rasuli was just bluffing and that his threats were irrelevant. So the next day when he wanted to fool me and asked me to pull my shirt over my face when Mohammadi or Manuchehri came in I did not listen to him. Instead when Manuchehri came into his office I greeted him, and he shook hands with me. I did the same thing with Mohammadi. As a result, Rasuli realized that his trick was no longer working and that he could not accomplish anything by his empty threats.

Troubles Caused by Afrakhteh

They took me back to my cell and brought a few sheets of blank paper. Rasuli came in too and wanted me to write everything I knew about Vahid and Hasan. I told him that I was very tired and was unable to concentrate but promised to write the next morning. However, he did not agree and ordered the guard not to let me go to sleep until I wrote everything about Hasan and Vahid. After Rasuli left, I wrote a page and handed it over to the guard and told him that I would write the rest the next morning and went to sleep. The next morning, when I went to Rasuli's office, he asked me if I had written what he had asked for. I said that I had, but he took a quick look at my papers and tore them up because those were not the things that he wanted me to write and ordered me to sit down and write again this time without his beating me up like in the past,

Rasuli explained to me all information that Vahid had disclosed about me, the assassination of Sha'aban Bimokh, the explosion t the Shah Abbas Hotel in Isfahan, the team house in Mashhad, and so on. I realized that Vahid had said everything. Well, the people who normally leak out information to the police always have a good memory. With all this said, I told Rasuli that I had nothing new to add to what Vahid had said.

He asked, "Who was that boy who was to meet you at the Shah Mosque? Vahid said that you never wanted him to see you and Vahid together. This was the arrangement you had made with him. Vahid also described the appearance of that young man as heavy-set, huge, and strong, and said he looked like a worker."

The truth of the matter was that one day Vahid and I had decided to meet in the vicinity of the Shah Mosque (now Imam Mosque). When I was walking with him in that area, I saw one of my acquaintances coming towards us. As we walked I asked Vahid to distance himself from me in such a way that would not look suspicious so he would not see us together. He did as I had told him, and I met Murad Nankali face to face. We greeted one another and shortly thereafter separated and everyone went his way. Murad was killed later. I had decided to answer the questions related to the confession made by Vahid without hesitation. Therefore, when Rasuli asked me, without any hesitation I said that the young man's name was Murad Nankali and currently he is in your custody in prison. I didn't mention that I was aware that Murad was killed in the JCCT prison. I also attributed some of the charges against me to Murad and insisted that he should be brought to face me so that I could prove my point.

As Rasuli was reading the notes written by Vahid, he asked, "What happened to that copy machine that was in a house in the vicinity of Seyyed Nasr al-Din neighborhood?" This was something that only Vahid knew about. I had told him that I had an extra printing machine in a house in the Seyyed Nasr al-Din area that he should take care of if anything happened to me. I told Rasuli that I had mentioned this before. It was the same copy machine that the police found in my brother's house. "In fact, if I am not wrong, you arrested my brother because of this machine. So when you discovered the machine yourselves, I saw no need for further explanation about it." In fact, this was a lie because these two copy machines were two different cases and had nothing to do with one another. I assembled my lies in such an organized manner that it was hard to discover any discrepancies. Even though Rasuli was angered by my answer, he didn't ask me any more questions about it and did not follow up.

One night around midnight in the month of Azar/December, they called me for more interrogation. Instead of taking me to the interrogation office, they took me to the office of the night officer. I noticed that Rasuli, Major Vaziri[187] (the head of the prison), and a suspect whose head was covered were present in that room. They both threatened that they would kill me soon and no one would ever find out because I had died once already and the newspapers reported my death. Of course it was not hard for me to believe that they would in fact do such a thing. Seeing a suspect who had covered his head, I concluded that they had discovered some new information about my activities and connections.

Rasuli came in front of me and bombarded me with curse words. "How are you, little pimp? Why don't you confess and set yourself and us free once and for all? I thought that you were truthful at least with me. But I have now realized that you have told me nothing at all. What you have given me is only a handful of insignificant information, but there are lots of other things that you have not revealed yet. You fool! Didn't I tell you to be honest with me?" He then turned to Major Vaziri and asked him to tell me that he was in Isfahan during the past three days and just returned from that city today.

---

[187] Major Vaziri was the director of the JCCT headquarters and must not be confused with Colonel Vaziri, who was the director of the Evin compound.

Rasuli said that Ezzat had not yet confessed to anything about his ties with people in Isfahan. He then added, "To prove to Ezzat that I was not bluffing I want you to be a witness to see tonight what I will do to him if he fails to talk."

I had told Vahid earlier that I had some friends who worked in such industrial complexes as the [Iran] metallurgy factories in Isfahan and Arj, and in case of need, I could have them help to distribute declarations there. So when Rasuli asked about my connections in Isfahan and what kind of activities I carried out there, I quickly remembered something and I reminded him that I had told him earlier that Abbas Agah worked in the Arj factory and that he was also a member the same mosque, and that I had told Vahid that if he had declarations to distribute he could count on Abbas. At the time Abbas was also in prison, and I was aware that he had once worked in that industry.

Rasuli asked, "And what about the Iran Metallurgy Industry?"

I told him, "When I was working in Mosaddeqi's shop and we printed and sold Imam Khomeini's treatise, there was a certain Hasan Hosseini who frequently visited our shop and who said that he worked in the Iran Metallurgy Industry in Isfahan. Hasan always carried a handbag that contained the letterhead of the Iran Metallurgy Industry of Isfahan. I never went to Isfahan to see him, and he always contacted me. I gave him a copy of Imam Khomeini's book titled *The Islamic Government* (*Hukumat-e Islami*) and some of his declarations.

Rasuli asked me to write down and describe his physical appearance. Since this person never existed, I just wrote down an imaginary description of a man his age. So Rasuli sent a couple of agents to Isfahan to do an investigation about him and if possible, find him and issue an arrest warrant for him.

Then Rasuli turned to me and said, "Ezzat! Please tell us the truth. What were you doing in Isfahan?"

I said, "Nothing! I had no activity is Isfahan."

418

He said, "Yesterday as I was driving through Shah Abbas Avenue in Isfahan, suddenly a young man of about twenty-five or twenty-six years of age jumped in front of my car. I was a little afraid as I thought that he might want to assassinate me. But quickly I controlled myself and said to myself, 'We were always risking our lives and ready to sacrifice ourselves for His Majesty, and therefore must always be prepared to die.' So I removed my pistol and I was ready to defend myself and either kill him or get killed myself. I pulled down the side window of my car and asked him what he wanted. He asked me whether I was Mr. Rasuli or not. When I told him that I was, he said that he had a request to make. I allowed him and he said, 'I had a friend by the name of Ezzat Shahi and we collaborated in anti-government activities. He used to give me books and declarations to distribute and planned to recruit me for the MKO. I heard that he has been arrested but did not say anything about me in his confession. I regret that I worked with him. Now I have changed my mind and want to marry and go on with my life. I am afraid that when I get married the police might come after me and arrest me and make my family life miserable. Now that I put myself at your disposal, if you want to arrest me you might as well do it now.'"

Rasuli then continued, "I was so impressed with his straight honesty that I asked him to come into my car. I gave him a piece of paper and a pen for him to write down his confession and that he was remorseful for what he had done. He wrote a detailed account of his activities. I then told him that he was free to go and assured him that no one would ever bother him. I also warned him against being deceived by anti-government activists and told him to go and enjoy his life. I could have easily arrested him but acted like a real man and released him. You see! We are not hostile to people. I was so brave not to take him to the prison. We have enmity with no one."

I asked Rasul the name of that person and he got angry and said, "Do you want to interrogate me? Look Ezzat! My purpose is to help those young men like him who have no-where else to turn for help. What you have to do is to identify men like him so that I can help them. So I want you to name anybody you know who is in such a condition."

Rasuli's story was an obvious lie. I told him, "If you can prove that I knew that man, I could introduce fifty men like him to you. It is true that I am a simple and uneducated man, but as a Persian proverb goes, 'Even though I may be dumb, I am not stupid.' Perhaps what you are saying is not a bluff, but what you are saying sounds like a bluff and does not make sense. First of all, even in Tehran you normally do not go anywhere without bodyguards. How could you then have gone to Isfahan without one? Secondly, it is impossible for a person of your caliber to just free that man in such a simple way, especially after he mentioned my name! And suppose you are telling the truth: then why don't you free the people in this prison who are in the same situation as that young man? Thirdly, why aren't you mentioning his name to me to see whether I knew him or not? And finally, I swear that you know that this story is nothing but a lie."

When Rasuli heard what I said, he said, "Anyway, this is just one case. Perhaps later I could tell you his name but not now."

I said that I had been honest with him and that whatever I told him was the truth anyway.

He said, "You were not truthful even with God, much less with us who are your enemy."

I said, "You have beaten and tortured me as much as you could. I have told you everything that I could. Even if you keep me in the prison for the next twenty years, I will still live in peace. I swear by your soul Mr. Rasuli's! If I knew such a person I would tell you so that he would be arrested and would experience prison as I have. Then when he goes back to socie-ty, he would not repeat the same mistakes."

Rasuli asked me whether I wished to see Vahid. Of course, I really wanted to see him, but in light of all the lessons

420

I had learned in situations like that, I knew that I was not supposed to show any interest in that kind of suggestion so as not to provoke their curiosity and sensitivity. I said, "I don't want to see him. He is worthless and I am more comfortable this way."

He asked why, and I said, *"Because he is a traitor."*

Again he asked, "Ezzat! How is it possible that you resisted torture and never revealed Vahid's name, but now you take such a strong position against him?"

I said, "Until now we shared the same aspirations and ideology and both had the same objectives. But there is nothing common between the two of us any longer. He chose a path that I oppose and therefore I am his enemy. My enmity with him is not because of his communist orientation, but because of his collaboration with the police."

He said, "So you no longer trust one another and are each other's enemies, right?"

I said, "If I were not his enemy, then I would not be in your claws right now."

Rasuli said, "But I want to help you! Don't always think that everything will stay like this. It is possible that in four years we will exchange places and you will be in my seat. If I fall into your hands, I would then expect you to treat me nicely."

I said, "First of all, this is only a possibility! Secondly, if such a change takes place and a person of your caliber falls into my hands I will release him right on the spot. I know that you do not understand what you are doing even as we speak. You guys are all doing these things for money. I know that you have no faith in your duties. This is just like the time when the Russians, Americans, and British attacked Iran, and all high officials covered their heads with a *chador* and ran away. If the same thing were to happen right now, you would definitely do the same thing."

Because I was saying these things in front of Major Vaziri and another prison officer, Rasuli was really embarrassed, and he kept on signaling to me to stop talking, but I did not pay attention until he interrupted me and said, "Tell us about the activities that you carried out in Isfahan."

I said, "I had no activity in Isfahan. The only thing that I know about Isfahan is about the operation in Shah Abbas Hotel. I was not involved in the operation, but I know that Vahid Afrakhteh and Mohsen Fazil took part in it." I knew that Vahid had talked to the police about this operation in detail. So by repeating this for Rasuli, I wanted to attract his attention and show him that I was honest and prove to him that I was telling the truth.

Rasuli called for tea for all of us, and after a few minutes they brought it. A cup of tea was given to the suspect in the room who had covered his face with his shirt. Rasuli didn't want to give up and never lost hope and questioned me for so long that night. While drinking tea, he again returned to questions about Vahid, hoping to provoke me against him. He said, "Tell us everything that you know about Vahid."

I said, "I do not know anything about Vahid. He worked with me for about a year, but we did not do much. Then I was arrested and imprisoned. I haven't had any contact with him since then. Of course you told me he has also been arrested, but I am not sure if this is true or is another trick to break prisoners' morale. And if he has truly been arrested, then he would tell you everything and it is not my business to talk about him or on his behalf."

Rasuli asked, "Now, do you want to meet him?" I said no, because I didn't like him.

Rasuli offered me a cup of tea and a cigarette. I declined. I was so stressed out by what was going on there. I was shaking, especially when I took the tea cup to drink. I had a gut feeling that the suspect whose head was covered was somehow related to my case. I was really anxious lest my interrogators would discover the truth that night. I wanted to hint to the guy that I had said nothing [about him], and so he was not supposed to say anything about me. I wanted to boost his morale. When the suspect finished drinking his cup of tea, Rasuli told him to remove his cover and show his face. He uncovered his head, and I was shocked to see that he was Vahid Afrakhteh! We looked at each other and smiled. I placed the cup of tea that was in my hands on the table and said, "Is it you?!"

He said, "Yes. How are you Ezzat?"

Rasuli said, "If you two want privacy to talk to each other, then I can go out!"

I said that I had nothing to talk to him about. Then Vahid stood up and came toward me. He hugged and kissed me and asked about my health.

Then Rasuli turned to Vahid and asked him, "What kind of person do you think I am?"

Vahid said, "You are a nice man!"

Rasuli said, "Then tell this boorish man."

Vahid said, "I do not think that there is any other interrogator better than Mr. Rasuli."

I said, "Of course. I think that I know him better than you. You don't need to describe him for me."

Again Vahid came and kissed my face, and we sat down to talk. That night Vahid had on casual clothes, a pair of corduroy trousers and a pullover. He began to advise me to confess and assured me that Rasuli would help me. He also told me that I was in a very bad situation, and they would definitely execute me. So he insisted that I should stop resisting and save my life.

In response, I said, "You know me very well, Vahid. So do not frighten me of execution."

He said, "Ezzat! I know that you have not said anything. But those members of the MKO who are out there in the society are not worthy of all your sacrifices."

Rasuli asked Vahid, "How do you know that he has said nothing?"

Vahid turned to me and said, "Ezzat! I have told Rasuli everything that I knew about you, but I know you well. Even

423

when we were working together, you never told me anything about your other activities and plans."

He then turned to Rasuli and said, "Mr. Rasuli! Even while Mr. Ezzat was outside prison working with us, he dealt with us as if we were SAVAK agents. He never shared with us any of his information."

Rasuli asked, "Were you superior in rank to him in the MKO?"

Vahid said, "Yes, I was, but we had our own differences. Ezzat wanted to separate from us and form his own group. It was because of this reason that he never introduced to us the other activists whom he knew. Ezzat knew a lot of freedom fighters, even the ones who were not religious."

I said, "Suppose everything you say is true. So it is obvious that you were following me closely and had a plan to assassinate me, as you took my weapon from me and threatened me once when we had all gone hiking together. Well, it was you who designated somebody to follow me everywhere I went. Therefore, you must know everything about me, and I am sure you have already told all that to your interrogators. So I don't really have anything more to say. Let me just remind you that if I did not share everything I knew with you and others when we were out of prison, it was because I could predict a day like this and did not trust you. Of course, I have not yet disclosed everything about my activities, and this has nothing to do with you. My activities and charges against me are clear to the police. I have been in prison for three years now. I have never asked anyone to have sympathy for me, so leave me alone the way I am."

Our discussion was becoming more intense and fierce, and we were almost fighting each other. Rasuli asked, "You fool! Tell me, is Vahid telling the truth that you wanted to form our own group?"

I said, "Yes."

He asked, "Which people did you want to form the group with?"

I mentioned the names of seven or eight of my friends who were all in prison, although these people I mentioned were not even aware of this matter. I said, "I wanted to form a group in coalition with the Khamseh Tayibeh group."

He asked, "Who were the members of this union?"

I said, "Kachu'i, Kabiri (Hasan and Ali Reza), Hossein Jannati, Akbar Mahdavi, Asghar Mahdavi and a few others."

Rasuli was pleased. So he brought a few blank sheets of paper and said, "I don't want you to explain anything; I just want you to write me the names of these individuals."

I told him that I couldn't recall the names of all those people. "If you just want me to list some names, I can write down the name of the entire nation and it won't take more than thirty pages." Up to now the names that I have been writing down belonged to people who were already dead. You could check to make sure for yourself. There is nothing that I have written that can help you."

I was really fed up and angry. Rasuli said, "All right. There is no problem. For the moment, just take the papers and go to your cell and write down the names."

I said, "It is dark in my cell, and it is not possible to write anything. It is better that you take me to the interrogator's office in the morning so that I can write there."

Vahid said, "No! They are not going to execute you."

I said, "In fact I want them to kill me. You are a fool if you think that they are not going to execute you no matter what you do or how well you serve them!"

Rasuli said, "No! We are not enemies with anyone. If someone commits a mistake but admits his error and is regretful and willing to repent, we must be crazy to execute him. These are the young people of this country who can serve their nation and country in the future. This is the truth of the matter. If you apologize and serve the country, the Shah, and his [White Revolution], you will be pardoned. Even though you killed an American, it is not the end of the world. We can easily ignore that or accuse another person of that crime. The crime of a person who assassinated an American general is not worse than the crime of attempting to assassinate His Majesty, the Shah. [Parviz] Nikkhah[188] was not executed for this, and in fact it was the Shah himself who pardoned him. Look at him now, how he is properly and sincerely serving the regime and his country."

I said, "He is not serving the regime, but he is rather a traitor to the regime."

I then pointed at Vahid and said, "Do you think that this guy is stupid enough to accept these words? I am sure that if he had killed the Shah or ten Iranians, it would be possible for him to be forgiven. But this would not be the same if he had killed one American! It would be foolishness to think otherwise!"

By making such a statement I wanted to prove to Rasuli that in a regime like the Shah's, the life of one American was more precious than the lives of 100 government agents and even worth more than the life of the Shah. I wanted to inform him that he had no power to free someone who had killed an American.

When Rasuli realized that the argument was getting heated and he did not have any answer, he told me to get up and get out and take Vahid with me, too.

I didn't want to go in Vahid's company so I asked him to leave by himself first. Vahid extended his hand to shake

---

[188] Parviz Nikkhah (b. 1318/1939) was initially a member of the Tudeh Party's youth branch. He continued his education in England and was a member of the Confederation of Iranian Students. He returned to Iran in 1342/1963 and formed a study group. The group was arrested and accused of plotting to assassinate the Shah, which the group had nothing to do with. Even though he was condemned to ten years in prison, he wrote to the Shah and asked for his pardon. He was released then and was hired by the National Iranian Television Corporation while he worked as one of the theoreticians of the regime. After the Revolution he was arrested and condemned to death, and was executed in the final days of 1357/1978. See Mehdi Khanbaba Tehrani, *Memoirs,* pp. 122. *Terror-e Shah: Hadeseh-ye Kakh-e Marmar be ravayat-e Asnad-e SAVAK*, Tehran, 1383/2004.

hands with me, but I pulled my hand away. He hugged and kissed me and wished me good luck, but I told him to get lost and stop talking nonsense. I never wanted to hear anything from him again. So he left and I too, went away.

A Meeting with Vahid, Karimi, and Abrari

During my interrogation, I always tried not to say much to my interrogators. From morning till noon, I only wrote a page or a page and half, and it was always the same things that I had written before. Every once in a while the interrogator came and asked why I was not busy writing, and I always responded by saying that I could not remember anything because those incidents had occurred about five or six years ago and that I had to put a lot of pressure on my brain in order to remember something. Jokingly sometimes I would ask my interrogator if he could remember what he had for dinner yesterday! My purpose in behaving like that was to deliberately cause trouble so that they would take me to interrogator's office because it was there that I could meet and get to know other prisoners. By listening to their interrogations I could gather a lot of useful information about them and the conditions outside of prison. Of course, they never brought any prisoners who knew me or whose case was linked to mine in one way or the other.

Here, I adopted the same technique that I used in my previous interrogations. I started my story talking about an activist who was already dead and ended it with another who had been executed. Sometimes I mentioned the names of people who were already in prison or had left the country. I even took the upper hand in relation to Rasuli. One day I told him that I had given him information that I had never disclosed to any other interrogators because I wanted to be truthful and honest with him, but I was tired of everything and wished that he would send me to be executed and set me free once and for all.

He said, "No! It is not possible."

He was well aware that I was bluffing, but there was nothing he could do. On the 30th night of the month of Azar 1354/ December 21, 1976, they covered my face as they were taking me to the interrogator's office. When they told me to uncover my face, I saw Vahid and Ahmad Reza Karimi[189] sitting in one corner of the office and in the other I saw Hasan Abrari.[190]

Hasan, Vahid, and I had a joint dossier, but I was not aware that Hasan had been arrested too, and I was surprised to see him. He had been beaten severely, and his feet were also injured. Rasuli turned to me and said, "Mr. Ezzat! Here is Mr. Hasan, and he too has become a Marxist!"

Since Vahid had adopted the Marxist ideology, and Hasan was his subordinate and under his command, Rasuli's statement was not shocking to me. I encountered them in a very casual manner. In fact, I never even greeted them. Vahid came and sat by my side. He greeted me, asked about my health, and offered me a cigarette, and I turned it down as I always did. Ahmad Reza Karimi was so close to Rasuli that he

---

[189] Ahmad Reza Karimi (b. 1330/1951) joined the MKO while studying law at Tehran University. He participated in many sensitive operations and in the meantime learned much about the organization and had access to information. For this reason when he was arrested in 1352/1973 and couldn't stand torture, he dealt a heavy blow to the MKO. After the Revolution he was arrested, and after his trial was condemned to a few years in prison. See *Mehr Iran*, # 4362, pp. 2 and 7. See also Shams Al Ahmad, *As Cheshm-e Bradar*, Qom, 1369, 2000, p. 113.

[190] Mohammad Hasan Abrari (b. 1319/1940) joined the MKO when he was studying law at Tehran University. He dropped out of college in his junior year and went underground. He was very polite and observant of religious commands. He resisted the split in the MKO and opposed the Marxist faction strongly. His wife was killed by the Marxist faction of the MKO, and Vahid Afrakhteh led the police to Hasan's safe house. When the police surrounded him, he tried to take his cyanide capsule and commit suicide, but the police stopped him and in the process dislocated his shoulder. Hasan went through every imaginable kind of torture but never gave out any information to the SAVAK. Finally, after a year in prison, they executed him. See, Asadullah Tajrishi, *Recorded Memoirs*, tape #3, 18–20, Marziyeh Hadidchi, *Memoirs,* pp. 163–165. See also Rouhani, pp. 419.

could even pick a cigarette from his pocket. Vahid told me, "I am aware how bad you have been tortured. But tell Hasan to talk so that he won't be beaten up."

I said, "That is none of my business. You were Hasan's superior and you were the person who brought him to the organization. So tell him yourself."

He said, "At the moment Hasan does not trust my words."

I asked Vahid, "Why should you have committed treason to the extent that even he could not trust your words any more?!"

By saying this, I had two objectives in mind. First, I wanted to convey to Hasan that Vahid was really a traitor and he should not submit to his pressure and that he should not say anything. The second thing was that I wanted to inform Hasan that I had not disclosed any information about him.

Vahid asked Hasan a few questions and received answers. He also asked what other members of the MKO had said about him.

Hasan said, "In the beginning, they all considered you a hero. They thought that you had not leaked any information to the police. But later on when the weapons storage was discovered, everybody realized that you had collaborated with the police."

Vahid laughed. What he meant was that the people outside prison were so stupid that they made an idol out of him and spoke highly of him. He then asked what they were saying about Samadiyyeh Labbaf.

Hasan said, "People used to say that Samadiyyeh Labbaf had fallen in love with a girl who worked under Vahid. He wanted to kill Vahid to get her. So he argued with Vahid, who shot Labbaf in the hand. After that, Vahid put himself at the disposal of the police and began to collaborate with them."

I never believed this story, and I was sure that it was a lie. Vahid asked about Khalil Dezfuli, and Hasan said, "As long as Khalil had not conducted an interview, he was the symbol of resistance for everyone else. But after that interview, it became clear to everyone that he was just a shady person from the beginning."

Hasan Abrari also talked about Sharif Vaqifi and said, "I was not aware that he had been assassinated until Khalil conducted the interview. I then asked my superior about that incident, and he told me that they intended to print and distribute a declaration entitled "Changes in Ideological positions of the MKO" (*"Taghyir Mavaze'-e Ideological"*) to explain why they thought Sharif had committed treason. However, he never told me anything more than this because I was against adopting Marxism as the organization's ideology. Hasan added, "You are aware that I never accepted the deviated ideologies of these guys. So they never trusted me, nor did they inform me of their operations."

From these questions and answers, I concluded that Hasan was fully religious and that Rasul's attempt to introduce him as a Marxist was meant to destroy his reputation. I had to help Hasan. I told Rasuli that Hasan Abrari was tired and could no longer talk, and that he should be given some food or a glass of milk and allowed to rest.

I had a very strange feeling in my heart at that moment and sympathized with Hasan. I thought that we would never see each other again. At the risk of being tortured again I decided to talk to him for a little while. I considered him my brother. Therefore, I greeted him and asked about his health. Rasuli jumped into our conversation and said, "You fool! Why weren't you talking to him all this time? Did you just remember that you were supposed to greet him?"

I said, "I thought that he was a communist, but now I am sure that he is a religious person."

Rasuli was angry because we exchanged greetings with each other. He said, "Even though you do not listen to our words, we will listen to yours." He thus ordered a glass of milk and an injection of anti-fever drug Novalgin for Hasan. Rasuli, Vahid, and Karimi were all seated and were discussing things that were happening outside prison. Rasuli asked me to leave his office, and although I wanted to stay, he insisted that I should leave because he didn't want me to collect more information from his conversation with others in his office. He said, "Get up and get lost, but whenever you are ready to tell me more, let me know and I will put you together with these guys in one cell."

I told him that I had nothing to say since I had already told them everything I knew. He faced Vahid, Ahmad Reza, and Hasan, and then he said, "Do you see this son of a——! He has not confessed to anything and he has resisted torture ever since he was brought here. Now I want to get words from him by flirting with him!"

I told him, "Be very careful. Even with torture, you still won't get any information from me because as I have said, I have nothing more to tell you."

He asked, "How long have you been in solitary confinement?"

I said, "For almost two years."

By saying this, I just wanted to give moral support to Hasan. I wanted him to know that even if he were sent to solitary confinement, he should not be stressed out and feel bad. He should also know that the beatings, whippings, and torture were all things that could be bearable.

Pain in the Neck

A few days later, Rasuli took me for interrogation and asked me to write down every issue that had been discussed in the office of the commanding officer of the prison. Again I wrote that I knew Abbas Agah[191] from the Arj factory and Hasan

---

[191] Abbas Agah (b. 1325/1946) became an orphan at a young age, when he started working. In 1346/1967 he was hired by Arj Industrial Corporation, where he met Amir Murad Nankali and started his political activities. He joined the MKO in 1350/1971. He was active among the workers of Tehran and distributed declarations among them and played a leading role in organizing labor strikes. In 1352 he was arrested, tortured severely, and sentenced to three years in prison. After the Revolution he was one of the

Hosseini from the Iran Metallurgical Industry in Isfahan. Rasuli was happy to see that I was writing something. Early on he bragged and told 'Azodi, "Ezzat has confessed to all these things without even being beaten!" He wanted to claim credit for his style of interrogation over methods used by the other interrogators. He took me for interrogation several times, and I wrote the same things all over again until he got disappointed and decided to change his method. From that time on he started a character-assassination campaign against me to destroy my reputation. In a sense, his problem with me became increasingly personal, and he was determined to push me so much that I either took a position against him or collaborated with him.

Rasuli was originally from the city of Masjid Suleiman in Khuzistan province. He brought two new prisoners from Ahwaz to the JCCT Prison and sent one of them to my cell. In the meantime, Assadullah Tajrishi, a member of the MKO's Islamist faction, was also in my cell.

The guest that Rasuli brought to the JCCT Prison for me was really a pain in the neck. He was a mendacious and corrupt soul. Hooshang J. was an eleventh-grade student. Words cannot describe how morally corrupt and physically filthy he was. I did not sleep well even one night while he stayed in my cell. At night he tried to come into my bed and ask me to have sex with him, and I was so afraid that the guards would see him and accuse me too and destroy my reputation. This was the worst torture of all, and often I stayed up all night and wrapped my blanket tightly around my body. He had the appearance of a monkey, with a hairy body and long hair on his head. His entire body and hair was full of lice.

One day when he was taken for interrogation, Rasuli noticed that Hooshang was taking lice from his body and throwing them into the air conditioner. He shouted at him and

---

MKO's candidates for the national parliament. He left the country along with other members of the organization in 1365/1985 where he continued his activities. See *Bamdad*, #236, p. 13.

became very angry. He then took him out of the cell and placed him on a chair out under the sun. He resisted taking a shower. Tajrishi and I took him out and forced him to take a shower. We would just rub soap over his head and body, but he would want to get out of the shower room without taking a shower. He really drove me crazy. There was nothing that tortured me more than the presence of this guy. He always had his hands inside his trousers and would take out the lice and throw them on the floor. I fought with him many times about his hygiene, as I was frustrated of his filthiness. He always had a runny nose and said that his nose had been injured in a boxing match. We had to tear a pair of pants into pieces and have him clean his nose. Otherwise he would just rub it on the walls. I don't think that this man ever experienced what it means to be clean. He was dirtier than a pig.

So for the sake of my health, I tried as much as I could to prevent him from doing these filthy things. On a few occasions I pretended that I was sick and went to the health center and got some nose drops and other medications and gave them all to him. Sometimes he started crying for his mother like a baby, or asked me to write his will, or a letter to the court that he could use for his defense.

When I was in the mood, I teased him. Once I took a piece of soap from the bathroom and told him that he should write as I told him, and he agreed. I told him to write, "I am the Devotee of His Imperial Majesty, King of kings, may he be sacrificed for me!" and he wrote exactly as I said. The poor man was mentally retarded and wrote whatever I told him to write, "Down with the Shah and his regime," "May the flag of Iran remain eternally glorious." And at the end of his letter I wrote, "If you have no sympathy for me, at least have mercy on my mother and her tearful eyes." I told him that he should be careful not to mention those words here, but he should only say them in the court. This strange fellow was reportedly arrested because of immoral behavior in public and for his appearance. Apparently, every day he appeared in a different form of appearance, sometime with long hair, and sometimes cut short, so finally the police became suspicious and arrested him.

Several times I asked Rasuli to take this man out of my cell, but he refused, saying that they did not have vacant cells and there was no space in the other cells and that I had to put up with him.

Out of frustration I said that I was afraid that I might kill this man, and Rasuli said, "I can't do a damn thing." A few times I fought with Hooshang and kicked him out. Another day I came out of the cell and told him, "This place is either yours or mine."

I sat in the corridor for almost two hours. No matter how many times I asked the authorities to take Hooshang out of my cell, no one paid attention. One day an idea came into my mind, and I decided to take this trouble back to Rasuli. So one afternoon when I returned from my interrogation, I told Hooshang that I had taken my request to Rasuli. I told him that exactly at midnight when the prison telephone would be available they would call his mother so that he could speak with her. That night one of the guards who was kind to me was in charge of the ward. I called him and said, "Mr. Rasuli wants to see this fellow. He told me that I should send him up at midnight to talk with his mother over the telephone."

The guard sent him up. When he went to Rasuli's room, Rasuli was very surprised and asked Hooshang what he was doing there.

Hooshang said, "Mr. Rasuli! You told Ezzat that I should come to you in order to talk with my mother over the phone."

Rasuli was so angry and told him to get lost before he killed him. Rasuli then came after me and said, "You fool! What sort of trick is this that you are playing on this guy?"

I told him, "You did not respond to my request, and I just wanted to prove to you to how much this man disturbed me every night."

He said, "What do you want me to do?"

I said, "Let him go. He is not even worthy of being jailed. He was willing to be raped a hundred times so that he could be released. He was ready to surrender his body for the sake of being freed. He once told me that if he were freed, he would be willing to work for SAVAK. I asked what exactly he wanted to do and he said that he would wander in the streets and if he saw anybody who is suspicious, he would follow him and call SAVAK to come and arrest him!"

I told him that even before he could pull his pants up, the suspect would have already run away. I told him that he was not fit for that kind of job. Finally one day we had a fight and I beat him up and threw him out of the cell. The guards came and slapped me on the face and took him away from me. This was how I was able to save myself from this man and all the hardships that I suffered because of him.

Cell Number 20

At the JCCT Prison, no one was allowed to announce his name loudly. Even the guards had no permission to call prisoners by their names in a loud voice because they didn't want the prisoners to know each other's identity. For instance if a guard ever called a prisoner by name in a loud voice to take him from one cell to another, he would be punished because other prisoners could find out that a certain person was also in prison. Therefore, usually the guards knocked on the doors or opened the small windows and called the inmate to take him out and transfer him to another cell.

As for Rasuli, whenever he entered the cell, he would shout my name, saying, "Mr. Ezzat! How are you? We have not heard from you for a while." By doing so he wanted to give other prisoners the impression that we had good relationship and I was complying and collaborating with him. He wanted to ruin my reputation and have the other prisoners to hate me. The old prisoners knew me well and Rasuli too, so

435

his trick had no effect on them. But for the new prisoners, it was possible for them to be easily fooled.

There was a prisoner by the name of Mostafa Madani[192] who was arrested because of his connection with the Tudeh Party. He had spent the first year of his term in prison. Later on he joined the Fidayan-i Khalq Organization and was the spokesman for the Fidayan-i Khalq guerrillas and their candidate in the elections for the national parliament. Madani was in Ward One for a while. Rumor had it that SAVAK took a number of vagabonds and criminals to this ward to give political prisoners a hard time. Madani heard of this rumor. He requested and was sent to cell number 11, but that cell was full. They had placed eleven prisoners there, whereas it could house only five prisoners. So he stayed in the hallway and had nowhere to go. Rasuli came and asked why he was not sent to a cell, and he said that there was no room in any of the cells. So in a loud voice for everyone to hear, Rasuli said, "Take him to cell number 20 to stay with Ezzat Shahi so that Ezzat can take care of him!" Other prisoners knew me well, but Madani was suspicious as to why Rasuli had assigned him to my cell. Assadullah Tajrishi was still in this cell with me.[193]

---

[192] Mostafa Madani was a graduate of Tehran Polytechnic University. Along with Mostafa Sho'aiyan and Behrooz Rad, he formed a group named Proseh (Process), later known as Jarayan/Current. The nature of their activities was more intellectual and gradually became interested in Maoist ideology. Toward the end of the 1340's/1950's, when Shoa'aiyan established the National Democratic Front of the Peoples of Iran, Madani also joined them. A number of members of this group were arrested in 1351/1972 and Mostafa was sentenced to eight years in prison. In Aban 1357/November 1978 he was released from prison along with many others and joined the Fidayan organization and was nominated as a candidate for national parliament. After the split in the Fidayan organization in Mehr 1358/September 1979 he took leadership of the Fidayan Minority Faction. After coming into armed conflict with the government in Dey 1360/December 1982 he, along with some others, fled the country.

[193] Asadollah Aqa Mohammad Tajrishi (b. 1316/1937) became interested and involved in political activity from a young age by distributing treatises by Imam Khomeini. He was arrested in Qom on 15 Khordad, 1342/June 5,

As Madani was crawling on the floor, he came towards me. He had been tortured and his feet were swollen, but he was still able to walk. To avoid more torture, he pretended to be sick and crawled on the floor. By the time he entered our cell, we had already eaten our supper. Sometimes they gave us fruit after supper. That night, they brought us oranges. Tajrishi always ate his orange without peeling it off and said that the peel had special vitamins. When Madani came to our cell, I gave him a blanket and held him by the arms to help him sit down.

Just at this moment, Rasuli came into the cell. He offered a handshake and asked about my health. He removed his pack of cigarettes and asked me if I wanted one. I refused as usual, but he insisted that I should take one anyway. Since I was not a smoker, I had collected my daily ration of cigarettes and had about twenty cigarettes with me. Sometimes I offered the guard my share of cigarettes or distributed them among the prisoners. Often I hid them in the cracks of the bathroom wall so that prisoners could find them.

Since I always used to tell him that I had not committed any crime and that I had been arrested by mistake, Rasuli said, "Ezzat! This fellow is also totally innocent, just like you! He has not committed any crime!" Then he went away, but his statement made Mostafa doubt me and become suspicious of my relationship with Rasuli. So when I asked his name, his birthplace, and the reason for his arrest, he treated me like an interrogator and answered my questions briefly: "Mostafa! Madani! From Damavand! I don't know [the reason for my arrest]!"

1963. Initially he was influenced by Fidayan Islam but when he moved to Tehran, he joined the MKO. He was arrested along with Hasan Abrari in his dry-cleaning store and spent two months under torture in the JCCT Prison, and then was transferred to Evin. After the Revolution he was appointed by Mir Hossein Mousavi, the Prime Minister, to several key positions, including the adviser to the minister of labor. For his observation on Ezzat Shahi see his *Interview, Oral History Archives,* tape # 4, Tehran, 1373/1994.

Since I had carried out some operations in Damavand and knew some people there, I asked him if he knew some people in Damavand.

He said, "I know no one because I have lived in Tehran my entire life."

I told him that we had already eaten supper, but there was some bread and cheese. He said that he could not eat because he suffered from an ulcer, and that they gave him milk downstairs. I called the guard immediately and told him to bring him some milk. I also requested that he bring us jam and butter from the other cells if they had any extra. The guard brought everything that I requested from the adjacent cell. In that place, Vahid's sister and brothers stayed.[194] They lived in good conditions, and their cell was more like a hotel than a prison cell. They were visited by their family members twice a week and had everything prepared at home and brought for them. The sister of Vahid had confessed to everything and had revealed the names of everyone that she knew.

I peeled the orange and realized that it was sour and thought that it was not good for him. I offered it neither to him nor to Tajrishi. I ate it myself. His suspicion increased. Perhaps he thought that I was an ordinary [non-political] prisoner and had no sympathy for him. That night, he did not sleep until morning. He was afraid and kept on looking around the cell. He checked under his blanket to see if there was any equipment for torture, but he found nothing. He was afraid that I was going to torture him. When the lights were switched off, I slept next to the door of the cell. Tajrishi slept in the center, but Mostafa sat in the corner. He could not sleep because of his fear. I told him to sleep several times, but he said that he could not sleep.

---

[194] Nahid Afrakhteh was an accounting student at Farah University (now al-Zahra) before the Revolution. She was single when she was arrested in connection with her brother's activities. See *Interview with Roqayyah Vaqifi*, Tehran, Shahrivar 19, 1383/September 9, 2004.

The next day when I went for my interrogation, Madani asked Tajrishi why he was in prison. He never asked me this question. This is because Tajrishi's feet were injured and were in bad shape as a result of torture, but my feet were fine. Tajrishi told him that he was arrested because of his affiliation and activities with the MKO. He was happy that he had found a friend there that could help him against me! When I returned from the interrogation, I decided to pull his leg, and like an interrogator, I asked, "Will you tell me why you were arrested or not?"

He didn't answer my question, but said that he had been in prison in the past.

I asked, "Which group were you with in prison?"

Again he did not answer. I mentioned the names of some prisoners and he confirmed that he knew them. I told him that my case was similar to that of those whom he knew. He still thought that I was just a non-political prisoner. If only I knew what he thought about me, I would have teased him more.

There were some lice in all cells but our cell was particularly dirty and unbearable. I had told the guard several times that we wanted our cell to be exterminated, but they never listened. I asked them to call the prison director to our cell, and Major Vaziri came. I talked to him in an angry voice and said that we were not animals so as to live in this condition, and that they should have our cell sprayed at least once a month.

He said that he had ordered this cell to be sprayed and even paid for it. I told him that our cell had not yet been sprayed and that those people had fooled him. Other prisoners came to our cell to see what was going on. Major Vaziri went away, and in the afternoon they came to spray our cell. This kind of attitude towards prison authorities didn't seem normal to Mostafa, and he was shocked and wondered how a prisoner like me could talk like that to the prison director. So his suspicion towards me began to fade away.

The next morning, I held Madani by his arms and walked him to the bathroom. He could not walk. While I was holding him up to wash his hands, one of the guards saw us and said, "You guys are having a good time! You will increase the number of prisoners in the prison!" I lost my temper and slapped him very hard on the face. I told him, "You asshole!! Why are you insulting me? You are a pervert." Then I held Mostafa by the arms and took him back to the cell. I told the guard in charge of the keys that I wished to see prison director to report this guard whose mind was in the gutter. He thought that everybody was as filthy as him. The deputy prison officer, together with the other police, came to me and begged me not to report the matter. They didn't want the guard to be in trouble. Some of these guards were my friends, and so I never wanted to let them down. I accepted their apology under one condition, that I should not see that idiotic guard near me.

I don't know whether it was by mere chance or there were other reasons that the same guard was not given a shift there for two or three weeks. After this incident, Mostafa Madani became my friend. He asked me what I did and why I was arrested. I told him that I worked with the MKO. I was surrounded by the police, and after I was shot, they arrested me, and I had been in prison for three years, and there was a high probability that I would be executed. I also mentioned some of the prisoners who shared charges with me. He realized that his thoughts about me were all wrong. He also told me about himself and his case. I gave him some advice about resisting the torture and whippings of the interrogators.

He then told me, "The first night I came here, I didn't sleep out of fear that you were going to abuse me sexually!" Mostafa was bald. When he told me this, I laughed and hit him on the head and said, "What an unfortunate man you are! You ugly man! Was this what you expected?! Aren't there more handsome guys than you in the world? In fact, you are so ugly, why would I ever want to do such a filthy thing with you?!" And all of us laughed after that joke.

The Prince and the Beggar

I was still in the JCCT Prison during the last days of the year, but there was no more torture or beatings. On the 25th of the month of Isfand, 1354/March 15, 1976 Rasuli came, and after collecting daily statistics of the number of prisoners, he told me to pack my belongings. I thought that he wanted to transfer me to the general cell, but I saw another group of people gathered in the prison officer's room. They then transferred all of us to Evin Prison. I stayed at Evin Prison until the last days of the month of Farvardin/ April of that year. This was a temporary transfer because reportedly many interrogators and guards at Qasr had gone for vacation during the Persian New Year (*Nowruz*) holidays.

When I returned to the JCCT Prison I spent four or five nights in solitary confinement. Then I was then taken to cell number 3 located in Ward Six. I stayed there until the 25th of the month of Khordad, 1355/June 15, 1976. They took me for interrogation two or three times, but nothing important happened. It was just a repetition of previous meetings. They wanted me to complete what I had written, but I could not write anything. I answered their questions orally. I did not have any particular objection or complaint for being in the JCCT Prison. In fact, because of what I had gone through in Qasr and Evin, the oppressive environment, and narrow-mindedness of the people, I felt more comfortable in the JCCT Prison. I had an opportunity to pass on my experiences in political activity and the ways to resist torture and beating to the young and new prisoners. In the JCCT Prison, my biggest fun was to go to the bathroom and take a shower. Most of the time, we only lay down, slept, or talked to each other. But in Qasr and Evin Prisons, we washed our utensils and dishes and mopped the floor.

This time when we were brought back to the JCCT Prison, another trouble-maker was sent to my cell (#3 in Ward

Six). He had a bachelor's degree and belonged to the MKO. He pretended to be crazy, and every night he disturbed others and didn't let them sleep. Sometimes he said that he would behead everyone in prison. Other times he would say that he wished he were a bird so that he could fly out of a crack on the wall. He had lost his senses and didn't seem to be a rational person. Sometimes he said that he wanted to collaborate with SAVAK, or leave prison and get married. I was so frustrated by his behavior that a few times I got into a fight with him and beat him up. Sometimes I asked the night commanding officer to take him away or else I would beat him up. The other guys feared to beat him, but I did so and never feared anything.

In the last days of the month of Khordad, 1355/June 1976, again Rasuli came after me. He told me that Mr. 'Azodi, Hossein Zadeh, and Dr. Javan wanted to talk to me. I told him that they should leave me alone, and as I said so many times, I have nothing more to say or write. I told him since he was my interrogator, they could tell him anything, and then he could convey to me whatever he could.

Rasuli said, "I hope you aren't resented, and it's all right with you that I plan to send you to Evin Prison so that you can meet them there."

After two days, they sent me to Evin Prison. Unlike previous times, this time they did not take me to the communal ward upstairs, but they sent me to solitary confinement.

What I experienced in this cell was drastically different from my previous experienced in solitary confinement. The services and facilities they put at my disposal were unexpected and strange. First they sent me to take a shower, which I did. Then they shaved my hair and beard and offered me new clothes. They really took good care of me there. I became very suspicious. I guessed that they had some new plans for me. They allowed me to take a shower three times a day and shave my beard every other day. They served me breakfast, lunch, and dinner on time and regularly. They even offered me a pack of cigarettes a day. Sometimes they even left the door of the cell open and told me to feel free!

I was not comfortable with this kind of treatment and favors that I received. So I requested a meeting with the prison director, Captain Ruhi. He called me to his office and gave me a warm welcome. We drank tea together and spoke a lot. I told him that I swore by God that they had brought me here by mistake!

He asked, "And how is that so?"

I said, "Because I was once in Evin Prison in the communal ward on the upper floor, but I was never treated by the authorities like this before. Their attitude and behavior towards me is very strange and unexpected. I think there is a yet another mistake here. I am not sure if I should be here in this ward and expect to be treated like this.

He asked me who my interrogator was, and I said Rasuli, 'Azodi, and Mohammadi, and all three of them have interrogated me from time to time. He asked me to leave and said that he was going to make a phone call to ask about this issue and then inform me.

Two hours later, they came after me and told me to gather my belongings. I was taken to cell number 2 in Evin Prison. I never found out the reason that I was taken to that special cell in the first place and never understood why they treated me—a beggar—like a prince for a few days. Perhaps they just had another plan to ruin my reputation.

*   *   *

CHAPTER NINE

Ideological Boundaries

When the Masks Were Removed

In the communal ward they placed me in that same cell, number three, where I was before. Mas'ud Rajavi had just returned from the JCCT Prison and was also in that cell. We spent the first two days in talking about formalities and asking about each other's condition and health. Soon, however, we began to talk about essential questions.

When the organization adopted Marxism as its ideology and issued public declarations, some uncertain questions were settled. Those who performed daily prayers for expediency stopped doing so and announced that they had adopted Marxism two or three years ago. They said that Mas'ud Rajavi had told them that they should not announce that change because if they did so, the organization would receive heavy blows from several directions. So he ordered them to keep up the religious appearance and continue to perform prayers to protect the organization and prevent its destruction. During that two-year period, they skillfully hid their belief in Marxism, even attending the Qur'an recitation sessions and fasting during Ramadan.[195]

Dr. Shaybani, who was a very pious man and remained so and who took very proper positions in dealing with the police and resisted torture, no longer showed any respect toward the Mujahidin and expressed his opposition. But in the month of Ramadan, he asked to have access to a copy of the Qur'an, and *Mafatih al-Jinan*—a widely read Shi'a prayer book—for

---

[195] According to Kachu'i, after 1352/1973 the higher-ranking members of the MKO knew what was going on in prison and how many of their members had turned Marxist. They never declared that openly and indeed many Marxist members of the organization continued to perform daily prayer. See *Interview with Kachu'i*, Winter 1358/1979.

an hour every day. The rest of the time, each prisoner was assigned a ten-minute time to have and read them. The way it worked was that at night, I recited the Qur'an and then I passed it to another person who would have it for ten minutes and then passed it to others. Even those MKO members who hid their Marxist tendencies took the Qur'an and recited that when it was their turn. Someone like Hasan Rahi, who had no faith in the Qur'an, would take it and keep himself busy with it for ten minutes just to mislead us.

When I was in the JCCT Prison, I knew that Mohammad Damavandi, Bahman Bazargani,[196] Mahmud Tariq al-Islam,[197] and Nasir Jowhari[198] had adopted Marxism. But we were not aware that Hasan Rahi had also turned Marxist. Hasan and Hanif Nezhad were arrested in 1350/1971 and were both sentenced to ten years behind bars. He declared his adoption of Marxism while he was in Mashhad Prison. Others knew about this, but I was not informed. As a senior prisoner, Rahi had been appointed at Evin Prison in charge of distribution of tea, sugar, and bread. Whenever I entered their cell, I found them performing prayers. At first I asked Rajavi, if these men were Marxists why they were performing daily prayers. Mas'ud told me to leave them alone and mind my own busi-

---

[196] On Bahman Bazargani's observations on this period see Lutfullah Maysami, *Anha ke gereftand*, pp. 38, 121, 125–127. He graduated from Tehran Poly-technical School of Engineering. He was a member of the central cadre of the organization after 1348/1969 who adopted Marxism in prison but did not go public until later.

[197] Mahmud Tariq al-Islam (b. 1327/1948) joined the MKO while he was a student at the University of Tehran. He also adopted Marxism in prison and became so radicalized that he received the epithet *Tariq al-kufr*! After the Revolution he joined the Marxist group, the Rah-e Karegar, and as a result of his activities against the new regime he was arrested and executed.

[198] Mohammad Ibrahim Jowhari (b. 1326/1947) was a student at Tehran Poly-technical School of Engineering. In 1352/1973 he adopted Marxism and after several clashes with the police he was injured and arrested in 1352/1974. He received a life term but he was released after the Revolution and joined the Rah-e karegar group, but soon fled the country and settled in Europe. See, *Tarikhche-ye mukhtasar-e goruhakha*, pp. 121–122.

ness, but I confronted him and said that they should stop pretending they were Islamist, should leave religion alone, and not betray and dishonor it; or else, I would publicize their hypocrisy. Rajavi knew my position, so he said, "These guys do not know anything about religion, and we do not have the time or the energy to teach them about religious matters. We will talk to them in due course when we have time. Let them do their own investigation about religion and at their own pace."

I told Mas'ud that I felt responsible before God and I wanted to let them know that they should stop performing daily prayer and do their own research for as long as they wish. If they decided to return to religion then, they could do so and resume their prayer and rest assured that God would forgive them for not praying during the period while they searched for the truth of religion.

Mas'ud and his clique were not willing to accept my advice and argued with me. He told me that I was nobody and should mind my own business, and what went on there was none of my business! I told him that I was a believing and practicing Muslim and I had a duty to voice my opposition to what they were doing.

When I realized that I could not do anything through the organization, I decided to act independently. I went to those who had turned Marxist and asked them why there were performing daily prayer and warned them that they could not take religion and its pillars lightly and must stop abusing religion. Otherwise, I would confront them personally.

A few days later, several Mujahidin members, including Jowhari, Hasan Rahi, Bazargani, Tariq al-Islam, Damavandi, and a few other who had become Marxists left our cell for another one. They formed their own group, and I heard that they stopped praying. Obviously after this incident they started criticizing and attacking me, calling me backwards and reactionary. As they continued their attacks and insisted on their ideological position, I decided to separate myself and work independently. I talked to a few others and they supported my

447

idea. Among the people was a young man named Behzad Nab-avi.[199] Nabavi was so closely allied with the Mujahidin that he would not take a step without their permission and approval. But he was an open-minded person, and after I spoke with him for some time, he found my argument sound and convincing and joined me and supported my thought and position. Thus, a separate current independent of the Mujahidin came into be-ing. The Mujahidin were angry and voiced their frustration that "these college graduates and engineers are so stupid that an uneducated and simple man [like me] can fool them."

We decided that all members in this current should take charge of disseminating their views independently and recruit members from among prisoners at Evin and Qasr Prisons. I was placed as the head of this current and wanted its members to be free and not to follow the Mujahidin blindly. I advised everyone to rely on their own intellect and objective judgment. I shared my experiences. Individuals of all walks of life, from university students to college graduates, must have found my experiences useful enough to follow me and express their sup-port for this current. That was how I severed my connection with Rajavi and even avoided greeting him when we met. It was obvious that our paths were separated after that. Obvious-ly, the Mujahidin did not sit idle, but increased their activities against me and the new group. They started labeling me and calling me names and accusing me, claiming that I was not after all against the Mujahidin and their ideology, but did all these things to save myself from execution. They even accused me of collaborating with SAVAK and of being determined to destroy revolutionaries and genuine revolutionary groups and

---

[199] Behzad Nabavi (b. 1321/1942), a graduate of Tehran Polytechnical School of Engineering, joined the National Front III, joined Sho'aiyan and Nader Shaygan in the People's Democratic Front of Iran, and was arrested in 1351/1972. In prison he joined the MKO, but after the Revolution left the organization. He was appointed as a member of the National Council of Islamic Revolutionary Committee, Minister of Heavy Industry, deputy of Tehran in the national parliament, and several other positions. He estab-lished the Revolutionary Islamic Mujahidin Organization in 1359/1980.

break the spirit and morale of the revolution and deviate it from its straight path!

To the Marxists, they described me as an anti-Marxist element, and to Islamist groups as collaborator with SAVAK, and thus tried to boycott me. A number of people accepted and believed these accusations and never spoke to me again. Some did not accept these charges and accusations against me but remained quiet. Still some others did not talk to me and avoided me out of fear, but they knew my background and my dealings with the police. Some prisoners knew me from my days in Qasr Prison and in their heart could not accept what they heard about me, but their blind obedience toward the organization did not prevent them from joining the boycott. Between me and the organization they had to choose one or the other. They could not turn their backs on the MKO; therefore, they joined the others and boycotted me. They stopped greeting me when they came across with me in the hallways.

The oppressive environment of prison, boycotts, and seclusion was truly unbearable. Some prisoners did not speak with me in front of the others because the organization had ordered them not to, but when they got a chance they would start brief conversations with me. For instance, once when I was washing my hands in the bathroom, one of the MKO members came in. He first inspected the toilets, and when he saw that no one else was there, he started to talk to me. As soon as someone came in, he stopped and busied himself with cleaning the bathroom.

To show that the MKO had deviated from fundamental doctrinal principles and strategies for revolutionary struggle, we were prepared and willing to hold debates with them in the presence of the other prisoners. Yet they prevented this and sabotaged all our efforts and never permitted us to discuss our views with others so that they could judge for themselves.

The most important issues that we believed needed urgent attention were the reflection of ideological transformation of the organization and adoption of Marxism outside prison, as well as their attitude toward Marxist groups inside prison. Disagreements over these vital issues brought me into face-to-face conflict with the MKO leadership. Not only were they not against deviationist groups and unwilling to condemn them openly, but they tried to justify their move. At best, they only stated that those people were *opportunist traitors* but never thought of them as non-Muslim, much less infidels. The application of the term *opportunist* to the *deviationist* group found widespread acceptance from that point on. Whereas we believed that they were in fact Mujahids who had turned communist, and therefore they were apostates (*murtad*), the Mujahidin were afraid to identify them as apostates because they feared that the same term would be applied to all leftist groups and would prompt them to turn against the organization and weaken or destroy it.

The leadership of the MKO avoided debate and argued that the rank and file of the membership of the organization could not understand and digest that sort of reasoning. This was an excuse that they exploited to use to isolate and boycott me and those who thought like me. In contrast to them, however, leftist groups were willing to sit down and debate with us because they knew me well and were aware that we used reason and did not advocate elimination of those who thought differently from us. I often talked to many leftist prisoners and often went to visit them in their cells.

When the MKO members observed my relationship with other leftist groups, they started to provoke them against me. They told them that I [Ezzat] considered them to be impure, and for this reason they had boycotted me! Their objective was to introduce me as an anti-Marxist element. I tried to nullify this assumption among the leftist groups and maintained normal and cordial relationships with them. I took walks with them, shared cigarettes with them even though I was not a smoker, and listened to their problems and complaints and ate with them. In all objectivity, the leftist prisoners never believed what they were told against me and had no problem with me. They always defended me as an honest man and someone whose positions are transparent. They appreciated that I criticized them to their face and not behind their back and praised this as a virtue. They knew that we had different belief systems, yet we had mutual respect toward each other. They said, "The good thing about Ezzat is that he is straightforward and transparent. He does not play political games with us. He has his views, and we have our own. He is not against our work, and we have seen nothing bad at all in him. He respects us and so we respect him."

Among the leaders of the left I often spoke with leaders of the Fidayan-i Khalq, including people like Asghar Izadi, Fariborz Sanjari, Ali Mehdizadeh, Shaltuki, Abdullah Anduri, Bizhan Farhang Azad, and Dr. Gholam Ibrahimzadeh (from the Setareh-i Sorkh group). Most of the time, they were the ones that initiated conversation with me. Sometimes when there emerged a quarrel or a disagreement between them, they would ask me to mediate to calm things down. I even offered them advice because they believed in my objectivity. I often warned them that prison is not the right place to quarrel because the enemy would take advantage and that they must try as much as they could to solve their problems among themselves and not allow the others to learn of these issues.

Amongst the Marxist leaders who were members of the MKO before the split and who spoke with me regularly were Bahman Bazargan, Kazim Shafi'iha,[200] and Nasir Jowhari. I dealt with them from a position of power and told them that I was not against their adoption of Marxism and that they should listen to my criticisms objectively and honestly. I always told them that after all these years of struggle, if they concluded

---

[200] Kazim Shafi'iha (b. 1327/1948) joined the MKO while studying at Tehran University. He went to Lebanon for training, and when he returned he participated in several operations and was arrested. In 1352/1973 in Mashhad Prison he adopted Marxism. After the victory of the Revolution he joined the Fidayan-I Kahlq organization. See Nejat Hossein, pp. 92–102, *Tarikhche-ye Mukhtasar-e Guruhak-ha*, pp. 145–146, and, Maysami, *Anha ke Raftand,* pp. 195.

451

that religion could not fulfill their needs for struggle and that was the reason they turned to Marxism, then that was a sign of their sincerity, and they didn't have to be ashamed! But my point was that for the sake of attaining their goals, they should not commit every crime that they thought might help them reach their objectives, like killing [Majid] Sharif Vaqifi. That was not a revolutionary manner in which to deal with their opponents. "My point is that when you guys reached the conclusion that Marxism is the only way forward and that religion is reactionary, why didn't you join other Marxist groups like the Fidayan-i Khalq and enter into a coalition with them, or at least adopt a different name instead of still using the name of the Mujahidin-i Kahlq? Had you done so, I would have dealt with you in the same manner that I dealt with the rest of the Marxist groups."

Unfortunately, they started the organization as a religious one, and the society welcomed and supported them financially at a time that religious groups had no quarrel with the Marxists, and in fact they fought together against the regime. But they took advantage of those privileges and turned the organization into a Marxist one. This was a big blow to the religious resistance groups and at the same time created an anti-Marxist environment that they became a victim of. I told the leaders of the deviationist current that despite all this, "If you condemn such deviation and remove the name of Mujahidin-i Khalq from your group and carry out your operations under a different name, then I will stop my opposition toward you and treat you like all other Marxist group."

The Verdict (*Fatwa*) Denouncing the Marxists

After the ideological transformation of the Mujahidin was declared and the apostasy of some of its members came into the open, they began to face a lot of problems in prison.[201] There

---

[201] Habibullah Asgar Awladi (b. 1311/1932) started his activities with Ayatullah Seyyed Abulqasim Kashini during the 1950's. He was arrested

were some clergy members and jurists who had been transferred from the other prisons to Evin at this time. After learning about the new development, they felt betrayed and guilty
to have provided material and spiritual support for the MKO.
They especially felt ashamed that they had given the *khums*
(one-fifth of a believer's net assets allocated in the name of the
Twelfth Imam and paid to his deputies, i.e. the *mujtahids*) to
the Mujahidin organization who eventually turned to Marxism.

During the first days of the year 1355/1976, several
'ulama and jurists like Hossein Ali Muntazeri, Rabbani Shirazi, Ayatullah Seyyed Mahmud Taleqani, and Akbar Hashimi
Rafsanjani discussed the issue among themselves and decided
to do something about it. After much debate and deliberation
they decided to issue a legal verdict (*fatwa*) that later on
caused much controversy. This *fatwa*, issued in the month of
Khordad 1355/June 1976, was composed of two central points.
One was concerned with denouncing the communists and declaring them as ritually impure (*najis*). On the basis of this
clause, eating and/or any kind of association with the Marxist
prisoners was to be impermissible (*haram*). The second issue
was about the Mujahidin. The second clause of the *fatwa* dealt
with the status of the members of the organization. It stated
that those who were killed or executed in the past and who
adopted Marxism consciously and by their own choice should
no longer be considered believers or called martyrs (*shahid*). If
they chose Marxism unconsciously and got killed or were executed, the authors of the *fatwa* would remain silent and pass no

several times until 1343/1964 when Prime Minister Mansur was assassinated. He was one of the founding members of the Islamic Coalition Party. In
prison he led anti-Mujahidin activities and signed the famous *fatwa*. He
was released in 1355/1976 and went back to his business in the bazaar.
After the Revolution he revived the Islamic Coalition Party and held important positions in several cabinets, including the Minister of Trade, Director of the Awqaf Foundation, and Ayatullah Mahdavi Kani's deputy in
the Office of Logistics [of War]. See *Jumhuri Islami*, # 60, p. 5, and
Kayhan, # 18, 1380/1981.

judgment about them. However, those who survived and continued the path of the [previously Marxist] Mujahidin were no longer recognized as believers and should not be considered martyrs even if they get killed unless they refuted their [Marxist] ideology and separated their path from the communists. It was decided that this *fatwa* would be conveyed orally to all cells and from one prison to the other.

The MKO considered the clergy as the second echelon in the struggle and expected to come into conflict with this group sooner or later. They knew that a day would come when their differences would come out into the open. When this *fatwa* became public, the MKO concluded that the clergy opposed them and refuted their principles and doctrines, and since they did not acknowledge their comrades who were killed in the course of struggle as martyrs, they felt obliged to take a position against the clergy. They declared that the clergy were part of the *petit-bourgeoisie* and were wealthy reactionaries, agents of the CIA and not suited for struggle.

Inside prisons, some prisoners supported the clergy and their affiliates in the bazaar and among the workers. This group advocated an alliance with the clergy and tried to distance themselves from the communists. Those members of the Mujahidin who remained under Rajavi's leadership declared their opposition to the clergy because in their view the *'ulama* were reactionary and in the service of the wealthy capitalist class. Rajavi declared that the *fatwa* was arranged by Rasuli and therefore the clergy were only fulfilling the wishes of SAVAK. As a result the situation in prisons became very tense and polarized, and many activists could no longer stand the situation and gave up the struggle altogether.

The Mujahidin and the Supporters of the *Fatwa*

This verdict (*fatwa*) issued by a number of the clergy in prison resulted in different and sometimes conflicting consequences. At that time I was in the JCCT Prison and remained completely unaware of the situation. Around the middle of the year in 1355/1976 a few Islamist activists including people like Ka-chu'i, Asgar Awladi, Araqi, Lajevardi, Haidari,[202] Badamchi (Badamchiyan),[203] Qurayshi, Mohammad Mohammadi Gorga-ni, Abbas Mudarresifar,[204] and Jalil Rafi'i were transferred from Ward One to Ward Two. Some of them were already in cell number two. When these individuals came, they began to discuss the content and objectives of the *fatwa*. This group be-came known as *advocates of the Verdict* (*ashab-e fatwa*). To their list of members we must also add some members of Dr. A'azami's group, whose members were mostly from Lorestan Province. They advocated complete detachment from the communists in every respect and separated their dining room, food, and schedule of activities from them.

The MKO members took a strong position before ad-vocates of the *fatwa*. Rajavi and other leaders of the organiza-tion declared their rejection of the verdict and condemned it strongly. Rajavi stated, "We are standing against this *fatwa* because it is anti-human, against the aspirations of the people and their struggle. We will fight against it just as we are fighting against the regime. We shall shed our blood in our

---

[202] Abu'lfazl Haji Haidari (b. 1319/1940) joined the Islamic Coalition Party in the bazaar of Tehran. He was arrested in 1343/1964 on charges related to the assassination of Hasan Ali Mansur and remained in prison until 1355/1976. See Ahmad Ahmad, *Memoirs*, p. 266.

[203] Asadullah Badamchiyan (b. 1320/1941) grew up in a family of political activists. He joined the Islamic Coalition party and supported Imam Kho-meini after 1342/1963. Between 1963 and 1356/1977 he spent years in prison on and off. He taught the Arabic language to prisoners. He was re-leased in 1977 and played an active part in organizing pre-Revolution demonstrations and led the committee to welcome the return of Imam Khomeini in 1978. After the Revolution he held several important positions including Deputy Minister of Justice on Social Affairs, and member of the national parliament.

[204] Abbas Mudarresifar (b. 1317/1938) was arrested in relation to the assas-sination of Mansur in 1343 and was sentenced to life in prison. Later he joined the Mujahidin and currently lives abroad. For more information on his life and activities see Ahmad Ahmad, *Memoirs*, pp. 434.

fight and struggle against this counter-revolutionary move even if we lose our lives."

Behzad Nabavi, Mehdi Khumsi, Sadiq Nowruzi, Hossein Montazer Haqiqi, and two or three other friends advocated reconciliation and unity and wished to mend the relationship between these two groups. But Behzad made a strategic mistake here that he had to pay a high price for. He decided to take measures to put a stop to the MKO leadership's dictatorial and monopolistic attitude and end their hegemony. Behzad was the cellmate of Ahmad Hanif Nezhad (the younger brother of Mohammad, the founder of the original MKO) and they trusted each other. Behzad took advantage of this relationship and provoked Ahmad to claim that he was the *true Mujahid and heir to Mohammad Hanif Nezhad* and to take measures to isolate Rajavi and his associates. Behzad's trick failed because he had overestimated Ahmad, and after this conversation ended, Ahmad told Mas'ud Rajavi and Musa Khiyabani everything that Behzad had told him and intended to accomplish by this trick. These two MKO leaders became very angry, and they boycotted Behzad and ruined his reputation. They made accusations against him and even claimed that they had helped Behzad to re-enter Islam. In short, deep hostility began to develop between the leaders of the MKO and Behzad Nabavi.

I knew the advocates of the *fatwa* and had friendships with some of them. I was also well versed in the MKO's ideology and had worked with them for a long time. I was absolutely certain the two groups could never work together under any circumstances. Even if the MKO acted upon the *fatwa* (of course that was impossible), the supporters of the *fatwa* could never get along with them. I knew both sides very well. Individuals like Lajevardi and Kachu'i did not even consider the Mujahidin to be Muslim and asserted that they performed prayer to convince others that they were Muslims but in reality they were communist! Right or wrong, *the fatwa became a pretext and separated the two groups once and for all.*

456

In the early days of this split, prison authorities scattered the advocates of the *fatwa* into different cells, and only the police knew their numbers and the cells they stayed in. It was only during mealtimes that they all gathered in one place and sat together to eat. There were eleven of them. Even though I agreed with many of their views, I did not support the tactics they used against Mujahidin and the Marxist groups. I did not condone their manner of dealing with the rest of the prisoners either. While I fully supported their separation from the leftist groups, I did not support their fanaticism and reactionary views on certain issues. For example, I did not agree that if a Marxist touched me or my clothes with his wet hand, I would become impure and should wash my hands immediately and change my clothes! In my opinion such issues belonged to the domain of intellect and emulation. My understanding and analysis was that the *fatwa* at that particular historical juncture was more a subjective political position than a religiousone. In my opinion it was a kind of intellectual boycott, but since we were in a situation such that we could not think objectively and understand, we resorted to emulation. Since the clergy said all leftists were infidels and hence impure, we simply repeated what they said. However, I did not support the idea of avoiding and isolating the leftists, nor did I believe that my belief and attitude would violate the sanctity of religion. Thus, I argued that even if one believed in the ritual impurity of the Marxists, one should not wash one's hands in front of them, but wait until they went away. The MKO members also used to consider the way the people of the *fatwa* dealt with the communists and Marxists as inhumane. I was in total disagreement with the advocates of the *fatwa*, and the Mujahidin also considered the anti-communist *fatwa* counter-revolutionary and inhumane. People like Behzad Nabavi who struggled to bring unity and wanted to create an environment of mutual respect and recognition did not accomplish anything. Jokingly, they became known as the Welding Group because they wanted to bring together conflicting forces of revolution and forces of reaction

This situation continued for a while until Kachu'i and his friends came up with a plan to gather all the MKO members in one room, close the door behind them, and boycott them. The Mujahidin discovered this plan, so they went to different cells and started seeking support, especially from the people who did not fully back the other group. These activities created anxiety and concern among members of both groups and in a way among all prisoners. The Mujahidin members also committed a great mistake on their part. They sent a man named Hossein Durrgushi to talk to Major Afshar. He complained that a group of prisoners constantly went from one cell to another, ate separately, and disturbed everyone. At the end he requested that authorities place those prisoners in one cell and end the turmoil. After two or three days, Major Afshar called Asgar Awladi and asked him about the situation and why his friends were disturbing other prisoners. Asgar Awladi told him that they had no differences or conflicts with any group. The reason they wanted to be in one cell was because in his group they had the same charges and had been separated from the Marxist groups as well as from the Mujahidin while they were in Mashhad and Qasr Prisons. They wanted to be separate from them in this prison too and were not willing to sit with them for meals. Major Afshar accepted this request and promised to put all of them in one cell.

The great mistake that the Mujahidin made was to get prison authorities involved in this dispute because it was the police who benefited the most from these conflicts and tried to promote group differences and conflicts. A few days later a police officer came to us, and since it was Ramadan he ordered all those who fasted and prayed to go downstairs and gather in one cell so that they would not disturb those who did not fast or wake up for *suhur* and morning prayer. Obviously, the message he meant to convey was that Rajavi and his supporters did not pray or fast. With this message he promoted further differences and conflicts and worsened the situation.

A Party to Celebrate Freedom

Kachu'i's group intended to take me to their cell after this incident. People like Ghayuran, Morteza Tajrishi, Asgar Awladi, Badamchiyan, and Kachu'i came after me one by one and invited me to join them in their cell. They hoped to convince a few well-known prisoners to join their camp so that they could use them to propagate their group and mobilize support for it. However, since I did not agree with their positions, I declared that I was their friend, but I disagreed with them on many points, and it was not right for me to join their group, especially because I had heard that the regime planned to release some of the advocates of the said *fatwa*. However, I told them that I would visit their cell and meet them and share meals with them from time to time. I also informed them that although I did not approve of the Mujahidin's allegations against the supporters of the *fatwa*, I had no intention of joining them.

Several members of this group had been in prison since the assassination of Hasan Ali Mansur. They had served at least ten to twelve years behind bars. They were getting old and could not tolerate the prison environment any longer. The regime was certain that if these individuals were released, they would not join guerrilla groups because they were not capable of living and operating underground. The most they could do was to join Qur'anic study groups and prayer sessions with like-minded friends. In addition, the regime knew that since these individuals opposed the MKO, if they were set free, they would work against that organization outside prison, and therefore, they were no longer a threat to the regime. The regime wanted to release these men from prison in order to ease domestic and international pressure that pushed for liberalization of Iran's political environment. So people like Asgar Awladi, Anvari, Haidari, 'Araqi, and others were transferred to Qasr Prison and then pardoned and released on the occasion of the celebration of the anniversary of the 15th of the month of Bahman, 1327/February 4th, 1949 that marked the failed assassination attempt on the life of the Shah. Had I joined this group I would have been released along with them. At that particular time, however, I believed my presence in prison was more important and that I had to complete my prison term. I had formed a group that was completely independent of both the MKO and the Marxist groups. I had also chosen a specific tactic and strategy. So had I been released at that time, it would have been harmful to my group psychologically and dealt a severe blow to its members.

In Between the Lines

In any case, I did not join the *fatwa* group and refused to move into their cells. The Mujahidin members actually wished that I had joined that group and openly told me that I belonged to them and would be more comfortable if I joined them. They told me that I had nothing in common with the MKO as I did not share their ideology and strategy. Mas'ud Rajavi sent me a letter in which he stated that I should join my *friends* in that group. I told him that I would not allow anyone to make decisions for me. I would do as I pleased and would join any group that I chose, and that they could not kick me out. I could join that group whenever I felt like it or leave it anytime I wished. Having been disappointed, they sent Mehdi Bukhara'i[205] and Majid Mo'ini[206] to convince me to join the supporters of the

---

[205] Mehdi Bukhara'i was the younger brother of Mohammad Bukhara'i, who was involved in the assassination of Mansur. He was a high-ranking member of the MKO. He was arrested and imprisoned after a series of operations in 1353/1974 and remained hospitalized for seven months. After the victory of the Revolution he continued his activities with the MKO and finally was arrested after a series of armed operations and was executed. See Javad Mansuri, *Memoirs,* pp. 136 & 157. See also Ahmad Ahmad, *Memoirs,* pp. 424–428.

[206] Majid Mo'ini (b. 1326/1947) was a high-ranking member of the MKO who was arrested in 1351/1972 and tortured frequently but resisted extremely well. He resumed his activities on the side of the MKO after the victory of the Revolution. According to Javad Mansuri he adopted Marx-

fatwa. They argued that I would be better off with them, and staying in prison would prompt the Muhjahidin to make my life miserable. I confronted them harshly and said that where I stayed was none of anyone's business. When they failed they decided to use other means. They sent two Marxist prisoners to my cell to stay with me to provoke me and kick me out of the cell. However, I stayed in the cell with my Marxist inmates. Other than Rajavi, some other leaders of the organization also came to this cell from time to time. They hoped that I would come into conflict with my leftist inmates. My two Marxists cellmates said that they wanted to leave my cell, but the Muja-hidin told them to stay. I told them that I had no problem with them staying in my cell, and soon became friends with both of them. We often took walks and talked together. I even had my bed next to one of them at night. During the day, I normally went out of the room and busied myself reading a book or watching a movie in the television room. Whenever I went back into the cell, I found my cellmates with a group of their friends and whispering but they stopped that when I entered as though a SAVAK agent had entered the room. Everyone kept quiet. I, too, intentionally stayed there for an hour or so, moved around, or made myself busy with my books, and then left.

I had a few supporters in every cell and four of them in my own cell. The Mujahidin tried hard to kick me out of that cell, but they failed. My supporters and I had told them that group-living had its own principles, and we would respect them as long as they did not contradict our own principles, and whenever they were against our principles and religious beliefs we would speak out and not be afraid to express our disagree-ment.

At Evin Prison, they hardly allowed visitors, and when they did, visitors normally brought fresh fruit that the prisoners shared with everyone. But when the visitors of prisoners in cell

---

ism and was killed in a clash with government forces. See Mansuri, *Mem-oirs,* p. 80, and Behzad Nabavi, *Interview,* Tehran, n.d.

number two brought fruit for them, they would give them only to Mujahidin members and accepted fruit from them alone. They also tried to share some of their fruit with theMarxists "for humanitarian reasons," but this was an insult, and the leftist groups did not accept their offers.

The Mujahidin also shared their fruit with the Marxist groups but never with inmates of cell number two. One day Hossein Montazer Haqiqi had some visitors. When he returned, he brought some fruit to share with everyone, including the inmates in cell number two. At that time [Mohammad Ali] Raja'i [207]was in charge of cell number one and shared our perspective. At Hossein's request he distributed the fruits and gave some to the inmates in cell number two. But they did not accept and sent it back. To make the story short, fruit distribution became a source of tension. For example, in cell number four out of nineteen inmates only ten, including Behzad Nabavi, accepted the fruit and the rest sent it back. The rest of the fruit esd left in cell number one until it spoiled.

One of the inmates named Shahpour Khushbakhtiyan[208] was a medical technician and knew how to dress wounds and injuries of inmates. When someone was injured while exercising or playing games, he was there to help. One day one of the inmates from cell number one went to him. Shahpour dressed his wound, and the man gave him two apples. He ate one and gave the other one to the man in charge of fruit in Rajavi's cell. This single apple caused a crisis between Shahpour and Rajavi and his friends to the extent that they had

---

[207] In an interview in 1358/1979 Ezzat Shahi stated, "The MKO reported Raja'i to the SAVAK. Raja'i was in contact with Hanif Nezhad and his wife (Pooran Bazargan) and was arrested in 1353/1974. He resisted under torture and was sentenced to a five-year prison term.

[208] Shahpour Khushbakhtiyan (b. 1327/1948) studied electrical engineering at the Science and Technology University. He was arrested in 1352/1973 and released in 1356/1977 and joined the Revolutionary Guard Corps. He held several positions in the Corps and then moved to the private sector. See *Interview*, Azar 1383/December 2004.

a fight and even threatened to kill him. They in fact were really bullying him and kept on telling him that *"He who is provoking you and hiding behind you must be man enough to come forward himself!"* They meant that Shahpur was a puppet in someone else's hand, and that *"someone else"* was I. It was obvious that they had me in mind. I decided that I could no longer remain quiet, so I opened the door and entered their cell where the fighting was. When I entered they stopped fighting and became quiet. So I left. Hardly had I stepped out of that cell when the argument began again. I opened the door and entered their cell again and looked sternly into their eyes. This time I decided to stay for a while. The fight ended and everybody went about his business.

These sorts of attitudes and games were nauseating and truly tragic and childish. Sometimes I told myself how unfortunate we were that these people wanted to rule over our country tomorrow and prayed that God would not allow that to happen. I remember that the inmates in cell number two observed and celebrated religious occasions such as the *Eid of Mab'ath* (Prophet's appointment), *Eid al-Azha, Eid Ghaadir Khum, Eid al-Fitr,* and Persian New Year (*Nowruz*) and invited the Mujahidin but they never attended. In fact the Mujahidin members never observed religious festivals and *Eids.* I remember on the eve of *Nowruz* in the year 1356/March 21, 1977, prisoners from cell number two went to visit the Mujahidin members. The Mujahidin members did not welcome them, nor did they pay the "people of *fatwa*" a visit in return. Instead they went to visit the Marxist prisoners a few times and celebrated the Persian New Year with them but never invited the prisoners from cell number two, the supporters of the *fatwa.* The people of *fatwa* attended the ceremonies organized by the Mujahidin as a gesture of respect, but the Mujahidin did not respect them and never visited them.

On the 11th of the month of Ordibehesht/May 1—Labor Day—a dispute broke out amongst leftist groups, and they could not conduct a ceremony. The Mujahidin who did not arrange the celebration of other occasions observed Labor Day, and leftist groups participated in this celebration and indulged in food and fruit in the name of the working class. We did not attend this ceremony while our own workers lived in such poor conditions and never could afford good food and fruit. The Mujahidin members had boycotted cell number two and forbidden any kind of contact with our cell. For instance, if the prisoners in cell number two asked for a nail-clipper, the Mujahidin refused to give it to them. But they provided anything that the Marxists asked for.

Dr. Shaybani had managed to sneak in one holy Qur'an and *Nahj al-Balaghah*. Since no other book was available, we had divided the *Nahj al-Balaghah* into six parts and made a cover page for each part separately, and each cell took turns a few hours a day reading it and then passed it to another cell. The Mujahidin could not prevent this because the book did not belong to them. Even when they wanted to pass by or borrow these books from us in cell number two, they did so through the small window in the door of the cell to avoid encountering us face to face. The strangest thing was that the Mujahidin called prisoners in cell number two impure (*najis*), infidels, and counter-revolutionaries, yet they never said these things to the Marxists.

The Mujahidin kept two of their members in each cell so as to watch and harass anyone who had ties with the prisoners in cell number two where the people of the *fatwa* stayed. They had also placed two of their members in our cell so that they could spy on me and encourage me to join the advocates of *fatwa*. One of those leftist elements was a man named Mohammad Ali Malakutiyan. He was very shrewd and rude. In every cell, one or two people were put in charge of daily cleaning and washing of the utensils, and serving food. Because they knew that I observed the rules that pertained to ritual purity, they appointed two Marxists as the leaders of our cell so they could clean and dry the utensils of the cell. I ate my food there with them. The Mujahidin sarcastically told me that if I believed these guys were ritually impure, why I was willing to use their utensils and eat with them! I told them that I observed the Qur'anic injunction that commands us not to spy on each other, and since I did care how the Marxists cleaned the utensils, those days that they were in charge of cleaning and washing, I did my own part and washed my utensil the way I was commanded too. On such days, I normally went to other cells and ate with Islamist groups. The Mujahidin criticized me for doing that. Even before the *fatwa*, I was very careful not to annoy Marxist prisoners with nonsense behavior while I observed my religious duties the way I was supposed to in a subtle way. I was particularly careful to behave in such a way as to win the friendship of the leftists and not to do something to repel them. I respected them, and I was also a friend to many of them. They knew and appreciated my manner and etiquette. They in turn were very considerate. For instance one of my feet was injured and an extra piece of flesh had grown on it, so I had a special pair of slippers and nobody ever wore them, even when I was not around. But if one of them wore my slippers by mistake one day, I would not go for a walk that day in order not to embarrass him. When I washed my clothes, I did not hang them on the same rope that the Marxist prisoners did theirs. Instead, I would take my clothes to the courtyard and hang them there to dry. Often Marxist prisoners played chess or backgammon or read Marxist books, and in situations like that I went to a secluded corner of the ward and remained quiet so that I wouldn't disturb them. When I went to sleep, I would cover my head with my blanket and pretend to fall asleep so that they wouldn't feel uncomfortable.

In the commune we usually washed all utensils together. But since the people of *fatwa* considered Marxist prisoners ritually impure, they often tried to have their food before them so that their food was not touched by them. They had a teapot that they brought to have their tea because they didn't want to take tea from the kettle that was touched by the Marxists! Even if the Marxists washed the cooking pot and utensils really well, the people of *fatwa* would wash them again. No matter how hard I tried to tell them that such actions were exploited by SAVAK, they would not listen and did as they wished.

The Boycott

Before the ideological transformation of the MKO they counted on the leftist groups and respected them. They established cordial relationships with them, and anyone who opposed such relationships was punished and boycotted immediately. This relationship continued at Evin, and the leadership used any means to punish those who opposed this policy. The prison became a place for accusation and counter-accusation and rumors. The Mujahidin labeled their opponents one way or the other to discredit them. If a person was a bazaar merchant, they called him *petit-bourgeois, capitalist pig*, and *greedy*. They labeled university students and intellectuals as those whose characters were not purified yet and were marred by intellectual disease. Others were labeled as police and SAVAK agents, while some others were criticized for having *petit-bourgeoisie* traits. About those prisoners who had solid characters and could not be labeled with any derogatory epithet they would say that since the police are so sensitive to them, they should be avoided. Those who were waiting for trial were accused of asking the regime for pardon. About those who had been transferred from the JCCT Prison, they claimed that they had collaborated with the police. In short, spreading rumors and innuendo was the name of the game.

There was a systematic effort to boycott anyone who was not in full support of the MKO. For instance if a boy and a girl were arrested together or a female activist removed her scarf, they were called progressive and revolutionary, but if a person did not shave his beard, he would be called reactionary and they would not even exchange greetings with him, nor did they ask for their opinions. And if they had to sit with such a prisoner for the meal, no one was willing to share his plate

466

with him. This was the worst insult to a political prisoner and usually he could not bear the situation for too long in such an environment. If he was not strong enough, he would soon lose his faith. Through these tactics the Mujahidin exploited others and recruited them to their own ranks. Then abruptly a person who was referred to as police and a SAVAK agent a short time ago would become a friend to all of them. If a prisoner remained firm in his position and was not willing to collaborate with them, he was boycotted until he got frustrated and apologized. In such situations the Mujahidin claimed that the man has discovered the truth!

Some prisoners who went through these processes with the Mujahidin became disappointed after a while and joined the left. The left instead paid special attention to him and provided whatever he needed. Then the Mujahidin claimed that they knew all along that that guy was not a believer and had predicted that he would eventually join the left! Hearing all these, the simple-minded members of the organization thought that the leadership had special wisdom and knowledge that they could predict all this. They did not realize that all this was orchestrated by the MKO leadership.

In some other cases that an activist did not agree to join either the Mujahidin or the left and wanted to remain independent, both sides pressured him so much that he got frustrated and did everything he could to be pardoned by the regime and released from prison. Many who wrote letters to authorities and asked for forgiveness and expressed regret went through these experiences. Even in such situations, the Mujahidin claimed that so-and-so was weak from the beginning and that it was obvious that he could not continue the struggle, and that he deserved to be boycotted. This sort of propaganda did not allow other prisoners to think logically and objectively. The truth was always buried under false claims and propaganda.

After 1355/1976 the number of prisoners who wrote letters to seek pardon increased. Most of the letters were written by members of the leftist groups. There was hardly any prisoner from among the Islamist groups who ever wrote such letters. But from that year on and as a result of the oppressive and dictatorial environment in prison, even religious prisoners started writing letters to authorities and asked for pardon. The police did not treat these requests in an objective manner. Sometime they released a prisoner after receiving the first letter from him. Sometimes police forced the petitioner to spy for them in prison. Other times they released people for different reasons and justified that. SAVAK also exploited the occasion, and forced petitioners to give interviews and appear on national television and praise the regime, thus totally destroying the reputation of many well-known activists. *The problem was that nobody asked why individuals who spent most of their lives in political struggle, went to prison, and experienced so much hardship and torture, would change so suddenly and so much to the extent that they would scorn the idea of revolutionary struggle, despise all revolutionaries, and worst of all, be willing to collaborate with SAVAK.*

There was also a group of prisoners who never changed their attitude and mind no matter how long they suffered from boycotts and dictatorial measures that dominated the prison environment. This group posed the greatest challenge to the Mujahidin and was the most serious problem they faced. They couldn't do anything about them, nor could they label them as counter-revolutionaries or reactionaries. In addition, within the organization also there were some members who opposed the leadership, but they could not be independent. So they pretended to be obedient and faithful to the organization. There were also individuals who were totally indifferent and had no particular position of their own. The leadership of the organization tolerated them and those who disagreed with them but did not openly express anger or take a position against them. Whenever somebody asked the reason for this attitude, the leaders said to "leave them alone, let them live the way they please."

468

Amongst the members of cell number two, it was only Badamchiyan who was fluent in the Arabic language. Since there was no textbook available in prison, he taught Arabic to the prisoners. The Mujahidin did not allow their members to take part in these classes. In fact they were totally against learning Arabic because they feared that if their members learned the language they would no longer accept their shallow understanding of the Qur'an and what they presented as "commentary" of the sacred text. When the Mujahidin recited a verse from the Qur'an, they would give a fully Marxist interpretation of the verse. Anyone who knew some Arabic could easily realize how deviated and eclectic their thoughts were. So the Mujahidin boycotted all those who attended Arabic classes.

Behruz Zufan was one of my cellmates. He opposed the tactics of the prisoners from cell number two (supporters of the *fatwa*) but he had a few friends among them and associated with them. When they needed anything he provided it for them. Since he did not have much to do during the day, he attended Badamchiyan's Arabic classes for a while. He was an emotional and generous man and was very attached to his family and his fiancée. He often thought about his life before being arrested and imprisoned and often dreamt of his mother and talked to her in his sleep. The Mujahidin boycotted him after he attended the Arabic classes. He had trouble sleeping and suffered from a sleep disorder and often moved his hands and legs involuntarily. So people gossiped about him behind his back and accused him of lacking manner and discipline, so he was thus boycotted. He could not take the accusations that were made against him and after a while he got sick. His physical and spiritual health deteriorated steadily. Nobody from among the Mujahidin was willing to help him or take care of him. In fact it was two Marxist cellmates who attended to him and gave him food and helped him. After a few days Musa

Khiyabani[209] spoke with Behruz and told him that if he cut his ties with the prisoners from cell number two he could count on the Mujahidin's support. He warned him that if he still wished to maintain his relationship with the people of the *fatwa* then he should not expect Mujahidin's support and friendship and he would be boycotted. Since he could not put up with all these troubles, he stopped attending the Arabic classes and never went to cell number two after that. The Mujahidin then became his friends and treated him as before.[210]

The Rabbani,[211] Ezzat Shahi, and Rasuli Triangle!

The position that the MKO adopted in relation to the leftist groups and their boycotting of the people of the *fatwa* prompted some members of the clergy to take a strong position against the Mujahidin and issued a strong warning against their relationship with the Marxists. In such a situation SAVAK, too, tried to take advantage of this golden opportunity for its

---

[209] Musa Khiyabani (b. 1326/1947) joined the MKO while at Tehran University where he was studying physics. He received military training in Lebanon and Jordan, and when he returned to Iran he was arrested and imprisoned. He was released in 1357/1978, and married Azar Reza'ie. A close friend and ally of Rajavi and the most influential member of the MKO after the Revolution, he was nominated for the parliament elections but was not elected. He was killed on 19 Bahman, 1360/February 8, 1981 when the police invaded his safe house in northern Tehran. See Maysami, *Anha ke Raftand*, pp. 53, 95–96, & Nejat Hosseini, pp. 59 & 92–102.

[210] The practice of boycotting those who disagreed with the MKO leadership did not end in Iran but continued in the Ashraf Camp in Iraq. Many important members like Hadi Shams Hai'iri and Ali Zarkash, who had served the organization, became victims of that practice.

[211] Abd al-Rahim Rabbani Shirazi (b. 1311/1932). He entered the Shiraz seminary at the age of seventeen, and then continued in Qom and studied with Ayatullah Burujerdi and Mihaqqiq Damad and reached the rank of *mujtahid* in 1327/1948. Before the Revolution he was imprisoned on and off. After the victory of the Revolution, he was appointed by Imam Khomieini as his representative, first in Kurdistan and then in Shiraz, and finally elected to the national parliament. He was killed in a car accident in 1360/1981. See Marziyyeh Hadidchi, *Memoirs*, pp. 78–79.

own objectives. Sometimes Rasuli took me to the interrogation room often for no particular reason and left me there alone for a few hours until a guard came and took me back to my cell. Whenever I returned, I had to explain to my cellmates the reason for spending time in the interrogation room. But unfortunately no one accepted my explanation. It was obvious that Rasuli used this trick to create doubt about me among my cellmates and cause conflict between us. It was during the last days of 1355/1976 and early days of 1356/1977 that I was called to the interrogation room again. Rasuli was there along with Rabbani Shirazi. I greeted them and sat down. I didn't speak with Rabbani and pretended that I did not know him at all. Rasuli asked me why I did not speak to Rabbani. At that moment Rabbani got up and came toward me. He embraced and kissed my cheeks and asked about my health.

I had known Rabbani for a long time before our arrest. We were also together in Qasr Prison. Apparently, the reason for this meeting with him was that Rasuli had told him that in cell number two, everyone had become a communist except Ezzat, who was the only religious person there. Rabbani had told him that Ezzat was not alive and pretended not to know that I was alive. Rasuli had told him that I was alive but a little sick and had asked if Rabbani wished to see me, whereupon Rabbani had said that he would love to see me after a long time.

In the interrogation room, Rabbani told me that he wanted to visit me when he heard that I was sick and I told him in a low and cold tone of voice that I was sick and did not want to see anybody. He understood what I meant. Rasuli then decided to leave and left us alone to chat. He told the guard to take him back to my cell when were done. I guessed that Rasuli had planted a microphone in the room to listen to our conversation. So I whispered in his ears some important issues I wished to share with him but spoke aloud when I talked about other insignificant issues. Just to be sure, we changed our seat-

471

ing positions. We guessed that the microphones might have been placed on the chairs or on the table close to us.

The first thing that I told Rabbani was that Rasuli, who was now referring to him as an "Ayatullah," was the same person who two years ago beat him up and whipped him. I emphasized that that he should not think of Rasuli as his friend simply because he called him an "Ayatullah" and that there was a great probability that this was just a trick.[212] I warned him against falling into this trap and writing or saying things about other prisoners. I also warned him not to be fooled, because SAVAK intended to use him to discredit other clergy members and to be aware that once they attained their objectives they would trash him like others.

Rabbani assured me that he was careful and told me to request to be transferred to his cell because he had heard that I was uncomfortable in my cell. I rejected the idea and asked him not to make such a request and said that I was comfortable in my cell and that is where I could stand against the Mujahidin. I also emphasized that the ideological transformation of the Mujahidin would ultimately serve our interests despite its harms. It was better that this happened now than in two or three years in the future because if at the moment only a hundred people turned to Marxism, in three or four years' time two thousand people would have joined them and become Marxist.

Rabbani whispered in my ear that those clergy members in prison believed that since the Islamist groups and individuals received a heavy blow from the communists, it was not appropriate for them to associate with Marxist elements and that they should live separately because from the point of view of the clergy the communists were infidels and hence impure (*najis*). This was what the *fatwa* had denoted. Mr. Rabbani in-

---

[212] This interview was conducted in Bahman 1358/February 1979 while Rabbani was still alive. Ezzat Shahi emphasized that he did not intend to insult him or anyone else, but reported the atmosphere that prevailed in prison then.

sisted that we had to treat the Islamist members of the Mujahidin in a normal way because people like [Ayatullah] Taleqani
and Montazeri did not consider the Mujahidin members to be
one hundred percent Islamic. If the Mujahidin accepted their
mistakes, it was permissible to maintain a relationship with
them. And if they wished to commit themselves to Marxism,
then the believing members would leave them and join the Islamist forces.

I told Rabbani to keep his morale high and not to conclude that we couldn't do anything or find a solution. In fact
the moment was right and the best opportunity for us to do
something. For one thing, the clergy who were the symbols of
Islam and were knowledgeable should sit down and analyze
the situation to find out the reasons the young people turned to
Marxism. The clergy should also criticize their own positions
and actions and discover their responsibility in the process. I
also suggested that they should read the Mujahidin's declaration on the ideological transformation (*taghyir Mavazi'-e ideolozhic*) and analyze their criticism of religion and provide responses to those criticisms. This was an important task that the
clergy should accept at that juncture.

As we were talking, Rasuli came in. He also started
talking against the Marxists and praising the clergy. In order to
teach Rabbani how our stand should be against the activities of
SAVAK and their defense of religion, I confronted Rasuli
harshly and said, "Please don't give us advice, as you are not
qualified to defend religion. If you say that you are a Muslim, I
will not accept that. If you believed in Islam, there would be
no reason for us to fight with you. We do not consider the
Shah or his regime to be Muslim. Your views are drastically
different from ours. In fact, we believe that you promoted
Marxism in this country. If the regime allowed religion to be
introduced the way it should be, then there would no longer be
any chance for the growth of Marxism. Your regime indeed
has promoted a materialistic culture, and your education system contains many elements of a Marxist system of education.

473

And you give the proponents of Marxism a free hand while you arrest and sentence to six years of prison any student who wishes to read a treatise by Dr. Shari'ati."

Incidentally around the same time they distributed copies of a journal titled *Javanan-e Rastakhiz* in our ward. It was published by the Shah's Resurrection Party (*Rastakhiz*) and I also read that. A university professor had written an essay titled "A Dynamic and a Static Civilization." At the end of the essay he had concluded that God is a product of human imagination and does not exist, and Heaven and Hell are created by man's imagination, and that man made these up to avoid the agony of death.

I told Rasuli that this was the ideology of his party, and he believed in that. The author could not have published such an essay in any other publication. I argued that that was the reason I believed the government itself promoted Marxism, and this was the Shah's party, and this was its ideology.

Upon hearing that, I got into a heated debate with Rasuli. Rabbani told me to take it easy and cool off. I did not give up, however. Rasuli couldn't say much, and threatened to put me on trial again and have me executed. I told him to stop threatening me and get lost, or have me executed and set me free. He simply continued to curse me and asked me to shut up. What was new to me was Mr. Rabbani's position.

I did not know if the Mujahidin were aware of the defections of many of their members. For instance, Hossein Javanbakht was an inmate in our cell, and he exchanged views with Seyyed Mohammad Ali Qurayshi, who was in cell number one, while they were going to court. Javanbakht was not in a good position at all. Several times I told the MKO leaders that they should watch him, but they ignored me. After his trial, however, the Mujahidin's attitude toward him changed. They appointed him as the head of the cell. I was puzzled about this change of attitude. After some investigation it turned out that he had spied for the Mujahidin and as a result they had made a deal with him.

474

SAVAK at Evin Prison had become very active. Every day or night they took three or four fellows for interrogation. Some of them reported everything that was going on in the cells. Mas'ud Rajavi was one of the prisoners that they picked for interrogations several times. They put at his disposal books and pamphlets to read. It turned out that on one of those occasions he had read the pamphlet on the ideological transformation of the organization (*taghyir-e mavaze'e ideolozhic*). When he came back from interrogation, however, he denied that anything important had happened there and said that he had been at the health center to take some medicine for his headache. It was only the leaders of the organization who knew what he was doing, but the other members had no clue at all. Whenever Rasuli took me for interrogation, he always insisted that no one should know what went on, but I always told him that I had nothing to hide and would share my encounter with everybody else.

Even though I didn't get along with the leaders of the organization (including Mas'ud Rajavi), to be on the safe side I always shared with them whatever happened in the interrogation. If others asked me a question, I told them that I had shared everything with Rajavi and they should ask him. But soon I realized that he shared things with others in a selective way and did not tell others anything that was not in their interest. After that I decided to share with everyone what I went through during the interrogation. So whenever I came from the interrogation and someone asked me what had happened, I would share every detail with him. Sometimes during lunch when everybody was present I gave a short report to all.

After my meeting with Rabbani and Rasuli, I told Rajavi everything in a private meeting. I told Mas'ud that I would not share what Rabbani had said with others because the whole issue was about him. I asked him to do something before this matter spread around, because people listened to clergy, and whatever position they might take would have serious ramifications. Rajavi dismissed my warning and said that he did not acknowledge the clergy and did not care what they said or did. "Let them do whatever s—— they wanted to do, and we do not care. We follow our own path."

The MKO did not care to find a proper solution for their conflict with the clergy. They often cursed Rabbani, Talaqani, Montazeri, and the rest of the clergy and labeled them as stupid, counter-revolutionaries, and reactionaries. Their position against Taleqani was harsher. They claimed that his betrayal was more dangerous than Rabbani's and Montazeri because the latter lacked political awareness and knowledge. He claimed that they did not understand anything and were his enemies. He was angry at Taleqani because he claimed to support the Mujahidin, yet like others he had also signed the *fatwa*. Since he had done that consciously, his treason wass much more important and he was guiltier than others. Since Taleqani was sick and SAVAK respected him and fed him kabob every day, the Mujahidin claimed that he was bribed and fooled by SAVAK. They even went so far as to accuse him of collaboration with the police!

Since I did not intend to do anything to harm the organization, I never shared their position against Taleqani with others. When they failed to kick me out of the cell and send me to cell number two, they began a campaign to discredit me. They went to the Marxist prisoners and told them, "A triangle composed of Rasuli, Rabbani, and Ezzat has been formed. They plot against the Mujahidin and Ezzat carries out their plans." They warned the other prisoners not to tell me anything about their activities. They probably wished to accuse me of being a SAVAK agent, but nobody could believe them.

Rasuli was very upset about my position and wanted to ruin my reputation among the prisoners and discredit me. Whenever he wanted to visit our cell, he talked in a loud voice before entering the cell, and when he entered he shook hands with everyone. I didn't want to see him and shake hands with him, so whenever he came I quickly ran to the toilet and sometimes stayed there for fifteen minutes until he left. Rasuli noticed my behavior and one day when he came to our cell he asked about me, wondering why I went to the toilet whenever he came to our cell. He finally sent someone to come and take me to him. I washed my hands and went back to the cell. I entered the cell but I didn't greet him. I got myself busy drying my hands with a towel. Rasuli said, "How are you, you foolish pimp?"

I said, "I am fine."

He said, "How is it that whenever I come to this cell, you go to the toilet?"

I said, "I don't know. I am also wondering why whenever I hear your voice I feel like going to the toilet."

He was really embarrassed in front of thirty prisoners that were present there. The guys too were afraid, and they expected him to whip me, but that was not the case. Rasuli hurled a few curse words at me and then went away.

Later when I saw him, he said, "You stupid pimp! Why is it that whenever you see me, you always embarrass me? Even when I don't want to beat you, why do you behave with me in this manner?"

I said, "Mr. Rasuli! Whenever you come to the cells, please don't look for me! I don't want to see you face to face."

He didn't beat me up again because he knew that I would still talk back and might be rude to him, and beating made no difference at all to me. When he threatened to take me to the basement [for torture] in front of others, I told him, "You cannot beat me more than you have already beaten me in the past. I have become accustomed to being beaten by you." So he could no longer threaten me with torture. When he tried to scare me by the threat of solitary confinement, I said that I loved it more than my cell because I felt much closer to God in solitary cells and enjoyed praying there much more. I begged him to send me there for God's sake, but he said that I must stay in my cell number two so that the Mujahidin could skin me alive!

A few days later they called me and Behrooz Zufan for another round of interrogation. When we entered the room, we saw Rabbani there. By doing this, the police wanted to prove to the prisoners that they were in full control in prison. They wanted to ruin my reputation before the other prisoners. I only exchanged brief greetings with Rabbani. Rasuli brought up a few irrelevant issues that were not important, and I answered him one by one. Because this time, as always before, I had answers for any questions he raised, he became angry. Again Rasuli said, "You have not yet told us everything you know. You have to sit down and write everything from the beginning to the end, especially your analysis on the ideological transformation of the organization and its adoption of Marxism." My answer was the same as always, that I had nothing more to say or to write.

Then they took my friend Behrooz and I to two separate cells. They dropped him in his cell and didn't go after him later. I was in my new cell less than one hour, and Rasuli came after me and stayed there till twelve-thirty a.m. He beat me up with a whip,and cursed me, and finally we both got tired. I told him that I was exhausted and had a terrible headache. Before he left he said that he would send me to solitary confinement again and have me there until midweek when he would call me for more interrogation. Again I had to tell him that I didn't have anything to say and it didn't make any difference which cell I was sent to, and I could not understand his games. He only told me to shut up and left.

When I left his office for my cell, Behrooz also joined me. I told him he could give whatever information he wanted to give to SAVAK and assured him that I would admit everything he said. Even though Behrouz and I had some connections in the past, his charges and interrogation had nothing to do with me because I had not been asked anything about him. So if he were to be interrogated, it was about himself.

When we entered the cell, Behrouz described for everybody that nothing had happened in the interrogation room and he was not questioned. I explained the remaining part. I told him what Rasuli wanted from me and that he was going to call me for more interrogation on Wednesday. Since I had differences with the Mujahidin and did not accept their position, my cellmates did not accept my words. But they listened to Behrouz and accepted everything he said. They also believed him that he did not take a position against the Mujahidin and that he slept for three hours in the interrogation room and no one came to interrogate him. On Wednesday, no one called me for any interrogation.

Members of Cell Number One

The Mujahidin initiated an extensive and poisonous propaganda against the prisoners of Ward One. They stated, "Ward One belongs to traitors, the reactionaries, and the collaborators of SAVAK." If an MKO supporter was transferred to that ward, they wrote many letters to prison authorities and requested the return of their comrade to their cell. They spread the idea that "Ward One belongs to traitors, those who could no longer continue the struggle, and those who had decided to collaborate with the police in order to be released from prison. They claimed that the prisoners of Ward One wanted to stand against the Marxists, who were the real fighters and revolutionaries." Sarcastically, they referred to Ward One as the Ward of "freedom seekers!" When some of the Mujahidin members were transferred to that ward, it was as if they were taken to Hell. They hated the prisoners of this ward even more than they hated SAVAK. In contrast, we really wished to be transferred to Ward One so that we could remain immune from disturbances caused by the Mujahidin. They had created a prison within the prison, so much so that when SAVAK wanted to punish people like us, they would threaten to send us to Ward Two where the Mujahidin stayed so that they would take care of us, as though they were Angel Israel in charge of taking our souls.

One day in the month of Ordibehesht 1356/April 1977, the guard came to me and told me to pack my belongings. I thought that they wanted to take me to the JCCT Prison. I took my belongings and bade farewell to my friends. As I was walking down toward the exit gate of the prison, they stopped me and told me not to go in that direction! Instead they took me to Ward One. When I reached the guards' station, I refused to go further. I told them that I was ready to go to Ward Three or Four or even Qasr Prison, but not Ward One. The guard said, "Your comrades who share your ideology are all in Ward One, and you belong there." I still insisted and refused to go, but finally they took me there and dropped me there. The reason I refused to go to Ward One was the environment that prevailed there. There were some clergy members in that cell who had signed the *fatwa* against the Marxists. It was across Ward Two where the Mujahidin stayed and had condemned and taken a position against them. Since I did not condone the actions of the clergy on that *fatwa,* I didn't want to go to their ward. So in such circumstances, if I had gone to their ward, the Mujahidin would have accused me of being a "freedom seeker" and claimed that I was transferred there in order to be released soon!

The police insisted on carrying out that order. There was nothing that I could do, and so I had to go Ward One. In that ward, the clerics and Islamist prisoners stayed on the upper floor, while the secular or leftist inmates lived on the lower level. I chose to go to the lower level and join the non-clerical and secular prisoners lest others would accuse me of "seeking my release," but SAVAK did not leave me alone and forced me to go to the upper floor. On that floor there were clerics such as Mr. Montazeri, Rafsanjani, Taleqani, Lahuti,[213] and a

---

[213] Hujjat al-Islam Hasan Lahuti Ashkevari (b. 1306/1927) studied first in seminary in Qazvin, then in Qom, and studied with Ayatullah Burujerfi and Imam Khomeini and became a *mujtahid.* He was arrested in 1342/1963 and again in 1354/1975 and was tortured severely by the SAVAK. Initially he supported the MKO but after their ideological transformation turned

number of other religious leaders who had not gone through trial yet. I remained in this ward until the last days of the month of Shahrivar 1356/August 1977. In general I had fairly good relationshipa with the clergy in the ward, especially with Mr. Montazeri and Mr. Hashimi Rafsanjani, but I had nothing to do with the remaining ones because I didn't like their behavior.

In Ward One they took me to cell number five where Taleqani, Montazeri, and another man named Nafari stayed. This cell was called "the Great Hall." Some prisoners from Ward One had met the prisoners of Ward Two and told them to be very careful of Ezzat because he was a SAVAK agent and was brought to their ward in order to gather information about them. So for quite a while Taleqani was not comfortable with my presence in that cell. He was cautious, or as he said, he was practicing prudent dissimulation (*taqiyyah*). He stayed away from me and did not talk to me very much. But the rest of the clergy had a good relationship with me and showed me that they were pleased to have me there. Even though I hated being there, it was a golden opportunity for me to explain the prevailing condition in Ward Two and the general environment of prison and share my other experiences with these clerics. Apart from this, I also had some other plans to carry out in this ward. I had more time to take care of some personal business. I tried as much as I could to help the other people in their affairs.

Mr. Taleqani was an old man, and it was difficult for him to wash his own clothes, so sometimes I washed his clothes in the bathroom. A few time I noticed him rinsing again the clothes that I had already washed for him as a matter of precaution! He was suspicious and doubted my cleanliness. From that time onwards, whenever I washed his clothes, I told him to rinse them himself.

---

against them. He was elected as a member of the national parliament from Rasht. He passed away in 1360/1981.

I also had a lot of free time to read books and newspapers. I was one of the three people who asked Taleqani to conduct a three-hour seminar every week about the exegesis of the holy Qu'ran, but he did not accept our request, saying that the environment was not conducive and that if we attended the discussion, the Mujahidin members too would want to attend, and that would cause a quarrel between us.

SAVAK really respected Taleqani. They treated him like a political celebrity in his own right and not necessarily as a supporter of Imam Khomeini. On the contrary, they treated others like Montazeri very harshly and with disrespect. When they wanted to take him somewhere, they always blindfolded him. They never did this to Taleqani, and they always respected him. They did not disrobe Taleqani, but did not allow Montazeri to wear his clerical attire. If Montazeri became sick, they did not take him to the doctor, but not so for Taleqani. If he just had the slightest problem, they would take him to the doctor even three times in a week if necessary and provided anything he needed. Shaykh Montazeri could not be visited by anyone except his wife and children. But Taleqani's entire family was allowed to come and visit him. Montazeri's visitors brought him special Persian sweets from Isfahan (*gaz*), but prison authorities never delivered them to him. In contrast, everything that Taleqani's family members brought for him was always delivered to him immediately. Sometimes Montazeri's family gave their packages to Taleqani's family to pass on to Montazeri.

There were two groups of religious prisoners in Ward One at Evin Prison. There was a group that was on the upper floor with us. Another group was on the lower floor and supported the MKO. We were almost twenty-six people while the other group consisted of five people. We were completely different in terms of ideology and strategy. For example, if we arranged an event to celebrate an occasion, we would get together, talk, and have a good time and then leave for our cells. After that the five MKO members came and sat in a circle

482

around Taleqani, their backs to Montazeri, and asked questions from him. These five Mujahidin who attended these meetings were Hasan Enayat, Hamid Reza Eshraqi, Mostafa Fumani Hai'ri, Ali Reza Kabiri, and Vahid Lahuti.[214] In addition to these five people, we also had on the upper floor people like Seyyed Abbas Salari,[215] Alavi Khorasgani, Ahmad Hashimi Nezhad, Hadi Hashimi, Muhsin Du'agu Fayz Abadi, and Ali Javadi Raka'i. These individuals supported the Mujahidin members and were against the *fatwa*. The only difference was that these fellows were not as radical as the other Mujahidin members. For example, someone like Hadi Hashimi (the son-in-law of Shaykh Montazeri), believed that it was better for them to perform morning prayer silently or at a later time than to perform it loudly and disturb the Marxist prisoners or wake them up! They went so far as to say that they had no problem at all with the Marxist prisoners. These individuals never prayed under Montazeri. Instead they gathered in a different room and took turns leading daily prayer. Of course when I went to the ward, Hashimi Nezhad was transferred to Ward Two. None of these individuals had any connection with the MKO before coming to prison. They joined to support the MKO inside the prison. Whenever they entered the clerics' cell, they did not greet men like Montazeri and Hashimi Rafsanjani, and walked straight past them and sat around Taleqani.

In the year 1356/1977, when I was still in Qasr Prison, I heard that they had made a plan to perform the *Eid al-Fitr* prayer in the prison courtyard. On occasions like this Montaze-

---

[214] Vahid Lahuti, the son of Hasan Lahuti, entered political activity at the age of eighteen and joined the MKO and continued his activities along with the MKO against the revolutionary regime. He attempted suicide by jumping down from the tallest high-rise in Tehran (Plasco building) and died in the hospital.

[215] Hujjat al-Islam Seyyed Abbas Salari was Iran's *chargé d'affairs* in Argentina between 1360 and 1365/1981 and 1986, and was then promoted to the position of Iran's Ambassador.

ri led the prayers and even Taleqani[216] prayed behind him. But on that day several Mujahidin supporters rejected this arrangement and stated that if Montazeri was to lead the prayer, SAVAK would put more pressure on them and would send them into solitary confinement. Mr. Montazeri argued that if the police were to take anyone to the solitary cells, it was he, the prayer leaders, and the *mullas* who would be taken and not the five supporters of the MKO. However, they did not comply and a few days before the *Eid* announced that they would participate in the *Eid* prayer only if Taleqani led it. It was strange that they were not willing to recognize the status of Montazeri even as a simple prayer leader. Therefore, Montazeri did not lead the *Eid* prayer. However, if Talaqani had wished to shut them up, he could easily have done so, but he remained silent.

*   *   *

---

[216] Ayatullah Taleqani was a pious man, but I believe that he should not have submitted to such a situation. The MKO leaders took advantage of his kindness. Mas'ud was canny and shrewd and could butter up his worst enemy when he needed him. He used a flattering language when he talked to Taleqani, saying, "We are like your children; be kind to us!" Musa was a much more transparent, disciplined, soldier-like young man, but very honest. Both, however, abused Taleqani one way or the other.

CHAPTER TEN

The Last Supper

For the Sake of Human Rights

Early in 1356/1977 the question of the condition of human rights in Iran began to be discussed openly. There were rumors about the visit of the Red Cross representatives to prisons to investigate the condition of human rights and to talk to political prisoners. Therefore, the regime became anxious and tried to select a group of prisoners who were never tortured and have them talk to the Red Cross representatives. The regime was hoping to present an acceptable picture of prisons and the conditions of prisoners to the world public opinion.

Evin was not a prison in the ordinary sense of the term but a temporary detention center. So those prisoners who had gone through their trial and been convicted were no longer supposed to be kept there. It was in fact against the law to keep them after their trials. Therefore, the regime started transferring to Qasr Prison those prisoners who had already been tried and condemned. Its objective was to show to Red Cross representatives that the prisoners' living conditions were fine and they were treated well as the law commanded. The regime selected a certain number of prisoners from each cell and transferred them to Qasr. The transfer of prisoners was not carried out in a systematic way, but selected individuals were taken out of each cell.

On the Persian New Year's Eve in 1356/1977, prison officials started visiting all wards for inspection, or so they pretended. There was no mention of the Red Cross mission yet. They started checking the soles of our feet to make sure that injuries caused by torture were healed. They said that the age of torture had come to an end, and those who were injured would receive proper treatment. They even promised that those who had been injured badly would be sent abroad for plastic surgery. They stated that the introduction of torture was wrong and irresponsible and that the new leadership was determined to change the situation. A few days later they announced that they wanted to have a clinical check-up of the prisoners' hearts. They took people from different cells to the health center where they asked them to remove all their clothes except the underwear. One of the SAVAK agents played the role of a doctor. In reality he was not a physician and did not know anything about medicine and health. He just placed the stethoscope in his ears and ran it over each prisoner's heart, chest, and back. In reality this was just an excuse to examine each prisoner's body to see if there was any mark of torture.

While we were lined up waiting for our turn for the check-up I decided to make fun of the procedures and the man in charge. They said that I should remove my clothes. I only took off my t-shirt and pullover. They told me to also remove my trousers. I said, "My heart is in my chest, and if it fell down, the farthest it could go is my stomach and not farther down, and therefore there is no need to take off my pants." The interrogators who were in the room all laughed and said, "You fool! Are you making fun of us?"
I said, "You guys asked us to come here to check out our hearts. What has the heart got to do with the legs? If there is something else going on, let us know. If you want to check and treat any part of my body other than my heart, then tell me so that I can help you."

They said, "You idiot! Stop talking like a parrot. Just shut up and remove your trousers."

I removed my trousers, and just to make the matters worse I started removing my underwear when they asked me not to remove that! So I stood in front of the "doctor" wearing only my socks and underwear. They told me to also remove my socks and I refused. They insisted that I had to remove my socks. I knew what they were driving at, so I said "So just say frankly that you want to inspect my feet and don't use the excuse of checking up my heart."

The interrogator said, "You fool! If you already know what we want to do, then why are you disturbing us?"

They checked my feet all over and wrote my name on the list of prisoners who had torture marks on their bodies. After four days, they separated around fifty prisoners who had torture marks on their bodies from the rest of the prisoners. I was also among these fifty prisoners. We were from different cells, and this group included Islamist as well as Marxist prisoners. We were all transferred to Ward Three at Qasr Prison. They intended to have full control over Qasr Prison and run everything the way they wished and according the rules they set. They also planned to take over duties that were always performed by the prisoners themselves. For example, the police wanted to bring the "Worker of the Day" or "Community Assistant" that were appointed by a council of prisoners under its control and have them act as they ordered. But we did not accept these new rules. We resisted these changes and told them that we wished to do things the way we did in the past, and that the rules they set for us to observe were not in line with general rules and regulations of the prison itself. They tried to talk to and coax some prisoners to accept the new rules, but none of them complied. Of course those prisoners who had gone through their trials were afraid that their sentences might become harsher and were willing to accept some of the new rules, but most others were united in their decision to resist the full control of the police over the affairs of prison.

Finally prisoners decided to go on a hunger strike. This hunger strike was different from those in the past. One of the contentious issues was the quality of the food and its distributors. The police insisted that they should choose a person to serve us the meals. We did not accept this and wanted to have one of our men distribute and serve food. Consequently, on the days that a person of our choice served the food, people would eat. But on the days that the police-appointed men were to serve us the food, no one even tasted the food. Neither the police nor we wanted to retreat or reverse our position. We were aware that the police could not pressure us more. They could neither beat us nor torture us any longer.

Captain Saremi[217](the head of Ward Three) spoke to me for half an hour. He said, "You are the source of all these troubles. You have to make these prisoners accept the new conditions, and if you could do so, then you should also be the person in charge of the kitchen."

I said that I would not accept any responsibility because I suffered from a terrible backache.

He said, "Do you want to only eat and sleep and have the rest of the prisoners serve you or work in your place?"

I said, "This is not any of your business"

He said, "In fact, it is my business. You are a prisoner and I am the head of the prison. You have to listen to me and obey me."

I said, "Captain! I am not a person to be forced to do something. What you are doing and saying is against the rules and regulations of prison. Why don't you deal with us on the basis of those rules? We don't expect more than this from you. According to the rules, you personnel are supposed to bring the food and give it to the wards and clean the cells. Now, if we have chosen to serve ourselves and clean our own cells, it is because of our own health; otherwise this is your duty. You are in charge of taking care of us. No one can force us to do anything here. I have left the worldly life, wife, children, pleasures, and so on and have come to prison just because of my faith. So today, there is no way that a lowly prison guard can give me orders. I am not supposed to listen to what he is saying. You too, you are sitting here because of your faith in your job. Therefore, your way and mine are totally different.[218]

---

[217] He was arrested after the Revolution and was sentenced to two years in prison.

[218] In 1352/1973 when they transferred me to Qasr Prison, I had an argument with this officer over not shaving my beard. This was against their rules. I was sent to solitary confinement several times over this issue. To the end, I resisted and did not shave my beard.

Do you remember that you sent me to solitary confinement because of my beard but you could see that I did not shave it?"

Our argument and push and pull with the police continued until just a few days before the visit of the Red Cross representatives. Prison officials did not think it was appropriate to continue this situation, so they transferred us to a ward that was originally assigned to non-political prisoners and then transferred the inmates there to the Ghezel Ghal'ah Prison. In the afternoon of that same day, they sent around thirty prisoners to single cells. Since we had come from Evin Prison, they were afraid that we might provoke other prisoners and cause trouble. They assigned three or four of us to one cell and eight or nine people to larger rooms. They took some prisoners like me to the ward that was known as the "mental hospital" where criminals and drug addicts were kept, because they considered us to be trouble-makers and gang leaders. In that ward they didn't gave us clothes, money, or towels, let alone books and newspapers.

They had threatened the other prisoners not to talk to us or else face punishment and torture, but we managed to speak with some of them. One of them was a thief, another one was a club-wielder and highway robber. A third prisoner claimed to have deserted the army during the Zuffar War in [Oman][219] where the Shah's regime interfered. When he realized that I was a political prisoner, he said that he had been in prison one year and would be released soon. He asked me for connections outside prison so that he could join us when he went out. I didn't trust him and suspected that he might be a police agent. I told him that I had no ties and had been in prison for five or six years and had no idea what life looked like outside prison. The strange thing was that this same person

---

[219] The British government granted independence to Oman in 1346/1967 and appointed Sultan Qabus as the head of the new state. His opponents formed the "Front for the Liberation of Zuffar" that enjoyed the support of Iranian revolutionaries. The Shah supported Sultan Qabus and sent troops to fight with his opponents.

became a revolutionary and was assassinated later by the MKO.

The leader of the non-political ward was a man named Abbas. I asked him where he was from and he said from Darvazeh Ghar, a poor neighborhood in south Tehran. I had a friend in that neighborhood and asked him about Abbas. It turned out that Abbas was a neighbor of my friend. Gradually, we became friends and our conversation continued and developed even more than I had expected.

Besides the limitations on money and books, there were also restrictions on leaving our cells and taking fresh air in the courtyard. No one in our group had the right to walk in the hallway or talk to others. Despite these limitations, the non-political prisoners who numbered around twenty-two or twenty-three and were all either drug addicts, thieves, or highway robbers showed much respect to us because we were political prisoners. In spite of all the threats they faced and warnings they received from prison authorities, they were very friendly toward us and treated us very well and protected us from the police. They told us that the police had ordered them to intimidate the political prisoners, but they felt indebted to us and were always so humble before us. They had their own groups of four or five members and sat together with us at the same dining table. So we became part of their community. They gave us the best of what they had. Every day a different group would welcome us to their own dining table. They had heard or seen that when prison authorities wished to punish them and sent one of them to the political prisoners' ward, how nicely he was welcomed and that he was treated like a dignified and respectable human being. Now that we were guests in their ward, they wanted to pay us back, so they treated us so nicely. Part of this attitude was, of course, a reaction to the way we treated them. More importantly, their behavior was a reflection of the respect that the masses of people had for political prisoners and those who devoted their lives to political struggle. For example, they had appointed one of their members as a watchdog to inform us when officers came for inspection so that they could not see that ordinary prisoners slept on the floor while political prisons lay on the bed and that the two groups were engaged in conversation. If the police saw newspapers in our hands, they would confiscate them. When the leader of that cell, Abbas received a newspaper, he held that in such a way that we could read it even while we were lying down.

Since I was neither sick nor a drug addict, I had very few miscellaneous expenses. But the people in the cells near ours had many problems. A person like Mr. Ghayuran, who was so sick, needed special attention. Another person was Hushang Delkhah, a member of the Fidayan-i Khalq Organization, who had mental problems and smoked sixty or seventy cigarettes per day. There were three other guys who were so sick and were in great need of medicine, money, and cigarettes. We took care of their needs with the help of the non-political prisoners. I was the spokesman for those people. I spoke with the other prisoners, and they offered me what they could to meet the sick prisoners' needs. I also spoke to the prison director, Captain Habibi, and requested blankets, towels, bowls, and plates because we shared everything that ordinary prisoners had. However, most often prison authorities either ignored our requests or fulfilled them only partially.

Dealing with non-political and ordinary prisoners had its own delicate rules. Not everybody in the prison knew how to communicate with them. If only we could understand their language or talk on their level of logic, then we would be able to communicate with them and raise their political awareness. We realized this and tried as best as we could to deal with them in their own way. So they loved and respected us a lot. As a result of such behavior on our part, many of them returned to normal and decent life when they were released from prison. In contrast to us, the Marxist groups were not able to communicate and make connections with ordinary prisoners.

Interestingly, their failure had religious reasons, as they denied the existence of God and believed that Paradise and Hell are not real. When Marxist individuals or groups saw that the ordinary prisoners did not pray, they approached them, hoping to attract them to their own side. But they were disappointed. Even though thieves, drug addicts, and criminals never prayed, they believed in God, the Prophet, the Imams, and Heaven and Hell. They participated in mourning sessions for Imam Hossein in Muharram. So these prisoners never went to the ward where the Marxists stayed. Conversely, when they saw us accepting and enduring torture because of our faith in God, the Prophet, and the Imams, they showed even more love and respect to us.

Even though most of them never prayed, in the little time that we were there, they started to join us in prayer, or at least pretended that they prayed. Sometimes they would line up behind us to perform congregational prayers. Although the police had warned them not to join us and punished them when they caught them praying with us, they still did as they wished.

These were some of the virtues this group of prisoners possessed. But like any other social group, they possessed good and bad traits. For example, they were so abusive and used foul language in their conversations. Moral corruption and homosexual practices prevailed among them.

In our cell, there were small rooms with triple-decker beds. Not everybody slept on the beds since there were not enough for all of us. The right to use a bed depended on the seniority of the prisoners and the length of time of their terms. Older prisoners slept on the beds, while the new prisoners had to sleep on the floor. There was a wide carpet in the middle of the cell with two blankets on it. Seven or eight people would sleep on that carpet. They insisted that I should sleep on the bed, but I didn't accept, because I didn't want to break their routine orders. So I slept on the floor near the wall and not in the midst of so many people. Of course this was not a restful sleep but a torture because the floor was hard concrete, people moved every now and then, and some of them also smoked cigarettes even in the middle of the night.

With this kind of sleeping order, the night was a good time for them to do their filthy things. Immediately when the lights were switched off, they started flirting and kissing each other and having sex, as there were many among them who were homosexual. This was quite normal in that environment. The prison guards were all aware of this situation, but they never did anything to stop it. They were happy to get their bribes on time, play chess, and gamble and make jokes to kill time.

Sanitation and hygiene were another serious problem there. The number of bedbugs was disturbing, and they could be seen all over the bodies of the prisoners. Every day they took us out to get fresh air, where we took off our clothes and thoroughly shook them, and the ground would be covered with bedbugs. This method was not good enough to solve the problem, because the bedbugs traveled from the courtyard into the cells and into the clothes of the prisoners. I tried to tell other prisoners to shower a couple of times every day, and use to spray to repel them. Every day I took off my clothes and those of Mr. Ghayuran, and shook them off to get rid of the bedbugs. Ghayuran was paralyzed, and he couldn't move his back and his arm. He still suffered from these problems and so I had to help him whenever I could.

Change in Attitude towards Political Prisoners

On a Friday in the month of Ordibehesht 1356/May, 1977, I was busy in the courtyard trying to remove bedbugs from my clothes when the guard called me and took me to the office of the commanding officer of the prison. I went wearing clothes full of lice, and my finger was stained with blood from the lice. I thought that the prison officer had called me to his office to negotiate with me and find out if we were complying with the rules they set, and if so, they would send us back to the political prisoners' ward.

When I entered his office, I met Rasuli. I acted indifferent and did not show that I was surprised to see him in Qasr. He had not changed at all. The guard directed me and left us alone. Rasuli stood up and greeted me. I never greeted my interrogators in the past, especially Rasuli, because they were the ones who had to deal with us and not the other way around. I was not ever afraid of them, so I never flattered them. Rasuli asked me to come forward! Just as I was walking towards him, he too started walking towards me, extended his hands to greet me, and came forward to kiss me on the cheeks and wish me a happy New Year. I avoided his face, and his beard touched my forehead. We sat down and he asked about my health conditions, and then we started talking about different issues. He then said, "You know that authorities are not happy with you and your resistance and that they want to execute you. But I have been the one who has prevented this from happening up to this date."

I said, "It is obvious that if they were pleased with me and I were pleased with them, then this prison must not be where I am supposed to be. In such a case either you have become like me or I am the one who has become like you, and this is something that can never happen. The gap between us cannot be filled with anything. We have our differences, and it is obvious that we are displeased with one another. The fact that you are the interrogator and I am the person being interrogated shows our difference."

He said, "Leave these matters aside. The main point is that they just want to put you on trial."

I said, "Of course this is what I have been wishing for in order to free myself from you as quickly as possible."

Rasuli told me several times about the issue of my brother, and finally he said, "Ezzat! I want to arrange for your brother to be released on the occasion of the 28th of the month of Mordad/August 18."

I told him, "It is none of my business. In fact, it makes no difference to me what you are going to do with him. If you believe that he is innocent, then let him go, and if you think that he is guilty, keep him as long as you want. You guys made a mistake from the beginning. He was not supposed to have been brought to this place. Right now he has spent three years here. Even if you keep him here for another seven years, it will make no difference."

Rasuli said, "He has a wife and a child. We want to send her money."

I told him, "My sister-in-law is not in need of your money. She has survived the past three years, and she will do anything from here on that is necessary for her to live."

I never had visitors, but my brothers received many visitors. In all this time that we were in Qasr Prison and Ghezel Ghal'ah Prison, I never saw him. I had no information about him and his family. When Rasuli realized that there was no point in continuing the conversation, he asked, "Do you by any chance know why I am here?"

I said, "No! Of course I am not an angel who can know the unseen. But an interrogator can come at any time to see his prisoner."

He said, "Do you know that there is no more torture? For one year now no person has been tortured."

Since the middle of 1355/1976 no one had been tortured openly. This meant that if a person was tortured, he was destined to die. The people who were tortured were all killed. Every time a prisoner was killed, they announced that he was killed in a street clash with the police. They intended to kill the guerrillas outside prison so that they wouldn't have to explain to the Red Cross and avoid other problems. Rasuli's claim was true. Since we had heard that a large number of people had been arrested, I rejected his claim and said that they still tortured prisoners. He insisted that I was wrong and that they no longer tortured any prisoner. I said that most of the people the regime claimed had died in clashes with the police in fact

495

died under torture. The regime killed these prisoners and then announced that they were killed in clashes with the police.

Rasuli became very upset and shouted, "You Son of a——! None of these things are any of your business!"

I said, "And why should it not be my business? I am a prisoner just like them and I have the right to defend them."

He said, "Who the hell are you to defend them? You are supposed to be careful and make sure that you come out of this place alive. Now that the regime has planned to execute you, do you want to be a rational person or do you want to be a pain in the neck?"

I said, "All right. You didn't call me here to say these things. Tell me what brought you here."

He said, "The truth of the matter is that you have a golden opportunity. There are some foreigners who are supposed to hold talks with you. Be careful and make sure that you don't say anything concerning torture and the previous state of the prison. If you adhere to this, it is possible for us to change the opinion of the regime in relation to your case. Do you know what will happen to you if you say anything concerning matters of the past?"

I said, "Yes. They would publish what I might say in their magazines and ruin the regime's reputation." Of course I pretended not to know that the foreigners were representatives of the International Red Cross (RC).

He said, "No, Ezzat! You are just imagining things. It would be worse than this."

I asked, "So, what would they do?"

He said, "Things will be worse for you. They will give all your statements to the JCCT Prison. If you think that those guys will support you, you are dead wrong! They will give their report directly to the JCCT Prison director. So you would again have to face Mohammadi and Manuchehri. This time you won't make it. They will kill you. At that time, I will no longer have any power to defend you."

I said, "It is strange, but if this is the case, then I am going to say everything and let those people do as they wish. Didn't you just say that torture has been abolished? You were lying to me. So let them beat me up and torture me as much as they can. After all, they cannot torture me more than they have already done."

I then asked him why they would give the report to the JCCT Prison if they were all collaborating with them.

He said, "No, they are not collaborating with them."

I said, "And how am I supposed to know that this whole thing is not a joke? Perhaps SAVAK is using foreigners to come and hear what I am going to say. Your agents too know the English language. So whether these people are foreigners or not, it makes no difference to me. I will tell them whatever I am saying to you here and will report everything that you people have been doing during the time that I have been here."

I also told him that my situation was clear for all to see. If I lied to Red Cross representatives, it would be of no benefit, and so it was better for me to say nothing but the truth. In any case, if I lied to them, they would think that I was talking under pressure and that I was not prepared to tell the truth. I said, "You are fully aware that Palestinian groups and some of the activists who live abroad have talked or written about me in foreign countries. So if you people do not want me to talk about these things, then take me out of their path."

Rasuli was stressed out. He begged me to get along with him and said that if I did, my condition would change. He added that those people at the Red Cross wanted to interview me and that it was impossible to reject their request.

I said, "So I have no choice but to tell them the truth."

Rasuli was so annoyed and said, "The hell with you! Do whatever you wish to do!"

I got up and said, "If you have nothing else to discuss, I can leave!"

Again Rasuli said, "Listen, Ezzat! What do you think I came here to talk to you about? You know well that I have helped you a lot and tried hard all this time to save you from more trouble and torture at the hands of these people. Your situation is very critical. I really have sympathy for you. By doing what you are planning to do, you are only depriving yourself of any chance of survival."

He used this tactic and in a way reminded me of the threat of execution. I said, "First of all, you have to prove when and how you ever helped me! Secondly, you need to tell me why you sympathize with me! Thirdly, what you say and all the promises you make may convince others who may be afraid of losing their wealth, position, or family members. I have nothing to lose, not even a simple family member. Mr. Rasuli! Don't bother! Whatever you say will not force me to change my mind. I will do as I wish. You know better than anyone else that I will not change my mind or ideas because of empty promises you make. Since my first arrest, my only prayer to God has been to take me and free me from all these pains you have inflicted upon me. So do not try to frighten me by the threat of execution. Believe me, death is sweeter than this life for me. I wish you could only know how much I wish to die at the filthy hands of oppressors like you!"

Of course my words were politically motivated maneuvers. In fact, I didn't really want to die. Even though I never feared death, at that time I was aware of charges against me and my situation as a whole. I knew very well that they were not in a position to put me on trial and condemn me to death. I knew that they would not execute a prisoner after keeping him in prison for five or six years. So in such a situation I had to take a calculated position to render Rasuli's bluff null and void. I had to let him know that I was not afraid of death at all.

Because I knew that Rasuli was a very cunning interrogator, I always dealt with him in a very harsh way. This time I was even harsher than the other times. In fact, on that very same day, my finger was stained with blood from the bedbugs.

I showed my hand to him and said, "So are you saying that there is no more torture? Isn't this filthy and unsanitary condition you have created for us torture? How do you justify keeping political prisoners among a bunch of criminals and drug=dealers and addicts? Isn't that torture?

He said, "If only you had not broken the law and gone on a hunger strike, we would have not sent you to that ward!

I replied that we had never gone on a hunger strike but were only wishing to eat the food that was handled by our own group. That was in line with prison law. In fact, what prison officials did was against the law, and we didn't want to allow them to impose on us what was against the rules of the prison. I would be more willing to receive a hundred lashes a day than to live in a dirty place like this prison. Here we are denied access to clothes, newspapers, books, and the shower.

I told him that we had enough money of our own to meet our expenses in prison, but they even did not even allow us to buy what we needed with our money. I said, "God bless these thieves and criminals who provide for some of our needs. These guys are poor, and constantly engaged in violations of all moral and ethical rules, and they steal from each other, and with the money they buy us cigarettes, milk, and food. So if this is not torture, what should we call it, then?"

He said, "I am shocked! Do you mean that you do not have any money?"

I said, "No! They took away our money and brought us here. We do not have anything at all. These fellows are sick and are in need of cigarettes and milk."

Rasuli was not able to say anything more. He talked about other things, and when he wanted to go, he took 8000 *tumans* from his pocket and asked me to take as much as I wished. By offering me money, he wanted to bribe me.

I told him that I had not described our situation to beg for special favors, and that we did not need his money because we had our own money in Qasr Prison, and if he were truly sympathetic to us he should bring us our money. We were about eighteen prisoners who had been sent to several different wards. I told Rasuli if he really meant to help, he should at least put us all in one cell where we could keep it clean and maintain a reasonable sanitary standard and pray in a ritually clean environment.

Rasuli promised to speak to the commanding general who had the authority to change our situation. He asked us to wait a few days and he would see what he could do. Before he left he insisted that I should take some money from him, but I did not accept. As he was going out, he asked the commanding officer of the shift why he didn't give us money, and he said that they didn't have any money. Rasuli gave him 200 *tumans* and asked him to pass it on to the store so that we could buy milk, cigarettes, and whatever else we needed. He also promised to arrange for our transfer to the political prisoners' ward within a few days. When he wanted to leave, he came close to me in order to kiss me on the cheek, but I pulled back. He extended his hand, and we shook hands, and he left.

Then an idea came to my mind what to do with the money Rasuli had given to the store for our expenses. I thought since that money was given under my name, I should not allow others to waste it. Some of the Mujahidin, like Hasan Mehrabi, Javad Zargaran, Hosseini Khorasani, and Ansari and Hooshang Delkhah from the Fidayan-i Khalq group, smoked two packs of cigarettes every day. Others needed that money for medicine and food. I decided that we should make use of this money, and after quite a bit of push and pull I convinced the shift commanding officer and got the money from him. When I went to the cell, I told the people who were around what had happened between me and Rasuli. Hasan Mehrabi— one of the Mujahidin members—said, "Ezzat! You have done the best thing."

I gave 100 *tumans* to the prisoners in Ward Eight, and the other 100 *tumans* to the prisoners in Ward Six. I didn't take anything from that money because I did not need anything.

Most of the sick guys were the Mujahidin members. So they went and bought milk and cigarettes.

Meeting Representatives of the Red Cross

Two days after that meeting, Rasuli fulfilled his promise. They gathered us, the eighteen prisoners, and placed us into two cells. From Ward Five they brought to our ward ten other prisoners who were in a situation similar to outs. So there were twenty-eight of us there. There were all kinds or activists in this group, some from the Fidayan guerrilla organization, from the Mujahidin, and members of the Tudeh Party. Abbas Samakar, who was a member of the Golsurkhi group, was also among us. I told everyone about the incident of my meeting with Rasuli and taking the money. Some believed that I was too harsh with him and that I should have been a bit polite. I told them that I was ready for anything.

A few days after we settled into the new ward, representatives of the Red Cross arrived. It turned out that they had a list of prisoners and wished to find and talk to them. SAVAK tried hard to prevent access to us by transferring us from one ward to another or from one prison to another. Yet they were not able to hide me from these people. Most of the names had been given to them by the political activists abroad, especially by members of the Confederation of Iranian Students.

My name had also been mentioned in foreign newspapers. From the moment I was arrested, the regime reported that I had been killed in a confrontation with the police. But activists who lived abroad told the representatives of the Red Cross that the regime was lying and that I was alive and that I had been severely tortured. They had warned them that unless they acted quickly, the regime might execute me. So the Red Cross members insisted on seeing me. Prison authorities were also afraid to show me to the Red Cross members. So they transferred me to different locations several times, but at last they were forced to present me to them.

When the Red Cross representatives came to see me, I told them everything that had happened to me and other prisoners during the last five years. There was a man who translated my statements to them. One of the leftist prisoners was fluent in English and was the one in charge of controlling the accuracy of the translator. If I remember correctly, it must have been Abbas Samakar. I explained to them how a person was interrogated, how the court conducted its sessions, that verdict was issued in advance, and that SAVAK interfered in every stage of the process.

Concerning torture, I told them everything that I had gone through, from solitary confinement, the lashes of the whip by Hosseini, keeping me naked for many days and nights in a dark and cold environment, special torture techniques like crucifixion, the Apollo, and so on. I also told them the reason why we were brought to that prison and that we never had any money to spend. At that point the translator turned to me and said that he could not translate my statements because if Rasuli asked him about it, he would have to report to him what I had said. He was concerned for my safety, but I told him not to fear and even asked him to add whatever he wished on my behalf.

My firm attitude toward the interrogators and my resistance to torture was very beneficial and helped everyone in the prison. On the one hand, it gave others hope and courage to speak up; and on the other hand, it proved wrong the claim by the Mujahidin members that I was a burned out and was seeking my release at any price. My explanations to the representatives of the Red Cross were so straight-forward, strong, and truthful that some prisoners became scared. They tried to dissociate themselves from me and told the shift officer, "You should know that Ezzat is talking only on his own behalf, and his words have nothing to do with us." These fellows didn't even have the courage to support my statement and blamed me for being too harsh. They said that they could not stand the possible negative consequences of my words for their situation once the Red Cross representatives left.

During those days I was in great pain because I had several teeth broken as a result of torture by Mohammadi, who kicked me in the face. I asked the commanding officer to send me for treatment. I did not have any income and asked if there was a budget in the prison for such expenses. They brought a dentist to check my condition and give an estimate of the cost. He gave an estimate of 500 *tumans*. Prison authorities contacted the Society for the Support of Political Prisoners for funding, but failed to collect anything. So I had to leave my teeth as they were. For the time being I had no choice but to accept and stand the pain.

The Failure of a Conspiracy

The thirty prisoners who had been taken to solitary confinement were transferred to Ward Number Three before the arrival of the Red Cross representatives. A few others also were transferred to Ghezel Ghal'ah Prison. We were the only twenty-eight prisoners who were left there, but after living among ordinary prisoners for a month, we were also moved to Ward Three. There, I again shared with the Mujahidin members the story of my encounter with Rasuli and the 200 *tumans* he gave us.

The prison was no longer the way it had been in the past. Everything had changed. No one cared about the affiliation or position of anyone else. Blind obedience was the rule of the game. No one had the courage to investigate and find out if a piece of news was true or false. The MKO had everything under its control. Three kinds of attitudes were discernible among prisoners. There were some who were honest and simple-minded, and believed whatever the organization said. For another group, truth or falsehood didn't matter; what was important for them was the rules, orders, and decisions made by the organization. The third group included people who cared for the truth and verified the things that the organization said. But they did not have the courage to reject the lies told by its leadership.

It was in such a situation that I found out that the Mujahidin in Qasr Prison had boycotted my brother. Since they could not deal with me, they decided to give my brother a hard time and harass him. The reason for boycotting him was the 200 *tumans* that I had received from Rasuli. Some prisoners who had not completely surrendered to the commands of the MKO asked me about the incident of the money. I told them that I had described everything to the entire community and later to the leadership of the organization and asked them what they had heard. One of them said, "People are saying that Rasuli came to see you and you kissed one another on the cheeks. Rasuli then told you that the regime was willing to set you and your brother free on the 28th of the month of Mordad. They also said that Rasuli gave you two hundred *tumans* and in return you cursed at the Mujahidin and expressed regrets for what you did in the past!"

I asked him who were saying these things behind my back, and he said they were the Mujahidin members. I asked him to go to Hasan Mehrabi and tell him, was he not the one who praised me and told me that what I had done with Rasuli was very appropriate? I said, "Tell him if he is telling the truth, he should come and see me face to face and say what he said behind my back." So these fellows went to the MKO leaders and reported what I had said. They ordered them not to spread this around, and they promised to fix things up, but were not willing to meet me. Some of those individuals were still unable to understand how the MKO leaders found out the details of my meeting and conversation with Rasuli. I explained and they understood that the only possibility was that they heard it from Rasuli himself, because besides Rasuli and me, nobody else knew about our meeting and our conversation. In that case they should question the leadership about their relationship with Rasuli

After this argument, the truth became obvious to everyone. However, the MKO leaders did not stop there, but rather continued to make accusations against me. They hoped that I would kneel down and beg them to pardon me! But this was not something that I could ever do, and that was their problem. I always dealt with them from a position of power. I therefore used their own tactics against them and told them that they probably had ties with the police and Rasuli. They had teamed up against me in order to ruin my reputation even though when Rasuli came forward to kiss my cheek, I avoided him and his beard touched my forehead. Moreover, I had given them the money that I received from Rasuli without spending a penny of it on my own needs. I asked them, if the money that came from Rasuli and SAVAK was *haram*, why did they take it? So why was it not a big deal when Mas'ud Rajavi took five hundred *tumans* from SAVAK and was kissed on the cheeks by Manuchehri and Tehrani?! When they realized that their tricks were turning against them, they stopped spreading gossip and shut up after that. Since I knew their temper and nature well, I was alert not to give them any excuse to make me the target of allegations.

While we were at Evin, we were not allowed to have visitors for a while. Rajavi pretended to be sick and asked Rasuli to allow him to see his visitors so that they could bring him medicine. Rasuli send him 500 *tumans* to pay for such expenses until he could set a visiting time for him.

Aborting a Rebellion

After going through these encounters, I decided that I would no longer have anything to do with the Mujahidin and tried to keep myself busy by studying the Arabic language and reading different books. My associations and friendship were limited to individuals like Behzad Nabavi, Sadiq Nowruzi, and Jalil Savadi Nezhad. The Mujahidin considered them as "conservative right" elements. Even though I had friendship with these

505

individuals, I also had differences of opinion with them. Nabavi and his friends believed that we should continue our own activities and at the same time acknowledge the MKO's principles and observe the organizational rules. My position regarding the Mujahidin, however, was very open and clear until Nabavi and his friends asked me not to talk openly against the MKO or take a position against them in public.

During those days, Sadiq Nowruzi, Savadi Nezhad, and I were studying Professor Amir Hossein Aryanpour's book *Sociology* (*Jame'eh Shenasi*). We had read most of the book and had only about fifty pages or so to finish it when the two friends told me that they would no longer continue unless I stopped criticizing the MKO. They argued that my position against the MKO would cause problems for them and turn them defenseless before accusations and attacks by others. I said that I didn't care if they continued reading the book with me, nor did it matter if I were left all alone. I said that I just did what my conscience demanded and that there was no guarantee that I would be alive in six months to express my opinion. After they insisted a lot, I promised not to volunteer to talk against the Mujahidin but emphasized that if others asked me questions I would tell them the truth as I understood it because I couldn't lie to anyone then. They told me if anyone came to me with questions about the Mujahidin I should refer him to them for a response. They did not realize that people came to me with questions only after they had exhausted all other possibilities. Even Parviz Ya'qubi[220] complained to Behzad Nabavi, "We don't know what to do with Ezzat. We cannot accuse him of any wrongdoing, nor can we isolate him.

---

[220] Parviz Ya'qubi (b. 1314/1935) one of the oldest members of the MKO, had been active in the National Front and Iran Freedom Movement before joining the Mujahidin in 1348/1969. He was arrested in 1351/1972 and condemned to ten years in prison. He was released in 1357/1978 and joined Rajavi in their activities against the Islamic Republic. He fled the country along with other leaders of the MKO to Paris. However, in 1363/1984 he left the organization in opposition to Rajavi and has been living in Europe since then. See Mansuri, *Memoirs*, p. 163, Maysami, pp. 89, 117, and 139.

We were able to easily isolate many others, but Ezzat has become a serious problem for us. He doesn't want to join us. His interrogation has been flawless, and he has not shown any weakness before the police. In fact, he has no ethical problem or any other kind of weakness. He has his own charisma and has some followers as well."

Finally, my book-club members threatened me that if I did not stop my anti-Mujahidin behavior, they would no longer continue friendship with me because they did not wish to be known as "anti-Mujahid."[221] I told them that they were free to do what they wished and I wouldn't stop them. Thus, our book-reading sessions came to an end. I finished the rest of the book by myself and reduced my contact and political activities with them afterwards. Of course, after some time, they also separated from the MKO, and toward the end of their prison terms took positions against them.

My situation in Ward Three continued routinely until the month of Shahrivar 1356/August 1977 when they came to transfer me to another prison. One day General Muharreri came to the prison to send me to another location. He said, "You have been fooled by other people and become a puppet in their hands. The Shah wishes to pardon you." In response, Behzad Nabavi said, "No, General! You do not understand! Right now our friends out of prison are all lawyers, high officials, and ministers. If we were puppets in other people's hands, then we too would have become lawyers and ministers like the Minister of Road and Transportation, who was my classmate." Sadiq Nowruzi was also angry and yelled at Muharreri and said, "Go to Hell!" I also spoke to him in a rude manner. Our confrontation with the General created tension. Major Yahya'i, the director of the prison, came and invited us to calm down. We expressed our anger at him too. They took

---

[221] Nabavi believed that the MKO were well-known and popular because of their long history of political struggle. That is why he called the group that he established after the Revolution "The Mujahidin of the Islamic Revolution."

us out and kept us in the courtyard until late afternoon. During lunchtime, we saw the special anti-riot police force came to the prison equipped with batons and tear gas, just in case. The head of SAVAK had informed them that we might start a revolt and asked for help because they were afraid that they might not be able to contain and control us. As a measure to punish us, later in the afternoon the police took a few prisoners to the general ward where criminals and drug addicts were kept. They also took me back to the JCCT Prison.

The Silent Tape

This time when they took us to the JCCT Prison, there was no longer interrogation or torture, and after only three days, we were sent back to Evin Prison. I spent a couple of days in Ward Two before I was transferred to Ward One. In this ward there were some supporters of the MKO who had been warned to avoid me, but a few of them came after me secretly. I asked them not to contact me, but first to contact the MKO and learn their positions, views, and characters, and then come to see me, as I was always available. I warned them not to follow orders blindly no matter where they came from and advised them to be alert so that they wouldn't be boycotted by the MKO, because they might not be able to endure.

One day one of the Mujahidin members who knew me came to me and asked if I knew anything about the cassette tapes. When I asked him which tapes he was talking about, he said the tape that contained a recorded conversation between me, Rasuli, and Rabbani about the MKO.

I asked him, "How do you know about the tape?"

He said, "Abrari and Vahid Afrakhteh were called, and the tape was played for them. So they heard the entire conversation."

I laughed and then told him, "I will not give you an answer, so that you can go and ask them the date of this meeting and the date these guys were executed." He was not convinced

508

by this answer, so he kept on insisting that I should give him the answer to his question right then and there.

I told him, "First of all, Vahid Afrakhteh was never brought to the ward, because by then he had assumed the function of an interrogator. Secondly, Vahid Afrakhteh and Hasan Abrari were executed in the month of Bahman, 1354/February 1975 and middle of Azar 1355/November 1976, whereas the said meeting took place during the last days of the year 1355/1976, that is, after the execution of these two fellows."

When I said this, he was so angry. I heard that he argued with the Mujahidin and criticized them for the way they handled things. He defended me and condemned them for treating me in an unethical and treacherous manner. After that he along with a few of his friends left the organization.

I was kept at the Evin Prison for about a month until the middle of the holy month of Ramadan, when I was transferred to the Qasr Prison.

Political Groups at Qasr Prison: 1356–1357/1977–1978

From Evin they took us to Ward Five and Six at Qasr Prison. At that time there were several groups at Qasr Prison. First of all, there were the communist groups. As usual, they were preoccupied with ideological propaganda and with their own work. The other group was composed of the Mujahidin members, who were fully obedient to Rajavi and Khiyabani and the rules and regulations of the organization. At the head of this group was Mohammad Reza Sa'adati.[222]

---

[222] Mohammad Reza Sa'adati (b. 1323/1944) studied electrical engineering at Tehran University, and held several respectable positions in the government and private sector before joining the Mujahidin in 1347/1968. He was arrested in 1351/1972 and received life in prison. He was released in 1357/1978 and resumed his activities with the MKO. It was during this time that he was arrested while passing some classified information to Soviet agents and was sentenced to fifteen years in prison. However, Sa'adati was executed in 1360/1981 allegedly because of his involvement in the assassination of Mohammad Kachu'i, the director of Evin Prison. See, *Fasl*

509

The third group consisted of Maysami and his followers, who opposed the MKO and its leadership. There was also a small group just in Ward Two who believed that the Marxists were ritually impure and were convinced they should stay away from them. Sa'adati's group consisted of eighteen members who had their own agenda, and did not believe in the impurity of the Marxists. Sa'adati was transferred from Evin Prison in order to lead this group and united them against the Maysami group and the people of the *fatwa*.

With our arrival at Qasr, the number of the activists who had differences of opinion with the MKO and rejected its position reached thirty-five. The Maysami group also joined them. These two groups had also differed on some major issues, and each opposed the MKO from its own standpoint. But they managed to live together and tolerate each other because of their common opposition to the MKO.

During the summer of 1353/1974, Maysami lost both of his eyes and an arm when a bomb that he was making exploded in his hands. Despite that, he led his followers in this situation. There was a kind of emotional friendship between him and his supporters, whose number did not exceed eleven or twelve. In the beginning, Maysami's group consisted of around fifty or sixty people who considered themselves "the real Mujahidin" and who continued the path set up by the founders of the organization. Lutfullah Maysami[223] was the leader of this group and also had a claim on the leadership of the organization. Ma'ud Rajavi did not acknowledge

---

Nameh-ye Muta li'at Tarikhi, #5, pp. 139–165; Golpoor Chamarkuhi, pp. 32–40; and *Chesm Andaz-e Iran*, # 22, pp. 37–38.

[223] Lutfullah Maysami (b. 1319/1940) graduated from the School of Petroleum Engineering at Tehran University. He worked for the National Iranian Oil Company for a while before joining the Mujahidin in 1348/1969. He spent two years in prison. In 1353/1974 he was making a bomb when it exploded in his hands, and he lost his eyes and an arm. He was hospitalized, and after initial treatment was sent to prison to be released after the victory of the Revolution. He continued his activities by publishing *Rah-e mujahid*, and later *Cheshm Andaz-e Iran*. See Maysami, *Memoirs*

Maysami's leadership role or even his membership in the central cadre of the organization. Therefore, they had their own differences. Maysami was also on the same team with Nasir Johari and Simin Salihi. The MKO spread allegations about Maysami and claimed that he did not pray before being imprisoned and even while he was in solitary confinement. He only pretended to pray when he was in the general ward. However, I should say that from the moment I met him in Qasr, I saw him performing daily prayer and found him to be a practicing Muslim and observant of the injunctions of the *Shari'ah*.

Maysami had been boycotted by the MKO at Evin Prison. He criticized the MKO and differed with its leadership over sixteen or seventeen issues. His differences with Rajavi were also based on these criticisms. In the absence of MKO leadership in Qasr he announced that he was the "true Mujahid" and that he did not recognize the leadership of Mas'ud Rajavi. At Qasr Prison, the Mujahidin members initially began to acknowledge Maysami's leadership and followed him. When this news reached the Evin Prison, the MKO leadership there labeled Maysami as an opportunist, leftist, and traitor who was not qualified for the leadership of the organization. This news transferred from one prison to another through the family members of prisoners who paid regular visits to these prisons.

When SAVAK noticed this situation, from among Rajavi's supporters they selected and transferred Sa'adati to Qasr Prison—in my opinion as a calculated move by Rajavi to encounter and control Maysami's activities and challenge his claim for leadership. In Qasr, Sa'adati moved from one ward to the other and informed all Mujahidin members of the leadership's position against Maysami and gave them proper guidance. Sa'adati's activities against Maysami were effective to the extent that whoever supported Maysami was immediately boycotted. Thus, Sa'adati became the leader of the MKO in Qasr Prison. He managed to cultivate support from most of the Mujahidin members, and by 1357/1978 the number of

Maysami's supporters declined to seven or eight members, most of whom had joined Maysami before learning about the Mujahidin. Thus, the leadership of the MKO fell completely into the hands of Sa'adati, and Maysami's group began to go through many difficult days. When they took me from Evin to Qasr Prison, after greeting my fellow inmates, I asked about Maysami's health. I thought now that he had been boycotted by the Mujahidin, I should go and see him and find out how he was. I was told that he was in Ward Four. I requested to see him.

There were some closet-like spaces in Ward Four that used to be part of the bathroom and had been converted into cells. I found Maysami sitting in one of those cells engaged in a conversation with his followers. Perhaps they were debating how to deal with new prisoners. We were around thirty people who were transferred from Evin Prison. Some of these people were supporters of the Mujahidin and some opposed them. The group was the main subject of debate and discussion among other prisoners.

When we reached the door of Maysami's cell, the man who had brought me there told others that I wished to meet and greet Mr. Maysami. I was asked to wait a few minutes so I stopped outside his cell near the entrance door. I waited for some minutes, but nothing happened. It turned out that his friends had decided that he should not meet me. I lost my patience and asked them what was going on. I was told that at the moment I should go back to my ward and wait until he would call me to meet him.

I was really angry and said, "Have you created a Vatican-like system in prison? What is this nonsense arrangement? Who do you think you and Maysami are to give me an appointment to see him? The hell with you all! Who do you think you are?" I then quickly left that place. When I returned to my cell, I saw prisoners from other cells who had come to greet me. In fact, among them there were three followers of Maysami. I guessed that the least thing that they could do was to avoid shaking my hands and thus embarrass me. So in the same manner, I walked towards each one of them to greet and shake their hands; but when I reached them, I quickly avoided them. They were embarrassed, but I had no doubt that these fellows had a plan for me, but they could not do anything at all. The environment of the Qasr Prison at that time was very political and very subtle. A person needed to be alert and skillful in order to protect himself and stay away from trouble.

The people of the *fatwa* and those who supported the complete separation from the Mujahidin members were around twelve people. They had separated even their clothes and utensils from everybody else. They received their share of fruit that came in for everyone except that they did not take anything from the Marxist groups. Most of the people of *fatwa* were among my friends. The very same night I arrived at Qasr Prison they asked me to join them. To show them that I supported their position toward Marxist groups, I went to pay a visit to them. They were very happy and welcomed me warmly and were hoping that I would stay with them. But in the morning I went to eat breakfast in the company of the other prisoners where Maysami's followers and other opponents of the Mujahidin were also present.

This action created a lot of commotion. Maysami's followers, who were trying to join the MKO under the leadership of Rajavi and Sa'adati, made me their scapegoat and declared that they could not associate with anyone who was against the Mujahidin and warned everyone not to deal with me once and for all. They argued that I was not supposed to be in their group because I was against the Mujahidin! Amongst the prisoners opposing the Mujahidin several people, including Seyyed Kazim Bujnurdi, Abulqasim Sarhaddi Zadeh, Hossein Sharia'tmadari,[224] and a son of Ayatullah Kashani stood firm in my defense and were not willing to have me ostracized.

---

[224] Hossein Sharia'tmadari (b.1326/1947) graduated in microbiology, and joined Ayatullah Sa'idi and Mutahhari, and supported Imam Khomeini. He was arrested in 1354/1975 to be released in 1357/1978. He held several

Maysami's followers did not give up and insisted that I should join my old friends and keep quiet for a while until things got back to normal. They thought that such an action was in everybody's interest. I was angry and did not want to allow anyone to tell me what to do and which group to join or who to oppose. I made it clear that I was not "anti-Mujahid" as they thought, but opposed deviations in the Mujahidin's positions, and that there were groups in prison that opposed the Mujahidin much more strongly than I did. One more time I emphasized that if I learned of deviation from any party or group, and it didn't matter whether the group was the Mujahidin, the Marxists, or Maysami's, I would take a position against that group. I heard through my friends that Maysami's followers continued their activity against me. I asked them not to try to defend me and to leave things to me. This push and pull continued and eventually resulted in the separation of Maysami's eleven followers from us. Thus, the group that opposed the Mujahidin became independent of others.

During the time that prisoners were transferred from one location to another, authorities sent a few inmates to each ward to avoid congestion in one ward. They sent me to a cell where seventeen other inmates lived. Everyone there welcomed and accepted me there except one. It turned out that he was a member of Maysami's group who opposed my presence in the cell. I didn't want to create yet another conflict, so I respected his view and his feelings and decided to sleep in the hallway or in the courtyard. Soon the news of this encounter and my reaction spread throughout the Qasr compound and everybody realized how short-sighted and narrow-minded in fact Maysami's followers were. The reputation of the group was further damaged as a result. Shortly afterward, the fellow went to another cell, and I entered the cell. The situation continued for a while until most everybody turned against

positions in the government, including serving in the Revolutionary Guard Corps, National TV and Radio, and as the executive president of *Kayhan Daily* Newspaper. See his *Memoirs, Kayhan*, #14949, p. 3.

Maysami's group. The Mujahidin in other wards too began to support Sa'adati, and gradually most followers of Maysami also joined the Mujahidin in support of Sa'adati, who then acted as Rajavi's deputy in Qasr Prison. Maysami's group weakened as the days passed. Every day a member of that group would join Sa'adati, who now began to introduce criteria for membership in the organization to show that his group did not just accept every Tom, Dick, and Harry.

Those poor followers of Maysami left him one by one. They practically stopped doing anything, even reading books and mixing with others, and spent most of the day and night sleeping. They took their food and ate alone. In short, they followed an ascetic lifestyle to please Sa'adati so that he would admit them into the organization. Abulqasim Ithna 'Ashari and Hossein Jannati were among these who went through such a humiliating process in order to join Sa'adati and be accepted for membership in his group. Their state of mind was so messed up that if Sa'adati had ordered them to go and kill their fathers, they would have done that. Even though I had my own issues with Maysami, I did not condone this kind of treatment of his followers by Sa'adati and the organization.

Hossein Jannati was once a friend of mine and in a sense one of my supporters in the past. He was arrested after Vahid Afrakhteh set him up with the police. He was one of the supporters of Maysami in Qasr Prison and wanted to join Sa'adati's group. His humiliating situation was so hard for me to observe. He was not even permitted to greet me if we ever met accidentally. On day, I saw him in the bathroom, greeted him, and asked him to come and see me. We decided to meet at eleven o'clock that night in the courtyard when everybody else was asleep. We tried to hide in between the bushes of flowers and the wall so that no one would see us. I noticed that Hossein was very nervous and anxious. I told him that I could understand his situation, and I didn't mind if he was not comfortable talking to me that night, as we could meet later. He just left without saying a word and never expressed any interest in seeing me again. But whenever I saw him, I greeted him. This was probably quite embarrassing to him.

Unexpected Changes: The Regime is Surprised

Beginning in 1356/1977 political conditions in Iran began to change drastically. As I described before, under international pressure the regime of the Shah was forced to accept intervention by the representatives of the international human rights organizations and the Red Cross.

In order to expand economic and military relations with the West, the Shah was forced to comply with some of the demands of the human rights groups. With the victory of the Democrats in the U.S. presidential elections and under the leadership of President Carter in America, pressures on the Shah increased even more. To show his good intention and willingness to collaborate with the United States, the Shah started initiating his "liberalization policy" by releasing a number of political prisoners. SAVAK tried to execute this project. It had political prisoners sign a note and promise that they would no longer carry on anti-regime activities. Many prisoners were released as a result of this arrangement. The regime was no longer willing or prepared to increase the number of political prisoners. So the police and SAVAK tried to create clashes with armed guerrilla groups and kill them while fighting with them. Those who were arrested in the process were executed, but SAVAK announced that they were killed in street battles with the police. During that year the armed resistant fighters received a very hard blow from SAVAK. If a fighter was arrested, they would announce his death in the newspapers while he was still alive and was under interrogation. His comrades, thinking that he was killed, continued to operate as though nothing happened. They continued to live and carry out their operations in that same team houses as before. As a result, SAVAK and the police were easily able to discover their safe houses and arrest them or kill them on the spot and declare that they had been killed after heavy fighting with the police! Thus, the regime was able to provide justification for its action before the human rights groups and claimed that those who were killed during confrontations with the police were terrorists and criminals.

Despite some success in dealing with guerrilla groups, the regime was concerned about the unfolding of the revolution. It committed a grave mistake on Shahrivar 17, 1357/September 8, 1978 when its forces attacked demonstrators in Zhaleh Square and a number of people were killed. When the news reached the prisons, we felt helpless and wished that we could join the people and fight on their side. We had to show our solidarity with the people and could not afford to remain passive. So we decided to condemn this matter by going on a hunger strike for a whole week. We discussed this with the Marxist groups and they agreed. But the Mujahidin members under Sa'adati and those of Maysami made many excuses. They claimed that at that juncture self-preservation was essential and a hunger strike would create many problems. They even criticized us and said that now the "religious right" pretended to be revolutionaries!

To express solidarity with the people after the bloody suppression of Zhaleh Square we decided to prepare a declaration. The leftist groups rejected its content and said that they could not accept Imam Khomeini as the leader of people's struggle and of the revolution. They prepared another declaration in which they condemned the killing that took place at Zhaleh Square. To show solidarity with the Iranian people, they announced that they would go on hunger strike for a week. The MKO and Maysami's group approved the declaration and agreed to join the hunger strike. They told us that since Marxist groups compromised about the declaration and its content, we should also take a step forward and remove Imam Khomeini's name from our declaration. We categorically rejected the idea and insisted that Imam Khomeini's name had to be mentioned in it.

When we concluded that we were not able to agree on this issue, we decided to do as we wished. So we prepared an interesting declaration and sent it to the police headquarters, SAVAK, the Red Cross, and several newspapers. The communists too, prepared and gave out their own declaration, and the Mujahidin and Maysami's group also signed it. The Police informed senior authorities of all these developments. Through prisoners' family members we sent declarations to the newspapers.

In the declaration we published we wrote, "The leader of our struggle is Ayatullah Khomeini, and our war is against imperialism and the Royal Court." We also strongly condemned the massacre of the people by regime forces on Shahrivar 17/September 8.

This was a political declaration that was signed and published by a group of Islamist prisoners, and we distributed it. We did not want to convey the message that all religious prisoners approved of it, nor did everyone sign it. Since some of them were Mujahidin members and did not acknowledge Imam Khomeini's leadership of the movement, they refused to sign it. Instead, they signed the version that the Marxist groups had published and distributed.

This move really angered the MKO. A number of them joined us in the hunger strike reluctantly. Some others excused themselves by claiming that they suffered from an ulcer and could not go on a hunger strike. Some leftist prisoners joined us in the strike. For seven days we just drank three cups of tea daily with two cubes of sugar. The first days were hard for us because we were used to eating at certain hours. After the second day we got used to it, but toward the end we became very weak and spent most of the daytime sleeping. We had informed our families not to bring fruit when they came to visit us.

Incidentally, it was during this month that an earthquake occurred in Tabas, Khorasan. We wanted to help the people affected by the earthquake and those who were injured.

There was an urgent need to donate blood, so we decided to do that and also collect money for people in need of help. But we had a major problem, that we did not have enough volunteers that we could trust, so we decided and announced that we would place all the funds we collected at the disposal of the Red Cross. We planned to produce another declaration to that effect, but leftist forces disagreed and suggested that this issue must not be politicized. They agreed to donate blood and money as long as only the Red Cross was in charge. The Mujahidin, however, refused to donate blood but also tried to stop the leftist groups from joinging the effort simply because "This was the initiative of the religious right!" In response to them, the Marxist groups said that donating blood was a good thing and they did not have any political interest or objective in doing that, and they would donate their blood, and that was not such a big deal.

In any case, we informed the Red Cross of our decision. Each one of us wrote a letter and gave it to the prison officer to give to the Red Cross. We also informed the media through our families. Of the 200 letters that we wrote to the Red Cross, the police only delivered 40. When the representatives of the Red Cross came, they asked us the reason we didn't deliver the donated bags of blood to the police. We told them that we did not trust these police, as they might sell them or use them for other purposes. But since the Red Cross was an international organization and it enjoyed our confidence, we wanted it to at least supervise the operation.

Ironically, in order for the Red Cross to be able to deliver blood and other donations, it had to secure the permission of the government. The government denied permission to the Red Cross. Nevertheless, we took advantage of this situation and scored a political victory by publicizing the decision of the government and revealing the true nature of the regime.

519

Free at Last!

Just as the Revolution was unfolding at an unbelievably rapid pace, the regime tried to take certain measures to show that it was changing its policies toward the opposition. One such measure was to release a large number of political prisoners. We could not understand, nor were we able to analyze, the reasons for the regime's sudden change of heart. Nobody could even think of much less anticipate a regime change in any way or form. When the regime began to release prisoners with less serious charges, we thought that it did so to distract international pressure. We assumed that they were only doing that to reduce the congestion in the prisons, hoping that those who were released would go about their personal lives. But soon we noticed that the regime was beginning to release members of guerrilla groups and those who were involved in armed resistance against the government. We became very pessimistic toward this new situation. Our analysis was that the regime had learned lessons from General Pinochet, the Chilean dictator who released political prisoners and arranged for their assassination outside prison. So we concluded that the regime wanted to do the same, that is, to release prisoners and kill them in "accidents" or in street clashes, and in many other ways. The reason for this pessimism was our inability to analyze and understand the international political environment and the regime's vulnerability, and most important of all, our inability to believe that the regime would fall in the foreseeable future.

Knowing the seriousness of charges against me, I didn't expect the regime to release me anytime soon. Instead of thinking about being released, I was writing my will. I advised those who were set free to find each other out of prison, reorganize, and form armed groups, recruit new members, plan, and especially observe safety and security. I also shared my experience with them in terms of logistics and especially fund-raising. In short, during those days I spent most my days talking and preparing those who were about to be released. Every day, immediately after breakfast at seven a.m., I went to the courtyard outside Ward Six and talked to younger prisoners. Of course, unlike the past, at that time we had much more freedom of action in prison, and people went back and forth between different wards and met whomever they wished. In the afternoon too, the discussions continued, sometimes until twelve-thirty a.m. The prison had in fact become like a school where people exchanged and shared useful experiences with each other.

It was either the 3rd or the 4th day of the month of Aban, 1357/ October 25 or 26, 1978 near noontime, and we were busy saying goodbye to and seeing off a few friends who were about to be released. Suddenly one of them said, "O Ezzat! They are calling your name through the microphone."

I did not even imagine that they would ever release me from that prison. In fact, I didn't even hear my name when they mentioned it. At that moment my friends left other prisoners and came to congratulate me, jumping all over me. Many of them hugged me, and some warned me that this might be a trick, and the police might try to assassinate me when I go out. This was no longer a possibility. The release of members of armed groups convinced us that the regime was in a weak position and might actually collapse soon. People like Mehdi Taqva'ie and the other high-ranking members of the MKO had already been released, and so there was no need to worry.

Still, I couldn't believe that I was about to be released, so I didn't even begin to collect my belongings. I thought somebody was making fun of me. So I went on with my business as usual and kept talking with other people who were supposed to be released that day.

That day after offering the evening (*maghrib*) prayer, they again announced some names and my name, too, was mentioned. I expected everybody else's release, especially of prisoners like Safar Qahramani,[225] who had spent several decades in prison. In the midst of all this thought, I accidentally met Safar, who came to me and said "Ezzat! You too are about to leave us!"

I was very worried about him. He had really struggled and gone through so much hardship. He was from the city of Kahlkahl in Azarbaijan. He had been arrested for his membership in the Democrat Party of Azarbaijan but was accused of raping the wife of an army colonel. He had spent almost thirty years in prison. He did not have any education, could not even read or write, or even sign his name. The only thing that he did was smoke cigarettes. He had really suffered in prison, and sometimes was sent to exile at Khark Islamd, or Burazjan and other remote prisons. At the time of his arrest his wife was pregnant. For many years they even did not allow him to have visitors. Once in Burazjan they told him that he had a visitor. He went to meet his visitor but saw no one. He returned to his cell very angry and disappointed. A short time later a young girl of about seventeen accompanied by a young man appeared near his cell. She introduced herself as his daughter and the young man as her husband!

All those years in prison Safar stayed away from political activity. The Marxist groups tried very hard to attract him to their side because of his seniority in prison. They visited him on Labor Day and on New Year's day and spoke of him as their hero. But he avoided them because he thought that if he joined them, charges against him would be more serious. Sometimes he blocked the door of his cell by putting his bed

---

[225] Safar Qahramani (b. 1300/1921) was born in Azarbaijan and joined the Democrat Party in 1324/1945, and when the party was defeated, he fled to Iraq. After a while he returned to Iran in 1327/1948. Reportedly he got into a conflict with the *gendamrie* commander in Azarbaijan and was arrested. They accused him of having a relationship with the wife of the said commander. He was initially condemned to death, but his sentence was reduced to life in prison. He was released after thirty years in Aban 1357/November 1978. He died in 1381/2002. See his *Memoirs*, edited by Ali Darvishiyan, Tehran, 1378/1999.

against the door so that nobody could come in. During the last days I was at Evin Prison I met him. I got a chance to know his real nature and his soul. He said, "Ezzat! How lucky you are! You are being released from prison. You have someone to rely upon. You have God, you have Khomeini, and people will support you. If you go out, don't forget about us."

I told him, "Safar Khan! Nobody but God knows how long we will live. Now that you are old, turn to God and start praying. Seek forgiveness from God and purify your soul."

He said, "I have no problem with this. My only fear is that if I so that and the Communists see me praying, they will say that I got burned out and was begging the regime for pardon." We talked about many other issues and I continued my friendly relationship with him.

That night when they mentioned my name, I really felt miserable that we were being released and he would still remain in prison. I was sad and in a state of helplessness. I turned to God and said, "My Lord! This is not fair! I am prepared to remain in prison for a few more years. But this unfortunate man has the right to be freed after thirty years. My Lord! I am ready to remain here in order for him to be released. He has nothing else in life. He had no conviction for which he could stand prison."

I prayed for him from the bottom of my heart and became very emotional and burst into tears. As I was crying, the name of Safar was also mentioned to be released the same night! Only God knows how happy I was at that moment. When his name was announced, all prisoners uttered benediction to the Prophet (*salawat*) all at once. Marxist prisoners wanted to recite their anthem, but this was not possible. So after confirming my freedom, I bid farewell to the remaining prisoners and gathered my few belongings. It was ten o'clock at night that they took us to Baharestan Square. When I got out of the car, I looked at the sky and saw a star winking at me! Everyone went to his own home, but I was the only person without a home. I decided to go to my brother's house.

The Day of Awakening

After my release from prison, I did not know what I was supposed to do and where to start. I was confused. All those prisoners who had been released at that time were in the same state of mind as I was. I decided to share my experience with young activists so that they would not commit the same mistakes that the earlier generation had committed. Therefore, we held some meetings with my friends in cities like Qom, Qazvin, Damavand, and Tehran. In these meetings, I never talked about my personal life and struggle and the tortures I went through in prison, but I discussed the peculiarities of the Marxist groups, the MKO, and other leftist organizations and currents.

I knew Mr. [Mortaza] Mutahhari and was a little familiar with his writings and character. My years in prison created a gap in our relationship, and we were not in contact for a few years. I do not recall exactly whether he sent me a note and asked me to meet him, or I was the one who requested to meet him. In any case, I met him several times at his house and we discussed issues of mutual interest. He was very curious to learn about the clergy's views and attitudes toward the Mujahidin, the Marxists, and other groups in prison. He was also interested to know about the ideological transformation of the Mujahidin, the people of *fatwa*, and others. I explained to him everything I knew. He was saddened and disappointed about some of the issues I shared with him. Mr. Mutahhari said that we need to inform Ayatullah Khomeini about these issues. In my opinion, other than Imam Khomeini, Mr. Mutahhari was the only person among the clergy who properly understood the nature of the Mujahidin's eclectic ideology, and perhaps this was one of the reasons for his assassination.

After I had spent some time in confusion and an indecisive state, Mr. Kachu'i insisted that I join their group, which consisted of Kachu'i, Islami, Lajevardi, and others. They played an important role in organizing and leading mass demonstrations on the 9th (*tasu'a*) and 10th (*'ashura*) of the month of Muharram in Tehran in 1357/1978. They worked so hard to make these demonstrations peaceful and prevent the infiltration of terrorist groups into the ranks of demonstrators, and avoided conflict with forces of the regime. So I also joined them and I was active in making sure that these demonstrations were peaceful and orderly. To succeed in this, we used armbands. We did not have a formal structure and only used armbands assigned to the press and those who were in charge of order and the safety of the demonstrators. We also gave some armbands to the prayer leaders of each mosque to distribute among those they trusted so that the Marxist groups or provocateurs would not be able to infiltrate into the demonstration lines.

There were numerous demonstrations in different parts of Tehran in those days. Sometimes some Marxist groups and also MKO members tried to take advantage of the situation. They hid in a quiet corner, and when the lines of demonstrators approached, they joined the lines and started to shout their own slogans. People were aware of these maneuvers, and they refused to reply to their slogans. As a result, they separated themselves from the demonstrators.

One day there was a gathering at Behesht Zahra cemetery, and Mr. Mutahhari and a number of other *'ulama* were present. All of a sudden a banner was raised in the ladies' section. It belonged to the MKO, and one of their slogans was printed on it. I recall very well that Mr. Mutahhari went to the ladies section in a very respectful manner, told them that the occasion was not right for that kind of expression, and asked them to hand the banner over to him.

During the last days of the life of the old regime, people like Mr. Mutahhari, Beheshti, Mahdavi Kani, and Mufatteh were in the front line of the demonstrations and led demonstrators. The presence of these gentlemen in front of the demonstration lines was indeed a testimony to the religious nature of those events. Some other groups had in their lines individuals

525

like Abdul Reza Hejazi and Shaykh Nasrullah Shah Abadi to highlight their religious identity.

I participated in the demonstration on the 9th or 10th of Muharram even though I had severe pain in my leg. I walked from my brother's home on Atabak Avenue in central Tehran to Azadi Square and back home. I was so exhausted at the end. During these demonstrations the MKO was divided into two groups. One group was under the leadership of Lutfullah Maysami and had its own flag. To stir up people's emotions, they carried a picture of Maysami that showed his arm cut from the elbow. Another group came with a minibus in which Jalal Ganjeh'ie—a cleric—was giving a discourse explaining the meaning of the signs and symbols on the MKO's emblem. The funniest thing was that Seyyed Ahmad Hashimi Nezhad and Shaykh Akbar Goodarzi, who later on became the leader of the Furqan group, carried the Mujahidin's banners and placards.

As one of the people in charge of maintaining order of the demonstrations, I mingled with the people to prevent and abort any possible misconduct by the MKO or any other group. When these fellows noticed our presence in the midst of people, they took their banners and went away. During this time, I was not affiliated with any particular group or political current, but rather followed friends like Sadiq Islami and Lajevardi because I believed they were loyal followers of Ayatullah Khomeini. On the day of Imam Khomeini's arrival in Tehran, I was also in charge of maintaining security and order.

We found out that in Paris Seyyed Ahmad [Khomeini's son] had decided to place the Mujahidin in charge of airport security and the protection of Imam Khomeini. He really did not know the MKO very well. Reportedly, when Mr. Mutahhari found that out, he phoned Paris and informed Imam Khomeini, who instructed Mr. Mutahhari not to let that happen. He told him that the security should be maintained by the people themselves and no particular group should assume this duty. Therefore, the committee that was formed to welcome

Imam Khomeini did not allow the MKO to play any role in the process.

The MKO wanted to take control of security on that day and exploit the opportunity to propagate their organization and their ideology and future plans. They wanted to claim that Imam Khomeini had no one to rely upon, and it was the MKO that was able to provide and guarantee his safety and security. It was during this time that the Council of Revolution decided to form a committee that would take charge of welcoming Imam Khomeini from Paris. This committee had also been formed by the order of Imam Khomeini. It consisted of Mr. Mutahhari, Beheshti, Rabbani Shirazi, Taleqani, Mehdi Bazargan, Dr. Sahabi, Dr. Shaybani, and a few others. In the beginning they held secret meetings, but soon they publicized their activities and plans. They also made decisions on the course of the future direction of national politics and related issues. The headquarters of the committee were under the control of Mr. Beheshti, Sadiq Islami, Badamchiyan, Asgar Awladi, and Kachu'i from the Islamic Coalition Party, and a few members of the Freedom Front of Iran, including Mr. Bazargan, Sabbaghiyan, and Tavassuli. I knew every member of this committee. Kachu'i insisted I should join this group and I accepted.

Finally, the day of arrival of Imam Khomeini was decided and announced. Each one of us had been given a specific area to guard. My station was to control the eastern gate of Behesht Zahra cemetery, so I was not able to go to the airport.

During those days, I didn't have a place of my own that I could call home. I stayed at my brother's house on Atabak Avenue. On Bahman 12, 1357/February 1, 1978 I woke up very early in the morning and went from Atabak Avenue to Behesht Zahra on foot. I positioned myself at the eastern gate of Behesht Zahra until Imam Khomeini arrived there by a helicopter. I left my position and entered Behesht Zahra.

According to the schedule after his speech at the cemetery, Imam Khomeini was supposed to go to Refah School.

But perhaps because he was tired, or for other reasons that I didn't know, the schedule was not observed. So he was taken somewhere else and for two hours nobody knew where he was. Then it turned out that he had gone to the house of one of his relatives to rest.

The plan to settle Imam Khomeini at Refah School changed to settling him at Alavi School. Perhaps it was because this school was better equipped, and had separate entrance and exit doors that opened onto Iran Avenue and Shahid Diyalamah Street respectively. So people never had problems in going to see their leader.

While Imam Khomeini stayed in the Alavi school, groups of people went to visit him. I think Imam Khomeini chose this school deliberately because it belonged to the Hujatiyyeh group. The group did not endorse political activism and was against the revolution, or at least indifferent toward it. By settling at the Alavi School, Imam Khomeini in fact wished to convey a message that the age of [political] passivism was over.

Here, Imam Khomeini often stood beside a window and greeted visitors and responded to their expression of love and support. During the first three days, together with two other fellows, I was in charge of providing security at this window. We stood below the window in order to prevent anyone from climbing up. The gap of the window was small and was about one meter in height. The weather was cold during that time and I had the flu. I used to wear a woolen hat. One day the number of visitors was so large and they pushed their way to the window so hard that my hat fell on the ground and got lost under the steps of the crowd. The memories, emotions, tears, and excitement of those days will remain with me forever. Day by day, the number of visitors continued to grow.

The day that the regime announced the extension of the martial law for two more hours, Sadiq Islami and Lajevardi said, "We have to take mini-buses and go to the streets, demonstrate, and demand the end of te martial law." So we

528

did. People heard and obeyed Imam Khomeini's order and poured into the streets like a powerful flood. The military government retreated and ended the martial law.

An Analysis of the Victory of the Revolution

In my opinion we did not pay as high a price for the victory of the Revolution as we have been paying for its protection and preservation. We lost more martyrs in the course of defending the Revolution than we lost in the course of the Revolution itself. We struggled a lot and we are still struggling to defend the Revolution more than what we did for the victory of the Revolution itself. We attained the victory of the Islamic Revolution not by means of guerrilla warfare or armed resistance but through peaceful demonstrations. In fact, during those days guerrilla warfare did not have any outward expression and had been almost forgotten. Even the MKO, which analyzed the situation after Vahid Afrakhteh's betrayal and the arrest of many of its members, had concluded that the armed struggle started too early when our society was not prepared to accept it. Another group that came to the same conclusion was Paykar. It then advocated the necessity of political education for the workers and peasants nationwide, but it was too late by then, and the people toppled the regime of the Shah through peaceful demonstrations. Even the Fidayan-i Khalq guerrilla organization admitted that armed resistance was useless and that they should concentrate on peaceful political activities. Other members of the group that still insisted on the primacy of armed struggle remained a small minority. They carried out a few operations in rural areas but were discovered, and perpetrators were arrested by the people and handed over to the police. The Marxist Mujahidin also concluded that Iran was a religious country and the majority of the population were *petit-bourgeois* and far from being proletarian, and therefore were unprepared for revolution. They argued that to prepare the people for an ideal revolution, extensive political education would be needed. In short, none of these groups were able to accomplish much through armed struggle or political activities.

*　　　*　　　*

By God's will, Imam Khomeini's honesty and sound leadership, and the nation's many sacrifices, the Revolution achieved victory. Before the arrival of Imam Khomeini and the formation of the provisional government, many people were anxiously worried that history would repeat itself and the Revolution would fail in the same way that the movement for the nationalization of the oil industry had failed in the 1950's. Some were concerned that a *coup d'état* similar to the one in Mordad 1332/August 1953 would take place and bring the Shah back to power. As a result of these concerns many used caution and did not get engaged much in the process of revolution. But when they realized that history would not repeat itself and revolution was here to stay, they became more revolutionary than genuine revolutionaries, or as it is said, they became "more Catholic than Pope"! They claimed credit for the victory of the Revolution. In reality, however, they were a bunch of cowards and opportunist individuals. These were the very same people who did not allow Dr. Sharia'ati's books on the shelves of their mosques. Some of them even did not allow anyone to mention the name of Imam Khomeini on the pulpits of their mosques. Yet, to prevent divisions in the rank of supporters of revolution, Imam Khomeini let bygones be bygones and began to focus on the new environment and the next moves of the Revolution.

I recall that during the early days when demonstrations started, our slogans were not very strong and provocative. The first day we placed a member of the clergy to lead the demonstrations. On the second day when we sent someone to pick him up and bring him to lead the crowd, he refused to come and said, "Whoever wishes to say, 'Down with the Shah' should go himself and lead the demonstrators." When slogans became stronger and more radical, this person did not show up again.[226]

Even though America had realized that the continuity of the Shah's regime was no longer in their interest and that he must go, they were unable to find an alternative that could replace the Shah. They had high hopes in some prominent national or even religious leaders and counted on them. They never thought that a clerical figure like Imam Khomeini would have such mass support and the power to isolate and push all others out of Iran's political scene. In my opinion the reason Imam Khomeini appointed Mr. Bazargan as the Prime Minister of the provisional government was to nullify American plans. The United States initially thought that Mr. Bazargan's government was an acceptable candidate for the West. It didn't take too long for them to realize that Imam Khomeini had fooled everyone and was in fact preparing to establish an Islamic government. It was after that realization that several plots, including the Nowzheh *coup d'état,* and finally the war with Iraq were imposed on Iran.

*   *   *

---

[226] Some slogans were increasingly becoming provocative and threatening. For example, these two slogans were heard most often during Bakhtiyar's tenure in the office: "Woe unto you O Bakhtiyar, If the Imam Khomeini does not arrive! and "If Imam Khomeini is delayed, our guns will come out!"

CHAPTER ELEVEN

Playing with Fire

The Establishment of the Revolutionary Islamic Committee (*Komiteh*)

With the defeat of martial law, the failure of military government, and the declaration of the army's neutrality, for all practical purposes the Revolution had attained victory. All police stations surrendered without resistance. Since people were afraid that the police and royalist forces might try to take back control, they disarmed them all and confiscated all weapons from police and *gendarmerie* stations. Thus, most weapons of these centers and garrisons in Tehran were taken over by the people. Some officials of the regime fled the country, but many were also arrested by the people and brought to Madrasah Rifah. They were housed in the basement of a house adjacent to the *madrasah*. We were assigned to protect the place and guard the prisoners. We, the very same people who were prisoners a few months ago, became the new prison-keepers!

The night that Generals Nasiri, Rahimi, Naji, and a few other officers in charge of martial law were executed on the roof of Madrasah Rifah, the people of Tehran were not aware and they thought that a *coup d'état* was taking place. Many people came of their homes to protect the residence, but we assured them that there was nothing to worry about.

The *Komiteh* that was responsible for planning to welcome the return of Imam Khomeini was not abolished after the victory of the Revolution. Rather, it maintained its unofficial structure and was put in charge of security of the residence of the Imam. In the meantime, people continued to arrest important members of the political elite of the Shah and especially those who had a role in in the crimes that the regime had committed. They were brought to the Rifah school and put on trial there.

The provisional government headed by Prime Minister [Mehdi] Bazargan had its headquarters in the Rifah school. Many members of the National Front Iran Freedom Movement frequented the school, and a few members of the MKO like Rajavi and Khiyabani went there often. We warned Bazargan and others about them and also told Imam Khomeini what the MKO demanded. I also warned Mr. [Ayatullah Seyyed Mohammad] Beheshti. I am not sure if he did something or Khomeini issued an order, because after a few days the Mujahidin no longer came to Khomeini's residence. Whether they had contact with Bazargan and the Iran Freedom Movement, I am not aware.

One day at the Rifah School I saw Colonel Tavakkoli.[227] He was imprisoned during the regime of the Shah on charges of spying for the Eastern Bloc and sending some of the documents on NATO negotiations to the headquarters of the Warsaw Pact. I knew him when I was in Ward Six at Qasr Prison. He associated with Mr. Beheshti and sometimes even gave him orders about what to do. I notice that he acted like he was in charge in the school building, and I did not feel good about it. I asked Mr. Beheshti if he knew the Colonel, and he said he did. I asked if he knew anything about the Colonel's background. He said he did not, and just because he was in prison for a while, Mr. Beheshti trusted him. I explained for Mr. Beheshti a little of Colonel's background and that he was not a religious and ethical person and should not be put in charge of security and/or intelligence duties. Mr. Beheshti stated that the colonel had been in charge of the residence security from the beginning, since he was released from prison. I told Mr. Beheshti that it was my duty to tell him what I knew about him, and he knew what to do and to accept responsibility

---

[227] Colonel Nasrullah Tavakkoli received special training in France, Pakistan, and the United States. After the 1953 *coup d'état* he was imprisoned for six months. Also in 1351/1972 he was arrested and sentenced to six years in prison because of his anti-monarchist activities. He was released after two years. See *Kayhan*, #10644.

for it. After that conversation I did not see Tavakkoli again in the vicinity of the Imam's residence, nor did I find out where he went, what he did, what he is doing now, or even if he is still alive. My own guess is that he returned to the army and must have retired by now.

Incidents like this showed that the situation must return to normal very quickly and the security of the capital city must be given to experienced people, the army personnel must know their duties, and all files in the police and SAVAK archives must be protected. In the absence of an efficient police force, violations and abuse could have grown faster. Unfortunately, the police forces did not attend their stations; nobody was at his job. The army still did not know what its position was. Everybody felt insecure. There were a lot of weapons in people's hands and especially in the hands of those political groups that did not have sympathy for the new regime. It was not possible to let the situation go uncontrolled.

Ayatullah Khomeini chose Mr. Mahdavi Kani and [Murteza] Mutahhari and a few others to form several committees to protect people's lives and property and maintain order. This verdict became the foundational stone of the Provisional Islamic Revolutionary *Komiteh*.[228] The *Komiteh* asked the people to return the weapons they had confiscated during the Revolution. People returned a large amount of weapons and ammunitions to local mosques, but political and guerrilla groups kept most of what they had. The Rifah School had an unusual appearance in those days, as a large number of weapons of all kinds and ammunitions were piled in the middle of its front yard because we did not have a garrison yet to store them. So we kept them for a while, and stored some in many friends' houses, so that whenever we had time we would take them and hide them somewhere less accessible. Thus I was

---

[228] On Ayatullah Kani's statement about the establishment of the Central *Komiteh*, see *Interview with Urwat al-wuthqa daily newspaper*, Aban 5, 1358/October 27, 1979.

busy performing different functions in the Provisional and tried to do my best in every duty that was assigned to me.

I didn't think that the situation would remain so for very long as the *Komiteh* was meant to be a provisional one, but it seemed that it was there to stay for a while. Even for or five years after the victory of the Revolution, we still used the same letterheads of the Provisional *Komiteh* for our correspondence. One day I brought this to Mr. Kani's attention. He said that when he accepted the responsibility he assumed that within three months or so a government would take over and the country would resume normal life and he would go back to the seminary and continue his teaching and preaching career. Now, he added, "We realize that the affairs of the country are not that simple, and governing over it is not a simple task."

The first individuals who took the initial steps in the formation of the Provisional *Komiteh* were Sadeq Eslami, Mahdavi Kani, Baqeri Kani, Mutahhari, Nateq Noori, Behzad Nabavi, Mohammad Mousavi, Alviri, Khosrow Tehran, Ali Qannadha, Mostafa Qannadha, and I. Mahdavi Kani was appointed as the Head of the *Komiteh* and Behzad Nabavi was put in charge of public relations. Mutahhari did not get involved in duties related to the *Komiteh* because of his demanding scholarly and theoretical works. After Kani his position was given to Nateq Noori and then to Baqeri Kani.[229]

The functions of the *Komiteh* started with investigations, sending night guards to different neighborhoods, and the like. Initially people we knew were appointed to these tasks. We chose the National Parliament building (*majlis*) in Baharestan Square as the headquarters of the *Komiteh*. At that time Tehran was divided into fourteen municipal districts. We selected the most active mosque in each neighborhood and established a local *Komiteh* there. We appointed Mr. Buka'ie, 'Irfani, Khosrow Shahi, 'Amid Zanjani, Movahhedi Kermani, Iravani, and Mohammad 'Iraqi as the heads of each local

---

[229] For a detailed biography of Ayatullah Mahdavi Kani see *Kayhan, #14949, Jumhuri Islami, #362, Movahhid, p. 255, Ahmad Ahmad, pp. 332.

Komiteh in districts 7, 8, 9, 10, 11, 5, 12, and 14 (Shahr Rayy) respectively. Mr. Maleki headed the *Komiteh* in Shemiran. I was the only non-clergy in this group. Each *Komiteh* created several sub-*komitehs* and appointed their own men to take charge of the sub-*komitehs*. Therefore, we did not have much control over their operations. Our only specific instruction to them was not to act against the injunctions of the *Shari'ah*, and if they noticed any non-ethical behavior try to stop it and bring the perpetrators to the central *Komiteh* headquarters in Baharestan Square.

Before I accepted an official position in the central *Komiteh* I performed a variety of duties and did whatever I could to get things going. My friends called me the "All-Purpose Wrench." Wherever something went wrong, I went and fixed it as well as I could. After a while when the overall situation settled down I was placed in charge of the office responsible for issuing new identity cards for members of *komitehs*. This was a very important position. In the chaotic situation after the Revolution there were people who took advantage of the anarchic condition and forged identity cards in their own names and abused their authority. So it was essential to bring the situation under control by creating a central office in charge of recruiting for the *komitehs* and issuing official identity cards for each member. We designed three kinds of identity cards for *komiteh* members: one for the armed forces in charge of military operations, the second for the head of each *komiteh* in provincial centers and cities, and finally a third category for administrative personnel.[230]

The central *Komiteh* put many resources at the local *komitehs'* disposal, including funds for personnel salaries, but we were reluctant to arm them. We did not know many members of those *komitehs*. Members of the clergy who were ap-

---

[230] Ayatullah Mohammad Baqer Baqeri Kani was a member of the Assembly of Experts during it first and second terms and a deputy to Mr. Mahdavi Kani when the latter headed the central *Komiteh*. At the time of the writing of this memoir he was the vice chancellor of the Imam Sadeq University.

pointed as commanders of each *komiteh* did not know anything about weapons, and the ways to deal with counter-revolutionary forces. Their duties were limited to supervision over the personnel. The rank-and-file members often did not disclose the details of their day-to-day operations to the clergy. For example, total anarchy prevailed in the ninth district, where a certain Shaykh Nasrullah Shah Abadi divided that jurisdiction into two sections. He did not recognize Khosrow Shahi's authority in that district and settled himself in the Pamenar Mosque. He gathered all neighborhood thugs and vagabond in his *komiteh* and appointed thieves and criminals as revolutionary guards (*pasdar*) and many other unruly and rebellious elements. His men arrested individuals, confiscated their money and other belongings and their weapons, and then released them. They never informed us of their actions because they knew that we would ask for documents and reasons for such arrests. They even arrested members of the units attached to the office in charge of "Commanding the Good and Forbidding the Reprehensible" (*Dayereh-ye munkarat*).

The prevailing situation prompted us to establish the Central Council to supervise over and control the situation in the fourteenth district [of Tehran]. Once a week commanders of each local *komiteh* in that district would meet to coordinate their policies and actions. Often Mahdavi Kani or Baqeri Kani attended these meetings and emphasized the necessity of observing the rules of the *Shari'ah* in their behavior.

Sometimes they sent their deputies to attend these meetings. These meetings, however, did not solve any of the problems we faced. We continued to have problems controlling the actions and behavior of individual *komiteh* members, and we continued to receive many complaints about their misconduct. So we created a unit in the Revolutionary Corps (Sepah) to deal with violations of *komiteh* members and their possible actions that were against the injunctions of the *Shari'ah*. If a Corps member who was sent for a mission acted in an unethical or illegal manner, the unit assessed his behavior

538

and punished him, even sending him to prison. I was appointed to inspect these violations and in case of need, issued a verdict on behalf of the revolutionary prosecutor to arrest such a perpetrator. I also trained the Corps members how to behave when they went to a person's house and instructed them to confiscate only weapons, ammunitions, drugs, and documents. But sometimes they did not follow instructions and confiscated some personal items of the people, even food items like onions, potatoes, and baby formula. We also told them to make a list of the confiscated items so that nobody can claim more than what was confiscated. Despite that, they often did not produce a detailed list and complete report.

In addition to these [official] *komitehs* that existed in the mosques and district offices, there were also *komitehs* established in police stations so that police personnel who had retreated or resigned could be encouraged to return to work. Mr. Khomeini also had asked them to report to their duty, so in each police station a number of *komiteh* members settled. It was hoped that a sense of commitment and loyalty among police personnel and the remnants of the Shah's regime that were not committed to Islam and the Islamic Revolution would develop as a result of association with the young revolutionary Corps members. The second reason was to teach the young *komiteh* members the necessary discipline and order for organizational work.

In practice, however, these measures did not produce the desired result. *In police stations and army units the personnel were so disciplined that they obeyed the order of a superior officer, but members of the Komiteh were not used to such discipline. They would not give up sleeping even if a general came for inspection. They attended morning march with slippers and in their pajamas.* Therefore, after one year not only did this plan fail, but it created a backlash. Many *Komiteh* members lost their motivation and commitment, and the police personnel lost their discipline. The plan failed entirely, and *Komiteh* members were removed from police stations.

Destroying Documents of SAVAK

During my work in the inspection office of the central *Komiteh* I tried hard to protect the documents of SAVAK and appoint someone to this post that I could trust. These documents were kept in a location known as the Center for Documents, and a certain Javad Madar Shahi[231] was appointed as its director. He was a member of the Hujjatiyah group. Prior to the Revolution this group did not interfere in political affairs. Some of its members even collaborated with SAVAK. The presence of Madar Shahi in such a sensitive position provided an opportunity for those members of the Hujjatiyah group to take out and destroy their own files from the SAVAK collection. I even asked them to put the list of SAVAK agents at my disposal so that we could examine their records and if necessary arrest them. They did not cooperate with us in any form. We even requested access to the list of members of the Third Division of SAVAK, but they refused.

We did not arrest any SAVAK members on the basis of the information and records we collected about them. When a neighbor or relative identified someone as an agent, we arrested him. Some agents voluntarily came and introduced themselves, and we made a file for them. If we asked for some documents for the Center for Documents, they just gave us a summary of the file and did not mention in which department of SAVAK an agent functioned. The summary we received only contained a little personal information such as loans he received. They never identified the position of the agent, and whether he was an interrogator or a torturer. Many times we complained, but no one paid attention.

---

[231] Javad Madar Shahi was a longtime member of the Hujatiyah group in charge of its investigation committee. The main duty of this committee was to collect news and information about the activities of the Baha'i community. He was a member of the first congress of the National Front of Iran.

Two Different Perspectives

Many new leaders of the Revolution were not in favor of coercive measure against members of the former regime and especially against the people. I remember my occasional conversations with Mr. Mahdavi Kani about some of the challenges we faced. He always said that he preferred to see the Revolution defeated than to keep the new regime by use of force and through dictatorial means and oppressive measures. He envisioned the creation of a utopia by God's grace.

In my opinion this perspective and its dissemination paved the way for many terroristic acts and even a *coup d'état.* He was, for example, against the use of force in dealing with the Mujahidin. At that time, he opposed their arrest and incarceration. After a while when the MKO resorted to armed uprising against the Islamic regime, he believed that government policies pushed the Mujahidin to use violence against the regime and blamed the government. He often stated, "You did not give them a chance and forced them to carry out terroristic acts." Unfortunately, Mr. Mahdavi Kani did not have proper knowledge about the MKO and did not understand their real nature.

We believed that the reality was very different. Because I knew the MKO very well, I warned Mr. Beheshti, Mahdavi Kani, and Ardabili about the MKO plan for the destruction of the Islamic government and its leaders, and that they did not recognize the clergy at all, and that one day they would raise arms against it and all of them. I told them that I did not suggest that the regime should arrest and execute all members of the Mujahidin, but believed that they should arrest individuals like Rajavi and his close associates and have them confess on national television because such measure would nullify their support in the streets, and their supporters would disperse because they were willing to do anything just to survive. Some other individuals like Behzad Nabavi, who was in charge of public relations, opposed my suggested plan. He believed that the regime should not act as the judge, the jury, and the executioner before the MKO raised arms against it; therefore, he saw no reason for their arrest.

The Mujahidin and the Revolution

In the early days of the Revolution, the MKO took advantage of our structural and organizational weaknesses and took measures to organize its supporters and expand its organization. During the early days after the victory of the Revolution, the Mujahidin collected a large number of weapons and ammunition from different garrisons in Tehran and major cities. This was a very dangerous development that authorities did not pay much attention to. The younger generations that did not condone the positions and views of the clergy were attracted to the Mujahidin. For whatever reasons, the youth found the MKO attractive, and many male and female university and high-school students joined them. Most supporters of the Mujahidin were recruited from among this echelon of the society. Their supporters were active among university students and faculty members and through extensive propaganda attracted and recruited a large number of them to join this organization. Once they organized a huge gathering in a park in the Khazaneh district in southern Tehran where thousands of people attended. They repeated this kind of activity in different parts of the capital city. Perhaps even the supporters of the Revolution and Imam Khomeini were not able to mobilize such a large number of people for a single event. Of course, demonstrations that took place by invitation of Mr. Khomeini, such as those on the 22nd of Bahman/February 12 or the last Friday of Ramadan known as the "Day of *Quds*" were exceptional cases, and no one else had such wide appeal to the public. However, people did not respond as positively to other gatherings organized by members of the clergy. Those who attended such gatherings were often the old and politically weak and obsolete. In contrast, the MKO supporters were young and energetic and thus were able to collect a large amount of weapons and ammunitions in their homes and those of their friends and relatives. Indeed, they took full advantage of the chaotic situation of those days very well.

The Mujahidin adopted two different strategies during those days. On the one hand, they established contact with the High Council of Revolution, and on the other hand, worked to expand their social base and integrate them within the organization. They took advantage of any occasion to criticize and discredit the leaders of the Revolution. Their main gathering place was in the house of Abrishamchi on Iran Avenue, and often the MKO leaders spent the night there. Several times I asked authorities to allow us to arrest them and bring them to the negotiation table, but they rejected this suggestion.

*   *   *

To eliminate abuses in *komitehs* and prevent violations against people, we decided to issue identity cards for members of the *Komiteh*. As I mentioned before, we designed and printed three kinds of identity cards for security and armed forces, administrative personnel, and inspection teams. Bani Sadr and Mahdavi Kani both wrote to us and asked that we should issue permits for the central cadre of the MKO and their bodyguards to carry weapons. I have copies of their letters at my disposal. Since I knew the Mujahidin well, I rejected their demands, but when they continued to insist, I agreed but set certain conditions. I suggested that we should have information about their residence and activity centers, and someone from the government and business community should guarantee access to them and their residence whenever we needed so that we could have access to them. These conditions would have enabled us to have valuable information at our disposal on the basis of which we could then ask the Interior Ministry to issue permits for members of the central cadre of MKO to carry weapons. Several months passed by, and we did not issue a single permit. When the situation began to change as a result of the MKO's activities, issuing permits was set aside altogether.

During the early days after the Revolution the Mujahidin managed to provide a solid financial basis for their organization by different means, such as confiscating funds from banks and companies like Bell Helicopter, several multinational corporations like Sabet Pasal Company, and the Pahlavi Foundation. They stole a large number of large and expensive carpets from the Foundation and sold about fifty of them through Mohammad Zabeti's father, who was a carpet dealer in the bazaar. When we heard this news we arrested Zabeti's father and took back most of the carpets, but four or five pieces of extremely expensive carpets had already been sent out of the country. We have demanded the U.S. government return these carpets to the government.

Despite all this, the MKO was so arrogant to deal with the High Council of the Revolution from a position of power. They often went to visit the authorities and demand their rights! Except Imam Khomeini, Mutahhari, and Rabbani Shirazi, others were in favor of reconciliation with the Mujahidin. Rabbani Shirazi opposed them for personal reasons and because of experiences he had with them in prison. Taleqani favored them from the beginning. He declared that even the Marxists should be free and have a share in the government because they also had struggled for revolution, were imprisoned and tortured, and had played a role in defeating the former regime. He insisted that they should also have representatives in the High Council of the Revolution.

Khordad 30th, 1360/June 20, 1981

Sometimes when the Mujahidin demonstrated in parks or major streets, they were arrested and brought to the *Komiteh*, but no one was prepared to keep them, and we didn't know what to do with them. So we ordered the *Komiteh* members to release them on their way to the station. Sometimes they got into fights with the *pasdars* and were arrested and brought to the station. Knowing that our means were limited, they used foul language and criticized us. They refused to give us their names, but introduced themselves as "*mujahid*, son or daughter of the People." When we asked them questions, they refused to answer and said "it is none of your business." We just assigned a number to them and printed that on their outfit. Authorities insisted that we should treat them kindly. So we released them after getting a guarantee from them or their parents and relatives. On some occasions when they insulted us or Imam Khomeini we kept them for a few days and then called Abrisham-chi to come and get them.

The MKO leaders had told their supporters that Ezzat Shahi is a torturer in the *Komiteh*. They had poisoned the minds of these young people with propaganda against prosecutors and had told them that we were all torturers and former agents of SAVAK. They had presented such a picture about me to their supporters, whereas all those who could remember could testify that I didn't even slap one person in the face, and prevented others from the use of force against the arrested members of the organization. I disagreed with the idea of giving them a free hand in the society and believed that they should not be left free to do whatever they wished. I argued that we should arrest their leaders and keep them until the truth became obvious to everyone; otherwise, soon they would resort to terror and assassination, or as they said, would carry out "revolutionary execution." They would push the authorities to use force against them, and then use it to condemn the Revolution. My point was that if they were not controlled then, it would be too late to do anything against them later.

In order to nullify their propaganda, when we arrested them, despite all the insults they subjected us to, we treated them kindly and with utmost respect. Had we done otherwise, we would have given them enough ammunition to use against us. That was exactly what they were seeking to attain. Their reactions were not based on logic and intellect, but purely emotional. In response to any question we asked them, they insulted Mr. Khomeini and saluted Rajavi.

Although my duty was not to interrogate anyone, to prevent extreme measures by others, I tried to share the experiences I had in dealing with SAVAK. I only interrogated those who were engaged in and carried out armed operations. I treated them with kindness and friendship, talked to them like a friend, even bribed them with food or cigarettes. To show them my kindness I even joined them for lunch and then took a rest in their cells, while there was the possibility of being attacked or even killed by them. I had warned other *pasdars* to be alert and come to my rescue if I called them.

One day they brought in a female supporter of the Mujahidin. She cursed me for a while. I realized that she was very emotional and the organization took advantage of emotional young people like her. She had not really done much and only carried some blank papers used for writing messages and instructions. She continuously cursed Imam Khomeini and everybody else in the system. Her mind had been totally poisoned by Mujahidin propaganda. She called us "Fascist, SAVAK agents, mercenaries, and Phalange." I smiled at her and asked her to get up and go home, but she continued to curse. I asked for Mr. Baqeri's intervention. He began to counsel her, hoping she would come to her senses, but he failed to convince her and referred her back to me. I decided to teach her a lesson, so I asked the guards to bring a bed and pretended that I planned to whip her. She got very scared and asked for forgiveness. I pretended to insist that she should be punished with 100 lashes of the whip, whereupon she agrees to give her parents' address and telephone number, and we called her parents to come and get her, and they did.

I took firm positions against the Mujahidin's political strategies and views. The leaders of the MKO knew me very well and were aware that I was an obstacle in their way, so they sent me messages time and again that I deserved better and the authorities had usurped my rights, and that I should have been given a higher position. They wanted to convince me to resign from my position as the chief interrogator of the central *Komiteh*. They hoped that a shrewd and ruthless person would replace me and use force and violence against them so that they could use his treatment of their arrested members to spread propaganda against the government. Sometimes they got engaged in fighting with the *pasdars* and beat them up to the point of death. In such situations Mohammad Hayati, who knew me well, called me and asked me for help to stop such fights.

The point I wish to make is that the Mujahidin enjoyed this degree of freedom of action until 1360/1981, and authorities always advised us to avoid confrontation and conflict with them until Khordad 1360/June 1981 when they declared their strategy of "armed struggle" against the Islamic Republic. This was probably the most foolish mistake they committed because had they not done so, they could have fooled the people with their imposturous propaganda and infiltrated the system and probably brought its foundations under their own control.

Before that date, often Mohsen (Abulqasim) Reza'ie, a younger brother of Ahmad, Reza, and Mehdi, as well as his father Hajj Khalil, and Parviz Ya'qubi called the central *Komiteh* and asked for help on different occasions, and I always helped them as much as I could. But as the developments unfolded, the situation became increasingly critical, and the hypocritical nature of the Muahidin became more and more evident. One day, Mohsen and his father, along with Ya'qubi, called me and asked to see me. I invited them to come to the central *Komiteh's* headquarters, but they were hesitant. I agreed to go and meet them. This was a dangerous step, but I was willing to take the risk for the sake of the Republic. We decided to meet in Hajj Hhalil's store on the intersection of Inqilab Avenue (formerly Shah Reza) and Shemiran Road. He had a cooling and heating system business.

I walked toward the meeting place. They had arrived there half an hour before me. The entire neighborhood was under their control, perhaps because they thought I might be accompanied by *Komiteh* forces. We had planned to meet for about an hour, but our meeting took over two and a half hours. We had a lot to talk about. They wanted me to resign and stay away and said that the *Komiteh* is not a proper place for me to serve and that I deserve to be a minister or parliament member. They tried to provoke me and criticized the authorities, saying that they act like dictators and do not give them freedom of action and that the law is meaningless for them. I told them that the Islamic Republic doesn't owe me anything, and that my intention is only to serve the people, and I have no ambition to become a minister of parliament member. I told them that I was just waiting for the system to consolidate its power, and after that I would go about my own business. I defended Beheshti and others and said that Bani Sadr, who enjoyed their support, was not any less of a dictator than others. They said that in their opinion Bani Sadr would give them the freedom they wished. I told them that we were both critical of the government but the difference between us was that I tried to correct the wrongdoings of the authorities and they wished to topple the government. I reminded them that they were in fact more dictatorial than everybody else, as their behavior in prison demonstrated. I believed that those in charge of the government might not have much experience in running a country, but they were not traitors and would not betray the country. We should do our best to correct their errors and should not try to destroy them. Perhaps Raja'i was not the right man to become prime minister, but he was better than Bani Sadr. In short they insisted that I should leave the government because the presence of people like me would turn their deceptive analysis null and void.

The Mujahidin had told their supporters that torture prevails in *komitehs*, but when they came to us they realized that we neither tortured nor whipped nor insulted anyone, and patiently listened to their insults. When one of them was released, and went out and told the truth, the MKO leadership confronted him or her. They became angry that their assessment and analysis proved wrong. In other *komitehs* the same situation prevailed and often they delivered most of the individuals they arrested to the central *Komiteh*.

This meeting ended without any positive result. When I decided to leave, Ya'qubi asked me if I needed a ride, and I told him that I would walk back as I had come. They couldn't believe that in such a dangerous situation I would dare to walk without bodyguards. Hajj Khalil volunteered to drive me up to Torfeh Hospital, and I walked the rest of the distance to central *Komiteh* headquarters.

The Mujahidin organized demonstration on Inqilab Avenue, and a considerable number of people joined them. They shouted provocative slogans and declared armed struggle against the government. They had distributed declarations a few days before that date, but the government had not given them a permit for demonstration. After that date, Lajevardi, Beheshti, and Quddusi functioned as revolutionary prosecutors, and I was in charge of maintaining order in the capital. On the 30th of Khordad/June 20th they poured into streets in Inqilab Square, Tehran's Bus Terminal, and several other locations in Tehran. They set fires and attacked and injured many people. After that day we decided to arrest some individuals we had identified before and put them on trial, and the government decided to confront the Mujahidin. One of the people who was involved in stealing documents about the Nowzheh *coup d'état* was Javad Qadiri. I knew him before the Revolution. He was from Isfahan and had been imprisoned two times before the Revolution. He was one of the theoreticians and ideologues in prison and trained many prisoners. After the victory of the Revolution he and other Mujahidin knew my position. I was not hostile to them and greeted and talked to them whenever I saw them. I was on good terms even with Mas'ud Rajavi and always exchanged greetings with him.

Once I went to Sevvum Sha'ban Hospital to donate blood for those injured in the war [with Iraq]. I met Javad Qadiri there. He was there for another business and did not believe in donating blood. In fact the Mujahidin despised that sort of action. Their main concern was to confiscate property. When I encountered him we greeted each other and talked about the recent developments. He had a scooter motor cycle and wanted to go to Tehran University. He offered me a ride and I joined him. On the way I asked him what he was up to. He said that he was no longer with the Mujahidin and had joined Dr. [Habibullah] Payman's group. I laughed and blamed him for that, adding that the MKO was better for him than Payman's group. I was certain that he was lying. I asked him if he was willing to give an interview on national television and announce his detachment from the MKO. He said he didn't have anything to say in an interview. We joked around a little bit and then departed.

After the Nowzheh *coup d'état* one day Javad came to see me. I had heard that through Mohammad Razavi and the Islamic Revolutionary Mujahidin Organization (of Behzad Nabavi) he had found his way to the office of Prosecutor General of the army. A portion of the *coup d'état* files were kept in that office. Again he told me that he was no longer with the MKO and had joined the regime, working on the cases of those who engineered the *coup d'état*. He asked me if I had any information or record of the *coup* to share with him. I laughed and told him that if I had a goat, I wouldn't give it to him to take for herding in the country, let alone documents that pertained to the *coup*! He returned disappointed.

In a few telephone conversations I had with Mohammad Razavi I warned him that Javad was a dangerous person and had infiltrated the office or Prosecutor General of the army. Razavi got upset and in a pejorative tone of voice said, "You have developed hatred and a psychological complex against the MKO because of your relationship with them in prison, and now you wish revenge, and that kind of attitude creates a backlash, and we should try to attract them to our side." After a long conversation I convinced him and he admitted that Javad's behavior was questionable and suspicious. I told him that in light of the position he held, he should be suspicious of Javad. He said that he was suspicious of me and even of himself, but added that we should try to attract them despite some questionable traits they may have. In any case I finally added that he should be careful, and if he wished to bring them into the system, he should do so in a gradual process, rather than bringing in the MKO theoretician and placing him in such a sensitive position.

At the end I could tell that he did not believe me and we departed. When Javad became a fugitive and went underground, Razavi realized that I was right. He called me and apologized.[232] Later I heard somewhere that before Mr. Khamene'ie's assassination attempt by the Mujahidin, Qadiri[233] had said that the regime would collapse within a few days and the authorities had already packed their belongings, ready to leave the country! Exactly at that time I sent a message to Mr. Khosrow Tehrani, who was in the intelligence department of the prime minister's office and informed him of what Javad had said. I suggested that they should arrest Javad. We got a permit to search his house, but he had evacuated his residence and disappeared. Apparently, for a while he was hid-

---

[232] On Tir 19, 1359/July 9, 1980 the *coup d'état* planners intended to attack important centers in Tehran and Qom, including the central *Komiteh's* headquarters, Fawziyeh Seminary in Qom, Imam Khomeini's residence, the offices of the president and prime minister, the major guard's garrison, and many other important centers. They had intended to establish the Social-Democratic Government of Iran. The *coup* was discovered by the Revolutionary Guard Corps, the Air Force *Komiteh*, and other popular forces. Several senior officers and pilots were arrested as a result. Every major newspaper published detailed reports of the incident.

[233] Javad Qadiri, one of the earliest members of the MKO and a close collaborator of Rajavi in prison, infiltrated into the intelligence organizations and took a lot of information and documents about the *coup* out of the country. It was believed that he headed the MKO's intelligence operations and planned to assassinate Imam Khomeini by a certain Effat Ghanipoor, who was reportedly a distant relative of the Imam. She failed to carry out her mission. See,Golpoor Chanmar Kouhi, pp. 475–476, and 484.

ing in the house of Mr. 'Atraiyanfar (his brother-in-law), and then we heard that he had fled the country. Soon his sister went abroad and joined him.[234]

The Furqan Group

Another group that we encountered in the early years after the Revolution was the Furqan group. This was a self-made and self-proclaimed group. We tried to find out if they had any connection with the MKO, but there was no connection between the two. However, when I noticed that on the day of 'Ashura, Akbar Goodarzi carried the Mujahidin flag, I suspected that the Mujahidin had serious influence on this group.

Akbar Goodarzi was the leader of the Furqan group. I was present during his interrogation. He was from the small town of Aligoodarz in Lorestan province. He was from a poor family in that town. He had tried to enter the Qom seminary when he was young but was not admitted there. So he entered the Jami' Mosque in Tehran and received his education there. He stayed in the mosque overnight. After a while they kicked him out, and he went to Shaykh Abdul Hossein (Azarbaijani) Mosque in the bazaar but was kicked out from there after a short time.

These experiences disillusioned him and created a sense of inferiority in him. To compensate, he established the Furqan group. Most members of the group were from western parts of Tehran and also from Shemiran. The rank-and-file members of this group were good and zealous individuals and resisted quite well, but its leadership easily revealed all information about themselves and their organization once they were arrested and interrogated. They undertook activities in the

---

[234] In 1979 Akbar Goodarzi (b.1328/1949), the leader of Furqan group, rebelled against the Islamic Republic. He assassinated General Qarani. He was arrested and executed on Khordad 3, 1359/April 23, 1980.

name of religion and attracted the young and religious men who did not have sympathy toward the clergy. Everything they did was motivated by their religious zeal and faith. Even the man who assassinated Ayatullah Mutahhari truly believed that he would be rewarded on the Day of Judgment. The group thought and acted like the Khawarij in the early days of Islam. They addressed Goodarzi as "imam."[235]

I was present during the time when Goodarzi was interrogated. Once they brought an accused member of the group to ask him a few questions. I asked him to sit down and he refused. When I asked the reason, he said, "First our imam and leader Goodarzi should sit down so that I will feel comfortable in following him." The rank-and-file members of the Furqan group were truly simple-minded and pure but very naïve, shallow, and prejudiced. They were not aware of how things were on the leadership level. They were fully obedient to their leaders and would even kill their own fathers if they were ordered to do so. They were blindly obedient to the leadership, and their pure sentiments were exploited by them. According to their beliefs, the Islamic Republic was not a truly Islamic government on the model of the Prophet. Since they held Ayatullahs Mutahhari and Mufatteh responsible for the consolidation of the government's power, they had decided to assassinate them. In my assessment I found Goodarzi too ignorant to know

---

[235] The Furqan was established about two years before the Revolution. Their ideas and views were influenced by and primarily based on Dr. Ali Shari'ati's ideas. They followed his classification of the Shi'a believers as Safavi-Alavi (i.e. reactionary-progressive) groups. According to their view, all members of the clergy, except Ayatullah Taleqani, belonged to the first group. They started their activities by reading the Qur'an and adopted terror and assassination as their strategy. They assassinated Ayatullah Mutahhari and Mofatteh, General Qarani, and Hajj Mahdi Iraqi and his son Hesam. Most of its members were arrested in the fall of 1358/1979 and executed for their crimes. See Ja'fariyan, pp. 511 and 568–580. See also Chamar Koohi, 88–93.

[235] In 1979 Akbar Goodarzi (b.1328/1949), the leader of Furqan group, rebelled against the Islamic Republic. He assassinated General Qarani. He was arrested and executed on Khordad 3, 1359/April 23, 1980.

what he was talking about, and that he was not capable of planning assassinations. I believed other hands were guiding him from outside his organization, similar to Kolahi's role in the explosion of the headquarters of the Islamic Republican Party in Tehran.

The night that the headquarters of the Islamic Republican Party exploded, it was not planned for so many dignitaries to attend the meeting there. Often not more than ten to fifteen people gathered there for ordinary meetings. The rest were invited by Kolahi.[236] He had invited anybody who was important but not necessarily a member of the party (like Mohammad Montazeri). He had told them that Ayatullah Beheshti would deliver an important speech about economic issues and the challenges the country faced, and many people went there to hear him. Even Beheshti himself did not know why so many people had gathered there that night. After performing the night prayer, when he wanted to start his talk, suddenly a bomb that had been placed under the microphone exploded.

A few days before this incident, the Mujahidin had started extensive propaganda. Its main theme was that the Islamic republic's collapse was imminent, and people should prepare for its demise. Javad Qadiri also had reiterated the same message a few days before that. In such a short period of time several assassinations and explosions also took place, including the one that injured Mr. Khamene'ie, soon to be followed by the explosion in the prime minister's office that killed Mr. Raja'i and Mr. Bahonar on Shahrivar 7, 1359/August 29, 1980

It was very obvious that all these events had been planned and coordinated in advance. But the Mujahidin committed a big mistake and underestimated Imam Khomeini's

---

[236] Javad Mansuri stated that Hashem Kolahi belonged to Mohammad Reza Sa'adati's team who infiltrated the Islamic Republic Party and engineered the explosion in the party's headquarters in 1360/1981 where about 100–120 leaders were gathered to discuss the nomination of the next president. See, Mansuri, *Mokhtasari as....*

power. The government continued to function, and the presence of the Imam guaranteed that nothing spectacular would take place, and the Islamic Republic would survive against all odds. Taking all these considerations into account, it is difficult to admit that the Furqan group acted on its own and other forces (i.e. the MKO) had no share in those incidents.

The Hand of Destiny

It was in 1360 or 1361/1980 that one day a friend called me and said that he had seen General Sujdeh'ie[237] near the Niavaran Palace. He had gone to local bakery and bought a loaf of bread and was walking toward his home. He had followed the General to his house. He gave me his address. Immediately I sent a team to that address and ordered them to arrest the General and bring him to the central *Komiteh* headquarters. When they arrived there the General escaped through the roof of his house, but the team finally arrested him and brought him to the *Komiteh* headquarters. I interrogated him briefly and sent him to Evin Prison, where they put him on trial and executed him.

We identified two individuals who had infiltrated the *Komiteh*. One of them was a revolutionary guard (*pasdar*) who informed the team houses that were to be invaded by the guards and saved them. This man was tried and executed. Another guard was a former member of the Imperial Guard, and we did not know anything about his background. He trained our military personnel. Later he became the commander of the *Komiteh's* garrison. It turned out that he was involved in the Nouzheh *coup d'état*. He was also arrested and executed.

One day I heard that Major Afshar, the former deputy director of Evin Prison, had been arrested. He was from the

---

[237] Jalal Sujdeh'ie (b. 1307/1927) was in charge of the army intelligence department in Ahvaz and later served in the Imperial Guard Corps (Javidan). He was transferred to SAVAK in 1346/1967 and served in Zanjan and Isfahan and retired in 1357/1978. He was arrested after the victory of the Revolution and executed on Azar 9, 1360/November 30, 1981.

Caspian Sea region. He was not such a bad person. I had had several encounters with him in Evin while I was there. On one occasion when I was trying to take off the shell of a hardboiled egg and was hitting it on the wall, a guard accused me of sending Morse code to the adjacent cell and started a fight. Major Afshar saved me that day from the troubles the guard tried to cause.

Now that he was imprisoned I went to visit him. He said that they accused him of torturing prisoners before the Revolution and claimed that he prevented the delivery of water, food, and blankets to them. On the basis of these charges they had condemned him to life in prison. I went to Mr. [Mohammadi] Gilani and told him that Major Afshar was a good man and all charges against him were fabricated. He was not the type of a man to prevent delivery of water, food, or blankets to prisoners, as it was impossible to implement such measures in a prison with such a large population. With my explanation, his term was reduced to fifteen years.

Two months later I heard on the national radio that Major Afshar had been executed on the same charges. I was very disturbed and decided to find out the truth. It turned out that he was executed on the basis of reports written by Ahmad Reza Karimi. Karimi was like Vahid Afrakhteh. Before the Revolution he had placed himself in the full service of SAVAK. After the Revolution when he was arrested, reportedly Badamchiyan and Kachu'i had asked him to write his memoirs! To please them he had written false reports about some of the interrogators and authorities of the prison and even against the Mujahidin before the Revolution. Since I knew him well, I was certain that his reports were not true and reliable and he had written them to save his own life.

Hasan Farzaneh had reported many activists to SAVAK before the Revolution, including Kazim Zulanvar, Akbar Mahdavi, and myself. In prison the Mujahidin ignored him because of his weakness and sometime even beat him up. After a while he was exiled to Shiraz Prison. He joined the

Mujahidin when he was released. After the victory of the Revolution he was in charge of the labor department of the MKO and printed their declarations. He commanded a group that invaded the Bell Helicopter Company's headquarters and stole their property. He was also in contact with the human rights group that Hajj Khalil Reza'ie had organized in Hosseiniyyah Irshad. His position as one of the most important members of the MKO was surprising to me because before the Revolution, the Mujahidin hated him, Sa'id Shahsavandi, Mehdi Taqva'ie, and Sadeq Katouzian. However, after the victory of the Revolution things changed in the organization and he became an important member of the MKO. He was arrested, and as a result of his armed activities against the Islamic Republic was executed.

Sadeq Katouzian had a similar situation.[238] When he was arrested in 1351/1972, he was condemned to three years in prison. He was our friend, but the Mujahidin hated him. When I was released, all my friends came to visit me, but he did not come, although I sent him a message that I really wished to see him. A friend asked me not to insist and let him go about his life. He became a good friend of the Mujahidin.

One day I was passing across the 17th Shahrivar Avenue to the other side when a speeding car approached me but did not stop. I threw myself in another direction, but the bumper of the car hit me. I turned and looked at the driver, and recognized that it was Katouzian. He laughed sarcastically and drove away. I tried to arrange a meeting with him but failed.

In the early day after the Revolution we used to go to Behesht Zahra cemetery very often. One day I saw Sadeq there. He was distributing dates and bread, a custom that people observe in cemeteries to ask for prayers for their deceased ones. He pretended that he didn't see me. Another time when I

---

[238] Mohammad Sadeq Katouzian (b. 1330/1951) started his political activities when he was fifteen and was arrested in 1346/1967. He was introduced to Ezzat Shahi in 1347/1968 in the bazaar and through him joined the MKO.

visited the grave of a friend with Hasan Qorbani, Sadeq was visiting another grave nearby. When he noticed me, he did not even greet me and left quickly.

Khalil Faqih Dezfuli, who was a brother-in-law of Katouzian, was once arrested for some unknown reasons. I released him before his case became too complicated. I told him to give a message to Katouzian that I just wished to see him and had no intention of arresting him. I liked him and we were friends, and I really wished to give him some advice and hopefully save him. He could then decide if he wished to continue with the MKO. In response, he sent me a message saying, "Tell Ezzat to save himself first, stop collaboration with the government, and leave the *Komiteh*."

I did not have much information about Katouzian's activities after the Revolution. He had married Faqih Dezfuli's sister, and through this marriage become a relative of Abbas Modarresifar. Together they kidnapped three *pasdars* of the *Komiteh*, interrogated and then killed them, and burnt their bodies. Katouzian's father was a religious man. When his son was arrested he sent me a message and asked to meet me. I went to see him. He asked me to give his message that "In light of your activities you will be condemned to death soon. If you repent and die as a believing Muslim, I will visit your grave and pray for you. Otherwise, I will never visit your grave because I will not consider you a Muslim."

I went to see Sadeq and gave his father's message to him. He did not pay much attention to my advice and remained firm in his position. In response to his father's message, he said that he didn't care whether or not his father came to visit his grave. In any case he did not change and finally was executed.

Among other important people who were arrested was Shukrullah Paknezhad. I had known him since we were in prison. He was the leader of the Palestine Group and had a leftist orientation. In prison he associated more frequently with the Mujahidin than with other leftist groups. We were on good terms and greeted each other whenever we met, and sometimes got engaged in conversation. After his arrest and execution, counter-revolutionary groups spread rumors and stories about me that were totally false.[239]

Once a truckload of documents was stolen by Hedayatullah Matin Daftari from Evin Prison, and Paknezhad was implicated in that incident and was wanted because of his involvement in it. The *Komiteh* personnel arrested him two times and brought him to the central *Komiteh* headquarters in Baharestan Square. On both of those occasions I talked to him extensively. I told him that he was then too old for political activities and should go about his life. Since I knew that charges against him were not so serious as to lead to his execution, I released him. This was the last encounter I had with Paknezhad, and there was no other charge against him. After a short while the *Komiteh* guards arrested him for the third time but did not bring him to me. They took him directly to the office of the Revolutionary Prosecutor General, where he was tried and executed after a short time.

Once we received a report that someone was teaching Ayatullah Taleqani's commentaries on the Qur'an in a mosque in Tehran. After some investigation it turned out that under the guise of the Qur'an he was in fact involved in anti-religious activities. When more information came in I realized that Seyyed Ahmad Hashimian[240] was conducting those sessions. He

---

[239] According to Khanbaba Tehrani, "While Shukri [Paknezhad] was leaving the MKO's headquarters he was arrested and transferred to the central *Komiteh*. Ezzat Shahi greeted and welcomed him, and addressed him as "Shukri, the Mujahid." This showed that the regime in fact was fully aware of his affiliation with the MKO. See Khanbaba Tehrani, *Memoirs*, p. 80.

[240] Seyyed Ahmad Hashimian (b.1328/1949) joined the MKO while he was a university student. Upon the ideological transformation of the organization, he joined the Marxist branch of the MKO and in 1357/1978 became one of the leaders of Paykar group. Later he joined the Tudeh Party and was arrested shortly afterwards. See *Tarikhche-ye Mokhtasar-e Goruhakha*, p. 126. See also Ja'fariyan, p. 433.

had gotten married and lived in south Tehran. I sent a team from the *Komiteh* to his address and they brought him and his family to *Komiteh* headquarters. After a few rounds of interrogation we released them. Hashimian was from Qazvin and a longtime member of the MKO. In 1352/1972 he sent a message and asked to see me. We did not have much information about his position in the Mujahidin organization. I decide to meet him in Tehran's Shah Mosque (Imam's Mosque after the Revolution). He wanted to bring some documents for me. Several people advised me not to meet him there, so I didn't go to the mosque. Hashimian was an active member of the MKO that the regime was not able to locate and arrest. After the ideological transformation of the MKO he adopted Maoism and joined the Paykar group. Shortly after that he developed interest in the Tudeh Party and its ideology. With this background he was teaching the Qur'an, using religion for his anti-religious activities. I was present at his interrogation sessions and tried to talk to him and advise him to come to his senses. At the end I tried to tell him that with his background he would surely be executed if he were put on trial. It seemed to me that he was convinced, as he said, and that he was prepared to co-operate with us. He said that he no longer believed in armed struggle and was prepared to deliver all weapons he had hidden in his residence in Qazvin.

I sent Mr. Sa'adat and Mirbazel in his company to Qazvin. I told them to be very careful, and if he were sincere and cooperated with him, to treat him well and bring him back. It turned out that he had a large amount of weapons and ammunition in his house and delivered them all. He worked with us for a while and then the Revolutionary Guards Corps asked for his transfer and used his experience in some of the interrogation of other prisoners. They tried him. He spent three or four years in prison and was then released.[241]

---

[241] For more information on these developments, see, Seyyed Kamal al-Din Mirbazel, *Memoirs*.

Fire in the Parliament Building

In the Parliament building in Baharestan Square, there were two rooms where all weapons and ammunition that were collected after the Revolution were stored. Another room was assigned to store all the records and files that pertained to the Mujahidin and other leftist groups. During those years all weapons and ammunitions that were collected from people and political groups were dumped in these rooms without any consideration for security and safety measures. One day a fire broke out in these rooms and caused a massive explosion. On that day Abbas Yazdanifar[242] and Khalil Ashja' were commanding officers of the day. After some investigation, it turned out that electrical wiring of the building was outdated and had caused the fire.

My Marriage

During the years that I was involved in activities against the Shah's regime I avoided getting married. I believed that family life would prevent me from struggle, so I had to choose one or the other. I chose the struggle. Then I spent many years in prison until the Revolution began to unfold. After the victory of the Revolution I was preoccupied with many responsibilities, and as a result never had time to think about marriage and family life.

As I mentioned before, I was in contact with members of the Islamic Coalition Party from around the 1340's/1960's. After I was released I continued my association with them one way or the other. Among its members Javad Amani, who was close to me, and I spent many nights before the Revolution in his house on Mowlavi Avenue. One day Javad asked me if I

---

[242] Abbas Yazdanifar was a civil engineer and a member of the central committee of the Organization of Mujahidin Inqilab-e Islami under the leadership of Behzad Nabavi. At the time of writing these pages he was an instructor at the University of Science and Technology.

ever intended to get married. I told him that I was not prepared and did not have the means to start family life. He asked me to inform him when I decided, as he knew someone who was a good candidate for me. Since for over two decades I lived like a gypsy and moved from one apartment to another, I didn't want to subject my future wife to such a situation and thought of first finding a good place to purchase.

In 1359/1980 my brother decided to buy a house. I managed to secure a loan and became his partner in his plan. We bought a small house near Ahang and Shahid Mahallati Parkway for about 550,000. *tumans* (around $75,000) then. This was a two-story house, and each floor had a two-bedroom apartment. I took one floor and my brother had the other. Then I went to Javad and told him that I was prepared to get married. He had a cousin who until then had rejected many marriage proposals, and Javad was not sure if she and her family would accept me. He volunteered to speak on my behalf anyway. I told him that my brother and sister could meet them for details, but I wanted to see the candidate myself before they stepped in. Javad went on to prepare a meeting between us, but the girl's father did not want to give his daughter to someone like me. I knew Asadullah Badamchiyan and had spent some time with him in prison. He mediated on my behalf and put in a few good words about me. Also, Javad and his father tried, but the girl's father continued to oppose this proposal.

In any case these friends decided to arrange a meeting between the girl and me, and if she liked me and approved of me, then find a way to get her father's agreement. On the day we all agreed on, I went to the designated place near Amin Hozur Avenue. Javad was there before I arrived. He said that the girl's father was home for a religious occasion, so we could not go to his house. Instead, he told me to go to Mr. Nazifi's house on Iran Avenue and the girl and her mother would come there to meet me. I went there an hour later and they also arrived. We were introduced to each other. I was too shy to look at her face, so I gazed on the floor! Her mother had a rosary in her hand and was busy praying. Gradually we broke the ice and started talking. I told her about myself and my life and adventures, my health and physical condition, my experiences with different political groups, my poor financial situation and my only possession that was a house, and, in short, everything I could tell about myself. The only condition I set for her was to observe *hijab*, if she accepted me the way I was. I gave them enough time to think and let Javad know when they decided.

The girl was an instructor of the Arabic language at that time and asked me if she could continue her teaching career. I told her that each of us is entitled to our political views and free to follow his/her own path, and added that I would not impose my views on her and would expect the same from her. I said that I had no objection to her to continue her teaching career but only if she taught female students and also had enough time to manage the house and was prepared to cook, as I only liked homemade food. Luckily, she responded positively and accepted my conditions.

Other friends secured her father's agreement and made an appointment for me to go and see him. He was very open and frank and said that he didn't like me, but Badamchiyan and Javad's father had said so many good things about me that he had agreed to give his daughter to me. He added that he had two conditions, however. The first condition was that I should own my own house. I told him that I own a house in partnership with my brother. His second condition was that the engagement period should be short and I should move my wife to my house within two or three months. We agreed on all these conditions. This was the way that I started my family life. Thank God, I was lucky to have found a pious, content, and religious wife. I was grateful to God for this blessing.

My Financial Condition: Salary and Benefits

Until the end of 1359/1980 I did not receive a penny from the *Komiteh* and the government at all. Since I was single and had no particular expenses and spent my days and nights in the *Komiteh* I did not need any money. In the early days of 1360/1981 I went to Mutahhari Mosque in the company of a few friends. On our way back, Hajj Aqa Hossein Mirzai'e shoved two or three thousand *tumans* in my pocket. He said that the money was paid as the New Year gift and Mr. Mahdavi Kani had given it to him. This was a gift and not a salary. Until that date whoever served in the *Komiteh* had a choice to draw a salary. Some people did and some did not. After 1360/1981 it was decided that single members should be paid a salary of 1500 *tumans* and married one about 2000 *tumans* plus 300 *tumans* for each child. So I started receiving a salary beginning in 1360/1981. Interestingly, our telephone operator received 3000 *tumans* because he had gotten married before and had three children. In all fairness this amount was barely enough to meet the needs of a family, and if an emergency expense like medical expenses came up, we had trouble, especially because I had no other source of support like parents, real estate, or any other source.

From that date on I had to pay a portion of my income for my home mortgage. As long as Mr. Mahdavi Kani and Baqeri Kani were in charge of the central *Komiteh*, utmost effort was made to cut expenses. For example, in 1360/1981 the *Komiteh's* budget was 11 billion *tumans*. Until the fifth or sixth months of that year we only spent about 4.3 billion of that amounts. Before 1360/1981the *Komiteh* did not have a set budget. Most of its expenses were met through donations and gifts. Everybody was careful to spend as little as possible. Transportation needs of the *Komiteh* were met by using the automobiles that were confiscated from the police stations and officials of the previous regime.

Toward the end of 1360/1981 the *Komiteh* purchased a number of domestically assembled *paykan* automobiles for police patrol units. Local branches of the *Komiteh* also faced serious budgetary shortages. In some regions they did not even have cameras to take photographs of those who were arrested for different types of violations. We found ways to remedy the situation. We discovered a large amount of video tapes and sold them and spent the funds to buy cameras and other items we needed in the *Komitehs*. Some people like Seyyed Mahdi Darvazehi'e and Iravani criticized us for taking these kinds of measures and argued that we must treat that kind of property in accordance with the injunctions of jurisprudence. We did not understand those injunctions and deposited all funds into one account. The other problem was that these gentlemen argued that confiscated video tapes and alcoholic drinks were *haram*, and we should delete their contents and dispose of the drinks but return the containers to their owners. Sometimes we did accordingly, but most of the time did not observe those injunctions. They believed that our behavior was against the *Shari'ah*. It was a complicated situation, and some of the members of the *Komiteh* became disillusioned because they had spent a lot of time and energy to confiscate those items.

Prosecutor-General of the *Komiteh*

We did not face any problem in treating and sentencing the ordinary people who were arrested because of their illegal activities. But if a person was well known and/or had strong connection with powerful people, they came to his defense. Even if his crime and treason were obvious, we received hundreds of phone calls to release such an individual. Fortunately, Mr. Lajevardi, the prosecutor-general of the Revolutionary Islamic *Komiteh*, was in agreement with us and supported our decisions. When we arrested someone and were supposed not to allow anyone to visit him, we informed Mr. Lajevardi. Although we were pressured by very powerful people to release such an individual, we transferred him to the jurisdiction of the prosecutor-general and referred his connections to that office.

These differences of opinion and attitudes caused some conflicts between us and Mr. Mahdavi Kani and some other politicians and decision-makers in the *Komiteh*. They believed that we caused unnecessary difficulties for the people.

Before the establishment of the Revolutionary Guards Corps (*Sepah-e Pasdaran-e Inqilab-e Islami*) the authority to arrest and prosecute counter-revolutionary elements and criminals was given to the central *Komiteh*. With the establishment of the Corps more discrepancies and differences appeared, and they began to interfere in our duties. Sometimes when we planned to arrest a defendant, the Corps arrested him before we arrived. When we discovered a team-house and wanted to arrest its members, they also came and interfered. As a result of this situation several people lost their lives for no obvious reasons.

Then an important development took place. When the Revolutionary Guard Corps realized that we were firm in our positions and actions, they sent a clergy to Evin and Qasr Prisons to train and appoint him as Religious Prosecutor (*hakim-e shar'*).

One night, Mr. Mahdavi Kani called us for a meeting where Mr. Baqeri Kani and Ali Qannadha were also in attendance. In the middle of the meeting Mr. Ma'adikhah also joined us. Mr. Mahdavi said that he had made an agreement with Mr. Qoddusi, the prosecutor-general, that a branch of the seventh office of chief prosecutor should be established in the central *Komiteh*. Also it was suggested that an office should be established under a religious judge to handle the cases of defendants whose offences warranted a ten-year prison term or less. The cases of defendants with more serious offences, or confiscation of their property, were to be referred to authorities in Evin Prison. I welcomed this idea granted that a responsible individual should be appointed as religious judge and always be accessible. Sometimes a defendant was arrested at night and we could not wait until the next morning for the religious judge to come and decide his case. In other words, I insisted that such an individual must be available any moment we needed him.

A man named Habibullah Sultani was appointed as the Religious Judge (*hakim-e shar'*) of the seventh office of Chief Prosecutor in the central *Komiteh*. As we got to know him, we decided to ignore him and didn't take him seriously. The *Komiteh* had established its own garrison, and this man was in charge of teaching ideology and ethics. We did more investigation about him and discovered that he did not even believe in what he was preaching. Initially he wore clerical garb but soon began to wear the guard's uniform. One of the *pasdars* once told him that the respect people had toward him was because of his clerical garb, and wearing the guard's uniform was an insult to his status. He gave him a very rude response and we realized that he was in fact not that ethical after all. After that I did some more investigation about him and found out that he was once a religious judge in the Bazargan region of Azarbaijan, but had caused some scandals there, and fled when they tried to arrest him. It turned out soon that he did not even respect Imam Khomeini at all. With all this background he was appointed as religious judge in the *Komiteh* and issued verdicts to arrest and torture people. We decided to keep quiet for a while to assure authorities that we had no ill intention toward him. I just ordered my colleagues there to be careful and when someone was arrested and brought to them, they should take a list of his belongings so that they wouldn't make false claims later on.

Among the security personnel there were some who supported Behzad Nabavi and his organization and who had infiltrated the Revolutionary Guards Corps. Initially they were not taken very seriously. They took ward number 209 under their control and wished to work through that channel. They used double standards. When they arrested someone, if he was wealthy and they could take advantage of his status for their own interests, they did not deliver him to us. Knowing that we make a list of all the possessions of every defendant, they delivered him directly to the Corps. They were not as punctual as we were in cases like these.

One night Mr. Mahdavi Kani invited us for another meeting. Mr. Sultani was there too. He said that he had appointed Mr. Sultani to the position of chief interrogator while maintaining him in his position as religious judge. He asked us to help him. I disagreed with his decision because I believed he was not qualified. Mahdavi got upset and said that he had decided so and whatever Sultani said, we were expected to obey. I became angry and said that if that was his decision, let Mr. Sultani take over and with friends like Golab Bakhsh accept all responsibilities for the interrogation. In such a case, I had to leave my position. The more he insisted that I should stay, the stronger I objected to his proposal because I believed he was not qualified. Mr. Mahdavi became very angry and said that he was the representative of Imam Khomeini and whatever he said must be obeyed, and that he did not take no for an answer. I said that I respected him but he should not impose his views on me, and that I was free to choose to obey his order or leave my position and go about my own life. Mr. Kani said in that case anybody who could not work with Sultani was free to leave.

I thus concluded that it was more appropriate that I leave my position by my own choice rather than be kicked out by force. I wrote my resignation. After that encounter, they spread allegations that we were torturers and acted against the injunctions of the *Shari'ah*. I take God as my witness that we never tortured anyone, nor did we ever whip any defendant. If the defendant had committed armed robbery or rape, we did not treat him well, but we never mistreated political defendants, much less beating them. We sent them directly to Evin.

In the central *Komiteh* we had two categories of prisoners. One group, whom we kept on the ground level of the compound, was composed of those prisoners who had committed petty crimes. The other group, who had committed serious financial or political crimes, was assigned to another floor. As a result of the negative environment that was created against me in the *Komiteh*, several times Mr. Ali Mohammad Basharati and Mohammad Montazeri came for inspection. After visiting the ground-floor prison, Montazeri asked me if we had another prison. I told him that we did but would show it to him alone. He asked for the reason, and I said that on the other floor there were prisoners whose crimes were very serious, and we needed to interrogate them. We did not mix them with ordinary prisoners, but to collect information from them we never resorted to force or torture. We had our own way.[243] To make the story short, they created an environment against us so that they could accuse us of measures we never took.

One morning Sultani came in and I delivered everything to him. Despite my recommendation, none of my colleagues and friends was willing to collaborate with him. I told him that they could act as they wished after that. I counted that until that date we had arrested about 5000 people that included all kinds of criminals, prostitutes, thieves, political activists, and the like. We had delivered about 1300 to the Ministry of Justice or Evin Prison and released the rest after a month or two.

I told Sultani that all prisoners were at his disposal and he could act as he wished and that I was no longer willing to collaborate with him. None of my colleagues were willing to work with him either. He went to Mr. Baqeri Kani and complained to him. Baqeri asked me to meet him. He said that he had talked to Mr. Mahdavi Kani the night before and told him

---

[243] Among those who knew Ezzat Shahi before and after the Revolution was Ahmad Ali Borhani. In an interview he said, "As far as I know, Ezzat never tortured or even touched any prisoner, but used common sense to get information from them. Ezzat never even entered those domains. Before the Revolution he never volunteered to give information. After the Revolution he treated prisoners in a very clever way and always used experiences he had acquired during his political activities before the Revolution. See *Interview with Ahmad Ali Borhani*, Tehran, 1383/1984

that he could not work without me. He then said jokingly that he could go to south Tehran and recruit a few thugs to work with him. I told him that they deserved to work with thugs because they were cheaper and would be obedient to him. As a result of my insistence, Sultani left and never returned to the *Komiteh*, so I continued to stay and work there. After that when they brought any defendant to the *Komiteh*, we sent him directly to Evin. If someone's crimes were not serious, we delivered them to the third district *komiteh* on Vozara Avenue. I had a friend there, and he could handle cases like that. We authorized him to release such prisoners after they left their house deed as collateral so that they would return we they were recalled. Otherwise, he would send them to Evin.

The new situation awakened us to be more careful. I warned a few friends, Mr. Ahmad Sa'adat, Morteza Mirbazel, Mokhtar Ibrahimi, Hossein Daqiqi, Hossein Modabberi, Akbar Baratchi, and others that if we left, we must expect a catastrophic situation like the Monghol invasion in the sense that people who would replace us would be a bunch of opportunist elements who would want to trap us and cause trouble. In such a situation we would not be able to defend ourselves because our decisions and actions were based on common sense and there was no clear legal injunction to guide us to legitimize our behavior. For example, when we asked the defendants to bring collateral, we did not keep it, but attached everything to his file. Sometimes people brought their personal belongings such as motorcycles or automobiles. In our absence those items could have been confiscated by questionable people in power, and we would be responsible for their misconduct. So we decided to return all such properties to their legitimate owners. We contacted all those who were not involved in serious crimes or terrorist acts and asked them to come and get their properties back. We sent all records of individuals who had committed crimes of a political nature to Evin and obtained receipts for each case. Thus we were able to return a large amount of documents, property, and collateral to their legitimate owners.

While we were busy with these responsibilities we heard that the prosecutor-general's office was searching to find and arrest Sultani. He was initially given a great deal of authority as a religious judge (*hakim-e shar'*) with logistical support such as a house, an automobile, and bodyguards and was about to be appointed as the chief interrogator. Apparently, he had abused his authority and revealed his true character. After these revelations about him, the authorities asked us to stay and continue our services, but I felt that I could no longer function under those circumstances. Mr. Mahdavi Kani accepted my resignation. I put all things in order and organized all files and records and left the central *Komiteh*. I was unemployed for about three or four months, but I sent my colleagues to Evin to work there and saved them from unemployment.

Mr. Fallahiyan's Tenure[244]

Another development around this time was the resignation of Mr. Mahdavi Kani from his position as interior minister. He was replaced by Mr. Nateq Noori. He contacted me and insisted that I should resume my work in the central *Komiteh*. He promised to introduce substantial changes there and remove questionable individuals and appoint new people to important positions. I accepted and returned to work, but after three or four months he resigned and was replaced by Mr. Fallahiyan. Things went from bad to worse and we began to face many new problems.

---

[244] Ali Fallahiyan (b. 1328/1949) received his education in Qom and reached the rank of a *mujtahid*. Before the Revolution he was arrested and spent some time in prison. After the victory of the Revolution he held several important positions such as the chief religious judge (*hakim shar'*) in revolutionary courts in Abadan and Khorasan, the director of the dentral *Komiteh*, and member of national parliament. See, *Ettela'at*, 1368–1376/1988–2009), see also, Golpoor Chamar Kouhi, p. 242, *Abrar*, #226, p. 6.

Prior to that date Mr. Fallahiyan had worked with Mr. Mousavi Tabrizi in the prosecutor-general's office. Mousavi was an arch-enemy of Lajevardi and planned to remove him from Evin and appoint Fallahiyan in his place. They also pushed me to resign, but I didn't give up and insisted that as long as Imam Khomeini was pleased with my work, I would remain in my position. I asked them to kick me out if they could. Mr. Beheshti had asked Lajevardi not to pay attention and remain steadfast in his position. When they realized that they could not remove Lajevardi, they resorted to another trick. Lajevardi was tough and uncompromising. They said that Imam Khomeini had asked them to remove Lajevardi and appoint Hajj Ahmad Khomeini in his place because he was softer and had a friendlier attitude. Upon hearing this, Lajevardi resigned and left his position. His friends, especially Asgar Awladi and Sa'id Amani, heard this and confronted him. They told him to request a note from the Imam about his removal and replacement by Seyyed Ahmad Khoemini.

The next day Asgar Awladi and Amani met Imam Khomeini and informed him of the story. Reportedly he became very upset and denied he had issued such an order. Thus, Lajevardi was maintained in his position. Thinking that I was a member of Lajevardi's gang, Fallahiyan did not want to work with me, but Mr. Nateq Noori insisted that I remain in my position. It was a complicated situation.

A few months after my encounter with Fallahiyan and all the problems he created, Jamal Isma'ili, known as Isfahani, was appointed as the director of intelligence of the central *Komiteh*. He had functioned in the Revolutionary Guards Corps. Until then the *Komiteh* did not have an intelligence department. All arrests and interrogations were conducted by about twenty officers who functioned as interrogators, investigators, and intelligence officers. Mr. Isfahani knew me from the past. Before he came to the headquarters, he called me and asked to meet me. I accepted and went to see him. He said that he made his acceptance of the new position contingent upon

572

my willingness to work with him. I told him that I did not belong to any particular group and acted independently, and would continue to serve as long as our principles were respected. Otherwise, I would not collaborate with anyone, no matter who he might be.

After this meeting, Mr. Isfahani accepted the new position. He created an organizational chart that included positions for investigation and intelligence officers. In short, duties that we performed with 20 officers, he hired 150 people to perform. Interestingly, he did not assign any position to me! I felt that I no longer belonged to that office but continued to serve and asked my loyal friends to do the same so that we wouldn't be accused of ill intention or procrastination. In any case, they moved me and my friends around, and we were scattered in different departments. Meanwhile Mr. Fallahiyan sent me a note and appointed me as inspector-general of the *Komiteh*. When Isfahani heard that news, he confronted Fallahiyan, claiming that I was his subordinate, and any transfer should take place by his order! I heard his reaction and asked him to come and meet me. He came in and I confronted him for his arrogance, tore up Fallahiyan's note, and told him that I had not worked under anybody's command for four years, and that it didn't matter who I worked with as long as my views and principles were respected.

When Isfahani noticed my reaction, he apologized and insisted that I should stay and work with him, but I had decided to leave anyway. When Fallahiyan heard this story, he became even more hostile. He did not return my phone calls, nor did he give me an appointment to meet him. Instead he referred me to Isfahani for every minor request. So I became *persona non grata*, without any job or specific responsibilities. Yet, I didn't want to use my connection with Mr. Montazeri, Hashimi Rafsanjani, Rabbani Shirazi, and others to ask for their intervention.

Mr. Fallahiyan really did not know what to do with me. He couldn't stand me in the *Komiteh*, nor could he kick me

573

out. Had I resigned, the above-mentioned gentlemen would have become angry at him. Moreover, Nateq Noori had insisted that I should stay and function there. Fallahiyan's plan was to indirectly force me to resign, and if I did so, reject my resignation so that if I quit, he could claim that I left by my own choice. This situation did not change for about seven or eight months. I practically functioned as a secretary for Mr. Isfahani and answered telephone calls. Gradually he became so arrogant that even if he was in the office he would not answer his own phone calls, until I picked up the phone and gave it to him. Interestingly, I knew that he totally misunderstood and misinterpreted my humility. To keep him in that state of mind, every morning I mopped the floor of his office, and cleaned and dusted the furniture and the windows. My friends criticized me for doing all these things, but I did not want to give the impression that I was superior to others.

The situation frustrated Mr. Fallahiyan and another member of the clergy named Salehi who had just joined him. They did not know what to do. Salehi often expressed his frustration because of my silence and compliance. I never gave an idea or opinion and treated them with respect whenever I encountered them. I never objected to any decision they made nor complained about anything and even tried to help Mr. Isfahani. Some colleagues tried to take advantage of his lack of experience. They asked him for recommendations for personal affairs, and borrowed his car, and when they had an accident repaired it in the *Komiteh* repair shop. They knew that I did not condone the abuse, so they went to Isfahani's office when I was not there.

During Fallahiyan's tenure, several new functions were created for me. One of them was to produce a bulletin on the activities of the *Komiteh* and send it to high officials. The content of this bulletin was discussed in the National Security Council. Since Isfahani did not have enough time to read the bulletin carefully, sometimes outdated news was printed in it and caused embarrassment. Fallahiyan criticized Isfahani for his negligence. After that they asked me to control the content of the bulletin, and I agreed to do that. As long as I was in charge, no outdated news ever appeared in the bulletin.

My Resignation

Mr. Isfahani loved the spotlight and tried hard to become famous. He contacted authorities in powerful positions and gave instructions for their duties. He often called [Ayatullah] Ardabili, Rayy Shahri, Nateq Noori, and others and met them and aggrandized his services. Fallahiyan approved of this behavior because it served his purposes and enabled him to get a bigger budget. At that time, most work was done through personal relationship, rather than official instructions and rules. Personal relationship helped a great deal in obtaining funds and support from higher officials.

In meetings that Mr. Isfahani arranged with high officials, several people like Mr. Salehi accompanied him. He introduced each person in charge of a specific position, which often was not true. Several times he asked me to go with him but I declined. One day when he was going to meet Mr. Mousavi Ardabili, he asked me to go with him, but I refused. He asked for the reason for my reluctance. I said that I had no official position and there was no reason to attend such meetings. Right then he said that he would introduce me as his office manager. I took it as an insult and refused to continue the discussion. After a mild argument, I asked Isfahani and Salehi to leave me alone. They went to visit Ardabili. I was convinced that I no longer belonged to that office and must leave. The next day I had a conversation with Isfahani and informed him of my decision. I made sure that he understood that we were not a "gang" and that each member of my team served in one position or the other and I did not interfere in their work. At the end I told him that I would quit on the coming Saturday and was trying to wrap things up before that day.

Isfahani did not expect to hear such a decision. He couldn't even imagine that after eight months of patiently working, suddenly I would make such a decision. He said that he did not allow me to resign, but when I insisted he asked me for a two-week extension of my deadline so that he could take a short trip that was planned a while ago. I accepted his condition, but he never took the trip. In the meantime, I secluded myself and began to write a letter and explained the reasons for my resignation. I addressed the letter to Mr. Fallahiyan, and its tone and language were strong and aggressive, so much so that I was sure it would cause further conflict, but I didn't care. What was important for me was to say everything that must be said.

My Assessment of the Situation

In my resignation I dealt with and criticized the new situation that was unfolding and examined the mindset and currents of thought that Mr. Fallahiyan tried to establish in the *Komiteh*. With his tenure fundamental changes were introduced in the structure and overall policies of the *Komiteh*. What was most noticeable was an enormous amount of waste and increasingly unnecessary expenses in all aspects of its operation. To meet the new expenses a new budgetary policy was to be appropriated. In previous fiscal years only half of the available budget was spent in the *Komiteh*. But under Fallahiyan's administration, the entire annual budget was spent during the early months of the fiscal year, and the *Komiteh* faced a severe budget deficit the second part of the year. The annual budget of the *Komiteh* at that time was some 11 billion *tumans*. Under Mahdavi Kani and his brother Baqeri Kani, there was always a surplus at the end of the year that they returned to the government treasury. But under Fallahiyan during the first year that I worked with him more than 3 billion *tumans* was spent within three months and the rest of it shortly afterward, and the *Komiteh* faced a budget deficit.[245]

Fallahiyan argued the budget deficit was better than surplus, because the *Komiteh* could always request a higher budget from the government for the following year. Therefore, toward the end of the fiscal year his administration began to purchase unnecessary items. Once they bought a number of Mercedes Benz automobiles and gave them to young personnel of the *Komiteh*. Many of these automobiles were destroyed in accidents because the young drivers were not that experienced. The rest were auctioned off because they were no longer needed.

Fallahiyan and his associates wanted to structure the *Komiteh* on the model of the Central Intelligence Agency. They established garrisons, formed naval and air force units, and purchased helicopters and boats. Since there was no control or supervision over their decisions and activities, every official acted according to his own taste and desires and purchased things as he wished. Government and parliament did not have any role in the process. As a result, the *Komiteh* bought a large amount of weapons, and sent a number of *pasdars* to foreign-language classes so that they could negotiate arms deals with other countries. Only God knows what kind of deals they made during those years and how much was spent. This trend continued even after Fallahiyan moved to the Ministry of Information. In fact, under his tenure the Information Ministry looked and acted more like a commerce department that an intelligence organization.

Seeing and hearing about these sorts of excessive expenses and waste disturbed me very much, but I felt helpless and couldn't do anything. In the past there was some wooden and old furniture in the office of the director of the *Komiteh*. Mr. Fallahiyan got rid of it all and replaced it with glass desks and tables. He also had a treadmill that he used to exercise while he talked and worked.

---

[245] These figures are approximate and not the actual amounts.

I wrote all these issues in detail in my resignation letter and hoped that everyone understood that we were not a "gang" or an elite group in the *Komiteh* and that I considered any such attitude treason to the revolutionary regime. I also mentioned the wasteful policies some authorities followed and the luxurious lifestyle they had adopted, the bulletproof automobiles they had purchased, and bodyguards they had hired, and in short warned them all that these were not our objectives when we struggled and established the revolutionary government. I brought their attention to the financial difficulties our people experienced as a result of the war [with Iraq] and asked them to pay a visit to the cemeteries that they might take heed. Interestingly, they wasted all these resources and followed such a lifestyle, but when someone criticized them they would respond, "We are the representatives of the Vali Faqih, and we decide how to live and work, and others also should act as we decide."

I did not believe in such arguments, nor did I follow such a lifestyle. I acted on the basis of logic and reason. If I was ordered to do something that was against common sense and the command of reason, I refused to carry out the command. I did not accept or follow any unreasonable order just because they said they were the representative of the Vali Faqih (Imam Khomeini) and I should obey whatever they say. I also challenged them to go to the Vali Faqih, and if he condoned what they said and did, I would obey his order without question. I knew that this would never happen.

In any case, I signed and sealed my resignation letter and went to Isfahani's office and asked him to give the letter to Mr. Fallahiyan, but he asked me to take it to him myself. I told him that I acted as the chain of command required, and since he was my "superior officer" it was his duty to deliver the letter to Mr. Fallahiyan.

The War Front

After all difficulties I experienced in the *Komiteh* I concluded that the best place for me to serve was in the war front. But for several reasons I did not get a chance to go to the front. First of all was my physical condition. I was still in pain because of the injuries inflicted on me by SAVAK and was still limping. I couldn't be very useful in the front, especially because I wished to participate in the war actively. Moreover, I was critical of some policies regarding the continuation of the war. I believed that we could conclude the war with much better conditions. In consideration of mediation by notable political figures like the Foreign Minister of Algeria and Yasir Arafat, I believed that the time was right to end the war, granted that Saddam Hossein would be punished and Iran would be compensated for war damages. But some authorities were not content with such preconditions. They repeated a slogan and argued that "The road to Quds (Jerusalem) and the White House will go through Karbala!" Under the circumstances I did not believe in such slogans and argued that the fact that the Arab states approached us for peace was in itself a testimony to our victory. They would not take any further step. The demand for Saddam's punishment was just an ideal but was not a realistic expectation. The Arab states never agreed to do anything against Saddam. When he threatened their interests and those of the United States, they attacked Iraq and removed him from power. The continuation of the war with Iraq was not in our best interests. We lost a lot of our assets and heroes like [Mostafa] Chamran and many others like him. And finally another reason for my inability to go to the war front was my age and family attachments and responsibilities. I did my best to contribute financially to the war effort and provide material and logistic support.

Ups and Downs

In the middle of 1362/1983 when I quit my job at the *Komiteh* I was in a terrible financial situation. Had I been single, I would have tolerated the situation, but I was married and had a family to take care of. Several days I stayed home and did not go out at all. I was not willing to use my connections and ask for what was my legitimate right. I decided to rely on God and go through the crisis alone. It was not easy to stay home all day, so I often left home in the morning and went to the bazaar and met old friends.

Around this time I heard some people saying that we executed many young people and still dared come to the bazaar and roam around freely. It hurt me greatly to hear this sort of allegation but there was nothing I could do. I couldn't start a business in the bazaar because I did not have the capital. But I needed to keep myself busy and earn a living.

One day I went to a shop that my friend Ahmad Maleki owned. He bought and sold papers. I spent most of the day in his shop and worked like a store assistant. Whenever Maleki went out, he put me in charge, and I managed the store as though it was my own. I never asked for, nor did I receive, a penny as wage or compensation. Sometimes my friends went out for lunch. I made all kinds of excuses not to join them because I could not afford it, and my dignity did not allow me to let someone else pay for me.

One day Mr. Maleki asked for my reason for not going for lunch with them and I explained it to him. He convinced me to allow him to pay for my lunch. I accepted granted that I would pay him back when I made enough money and started to join the group for lunch after that.

I borrowed some money and resolved my family's immediate financial problems. There was always some money at home and I never let my wife find out my financial situation lest she get anxious. I suspect that she had sensed the situation but pretended that everything was normal, and she never asked me for anything extraordinary. Even for our wedding I just bought her a ring for 500 *tumans* and a wristwatch for 300 *tumans*. Until 1369–1370/1990–1991 I did not buy her anything else.

I also tried to preserve my dignity and keep my head high. I didn't like to let people find out I was in need. One of my brothers-in-law (Mr. Akbar Badamchiyan) was a carpet dealer, and when he found out that I was out of work, he tried to give my wife (his sister) some money, but she did not accept. He also wanted to give me money on a couple of occasions, and I thanked him but did not accept. Another time my other brother-in-law (Mr. Asadullah Badamchiyan) gave me a check in the amount of 150,000 *tumans* and insisted that I should accept it. Although I needed the money badly, I did not accept his gift. I knew that my wife's family was, more or less, aware of my financial situation. To change their perception, one day I went to my brother-in-law's store (Akbar Badamchiyan) and told him that I have a few hundred thousand *tumans* and wished to invest in the carpet business. As I predicted, he needed time to think about this suggestion, as I could guess. A few days later he agreed to help me, but I said that I had invested the money in the paper business. By this maneuver I believe I was able to change the perception of my brothers-in-law and all members of my wife's family.

This situation continued for a while until Mr. Maleki and a couple of other friends helped me and I bought a printing press machine to produce cover pages for books and notebooks. I rented a small shop from Mr. Hossein Talib for 2000 *tumans* a month and I started working. Thus I became a businessman. That profession had its own difficulties and politics. Paper was rationed back then. The co-ops that were in charge of the distribution and sales of paper were controlled by its president and board members. They did not like a person with a history of political activity, and even though I was in this business before the Revolution, they did not take into account my background and experience.

So I decided to turn to the [black] market. The official price of a roll of plastic at that time was around 700–800 *tumans*, but I had to pay double that price for it in the open market. Therefore, the cover sheets I produced cost me twice as much. I produced over 300 thousand book covers in a short time, but I was not able to compete with them. People who knew me did not believe that I was in that business to earn a living and thought that it was a means to cover up my political activities. Some even told me openly that I was a government spy or an agent of the Ministry of Information and Intelligence, and that the kind of business I started could not provide a reliable and sufficient source of income to meet my expenses. Some others jokingly told me that I was on the payroll of the said Ministry anyway and did not have to work to make a living. In short, I had to listen to all kinds of intimidating comments and hints and remain quiet.

It was very difficult for me to work on the press machine because of my age and health condition. A young and energetic worker could easily produce over 2000 cover sheets per day. Because of the pain in my leg and the bullets I had taken when I was arrested, I could hardly produce about 800 cover sheets. To compensate, I had to work long hours, often until ten p.m. after all other shops closed. Sometime I became very depressed when I reflected on my ordeal. Some nights when I worked alone, tears would gush forth and I cried in silence and wondered why I was in that situation. Sometimes I whispered as though I was talking to God, "O God! You know whatever I did and said was for Your sake and my silence is also for Your sake. But I do not know why I have to work that hard in my old age and do not understand why You subjected me to all these trials!"

Many people and friends came to me during those days with all types of business proposals and partnerships. I knew that they wished to use my political connections for their own benefit, and I never accepted such proposals. The general-manager of a plastic production factory made a lucrative suggestion. He was willing to put enough materials at my disposal and asked only for 20% of the profit. Another friend offered me five tons of plastic materials. I knew that they wanted to do me favors because of my political activities in the past. I thanked them but did not accept their help. Perhaps I was naïve. In the meantime, all the book covers I produced remained in the storage for over two years and did not sell. Thus, I lost quite a bit of capital in my paper business. Perhaps that was ordained to be my destiny. I spent another year in that business and made a small amount of money until I ran out of paper. Meanwhile, Mr. Talib decided to sell his store, and he preferred that I buy it from him. He asked 5 million *tumans* for it. Obviously, I did not have that amount. I asked him to give me twenty-four hours' time so that I could evacuate his store and he agreed. I took some of the furniture and store equipment to my brother's shop and the rest to other friend's storage rooms. I sold the press machine for 600 thousand *tumans* and received the amount in installment. Surprisingly, a month later the same machine was bought and sold in the bazaar for over one million *tumans*!

*   *   *

After closing my shop and selling all the equipment, I spent some time in the bazaar and worked in a printing press factory. Eventually, I began to print and sell letterheads and official forms and receipts for the Interest-Free Loan institution. Thank God, I managed to make a living.

I am content before my conscience. My only happiness is that I rebelled against injustice and struggled to see justice and equality established in our society. God knows best.

*   *   *

CHAPTER TWELVE

The Mujahidin-i Khalq Organization of Iran

Historical Background

The origin of the Mujahidin-i Khalq Organization goes back to student activists such as Mohammad Hanifnezhad,[246] Sa'id Mohsen,[247] Ali Asghar Badi'zadegan, 'Abdi, and a few others.

After the arrest of a few founding members of the Iran Freedom movement like Mehdi Bazargan, Ezzatullah Sahabi and several of its student members of such as Mohammad Hanifnezhad and Sa'id Mohsen in 1341/1962, an environment was created within which exchange of opinions and association with other political groups became possible.

The young and energetic students who did not see any positive results of parliamentary and reformist struggle began to express their opposition to the prevailing conditions.

After the uprising of 15 Khordad 1342/June 5, 1963 this generation concluded that peaceful and legal opposition would not be effective, and the idea of "armed struggle" came into being. Hence, in his declaration, Mehdi Bazargan declared that the Iran Freedom Movement would be the last group that remained loyal to the Constitution [of 1905–1906] and warned the government that it should expect opposition groups that would not believe in the constitutional and parliamentary struggle. It was in reference to this declaration that the

---

[246] Mohammad Hanifnezhad (b.1317/1937) graduated from the School of Agriculture at Tehran University, started his activities in student organizations, joined the Iran Freedom movement, and was arrested in 1341/1962. He founded the MKO in 1344/1965. After six years of activities, he was arrested and executed in Khordad 1351/June 1972.

[247] Sa'id Mohsen (b. 1318/1939) graduated from the School of Engineering at Tehran University and joined the National Front in 1340/1961 and a little later the Iran Freedom Movement. He spent some time in prison, and then worked at different jobs, eventually being hired by the Interior Ministry. He was one of the founding members of the MKO, and after six years of activity was arrested and executed in Khordad 1351/June 1972.

Mujahidin-i Khalq later announced that they did not believe in the Bazargan style of struggle and accused him of supporting capitalism. They regarded Bazargan's declaration as a turning point that marked the end of peaceful struggle and the beginning of armed struggle. The young prisoners agreed that after their release they would search for a new way to attain their goals. Once they were freed, they began to hold numerous meetings in which they studied political treatises, manifestos, and the history of liberation movements in different parts of the world.

Early in 1347/1968 the Mujahidin began to recruit members mostly on the university campuses. They identified prospective members in their gatherings or in social events like hiking and then accepted them for membership in the organization. They started training individuals in their book-reading sessions that included leftist literature as well as the Qur'an and the *Nahj al-Balaghah*, followed by writings by Ayatullah [Seyyed Mohammad Hossein] Tabataba'i, [Murteza] Mutahhari, and Rafsanjani and continued by reading and analyzing writings on the Palestinian resistance movement.

In the beginning of 1347/1968 some members of the organization began to express opposition to the degree of emphasis the organization placed on theoretical training. They argued that they did not wish to become philosophers and intellectuals, but demanded action. From the outset they had intended to adopt armed struggle as their strategy. This position was in conflict with the views of the more religious elements, but the majority argued that the ends justified the means. They began to promote opposition among the ordinary people and to that effect considered philanthropic activities such as helping the poor as counter-revolutionary. For example, they argued that if a car ran into an accident and the driver was killed, his family would suffer, and such suffering should be translated into opposition to the government.

With this mindset they used religion as long as it helped their cause and made some advancement in the process.

586

But later on they turned to Marxism and argued that it was the best guideline for struggle, and that religion was no longer able to help their cause. Their most important priority was struggle, especially struggle against capitalism and imperialism. In my opinion, theirs was not a struggle between the truth and falsehood. Their role models were popular movements and organizations such as the Front for the Liberation of Palestine, the Liberation Front of Algeria, and the Liberation Movement of the Viet Kong. Their objective was not to establish an Islamic government but one modeled after the Algerian example. They had concluded from the beginning that their ideal was not to establish a social system based on religion. However, they did not discuss it openly because such a position would have cost them popular support and ended in their isolation. Therefore, they believed that they should educate and lead the people and prepare them for accepting a new kind of social system.

Abd al-Reza Nikbeen Rudsari, known as "Hasan Nikbeen," and Abdi,[248] "the Engineer," was one of the founding members of the Mujahidin organization, who eventually turned left and adopted Marxism. He criticized the organization's dual [ideological] character. In his view, the organization was neither Islamist nor a Marxist organization, and religion was used only as its superstructure. He did not wish to, nor could he, continue his activities under such a situation and left the organization. His departure was the first heavy blow against the MKO. After that his name was deleted as a founding member of the organization. Parviz Ya'qubi, one of Mujahidin leaders, told me in prison that until 1350/1971, when he was arrested, he was in regular contact with and often met Ab-

---

[248] Abd al-Reza Nikbeen Rudsari, known as "Abdi" and "Hasan Nikbeen," joined Hanifnezhad and Sa'id Mohsen in 1342/1963. He was a theoretician and a founding member of the MKO. He wrote some of the early treatises of the organization, such as "What Is to Be Done?" and "What Is Struggle?" Shortly afterward he adopted Marxism and left the organization and was replaced by Asghar Badi'zadegan. His departure was a heavy blow to the organization.

587

di in Tehran. He worked in a company. Once Ya'qubi asked Abdi to return to the organization and resume his activities on the condition they keep their ideological stands independent of each other. Abdi did not accept his suggestion and never got engaged in armed activities. Apparently, he was once arrested in a demonstration in 1352–1353/1974–1975 and was sentenced to eighteen months in prison. When he was released, he left political life and got married, and his name never appeared anywhere in the Mujahidin's declarations or publications.

Abdi had a truly leading role in the translation of Marxist texts. Ya'qubi mentioned that after Abdi left, he went to meet Mehdi Bazargan and asked him to collaborate with the Mujahidin's struggle to develop their ideology, and they were even willing to pay him for that service. Mr. Bazargan refused, as he believed the Mujahidin were a deviated group. Bazargan told Ya'qubi that affiliation with the MKO demanded an underground lifestyle, and he wished to follow his own personal life as he pleased.

The Hijacking Operation

In their struggle to attain a status like that of the al-Fath organization, in 1349/1970 the Mujahidin decided to send their members to al-Fath training camps in Lebanon and Syria. In Aban/October of that year, a dangerous incident took place in relation to that plan. A few members of the organization established a base in Dubai in search of a way to enter Lebanon. Out of lack of experience and carelessness, they had taken some forged passports, birth certificates, and seals, and some communist literature there. They spent some time in Dubai wandering around. Toward the end of their stay in Dubai a few incidents of robbery was reported to the police. The authorities identified the Mujahidin members as prime suspects and arrested and imprisoned them. They searched their residence and found the forged documents. At that time the UAE was still under British control, and the police worked under British supervision. In prison with collaboration of the cleaning crew, the six arrested Mujahids[249] were able to contact their comrades and were told that a few people would come to Dubai to rescue them from prison. They also found out that the Iranian government had sent a team and an aircraft to transfer the arrested Mujahids to Iran. In the process of transferring the prisoners to the airport three other MKO members somehow found their way into the aircraft.[250] Before entering Iran territories over the Persian Gulf, the three-member rescue team hijacked the aircraft and through Kuwait took it to Iraq. The Iraqi government did not permit the aircraft to land at the airport, and the pilot was forced to land in the middle of the desert in Iraq. Since Iran and Iraq were not on good terms at the time, the Iraqi government welcomed the hijackers but soon arrested and imprisoned them because they were not willing to cooperate with the government and refused to give interviews to avoid revealing their identities. The Iraqi government became suspicious and concluded that the arrested individuals might be spies. They took them to a detention center and tortured them severely but failed to force them to reveal their identities. They only stated that they were Iranian citizens and wished to go to Lebanon or Syria. Finally, al-Fath interceded on their behalf and convinced Iraq to release them to go to Lebanon. During those years a total of thirty to thirty-two Mujahids were able to go to Lebanon and Syria, where they received military training in Palestinian bases and then returned to Iran.

---

[249] The six arrested Mujahids were Musa Khiyabani, Kazem Shafi'iha, Hossein Khoshroo, Mahmud Shamekhi, Jalil Seyyed Ahmadian, and Mohsen Nejat Hosseini. See Nejat Hosseini, pp. 92–96.

[250] The three included Abd al-Rasool Meshkinfam, Mohammad Sadat Darbandi, and Hossein Ahmadi Rouhani, who led the operation. See Nejat Hosseini, p. 143.

Shahrivar 1350/August 1971: A Heavy Blow

Toward the end of 1349/1970 a few members of [Bizhan] Jazani's group went to the Caspian Sea regions in northern Iran to study the strategic situation of the region for their future operations. They settled in the forest of the Siyahkal region. Several days later they ran out of provisions. They sent two people to the nearest town to purchase food and other items they needed. On their way, the rural police became suspicious of them, and a conflict broke out between them. The two individuals were injured or probably killed. When the rest of the team heard the news, they concluded that the police discovered their location, and out of desperation they came into a conflict with the police, and few of them were killed and the rest were injured and arrested. Perhaps if they had not miscalculated the subsequent events would have never taken place.

The group that was identified as the Siyahkal group in their trial changed their name to the Fidayan Guerrilla Organization (*Cherik-ha-ye Fadayee-ye khalq*). The emergence of this organization created a sense of inferiority among the Mujahidin. They reduced their theoretical and educational activities and turned more to action. For this purpose they needed weapons and ammunition. From that date on, Allahmorad Delfani began to be involved more and more in the MKO's activities.

The founding members of the MKO were introduced to Delfani in prison in 1341–1342/1963-1964. He was a former member of the Tudeh Party who later collaborated with SAVAK. Thanks to his friendship with the Mujahidin that started in prison, after his release from prison he infiltrated the MKO, won their trust, and began to associate with them.

After the Siyahkal incident the Mujahidin expanded their activities and initiated extensive terrorist operations during the celebration of 2500 years of Persian monarchy. For this purpose they needed arms and ammunitions, so they approached Delfani. He had promised to provide whatever they needed through his connections in Iran's western border regions, especially in Kurdistan. To further attract the trust of the MKO, he took several Mujahids to Kermanshah and showed them to a few armed men who belonged to SAVAK and claimed that they were under his command. After that, the Mujahidin trusted him completely and told him what they needed. On a couple of occasions, he actually gave them some arms and ammunitions. Interestingly, these weapons came from SAVAK, but he claimed he had brought them from Afghanistan or Palestine. Of course, SAVAK knew well what it was doing and always gave them sub-standard arms and often the wrong bullets. Delfani also taught the Mujahidin a few tactical lessons and security measures he had learned during his training in SAVAK. He advised them to use fake names and how to use telephones. Once he entered a garage accompanied by a woman whom he claimed was his wife. The lady carried some weapons under her veil (*chador*). The Mujahidin realized that women can play an important role in their activities, and they began to recruit women and placed them in their team houses.

Shortly before the celebrations marking 2500 years of Persian monarchy, Delfani contacted the Mujahidin to inquire about their plan during that event. They told him that they needed some weapons as they had planned some operations. SAVAK learned about the Mujahidin's plan and decided to abort their operations. One night SAVAK conducted extensive raids on several team houses. Had SAVAK known about the limited capabilities of the Mujahidin, it would probably have delayed its operations against them, waiting to get more information and to arrest more of its members. But SAVAK had found out that the Mujahidin received arms from Syria and Lebanon. So without any hesitation they attacked seven or eight team houses and arrested several members of the organization's central committee. Only a few leaders of the organization survived, including Hanifnezhad, Ahmad Reza'ie, and Seyyedi Kashani. He was the oldest leader of the MKO, and others called him "Seyyed Baba Kashani." Incidentally, Delfani disappeared after this date.[251]

The remaining members of the organization were caught by surprise but could not remain quiet after the arrest of their comrades. They decided to find a way to free them from prison. After much discussion and deliberation, they decided to kidnap Prince Shafiq,[252] the son of Princess Ashraf. They argued that since the Shah was helpless before his sister, he could not resist her pressure to make a deal with the Mujahidin and get her son released. They had planned to hijack another airplane and transfer Prince Shafiq to Palestine, Jordan, or Syria. This was the first operation of its kind. They had no previous experience in such operations and did not have an opportunity to receive training. They rented a car and started their operations.

Prince Shafiq was very athletic and resisted his kidnappers. Bullets were exchanged between the two sides. An old man who worked as a custodian of an adjacent building was killed. When the police arrived, the kidnappers fled the scene. The police recorded the automobile's license number, and after investigation it turned out that Badi'zadegan[253] had

---

[251] Allahmorad Delfani, from Kermanshah, was a member of the Tudeh Party. A sophisticated young man with a mysterious history of political activity, he reportedly spied for Iraq for a while, then joined the MKO and attracted the confidence of its leadership. He identified the leadership and many members of the organization and with a wealth of information and finally chose to work for the SAVAK. After the victory of the Revolution, the Mujahidin located Delfani and killed him.

[252] Shahram Pahlavinia (b. 1317/1937) studied political science, then entered the business world. He had shares in more than twenty business enterprises, including night clubs, construction companies, and distribution services, and became very wealthy. See, Mohammad Mehrayeen, *Memoirs.* See also *Fasl nameh-ye mutali'at Tarikhi,* #2, pp. 283–301.

[253] Ali Asghar Badi'zadegan (b.1319/1940) graduated from the School of Engineering at Tehran University, and after serving in the army, joined the faculty of that school as an instructor and taught chemistry. He was another founding member of the MKO who was arrested in 1350/1971 and after

rented the car. He was arrested shortly thereafter and tortured severely. He gave SAVAK some obsolete information. Soon the policed delivered him to SAVAK. Other members of the central committee, including Seyyedi Kashani, Alireza Tashayyud, and several others were arrested. They were on their way to blow up a power station that supplied electricity to Tehran. To mislead the police they had placed several bottles of alcoholic drinks in the trunk of their car and pretended to be drunk and even offered drinks to the police agents. The agents searched their car's trunk and found several backpacks and tennis shoes and arrested them. Tashayyud began to argue with the police and tried to disarm an agent. But the police shot Seyyedi Kashani and arrested the rest of the team. After this adventure Ahmad Reza'ie,[254] the only surviving member of the central committee of the organization, began to reorganize the remaining members of the organization.

A Vessel in a Storm

Between August and late October 1971, SAVAK inflicted heavy blows to the Mujahidin organization and created a critical situation for its leadership inside prison and outside of it. After Mohammad Hanifnezhad's arrest, extensive debates surfaced among members of the organization. Some believed that Hanifnezhad had not resisted torture and had put a lot of information at SAVAK's disposal. According to their argument, Hanifnezhad believed that if the Mujahidin could be so vulnerable and arrested so easily despite their activities and experiences, those with less experience would either turn to com-

---

much torture was executed in Khordad 1351/June 1972. See Deldam, p. 115, *Kayhan*, #10736–10737, and *Sharq*, #207–208.

[254] Ahmad Reza Reza'ie (b. 1325/1946) is another son of the Reza'ie family. He started his political activity at a young age and joined the MKO and became one of its most important leaders. A capable organizer and fundraiser, he was killed in 1350/1971 in a street clash with the police after killing three agents. He was the first martyr of the MKO. See Nejat Hosseini, p. 308, *Chesm Andaz-e Iran*, #12, pp. 36–40, and *Tarikhche-ye Paydayesh...*, p. 20.

munism or become passive and be destroyed. Therefore, in his opinion, it would be better for most activists to be arrested and have their will power tested, and then decide to continue the struggle. Otherwise, they had better leave politics and go about their own lives. Hanifnezhad's friends shared these arguments with me in prison. They claimed that he tried to convince all members that the MKO was done with and those who were active outside of prison were not capable of continuing the struggle inside prison, and that SAVAK knew everything about them. According to their claim, Hanifnezhad recommended that they should not bother to continue their struggle.

During the period that I associated with the Muhjahidin, the leading figures of the organization, such as Bahram Aram,[255] Mohsen Fazil, Vahid Afrakhteh, Abbad Javdani, Mohammad Yazdani (Yazdanian), and a few others believed that Hanifnezhad had betrayed them and had reported them to SAVAK. In my opinion, however, Hanifnezhad was the best and the purest of them all, and SAVAK had independently infiltrated the organization and collected information about its members, and if Hanifnezhad had shown weakness before SAVAK, he had their best interests in mind and wished to save them from torture and trouble.

There was also a second perspective that preferred to see the Mujahidin continue their struggle even if they turned to communism, for it would be better than becoming passive in prison and getting disillusioned. For the proponent of this view, continuation of the struggle was the most important thing. They did not see any problem in their collaboration with

---

[255] Bahram Aram (b. 1328/1949) started his political activity while he attended the Sharif Technical University in Tehran, joined Ahmad Reza'ie, and through him became a member of the MKO. He attended Dr. Shari'ati's lectures in Hosseiniyyah Irsah for a while but eventually played a leading role in the ideological transformation of the organization and became a Marxist. He was involved in the kidnapping and killing of Majid Sharif Vaqifi. He was killed in a street clash with security forces in Aban 1355/October 1976.

Marxist forces. Reza Reza'ie[256] supported this view, so he was willing to do anything to stay out of prison.

Some people also expressed doubt and were pessimistic about the manner of Reza Reza'ie's escape from prison. They argued that his escape was made possible as a result of his collaboration with SAVAK. I do not believe that was true, and his death in the hands of SAVAK in the spring of 1352/1973 proves my argument. He in fact fooled the SAVAK agents and fled. Other members of the MKO in prison had concluded that they should do anything it takes to go out of prison, revive their organization, and reorganize its members. However, if they were unable to do so they should join the Fidayan-i Khalq and put all their assets at their disposal.

SAVAK knew that a person of Ahmad Reza'ie's caliber could reorganize the MKO and provide effective leadership and concluded that they should stop him at any price. Some people believed that SAVAK arranged Reza Reza'ie's escape so that through him they could have access to Ahmad and arrest him. However, the Mujahidin members believed that Reza escaped to transmit his experiences to other members who were out of prison. It was with this plan in mind that Reza pretended to collaborate with SAVAK and fooled them, assuring them that he would persuade Ahmad and other Mujahids to introduce themselves to SAVAK. In any case, it is not actually known to what extent Reza Reza'ie's escape was engineered by SAVAK, but they took Reza out and stayed in his house a few nights so that they could arrest Ahmad. A few days later the SAVAK agents took Reza to a public bath on Buzarjomehri Avenue, where reportedly he was going to meet

---

[256] Reza Reza'ie (b. 1327/1948) joined the MKO while he was a student at the School of Dentistry at Tehran University. He received some training in Jordan but was arrested in 1350. He escaped from prison in 1350/1971 and resumed his activities. On Khordad 1352/June 15, 1973 he was injured in a clash with security forces and according to one report committed suicide to avoid arrest. See *Tarikhche-ye Goruhak-ha*, and Nejat Hosseini, pp. 305–307.

Ahmad. This bath had an entrance and a separate exit door. Reza fooled the agents and escaped through the other door and joined his brother Ahmad. Their collaboration did not last too long, because soon Ahmad's location was discovered, and fighting broke out between him and the SAVAK agents, and Ahmad was martyred. He was thus the first martyr of the organization. Shortly after that Reza Reza'ie who had gone to the house of his brother (Mehdi) was killed in an armed conflict with the police.

Reza Reza'ie and other leading members of the MKO did not advocate an "ideological struggle" per se. For them the struggle was the central goal, and they never claimed that they intended to establish an Islamic government. At most they talked about an egalitarian and classless society whose main objective would be struggle against imperialism. They declared that any group and ideological current whose main goal was to fight against imperialism would be their natural ally and they could work side by side with them. However, any religious or non-religious group that opposed them or their allies was considered reactionary and a natural ally of imperialism. Thus, individuals like Mutahhari and 'Allamah Tabataba'i fell into that category, and studying their books was forbidden for all members of the organization except members of the central committee. When I asked them about this position, they said that if such writings were of any use for the purpose of the struggle, these individuals should have been on the forefront of anti-imperialist struggle. They ruled out the effectiveness of such writings because of their position against communism. Therefore, in their opinion reading these books would be harmful and poisonous for the rank-and-file members of the organization. In prison they read books like *Man: A generation of Monkeys* and *How Man Became a Bugbear*. They also read Dr. Yadullah Sahabi's book titled *The Book of Evolution* but criticized that for its unscientific approach.

This was the status and position of the high-ranking members of the organization, most of whom were arrested and executed or were killed in clashes with the security forces. Outside prison the surviving members of the organization such as Farhad Safa,[257] Bahram Aram, Vahid Afrakhteh, Mohsen Fazil, and a few others wished to learn from the experiences of the old leadership and fill the vacuum that had been created in the organization and revive and reorganize it.

The Process of Ideological Transformation

Taqi Shahram[258] was among those members of the Mujahidin organization who were arrested in Shahrivar 1350/August 1971. He was sentenced to ten years and transferred to a prison in the city of Sari in Mazandaran. In prison he was introduced to Hasan Ezzati, a member of the group called The Red Star, also known as Toofan ("Storm"), and they became good friends. Together they won the friendship of Lieutenant Ahmadian, but SAVAK remained uninformed of their friendship. SAVAK's policy often was to send political prisoners in groups of ten or twenty to different prisons in such cities as Burazjan, Kermanshah, Shiraz, and Mashhad. It was a mystery

---

[257] Farhad Safa (b. 1326/1047) was raised by his grandfather, Ayatullah Fayz, and attended the School of Agriculture at Tehran University. He joined the MKO in 1346/1967. He was arrested in 1350/1971 and spent three years in prison. After his release he worked in Ahvaz, but soon came to Tehran and resumed his activity with the Mujahidin. After 1354/1975 he reorganized the Islamist faction of the MKO but was killed mysteriously in 1354/1975, reportedly during a clash with security forces. See Ahmad Ahmad, *Memoirs,* p. 366.

[258] Mohammad Taqi Shahram (b. 1326/1947) studied mathematics at Tehran University, where he joined the MKO and started his political activity. He studied Marxism in prison and associated frequently with the leftist groups. Later he adopted Marxism and played a leading role in the ideological transformation of the MKO. He also participated in the murder of Sharif Vaqifi. After the victory of the Revolution he established the Paykar group and rebelled against the Islamic government. He was arrested in 1359/1980 and executed in Tir 1359/July 1980 on charges of the assassination of Sharif Vaqifi and several government agents. See *Tarikhvhe-ye Paydayesh...,* pp. 29–32, Njeat Hosseini, pp. 320 and 414, Ahmad, *Memoirs,* pp. 462–463.

597

and quite unusual in this case why they sent Shahram, a *Mujahid*, and Ezzati, a *Marxist* to Sari prison. One night when Lieutenant Ahmadian was the commanding night officer in prison, he replaced the night guards and called the two prisoners into his office. He managed to escape with Shahram and Ezzati. Reportedly, Ahmadian had leftist tendencies. The three of them took a considerable amount of arms and ammunitions from the prison depot with them.

In 1352/1973 Shahram gathered Vahid Afrakhteh, Hasan Fazil, and other surviving members of the MKO around him to reassess the organization's situation. He had concluded that religion was not of much help in their political struggle and eventually would lead to conservatism and passivity. His ideas appealed to people around him and gradually created doubt in their minds about the effectiveness of religion as a political ideology. Shahram then wrote a treatise titled *Ideological Transformation of the Mujahidin-i Khalq Organization* and officially declared the Mujahidin as a Marxist organization. Those who were in prison at that time were not brave enough to openly declare their new orientation. If they performed daily prayer—often without making ablution—it was out of expediency and for political considerations. They pretended to read the Qur'an and *Nahj al-Balaghah*, but in reality they never read them. Among the leading members of this new perspective were Kazim Shafi'iha and Hasan Rahi[259]from Mashhad Prison, Zayn al-'Abidin Haqqani and Alireza Zemorrodiyan from Shiraz, and Ahmad Banasazi and Bahman Bazargani from the central committee of the organization. They openly declared their new Marxist position, rejected religion, and stopped performing prayers.

---

[259] Hasan Rahi (b. 1325) graduated from the School of Engineering at Tehran University and joined the MKO. He was arrested in 1350/1971 and received a ten-year prison term. He later adopted Marxism but did not publicize it until 1354/1975. He was released from prison in 1357/1978 and joined the *Rah-e kargar* group. See Ja'fariyan, pp. 433 and 737, *Tarikhche-ye Mukhtasar-r goruhak-ha*, p. 146.

The new Marxist Mujahidin were scattered in prisons throughout the country. SAVAK gathered and transferred most of them to Qasr Prison in Tehran, and took their leading members to Evin Prison to limit their contact. Gradually differences appeared among members of the new current. Some of them believed that they should continue to pray and adopt a wait-and-see attitude for another year or two. However, *the genie was out of the bottle,* so to speak. The ideological transformation of the organization had been declared, and the news spread around and attracted quite a bit of support outside prison. It was a "done deal" and there was no further need for covering it up.

Outside of prison and in reaction to this change, Islamist members of the organization like Majid Sharif Vaqifi,[260] Murteza Samadiyyeh Labbaf,[261] and Sa'id Shahsavandi began to oppose and resist the new changes. Expectedly, they were criticized and attacked by the new leadership. They labeled Sharif Vaqifi as a *petit-bourgeois* and took away his weapons. They sent him to work as a simple laborer in a brick factory outside Tehran so that *he could purify himself of petit-bourgeois traits.* There were some rumors that Majid had hit a

---

[260] Majid Sharif Vaqifi (b. 1317/1938) graduated in electrical engineering from Sharif Technical University in Tehran, where he joined the MKO. He was assassinated by a team composed of Vahid Afrakhteh, Mohsen Khamooshi, and a few others, who set fire to his body to prevent its identification.

[261] Murteza Samadiyyeh Labbaf (b. 1325/1946) joined the MKO while he was studying engineering at Tehran University. A sharp-shooter, he was in charge of the news and research department of the organization. He was the target of an assassination by the Marxist faction of the MKO but escaped their plan. He was arrested in 1353/1974 and managed to mislead the SAVAK for a while. Vahid Afrakhteh and Mohsen Khamooshi revealed his identity and gave much information about his activities to the SAVAK, as a result of which he was condemned to death and executed in Bahman 1354/February 1975. See, *Tarikhche-ye Mokhtasar-e Goruhak-ha*, pp. 171–192, Rouhani, pp. 366, 422, and 427–429. See also Ahmad Ahmad, *Memoirs*, pp. 335–336.

dead end and was disillusioned and had stopped performing daily prayers. Some said that he wanted to please the Central Committee members and pretended that he was still an Islamist. Samadiyyeh Labbaf, however, stood firm and severed his relationship with the Marxist group and joined Sharif Vaqifi. Labbaf and Majid were both from the city of Isfahan. When they met then, they decided to end their relationship with the Marxist group gradually and start a new phase in their activities. Unfortunately, under those circumstances the interest of the organization had priority over all other interests, principles, and considerations. The central committee tried to control and suppress all opposing views and actions.

It was decided that Sharif Vaqifi should marry Laila Zemorrodiyan who, in contrast to Majid, was a Marxist. Hoping to be able to influence her, Majid accepted this proposal and married Laila. Trusting his wife, he shared some of his aspirations and plans with her, not realizing that Laila shared them with Taqi Shahram and Bahram Aram. Laila's brother, Alireza, was the first Mujahid who contacted me through Majid Mehr Ayin. It was in such a manner that the Marxist faction of the organization found out all plans of the Islamist faction of the Mujahidin. Therefore, the Marxist faction decided to react and planned to purge Sharif Vaqifi and Labbaf. They arranged a rendezvous with Sharif on Adib Avenue and planned to kill him and announce that he was killed in a clash with the police. They disguised themselves as SAVAK agents and met Sharif at the designated place, shot him there, and then took his body out of town and set fire to it so that it couldn't be identified. In this bloody criminal act Taqi Shahram, Vahid Afrakhteh, and Hossein Siyah Kolah participated. They arranged another rendezvous with Labbaf in Nezam Abad district of Tehran. Around three p.m. Vahid Afrakhteh and another person whose name I do not know went to meet Labbaf. Vahid, who suffered from chronic anxiety, did not know that Labbaf had become suspicious. When they met, he began to shoot, and a bullet hit Labbaf's face, but he managed to escape the scene. Since we were in prison at that time and Labbaf did not have any friends in Tehran, he went to a relative's house that night. When the news spread, SAVAK sent a note to all the hospitals in Tehran and ordered them to report if an injured man came for treatment. Labbaf was forced to go to Sina Hospital that night, and hospital authorities reported him to the police.

I met Samadiyyeh Labbaf during his interrogation. When he was arrested, he did not give out any information. He stated that his activities were limited to writing and distributing declarations and denied that he had ever participated in military operations, whereas he participated in several operations around Mehrabad airport and killed a petit police officer there. Nobody accompanied him in that operation to find out about it. He tried and succeeded in fooling SAVAK. They hospitalized him and provided medical and dental care. Labbaf told SAVAK that the Marxist Mujahidin knew that he and Sharif wanted to surrender themselves to the authorities. To prevent that and protect the information I had, they planned to kill him, and the bullet mark on his face was a proof of his claim. He also assured them that he was willing to work for SAVAK. In short he completely fooled SAVAK and received special treatment, including a private room.

There was another person named Khalil Faqih Dezfuli. His father was a member of the clergy and prayer leader (*imam*) of a mosque. His sister, Batool, had been arrested during a conflict with the police, and his brother, Jalil, was a fugitive. Khalil had agreed to work for SAVAK and even participated in a nationally televised interview. He and Labbaf were kept in the same building. Sometimes SAVAK took them for a tour in town to locate and identify other activists. But Labbaf never identified anyone.

Labbaf also had another friend named Sa'id Shahsavandi, who was a religious activist. He was disillusioned after he witnessed the ordeal Labbaf and Sharif went through and feared that the Marxist Mujahidin might assassinate him

601

too. So he called SAVAK and asked them to arrest him. In a way, he asked for asylum. Despite all this, Labbaf resisted and for a while did not give out any information about his activities. With the arrest of Vahid Afrakhteh in 1354/1975 and his confession and subsequent collaboration with SAVAK, the situation changed drastically. Vahid gave much information about Labbaf's activities, including his involvement in killing a police officer. As a result, SAVAK began to torture Labbaf, and for a while they put him on shackles. I met him in prison in such a situation. He tried to convey a message to me, saying, "I am not a traitor and never revealed any information about anyone [to SAVAK], but be aware of Vahid. He is a traitor and has betrayed you, and me and many others." Eventually and after much resistance Labbaf was executed along with Vahid Afrakhteh and a few others.

Vahid Afrakhteh could not think that after all his services to SAVAK and betraying his comrades he would be executed. He tolerated all kinds of insult to save his life and became so intimate with SAVAK agents that he accompanied them in their missions and interrogation of prisoners. But charges against him were serious, especially his involvement in the assassination of two American military advisers in Tehran. This was an unforgiveable sin, and the regime was extremely angry about it. On the day of his execution at Chitgar military base, and when he realized that the situation was critical, he asked to meet his interrogator. He claimed that he remembered some information and wished to share it with him. His interrogator refused to see him and asked him to write down anything he wanted to share with him.

Sa'id Shahsavandi, who surrendered voluntarily and went to prison, showed a great deal of weakness and could not get along with his wife and her leftist views. He was disillusioned and lived an irresponsible life until 1357/1978. He spent his time in prison making yoghurt and earned the nickname of "Sa'id, the Yoghurt Maker." As a result of his behavior nobody took him seriously in prison, and everyone ignored him until he was released.

After officially declaring its ideological transformation to a Marxist organization, the Mujahidin carried out several operations, the most important of which was the assassination of two American military advisers, Colonel Schafer and Colonel Turner, followed by General Zandipoor's assassination. In both of these operations Vahid Afrakhteh played a leading role. The now-Marxist Mujahidin wanted to send a message out that they had freed themselves of the yoke of religion, and that thanks to their newly adopted ideology they could carry out such extraordinary operations.

The Origins of Ideological Deviation

The Mujahidin believed that only three groups in the society struggled against the existing regime. They were university students, the clergy, and the bazaar merchants. In their opinion, those three social groups did not believe in the power of the people, nor were they willing to jeopardize their own social standing and privileges. They argued that the clergy was totally dependent on the capitalist class and therefore could not lead the struggle, and that the bazaar merchants were concerned about their own interests and status before the threats of the dependent capitalist (*bourgeois comprador*) class. As to their own position, the Mujahidin stated that if they succeeded, they would nationalize industries and destroy capitalism, and argued that in the process capitalists and the clergy could unite against them. Therefore, they were determined not to let the clergy and their bazaar allies take the leadership of the struggle in their hand. Rather, they expected to use those two groups and have them accept the Mujahidin's leadership. In short, whenever it was in their interests, they used the clergy and the bazaar, and criticized them when they came into a disagreement. What was essential for the Mujahidin was that all social groups and classes that wished a change in the country's political system must accept their leadership.

The Mujahidin faced quite a few challenges and obstacles in articulating their ideology. On the one hand, they wished to attract and recruit intellectuals and university students, and on the other, they did not want to lose the support of the clergy and the bazaar merchants. The main concerns of the intellectuals and students were the economic system, infra- and supra-structures, social evolution, and other fundamental issues. Questions concerning such topics as revelation, miracles, *jinn*, and the like were not their concern. Had the clergy and the bazaar mercantile classes learned the views of the Mujahidin earlier, they probably would have declared them infidels from the beginning. Thus, the Mujahidin were torn between these two currents and social groupings, each one representing their social basis of support—one being intellectual and the other a populist. At the same time, they knew that by referring to the Qur'an and the *Nahj al-Balaghah* they could win the support of the clergy and the bazaar, but they would lose the support of students and intellectuals, who might turn to communism. So they concluded that the best way for them was to take the middle road to reconcile religion and communism. To do so they needed to provide *scientific* explanations for their ideology and prove God's existence through the *scientific* method. This became the basis of their eclecticism and eclectic ideology.

For some people who were concerned with questions about such topics as miracles and revelation, the Mujahidin argued that those issues could be explained and proven through science, but since science was not developed that far yet, it could not provide convincing elaboration for such metaphysical issues. Like many other questions to which science could not provide answers fifty years ago and are now accepted, there will be a time that science will provide answers to metaphysical questions as well. Later on, however, the Mujahidin did not even show an interest in these issues, as they argued that metaphysical questions did not solve any of the problems the society faced. Sometimes they went ahead further and said that they did not believe in such issues at all. I heard that after Hanifnezhad, Sa'id Mohsen, and Badi'zadegan were executed, their comrades held a memorial in Qezel Qal'eh Prison. During the session Hashimi Rafsanjani delivered a sermon in which he talked about the status of the *martyrs* and said that angels would welcome them to Heaven. After the memorial ended, the Mujahidin confronted him and criticized him for saying things that they did not even believe in, and stated that if Marxists and other leftist groups had been present, it would have been embarrassing to talk about such issues!

The Mujahidin collected religious taxes and alms and gave them to the leftist groups and communists. When they were confronted for such measures, they argued that the Prophet and Imam Ali would do the same thing if they lived in our time, as alms and religious taxes were measures toward fair and just distribution of wealth. They could be spent for any purposes and not just for religious causes. They tried to introduce modern heroes and symbols of martyrdom like [Ernesto] Che Guevara and apply Qur'anic verses to them, ignoring symbols like Abudhar [Ghifari], Salman [Farsi], Ammar Yasir, Bilal, and many others. The Mujahidin also approved of and supported the Fidayan-i Khalq Organization's activities, such as bank robberies, and justified and likened such operations to confiscation of properties of infidels in the early days of Islam.

This was the description of the prevailing situation in the early days of the Mujahidin's activities. After that they sent everyone to team houses, and no one could question their decisions. Each member was assigned to a function. They could not trust anybody and were not honest and sincere with the people. Their hearts were cold like an icebox. They told religious people that their goal was to establish a classless society based on *tawhid*, while they told the left that anti-imperialist struggle was their main concern.

These kinds of maneuvers and conclusions were the natural consequences of the Mujahidin's "scientific process" as they considered themselves the standard-bearers of *scientific struggle* and others as reactionaries. They tried to find correspondence between principles of dialectic materialism and verses of the Qur'an and apply them to those principles. Even in the Qur'an they were interested more in verses on *jihad* and *martyrdom*, and Chapter Nine ("Repentance," which mentions of the greater war to come) and Chapter Forty-Seven [("Mohammad," which was revealed when the Prophet fled Mecca)]. They did not show much interest in the Qur'an's ethical, moral, and humanitarian injunctions. They never believed in emulation [of a *mujtahid*], and argued that they could practice *ijtihad* themselves. In terms of faith and disbelief, they stated that the criterion for faith is not accepting and practicing the commands of religion, but struggling on the path of God, as "The path of God is the path of the people."[262] In other words, they translated the Qur'anic term *fi sabil'alLah* the same as "the path of the people!" And since Lenin and Stalin were on the path of the people, ultimately they were on the *path of God*. They argued that they could not believe that an ayatollah or a pious bazaar merchant who prays but does not struggle on the path of the people could go to Heaven, and popular leaders like Mao tse Tong, Ho Chi Minh, Che Guevara, and Fidel Castro, who sacrificed their lives for the people, will not go to Paradise. After a while, they said that they did not have an answer for questions related to Heaven and Hell.

With such a mindset the Mujahidin considered U.S. imperialism and its puppets like the Shah's regime as their prime enemy, followed by what they identified as domestic reactionary forces, including the clergy and the bazaar merchants. The assassination of American military advisers and

---

[262] They wrote the book titled *The path of the Prophets, the Path of the People.*

later of General Tahiri and Zandipoor was part of this strategy. Also, their aggressive attitude and insulting behavior toward Islamist forces and the clergy in prison was a reflection of this mindset.

The anti-American position of the Mujahidin was so extreme that communist groups called them more "anti-imperialist" than the communists! They considered all anti-imperialist forces as their natural allies regardless of the ideological stand of those forces, and viewed the enemies of America as their own enemies, and were determined to struggle against them. They labeled their opponents as reactionary, and for this reason they boycotted all books written by such scholars as Mutahhari, 'Allamah Tabataba'i, and Seyyed Qutb.

I did not believe that an individual like Taqi Shahram could change the ideology of an organization single-handedly, and reorient it to adopt Marxism. If other members of the leadership had not supported such a transformation, such a change would not have been possible. I did not believe that a *coup d'état* took place in the organization. Rather, in my opinion, such a transformation was the natural result of the nature of the Mujahidin's ideology. Sooner or later, they were destined to reach that end anyway. The most credit one can give Shahram was his ability to expedite the process. Even before Shahram started to act, Marxist ideology had penetrated deeply into the organization. The Mujahidin felt a natural strategic alliance with the Marxist forces. Shahram was only a catalyst in the process.

In reaction to the activities of the Marxist faction, some friends of Hanifnezhad decided to form a group to study Marxism and stop the spread of their ideas. When Dr. Sarukhani (who is now a sergeant) came to prison, he said that Hanifnezhad asked him not to disturb the communists and to leave them alone. Hanifnezhad had also told Reza Reza'ie that in case he found any aspirant outside prison, he should introduce him to the Fidayan organization. The question was whether the Mujahidin knew that Fidayan were communists. If they did, why did they justify communist activities? The fact that the Mujahidin gave priority to political struggle over ideological may indicate that their claim to advocate Islamic doctrine was just a baseless claim. In any case, the Mujahidin were doctrinally and in practice in strategic alliance with the Marxists and considered them anti-imperialists, and consequently natural allies. They argued that in that phase of the struggle, whoever opposed the Marxists deviated from the path of the struggle and must be boycotted, and that America was the only enemy to fight against.

The Mujahidin's other error and deviation in the period under review was their argument that whoever accepted their struggle against American imperialism would be counted as a member of the organization, regardless of being religious or non-religious. Some of their members even accepted that condition granted that religion played the central role in the organization's activities and that non-religious elements must not participate in the decision-making process. Clearly this was not logical, because if Marxist groups did not participate in the decision-making process, why would they agree to collaborate with the Mujahidin? Moreover, as the Marxist groups did not accept religious activists as their members, why should religious groups accept them as members of their group? Other Mujahidin members argued that their ideal model was al-Fath organization, and not all its members were religious or even Muslim. According to them al-Fath struggled as a national revolutionary organization. In short, they believed that since our country was occupied by a hostile force, fighting against it was a priority, and under the circumstances religion was not that important. These debates continued in prison and outside and the Mujahidin never had convincing answers for any of these questions.

Some observers believed that after 1350/1971 and the arrest of many leading and experienced members of the MKO, there remained no experienced person to guard the political direction and ideological integrity of the organization. According to this view, if the founding members of the organization were alive, such deviations would have not taken place. I, however, believe that even if the founders were alive, deviation would have taken place anyway, albeit with some delay. Many of the early texts of the Mujahidin were Marxist sources that were translated into Persian by Abdi, the Engineer. For example the book titled *Principles of Economics in a Simple Language* was a Marxist text. When some members criticized that book, they were told that it represented Asgarizadeh's personal opinions and not the official position of the organization. If that were the case, the Mujahidin's leadership would have not approved its publication. In any case after Abdi left, nobody continued his work. The Mujahidin continued to believe that Islam did not have a clear economic system, and religion could not provide a proper guideline for the economic life of the society.

In their book titled *Introduction to Cognition*, the Mujahidin accepted four principles of dialectic and added a fifth principle, *purposefulness of creation*, and claimed that they completed the principles of evolution. According to this view, life has a purpose, but they did not discuss this issue with the leftist group lest they would label them reactionary. But this argument convinced religious groups. They presented one opinion to leftist groups and another to religious forces. Other books that the Mujahidin read widely were *How Man Became a Bugbear* and *Sociology* by [Amir Hossein] Aryanpoor.

Gradually, the Mujahidin concluded that the *petit-bourgeoisie* ideology made their organization vulnerable and admitted that it is eclectic. They confessed that their struggle was "scientific" but their ideology was not, and these two were not in harmony with one another; whereas the Marxist groups' ideology and struggle are both "scientific" and that was the reason for their success. In conjunction with this argument, Taqi Shahram published a treatise titled *Let Us Raise the Flag of Ideology*, and with the publication of the treatise on the *Ideological Transformation* officially declared the MKO's adoption of Marxist ideology.

During the days after the victory of the Revolution and while the government was involved in fighting with the Kumleh, Democrat Party, and other counter-revolutionaries, the Mujahidin supported those groups and condemned the government's policies toward them. When Mas'ud Rajavi nominated himself for the presidential elections, these groups supported his candidacy. During the period of unrest in Kurdistan, their members were free to roam around there and even provided escorts for them. Those forces released their prisoners with the mediation of the Mujahidin.

The Mujahidin and the [Shi'ite] Clergy

The Mujahidin did not assign a role for the clergy in political struggle. They believed that they should not play a part in the Revolution because they could lead the struggle in the wrong direction. In their view the clergy relied on capitalist and/or *petit-bourgeoisie* classes and would fight against any force that might threaten their own interests. Of course, they were aware of the power of the clergy and were willing to use them as a means toward their own goal, but only as long as they would listen to revolutionary forces speak on their behalf. In other words, they respected the clergy as long as they served the Mujahidin's interests and objectives. They considered themselves as the defenders of *true Islam* and did not accept Mr. Khomeini's interpretation of religion.

They had a dual approach toward religion. On the one hand they were critical of religion because in their view religion was the social basis of the *petit-bourgeoisie*, and on the other hand they did not wish to create a conflict between them and the clergy. They considered such a conflict a dangerous threat to their own strategies and objectives, and if they couldn't prevent it, at least they tried to postpone it. This was a harmful perspective that took shape in the organization from the beginning. With this mindset they presented three kinds of approach toward social classes. One approach was based on what they termed as *scientific, materialistic, and socialistic* knowledge of the first echelon in the society that included university students and intellectuals. In relation to the second and third echelons, the Mujahidin's attitude was identical with those of the clergy and the working classes. However, they did not believe in prayer and Shi'ite rituals such as Muharram processions (*rozeh khani*) and just pretended in order to win the support of the clergy and the working classes. Moreover, the Mujahidin did not believe in miracles and the Twelfth Imam (the Mahdi). They argued that it was not *scientific* for the Twelfth Imam to live for 1400 years, and that the Imam of the Age (*Sahib al-zaman*) is in fact he who leads the struggle of that age. Rajavi did not accept the clergy's view that the Marxists were impure (*najis*) but stated that those who opposed people's struggle (such as Ayatullah Khansari) were impure, and not organizations and leaders like Ho Chi Minh or Che Guevara. In their opinion only imperialists were true infidels.

With this perspective toward religion and the clergy and their emphasis on the primacy of struggle, they accepted people of diverse views and ideologies for membership in their organization. It was thus that they accepted religious as well as Marxist elements such as Bahman Bazargani and Ahmad Banasazi in their organization.

During the early years of their activities, the Mujahidin enjoyed the support and financial backing of some members of the clergy, such as Mr. Taleqani, Montazeri, Hashimi Rafsanjani, Mahdavi Kani, Haqqani, Lahuti, and many others. Rafsanjani and Taleqani put a considerable amount of money at their disposal and gave them advice on religious and political matters. But Ayatullah Khomeini never agreed with or supported the Mujahidin. In 1350–1351/1971–1972 Rafsanjani and Taleqani wrote a letter to Khomeini and asked him to provide some funding for the organization, but he rejected their request. Khomeini did not believe in armed struggle at all and rejected the Mujahidin's ideology, but because of prevailing circumstances, he never expressed his opposition openly lest the enemy take advantage. After a while, he only allowed some financial support to be given to the families of political prisoners from the charitable contributions of his followers.

In the early days of 1352/1972 when some of the Mujahidin leaders were executed, Mr. Hashimi Rafsanjani was in Qizil Qal'ah Prison and learned about the Mujahidin's ideology. Even at that time I had some criticisms against the Mujahidin, and when I met Rafsanjani I shared them with him. He confronted me strongly and warned me against any effort to divide the Islamist forces and defended the Mujahidin as protectors of the Qur'an and *Nahj al-Balaghah*. In my opinion the reason that some members of the clergy were influenced by the Mujahidin was that, unlike the Mujahdin, they had never participated in armed struggle. When they realized that the Mujahidin were good organizers and engaged in military operations, they identified with them and expanded their friendship with them.

Other than Mr. Khomeini, Ayatullah Mutahhari also never approved of or supported the Mujahidin. He did not express open opposition to them. If somebody asked his opinion about the Mujahidin, he would share his views in private, but never took position against them openly lest the police take advantage of it.

Some members of the clergy, such as Seyyed Hadi and Seyyed Ahmad Hashimi Nezhad (the son-in-law of Mr. Montazeri), Mostafa Fumani, and Jalal Ganjeh'ie joined the Mujahidin in prison. Seyyed Hadi even shaved his beard, and Montazeri confronted him for that. Mostafa Fumani and Montazeri came into conflict because of some statements Fumani had wrongly attributed to him. Gholam Hossein Haqqani[263] also

---

[263] Gholam Hossein Haqqani (b. 1320/1941) graduated from Qom seminary. He was one of the founding members of the Institute for Social Justice and wrote a book titled *Islam: The Vanguard of Revolutions*. He joined Ayatullah Taleqani and was arrested in 1350/1971 and another time in

joined the Mujahidin hoping to guide them on the straight path.

Regarding the issue of the *fatwa* on the impurity of Marxist elements, SAVAK tried to educate the clergy and had extensive discussions with them. It also pressured them to take a position against the Mujahidin by writing articles in defiance of their strategy of armed struggle. However, the clergy refused to comply. They decided to use the pulpits against the Mujahidin and educate their audience when they were released from prison.

Whenever SAVAK met and talked to the clergy individually, they took different positions. After a while the clergy decided to have a spokesman and chose Rafsanjani for that position. After the MKO announced its ideological transformation and adopted Marxism, the clergy took position against them. Some of them claimed that they were aware of changes in the Mujahidin organization and they needed time to take a position against them. I do not know if this claim was true or not. Some suggested that Mr. Taleqani and a few others should meet the Shah and convince him to give more freedom to the opposition. They meant to tell the Shah that his oppressive policies against intellectuals and religious class had pushed the youth to go toward the Mujahidin and similar groups, and to argue that if the Shah gave some freedom to his opponents, the youth would not be attracted to the Mujahidin and their strategy of armed struggle. It was suggested that they ask the Shah to abolish the single-party system and demand more freedom so that they could educate people and possibly redirect opposition from the Shah to the Mujahidin. They planned to do so not through the Rastakhiz Party but on the pulpits in the mosques.

1354/1975. He held several important positions after the victory of the Revolution in the Revolutionary Guard Corps, and was the Secretary General of the Institute for Islamic Propaganda, and a member of the national parliament. He was killed in the explosion of the Islamic Republican Party's headquarters in Tehran in Tir 1360/July, 1981. See *Kayhan*, #10949, p. 11, *Islamic Republic Daily Newspaper*, # 671, p. 12.

The reason for such a proposal was that before he was arrested, Mr. Taleqani met Taqi Shahram in Mr. Ghayuran's residence. He also met other leading members of the Mujahidin in other locations. After 1354/1975 SAVAK no longer permitted such meetings to take place and arrested Mr. Taleqani.

I discussed these questions with Mr. Rafsanjani on another occasion and told him that the young activists were joining the Mujahidin one after another and the clergy should do something to stop that. He was not disturbed by this news and told me that the Mujahidin recruit one by one, whereas the clergy could line up supporters in the thousands each time they deliver a sermon from the pulpit.

In early 1357/1978 as a result of the Shah's liberalization policy, a less restrict environment was introduced in every prison. Prisoners began to enjoy more freedom, and as a result most people who entered prison did not pay attention to the clergy, but rather, they joined the Mujahidin and other leftist groups. The Mujahidin took advantage of the new situation and began to criticize the clergy more openly. The clergy did not try to stop the process and failed to attract the youth to their own side.

Shari'ati and the Mujahidin

The Mujahidin did not have a positive image of Dr. Ali Shari'ati and considered him to be a traitor. They called him a *petit-bourgeois* who sought reconciliation with the regime. When a few of his articles were published in several daily papers, the Mujahidin claimed that there were no logical reasons for the regime to publish anti-communist articles by Shari'ati and concluded that he had made peace with the regime. When Shari'ati's book titled *What Is to Be Done?* was brought to the prison, Rajavi and Khiyabani were in the library. Musa took the book, threw it to Mas'ud, and said, "Here is the Lenin of Iran." Shari'ati's books, like those of Mutahhari and Seyyed Qutb, were boycotted in prison. Later, when the Mujahidin were released they realized that Shari'ati had in fact attracted a large following. They took advantage of his popularity and claimed that they were also among Shari'ati's followers. Ironically, when Shari'ati's articles titled "A Return to the Self" were published in the daily *Kayhan*, because of the predominantly anti-communist themes of the articles, the Mujahidin accused him of collaboration with the regime!

The Mujahidin did not accept Shari'ati's political stand. Referring to his famous statement, "Those who were martyred acted like [Imam] Hossein, and those who survived must act like Zaynab," the Mujahidin argued that Shari'ati opposed their strategy of armed struggle, and therefore he was an obstacle before their revolutionary objectives. But after Shari'ati's death when they noticed his popularity among the youth, they tried to cash in on his assets and claimed to have been inspired by him in compiling their own revolutionary ideology.

*   *   *

The Final Word

In any case, my only intention of my struggle was to please God. I do not know how many mistakes and errors I committed in the process. I ask God for His forgiveness for my mistakes. When I was injured and was taken to the hospital I appealed to and sought refuge in God to help me. I realized that any opening on my way in fact was by God's grace. I always asked God to save me from my interrogators if He saw sincerity in my deed. I used to fast when my prayers were fulfilled and often recited the Qur'an. In a sense, I saw God's hand when my interrogators did not ask me some very sensitive questions. This may seem simplistic or fatalistic to some, but those who experienced what I did certainly understand what I am talking about.

If I am at peace today and can speak freely, it is because I do not owe anything to anybody, nor do I expect anything from anybody. I did not ask for nor receive a reward or high position in return for my struggle, and that is the reason I can speak freely and comfortably and defend what I did. I always believed that if we wish to guide others, we should practice what we preach. Otherwise, we cannot stop corruption and deviation.

At the time that Mr. Khomeini invited the clergy to live a simple life, it was because he could foresee corruption and preoccupation with the worldly life. I told several members of the parliament that Mr. Khomeini was no longer with us and we might forget his advice. I reminded them of Mr. Khameni'ie's advice to pay attention to people's needs. As he said, "With a dirty handkerchief you cannot clean a window." We must be clean in order to be able to help people.

Most of what I said [in this book] I had said in 1358/1979. My intention here was to give a warning about the abuse of the Revolution and its achievements. My other intention was to warn the youth so that they wouldn't join different groups and political currents blindly. I believe that if my experiences and those of others who were involved in political activities against the Shah's regime had been shared with the post-Revolution generation, many problems and tragic events that we faced could have been avoided and many lives would have been saved. At this moment, too, I write these lines with the same intentions that motivated me to speak out in the early days after the victory of the Revolution. It seems that once more the waves of hostility with the Islamic government are hitting the shores of revolution, and through distortion of the realities, they target the public opinion. I wrote these pages so that future generations would realize that this revolution did not achieve a victory to be destroyed easily. Many lives were lost and energies spent for that end, and I was only a drop in the ocean of people's struggle.

In writing these pages I relied on my memory, and naturally I might have committed many errors and mistakes. I appeal to my friends to bring such errors to my attention and share their criticisms with me. Throughout my life I have always tried to act upon what I preach. Up to this day, God had always been generously helping me. By His grace, I have been able to avoid many mistakes and deviations. I do not wish to justify what I did nor do I want to defend myself. If I achieved any success in this domain, it was by God's grace. I appeal to Him to shower me with His grace for the remaining years of my life and keep me on His straight path.

I remember that on my wedding night after I preformed two courses of prayer I asked my wife to pray to God to give us a child who could behave better than we did. Perhaps she didn't understand what I told her that day. She understood that statement twenty years later when she noticed that some children of notable people have been harming the reputation of their fathers.

I ask God to grant us and all followers of the Prophet and his immaculate progeny good ending by His grace.

*   *   *

General Index

A

A'azam Ruhi Ahangaran, 219
Abbas, 3
Abbas Agah, 337, 418, 431
Abbas Aghazamani, 97, 98,
  99, 104, 106, 108
Abbas Duzduzani, 98, 228
Abbas Farnam, 365
Abbas Fazilat Kalam, 380
Abbas Javdani, 126, 157, 183
Abbas Mudarresi Far, 27, 445
Abbas Samakar, 215, 501,
  502
Abbas Yazdanifar, 561
Abd al-Rasool Meshkinfam,
  589
Abd al-Reza Nikbeen
  Rudsari, 587
Abdi, 585, 587, 588, 609
Abdul Karim Qasim, 47
Abdullah Anduri, 290, 451
Abdullah Mahjum, 167
Abdullahi, 86
Abolqasem Sarhaddi Zadeh,
  95
Abu Dawud, 52
Abu Mazan, 52
Abu Sharif, 97, 99, 106, 107
Abudhar, 48, 129, 147, 295,
  605

Abudhar Ghifari, 48, 129
[Abul Fazl] Heidari, 27
Abulqasim Reza'ie, 280
Abulqasim Sarhaddi Zadeh,
  513
Adam and Eve, 200
Adil Jismi, 146
Afrakhteh, 126, 144, 148,
  153, 157, 168, 400, 403,
  411, 412, 415, 438, 509,
  600, 602
Afzali, 174
Ahmad Ahmad, 47, 82, 97,
  98, 99, 100, 104, 108, 110,
  112, 193, 222, 261, 296,
  455, 460, 536, 597
Ahmad Ali Borhani, 569
Ahmad Banasazi, 598, 611
Ahmad Hashimi Nezhad, 483
Ahmad Karrubi, 24, 25, 44,
  59, 384
Ahmad Mahdavi, 121
Ahmad Reza Karimi, 376,
  413, 428
Ahmad Sa'adat, 570
Ahmad Shahab, 27
Ahmad Zamani, 86
Ahvaz, 212, 555, 597
Akbar Badamchian, 581
Akbar Baratchi, 570
Akbar Izadpanah, 263, 291
Akbar Mahdavi, 142, 152,
  153, 161, 165, 166, 302,

335, 336, 338, 341, 425, 556

Alavi Khorasgani, 483

Alavi School, 186, 401, 528

Algeria, 48, 579, 587

Algerian National Liberation Front, 48

'Ali, 13, 15, 17, 18, 19, 22, 27, 38, 46, 60, 86, 87, 93, 100, 104, 106, 109, 110, 112, 113, 124, 149, 152, 153, 168, 179, 324, 425

Ali Akbar, 6, 153, 161

Ali Asghar, 6, 13, 119, 585, 592

Ali Asghar Ikbatani, 59

Ali Darvishiyan, 522

Ali Fallahiyan, 571

Ali Hasan Salamah, 52

Ali Jannati, 87, 212

Ali Javadi, 483

Ali Mehdizadeh, 451

Ali Mirza, 13

Ali Mohammad Basharati, 569

Ali Reza Beheshti Zadeh, 123

Ali Reza Kabiri, 483

Ali Reza Sepasi Ashtiyani, 97, 100, 104, 110

Ali Reza Zemorrodiyan, 124, 179

Aligudarz, 44, 552

Alireza Beheshtizadeh, 179

Alireza Kabiri, 337

Alireza Zemorrodian, 598

Allahmorad Delfani, 590, 592

Allahyar Salih, 57

'Allameh [Seyyed Mohammad Husayn] Tabatabai', 154

Amani, 18, 19, 20, 27, 45, 83, 85, 561, 572

American School, 58

'Amid Zanjani, 536

Aminabad, 13

Amir Abbas Huveyda, 32, 154, 155

Amir al-Mu'uminin Mosque, 98

Amir Asadollah Alam, 16

Amir Lashkari, 24, 40, 60, 84

Amjadiyeh, 51, 52, 54, 55

Ammar Yasir, 48, 129, 295, 605

Amr bil ma'aruf wa nahy 'an ilmunkar, 46

Ansar al-Hossein and Khamsah Tayyibah, 302

Ansar al-Mahdi Mosque, 388

Ansari, 500

Anwari, 83

Apollo, 217, 220, 316, 317, 318, 339, 414, 502

Aqa Salim, 207

al-Aqsa Mosque, 52

Arab Shahi, 82, 96

Arabtoxication, 268

Arak, 21, 68, 70, 104

Arash, 193, 219, 307, 319,
320, 321, 322, 329, 355,
365
Arif Avenue, 138, 141, 142,
145, 394
Arj factory, 418
Arman Mellat, 58
Art Festivals in Shiraz, 32
Aryanpoor, 609
Asadollah Alam, 17
Asadullah Badamchian, 455,
562, 581
Asadullah Tajrishi, 428
Asgar Awladi, 26, 27, 86,
452, 455, 458, 459, 527,
572
Asghar Badi'zadegan, 279
Asghar Bamiyeh, 13
Asghar Izadi, 451
Asghar Mahdavi, 341, 343,
425
Asghar Qatel, 12
ashab-e fatwa, 455
Ashja', 561
Ashraf Camp, 239, 470
Ashraf Dehqani, 120
Ashraf Khorasani, 60, 137
Ashraf Pahlavi, 123, 193
Ashraf Rabi'i, 86
Ashrafi Isfahani, 193
'Ashura, 19, 20, 525
al-Asifah, 68
Assadullah Lajevardi, 47
Association of Conscientious
Muslims, 37

Atabak Avenue, 15, 164, 526,
527
Ayatollah Kashani, 513
Ayatollah Khomeini, 518
Ayatullah [Ali] Meshkini, 155
Ayatullah Ahmad Jannati, 86
Ayatullah Ali Quddusi, 154
Ayatullah Ashtiyani, 261
Ayatullah Gholam Hossein
Ja'afari, 29, 32
Ayatullah Hakim, 17, 30, 76
Ayatullah Hossein Ali
Montazeri, 23
Ayatullah Ja'afari, 30
Ayatullah Kashani, 91, 149
Ayatullah Khamenei, 90, 98,
193
Ayatullah Khansari, 611
Ayatullah Kho'i, 17
Ayatullah Khomeini, 16, 17,
86, 261, 297, 524, 611
Ayatullah Mirza Hashim
Amoli, 57
Ayatullah Mohsin Hakim, 33,
95
Ayatullah Morvarid, 161
Ayatullah Musavi Tabrizi, 86
Ayatullah Rabaani Shirazi,
124
Ayatullah Sai'di, 49, 57, 59,
161, 513
Ayatullah Taleqani, 66, 160,
401, 484, 553, 559, 612
Azadi Square, 526
A'zam Fard Amiri, 167, 169

621

Burazjan, 522, 597
Burujerdi, 13, 17, 22, 57, 470
Buzarjumehri Avenue (now
15th Khordad), 33, 125,
595

C

Captain Ruhi, 443
Captain Saremi, 488
Captain Ta'ziyehchi, 224
Captain Zhiyan Panah, 230,
235, 242, 243, 347
Caspian Sea, 48, 73, 75, 78,
173, 556, 590
Central Kmiteh headquarters,
549
chador, 421, 591
*Chahar enqelab va do
geryesh-e maktabi dunya
dolati*, 47
Chahar Shanbeh Soori, 261
Chaim Weizman, 56
chain, 7, 41, 148, 242, 322,
578
Chamkhaleh, 76, 78
Chamran, 579
Charles De Gaulle, 22
Che Guevara, 48, 129, 605,
606, 611
*Cherik-ha-ye Fadayee-ye
khalq*, 590
Colonel Abbas Zamani, 203,
204
colonel Afzali, 32, 174

Colonel Mohammad Ali
Afzali, 174
Colonel Nasrullah Tavakkoli,
534
Commanding good and
forbidding the
Reprehensible, 46
Costa Rica, 224
Council of Revolution, 527
Cyanide capsule, 168, 428
Cyrus Crossroad, 166
Cyrus Nahavandi, 232,
263, 290, 291, 292

D

dagger, 41
dakhmat al'ulama, 161
Damavand, 44, 83, 93, 94,
126, 135, 338, 340, 437,
438, 524
Damavandi, 447
*Daneshjuyan Musalman
Jebhe Azadibakhsh Melli
Ira*n, 37
Daryush Furuhar, 46, 58,
147
David Ben Gurion, 56
Davud Abadi, 123
Davudi, 123
Dayereh-ye munkarat, 538
Delfani, 105, 590, 591, 592

Faridan, 43
Fascist, 546
Fatemeh Amini, 219
Fatemeh Hosseini, 193
al-Fath, 68, 126, 127, 142,
    187, 257, 588, 608
Fatimah Zahra, 322
fatwa, 452, 453, 454, 455,
    456, 457, 459, 460, 463,
    464, 465, 469, 470, 472,
    476, 480, 483, 513, 613
Fawziyeh Suare, 80
Fazil, 126, 136, 157, 422,
    594, 597, 598
Fidayan-i Khalq, 130, 131,
    132, 233, 239, 249, 380,
    451, 452
Fidayan—the Minority
    Faction, 436
Fidel Castro, 606
Firdawsi Avenue, 145, 146,
    202
Firdawsi Square, 39, 55,
    56, 254
Firuzkoohi, 157
*From Bayt al-Muqadas to
    Munich*, 52
Furqan, 22, 26, 526, 552,
    553, 555
Furqan group, 22, 26, 526,
    552, 553, 555
Furuhar, 58

G

Ganje'i, 389
gendarmerie, 7, 533
gendarmes, 6, 7
General [Charles]
    DeGaulle, 24
General Bahram Aryana,
    150
General Hossein Fardoost,
    350
General Ja'far Quli Sadri,
    193
General Kamangar, 228,
    235
General Manuchehr
    Hashemi, 371
General Muqadam, 31
General Nasir Alavi
    Moghaddam, 31
General Nasiri, 32
General Sujdeh'ie, 555
General Taheri, 112, 607
General Vaziri, 377
General Zandipoor, 203,
    206, 222, 603
Geneva, 56
Germany, 52, 96, 195, 215,
    290, 402
Gharbaltaq, 43

624

Ghezel Ghal'ah, 30, 87, 139, 215, 232, 489, 495, 503
Ghiyathi Road, 139
Gholam Hossein Haqqani, 612
Gholamreza Nejati, 257
Golab Bakhsh, 568
Golda Meir, 52, 54
Golestan Palace, 23
Golpeigan, 137
Golsorkhi, 206, 214, 215
Golsurkhi group, 206, 501
grand commune, 233, 240
Great Encyclopedia of Islam, 95, 96

H

Hadi Hashimi, 483
Hadi Mansuri., 293
Haji Ibrahim Davar, 391
Hajj Ahmad Khomeini, 572
Hajj Ahmad Mosque, 98
Hajj Ezzat Khalili, 297
Hajj Hadi, 83
Hajj khalil, 547
Hajj Mahdi 'Araghi, 20
Hajj Mohammad Baqir, 28
Hajj Sadiq Amani, 19, 20, 26, 27

Hajj Seyyid Taqi Khamushi, 20
Hakim-e Shar', 567, 571
Hamadan, 29, 261, 286, 302
Hamid Ashraf, 411
Hamid Okhovvat, 65
Hamid Reza Eshraqi, 483
Hamid Ukhuvvat, 25
Hamideh, 243, 244, 328, 341, 347, 348
Hanifnezhad, 22, 106, 585, 591, 593, 594, 605, 607
Haqqani Seminary School, 213
Harandi, 20, 27
Hasan Abad Square, 56, 150, 151
Hasan Abrari, 126, 134, 136, 138, 141, 146, 147, 157, 161, 183, 184, 335, 400, 428, 430, 437, 509
Hasan Ali Mansur, 19, 25, 95, 249, 455, 459
Hasan Enayat, 483
Hasan Ezzati, 597
Hasan Farzaneh, 123, 140, 164, 165, 167
Hasan Hossein Zadeh, 87, 91
Hasan Kalahduzan, 65

Hossein Talib, 581
Hossein the vinegar seller, 341, 342
Hossein Zadeh, 442
Hosseini Khorasani, 500
Hosseini, the Torturer, 308
Hosseiniyyah Irshad, 143, 209
Hosseinzadeh, 244, 245, 350, 358, 359
How Man Became a Bugbear, 596, 609
Hozhabr Yazdani, 224
Hu Chi Minh, 48
Hujat al-Islam Mohammad Jawad Hujjati Kermani, 95
Hujjatiyah group, 540
Human Rights Commission, 90
Human Rights group, 557
Human Rights Organization, 121
Hushang Delkhah, 491
Hushang Tahami, 196

I

I'dam Square, 43, 65
Ibn Muljam, 314
Ikhwan al-Muslimin, 97

Imam Hossein, 6, 20, 21, 56, 78, 173, 245, 247, 311, 393, 492
Imam Khomeini, 16, 17, 18, 19, 21, 22, 23, 24, 25, 29, 33, 37, 39, 44, 47, 57, 58, 85, 88, 100, 144, 161, 162, 176, 194, 210, 211, 312, 314, 400, 418, 455, 480, 482, 513, 517, 518, 524, 526, 527, 528, 529, 530, 531, 533, 534, 542, 544, 545, 546, 551, 554, 567, 568, 572, 578
Imam Sadeq University, 537
Imam Zadeh Yahya, 49, 179, 186
Imam Zaman, 154
Imami Kashani, 93
Imamzadeh Yahya, 159, 185, 186
Imperial Guard, 555
India, 51
Inqilab Avenue, 547, 549
Ipak, 121
Iraj Kashkooli, 291
Iran Agro-Business Company, 160

Iran Avenue, 403, 528,
543, 562
Iran Metallurgy Industry,
418
Iran National Party, 46
Iraq, 30, 34, 37, 47, 57, 96,
97, 109, 124, 126, 239,
244, 349, 388, 470, 522,
531, 549, 578, 579, 589,
592
Iravani, 536, 565
'Irfani, 536
Isfahan, 18, 19, 44, 58, 60,
86, 95, 136, 137, 138,
160, 179, 180, 181, 183,
210, 212, 274, 400, 413,
416, 417, 418, 419, 420,
422, 432, 482, 549, 555,
600
Isfahani, 189, 572, 573,
574, 575, 576, 578
Islamic Coalition Party, 2,
16, 18, 19, 20, 22, 25,
26, 27, 28, 37, 45, 46,
123, 232, 250, 261, 297,
298, 452, 527, 561
Islamic Nations Party, 2,
42, 95, 96, 97, 99, 102,
111, 232, 234, 298
Islamic Republican Party,
2, 22, 93, 96, 554, 613

Islamic Revolution and the
Social Mobilization, 47
Isma'ili, 196
Israel, 34, 35, 46, 48, 51,
52, 54, 55, 56, 110, 150,
350, 386, 479
istikhara, 29

J

Ja'afari, 29, 30, 34, 46,
149, 152, 163, 183, 189,
290
Ja'afari Bazaar, 46
Jack Turnerwill, 115
Jalal al-Din Farsi, 48
Jalal Ganjeh'ie, 139, 526,
612
Jalal Sujdeh'ie, 555
Jalaliyeh square, 13
Jalil Savadi Nezhad, 505
Jalil Seyyed Ahmadian,
589
Jamal Ismai'ili, 572
Jamilah Bou Pasha, 48, 129
Jannati, 162
Japan, 51, 150
Javad Madar Shahi, 540
Javad Mansuri, 82, 96, 97,
98, 99, 100, 106, 109,
139, 224, 243, 388, 460,
554

Kerala, 51
Kerman, 84, 95
Khalil, 147, 149, 196, 280,
  394, 395, 396, 397, 404,
  429, 430, 547, 549, 557,
  558, 561, 601
Khalil Faqih Dezfuli, 196,
  394, 504, 558, 601
Khalil Reza'ie, 280
Khameni'ie, 616
Khamseh, 26, 425
Khamushi, 400, 402, 405
Khan Ali, 167, 168
Khandaniha, 30
Khani Abad street, 60
Khark Islamd, 522
Khawarij, 553
Khiyabani, 270, 280, 284,
  293, 294, 509, 534, 614
Khodadadi, 286
Khomeini, 17, 18, 19, 20,
  21, 22, 23, 24, 44, 57,
  86, 91, 176, 418, 455,
  517, 523, 526, 527, 528,
  530, 531, 534, 539, 542,
  546, 572, 610, 611, 612,
  616
Khonsar, 5, 11, 13, 17, 137
Khorasan Square, 21, 82,
  90, 91, 165
Khosrow Golsorkhi, 115,
  193, 214

[Khosrow] Roozbeh, 115
Khosrow Shahi, 536, 538
Khuzistan, 386, 432
Khwansar, 348
knuckledusters, 41
Kolahi, 554
Komiteh, 533, 535, 536,
  537, 538, 539, 540, 543,
  544, 545, 547, 549, 551,
  555, 558, 559, 560, 564,
  565, 566, 567, 568, 570,
  571, 572, 573, 574, 576,
  577, 578, 579
Koorush Lasha'ie, 291,
  350, 412

L

Lahuti, 246, 480, 611
Laila Zemorrodian, 600
Lajevardi, 26, 46, 60, 82,
  83, 84, 86, 244, 245,
  286, 297, 455, 456, 524,
  526, 528, 549, 565, 572
Lake Tar, 83, 93, 126, 338,
  340
Land Reform, 44
Langaud, 76
Lashkari, 18, 40, 46, 56,
  57, 59, 60, 62, 65, 68,
  69, 82, 83, 84, 173

Lebanon, 47, 96, 100, 106, 126, 187, 451, 470, 588, 591
Leonid Brezhnev, 55
liberalization policy, 228, 516, 614
Lieutenant Ahmadian, 597
Lilian Tel, 57
The *Little Red Book*, 168
London, 414
Los Angeles, 150, 412
Lutfullah Maysami, 124, 257, 328, 446, 510

M

Ma'sumeh Shadmani, 324
Madar Shahi, 540
Madrasah Rifah, 533
Mafatih al-Jinan, 261, 445
Maghrib, 521
Mah Munir Farzaneh, 81
Mahbubeh Afraz, 157
Mahdavi Kani, 453, 525, 535, 536, 537, 538, 541, 543, 564, 566, 568, 569, 571, 576, 611
Mahdi, 154, 264, 611
Mahdi Iraqi, 18, 21, 27, 29, 250, 553
Mahdi Karrubi, 44
Mahjum, 166, 167

Mahmud Abbas, 52
Mahmud Tariq al-Islam, 446
Majid Mehr Ayin, 600
Majid Mo'ini, 460
Majlis, 536
Major Afshar, 377, 381, 458, 555
Major Pour Kumayliyan, 224
Major Vaziri, 354, 417, 421, 439
Maleki, 537, 580, 581
Malik Hossein, 52
Malik, Hujr ibn 'Adi al-Kindi, 48
Maliki, 84
Manizheh Ashrafzadeh Kirmani, 219, 411
Manochehr Moqaddam Salimi, 207
Manoochehr Vazifeh Khah, 414
Mansur, 22, 25, 26, 27, 28, 29, 46, 228, 243, 262, 263, 298, 452, 455, 460
Mansur Nahavandi, 263
Mansur Pour Kashani, 262
Mansur Zamani, 228, 243
Manuchehr Moqaddam Salimi, 206, 215

Manuchehr Nahavandi, 291
Manuchehri, 126, 196, 307,
  319, 321, 322, 328, 349,
  351, 355, 365, 369, 398,
  414, 415, 496, 505
Mao tse Tong, 168, 606
Maoist group, 112, 124,
  126
maqam-i amniyyati, 193
maraji', 85, 295
marja', 17, 21, 22, 312
Martial Law, 528, 533
Marxist, 22, 53, 59, 67, 77,
  78, 91, 105, 107, 112,
  114, 120, 129, 131, 132,
  133, 157, 183, 214, 218,
  261, 262, 263, 268, 269,
  279, 280, 282, 284, 288,
  289, 293, 341, 345, 352,
  366, 375, 377, 392, 400,
  405, 410, 428, 430, 445,
  446, 449, 450, 452, 453,
  457, 458, 460, 461, 462,
  463, 465, 469, 472, 473,
  476, 483, 491, 513, 517,
  518, 519, 522, 523, 524,
  525, 529, 559, 587, 588,
  594, 595, 598, 599, 600,
  601, 603, 607, 608, 609,
  611, 613
Maryam Azodanloo, 239

Marziyeh Hadidchi, 428
Mas'ud, 112, 115, 118,
  120, 125, 157, 257, 279,
  280, 294, 295, 388, 389,
  390, 391, 392, 445, 446,
  447, 456, 460, 475, 505,
  549, 610, 614
[Mas'ud] Ahmad Zadeh,
  115
Mas'ud Rajavi, 257, 294,
  456
Mashhad, 26, 47, 57, 67,
  68, 92, 126, 139, 156,
  157, 158, 159, 183, 184,
  185, 296, 301, 302, 335,
  341, 366, 416, 446, 451,
  458, 597, 598
Mashhad University, 183
Mawlavi Avenue, 33
Mawlavi aquare, 12
May 1: Labor Day, 463
Maysami group, 510
Mazandaran, 597
Mehdi Bazargan, 45, 66,
  157, 241, 268, 527, 585,
  588
Mehdi Bukhara'i, 460
Mehdi Khanbaba Tehrani,
  257, 426
Mehdi Rajabi, 280
Mehdi Taqva'i, 521, 557

Mohammad Razavi, 550
Mohammad Reza Fatemi,
  365
Mohammad Reza
  Moqaddam, 65, 84, 85
Mohammad Reza Pahlavi,
  30, 150
Mohammad Reza Sa'adati,
  509, 554
Mohammad Reza Shah, 58
Mohammad Sadat
  Darbandi, 589
Mohammad Sadeq
  Katouzian, 557
Mohammad Sadiq Amani
  Hamadani, 19
Mohammad Tafazzuli, 307
Mohammad Taqi Shahram,
  157, 597
Mohammad Taqi Shari'ati,
  246, 296
Mohammad Yaqini, 157
Mohammad Yazdaniyan,
  126, 157
Mohammad Zabeti, 544
Moharram, 245, 246
Mohsen (Abulqasim)
  Reza'i, 547
Mohsen Reza'ie, 284
Mohsin Fazil, 126, 157,
  158

Mokhbir al-Dawlah
  Square, 56
Mokhtar Ibrahimi, 570
Molotov cocktail, 55, 56
Monghul invasion, 570
Montazeri., 384, 483
Morteza Alviri, 83, 93, 125
Morteza Kashani, 147
Morteza Mirbazel, 570
Morteza Mutahhari, 18
Morwarid, 30
Mosaddeq, 16, 22, 150,
  289
Mosaddeqi, 35, 62, 65, 418
Mosque of Abulfath, 20
mosque of Hajj Abolfat'h,
  20
Mostafa Fumani Hai'ri,,
  483
Mostafa Fumani,, 612
Mostafa Hirad, 193, 329
Mostafa Javan Khoshdel,
  105, 106, 110, 187, 239,
  296, 301, 324
Mostafa Khomeini, 58
Mostafa Madani, 436, 440
Mostafa Sattari, 59
Mostafavi, 162, 329, 330,
  331
Mostazafan Foundation, 22
Mousavi Ardabili, 575

634

Musavi, 86, 162
mut'ah, 177
Mutahhari, 26, 261, 269,
  347, 513, 524, 525, 526,
  527, 535, 536, 544, 553,
  564, 586, 596, 607, 612,
  614

N

Nader Shaygan, 289, 448
Nahj al-Balaghah, 48, 87,
  98, 99, 268, 269, 280,
  366, 464, 586, 598
nahzat-e sarbedaran, 269
Najaf Abad, 137
najis, 453, 464, 472, 611
Nasir Jowhari, 446, 451
Nasir Khosrow Avenue,
  146
Nasiri, 32, 533
Nasser Nowzari, 193, 86
Nateq Noori, 536
National Democratic Front
  of the Peoples of Iran,
  436
National Front, 2, 18, 24,
  37, 38, 46, 58, 147, 296,
  412, 448, 506, 534, 540,
  585
National Front for the
  Liberation of Iran, 24, 38

National Iranian Oil
  Company headquarters
  (NIOC), 145
National Liberation Front,
  281
National Party of Iran, 58
National Security Council,
  574
National University of Iran,
  371
Navab Safavi, 19, 22
Nejat Hosseini, 157, 162,
  187, 470, 589, 593
Nejatullahi, 56
Nezam Abad district, 600
Ni'imatollah Hajj Amiri,
  60
Ni'matullah Shahi, 244,
  347, 348
Niavaran Palace, 555
Nikdavudi, 82
Nik-Khah, 426
Niknezhad, 20, 26
Niktab', 181, 321, 391
Noori, 23, 279, 280, 293,
  536, 571, 572, 574, 575
Nouzheh *Coup de etat*, 555
Nowruz, 42, 83, 441, 463
Nowruz Khan, 42
Nowzheh Coup d'état, 531,
  549, 550

488, 495, 499, 504, 509, 511, 513, 515, 534, 599
Qazvin, 480, 524, 560
qiblah, 312, 313, 314
Qishm Island, 58
Qiyam Square, 20
Qizil Qal'ah Prison, 32, 47, 82, 119
Qom, 11, 17, 18, 20, 21, 23, 24, 29, 44, 57, 67, 68, 72, 73, 85, 87, 88, 135, 137, 154, 162, 212, 213, 261, 264, 365, 368, 428, 470, 480, 524, 551, 552, 571, 612
Quddusi, 549
Quds, 542, 579
Queen, 273, 277
Qur'an, 6, 29, 34, 45, 53, 87, 90, 93, 97, 98, 107, 108, 123, 125, 128, 129, 143, 180, 261, 262, 267, 268, 269, 275, 280, 358, 374, 409, 445, 446, 464, 469, 482, 553, 559, 560, 586, 598, 604, 606, 612, 615
Quraysh, 130
Qurkhaneh Street, 161

R

Rabani Amlashi, 30

Rabbani, 193, 281, 453, 470, 471, 472, 473, 474, 475, 476, 478, 508, 527, 544, 573
Rabbani Shirazi, 193, 281, 453, 470, 471, 527, 544, 573
Rafi'i Qazvini, 261
Rafsanjani, 480, 573, 586, 605, 611, 612, 613, 614
Rahim Banai, 291
Rahmani, 231
Raihan, 121
Raja'i, 28, 193, 462, 548, 554
Rajabi, 59, 60, 231, 293
Rajavi, 118, 119, 120, 228, 239, 250, 253, 255, 257, 260, 268, 270, 271, 279, 280, 284, 293, 294, 295, 356, 383, 388, 389, 390, 391, 393, 404, 405, 408, 409, 445, 446, 448, 454, 455, 456, 458, 460, 462, 470, 475, 505, 506, 509, 510, 511, 513, 515, 534, 541, 546, 549, 551, 610, 611, 614
Ramazan, 279, 282, 295, 299, 304, 312, 314, 315, 316, 319, 325, 445, 458, 509, 542

Rasht, 73, 481
Rastakhiz Party, 206
Rasuli, 196, 307, 311, 321,
    322, 328, 340, 355, 365,
    367, 368, 381, 384, 385,
    386, 387, 388, 389, 390,
    404, 407, 409, 410, 411,
    412, 413, 414, 415, 416,
    417, 418, 419, 420, 421,
    422, 423, 424, 425, 426,
    427, 428, 430, 431, 432,
    434, 435, 436, 437, 441,
    442, 443,454, 470, 471,
    472, 473, 474, 475, 476,
    477, 478, 479, 494, 495,
    496, 497, 498, 499, 500,
    501, 502, 503, 504, 505,
    508
Red Army, 55
Red Cross, 485, 489, 495,
    496, 497, 501, 502, 503,
    516, 518, 519
Red Light District, 177
Refah School, 91, 100,
    527, 528
Resurrection, 18, 474
Revolutionary Guard
    Corps, 99, 100, 123, 244,
    462, 514, 551, 566, 613
Revolutionary Islamic
    Committee, 533

Reza Reza'ie, 595, 596
Reza Shah, 58
Reza'ie'yyeh, 291
risaleh-ye 'amaliyyeh, 17
Robab, 121
Robabeh Ashrafzadeh
    Dehqani, 120
Rockefeller, 57
Rubabeh Ashraf zadeh
    Dehqani, 81
Rudabeh Street, 167

S

Sa'ad ibn Abi Waqqas, 130
Sa'adti, 279, 509
Sa'id Mohsen, 585, 587,
    605
Sa'id Shahsavandi, 557,
    599, 601, 602
Sa'id, the Yoghurt Maker,
    602
Sa'idi, 58, 129, 196
al-Sa'iqah, 68, 142
Sabbaghiyan, 527
Sabet Pasal, 160, 544
Sabzavar., 269
Saddam, 579
[Sadeq] Qutbzadeh, 154
Sadiq Islami, 19, 526, 527,
    528

294, 296, 301, 313, 328,
347, 349, 366, 371, 386,
388, 391, 393, 394, 400,
401, 420, 426, 428, 431,
436, 437, 438, 446, 448,
451, 455, 461, 470, 483,
490, 509, 510, 522, 524,
525, 526, 533, 536, 538,
542, 549, 550, 551, 552,
554, 559, 569, 570, 585,
588, 592, 593, 594, 595,
597, 598, 599, 602, 613
Tehran University, 154,
296
Tehrani,, 193, 222, 365,
426, 559
Tokyo, 51
Toofan, 366, 597
Torfeh Hospital, 549
Tudeh party, 206, 218, 234,
366, 380, 412, 426, 501,
559, 560, 590, 592
Turkey, 25, 37, 57, 150
Twelfth Imam, 453, 611
Twelve Angry Men, 79

U

Ubeidullah ibn Ziyad, 6
'ulama, 30, 33, 85, 161,
453, 454, 525
Umar Khattab, 157

United Nations, 121
United States, 38, 330, 516,
531, 534, 579
"Unity, Struggle, Victory.",
208
Urumiyyeh, 291

V

Vahid Afrakhteh, 86, 125,
126, 127, 130, 131, 136,
142, 150, 156, 157, 165,
167, 183, 185, 196, 219,
335, 400, 403, 405, 410,
413, 422, 423, 428, 508,
509, 515, 529, 556, 594,
597, 598, 599, 600, 602,
603
Vahid Lahuti, 483
Vali Faqih, 578
Villa Avenue, 56
Vozara Avenue., 570

W

Warsaw Pact, 55, 534
Washington, 38, 58, 350
Westoxication, 268
White Revolution, 38, 43,
159, 161, 355, 425
Women's Prison, 3, 193,
195, 215, 216
wujuhat, 264

643